Charmaine Solomon

THE COMPLETE
ASIAN
COOKBOOK

Frontispiece: SAI LAN FAR CHOW HAR KAU (coral and jade prawns) *recipe page 384.*

Charmaine Solomon
THE COMPLETE
ASIAN
COOKBOOK

LANSDOWNE

TO REUBEN
WHO MARRIED ME BEFORE I LEARNED TO COOK

Published by Lansdowne Publishing Pty Ltd
Sydney, Australia

First published by Lansdowne Press 1976
Reprinted 1977, 1978, 1979, 1981, 1982, 1984, 1985 (twice), 1987, 1988
Reprinted by Weldon Publishing 1989, 1990
Revised edition first published 1992
Reprinted by Lansdowne Publishing Pty Ltd 1993, 1994, 1995, 1996, 1997, 1999

© Copyright text: Charmaine Solomon 1976
© Copyright design: Lansdowne Publishing Pty Ltd 1976,1992
Photographers: Reg Morrison, Rodney Weidland
Designer: Bruno Grasswill
Cover design: Kathie Baxter Smith
Editors: Peter and Wendy Hutton

Typeset in Australia by David Graphic Typesetting
Revisions by Post Typesetters
Printed and bound in Singapore by Kyodo Printing Co Pte Ltd

National Library of Australia Cataloguing-in-Publication data

Solomon, Charmaine.
    The complete Asian cookbook.

    Rev. ed.
    Includes index.
    ISBN 1 86302 185 X.

    Cookery, Oriental. 1. Title.

641.595

PREFACE

Good cooking is one of the creative arts. Early in life I was fortunate enough to learn from the accomplished and dedicated cooks around me — mother, grandmothers, aunts — that it is one of the most rewarding ways to express oneself and give enjoyment to others at the same time. What's more, I found, it's fun!

I also discovered that there is no real mystery about being able to cook well — no magic potions or charms, just a healthy interest in good eating and in getting the most pleasure possible from each meal. A reliable cookery book is also a great help. I love cooking, but I'm bored stiff by the idea of preparing the same kind of food day in, day out. For me, and I hope for you, the excitement of cooking is to be found in creating new dishes, playing variations on old and familiar ones, and in trying recipes from other countries. Presenting such meals to an appreciative family and friends becomes an experience to be shared and remembered with pleasure.

My aim in writing this book has been to make it possible for keen cooks everywhere to explore the cooking of Asia — and to prove that *real* Eastern meals can be produced in a Western kitchen. But because we have to manage without those ubiquitous servants who do most, if not all, of the cooking (and the washing up!) in many Asian homes, I have tested and re-tested these recipes to preserve their flavour and character while cutting down on the traditional preparation time and effort.

Food, of course, crosses geographic and political boundaries, and dividing lines between one culinary tradition and another are frequently imprecise. I was going to call this book 'Southeast Asian Cooking', but that would (by definition) have excluded India, Korea, Japan, China and Sri Lanka; 'Oriental Cooking' suggested China and Japan but not India; 'Far Eastern Cooking' seemed to leave out India and Sri Lanka, and was in any case a European notion. Hence my choice of 'Asian'. Perhaps arbitrarily it draws a line on the western side of the Indian subcontinent, and leaves out the interesting cuisines of Afghanistan and Iran and Turkey, but the line had to be drawn somewhere!

For reasons of convenience, and not through political ignorance or bias, I have grouped the foods of India, Pakistan, Bangladesh and Kashmir within one chapter. The chapter on China draws heavily on my on-the-spot experiences in Hong Kong, but in addition to the world-famous Cantonese cuisine the cooking of other mainland provinces is well represented. Much of Singapore's excellent Chinese food is also found in Hong Kong, so to avoid repetition I have made a particular feature of the island republic's Nonya dishes. Many dishes in Malaysia and Indonesia are the same, or are strikingly similar, so again I have tried to choose those that seem most representative of each country — if you can't find a favourite recipe in the Malaysian chapter, try Indonesia, and vice versa.

For those of you who are unfamiliar with some of the ingredients and methods used in the recipes that follow, the introduction to each chapter provides much useful information, both general and specific. Besides being practical in terms of what you'll need in the way of special ingredients and utensils, the introductions try to evoke some of the colour and flavour of every country visited in this culinary tour. In some cases, the names commonly used in Australia for ingredients or kitchen equipment mean something else in the United States or are not used there at all — hence the list of synonyms and equivalents on page 484. There is also an extensive alphabetical glossary starting on page 485.

I hope that in using this book you may share some of the pleasure that I have had in putting it together. Start tonight, and dine abroad in the Asian country of your choice. Enjoyment and a whole new world of cooking — and a touch of adventure! — await you.

Charmaine Solomon

CONTENTS

HUNG SHIU SAY SAW (heavenly braised vegetables) *recipe page 412*

ACKNOWLEDGEMENTS

This book represents the work, time and generous help of many people. I cannot ever hope to thank them enough, but I'm going to try.

Had my husband, mother and children not cheerfully taken on so much of what I normally do in order to give me time to travel, research, test recipes and write them, this book could not have been completed. My husband, in particular, worked alongside me on many occasions, encouraging me when I felt the task was too great, and helping me develop some terrific recipes. He continued to love me when I was so completely absorbed in my work that, even though physically present, I was hardly there at all.

My talented aunt, Constance Hancock. Formerly of Akyab, Burma, and now of Dorset, England, Connie has always been an inspiration. When I asked her to help in making the Burmese chapter a complete and authentic guide to Burmese cookery, she responded with an enthusiasm and verve typical of everything she does; wrote reams of instructions, information and recipes; and put me in touch with Mrs Ida Htoon Phay, a recent arrival from Burma, a scholar and eminent lawyer as well as a good cook, whose practical help in testing recipes, translating titles and lending Burmese treasures for photography was invaluable.

My good friends Carmel Raffel and Margaret Turner, who willingly offered to type my manuscript and worked long hours on doing so when it seemed I could not possibly get it done on time.

Reg Morrison, pictorial editor and the most painstaking photographer I have ever worked with. This is the third book we have done together, and each time he puts as much thought, patience and imagination into the photographs as he has before. Not only a work associate but also a family friend, he has been on the testing panel for many of the recipes that follow.

Clair Bean, who assisted in preparing the food for photography. The pictures represent weeks of working long hours, and I am grateful for her unflagging support.

Peter and Wendy Hutton, my enthusiastic editors, who worked so hard and lovingly on this book. Meeting them there was instant rapport. Because they lived in Southeast Asia for many years and have a working knowledge of the food and cooking of the area, I could not have been luckier.

Bruno Grasswill, art director and designer of this book, with whom it is a joy to work. No artistic temperament, and lots of Gallic charm.

Judith Dine, who put such developed effort into the unloved but vital task of indexing.

Kevin Weldon, for asking me to write three cookery books and having faith in my ability to complete a book of this magnitude.

Rodney Weidland, photographer, and Margaret Alcock, stylist, for cover photographs and photos on pages 43, 59, 66, 70, 90, 95, 103, 134, 139, 162, 175, 191, 227, 238, 247, 294, 302, 322, 350, 379, 386, 410, 447.

I'd also like to thank those who helped with the following chapters:

India: Ike Sassoon, Maude Sassoon and Mohini Bhuller of Bombay; Mr I. C. Khanna of the Government of India Tourist Office, Sydney.

Sri Lanka: All the dedicated cooks I have known and learnt from over the years; Anne and Earle Abayasekara and their family.

Thailand: Sherry Brydson, Douglas and Verna Greve, Harriet Muller, Mom Luang Terb Xoomsai of Bangkok; Messrs Phairot and Pannaram of the Tourist Organisation of Thailand in Sydney.

Vietnam: Le Thang Tien.

Laos: Vatsana Souvannavong.

Cambodia: John Lee Kha, Miss Lyna, Miss Chantou Boua.

Indonesia: Mike Schuetzendorf, Yanto Rukmito and Nora Suryanti of Jakarta.

Singapore: May Leong, Wadhu Sakrani, Mrs Lee Chin Koon, Chef Nogawa.

Malaysia: Karl Waelti, Miss Mastura Vaiduri Badrullah of Kuala Lumpur.

The Philippines: Cris Cuevas, Mrs Rixsa Cornista, Mrs Lourdes Rosales, Mrs Nita Jones.

Korea: Soojin Kim for her help in checking and authenticating recipes, translating titles and preparing the Korean dishes illustrated on pages 438 and 443.

Japan: Keiko Terada, teacher and guide, who also prepared the exquisite tray of sushi illustrated on page 482; Jo and Bob Allen, Mona Allen; Susan Kurosawa; Tetsu Kurosawa.

China: Annie Wu, James T. Wu, Chef Lai Tai, Willie Mak, Herbert and Helen Ebert, all of Hong Kong; Lynette Tung, David and Pat Fong, Jan Fong, all of Sydney.

My thanks also to: Ken Bickle, John Boddinar, Glen Bowden, Anne Christie, Haley Epstein, Gerri Ettinger, Margaret Fulton, Valerie Jansz, Mr and Mrs Geoffrey Mottershead, Graham Sims, Dr J. Chapman, A. Rodd of the Royal Botanic Gardens, Mrs R. Whitmont and Lynn Wickramasinha of Sydney; Saul and Shirley Solomon of San Francisco; Moira Isaacs of London.

Joan Bowers Interiors Pty Ltd; Breville; Corso de'Fiori; Finnish Importing Co. Pty Ltd; Global Village Craft Pty Ltd; Handicrafts of Asia; Hong Kong Tourist Association; Incorporated Agencies Pty Ltd; Japan National Tourist Organisation; Consulate of the Republic of Korea; Kosta Boda (Aust.) Pty Ltd; Noritake (Aust.) Pty Ltd; NSW Fish Marketing Authority; Royal Doulton Australia Pty Limited; Saywell Imports; Shea and Associates; Singapore Airlines; Singapore Tourist Promotion Board; Wengar & Co. Pty Ltd.

Charmaine Solomon

INTRODUCTION

Just as France has its robust country fare as well as its subtle *haute cuisine*, so too does Asia have a range of culinary delights that can be simple, complex, delicious, fiery, mild, tantalising — and compulsive! Not all Asian food is exotic or wildly unusual. Much of it (the noodle and rice dishes) is as commonplace as the pastas and potatoes of the West. Many of the ingredients are also familiar to anyone who knows their way around an average kitchen. The main differences have arisen just as they have arisen in other parts of the world — through the use of available ingredients. Thus there is a reliance on some herbs and spices less well known in the West (ginger and cardamom, for example); there are the nutritious by-products of the soy bean; the protein-rich fish sauces and shrimp pastes.

True, some of the more unusual ingredients take a little getting used to. But once you have overcome whatever resistance you may have towards the *idea* of raw fish or freshly ground chilli paste or dried seaweed, you'll find that these (and other) ingredients are no less delicious than — and certainly as exciting as — those you use in your favourite Cordon Bleu dishes.

The introduction to each country chapter will give you a good idea of what to expect in the way of out-of-the-ordinary ingredients. Almost without exception, those called for are now readily available in the West; in the rare cases when they are not, or are out of stock, there are generally suitable substitutes.

Those of you who are already familiar with some of the Asian cuisines will, I hope, find recipes to interest and excite you in these pages; and I think you will be tempted to explore cuisines with which you are less well acquainted. For those who are coming to Asian cooking for the first time, or whose previous experience with Asian food has been limited to restaurant fare, I have taken care to ensure that the essential steps have been made clear and precise. The recipes here are, with occasional minor modifications, the same as the ones used in Asian homes where there is generally much less in the way of modern conveniences — refrigerators, electric or gas stoves, electric blenders and mixers — than there is in Western kitchens, so there's no reason at all why you should be worried about cooking Asian food if you have the few essential implements and utensils.

In the pages immediately following are special sections devoted to the use of cooking oils, the best ways to prepare rice (and the types to buy), the making of coconut milk, the handling of chillies and several other worthwhile tips that apply to many of the recipes.

A brief note on spelling and pronunciation: For most countries the names of the recipes have been given in the dominant or most common language or dialect of the country concerned, followed by the English name in smaller type. In the case of China, the dialect used is Cantonese, for the cooking of Kwangtung Province is the Chinese cuisine best known in the West. Filipino names are generally given in Tagalog, although there are a few Spanish names as well. The names in India are mostly in Hindi (though don't be surpised to see the word 'mutton' — it was adopted by the Indians from the British in the same way that the latter adopted 'topee' and 'pukka' and a dozen other Indian words).

In Malaysia and Indonesia, some years ago, a new unified system of spelling was introduced. The 'ch' in Malay and the 'tj' in Indonesian were replaced by the letter 'c' — thus *blachan* became *blacan* and *tjumi-tjumi* (squid) became *cumi-cumi;* the letters 'oe' in Indonesian became the letter 'u' — thus *ulek* instead of *oelek;* and the letters 'dj' in Indonesian became the letter 'j' — thus *bajak* instead of *badjak.*

Generally, the letter 'a' in Asian words is pronounced as the 'a' in father, never as in cat; the letter 'u' is rather like the 'oo' in look, never as in duty; and the letters 'th' are generally pronounced like an ordinary 't' (slightly aspirated), never as in breath or breathe.

The pronunciation of Burmese names can be confusing. Just remember that the letters 'ky' are pronounced somewhere between a 'ch' and a 'j', so that *kyazan* is spoken as 'chahzan' and *kyetha* as 'chetha'. The letter 'k' in the middle of a word is silent; and the letters 't' and 'ke' at the end of a word cut short the preceding vowel, e.g. *lethoke* sounds like 'letho' and *gin thoke* sounds like 'jin tho'.

I have frequently used the local name for an ingredient in addition to the English name. As an example, you will find 'dried shrimp paste' also referred to as *blacan* (Malaysia), *trasi* (Indonesia), *ngapi* (Burma) and *kapi* (Thailand). There is a comprehensive list of local names in the glossary, starting on page 485.

EATING FOR HEALTH

Most Asian food is healthy food. A Japanese diet, for instance, is a guarantee against heart disease, overweight and gout. On Chinese food, especially steamed and stir fried dishes, it is possible to reduce both weight and cholesterol count. Even the spiced food of India and Southeast Asia is beneficial. Many of the spices and ingredients such as garlic and ginger have been proved to have health-giving properties.

However, with today's emphasis on weight control I have made modifications in the quantity and type of fat used for cooking. I have found it is possible to get very good results using almost half the amount of fat called for in many traditional dishes.

Ghee, which is clarified butter, is the main cooking medium in North India. It keeps without refrigeration because it is pure butter fat with all the milk solids removed. It is essential both for flavour and for its ability to reach high temperatures without burning. I use it for flavour, but substitute light oils for a proportion of the ghee.

In some recipes it is not possible to use substitutes without spoiling the end product — for instance, in Indian sweetmeats or biscuits such as *nan khatai*. So don't substitute margarine or vegetable shortening in these recipes, for you will not get the desired results. In any case, with sweetmeats such a small amount is consumed that it cannot harm health or digestion — unless, of course, discretion and self-control desert you!

In the food of Thailand, the Philippines and certain other Southeast Asian countries, lard is used as a cooking medium. In my kitchen I substitute a light vegetable oil. The flavour will be slightly different, but the way it sits on your stomach will be different too.

Coconut oil, used almost exclusively in Sri Lanka, Malaysia and other coconut-growing countries, is a highly saturated oil. You cannot duplicate its flavour but if you are battling a health problem you can substitute corn, safflower or sunflower oil. In using coconut milk, cut down on the quantity and substitute a similar amount of skimmed milk.

All of these recipes are adaptable to low fat diets with very little sacrifice of flavour since most of the exotic tastes come from herbs, spices and sauces.

RICE

One of the oldest grains in the world, and a staple food of more than half the world's population, rice is by far the most important item in the daily diet throughout Asia.

There are thousands of varieties. Agricultural scientists involved in producing new and higher yielding strains of rice will pick differences that are not apparent to even the most enthusiastic rice eater. But, from the Asian consumer's viewpoint, the rice has qualities that a Westerner would not even notice — colour, fragrance, flavour, texture.

The average Asian can tell blindfold, merely by smelling a dish of cooked rice, what kind of rice it is.

Rice buyers are so trained to recognise different types of rice that they can hold a few grains in the palm to warm it, sniff it through the hole made by thumb and forefinger, and know its age, its variety, even perhaps where it was grown. Old rice is sought after and prized more than new rice because it tends to cook fluffy and separate, even if the cook absent-mindedly adds too much water. Generally speaking the white polished grains — whether long and fine or small and pearly (much smaller than what we know as short grain rice) — are considered best.

The desirable features of rice are not the same in every Asian country. In India and Pakistan, Sri Lanka and Burma, fluffy, dry rice is preferred. Long, thin grains are considered best and rice is cooked with salt. The most deadful thing a cook could do is forget to salt the rice.

In Malaysia, Indonesia, Thailand and Vietnam rice is preferred dry and separate, but it is cooked without salt.

Further East, medium or short grain varieties come into their own. In Laos, Cambodia, China, Korea and Japan the requirement is rice that is perfectly cooked but not dry and fluffy. Glossy, pearly grains are desired, each one well defined and separate, but with a tendency to cling together so that it can easily be picked up with chopsticks. Again, no salt is used. Laotians are different from all other rice eaters in that they prefer sticky or glutinous rice to other varieties, whereas in most countries it is used only for sweets or leaf-wrapped snacks.

During World War II, when popular kinds of rice were in short supply, the rice distributed on the ration was extremely unpopular because it had a strong (though not unpleasant) aroma. 'Ha!' said the householders. 'How can we eat this? It is the rice we used to give to the dogs.'

Yes, at least three different kinds of rice used to be bought regularly in a household: rice for the master and his family, usually white and polished; unpolished rice for the servants, despised by the moneyed class, though research has shown it is by far the more wholesome; and rice for the animals, a cheap variety with a smell considered unpleasant.

However, every kind of rice is treated with respect that is almost reverence, for the rice crop is literally a matter of life and death in the crowded lands of Asia. I remember, as a child, once making the mistake of climbing on to the large wooden chest or 'rice box' in which the month's supply of rice was stored. And I remember, too, my *ayah* (native nurse), who almost never rebuked me, telling me sternly to get off and show proper respect for the rice. Rice figures largely in religious ceremonies, is a symbol of prosperity and fertility, and a number of superstitions have grown up around it.

Even the Western world has adopted some of the symbolism of rice, for example the throwing of rice at weddings. But where the Western rice eater is concerned, the choice that has to be made is comparatively simple. Rice is sold either packaged or in bulk and there is polished white rice — long, medium or short grain; unpolished or natural rice — medium or long grain; and in many countries it is possible to buy an aromatic table rice grown in Bangladesh, called Basmati rice. In some parts of India this is known as Dehra Dun rice. Patna rice, which is more commonly known, is also a table rice with long fine grains, but does not have the aroma that distinguishes the true Basmati. However, Basmati is expensive. In dishes where spices and flavourings are added and cooked with the rice, any type of long grain rice may be used.

In each recipe in this book the type of rice best suited is recommended, but as a general rule remember that medium or short grain rice gives a clinging result and long grain rice, properly cooked, is fluffy and separate.

To wash or not to wash. Among Asian cooks there will never be agreement on whether rice should be washed or not. Some favour washing the rice several times, then leaving it to soak for a while. Other good cooks insist that washing rice is stupid and wasteful, taking away what vitamins and nutrients are left after the milling process.

I have found that most rice grown in Australia does not need washing but that rice imported in bulk and packaged here picks up a lot of dust and dirt and needs thorough washing.

If rice must be fried before liquid is added, the washed rice must be allowed enough time to thoroughly drain and dry, from 30-60 minutes. Rice to be steamed must be soaked overnight. Rice for cooking by the absorption method, without previously being fried, may be washed or not, drained briefly and added to the pot immediately.

To cook rice perfectly. Though details are given in every rice recipe, here is a general rule regarding proportions of rice and liquid.

Long grain rice: 2 cups water for first cup of rice, 1½ cups of water for each additional cup of rice.

> 1 cup rice — 2 cups water
> 2 cups rice — 3½ cups water
> 3 cups rice — 5 cups water
> . . . and so on.

Short or medium grain rice: 1½ cups water for the first cup of rice and 1 cup water for each additional cup of rice.

> 1 cup rice — 1½ cups water
> 2 cups rice — 2½ cups water
> 3 cups rice — 3½ cups water

Bring rice and water to a bubbling boil over high heat, then turn heat as low as it will go, cover pan tightly and cook for 20 minutes. Remove from heat, uncover pan and let steam escape for a few minutes before fluffing rice with fork. Transfer rice to serving dish with a slotted metal spoon, for a wooden spoon will crush the grains.

You will notice that long grain rice absorbs considerably more water than short or medium grain, so the two kinds are not interchangeable in recipes.

COCONUT MILK

I have heard many people refer to the clear liquid inside a coconut as 'coconut milk'; I have even read it in books. So, at the risk of boring those who already know, let's establish right away what coconut milk really is. It's the milky liquid extracted from the grated flesh of mature fresh coconuts or reconstituted from desiccated coconut (dried shredded coconut).

Coconut milk is an important ingredient in the cookery of nearly all Asian countries. It is used in soups, curries, savoury meat or fish mixtures and all kinds of desserts. It has an unmistakable flavour and richness and should be used in recipes that call for it. This should present no difficulty, for even in countries where fresh coconuts are not available it is simple to make.

Before I start to cook I make all the coconut milk I am going to need. I strongly recommend this routine so that you're not stopped in your tracks in the middle of a recipe.

Coconut milk is extracted in two stages. The first yield being the 'thick milk', the second 'thin milk'. Use a mixture of first and second extracts when a recipe calls for coconut milk unless thick milk or thin milk is specified. Sometimes they are added at different stages of the recipe. In some recipes you use 'coconut cream'. This is the rich layer that rises to the top of the thick milk (or first extract) after it has been left to stand for a while.

Using desiccated coconut: Many cooks use desiccated coconut for making milk. Nine times out of ten I do, too. It is much easier and quicker to prepare than grating fresh coconut, and in curries you cannot tell the difference.

Put 2 cups desiccated coconut in a large bowl and pour over 2½ cups hot water. Allow to cool to lukewarm, then knead firmly with the hand for a few minutes and strain through a fine strainer or a piece of muslin, squeezing out as much liquid as possible. This should produce approximately 1½ cups *thick* coconut milk.

Repeat the process using the same coconut and 2½ cups more hot water. This extract will yield approximately 2 cups *thin* coconut milk. (Because of the moisture retained in the coconut the first time, the second extract usually yields more milk.)

Using a blender: With an electric blender you save time and a lot of hard work. Put 2 cups desiccated coconut and 2½ cups hot water in blender container, cover and blend for 30 seconds. Strain through a fine sieve or piece of muslin, squeezing out all the moisture. Repeat process, using the same coconut and 2½ cups more hot water.

Sometimes a richer milk is required. For this, hot milk replaces the water and only the first extract is used. However, a second extract will yield a flavourful and reasonably rich grade of coconut milk that can be used in soups, curries or other dishes.

Using fresh coconut: In Asian countries, fresh coconut is used and a coconut grater is standard equipment in every household. Grating fresh coconut is easy if you have the right implement for the job. There are various types of coconut graters; the most successful one, and the easiest to use, screws on to the edge of a table, like a mincing machine. It has a number of curved, serrated blades that meet at a central point like a citrus juice extractor. By turning the handle with one hand and holding a half coconut in position with the other, it is possible to grate all the white flesh with no danger of slipping knives or skinned knuckles. (See picture page 16).

However, if you are able to get fresh coconuts and do not have this sort of implement, use the electric blender both to pulverise the coconut and to extract the milk. First crack the nut in two by hitting it with the back of a heavy kitchen chopper on the middle of the nut. Once a crack has appeared, insert the thin edge of the blade and prise it open. Save the sweet liquid inside for drinking. Put the two halves of the nut into a low oven and in 15 or 20 minutes the flesh will start to come away from the shell. Lift it out with the point of a knife, and peel away the thin dark brown skin that clings to the white portion. Cut into chunks, put into container of electric blender with 2 cups milk or water and blend at high speed until coconut is completely pulverised. Strain out liquid, repeat using more water and the same coconut.

To extract fresh coconut milk by hand, grate the pieces of white meat finely and to each cup of grated coconut add a cup of hot water, knead thoroughly and strain out the liquid. Repeat process a second and even a third time, adding hot water.

CHILLIES — HANDLE WITH CARE

Fresh chillies are used in most Asian food, particularly that of Southeast Asia. If mild flavouring is required, simply wash the chilli and add it to the dish when simmering, then lift out and discard the chilli before serving. But if you want the authentic fiery quality of the dish and decide to use the chillies seeded and chopped as the Asians do, then equip yourself with disposable plastic or well-fitting rubber gloves. (Loose, clumsy gloves are difficult to work in.)

Remove stalk of chilli and make a slit to remove the seeds, scraping them out with the tip of a small, sharp knife; or, cut the chilli in two lengthways and remove the central membrane together with the seeds. The seeds are the hottest part of the chilli. If you wish to make some of the fiery hot sambals, the chillies are used seeds and all — generally ground or puréed in a blender (e.g., *sambal bajak* and *sambal ulek* in the Indonesian chapter).

If you handle (i.e., cut or chop) chillies without gloves, after doing so wash your hands thoroughly with soap and warm water. Chillies can be so hot that even two or three good washings do not stop the tingling sensation, which can go on for hours. If this happens, remember to keep your hands well away from your eyes, lips or where the skin is especially sensitive — and in particular, don't touch young children.

Dried chillies: There are large and small dried chillies; those called for in any of the following recipes are the large variety. If frying them as an accompaniment to a meal, use them whole, dropping them straight into hot oil. If they are being soaked and ground as part of the spicing for a sambal, sauce or curry, first break or snip off the stalk end and shake the chilli so that the seeds fall out. They are safe enough to handle until they have been soaked and ground, but if you handle them after this has been done, remember to wash your hands at once with soap and water. Dried chillies, though they give plenty of heat and flavour, do not have as much effect on the skin as fresh chillies with their volatile oils.

KNOW YOUR ONIONS

This indispensable bulb, used all over the world, varies from country to country and from season to season. Onions range from tiny red onions of pickling size to those as large as grapefruit. As a result, when a large onion is stipulated it could mean different things to different people.

To introduce some uniformity in judging the size of onions, here is a guide. A large onion is one that weighs over 250 g (8 oz); a medium onion is about 125 g (4 oz); a small onion weighs in around 60 g (2 oz). Weigh some onions to get an idea of the sizes and it will save you much deliberation.

Flavour and pungency also vary tremendously, but I expect your discretion and judgement as a cook to tell you when to increase or decrease the quantity. The small purple shallots so widely used in Asian countries are not easily available in Australia, so recipes have been tested using the common white or brown onion. If you do get hold of some shallots use them by all means, but in a smaller quantity than onion, and be sure to cook them very carefully and not let them burn.

Spring onions are also useful in Oriental food and usually both white and green parts go into the recipe unless otherwise stated. Strangely, in Australia the spring onion is called a shallot; spring onions are also known as green onions or scallions in the United States. Those best for the purpose are straight, without a large, well-developed bulb.

CUTTING A CHICKEN FOR CURRY

I have often referred to cutting a chicken into 'curry pieces'. This is simply cutting the pieces smaller than joints so that the spices can more readily penetrate and flavour all the meat. A 1.5 kg (3 lb) chicken, for instance, can be jointed, then each thigh cut into two with a heavy cleaver; the breast is divided down the centre, then each half cut into 2 pieces; wings are divided into two, cutting at the first joint and leaving the wing tip attached to the second joint; the back is cut into 4 pieces and used in curry, though not counted as serving pieces because there is very little meat on them. Neck and giblets are also included to give extra flavour.

CUTTING A CHICKEN
THE CHINESE WAY

After cooking, a whole chicken is divided through the centre lengthways with a sharp, heavy cleaver. Then turn each half, cut side down, on a sturdy wooden chopping board and chop crossways into 3.5

cm (1½ inch) strips. Reassemble on serving plate. If this seems a formidable task, start by cutting off the drumstick, thigh and wing. Chop each of these into two pieces. Then use the cleaver to cut the chicken through. With a good Chinese cleaver this is not as difficult as it sounds.

CUTTING FISH STEAKS
INTO SERVING PIECES

Depending on the size of the fish, each steak may need to be cut into 4, 6 or 8 pieces. Once again, smaller portions are better, for they allow flavours to penetrate and you can allow more than one piece per person. The accompanying sketch shows how to divide fish steaks — small ones into 4 pieces, medium-sized ones into 6 pieces and really large steaks into 8 pieces.

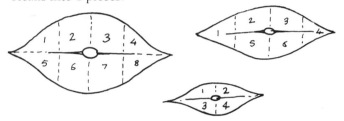

HOW TO PREPARE A
PINEAPPLE FOR EATING

To peel a pineapple without wasting much of the edible portion, cut off a thin layer of skin with a sharp (preferably stainless) knife. The 'eyes', placed neatly in spiral rows, will be clearly seen. Cut out the eyes, 3 at a time, in a series of diagonal cuts. This is not only an economical way to prepare a pineapple, but also decorative.

INTRODUCTION TO THE REVISED EDITION

In 1975, with two small books on the subject to my credit, I was asked to write this book — over 500 pages on the cooking of Asia. It was a formidable task, but I could not resist the challenge of sharing the culinary traditions of Asia with people who live in western countries and cook in western kitchens.

The Complete Asian Cookbook was first published in 1976 and has been reprinted almost every year since then. It has also been translated into German, French and Dutch.

We now bring you an updated edition, for in the intervening years I have learned a great deal, and continue to learn. The recipes are still used all the time in my own kitchen, but things do not remain static; ingredients have become available internationally which at one time were only sold where they were grown.

Cooking is a living, developing art. New cooks bring fresh ideas to a cuisine, and experienced cooks find there are better and easier ways of achieving the same results. I am glad to be able to share with readers ways of making Asian cooking in western kitchens even easier.

The world is changing rapidly, and in no way has it changed more rapidly than in the spread of popularity of Asian cooking through travel and immigration. Witness the way Japanese, Thai and Vietnamese restaurants have mushroomed in diverse places. Chinese restaurants, of course, seem always to have been there in most countries. With the movement of migrants and refugees has come an abundance of Asian ingredients throughout the western world, bringing authentic Asian flavours within everyone's grasp.

While I still use the recipes I wrote so many years ago, I find there are ways to cut down preparation time by taking advantage of modern appliances. Food processors have become commonplace, for instance, taking much of the work and most of the tears from chopping onions.

Recipes taste even better now because it is possible to buy fresh ingredients which were not available when the original book was written. For instance, I can now buy lemon grass at suburban greengrocers or purchase a plant at a nursery and grow my own supply. If this had been the case when I was writing this book, I would never had thought of resorting to dried lemon grass. For those who still cannot obtain it, don't worry, a thinly peeled strip of lime or lemon zest is a good substitute.

In my original recipe for laksa (prawn soup, which is a specialty of Singapore and Malaysia) I can now include laksa leaf, also known as Vietnamese mint, Cambodian mint, daun kesom, phak pheo.

Its botanical name is *polygonum odoratum*, and it is not a member of the mint family at all. You won't find it in the first edition because in those days it was not grown outside Southeast Asia, but ten years or so later, here it is — in markets, plant nurseries and Asian greengrocers. Its distinctive flavour and tingling taste are an essential part of laksa.

From having to buy galangal (laos, lengkuas, kha) in dried form, we can now find it fresh, frozen or pickled in brine. On this subject, when a teaspoon of dried laos powder is called for in the original recipe, I would advise the use of a tablespoon of chopped galangal in brine instead. Unfortunately, galangal is not one of those ingredients which has an acceptable substitute. There is nothing with a flavour quite like it, and while it may be omitted, when available it adds a certain something. Galangal is available in Asian groceries in most major cities. Also available, fresh or frozen, are fragrant pandanus leaves, curry leaves and kaffir lime leaves.

After buying cellophane (bean starch) noodles for years in large packets and nearly blistering my fingers trying to cut off the amount I needed with a pair of scissors, it is a joy indeed to be able to purchase them already divided into small 50 g skeins.

The vexed question of the Great Saffron Rip-off continues. My warning in the glossary that there is no such thing as cheap saffron still holds good; but now the producers of spurious "saffron" charge so much that anyone could be forgiven for thinking they are getting the real thing. Buyer beware! Buy only from reputable dealers, preferably a chef's supplier. Saffron will last indefinitely, stored airtight in the freezer. To make it go further, toast lightly in a dry pan for a minute or so, taking care not to let the delicate strands burn. Turn onto a saucer, crush to powder with the back of a spoon, and dissolve in hot water before adding to a dish and letting it release its unique flavour.

Yet, there are some things which never change. While many new curry pastes, powders and garam masalas have appeared on the shelves, I have yet to find one which comes anywhere near the quality of what you make yourself. I urge you to try the Thai curry pastes in the chapter on Thailand, and the garam masala in the Indian chapter. Compare them with commercial products and judge for yourself.

When I wrote *The Complete Asian Cookbook*, the only way to obtain good coconut milk outside the countries where coconuts grow was to extract it from desiccated (dried, shredded) coconut; so I gave detailed instructions for this procedure. Since there are still areas where canned coconut milk is not available, the instructions are there, on pages 11 and 12. Nowadays, however almost every supermarket in major cities carries coconut milk in cans, and using canned coconut milk certainly saves time and effort.

Make sure the coconut milk you buy is the unsweetened variety. Read the ingredients listing — there should be only coconut and water. It is better to avoid those brands which contain a stabilizer and preservatives. My method of choosing a good brand is to buy a few different cans, open them all at the same time and assess them. Some contain milk that is thick, rich and white. Other kinds of milk are thinner but still very good. The should all smell and taste fresh and pleasant and naturally sweet. Occasionally you may find a can which has grayish, oily contents and smells somewhat rancid. These I would avoid. Thankfully, quality is generally good and it is years since I had to throw out an unsatisfactory can of coconut milk. Having noted the brand which is best, what to do with all the cans you've opened? Stir with a spoon to disperse the richness evenly, and pour the contents of each can into an ice-cube tray. Freeze. When frozen solid, pop the cubes out of the trays and into freezer bags and use as required.

Delicious as it is, we must remember that coconut milk is full of saturated fat and is not to be indulged in recklessly. With this in mind, I suggest that only where "coconut cream" is required should canned coconut milk be used undiluted. Where "thick coconut milk" is called for, dilute the bought product with half its volume of water, that is, one cup of canned coconut milk to half cup of water. Where "coconut milk" is called for, dilute with an equal amount of water. Where thin coconut milk is specified, dilute canned coconut milk with two parts by volume of water.

Remember those cubes of frozen coconut milk? Use two or three to a cup of water to make up the amount of liquid called for in the dish. The sauce won't be as rich and smooth, but if you cook and eat Asian food frequently, it makes sense to cut down on the proportion of fat.

In the original edition, I included two pages on "Where to buy Asian ingredients". Today, this is hardly necessary, because any aficionado of Asian food knows in which corner of the supermarket or delicatessen he or she will find a good selection, and indeed there is often more than one Asian grocer in any suburban shopping centre.

It is all very well to be able to cook, but for me, writing down recipes so other people can get the same results was no simple task. It meant cooking over again the familiar dishes, this time weighing and measuring instead of shaking a bottle of sauce or spice or seasoning over the dish until it tasted as it should. It became a labour of love, and required discipline, but I'm glad I had to do it. The result is that every dish can be successfully recreated from this book, and I can pass on to my children and to their children the legacy of a tradition of Asian cuisine; a cuisine whose magic is woven through a host of my childhood memories, and years of living in Asian lands.

GUIDE TO WEIGHTS & MEASURES

NOTE: For successful cooking use either metric weights and measures **or** imperial weights and measures — do **not** use a mixture of the two.

WEIGHT, VOLUME AND LIQUID MEASURES

In all recipes, imperial equivalents of metric measures are shown in parentheses, e.g. 500 g (1 lb) lean beef. Although the metric yield of cup or weighed measures is approximately 10% greater, the proportions remain the same.

Lists of ingredients in this book have been designed to cater for cooks using either American Standard measures or metric measures, as can be seen from the following example:

> 1.5 kg (3 lb) chicken
> 3 cups water
> 2 large onions
> 5 tablespoons flour
> ½ cup milk

This listing can be read in two ways:

American	Metric
3 pound chicken	1.5 kilogram chicken
3 AMERICAN cups water	3 METRIC cups water
2 large onions	2 large onions
5 AMERICAN table-spoons flour	5 METRIC tablespoons flour
½ AMERICAN cup milk	½ METRIC cup milk

It must be stressed that the quantities given in the American and metric ingredients listings are in proportion, but they are NOT exact conversions — the metric yield is approximately 10 per cent greater than the equivalent American Standard yield. Therefore, to use this book successfully, follow American Standard quantities **or** follow metric quantities **but** do **not** use a mixture of the two.

Using metric measures

The metric measuring cup specified in this book has a capacity of **250 millilitres** (250 ml). Clearly graduated metric measuring cups and jugs can therefore be used for all liquid and dry cup quantities given in the recipes. Note that:

¼ metric cup	=	60 ml
½ metric cup	=	125 ml
¾ metric cup	=	185 ml
1 metric cup	=	250 ml = ¼ litre
2 metric cups	=	500 ml = ½ litre
3 metric cups	=	750 ml = ¾ litre
4 metric cups	=	1,000 ml = 1 litre

The American Standard teaspoon and tablespoon can be used for measuring metric quantities. The American teaspoon has exactly the same capacity as the metric teaspoon specified in this book:

1 metric teaspoon = 5 ml = 1 American teaspoon

Grating coconut for **extracting milk** (*instructions page 11, 12*).

INDIA &
PAKISTAN

Indian spices, dried Bombay duck (*foreground*) and various lentils, fresh chillies, coriander herb and okra (*background*).

Most Westerners, asked what food they associate with the Indian subcontinent, will say 'curry', but not every spiced dish is a curry, and curry is not just one dish. It embraces a whole range of dishes, each distinctly different according to the spices and herbs used in varying combinations.

Spices, imaginatively used, are the outstanding feature of Indian and Pakistani cookery — subtle or pungent, hot or mild, there is something to suit every palate.

Much of the cooking of northwestern India and Pakistan (formerly West Pakistan) is so similar that I, for one, would hesitate to say which dishes belong to one country and which to the other. Pakistan, being a Muslim country, uses no pork; but it boasts a diet rich in other meats and has as many sumptuous *biriani* and *pilau* as does the celebrated Moghul cuisine of the neighbouring Indian provinces; lamb is predominant in both areas, and both use spicing and ingredients such as yoghurt and ghee in dishes that are elaborate without being hot; both, too, rely more heavily on wheat-flour *chapati* than on rice.

Bangladesh (formely East Pakistan) is more than 1,500 kilometres (900 miles) from Pakistan. With the eastern Indian province of Bengal, of which it was once a part, it shares more pungent spicing, a tendency to cook in mustard oil rather than ghee, and emphasis on a variety of seafood instead of the fat lamb popular in northwestern India and Pakistan.

The culinary offerings of southern India are different again. The coconut plays a commanding role, rice largely replaces wheat, mustard seeds are widely used as a spice, and chillies come into their own — as anyone who has tackled a really hot Madras or Mysore curry will readily acknowledge!

Throughout the subcontinent, different religions impose food taboos that are rigidly adhered to. Hindus will not eat beef. Muslims will not eat pork. Buddhists will not take life and so will not even crack an egg. And many Indians are strictly vegetarian, enjoying a cuisine that is in a class by itself — and could convert the most dedicated meat eater! It included superb curries; *bartha* (purees) and *bhaji* (fried vegetable); *pakorha* (fritters) and *vadai* (rissoles of lentils and pulses); home-made bread with spiced vegetable fillings; high-protein dishes based on lentils and home-made cheeses; and rich sweetmeats made with vegetables and fruit.

When I think of Indian sweets I think of an Indian sweetmaker I knew. He was over six feet tall, had a ruddy complexion, dark hair and dark flashing eyes. I guessed his age at around sixty, but he stood erect and looked strong and healthy, and he was one of the proudest, most dignified men I have ever met.

I cannot remember ever seeing him smile. While not surly, he saw no reason to smile at his customers. Was it not enough that they were able to purchase the exquisite work of his hands?

His shop, which nestled close to a Hindu temple covered by stone carvings of gods, goddesses, mortals and animals, was stark and unrelieved by any kind of decoration. Inside there was only a glass showcase to protect the sweetmeats from the ever-present flies. Further inside, partly hidden by a curtain, was the small stone fireplace on the stone floor where he squatted on his heels to prepare his delicacies. In the bazaar area were a variety of lesser sweets, but he made only the expensive, exquisite, rich varieties and his clientele knew they were privileged to taste the work of a master craftsman and cheerfully paid his high prices.

Eastern sweetmakers are a race unto themselves. They guard their secrets as jealously as they guard their money and yet, somehow, the secrets leak out. Recipes, good and not quite so good, are printed in cookbooks. But they are no great'threat to the sweetmakers, for who would take the trouble to make these morsels? As long as I lived in the East, I was content to buy the sweetmeats. But when we settled in a Western country where such sweets were unobtainable, I knew it was necessary to do something about it.

And so began the search for recipes, the repeated experiments, the ultimate triumph. Was it worth it? Oh yes! Once you have tasted rose and cardamom-scented *rasgula, barfi, gulab jaman*, you will not rest until you know that you can make the glorious confections yourself. If you have a sweet tooth and a taste for the exotic, you will enjoy the recipes in that section as much as I do.

SERVING AN INDIAN MEAL

In southern India, banana leaves are often used as plates, but more universal is the *thali* service — the *thali* being a circular metal tray on which are placed a number of small bowls called *katori*, also made of metal. Rice or *chapati* are placed directly on the tray; curries and other accompaniments are served in the bowls. The food is eaten with the fingers of the right hand only, for it is considered impolite to use the 'unclean' left hand to touch food.

Some orthodox Hindus feel that spoons, forks and plates that are used again and again are quite unhygienic, but in most Indian cities Western customs have taken over and food is served on dinner plates and eaten with dessertspoon and fork.

Rice is served first in the centre of the plate, then various curries and accompaniments are placed around it. The rice is the base, and only one curry should be tasted with each mouthful of rice in order to appreciate the individual spicing of each dish.

The matter of proportions is all-important. One needs to forget the Western idea of a large amount of meat or fish with a small amount of rice. Rice is the main part of the meal and curries of meat, fish or vegetables should be served in much smaller portions. There is wisdom in this too, because when food is spiced it needs the bland background of rice to delight the palate and placate the digestion.

When eating Indian breads with a meal, there is no choice but to eat with one's fingers. Tear off a piece of *chapati* or *paratha*, use it to scoop up the accompaniment, fold it over neatly, then eat it. Just as Chinese or Japanese food tastes better eaten with chopsticks, Indian food tastes better eaten with the fingers. Fingerbowls are provided, of course.

What to drink with an Indian meal has always been the subject of much argument. Cold water is the most authentic, but many Indians prefer a sweet drink such as *sharbat gulab* or *falooda*. These are certainly effective in quenching fiery spices. For those who want an alcoholic beverage, a chilled lager or shandy, or wine cup using a semi-sweet white wine or rosé wine is permissible, but fine dry wines and curries just do not go together. One warning: carbonated or 'fizzy' drinks, including lager beer, tend to exaggerate the burning sensation of a really hot curry; so does ice-cold water.

UTENSILS FOR COOKING

Believe me, the Western housewife with her gas and electric appliances can cook any kind of food with less effort than the Indian housewife with her primitive equipment.

The brass *degchi* used throughout India is like a saucepan without handles. The sides are straight and have a horizontal rim. The flat lid fits over the rim of the pan, and is sometimes sealed with a flour and water paste, making a sort of oven or steam cooker out of the pan, for what is called *dum* cooking. Hot coals are put on the lid to provide cooking heat from above as well as below, for ovens are almost unknown in the average Indian household. Nowadays the *degchi* is also made from aluminium.

Saucepans with well-fitting lids are just as suitable as a *degchi*, and a casserole in the oven is the answer to *dum* cooking. Wooden spoons substitute for the coconut-shell spoons mostly used in India, and a deep frying pan takes the place of the *karahi,* a rounded pan used for frying. A griddle or heavy iron plate replaces the *tawa* on which *chapati* or *paratha* are cooked; even a heavy frying pan will do. The ever-present grinding stone for spices, and the coconut grater, are replaced by the versatile electric blender; failing that, use a mortar and pestle for spices.

YOUR INDIAN SHELF

These ingredients will put the whole range of Indian spice dishes at your fingertips. Fresh ingredients are not included, only those that have a good shelf life. Buy in small quantities and store in airtight jars away from heat and direct sunlight.

black cummin seeds
black mustard seeds
black peppercorns, whole and ground
besan (chick pea flour)
cardamom, whole pods and ground
cinnamon sticks
chilli powder
cloves, whole and ground
coriander, seeds and ground
cummin, seeds and ground
curry leaves
creamed coconut
desiccated coconut
fennel, seeds and ground
fenugreek, whole seeds and ground
garam masala (recipes page 35)
ghee
mace, ground
nutmeg, whole
panch phora (recipe page 22)
rose water or rose essence
Spanish saffron
turmeric, ground

Optional extras
amchur
asafoetida
aromatic ginger, ground
tandoori mix

OTHER INGREDIENTS

Besides the all-important spices there are a few ingredients used in Indian and Pakistani cooking that may be unfamiliar but that are readily available or, if not, can be made at home:

PANIR: Home-made cream cheese. Bring milk to the boil, stirring occasionally to prevent a skin forming on top. As the milk starts to rise in the pan, stir in lemon juice in the proportion of 1 tablespoon to 2½ cups milk. Remove from heat and let stand for 5 minutes, by which time firm curds will have formed. Strain through muslin. Let it hang for at least 30 minutes, then press to remove as much moisture as possible. If it has to be very firm, weight it down and leave for some hours in a cool place. This is necessary when it is cut into cubes and cooked with vegetable dishes, such as in *mattar panir* on page 76. It may be added to any of the vegetable preparations for extra nutrition.

KHOA: Unsweetened condensed milk made by boiling milk quickly in a shallow pan (such as a large, heavy frying pan) to allow for as much surface evaporation as possible. It must be stirred constantly. When ready, *khoa* has the consistency of uncooked pastry. Four cups of milk yield about 90 g (3 oz) of khoa. It is an ingredient in Indian sweetmeats.

MALAI: Thick cream. This is not the separated cream sold commercially, but is collected from the top of the milk. The milk is kept boiling steadily in a wide pan, usually with a fan playing on the surface to cool the top of the milk and hasten formation of the skin. When cool, the skin is removed and the process repeated. It is possible to buy this type of cream from Lebanese shops, where it is called *ashtar*.

PANCH PHORA: 'Panch' means five in Hindi, and *panch phora* is a combination of five different aromatic seeds. These are used whole and, when added to the cooking oil, impart a flavour typical of certain Indian dishes. Combine 2 tablespoons each of black mustard seed, cummin seed and black cummin seed, 1 tablespoon each of fenugreek seed and fennel seed. Put into a glass jar with a tight fitting lid. Shake before use to ensure even distribution. No substitute.

OILS FOR COOKING: Different oils used in various parts of India give the cookery of each region its distinctive flavour. *Til* (sesame) seed oil and coconut oil are much used in southern India, and in Bengal the favourite cooking medium is mustard oil. It is up to your personal taste what type of oil you use, but olive oil is not used in Indian cooking. A tasteless oil such as maize or sunflower oil is best, and may be flavoured with ghee.

GHEE: Clarified butter or pure butterfat. It is what gives the rich, distinctive flavour to north Indian cooking. Having no milk solids it can be heated to much higher temperatures than butter without burning. It is sold in cans, packets or tubs.

If you find it difficult to buy ghee, make your own by heating butter in a saucepan until it melts and froths. Spoon off foam from the top and pour the melted butter into a heatproof glass bowl, discarding the milk solids in the pan. Leave to cool to room temperature, then chill until set. Spoon off the fat from the top, leaving residue. Heat the fat again, then strain through fine muslin to remove any remaining solids. This will keep for three or four months without refrigeration.

YOGHURT: In India this is called *dahi* or curd and is always unflavoured. Natural yoghurt should be used, and if possible choose one with a definite sour flavour. I have found that goat-milk yoghurt or Greek yoghurt is most suitable.

SABZI PILAU (rice with vegetables) *recipe page 24*

NAMKIN CHAWAL
PLAIN SAVOURY RICE

Rice is the staple food in southern, central and eastern parts of India and when eaten at an Indian meal forms the major part of the meal. Served Indian-style, this quantity will serve two.

Serves: 2-4
1¼ cups long grain rice
2 teaspoons ghee
2½ cups hot water
1 teaspoon salt

Wash rice well if necessary. Drain in colander for 30 minutes. Heat ghee in a heavy-based saucepan with a well-fitting lid. Add rice and fry, stirring for about 2 minutes. Add hot water and salt, stir and bring quickly to the boil. Turn heat very low, cover tightly and cook, without lifting lid or stirring, for 20-25 minutes. Lift lid to allow steam to escape for a minute or two, then lightly fluff up rice with fork, taking care not to mash the grains, which will be firm and separate and perfectly cooked. Dish up using a slotted metal spoon rather than a wooden spoon, which will crush the grains. Serve with curries or other spiced dishes.

KITCHRI
SAVOURY RICE AND LENTILS

Serves: 4-6
1 cup long grain rice
1 cup red lentils
2½ tablespoons ghee
2 medium onions, finely sliced
5 cups hot water
2½ teaspoons salt
1½ teaspoons garam masala (page 35)

Wash rice and drain well. Wash lentils well, removing any that float to the surface, then drain thoroughly.

Heat ghee in a saucepan and fry onion gently until golden brown. Remove half the onion and reserve. Add rice and lentils to pan and fry, stirring constantly, for about 3 minutes. Add hot water, salt and garam masala. Bring to the boil, cover and simmer over very low heat for 20-25 minutes or until rice and lentils are cooked. Do not lift the lid or stir during cooking time. Serve hot, garnished with reserved fried onion.

Note: This is a soft kitchri with the consistency of porridge. If a drier, fluffier result is desired, reduce water to 3½ cups. Also, whole spices, i.e. small cinnamon stick and a few whole cloves, cardamoms and peppercorns may be used instead of garam masala.

SABZI PILAU
RICE WITH VEGETABLES *(picture page 23)*

Serves: 5-6
2 tablespoons ghee
2 tablespoons oil
2 medium onions, finely sliced
1 clove garlic, finely chopped
2 cups long grain rice
4 cups hot water
2 teaspoons salt
1 teaspoon garam masala (page 35)
2 carrots cut into matchstick pieces
12 green beans, thinly sliced
½ cup diced red or green capsicum
1 small potato, peeled and cubed
½ cup fresh or frozen peas

Heat ghee and oil in a large, heavy saucepan with a well-fitting lid. Over low heat cook onion for 10 minutes or until soft and pale golden. Add garlic and continue cooking for 2 minutes. Add rice, raise heat to medium and fry for 2 minutes. Add hot water, salt, garam masala. Bring to the boil over high heat and when bubbling turn heat very low, cover pan and cook for 10 minutes. Add vegetables (do not stir) and sprinkle with an extra teaspoon of salt. Replace lid and cook for a further 10-15 minutes until vegetables are tender but not overcooked. Leave pan uncovered for a few minutes then fluff up with fork, mixing the vegetables through the rice. Use a slotted metal spoon to pile rice on serving dish. If liked, garnish with fried almonds and sultanas. Serve with curries.

MATTAR PILAU
RICE WITH FRESH GREEN PEAS

1 tablespoon ghee or oil
4 whole cloves
1 small cinnamon stick
2 cardamom pods
1 teaspoon cummin seeds
½ teaspoon ground turmeric, optional
1¼ cups long grain rice
1¼ cups shelled green peas
2 teaspoons salt
2½ cups hot water

Heat ghee in a heavy saucepan and fry the cloves, cinnamon, cardamom and cummin over medium heat for 1 minute. Add turmeric and rice and fry for 2 minutes, stirring. Add peas, salt, water and bring to the boil over high heat, then turn heat very low, cover tightly and cook for 25 minutes without lifting lid or stirring. Fork up and remove whole cloves, cinnamon and cardamom. Serve hot with vegetable or meat dishes.

PARSI PILAU
SPICED RICE, PARSI STYLE

Serves: 5-6
2½ cups long grain rice
½ teaspoon saffron strands
2 tablespoons boiling water
2 tablespoons ghee
4 cardamom pods, bruised
1 small cinnamon stick
4 whole cloves
10 black peppercorns
4 cups hot water
2½ teaspoons salt
rind of 1 orange, finely grated
2 tablespoons sultanas
2 tablespoons blanched sliced almonds
2 tablespoons blanched halved pistachios

If rice needs washing, do so and leave to drain and dry thoroughly. Soak saffron in boiling water for 10 minutes. Heat ghee in heavy saucepan and gently fry cardamom, cinnamon, cloves and peppercorns for 2 minutes. Add rice and continue stirring and frying for 2 or 3 minutes. Add hot water, salt, soaked saffron strands and liquid, orange rind. Stir well and bring quickly to the boil, then turn heat very low, cover tightly and cook for 20 minutes. At end of this time scatter sultanas over surface of rice, replace lid and continue cooking for 5 minutes longer. Serve garnished with almonds and pistachios. This is very good served with dhansak, a famous Parsi dish of meat or chicken cooked with lentils and vegetables (page 47).

KESAR PILAU
SAFFRON AND LEMON SWEET PILAU

Serves: 4-6
1 tablespoon ghee
6 cardamom pods, bruised
4 whole cloves
1 small stick cinnamon
1¼ cups long grain rice
2 cups hot water
¼ cup lemon juice
1 tablespoon sugar
1 teaspoon salt
¼ teaspoon saffron strands
2 tablespoons very hot water

Heat ghee in a heavy saucepan and fry cardamom pods, cloves and cinnamon for 3 minutes. Add rice and fry, stirring, for 4 or 5 minutes over low heat. Add water, lemon juice, sugar and salt, stir well and bring to the boil over high heat. Turn heat low, cover and cook 10 minutes. Meanwhile pour hot water over saffron strands and allow to soak for 5 minutes. Press the strands between your fingers to extract as much colour as possible. At end of the 10 minutes lift lid of pan and sprinkle saffron water and strands over the rice. Do not stir. Replace lid and cook for a further 10 minutes. Uncover, allow steam to escape for a few minutes, remove whole spices. Fluff rice gently with fork before serving.

JHINGA PILAU
SPICED PRAWNS AND RICE

Serves: 4
500 g (1 lb) raw prawns
1½ cups long grain rice
2 tablespoons ghee
2 tablespoons oil
1 medium onion, finely sliced
3 cloves garlic, finely grated
½ teaspoon finely grated fresh ginger
4 cardamom pods, bruised
4 whole cloves.
small stick of cinnamon
1 teaspoon garam masala (page 35)
½ teaspoon chilli powder, optional
2 fresh red chillies, sliced
1½ teaspoons salt
3 cups hot water
sliced cucumber and fresh coriander
   leaves to garnish

Shell and de-vein prawns. If rice needs washing, allow it to dry well. Heat ghee and oil in a large saucepan with a well-fitting lid. Put in the prawns and fry quickly until they change colour, then remove them from pan. Put in onion, garlic and ginger and fry for a few minutes, stirring frequently. Add whole spices and fry for a minute or two longer, then turn in the rice and fry, stirring, until it is coated with the ghee. Add garam masala, sliced chillies, chilli powder, salt, prawns and hot water. Let it come to a boil then reduce heat to very low, cover tightly and cook for 20 minutes without lifting lid. Serve hot, garnished with thin slices of cucumber and sprinkled over with chopped fresh coriander.

YAKHNI PILAU
RICE COOKED IN STOCK WITH SPICES

Serves: 4-6
1 x 1 kg (2 lb) chicken or 3 lamb shanks
4 cardamom pods
10 whole black peppercorns
4½ teaspoons salt
1 onion
3 whole cloves
2½ cups long grain rice
5 tablespoons ghee
1 large onion, finely sliced
¼ teaspoon saffron strands or 1/8
   teaspoon powdered saffron
2 cloves garlic, crushed
½ teaspoon finely grated fresh ginger
½ teaspoon garam masala (page 35)
½ teaspoon ground cardamom
3 tablespoons rose water
¼ cup sultanas
¼ cup fried almonds
1 cup hot cooked green peas
3 hard-boiled eggs, halved

Make a strong, well-flavoured stock by simmering chicken or lamb in water to cover, with cardamom pods, peppercorns, 2 teaspoons salt and the onion stuck with cloves. Simmer for approximately 2 hours. Cool slightly, strain stock and measure 4 cups. Remove meat from bones, cut into bite-size pieces and set aside.

Wash rice thoroughly in water, drain in a colander and allow to dry for at least 1 hour. Heat ghee in a large saucepan and fry sliced onion until golden. Add saffron, garlic and ginger and fry for 1 minute, stirring constantly. Add rice and fry 5 minutes longer over a moderate heat, stirring with a slotted metal spoon. (This prevents breaking the long delicate grains of rice which add so much to the appearance of this dish.) Add hot stock, garam masala, cardamom, remaining salt, rose water, sultanas and reserved chicken pieces, stir well. Cover pan with a tightly fitting lid and cook over a very low heat for 20 minutes. Do not uncover saucepan or stir rice during cooking time.

When rice is cooked, remove from heat and stand, uncovered, for 5 minutes. Fluff up rice gently with a fork and place in a dish, again using a slotted metal spoon. Garnish with almonds, peas and eggs and serve hot accompanied by pickles, cucumbers in sour cream or yoghurt, and crisp fried pappadams. A curried dish can also be served if liked.

MOGLAI BIRIANI (Moghul biriani) *recipe page 28.*

MOGLAI BIRIANI
MOGHUL BIRIANI *(picture page 27)*

Biriani is a very rich pilau, usually layered with a spicy mutton or chicken savoury mixture and steamed very gently so that the flavours blend.

It is the masterpiece of many Eastern cooks and the central dish at festive dinners. Here is a recipe for a lamb biriani, suitable for serving at a party. Halve all quantities for a smaller number of people, but cooking times remain the same.

Serves: 12-14
Cooking time: 2½ hours
Oven temperature: 160-170ºC (325-350ºF)

1 x 2 kg (4 lb) leg of lamb, boned
5 tablespoons ghee
3 large onions, sliced
6 cloves garlic, chopped
1½ tablespoons finely chopped fresh
   ginger
6 tablespoons curry powder or paste
4 teaspoons salt
2 tablespoons lemon juice
1 teaspoon garam masala (page 35)
1 teaspoon ground cardamom
2 fresh red chillies
½ cup chopped fresh mint
4 ripe tomatoes, peeled and chopped
3 tablespoons chopped fresh coriander
   leaves
yakhni pilau (page 26)
1 tablespoon extra ghee

Lamb Savoury: Trim all excess fat from lamb and cut lean lamb into large cubes. Heat ghee in a saucepan and fry the onion, garlic and ginger until soft and golden. Add curry powder and fry 1 minute longer, then add salt and lemon juice. Add cubed lamb and fry, stirring constantly, until it is thoroughly coated with the spice mixture. Add garam masala, cardamom, whole chillies, mint and tomato.

Cover and cook over a very low heat for approximately 1 hour, stirring occasionally. When lamb is tender and gravy very thick and almost dry turn off heat and remove whole chillies. Sprinkle with chopped coriander leaves.

Pilau (page 26): Double all quantities and leave cooking times the same. Make a strong stock using lamb shanks. Measure 8 cups stock.

When pilau is cooked, allow to cool slightly. Melt extra ghee in a large ovenproof casserole and put in one-third of the pilau, packing it in lightly. Spread half the lamb savoury over, taking it right to the edges of the casserole. Cover with half the remaining pilau. Repeat layers. Put lid on casserole and put in a moderately slow oven for 20-30 minutes. Leave biriani in the dish or turn out on a large serving tray.

To serve, garnish as for pilau. For special occasions, add blanched pistachio nuts and edible silver leaf to the garnish in traditional Indian style.

KEEMA MATTAR PILAU
MINCED MEAT AND PEAS WITH RICE

A wholesome one-dish meal, needing only pickles, sambal or raita as an accompaniment.

Serves: 6

2 cups long grain rice
3 tablespoons ghee or oil
1 teaspoon cummin seeds
1 medium onion, finely chopped
1 clove garlic, crushed
½ teaspoon finely grated fresh ginger
6 whole cloves
250 g (8 oz) minced lamb or beef
2 cups shelled green peas
4 cups hot water
3 teaspoons salt
1 teaspoon garam masala (page 35)

Wash rice if necessary and leave to drain. Heat ghee in a large heavy-based saucepan with a well-fitting lid. Fry the cummin, onion, garlic, ginger and whole cloves until onion is soft and golden brown. Add meat and fry over moderately high heat until meat is browned. Add peas and half cup water, stir well, cover and cook until peas are half done. Add rice and hot water and stir in the salt. Bring quickly to the boil, cover, turn heat very low and cook for 10 minutes. Uncover and sprinkle with garam masala but do not stir. Replace lid and continue cooking for a further 10 minutes or until liquid is all absorbed and rice is cooked through. Serve hot.

KORMA PILAU
RICE WITH SPICED LAMB IN YOGHURT

Serves: 6-8

1 quantity korma (page 60)
1 quantity pilau (page 26) using lamb
   stock or water in place of chicken and
   cooking rice for 15 minutes only

Extra ingredients:
¼ teaspoon saffron strands
¾ cup hot milk
2 tablespoons rose water or few drops rose
   essence
3 drops kewra essence, optional
ghee
slices of firm ripe tomato
1 cucumber, thinly sliced
1 onion, thinly sliced
2 fresh green chillies, thinly sliced
3 hard-boiled eggs, sliced or quartered
3 tablespoons slivered fried almonds

Prepare korma. While pilau is cooking soak the saffron strands in the hot milk and press to diffuse as much as possible of the yellow colour. Mix in the flavourings.

Grease a large ovenproof casserole with ghee and arrange pilau and lamb korma in layers. Sprinkle each layer of rice with the saffron and milk mixture. Finish with a layer of rice. Cover the casserole and cook in a slow oven 150°C (300°F) for 30 minutes. Garnish top with the remaining ingredients and serve hot.

Alternatively, cook pilau for full 20 minutes. Remove two-thirds of the rice from pan in which it was cooked, sprinkle the rice left in the pan with a third of the milk. Put in half the lamb korma, spreading it to sides of pan. Cover with half the rice, sprinkle rice with half the remaining milk. Make a layer of the remaining korma and cover that with the rest of the rice. Sprinkle remaining milk over, cover tightly and leave on *very* low heat for 25-30 minutes. In India they put coals on the lid of the degchi.

CHAPATIS
(*picture page 31*)

Flat discs of unleavened bread, with a delight-ful flavour and chewy texture.

Yield: 20-24

3 cups fine wholemeal flour or roti flour
1-1½ teaspoons salt, or to taste
1 tablespoon ghee or oil, optional
1 cup lukewarm water

Put flour in mixing bowl, reserving about half cup for rolling chapatis. Mix salt through the flour in the bowl, then rub in ghee or oil, if used. Add water all at once and mix to a firm but not stiff dough. Knead dough for at least 10 minutes (the more it is kneaded, the lighter the bread will be). Form dough into a ball, cover with clear plastic wrap and stand for 1 hour or longer. (If left overnight the chapatis will be very light and tender.)

Shape dough into balls about the size of a large walnut. Roll out each one on a lightly floured board (using reserved flour) to a circular shape as thin as a French crepe. After rolling out chapatis, heat a griddle plate or heavy-based frying pan until very hot, and cook the chapatis, starting with those that were rolled first (the resting between rolling and cooking seems to make for lighter chapatis). Put chapati on griddle and leave for about 1 minute. Turn and cook other side a further minute, pressing lightly around the edges of the chapati with a folded tea towel or an egg slice. This encourages bubbles to form and makes the chapatis light. As each one is cooked, wrap in a clean tea towel until all are ready. Serve immediately with butter, dry curries or vegetable dishes.

Note: In India, the chapatis are cooked on the tawa or griddle and are held for a moment or two right over the fire. This makes them puff up like balloons. You can do this over a gas flame, holding them with kitchen tongs.

DHAL CHAPATI
CHAPATIS WITH LENTIL AND SPINACH FILLING

Makes:8

1 quantity chapati dough (page 29)
1 cup red lentils
3 cups shredded spinach
2 tablespoons oil or ghee
1 onion, finely chopped
1 clove garlic, finely chopped
1 teaspoon ground cummin
½ teaspoon garam masala (page 35)
1 teaspoon salt or to taste
squeeze of lemon juice
1 tablespoon ghee for cooking

Make chapati dough, using a generous measure of water as you need a pliable dough instead of a firm one. Add the water all at once, it is easier than working it in a little at a time. If dough becomes too soft don't worry, just sprinkle on a handful of flour and knead it in and repeat if necessary until the right consistency is obtained. Knead dough and set aside while preparing filling.

Put the lentils into a saucepan, add water to cover by 12 mm (half inch) and bring to the boil. Cover and cook 5 minutes, then stir in the shredded spinach and continue to cook until lentils are tender enough to be mashed when stirred with a wooden spoon. If necessary add more water. In another pan heat ghee or oil and fry the onion until soft and golden. Add garlic and spinach to the pan and fry, stirring until the mixture is well blended. Add garam masala and salt and a squeeze of lemon juice and mix well. Fry until it is quite dry and no liquid remains, stirring constantly and keeping heat low or mixture will stick to pan. Allow to cool. Taste and adjust seasoning.

Form chapati dough into 8 balls, press them out slightly to the size of a small saucer and put a spoonful of the cooked lentil mixture in the centre. Bring edges of the dough together and pinch well to seal. On a floured board roll out chapatis very gently with a floured rolling pin. They must be thin, but not so thin that the dough breaks and lets the filling out. They should be the size of a bread and butter plate, or a little larger.

Heat a griddle until very hot, spread a little ghee on it and cook the chapatis, one or two at a time depending on the size of your griddle. While cooking press gently with frying slice. Turn and cook other side. Both sides should be golden with brown spots here and there. If while cooking the first side the uppermost side is spread with extra ghee the chapatis taste richer. Keep the cooked chapatis covered with a clean cloth and when all are cooked serve hot with extra dhal and spinach filling, or other accompanying dishes.

PURI *(top left)*, CHAPATI *(top right)* and rolled dough for PARATHA. *Recipes pages 29-34*

PARATHA
FLAKY WHOLEMEAL BREAD *(picture page 31)*

Probably the favourite variety of Indian bread, parathas are rich, flaky and deliciously flavoured with ghee. Kebabs and parathas is a combination which is quite famous. A dear friend of my grandmother taught me her method of rolling and folding the parathas — the easiest and most successful one I've tried; see illustration, page 31.

Makes: 12-14
1½ cups fine wholemeal flour
1½ cups plain white flour or roti flour
1½ teaspoons salt
6-8 tablespoons ghee
1 cup water
extra ghee for cooking

Sieve wholemeal flour, white flour and salt into a mixing bowl and rub in 1 tablespoon of the ghee. Add water, mix and knead dough as for chapatis (page 29). Cover dough with clear plastic and set aside for 1 hour.

Divide dough into 12-14 equal portions and roll each into a smooth ball. Melt ghee over a low heat and cool slightly. Roll each ball of dough on a lightly floured board into a very thin circular shape. Pour 2 teaspoons of the melted ghee into the centre of each and spread lightly with the hand. With a knife, make a cut from the centre of each circle to the outer edge. Starting at the cut edge, roll the dough closely into a cone shape. Pick it up, press the apex of the cone and the base towards each other and flatten slightly. You will now have a small, roughly circular lump of dough again. Lightly flour the board again and roll out the dough very gently, taking care not to press too hard and let the air out at the edges. The parathas should be as round as possible, but not as thinly rolled as the first time.

Cook on a hot griddle liberally greased with extra ghee, turning parathas and spreading with more ghee, until they are golden brown. Serve hot with grilled kebabs, sambals and podina chatni.

Note: The wholemeal and plain or roti flour can be replaced by 3 cups plain white flour.

GOBI PARATHA
PARATHAS WITH CAULIFLOWER FILLING

Makes: 8
2 cups roti flour or plain white flour
½ teaspoon salt
⅔ cup warm water
2-3 tablespoons ghee for cooking

Filling:
1 cup finely grated cauliflower
2 teaspoons finely grated fresh ginger
1 teaspoon salt
1 teaspoon garam masala (page 35)
chilli powder to taste, optional

Mix flour and salt together in a large bowl, add the water all at once and knead hard for 10 minutes. Dough should be firm but pliable. Cover and leave for at least 30 minutes. Divide dough into 8 equal portions and roll each into a ball. Flatten out to a circle about 10 cm (4 inches) in diameter, put a spoonful of filling in the middle of each and draw ends together, pinching them firmly to join. Flatten between the hands to a round shape. On a lightly floured board roll out very lightly and carefully to a circle the size of a breakfast plate. Do not press too hard on the rolling pin or the filling will break through the dough. If this does happen take a small piece of dough, press flat and place it over the break. Roll gently to join. When all the parathas are filled and ready to cook, heat a heavy griddle or thick, heavy frying pan until very hot. Melt the ghee in a small saucepan and have it within easy reach.

Put a teaspoon of melted ghee on the griddle, spread it with a frying slice and put a paratha on it. Spread another small teaspoon of melted ghee on top of the paratha. Turn the paratha over and cook other side, pressing gently with frying slice. Paratha should be cooked until nicely golden on both sides. Serve at once, accompanied by a raita.

Filling: Prepare filling only when ready to use it. Combine all the ingredients in a bowl and mix well. Use only the tender flower heads of the cauliflower and make sure there are no large pieces, for these will make the parathas difficult to roll out.

NAAN
PUNJABI LEAVENED BREAD

Makes about 8 loaves

30 g (1 oz) fresh compressed yeast or 1
    sachet dried yeast
¾ cup lukewarm water
3 teaspoons sugar
¼ cup yoghurt
1 egg, beaten
¼ cup melted ghee or butter
2 teaspoons salt
about 3½ cups plain white flour
extra melted butter
2 tablespoons poppy seeds or black
    cummin seeds

In a small warm bowl sprinkle yeast over quarter cup warm water and leave for a few minutes to soften, then stir to dissolve. Add 1 teaspoon of the sugar, stir, then leave in a warm place for 10 minutes or until it starts to froth. This is to test whether the yeast is live. If it does not froth start again with a fresh batch of yeast.

Stir yoghurt until smooth, then mix with the rest of the sugar, the remaining half cup lukewarm water, egg, melted ghee and salt. Stir in the yeast mixture. Put 2 cups flour into a bowl, make a well in the centre and pour in liquid mixture, beating well with a wooden spoon until it is a smooth batter. Add remaining flour a little at a time and when it gets too stiff to use the spoon, knead with the hands until a stiff dough is formed. Knead for 10-12 minutes or until dough is smooth and elastic, using as little extra flour as possible. Form dough into a ball, let it rest on board while preparing bowl. Heat bowl by running warm water into it and leaving for a few minutes. Dry bowl well, grease it, then put dough in bowl and turn it over so that top is greased. Cover with a cloth and leave in a warm place until doubled in bulk and a finger pushed into the dough leaves an impression. Punch down dough and divide into 8 balls, leave to rest 10 minutes.

Preheat oven to very hot — 230°C (450°F). Put two ungreased baking trays into the oven to preheat.

Pat dough into circles keeping them thin in the centre and thicker around the rim then pull one end outwards, making a teardrop shape. They should be a handspan long and little more than half that much wide at the base. Brush with melted ghee and sprinkle with poppy or black cummin seeds.

Put 2 or 3 loaves on each baking tray. Bake about 10 minutes or until golden and puffed. If naan is not brown enough, put under a preheated grill for a minute or two. Serve warm or cool with tandoori chicken, lamb kebabs, korma or boti kebab, and with kachumbar as an accompaniment.

PURI
DEEP-FRIED WHOLEMEAL BREAD *(picture page 31)*

Proceed as for chapatis (page 29). When all the dough is rolled out heat approximately 2.5 cm (1 inch) of oil in a deep frying pan. When a faint haze rises from the oil, fry puris one at a time, over a moderate heat. Spoon hot oil continually over the cooking puri until it puffs and swells. Turn over and fry other side in the same way. When both sides are pale golden brown, drain on absorbent paper. Serve immediately with curries and bhajis.

Note: Puri is pronounced 'poo-ree'

KACHORI
PURIS WITH FILLING

Makes about 18

1 quantity dough for chapatis (page 29)
1 cup dry potato or lentil curry, smoothly
    mashed
oil for deep frying

Prepare the dough for puris and let it rest. Divide into about 18 equal-size balls, roll and fill as for chapatis filled with lentils and spinach (page 30). Instead of cooking on a griddle, heat oil in a frying pan and deep fry the kachoris. Drain well on absorbent paper.

ALU PURI
POTATO PURIS

Makes about 20
250 g (8 oz) boiled, mashed potato
2 cups plain white flour
2 teaspoons salt
¼ cup lukewarm water
oil for deep frying
1 tablespoon ghee, optional

Use floury potatoes and mash until very smooth. Allow to cool, then mix in flour and salt sifted together. Knead, adding water as necessary to make a firm but not dry dough. The more the dough is kneaded, the lighter the puris will be, so knead for at least 10 minutes or until dough becomes smooth and non-sticky. Cover and leave to rest for 30 minutes to 1 hour.

Divide mixture into 20-24 equal-size balls, and roll each one out on a floured board to the size of a saucer. When all are rolled out, heat enough oil in a deep pan (a karahi, shaped like a wok, is ideal because it requires less oil) and add the ghee for flavour. As soon as the oil starts to show a haze on the surface slip in one puri at a time and with a frying spoon splash oil over the top of it to make it puff like a balloon. When underside is pale golden brown, turn and cook the other side. Drain on absorbent paper and serve warm with lentils, vegetables, or meat curries that do not have a lot of thin gravy.

CURRY POWDERS AND PASTES

Curry powder, as it is sold commercially, is almost never used in India or other countries where curry is made and eaten every day. Rather, the individual spices are freshly ground each day on a masala stone and added to the food in many different combinations and proportions. Even when there is a grinding mill in the town and housewives, yielding to the pressures of modern living, have a month's supply ground at a time, the dry ground spices are kept separate.

There are many good curry mixtures sold commercially, but there are also many that lack good flavour because of a skimping on the more expensive spices and a reliance on 'fillers' such as rice flour to make up the bulk. If using curry powder, make sure it is fresh by buying from a store where the turnover is quick — preferably a store specialising in spices. Buy in small quantities so it does not stay on your shelf for too long. And look for a brand in a bottle or tin, because cardboard containers absorb a lot of the essential oils of the spices.

In most of the recipes in this book I have used the individual spices to allow for as much variation as possible. Spicing is an art you can learn, and eventually you can tailor your curries to your own taste and not rely on a ready-mixed formula.

However, if you cannot obtain the spices mentioned or have a liking for a particular curry mixture, substitute a similar quantity of the blend for the combined amount of turmeric, coriander, cummin, chilli, fennel and fenugreek used in the recipe. Curry powder does not include the fragrant spices such as cardamom, clove and cinnamon, so these must be added separately.

A curry paste I like to buy or make is green masala paste, based on fresh herbs. Because these are not always in season it is a good idea to make a batch when they are plentiful and preserve them in oil for use later on. I include a recipe for this. It can take the place of fresh ginger and coriander leaves and even part of the garlic in a recipe, or it can be used as an extra flavour accent.

Spices are the soul of Indian cooking. Another important ingredient and time-saver is garam masala, a mixture of ground spices, which is added to many types of Indian dishes. Sometimes it is added with other spices at the frying stage, but more often it is sprinkled on during the last few minutes of cooking. If stored airtight and away from heat and light, garam masala will keep for six months or longer and amply repay the effort of making it. Here again, if you find a good commercial garam masala, by all means use it — but if you are a real enthusiast about spice cookery, you owe it to yourself to try a home-made blend or two. They are so marvellously adaptable to your own taste. The recipes that follow will give you a good selection to choose from.

Roasting the spices brings out their flavour and also makes them easier to grind. If a blender is not available, use a mortar and pestle to pound spices to a powder. If spices are still warm and crisp after roasting this process is made much easier.

GARAM MASALA
GROUND MIXED SPICES

There are many versions of garam masala, some using hot spices, such as pepper, and others only the fragrant spices. Here are some combinations to choose from according to your own personal taste. Made from good quality spices and stored airtight, garam masala will keep its flavour and fragrance for months.

No. 1 GARAM MASALA

4 tablespoons coriander seeds
2 tablespoons cummin seeds
1 tablespoon whole black peppercorns
2 teaspoons cardamom seeds (measure
    after removing pods)
4 x 7.5 cm (3 inch) cinnamon sticks
1 teaspoon whole cloves
1 whole nutmeg

In a small pan roast separately the coriander, cummin, peppercorns, cardamom, cinnamon and cloves. As each one starts to smell fragrant turn on to plate to cool. After roasting, peel the cardamoms, discard pods and use only the seeds. Put all into electric blender and blend to a fine powder. Finely grate nutmeg and mix in. Store in glass jar with airtight lid.

No. 2 FRAGRANT SPICE GARAM MASALA

3 x 7.5 cm (3 inch) cinnamon sticks
2 teaspoons cardamom seeds (measure
    after removing pods)
1 teaspoon whole cloves
1 teaspoon blades of mace, or
    ½ nutmeg, grated

Roast spices separately and grind in a blender or with mortar and pestle; add grated nutmeg, if used.

No. 3 KASHMIRI GARAM MASALA

2 teaspoons cardamom seeds (measure
    after removing pods)
1 teaspoon black cummin seeds
1 teaspoon whole black peppercorns
2 x 5 cm (2 inch) cinnamon sticks
½ teaspoon whole cloves
quarter of a nutmeg, grated

Roast spices separately and grind to a fine powder. Add nutmeg. Store airtight.

MADRASI MASALA
MADRAS-STYLE CURRY PASTE

1 cup ground coriander
½ cup ground cummin
1 tablespoon each ground black pepper,
    turmeric, black mustard, chilli powder,
    and salt
2 tablespoons each crushed garlic and
    finely grated fresh ginger
vinegar for mixing
¾ cup oil

Combine ground spices and salt in a bowl. Add garlic and ginger and sufficient vinegar to mix to a smooth, thick puree. Heat oil in saucepan and when very hot turn in the spice mixture and reduce heat. Stir constantly until spices are cooked and oil separates from spices. Cool and bottle. Use about a tablespoon of this paste for each 500 g (1 lb) of meat, fish or poultry, substituting it for the garlic, ginger and spices in a recipe.

TAAZA MASALA
GREEN MASALA PASTE

A spice paste based on fresh coriander leaves, mint, garlic and ginger. Added to any curry or spiced preparation, it will give extra flavour.

1 teaspoon fenugreek seeds
5 large cloves garlic
2 tablespoons finely chopped
   fresh ginger
1 cup firmly packed fresh mint leaves
1 cup firmly packed fresh coriander leaves
½ cup vinegar
3 teaspoons salt
2 teaspoons ground turmeric
½ teaspoon ground cloves
1 teaspoon ground cardamom
½ cup vegetable oil
¼ cup sesame oil

Put fenugreek seeds in water to soak overnight. They will swell and develop a jelly-like coating. Measure 1 teaspoon of soaked seeds and put into container of electric blender with garlic, ginger, mint, coriander and vinegar. Blend on high speed until very smooth. Mix in salt and ground spices. Heat oils until very hot, add blended mixture, bring to boil, turn off heat. Cool and bottle. Oil should cover the top of the herbs. If there is not quite enough oil, heat a little more and add it to the bottle.

MACHCHI MOLEE
FISH COOKED IN COCONUT MILK

Serves: 4
500 g (1 lb) firm fish fillets or steaks
½ teaspoon ground turmeric
1 teaspoon salt
1 tablespoon ghee or oil
1 medium onion, finely sliced
2 cloves garlic, finely chopped
1 teaspoon finely grated fresh ginger
8 curry leaves
2-3 fresh red or green chillies, slit and
   seeded
2 cups thin coconut milk
1 cup thick coconut milk
lime or lemon juice to taste

Wash the fish, rub with turmeric and salt and set aside. In a saucepan heat the oil and fry the onions, garlic, ginger, curry leaves and chillies until onions are soft. Keep stirring and do not let them brown. Add the thin coconut milk and stir while it comes to simmering point. Add the fish and bring slowly to simmering point, cook uncovered for 10 minutes. Add thick coconut milk, heat through and remove from heat before adding lemon juice and salt to taste. Serve with white rice.

MACHCHI TAMATAR KI KARI
FISH CURRY WITH TOMATO

Serves: 4
500 g (1 lb) fish fillets or steaks
2 tablespoons ghee or oil
1 medium onion, finely chopped
2 cloves garlic, finely chopped
2 tablespoons chopped fresh coriander
   leaves or mint
1 teaspoon ground cummin
1 teaspoon ground turmeric
½-1 teaspoon chilli powder to taste
1 large ripe tomato, chopped
1 teaspoon salt
1½ teaspoons garam masala (page 35)
lemon juice to taste

Wash the fish and cut into serving pieces. Heat the ghee or oil in a saucepan and on low heat fry the onion, garlic and coriander, stirring, until onion is soft and golden. Add the cummin, turmeric, and chilli powder and stir until the spices are cooked. Add the tomato, salt and garam masala and fry, stirring, until tomato is cooked to a pulp. Add lemon juice and check whether more salt is needed. Put the pieces of fish into the tomato gravy, spooning it over the fish, cover and simmer for 10 minutes, or until fish is cooked. Serve with rice.

PATRANI MACHCHI
FISH STEAMED IN BANANA LEAVES *(picture page 59)*

Serves: 4

4 whole fish or 750 g (1½ lb) fish
    fillets
salt
1 large lemon
2 medium onions
1 teaspoon finely chopped fresh ginger
2 cloves garlic
2 large fresh green chillies, seeded and
    chopped
½ cup chopped fresh coriander leaves
1 teaspoon ground cummin
½ teaspoon ground fenugreek
½ cup fresh grated or desiccated coconut
2 tablespoons ghee or oil
2 teaspoons salt
1 teaspoon garam masala (page 35)
banana leaves or foil

Wash the fish, dry with paper towels and rub over with salt. Leave while preparing masala.

Peel the lemon, removing all the white pith. Cut lemon in pieces and discard all seeds. Put into container of electric blender with one onion, roughly chopped, ginger, garlic, the chillies, fresh coriander, cummin and fenugreek. Blend on high speed until puréed, then add coconut and blend again.

Heat oil and fry remaining onions, finely chopped, until soft and golden. Add blended mixture and fry, stirring, for a few minutes. Remove from heat. Add salt and garam masala. Coat each fish or fillet with the mixture, wrap securely in banana leaves or foil and steam over gently simmering water for 30 minutes, turning parcels once. Serve in the leaf parcels. Have a bowl or plate to collect leaves as each person unwraps the fish.

MACHCHI KARI
FISH CURRY

Curry any kind of fish, but strong curries are particulary suited to strongly flavoured fish with dark flesh such as kingfish, tuna, trevally or small fish such as sardines or anchovies. Fenugreek is almost always used in a fish curry, particularly with strongly flavoured fish.

Serves: 4

500 g (1 lb) fish steaks or fillets or small
    whole fish
2 tablespoons oil
6-8 curry leaves
1 medium onion, finely sliced
2 cloves garlic, finely sliced
1 tablespoon finely grated fresh ginger
1 tablespoon ground coriander
2 teaspoons ground cummin
½ teaspoon ground turmeric
½-1 teaspoon chilli powder
½ teaspoon ground fenugreek
2 cups coconut milk
1½ teaspoons salt or to taste
lemon juice to taste

Wash fish well. If small fish are used, clean and scale them. If large steaks or fillets are used, cut them into serving pieces. Heat oil and fry the curry leaves until slightly brown, then add onion, garlic and ginger and fry until onion is soft and golden. Add all the ground spices and fry, stirring, until they smell aromatic.

Add coconut milk and salt and bring to the boil, stirring. Simmer uncovered for 10 minutes, then put in the fish, ladle the liquid over it and simmer until fish is well cooked. Remove from heat and stir in lemon juice to taste.

KHATTAI WALI MACHCHI KARI
SOUR FISH CURRY

Serves: 4
500 g (1 lb) fish fillet, steaks or whole
    small fish
1 tablespoon tamarind pulp
½ cup hot water
1 medium onion, chopped
3 cloves garlic
1 teaspoon chopped fresh ginger
1 tablespoon ground coriander
2 teaspoons ground cummin
1 teaspoon ground turmeric
1 teaspoon chilli powder
½ teaspoon ground fenugreek
3 tablespoons oil
1 tablespoon vinegar or lemon juice
1 ½ teaspoons salt

Wash fish and cut into serving pieces, or clean small fish. Soak tamarind pulp in hot water for 10 minutes, then rub the pulp off the seeds and dissolve in the water. Strain and discard seeds and fibres. Put onion, garlic and ginger in container of electric blender with a tablespoon of the tamarind liquid, and blend to a smooth purée. Mix in the ground spices. Heat oil in a saucepan and fry the blended mixture stirring until it thickens and darkens. Add the rest of the tamarind liquid, vinegar and salt and enough hot water to just immerse fish. When this comes to the boil put in the fish and simmer very gently until cooked.

TALI MACHCHI (1)
FRIED FISH (1)

Use tuna, jewfish, spanish mackerel, kingfish or any firm fish.

Serves: 4 .
750 g (1 ½ lb) fish steaks
2 cloves garlic
1 ½ teaspoons salt
1 teaspoon finely grated fresh ginger
½ teaspoon ground turmeric
½ teaspoon ground black pepper
¼ teaspoon chilli powder, optional
lemon juice
oil for frying
fresh coriander leaves to garnish
lemon wedges to garnish

Wash fish and dry on paper towels. Crush garlic with salt, mix with ginger, turmeric, pepper, chilli powder and enough lemon juice to make a paste. Rub this well over the fish on both sides, cover and leave for 20 minutes. In a large frying pan heat just enough oil to cover base of pan and when hot put in the fish steaks. Fry on medium heat until cooked on one side, then turn slices carefully with a fish slice and fry other side. Serve on platter garnished with coriander leaves and lemon wedges.

TALI MACHCHI (2)
FRIED FISH (2) *(picture opposite)*

Serves: 4
500 g (1 lb) firm white fish fillets
3 tablespoons plain flour
3 tablespoons besan (chick pea flour)
1 ½ teaspoons salt
1 teaspoon garam masala (page 35)
½ teaspoon ground turmeric
oil for frying
1 egg, well beaten

Wash and dry fish fillets. Mix flour, pea flour, salt, garam masala and turmeric together. Heat oil in deep frying pan until smoking hot. Dip fish fillets into beaten egg then lightly coat with the flour mixture. Fry quickly until golden brown on both sides. Drain on absorbent paper and serve immediately with boiled rice, pickles and brinjal bartha (page 80).

TALI MACHCHI (fried fish) *recipe above*

A DUM MACHCHI

FISH

whole fish
uice
1 tablespoon finely chopped fresh ginger
3 cloves garlic, finely chopped
1 fresh red chilli, seeded and chopped
1 teaspoon ground cummin
1 teaspoon garam masala (page 35)
1 cup yoghurt
fresh coriander leaves and red chillies to
garnish

Buy the fish cleaned, scaled and with head removed. Wipe out cavity with kitchen paper dipped in coarse salt and wash well. Rub inside cavity with a little salt and lemon juice. Heat oil and gently fry ginger, garlic and chilli until soft. Add cummin and garam masala and fry for 2-3 minutes. Remove from heat, stir into yoghurt and add salt to taste. Dry fish on paper towel, make diagonal slits in the flesh on each side and put into a greased baking dish. Spread the marinade on both sides of the fish and inside the cavity. Leave to stand at room temperature 30 minutes, then bake in a moderate oven 35 minutes or until flesh is white and opaque at the thickest portion. Garnish with coriander leaves and chilli, and serve hot.

MACHCHI KEBAB
GRILLED FISH ON SKEWERS

Use fish of a good thickness, such as snapper, hake, jewfish and similar varieties, for it is difficult to thread very thin slices of fish on skewers.

Serves: 6
1 kg (2 lb) firm white fish fillets
2 teaspoons finely grated fresh ginger
3 cloves garlic, crushed
1½ teaspoons salt
4 teaspoons ground coriander
1 teaspoon garam masala (page 35)
½ teaspoon chilli powder
1 teaspoon dried mango (amchur) or 3
  tablespoons lemon juice
1 cup yoghurt
2 tablespoons plain flour

Wash the fillets and dry them on kitchen paper. Cut fish into 4 cm (1½ inch) pieces. Make a marinade of all the other ingredients mixed well together, put the fish pieces in and mix gently but thoroughly so that each piece is coated with marinade. Leave 15 minutes at room temperature, or longer in the refrigerator. Preheat griller and while it is heating thread pieces of fish on bamboo skewers, 4 or 5 pieces on each. Make sure all the skin is on one side of the skewer.

Put skewers on griller tray and grill 10 cm (4 inches) away from heat with skin side upwards, for 4 minutes. Turn skewers and grill other side for 4-5 minutes, depending on thickness of fish. Do not overcook. Serve kebabs immediately accompanied by rice or chapatis, and onion sambal (page 89).

JHINGA MOLEE
PRAWNS IN COCONUT MILK

A molee is a South Indian preparation in which the main ingredient is cooked in rich coconut milk. It is also used in Sri Lanka and among Malays, and is often called a 'white curry'. It is deliciously mild. Coconut milk being the main ingredient, the pan must not be covered at any time during cooking and the liquid should be stirred while coming to the boil to prevent curdling.

Serves: 4
750 g (1½ lb) large raw prawns
1 tablespoon ghee or oil
2 medium onions, thinly sliced
2 cloves garlic, crushed
1 teaspoon finely grated fresh ginger
2 fresh red or green chillies, slit and
   seeded
1 teaspoon ground turmeric
8 curry leaves
2 cups coconut milk
1 teaspoon salt
lemon juice to taste

Wash prawns well. Shell and de-vein if liked, but some local cooks say the prawns should be in their shells, for they retain more flavour this way. Heat ghee and fry the onions, garlic and ginger until onions are soft but do not let them brown. Add chillies, turmeric and curry leaves and fry 1 minute longer. Add coconut milk and salt and stir while bringing to simmering point. Simmer uncovered for 10 minutes, then add prawns and cook for 10-15 minutes. Remove from heat and add lemon juice to taste.

JHINGA KARI
SOUTH INDIAN PRAWN CURRY

If cooked prawns are used in this recipe, add them during the last 10 minutes. The paprika is used to give the curry the desired red colour, which in India would come from the large number of chillies or chilli powder used.

Serves: 4-6
1 kg (2 lb) raw prawns
1 tablespoon desiccated coconut
1 tablespoon ground rice
2 cups coconut milk
2 tablespoons ghee or oil
12 curry leaves
2 medium onions, finely chopped
5 cloves garlic, finely chopped
3 teaspoons finely grated fresh ginger
2 tablespoons Madras curry powder
   or paste
1 teaspoon chilli powder, optional
2 teaspoons paprika
1½ teaspoons salt
2 tablespoons lemon juice

Shell and de-vein prawns. Put desiccated coconut into a dry pan and toast over medium heat, shaking pan or stirring constantly until coconut is golden brown. Remove from pan and do the same with the ground rice. Put both into blender container with about half a cup of the coconut milk and blend until smooth and coconut is very finely ground.

Heat ghee in a saucepan and fry the curry leaves for 1 minute. Add onions, garlic and ginger and fry until golden brown, stirring with a wooden spoon. Add curry powder, chilli powder and paprika and fry on low heat, stirring. Do not let the spices burn. Add blended mixture, coconut milk and salt, stir while bringing to simmering point. Do not cover. Simmer gently for 15 minutes, stirring occasionally. Add prawns, stir to mix, simmer for further 10-15 minutes or until prawns are cooked and gravy thick. Stir in lemon juice. Serve with rice.

JIIINGA BHAJIA
PRAWN FRITTERS

Makes about 20
250 g (8 oz) raw shelled prawns
1 small onion, finely chopped
1 clove garlic, crushed
½ teaspoon salt
1 teaspoon finely grated fresh ginger
1 tablespoon finely chopped fresh
   coriander leaves
¼ teaspoon ground pepper
½ teaspoon ground cummin
½ teaspoon garam masala (page 35)
2 tablespoons besan (chick pea flour)
2 tablespoons plain flour
oil for deep frying

De-vein and wash the prawns. Drain thoroughly, then chop very finely. Combine prawns in a bowl with onion, garlic crushed with salt, ginger, coriander, pepper, cummin and garam masala. Mix the chick pea flour and plain flour well and put on a sheet of paper. Form small balls of the prawn mixture and roll in flour. Heat oil for deep frying and when a faint haze appears over the surface drop prawn balls into the oil, a few at a time, and fry over medium heat, spooning oil over the bhajias all the time, until they are golden brown all over. Drain on absorbent paper and serve hot.

TISRYA DUM MASALA
SPICY STEAMED MUSSELS *(picture opposite)*

Serves: 4
1 kg (2 lb) fresh mussels
3 tablespoons ghee or oil
2 large onions, finely chopped
4 cloves garlic, finely chopped
3 teaspoons finely chopped fresh ginger
3 fresh red chillies, seeded and chopped
½ teaspoon ground turmeric
3 teaspoons ground coriander
pinch chilli powder, optional
½ teaspoon salt
1 cup water
1 tablespoon chopped fresh coriander
   leaves
lemon juice to taste

Scrub mussels well and beard them. Heat the ghee in a large, deep saucepan and fry onions, garlic and ginger on medium heat until the onions are soft and golden. Add chillies, turmeric, coriander and chilli powder and stir for 3 minutes. Add salt and water, bring to the boil and simmer, covered, for 5 minutes. Add the mussels, cover and steam for 10-15 minutes or until the shells have opened. Remove from heat, sprinkle in the coriander, taste and add more salt if necessary. Add lemon juice to taste. Spoon the gravy over and into the mussell shells and serve immediately with white rice.

Note: Do not use any mussels that are not tightly closed when raw, and discard any that do not open during cooking.

TISRYA DUM MASALA (spicy steamed mussels) *recipe above.*

MURGII BIRIANI
MUSLIM-STYLE CHICKEN BIRIANI

For biriani, always use long grain rice. Basmati rice with its thin, fine grains is the ideal variety to use in this festive dish.

Serves: 6

Chicken Savoury:
1.2 kg (3 lb) chicken or chicken pieces
5 tablespoons ghee or oil
2 tablespoons blanched almonds
2 tablespoons sultanas
4 small potatoes, peeled and halved
2 large onions, finely chopped
5 cloves garlic, finely chopped
1 tablespoon finely chopped fresh ginger
½ teaspoon chilli powder
½ teaspoon ground black pepper
½ teaspoon ground turmeric
1 teaspoon ground cummin
1 teaspoon salt
2 medium tomatoes, peeled and chopped
2 tablespoons yoghurt
2 tablespoons chopped mint leaves
½ teaspoon ground cardamom
5 cm (2 inch) piece cinnamon

Biriani Rice:
500 g (1 lb) basmati rice
2½ tablespoons ghee
1 large onion, finely chopped
a good pinch powdered saffron or
  saffron strands
5 cardamom pods
3 whole cloves
2.5 cm (1 inch) piece cinnamon
½ teaspoon powdered aromatic ginger
  (kencur)
2 tablespoons rose water
1½ teaspoons salt
4 cups strong chicken stock

Chicken Savoury: Cut chicken into serving pieces. Heat half the ghee in a small frying pan, fry almonds until golden, drain. Fry sultanas a few seconds and set aside. Fry peeled and halved potatoes until brown, drain and reserve.

Pour any ghee left in pan into a large saucepan, add remaining ghee and fry onion, garlic and ginger until onion is soft and golden. Add chilli, pepper, turmeric, cummin, salt and tomato. Fry, stirring constantly for 5 minutes. Add yoghurt, mint, cardamom and cinnamon stick. Cover and cook over low heat, stirring occasionally until tomato is cooked to a pulp. (It may be necessary to add a little hot water if mixture becomes too dry and starts to stick to pan.) When mixture is thick and smooth, add chicken pieces and stir well to coat them with spice mixture. Cover and cook over very low heat until chicken is tender, approximately 35-45 minutes. There should be only a little very thick gravy left when chicken is cooked. If necessary cook uncovered for a few minutes to reduce gravy.

Biriani Rice: Wash rice well and drain in colander for at least 30 minutes. Heat ghee and fry onion until golden. Add saffron, cardamom, cloves, cinnamon stick, aromatic ginger and rice. Fry stirring, until rice is coated with the ghee. Add rose water and salt to hot stock, pour over rice mixture and stir well. Add chicken savoury and potatoes and gently mix into rice. Bring to boil.

Cover saucepan tightly, turn heat to very low and steam for 20 minutes. Do not lift lid or stir while cooking. Spoon biriani onto a warm serving dish. Garnish with the almonds and sultanas and serve immediately. Serve with onion sambal (page 89), cucumber raita (page 85) and hot pickles.

Note: If liked, more colour can be added to dish by garnishing with quartered hard-boiled eggs and cooked green peas.

KAJU MURGH KARI
CURRIED CHICKEN WITH CASHEWS *(picture page 55)*

This curry has a rich, thick gravy that makes it ideal for eating with the flat breads of India.

Serves: 6

1 chicken, about 1.75 kg (3½ lbs)
3 tablespoons ghee or oil
2 large onions, finely chopped
3 cloves garlic, finely chopped
1½ teaspoons finely grated fresh ginger
3 tablespoons curry powder
1 teaspoon chilli powder, optional
3 teaspoons salt
3 ripe tomatoes, peeled and chopped
2 tablespoons chopped fresh coriander
   or mint leaves
2 teaspoons garam masala (page 35)
½ cup yoghurt
125 g (4 oz) raw cashews, finely ground

Cut chicken into serving pieces. For curry, pieces should not be large, so separate drumsticks from thighs, wings from breasts, and cut breast into four. If large, the thighs and drumsticks can be chopped in halves using a heavy cleaver and cutting through the bone. The smaller the pieces of chicken, the better the spices can penetrate.

Heat ghee or oil in a large saucepan and gently fry onion, garlic and ginger until soft and golden, stirring occasionally. Long slow cooking at this stage is the basis of a good curry.

Add curry powder and chilli powder and stir for 1 minute. Add salt, tomatoes, chopped herbs and cook to a pulp, stirring with a wooden spoon. Add chicken. Stir well to coat chicken with spice mixture. Cover tightly and simmer on very low heat for 45 minutes or until chicken is tender, stirring with a wooden spoon every 15 minutes and scraping base of pan to ensure that spices do not stick. Stir in garam masala and yoghurt and simmer, uncovered, for 5 minutes. Last of all stir in the cashews and heat through. If liked, the curry may be sprinkled with extra chopped coriander or mint leaves before serving. Serve with chapatis, parathas, puris or rice.

Note: For a milder flavour, use paprika instead of chilli powder. It will give a good red colour without adding to the heat of the curry. The cashews can be ground in a nut mill or an electric blender, or very finely chopped.

DAHI MURGH
CHICKEN AND YOGHURT CURRY

Serves: 4

1 kg (2 lb) roasting chicken
1 medium onion, roughly chopped
3 cloves garlic, peeled
1 teaspoon finely chopped fresh ginger
½ cup fresh coriander or mint leaves
1½ tablespoons ghee or oil
1 teaspoon ground turmeric
1½ teaspoons garam masala (page 35)
1½ teaspoons salt
½ teaspoon chilli powder, optional
½ cup yoghurt
2 ripe tomatoes, diced
extra chopped mint or coriander leaves
   to garnish

Cut chicken into serving pieces, or use chicken pieces of one kind — drumsticks, thighs or half breasts. Put into container of electric blender the onion, garlic, ginger, fresh coriander or mint. Blend to a smooth purée. Heat oil in a heavy saucepan and fry the blended mixture, stirring, for about 5 minutes. Add turmeric, garam masala, salt and chilli powder and fry for a further minute. Stir in yoghurt and tomatoes, and fry until liquid dries up and the mixture is the consistency of thick purée. Add chicken pieces, turning them in the spice mixture so they are coated on both sides, then turn heat low, cover tightly and cook until chicken is tender. If liquid from chicken has not evaporated by the time the flesh is cooked, uncover and raise heat to dry off excess liquid, stirring gently at the base of pan to prevent burning. Garnish with chopped herbs and serve with rice or chapatis.

DHANSAK
CHICKEN OR MEAT WITH LENTILS *(picture opposite)*

A Parsi dish, dhansak is served every Sunday in many Parsi homes and plays an important part at festive meals. The list of ingredients looks formidable, but the recipe consists of just five parts — meat or chicken, lentils, vegetables, a blended masala and a dry masala. Prepare each component separately and have it ready, then combining them becomes a simple matter. This dish is served with rice, onion kachumbar and other accompaniments, and is a very hearty and filling meal.

Serves: 8-10

Lentils:
1 cup toor dhal or yellow split peas
½ cup each chick peas, moong dhal and
   red lentils

Vegetables:
1 medium eggplant
slice of pumpkin, peeled
1 large potato, peeled
2 medium onions, peeled
2 ripe tomatoes, peeled
2 cups spinach leaves

Meat:
1 x 2 kg (4 lb) chicken or 1.5 kg (3 lb)
   lamb, boned

Blended Masala:
6 dry red chillies, seeded
¼ cup hot water
6 fresh green chillies, seeded
1 tablespoon chopped fresh ginger
10 cloves garlic, peeled
½ cup fresh mint leaves
½ cup fresh coriander leaves

Dry Ground Masala:
1 tablespoon ground coriander
2 teaspoons ground cummin
2 teaspoons ground turmeric
½ teaspoon ground cinnamon
½ teaspoon ground cardamom
½ teaspoon ground black pepper
½ teaspoon black mustard seeds, bruised
¼ teaspoon ground fenugreek
¼ teaspoon ground cloves

For Cooking:
3-4 tablespoons ghee or oil
4 medium onions, finely sliced

Wash lentils and soak overnight. Roughly chop vegetables. Put chicken, cut into joints, or lamb cut into large cubes, into a large pan with all the lentils and sufficient water to cover. Add 1 tablespoon salt and bring to the boil, cover and simmer for 15 minutes. Add vegetables and continue cooking for 30 minutes or until meat is almost cooked. Remove pieces of chicken or meat and set aside, strain lentils and vegetables through a sieve or purée in electric blender.

Ingredients for blended masala should be reduced to a smooth paste in electric blender.

Ingredients for dry ground masala should be combined in a bowl.

Heat the ghee in a large saucepan and when very hot throw in the sliced onions and fry, stirring frequently, until the onions are brown. Remove from the pan and set aside. To the ghee remaining in pan add the blended masala and the dry ground masala. Fry, stirring constantly, until they are well cooked and give out a pleasing aroma. Add half the browned onions, the chicken or meat, and the lentil/vegetable purée. Bring to the boil once more, simmer for 20-30 minutes, adding salt if necessary. Serve garnished with the rest of the fried onions.

Ingredients for DHANSAK (meat with lentils). *Recipe above.*

BHUNA MURGH
CHICKEN DRY CURRY

Serves: 4-5

1 x 1.25 kg (2½ lb) chicken
3 tablespoons oil or ghee
10 curry leaves, finely crumbled
½ teaspoon black mustard seed
1 large onion, finely chopped
2-3 cloves garlic, finely chopped
1 tablespoon finely chopped fresh ginger
2 teaspoons curry powder
1 teaspoon tandoori mix (see Glossary)
1 teaspoon ground cummin
½ teaspoon garam masala (page 35)
½ teaspoon amchur (dried mango) or
    1 tablespoon lemon juice
1 teaspoon chilli powder or paprika
2 teaspoons salt

Cut chicken into pieces for curry. Heat oil and fry the curry leaves and the black mustard for 1 minute. Add onion, garlic and ginger and fry slowly until onions are golden brown, stirring from time to time. Add curry powder, tandoori mix, cummin, garam masala, amchur and chilli or paprika. If using lemon juice instead of amchur do not add at this time. Fry, stirring, for 1 minute, then add salt and lemon juice if used. Add chicken and turn pieces until they are coated with the spice mixture. Cover pan tightly and cook over low heat until tender. Stir occasionally and if necessary add a very little hot water, about quarter to half cup. Serve with chapatis, parathas or rice.

MOGLAI MURGH
CHICKEN, MOGHUL STYLE

Serves: 6

1 x 1.5 kg (3 lb) roasting chicken
3 cloves garlic, crushed
1 teaspoon finely grated ginger
1 teaspoon ground turmeric
½ teaspoon saffron strands
¼ cup boiling milk
3 tablespoons ghee or oil
2 large onions, finely sliced
2 teaspoons garam masala with pepper
    (page 35)
1 teaspoon garam masala with fragrant
    spices (page 35)
2 teaspoons salt
½ cup hot water
2 tablespoons ground almonds
½ cup cream
2 tablespoons chopped fresh coriander
    leaves, optional

Cut the chicken into joints. Combine garlic, ginger and turmeric and rub well all over chicken. Soak saffron strands in milk for 10 minutes.

Heat ghee in a large heavy pan and fry the onions until golden brown, then remove from pan and reserve. Add chicken pieces to pan, a few at a time, and brown lightly on both sides. When all are done return them all to the pan, sprinkle with both kinds of garam masala and the salt. Add saffron soaked in milk, the hot water and half the browned onion. Cover and cook until chicken is tender, turning pieces of chicken halfway through cooking. Remove chicken to a warm serving plate, add almonds and cream to liquid remaining in pan and heat through, stirring well. Spoon over chicken and serve, garnished with remaining onions and the coriander leaves if used. Serve with rice or chapatis.

BUHARI MURGH
SPICED DEEP-FRIED CHICKEN

*Named in honour of a favourite Muslim
restaurant, where the fried chicken was like
no other fried chicken we have ever tasted,
this recipe evolved out of a nostalgic
determination to try to duplicate the original.*

Serves: 4
2 x 500 g (1 lb) frying chickens
3 spring onions, roughly chopped
4 cloves garlic, peeled
2 teaspoons finely chopped fresh ginger
2 tablespoons lemon juice
2 tablespoons chopped fresh coriander
 leaves
2 teaspoons sesame oil
2 teaspoons peanut oil
2 teaspoons ground coriander
1 teaspoon ground cummin
1 teaspoon paprika
½ teaspoon chilli powder
1½ teaspoons salt
oil for frying

Cut each chicken in halves down the centre. Put onions, garlic, ginger, lemon juice, fresh coriander leaves and both oils into container of electric blender and blend to a smooth purée. Add ground spices and salt. Rub this mixture well into the chickens, cover and refrigerate overnight.

Put chicken on deep plate and steam for 30 minutes. Pat dry without removing spices. At serving time heat oil for deep frying and when very hot fry the chickens for 2 minutes or until brown all over. Serve with spiced pilau rice and onion sambal.

Note: Any juices that collect in the plate when steaming chickens can be added to the liquid when cooking the rice.

MASALA MURGH
GRILLED MASALA CHICKEN

*An easy way to cook spiced chicken, using
some of the excellent masala mixtures
available in paste and powder form.*

Serves: 4-6
1 chicken, about 1.25 kg (2½ lb), or
 6 large drumsticks
3 teaspoons tandoori mix (see Glossary)
3 teaspoons green masala paste (page 36)
1 teaspoon salt
3 teaspoons sesame oil
3 teaspoons ground rice
½ teaspoon garam masala (page 35)
1½ tablespoons water

Cut chicken into serving pieces and score diagonally with a sharp knife, cutting through skin and flesh halfway to the bone. Combine all remaining ingredients and rub well all over the chicken and into the cuts. Marinate for 30 minutes. Chicken can be covered and marinated overnight in the refrigerator. Preheat grill and put chicken on the rack with skin downwards. Position rack at the furthest point from the heat and grill for 10-15 minutes. Turn chicken pieces over and grill for a further 10-15 minutes. Serve hot, accompanied by rice or any of the Indian breads, and a sambal or raita.

MURGH TIKKA
SKEWERED BARBECUED CHICKEN

Serves: 4-6
500 g (1 lb) chicken breasts or thighs
1 medium onion, roughly chopped
1 clove garlic, sliced
2 teaspoons finely chopped fresh ginger
2 tablespoons lemon juice
1 teaspoon ground coriander
½ teaspoon ground cummin
1 teaspoon garam masala (page 35)
3 tablespoons yoghurt
1 teaspoon salt
2 tablespoons chopped fresh coriander or
   mint leaves

Bone the chicken and remove skin. Cut chicken meat into bite-size pieces. In container of electric blender put the onion, garlic and ginger and blend until smooth, adding the lemon juice if more liquid is required. Mix with the ground spices, yoghurt and salt and marinate the chicken in this mixture for at least 2 hours at room temperature, or refrigerate overnight if possible. Thread chicken on bamboo skewers and cook over glowing coals or under a preheated griller until cooked through. Serve with onion and tomato sambal and puris or chapatis.

CHICKEN EVEREST

This is one of my husband's successful variations on a traditional Indian theme — which accounts for the lack of an Indian name and the presence of soy sauce. Using ground rice in the marinade gives the chicken a crisp coating.

Serves: 6
1 x 1.5 kg (3 lb) roasting chicken
2 cloves garlic, crushed
2 teaspoons finely grated fresh ginger
1½ tablespoons curry powder
1 teaspoon paprika
2 teaspoons salt
½ teaspoon ground black pepper
1 teaspoon garam masala (page 35)
1 teaspoon amchur (dried mango) or 2
   tablespoons lemon juice
½ teaspoon ground curry leaves
2 teaspoons light soy sauce
2 tablespoons oil
2 tablespoons ground rice
little warm water
2 tablespoons finely chopped spring
   onion
2 tablespoons chopped fresh coriander
   leaves

Wash and dry chicken well. Combine all other ingredients with sufficient warm water to make a paste of spreading consistency. Rub this paste inside and outside the chicken, leave for 1 hour. Roast in a preheated moderate oven 170°C (350°F) for 1-1¼ hours or until chicken is done. If bird browns too much during cooking, cover with foil. Serve warm or cold with rice, bread, or a salad.

MURGH MUSALLAM (whole chicken in spices and yoghurt) *recipe page 53.*

TANDOORI MURGH
SPICED ROAST CHICKEN

Tandoori chicken, perhaps the most publicised of all Indian chicken preparations, takes its name from the tandoor or clay oven in which it is cooked. Shaped like one of Ali Baba's jars and usually buried in earth, the tandoor is heated by white-hot coals within. The chicken is threaded on a very long skewer, which is lowered into the oven, leaving the bird to cook over the coals. Try this version cooked in a gas or electric oven — it does not have quite the same flavour as when cooked over coals, but is too delicious to miss.

Serves : 4

2 small roasting chickens, about 500 g
  (1 lb) each
½ teaspoon saffron strands
1 tablespoon boiling water
4 cloves garlic, peeled
1 tablespoon finely chopped fresh ginger
1 tablespoon lemon juice
½ teaspoon chilli powder
1 teaspoon paprika
1½ teaspoons garam masala (page 35)
2 teaspoons salt
2 tablespoons ghee

Skin the chickens, then make slits in the flesh of the thighs, drumsticks and breast, to allow spices to penetrate. Soak saffron in boiling water for 10 minutes and put into small blender jar with garlic, ginger and lemon juice. Blend until smooth. Scrape out blender jar and mix all other ingredients except ghee with the blended mixture. Dry the chickens inside and out with kitchen paper, then rub the spice mixture all over the chickens, especially in the slits made in the flesh. Cover and leave to marinate for 2 hours at least, or preferably refrigerate overnight.

Preheat oven to 200°C (400°F). Put ghee in a roasting pan and heat in the oven for a minute to melt the ghee, then spread ghee over the base of the pan. Put chickens in the roasting pan, side by side but not touching, with the breasts downwards. Spoon the melted ghee over the birds. Roast in hot oven for 20 minutes. Baste with ghee, turn birds on one side and roast for 15 minutes. Then turn on other side, baste again and continue roasting for a further 15 minutes. Turn birds breast upwards, baste well with ghee and pan juices and cook for a further 10-15 minutes, basting every 5 minutes. Serve hot with parathas or naan roti and an onion salad.

Note: If oven has a rotisserie, it is ideal for cooking tandoori chicken, but it will still be necessary to baste the birds because the skin has been removed.

KESAR MURGH
SAFFRON CHICKEN

Serves: 4-6

1 x 1.5 kg (3 lb) roasting chicken
3 tablespoons ghee
1 large onion, finely chopped
3 cloves garlic, finely chopped
1½ teaspoons finely grated fresh ginger
3 fresh red chillies, seeded and sliced
¼ teaspoon saffron strands
½ teaspoon ground cardamom
1½ teaspoons salt

Cut chicken into small serving pieces, dividing breast into quarters, separating thigh from drumstick and disjointing wings.

Heat ghee in a heavy saucepan and gently fry onion, garlic, ginger and chillies until onion is soft and starts to turn golden. Stir frequently. Pound saffron with mortar and pestle and dissolve in a tablespoon of very hot water. Add to pan with cardamom and stir well, then add chicken. Increase heat and turn chicken pieces for 4 or 5 minutes until each piece of chicken is golden and coated with the saffron mixture. Add salt, cover and cook over moderate heat for 10 minutes or until chicken is tender. Uncover pan and continue cooking until almost all the liquid evaporates.

Especially suitable for serving with parathas (page 32) or rice.

MURGH MUSALLAM
WHOLE CHICKEN IN SPICES AND YOGHURT *(picture page 51)*

A North Indian speciality, delicately spiced and delicious when served with parathas and raita or salad.

Serves : 6
1 x 1.5 kg (3 lb) roasting chicken
¼ teaspoon saffron strands
1 tablespoon hot water
½ teaspoon each ground black pepper, ground turmeric, ground cummin and chilli powder
¼ teaspoon each ground cardamom, cloves, cinnamon and mace
2 cloves garlic, crushed
1½ teaspoons salt
2 tablespoons yoghurt
3 tablespoons ghee or oil
2 medium onions, finely sliced
1¼ cups hot water or stock

Wash and dry chicken inside and out, removing neck and giblets and cutting off wing tips. These can be used for making stock.

Soak saffron strands in hot water 10 minutes, pressing saffron strands between the fingers to diffuse flavour and colour. Mix saffron and soaking water, all the ground spices and the garlic crushed with salt, into the yoghurt. Rub a tablespoon of the mixture inside the cavity of the chicken. Rub some of the mixture over the chicken. Leave chicken to marinate for 1 hour.

Heat ghee in a large, heavy saucepan and fry onions until golden. Remove onions to a plate, put in the chicken and brown it lightly on all sides. Return onions to the pan and stir remaining chicken marinade into the hot water or stock, pour into pan and bring to boil. Turn heat low, cover and cook for 45 minutes or until chicken is very tender. Turn chicken from time to time so it cooks first on one side and then the other, on its back and, for the last 10 minutes, breast downwards. Liquid should evaporate almost completely. Serve hot.

MURGH KALEJA KARI
CHICKEN LIVER CURRY

Serves: 4
500 g (1 lb) chicken livers
2 tablespoons ghee or oil
1 medium or large onion, finely chopped
2 cloves garlic, finely chopped
2 tablespoons finely grated fresh ginger
½ teaspoon ground turmeric
1 teaspoon chilli powder
3 teaspoons ground coriander
2 teaspoons ground cummin
1 teaspoon garam masala (page 35)
1 ripe tomato, chopped
1 teaspoon salt
½ teaspoon ground black pepper

Wash and drain the chicken livers. Cut each one in half, and discard any yellow spots. Heat the ghee or oil and fry the onion, garlic and ginger until onion is soft and golden brown. Add turmeric, chilli powder, coriander and cummin. Fry, stirring, for 2 minutes, then add the garam masala, tomato and salt and cook, covered, until tomato is pulpy. Stir and mash tomato with wooden spoon to speed the process. Add chicken livers, stir well, sprinkle pepper over and cook, covered for 15-20 minutes. Serve hot with rice and other accompaniments.

BADHAK VINDALOO
HOT AND SOUR CURRY OF DUCK

Serves: 4
1 x 2.5 kg (5 lb) duck
6-10 dried red chillies
½ cup vinegar
6 cloves garlic
1 tablespoon finely chopped fresh ginger
1 tablespoon ground coriander
2 teaspoons ground cummin
1 teaspoon ground turmeric
½ teaspoon ground black pepper
2 tablespoons ghee or oil
2 teaspoons salt
1 tablespoon sugar

Cut the duck into serving pieces. Remove stalks and seeds from dried chillies and soak in vinegar for 5-10 minutes. Put chillies, vinegar, garlic and ginger into container of electric blender and blend until smooth. Scrape mixture out of blender into a large bowl and mix in the ground spices. Add pieces of duck washed and well dried on paper towels, and turn them over in the mixture until they are well coated. Cover and leave for 2 hours at room temperature or overnight in the refrigerator.

In a large pan heat the ghee or oil and fry the pieces of duck lightly, add salt and a little hot water together with any marinade left. Cover and simmer on very low heat until duck is tender, about 1½-2 hours. Stir occasionally and turn duck so that it does not stick or burn. Add more water if necessary during cooking. At end of cooking time stir in sugar. Serve with rice.

BADHAK BUFFADO
SPICED DUCK WITH CABBAGE AND POTATOES

Serves: 4-5
1 x 2 kg (4 lb) duck
2 tablespoons oil
1 large onion, sliced
4 whole cloves
4 cardamom pods
1 small stick cinnamon
1 teaspoon finely grated fresh ginger
1 teaspoon ground turmeric
½ teaspoon ground pepper
2 teaspoons ground coriander
2 fresh red or green chillies
2 teaspoons salt
2 cups hot water
2 tablespoons vinegar
4 potatoes, peeled
half a cabbage, cut into wedges
1 cup fresh or frozen peas

Cut the duck into serving pieces. Heat oil in a large, heavy saucepan and fry onion and whole spices until onion is golden. Add ginger, turmeric, pepper and coriander and fry for a minute or two longer, then add the duck and fry until the pieces are slightly browned. Add the whole chillies (seed them if a less hot flavour is preferred), salt, water and vinegar. Cover tightly and simmer for 45 minutes or until duck is almost tender. Skim off any excess fat. Add potatoes and cook 10 minutes, then add cabbage and cook for a further 10 minutes. Lastly add peas, taste and adjust seasoning if necessary, cover and cook until peas are done. Serve hot.

KAJU MURGH KARI (curried chicken with cashews) *recipe page 45.*

ANDA KARI
EGG CURRY

Serves: 4-6
6 eggs
2 tablespoons ghee or oil
2 medium onions, finely chopped
3 cloves garlic, finely chopped
2 teaspoons finely grated fresh ginger
3 teaspoons ground coriander
2 teaspoons ground cummin
1 teaspoon ground turmeric
½ teaspoon chilli powder
2-3 ripe tomatoes, diced
1 teaspoon salt or to taste
½ cup hot water
½ teaspoon garam masala (page 35)

Hard boil the eggs, cool quickly under running cold tap, then shell and set aside. Heat ghee or oil and fry onions, garlic and ginger until soft and golden brown. Add coriander, cummin, turmeric and chilli and fry for a few seconds, then add tomatoes and salt and stir over medium heat until tomatoes are soft and pulpy. Add hot water, cover and simmer until gravy is thick, then stir in garam masala and the halved eggs and heat through. Serve with rice.

MOOTAY MOLEE
EGGS IN COCONUT MILK GRAVY

Among the South Indian Tamils, this is a favourite way of serving eggs.

Serves: 4-6
6 eggs
1½ cups thick coconut milk
2 cups thin coconut milk
2 tablespoons ghee or oil
1 large onion, sliced finely
3 cloves garlic, finely chopped
2 teaspoons finely grated fresh ginger
3 fresh green chillies, seeded and sliced
6 curry leaves
1 teaspoon ground turmeric
1 teaspoon salt or to taste
2 tablespoons lemon juice

Hard boil the eggs, cool under running cold water, shell and set aside. Extract the coconut milk as described on page 11, and keep the first extract or thick milk, and the second extract or thin milk, separate.

Heat the ghee and fry onion, garlic, ginger, chillies and curry leaves on low heat until the onions are soft. Do not let them colour. Add the turmeric and stir for a minute, then add the second extract of coconut milk and simmer gently, uncovered for 10 minutes. Add the thick coconut milk and salt and stir constantly as it comes to simmering point, then put in the eggs cut in halves and simmer, uncovered, for 6 or 7 minutes. Remove from the heat, stir in lemon juice to taste and serve with rice.

AKOORI
PARSI SCRAMBLED EGGS *(picture page 90)*

Serves: 4-6
6-8 eggs
4 tablespoons milk
¾ teaspoon salt
¼ teaspoon ground black pepper
2 tablespoons ghee
6 spring onions, finely chopped
2-3 fresh red or green chillies, seeded and
   chopped
1 teaspoon finely grated fresh ginger
⅛ teaspoon ground turmeric
2 tablespoons chopped fresh coriander
   leaves
1 ripe tomato, diced, optional
½ teaspoon ground cummin
tomato wedges to garnish
sprig of fresh coriander leaves to garnish

Beat eggs until well mixed. Add the milk, salt and pepper. Heat ghee in a large, heavy frying pan and cook the spring onions, chillies and ginger until soft. Add turmeric, coriander leaves and tomato if used and fry for a minute or two longer, then stir in the egg mixture and the ground cummin. Cook over low heat, stirring and lifting the eggs as they begin to set on the base of the pan. Mix and cook until the eggs are of a creamy consistency — they should not be cooked until dry. Turn on to a serving plate and garnish with tomato and coriander. Serve with chapatis or parathas.

MUTTON KARI
LAMB CURRY

If your experience with curry has been cold meat re-heated in a curry sauce, be assured that this dish, fragrant with spices and herbs, bears no resemblance to the pallid impostor of your acquaintance. This is curry in its simplest form, using a commercial curry powder — but make sure it is fresh and of good quality.

Serves: 6-8
1.5 kg (3 lb) boned shoulder of lamb
2 tablespoons ghee or oil
2 large onions, chopped
4 cloves garlic, chopped
1 tablespoon finely chopped fresh ginger
2 tablespoons curry powder
3 teaspoons salt
2 tablespoons vinegar or lemon juice
3 large tomatoes, chopped
2 fresh chillies
2 tablespoons chopped fresh mint leaves
1 teaspoon garam masala (page 35)
1 tablespoon chopped fresh coriander or
   mint leaves

Cut lamb into cubes. Heat ghee in a saucepan and gently fry onion, garlic and ginger until soft and golden. Add curry powder, salt and vinegar, stir thoroughly. Add lamb and cook, stirring constantly, until lamb is coated with the spice mixture. Add tomato, chillies and mint. Cover and cook over low heat for 1¼ hours or until lamb is tender, stirring occasionally. The tomatoes should provide enough liquid for the meat to cook in but, if necessary, add a little hot water, approximately half cup, just enough to prevent meat from sticking to pan. Add garam masala and chopped coriander leaves for the last 5 minutes of cooking time.

SEEKH BOTEE
SKEWERED MUTTON CURRY

Serves: 4-6

1 kg (2lb) lamb or mutton
thin slices of fresh young ginger
3 tablespoons ghee or oil
1 large onion, finely chopped
3 cloves garlic, finely grated
1 tablespoon ground coriander
2 teaspoons ground cummin
½ teaspoon ground fennel
½ teaspoon ground turmeric
½ teaspoon ground black pepper
2 teaspoons salt
1 ripe tomato, diced
2 green chillies, sliced
½ teaspoon ground cinnamon
½ teaspoon ground cardamom
¼ teaspoon ground cloves

Cut lamb into small cubes and thread on thin bamboo skewers cut in 10 cm (4 inch) lengths, alternating each piece of meat with a thin slice of ginger. Cut the ginger from a slender root so the slices will not be too big, or cut large slices in pieces.

Heat ghee or oil and fry onion over medium low heat until soft, stirring occasionally. Add garlic, stir and fry until onion is golden brown. Add coriander, cummin, fennel, turmeric and pepper and fry for 1 minute, then add salt and tomato and stir for 3 minutes longer. Add chillies and skewered meat and fry until meat is lightly browned. Turn heat low, cover and cook until meat is tender. Liquid from the meat will eventually be re-absorbed, leaving the gravy very thick. Stir occasionally to prevent spices catching on the base of the pan.

Ten minutes before end of cooking time sprinkle cinnamon, cardamom and cloves over the curry. Stir well and leave on very low heat. Serve hot with rice and accompaniments.

ROGHAN JOSH
LAMB IN SPICES AND YOGHURT

Serves: 6

750 g (1½ lb) lean lamb
3 dried red chillies, seeded
½ cup hot water
6-8 cloves garlic
1 tablespoon finely chopped fresh ginger
2 tablespoons desiccated coconut, toasted
2 tablespoons blanched almonds
1 tablespoon ground coriander
1 teaspoon ground cummin
1 teaspoon poppy seeds
½ teaspoon ground fennel
½ teaspoon ground cardamom
¼ teaspoon ground cloves
¼ teaspoon ground mace
½ teaspoon ground black pepper
4 tablespoons ghee or oil
1 medium onion, finely chopped
4 cardamom pods, bruised
½ teaspoon ground turmeric
½ cup yoghurt
2 ripe tomatoes, peeled and chopped
1½ teaspoons salt
1 teaspoon garam masala (page 35)
2 tablespoons chopped fresh coriander
   leaves

Cut the lamb into large cubes. Soak chillies in the hot water for 5 minutes. Put garlic, ginger, coconut (shake in a dry pan over medium heat to toast), almonds and chillies together with 2 tablespoons of the soaking water in container of electric blender. Put ground coriander, cummin, poppy seeds and fennel in a small pan and shake over low heat for a few minutes until spices darken slightly in colour and give off an aromatic smell. Add to the ingredients in blender. Blend for a few seconds until smooth. Remove from blender container and add the ground cardamom, cloves, mace and pepper. Set aside.

Heat ghee in a large heavy saucepan and fry the chopped onion, stirring, until onion is golden brown. Add bruised cardamoms, turmeric and the blended spice mixture and fry, stirring until well cooked and the ghee starts to separate from the spices. Add the yoghurt, a spoonful at a time and stir it in. Add tomatoes and salt, stir and fry for a further 5 minutes, then add the cubed lamb and cook over high heat, stirring and turning meat so that each piece is coated with the spice. Turn heat very low, cover and cook for 1 hour or longer. Lamb should be very tender and liquid almost absorbed. Stir occasionally to ensure that spices don't stick to base of pan. Sprinkle with garam masala, replace lid and cook 5 minutes longer. Serve sprinkled with coriander leaves and accompanied by plain rice or a pilau.

PATRANI MACHCHI (fish steamed in banana leaves) *recipe page 37.*

KASHMIRI ROGHAN JOSH
LAMB IN YOGHURT AND SPICES, KASHMIRI STYLE

Serves: 6

1 kg (2 lb) lean, boned lamb
½ cup yoghurt
2 tablespoons ghee
peppercorn-size piece of asafoetida,
  optional
2 teaspoons salt
1 teaspoon ground dried ginger
about 2 cups hot water
1 teaspoon chilli powder, or to taste
1 tablespoon finely grated fresh ginger
2 teaspoons Kashmiri garam masala
  (page 35)
2 tablespoons chopped fresh coriander
  leaves

Trim excess fat from lamb and cut meat into large cubes. Combine the yoghurt, ghee, asafoetida dissolved in about a tablespoon of hot water, salt and dried ginger. Mix with the lamb in a large heavy saucepan, cover and cook, stirring occasionally. After some time the juices given out by the lamb will evaporate and the spice mixture start to stick to base of pan. Add half cup hot water, the chilli powder and grated fresh ginger and stir well with wooden spoon, scraping the dried mixture from base of pan and incorporating it with the liquid added. Continue to cook, covered, until again the liquid evaporates and mixture sticks to pan. Add half cup more hot water and repeat first process. Do this until meat is very tender, adding no more than half cup water at a time. When liquid evaporates and meat is done, sprinkle with Kashmiri garam masala and fresh coriander. Replace lid and leave on very low heat for 10-15 minutes longer. Serve hot with rice, chapatis or parathas.

KORMA
LAMB WITH SPICES AND YOGHURT

Serves: 6

1 kg (2 lb) boned leg of lamb
2 medium onions
1 tablespoon chopped fresh ginger
2 large cloves garlic
¼ cup raw cashews or blanched almonds
2-6 dried chillies, seeded
2 teaspoons ground coriander
1 teaspoon ground cummin
¼ teaspoon ground cinnamon
¼ teaspoon ground cardamom
¼ teaspoon ground cloves
½ teaspoon saffron strands
2 tablespoons boiling water
1 tablespoon ghee
2 tablespoons oil
2 teaspoons salt
½ cup yoghurt
2 tablespoons chopped fresh coriander
  leaves

Cut lamb into large cubes, trimming off excess fat if any. Peel onions, slice one finely and set aside. Chop other onion roughly and put into container of electric blender with ginger, garlic, cashews and chillies. Add half cup water to blender jar, cover and blend on high speed for a minute or until all ingredients are ground smoothly. Add all the ground spices and blend for a few seconds longer.

Put saffron strands into a small bowl, pour the boiling water over and allow to soak while starting to cook the masala (ground spice mixture).

Heat ghee and oil in a large saucepan and when hot put in the sliced onion and fry, stirring frequently with a wooden spoon, until soft and golden. Add the blended mixture and continue to fry, stirring constantly until the masala is well cooked and the oil starts to separate from the mixture. Wash out blender container with an extra ¼ cup water, add to pan together with salt and continue to stir and fry until the liquid dries up once more. Add the meat and stir over medium heat until each piece is coated with the spice. Stir the saffron, crushing the strands against side of the bowl, then add to the pan. Stir to mix well. Add yoghurt and stir again until evenly mixed. Reduce heat to low, cover and cook at a gentle simmer for 1 hour or until meat is tender and gravy thick. Stir occasionally taking care that the spice mixture does not stick to base of pan. When lamb is cooked, sprinkle with fresh coriander leaves, replace lid and cook for 5 minutes longer. Serve hot with rice.

BADAMI GOSHT
SPICED LAMB WITH SAFFRON AND ALMONDS

This dish, flavoured only with sweet spices and using no chilli at all, will be popular with everyone, even children. A good introduction to spicy food.

Serves: 6-8
1 x 1.5-2 kg (3-4 lb) leg of lamb
½ teaspoon saffron strands
3 tablespoons boiling water
3 teaspoons salt
1 cup yoghurt
2 tablespoons ghee
2 tablespoons oil
1 small stick cinnamon
6 cardamom pods, bruised
6 whole cloves
1 large onion, finely chopped
4 cloves garlic, finely chopped
2 teaspoons finely grated fresh ginger
2 teaspoons ground cummin
2 tablespoons ground almonds or
    25 whole blanched almonds
1 tablespoon chopped fresh mint,
    optional

Ask butcher to bone the lamb. Trim skin and excess fat from meat and cut meat into 5 cm (2 inch) cubes. (The bones can be used for making stock. Serve parsi pilau with the lamb, and cook the rice in the stock.)

Soak saffron strands in the boiling water until soft, about 10 minutes, then press strands between fingers to diffuse as much colour and fragrance as possible. Stir saffron and salt into the yoghurt in a large bowl, add lamb and mix well, cover and let stand at room temperature while preparing the rest of the ingredients.

Heat ghee and oil in a heavy saucepan with a well-fitting lid. When hot add the cinnamon, cardamom, cloves and fry over medium heat for a minute or two. Add the onion, garlic and ginger and continue frying and stirring until onion is soft and golden, about 10 minutes. Add ground cummin and fry for a minute longer.

Drain lamb from yoghurt marinade and add to the pan, turning pieces of lamb so that they come in contact with the heat on all sides. Add the marinade and ground almonds. Stir half cup water into any marinade remaining in bowl and add to pan. Stir well, reduce heat to low, cover and cook 1 hour or until lamb is tender and gravy thick. Towards end of cooking stir with wooden spoon to ensure gravy does not stick to the bottom of the pan. Sprinkle with mint, replace lid for 5 minutes, then serve hot with rice. A light, slightly sweet rice dish such as Parsi pilau (page 25) goes particularly well with this.

Note: If ground almonds are not available, soak the whole almonds in half cup boiling water until the water cools, then pulverise in electric blender.

RAAN
ROAST LEG OF LAMB, KASHMIRI STYLE

Serves: 8
1 x 2.5 kg (5 lb) leg of lamb
1 tablespoon finely grated fresh ginger
4 cloves garlic, crushed
3 teaspoons salt
1 teaspoon ground cummin
1 teaspoon ground turmeric
½ teaspoon ground black pepper
½ teaspoon ground cinnamon
½ teaspoon ground cardamom
¼ teaspoon ground cloves
½ teaspoon chilli powder, optional
2 tablespoons lemon juice
¾ cup yoghurt
2 tablespoons each blanched almonds
    and pistachios
¼ teaspoon powdered saffron or
    ½ teaspoon saffron strands
3 teaspoons honey

With a sharp knife remove skin and any excess fat from lamb. Using point of the knife make deep slits all over the lamb. Combine ginger, garlic, salt, ground spices and lemon juice. (If mixture is too dry to spread, add very little oil.) Rub spice mixture well over the lamb, pressing it into each slit.

Put yoghurt, almonds, pistachios and saffron powder into blender container. If saffron strands are used, soak for 10 minutes in 2 tablespoons hot water and use water as well. Blend together until smooth, then spoon the purée over the lamb. Drizzle the honey over, cover and allow lamb to marinate at least overnight in the refrigerator, or two days if possible.

Allow 30 minutes per pound cooking time. Preheat oven to very hot, 230°C (450°F), and roast lamb in a covered baking dish for 30 minutes, then reduce heat to moderate, 170°C (350°F) and cook for a further 1¾ hours or until lamb is cooked through. Uncover lamb and cool to room temperature. Serve with namkin chawal, page 24.

QABARGAH or KAMARGAH
LAMB CHOPS IN SPICY BATTER

A Kashmiri method of preparing lamb, first simmering it in milk and spices, then frying in batter.

Serves: 4
8 small lamb chops or cutlets
1½ cups milk
½ cup water
1 teaspoon salt
8 cardamom pods, bruised
8 whole cloves
small stick cinnamon
½ teaspoon whole black peppercorns

Batter:
⅓ cup besan (chick pea flour)
1 teaspoon ground coriander
½ teaspoon salt
¼ teaspoon ground cardamom
¼ teaspoon chilli powder
pinch each of ground cinnamon,
    nutmeg, cloves and turmeric
⅓ cup water
2 teaspoons melted ghee
oil or ghee for frying

Put lamb chops in a saucepan with the first group of ingredients and bring to the boil. Reduce heat and simmer, covered, until meat is tender and the liquid evaporates. Cool while preparing batter. Mix all ingredients for batter, beating with a wooden spoon until smooth. Let stand for 30 minutes.

Heat enough oil or ghee for frying. Dip chops into batter, coating them thinly, then slip into the hot oil and fry until golden brown on both sides. Drain well on absorbent paper. Serve hot with Indian breads and vegetables.

LAMB KEBABS
(picture opposite)

Let me confess that this is not a traditional Indian recipe — no Indian cook would use oregano or soy sauce. It evolved when I was in an unorthodox mood, and proved so delicious that I wrote it down and have used it frequently. Strangely enough, the kebabs still have an Indian flavour.

Serves: 6-8
2 kg (4 lb) boned leg of lamb
1 large clove garlic
2 teaspoons salt
1½ teaspoons finely grated fresh ginger
1 teaspoon freshly ground black pepper
1 teaspoon ground turmeric
1 teaspoon ground coriander
1 teaspoon ground cummin
1 teaspoon crushed dried curry leaves
1 teaspoon crushed dried oregano leaves
1 tablespoon light soy sauce
1 tablespoon sesame oil
2 tablespoons peanut oil
1 tablespoon lemon juice

Trim excess fat off lamb, cut meat into 2.5 cm (1 inch) cubes and put in a large bowl. Crush garlic with salt and combine with remaining ingredients, mixing well. Pour over lamb and stir, making sure each piece of meat is covered with the spice mixture. Cover bowl and refrigerate at least 3 hours, or as long as 4 days.

Thread 4-5 pieces of meat on each skewer and cook under a hot grill, allowing about 5 minutes on each side. When nicely brown, serve hot with boiled rice or parathas, accompanied by onion sambal (page 89) and podina chatni (page 88).

LAMB KEBABS, *recipe above.*

SEEKH KEBAB KARI
SKEWERED LAMB IN SPICES

These kebabs are marinated in a spice mixture and fried in ghee before being simmered in curry.

Serves: 4-6
750 g (1½ lb) lamb
thin slices of fresh young ginger
bamboo skewers

Marinade:
2 teaspoons ground coriander
1 teaspoon garam masala
1 teaspoon ground cummin
½ teaspoon ground dried ginger
½ teaspoon ground turmeric
⅛ teaspoon grated nutmeg
4 cloves garlic, crushed
1 teaspoon salt
1 tablespoon oil
1 tablespoon lemon juice

Curry:
3 tablespoons ghee or oil
1 medium onion, finely chopped
4 cloves garlic, crushed
1 small stick cinnamon
4 cardamom pods, bruised
4 whole cloves
1 teaspoon chilli powder, optional
½ cup hot water
½ teaspoon black cummin seeds
½ teaspoon garam masala (page 35)
2 fresh green chillies, seeded and sliced,
   to garnish
2 tablespoons chopped fresh coriander
   leaves, to garnish

Cut lamb into 2.5 cm (1 inch) cubes. Mix together the ingredients for the marinade, adding more oil if necessary to make it into a spreading consistency. Put cubes of lamb into the marinade and mix, rubbing the marinade well into the lamb. Leave overnight if possible, or at room temperature for 2 hours. Thread lamb cubes on skewers alternately with slices of ginger. If ginger is very strong use fewer slices, say one slice of ginger to every two or three cubes of lamb.

Curry: Heat ghee in a large saucepan or frying pan and fry the skewers of lamb, a few at a time, over high heat until they are browned on all sides. Remove from pan, reduce heat and fry onion and garlic gently, stirring constantly, until they are golden brown. Add whole spices and fry for a minute longer, then add chilli powder and fry for a few seconds. Return meat to pan. Add water, stir well to loosen any spices on base of pan, cover and simmer gently until meat is tender. When almost done and curry is reduced and thick, sprinkle with black cummin seeds lightly roasted in a dry pan over medium heat. Sprinkle with garam masala. Stir, leave for a minute or two longer, then serve hot garnished with chillies and coriander leaves. Serve with rice and accompaniments or with any of the Indian breads.

KEEMA SEEKH KEBAB
MINCED MEAT ON SKEWERS

Serves: 4-6
500 g (1 lb) minced lamb or beef
2 tablespoons besan (chick pea flour)
1 medium onion, finely chopped
1 clove garlic, crushed
2 tablespoons finely chopped fresh
   coriander leaves
1 teaspoon finely grated fresh ginger
1 teaspoon salt
1 teaspoon garam masala (page 35)
¼ cup yoghurt

Combine minced meat with all other ingredients except the yoghurt. Mix thoroughly and knead well until the mixture becomes very smooth. Form portions of the mixture into sausage shapes around skewers. (Use skewers that are square or rectangular in cross section, because the minced meat mixture will slip on round skewers.) Beat the yoghurt slightly and coat the meat with it, then place over barbecue or under preheated griller until browned on all sides and cooked through. Serve with rice or Indian bread, vegetables and other accompaniments.

KASHMIRI KOFTA KARI
CURRIED MEATBALLS, KASHMIRI STYLE *(picture page 66)*

A feature of Kashmiri Brahmin cooking is the absence of onions and garlic, both of which are supposed to inflame the baser passions. Kashmiri Brahmins also do not eat beef, so if this dish is to be made in the true Kashmiri tradition, use minced lamb.

Serves: 6
750 g (1½ lb) lean minced lamb
1 teaspoon finely grated fresh ginger
2 fresh chillies, finely chopped
1 teaspoon ground coriander
½ teaspoon chilli powder
2 teaspoons garam masala (page 35)
2 teaspoons salt
½ cup yoghurt
3 tablespoons ghee
1 tablespoon dried milk or khoa (page 22)
1 teaspoon sugar
½ teaspoon ground black pepper
¼ teaspoon ground cardamom

Put the lamb into a bowl with ginger, chillies, coriander, chilli powder and 1 teaspoon each of the garam masala and salt, adding 1 tablespoon of the yoghurt to moisten the spices and help distribute them evenly. A teaspoon or so of the ghee can also be added if the lamb is very lean. Mix well and form into small oval shapes.

Heat ghee in a heavy saucepan, add the dried milk, sugar, remaining yoghurt, garam masala and salt. Fry in the ghee, then add half cup hot water, bring to the boil and add the koftas. Simmer, covered, until no liquid remains. Turn koftas over, add half cup more hot water and the pepper, cover and simmer until liquid is absorbed once more. Sprinkle the dish with cardamom and serve with Indian breads or rice. Cover after adding cardamom so its fragance will not dissipate.

BOTEE KEBAB
MUTTON KEBAB

Serves: 4-6
500 g (1 lb) mutton
2 tablespoons desiccated coconut
1 large onion, roughly chopped
2 cloves garlic, peeled
1 teaspoon chopped fresh ginger
¼ teaspoon each ground nutmeg,
   cinnamon, cloves and cardamom
½ teaspoon coarsely ground black pepper
1 teaspoon poppy seeds
½ cup yoghurt

Trim mutton of excess fat but leave a thin layer, for it gives a delicious crisp layer when grilled. Cut meat into bite-size cubes. For Eastern cooking, meat is cut smaller than it is for Western-style kebabs. For one thing the flavours penetrate better; for another no knives are used at the table.

Toast the coconut in a dry frying pan over medium heat, stirring constantly, until it is a golden brown colour. Set aside to cool.

Put onion, garlic and ginger into container of electric blender and grind to a smooth purée. Add spices, toasted coconut, poppy seeds and yoghurt and blend again for 1 minute or until coconut is finely ground. Pour over the pieces of meat in a bowl and rub well into the meat so that every piece is well covered with the spice marinade. Cover and leave in the refrigerator overnight or at room temperature for 2 hours. Thread the pieces on bamboo skewers and cook under a preheated griller or over glowing coals until brown. Serve with chapatis, parathas or rice, accompanied by onion sambal (page 89) or other salad type of relish.

DOH PIAZA
SPICED LAMB WITH ONIONS

The name of this dish translates literally as 'two onions', and it has never quite been settled whether this means the onions are added in two forms — raw and fried — or at two different stages of cooking, or means the dish has twice as much onion as most other preparations of this type.

Serves: 8-10

1.5 kg (3 lb) shoulder of lamb or mutton
1 kg (2 lb) onions
6 cloves garlic
1½ teaspoons finely grated fresh ginger
3 tablespoons yoghurt
1-2 teaspoons chilli powder, or to taste
1 teaspoon paprika
3 tablespoons chopped fresh coriander
   leaves
2 tablespoons ground coriander
2 teaspoons black cummin seeds
3 tablespoons ghee
3 tablespoons oil
8 cardamom pods
1 teaspoon garam masala (page 35)

Cut meat into large cubes. Slice half the onions finely and chop the rest. Put the chopped onions into container of electric blender with garlic, ginger, yoghurt, chilli powder, paprika, coriander leaves, ground coriander and black cummin seeds. Blend until smooth.

Heat ghee and oil in a large heavy pan and fry the sliced onions, stirring frequently, until evenly browned. Remove from pan. Add cubed meat to pan, not too many pieces at one time, and fry on high heat until browned on all sides. Remove each batch as it is browned and add more. When all the meat has been done and removed from pan, add a little more ghee or oil if necessary and fry the blended mixture over medium heat, stirring all the time, until it is cooked and gives out an aromatic smell. Oil should start to appear around the edges of mixture. Return meat to pan, add cardamom pods, stir well, cover and cook on low heat until meat is almost tender. Stir occasionally. It might be necessary to add a little water, but usually the juices given out by the meat are sufficient. When meat is tender and liquid almost absorbed add garam masala and reserved fried onions, replace lid of pan and leave on very low heat for a further 15 minutes. Serve with rice or Indian breads.

ALU GOSHT KARI
MEAT AND POTATO CURRY

Serves: 6-8

1.5 kg (3 lb) skirt or other lean stewing
   steak
¼ cup oil or 2 tablespoons ghee
1 teaspoon black mustard seeds
½ teaspoon fenugreek seeds
6 cloves garlic, chopped
1 tablespoon finely chopped fresh ginger
3 medium onions, finely sliced
1½ teaspoons ground turmeric
2 tablespoons ground coriander
1 tablespoon ground cummin
2 teaspoons chilli powder
3 teaspoons salt
2 tablespoons vinegar
2 teaspoons garam masala (page 35)
2 tablespoons extra vinegar
750 g (1½ lb) potatoes, peeled and cubed
2 tablespoons chopped fresh coriander
   leaves, optional

Trim steak of fat and gristle and cut into small cubes. Heat oil in a large saucepan and fry the mustard seeds until they pop. Add fenugreek seeds, garlic, ginger and onion and fry over medium heat, stirring occasionally with a wooden spoon, until onions just begin to brown. Add turmeric and fry for a minute longer. Add coriander, cummin and chilli powder and stir for a minute or so, then add salt and vinegar and stir until liquid dries up. Sprinkle in the garam masala and mix well. Add the cubed meat, stirring so that all the pieces are coated with the spice mixture. If there is much of the spice sticking to the base of the pan, add the extra vinegar and stir, scraping as much as possible from the base of the pan. Reduce heat, cover with well-fitting lid and let meat and spice mixture simmer for 1½-2 hours or until meat is tender. Depending on the type of meat used, it may be necessary to add a little water. Add the cubed potatoes, cover once more and cook for 20-25 minutes or until done. Sprinkle with fresh coriander leaves and serve hot with rice or Indian bread.

KASHMIRI KOFTA KARI (curried meatballs, Kashmiri style) *recipe page 65.*

NARGISI KOFTA
EGGS IN MEATBALLS *(picture page 70)*

Named for their resemblance to the yellow and white flowers of the narcissus, these meatballs are fried, then simmered in curry and served as a main dish. For picnic fare try them just fried and served with a salad.

Serves: 6

Meatballs:

7 small eggs
500 g (1 lb) twice-minced lamb or beef
1 small onion, finely chopped
2 cloves garlic, finely grated
½ teaspoon finely grated ginger
1 fresh green chilli, finely chopped
1 teaspoon salt
1 teaspoon garam masala (page 35)
½ teaspoon ground turmeric
½ cup water
1½ tablespoons besan (chick pea flour)
1 tablespoon yoghurt
ghee or oil for frying

Curry:

1 tablespoon ghee or oil
1 medium onion, finely chopped
5 cloves garlic, finely grated
2 teaspoons finely grated fresh ginger
1 teaspoon garam masala (page 35)
1 teaspoon ground turmeric
½ teaspoon chilli powder
2 large ripe tomatoes
1 teaspoon salt
½ cup yoghurt
½ cup hot water
2 tablespoons chopped fresh coriander
   leaves

Put 6 eggs into a pan of cold water and bring slowly to simmering point. Stir eggs gently for first 5 minutes to centre the yolks. Simmer for a further 10 minutes, then run cold water into the pan until the eggs are cold. Shell them and set aside.

Put meat into a saucepan with the onion, garlic, ginger, chilli, salt, garam masala, turmeric and water. Stir well, bring to the boil, then cover and simmer 20-30 minutes or until meat is well cooked. Stir in chick pea flour and continue cooking until all the liquid has been absorbed. Cool the meat mixture, then knead it until very smooth, adding a little yoghurt if necessary to moisten it.

Divide into 6 equal portions and mould each one around a hard-cooked egg. Beat remaining egg. Dip koftas in beaten egg and fry in hot oil until golden brown all over. Drain on absorbent paper. Cut in halves with a sharp knife, spoon some of the curry over and serve hot.

Curry: Heat ghee or oil and fry onion until soft and pale golden, then add garlic and ginger and fry, stirring, until onions are golden brown. Add garam masala, turmeric and chilli powder, stir for a few seconds, then add tomatoes and salt. Cover and cook to a pulp, stirring occasionally. Mash the yoghurt smoothly, mix with the water and add to the simmering curry. Stir well and cook uncovered until thick. If koftas are prepared beforehand they can be put into the sauce to heat through, then cut in halves and served with rice or chapatis. Garnish with fresh coriander leaves.

ALU CHAP
SPICY POTATO RISSOLES

Serves: 4
1 kg (2 lb) potatoes
1 teaspoon salt
2 tablespoons finely chopped mint leaves
2 spring onions, finely chopped
1 fresh green chilli, seeded and finely
    chopped
1 egg, beaten
breadcrumbs for coating
oil for frying

Filling:
250 g (8 oz) minced meat prepared as for
    samoosas (page 100)

Boil and mash potatoes smoothly. Mix in salt, mint, spring onions and chilli. Divide mixture into 8-10 portions and shape each into a flat circle. Put a spoonful of the meat filling in the centre and close the potato around it, shaping to a thick round patty. Dip in beaten egg, then in breadcrumbs and fry in hot oil until golden brown.

KEEMA KARI
MINCED MEAT AND SPLIT PEA CURRY

Serves: 4-6
½ cup split peas
2 tablespoons ghee or oil
2 medium onions, finely chopped
2 cloves garlic, finely chopped
1 teaspoon finely grated fresh ginger
1 teaspoon ground turmeric
½ teaspoon chilli powder
1 tablespoon chopped fresh coriander or
    mint leaves
4 small ripe tomatoes, chopped
2 teaspoons salt
500 g (1 lb) minced meat
2 teaspoons garam masala (page 35)

Wash split peas and soak while preparing other ingredients. Heat ghee or oil and gently fry onions, garlic and ginger until soft. Add turmeric, chilli powder, coriander or mint, tomatoes and salt. Stir over medium heat for a few minutes, then add meat and drained split peas. Stir until well mixed, then cover tightly and cook for 40 minutes or until meat and peas are tender, stirring from time to time and adding a little hot water if liquid evaporates.

Add garam masala and cook until liquid evaporates and mixture fries in the fat left in the pan. At this stage stir frequently so it does not burn. Serve this dry curry with Indian bread and other accompaniments such as vegetable preparations, sambals, chutneys.

KEEMA MATTAR
MINCED MEAT WITH FRESH PEAS

Serves: 4-6
2 tablespoons ghee
1 large onion, finely sliced
2 cloves garlic, crushed
½ teaspoon finely grated fresh ginger
1 teaspoon ground turmeric
½ teaspoon chilli powder
500 g (1 lb) minced meat
½ cup yoghurt
1 cup fresh green peas
1 teaspoon garam masala (page 35)
1½ teaspoons salt
2 tablespoons finely chopped fresh
    coriander leaves
1 fresh red chilli, finely sliced

Heat ghee and fry onion until soft. Add garlic and ginger and fry until onion is golden brown. Add turmeric and chilli powder and stir for a few seconds, then add meat and fry, turning meat constantly until colour changes. Break up any large lumps of meat. Stir in the yoghurt and peas, cover and cook for 15 minutes. Add garam masala and continue cooking until meat and peas are tender. Serve garnished with coriander leaves and chilli.

GOANI KEBAB
GOANESE KEBAB CURRY

Serves: 6
500 g (1 lb) lean lamb
500 g (1 lb) pork
thin slices fresh ginger
2 tablespoons ghee or oil
1 large onion, finely chopped
4 cloves garlic, finely chopped
2 fresh red or green chillies, seeded
1 tablespoon ground cummin
2 tablespoons black mustard seed, ground
2 teaspoons chilli powder, or to taste
2 teaspoons garam masala (page 35)
½ cup vinegar
½ cup water
2 teaspoons salt
½ teaspoon ground black pepper

Cut both meats into cubes and thread on bamboo skewers alternately with thin slices of tender ginger. Heat ghee or oil in a saucepan and fry the onion, garlic and chillies until onion is soft and golden brown. Add the ground spices and continue stirring and frying for 1 minute. Add vinegar, water, salt and pepper. Let the mixture come to the boil, then put in skewers of meat, turn to coat in the spice mixture, cover and cook on very low heat, until meat is tender. Stir and turn kebabs once or twice during cooking. When meat is tender, cook uncovered until gravy is thickened and dark. Serve with white rice and accompaniments.

SHIKAR VINDALOO
PORK VINDALOO

Because of the high acid content of this recipe, cook it in an earthenware, enamel or stainless steel vessel.

Serves: 6-8
1 kg (2 lb) pork
6-8 large dried red chillies
1 cup vinegar
2 teaspoons chopped fresh ginger
7 cloves garlic
2 teaspoons ground cummin
½ teaspoon ground black pepper
½ teaspoon ground cinnamon
½ teaspoon ground cardamom
¼ teaspoon ground cloves
¼ teaspoon ground nutmeg
2 teaspoons salt
2-3 tablespoons ghee or oil
2 medium onions, finely chopped
1 tablespoon brown sugar, optional

Cut meat into cubes. Soak chillies in vinegar for 10 minutes. Any kind of vinegar may be used, but if using double strength cider vinegar dilute with an equal quantity of water. (Ideally, coconut vinegar gives the correct flavour.) Put chillies and vinegar, ginger and garlic into container of electric blender and blend until smooth. Add ground spices and salt. Marinate the meat in this mixture for about 2 hours.

Heat ghee or oil and fry onions gently until soft and golden. Stir frequently and cook until all liquid from onions has evaporated and the oil comes out. Drain meat from marinade and fry, turning cubes, until meat changes colour, then pour in marinade, cover pan and simmer on low heat until meat is well cooked. Stir in sugar, if used. Serve hot with plain rice and accompaniments.

NARGISI KOFTA (eggs in meatballs) *recipe page 68.*

DHAL
LENTIL PUREE *(picture page 87)*

Any type of lentils can be used for this, but red lentils or moong are the quickest cooking types and do not need soaking. Other types of lentils should be soaked overnight before cooking.

Serves: 4-6
250 g (8 oz) red lentils
1 ½ tablespoons ghee or oil
1 large onion, finely sliced
2 cloves garlic, finely chopped
1 teaspoon finely grated fresh ginger
½ teaspoon ground turmeric
3 cups hot water
1 teaspoon salt, or to taste
½ teaspoon garam masala (page 35)

Wash lentils thoroughly, removing those that float on the surface. Drain well. Heat ghee and fry onion, garlic and ginger until onion is golden brown. Add turmeric and stir well. Add drained lentils and fry for a minute or two, then add hot water, bring to the boil, reduce heat to simmer. Cover and cook for 15 to 20 minutes or until lentils are half cooked. Add salt and garam masala, mix well and continue cooking until lentils are soft and the consistency is similar to porridge. If there is too much liquid, leave the lid off the pan to speed evaporation. Serve dhal plain or garnished with sliced onions, fried until deep golden brown. Eat with boiled rice, Indian breads, or as a light meal by itself.

SAME KA BHAJI (1)
SPICY FRIED BEANS (1)

Use any kind of bean — broad beans, French beans, stringless beans, snake beans; they all go well with this type of light spicing.

Serves: 4-6
500 g (1 lb) tender beans
1 tablespoon ghee or oil
1 medium onion, finely chopped
½ teaspoon finely grated fresh ginger
1 teaspoon ground turmeric
1 teaspoon garam masala (page 35)
½ teaspoon chilli powder, optional
2 teaspoons salt
2 ripe tomatoes, chopped, or ¼ cup hot water
squeeze of lemon juice

Top and tail beans, remove strings if necessary and cut them into bite-size pieces. Heat the ghee in a saucepan and fry the onion and ginger over medium low heat until onion is golden. Add turmeric, garam masala, chilli powder and salt and fry for 2 minutes. Add tomatoes or water and cook stirring, until tomatoes are cooked to a pulp and most of the liquid evaporates. Add beans and stir well, partially cover pan with lid and cook until beans are just tender. Do not overcook. Stir in lemon juice to taste.

SAME KA BHAJI (2)
SPICY FRIED BEANS (2)

A drier version, less acid in flavour because no tomatoes or lemon are used.

Serves: 4
500 g (1 lb) green beans
1 tablespoon ghee or oil
1 onion, finely chopped
½ teaspoon ground turmeric
½ teaspoon chilli powder
½ teaspoon garam masala (page 35)
1 teaspoon salt, or to taste

String beans and slice thickly. Heat ghee in a saucepan and fry onion until golden, then add turmeric, chilli and garam masala and stir for a few seconds. Add beans and salt and cook, stirring, for about 5 minutes. Cover and cook on low heat until beans are just tender.

SUKHE PHALLI KARI
CURRIED DRIED BEANS

Make this curry with Bengal peas, chick peas, haricot, lima or any favourite variety of dried beans.

Serves: 4
250 g (8 oz) dried beans
water
2 teaspoons salt
1½ tablespoons ghee or oil
1 large onion, finely chopped
2 cloves garlic, finely chopped
1 tablespoon finely chopped fresh ginger
1 teaspoon ground turmeric
1 teaspoon garam masala (page 35)
2 large ripe tomatoes, chopped
1-2 fresh green chillies, seeded and chopped
2 tablespoons chopped fresh mint
2 tablespoons lemon juice

Soak dried beans in plenty of cold water overnight. Drain, rinse and put beans into a large saucepan with water to cover and 1 teaspoon salt. Bring to the boil, cover and cook until tender. Add more hot water during cooking if necessary. Drain and reserve cooking liquid.

Heat ghee in large saucepan and gently fry the onions, garlic and ginger until soft and golden, then add turmeric, garam masala, tomatoes, chillies, mint, remaining teaspoon salt and lemon juice. Add the beans and stir well over medium heat for 5 minutes. Add 1 cup reserved liquid, cover and cook over low heat until tomatoes and chillies are soft and the gravy thick. Serve with rice or Indian breads as part of a vegetarian meal.

MATTAR CHILKA KARI
CURRIED PEA PODS *(picture page 74)*

When green peas are young and tender, save the pods after shelling the peas. They are delicious and sweet when cooked this way.

Serves: 4
pods from 500 g (1 lb) peas
1 tablespoon ghee or oil
1 medium onion, finely chopped
1 teaspoon finely chopped fresh ginger
1 teaspoon ground turmeric
1 teaspoon salt
1 teaspoon garam masala (page 35)
½ teaspoon chilli powder, optional
2 ripe tomatoes, diced
4 small potatoes, peeled and diced

Separate halves of the pods. Hold each half with the inner side towards you and bend stalk end inwards so that the fleshy part of the pod cracks. Then pull downwards, peeling off and discarding the thin, silk-like inner lining of the pod. Wash the pods and remove any strings from the edges.

Heat ghee and fry onion and ginger over low heat until onion is soft and golden. Add turmeric, salt, garam masala and chilli powder, stir and fry for a minute or two, then add the tomatoes, potatoes and pea pods.

Stir well, cover and cook until potatoes and pea pods are tender. It may be necessary to add a few spoonfuls of water if curry tends to stick to base of pan, but if it is cooked on low heat and stirred occasionally, the liquid from the tomatoes will be sufficient. This curry should be quite dry. Serve with chapatis, parathas or rice.

GOBI FOOGATH
SPICY FRIED CABBAGE

Serves: 6
half a large, firm cabbage
4 tablespoons oil
1 large onion, finely sliced
2 or 3 fresh green or red chillies,
  seeded and sliced
2 cloves garlic, finely grated
1 teaspoon finely grated fresh ginger
1 teaspoon ground turmeric
1½ teaspoons salt, or to taste
2 tablespoons desiccated coconut

Shred cabbage coarsely. Heat oil in a large saucepan and fry the onion and chillies until soft. Add garlic and ginger and fry, stirring, until golden. Add turmeric and cabbage, fry and toss cabbage in the mixture, then cover and cook over low heat for 10-15 minutes or until cabbage is tender but not too soft. Sprinkle with salt and mix well, then add coconut and stir to mix thoroughly. If there is any liquid in the bottom of pan leave cover off and stir over medium heat until all liquid is absorbed. Serve as an accompaniment to rice and curries.

PALAK BHAJI
SPICY FRIED SPINACH

Serves: 4-6
1 or 2 bunches of spinach (about 500 g
  [1 lb] after removing stalks)
2 tablespoons ghee
2 tablespoons oil
2 large onions, finely sliced
2 cloves garlic, finely chopped
1 teaspoon finely grated fresh ginger
1 teaspoon cummin seeds
½ teaspoon black cummin seeds, optional
½ teaspoon ground cummin
½ teaspoon ground coriander
½ teaspoon ground turmeric
¼ teaspoon chilli powder, optional
1 teaspoon salt, or to taste

Wash spinach well in several changes of water and remove tough stalks. Heat ghee and oil in a large saucepan and fry the onion until golden, then add garlic and ginger and fry, stirring, for a further minute or two. Add seeds, ground spices and salt and mix well, then turn in the spinach with only the water that remains on the leaves after washing. Toss in the spicy mixture, then turn heat very low and cook uncovered, stirring frequently, until the spinach is cooked. It may be necessary to add a little more water to prevent spinach sticking to pan. Serve with rice, chapatis or other Indian breads.

ALU MATTAR SUKHE
POTATO AND PEA DRY CURRY

Serves: 6
500 g (1 lb) potatoes
500 g (1 lb) fresh peas in the pod
2 tablespoons ghee
1½ teaspoons panch phora (page 22)
1 large onion, finely chopped
2 tablespoons chopped fresh mint
  or coriander leaves
1 teaspoon finely grated fresh ginger
1 teaspoon ground turmeric
1½ teaspoons salt
½ teaspoon chilli powder, optional
¼ cup hot water
1 teaspoon garam masala (page 35)
1 tablespoon lemon juice

Peel and dice potatoes. Shell the peas. Heat the ghee and fry the panch phora on low heat until seeds start to brown, then add onion and fry gently until onion is soft and starts to colour. Add chopped herbs and grated ginger and fry for a few seconds, stirring. Add the turmeric, salt and chilli powder and stir well. Add potatoes and peas, stir well and sprinkle with hot water. Turn heat very low, cover saucepan tightly and cook for 20 minutes, shaking pan occasionally. Sprinkle with garam masala and lemon juice, replace cover and cook for a further 10 minutes. Serve hot with rice or chapatis.

Preparing pods for MATTAR CHILKA KARI *(curried pea pods).* Recipe page 73.

MATTAR PANIR
PEAS WITH FRESH CHEESE *(picture page 83)*

Fresh home-made cheese is a favourite addition to vegetable curries, for it is an important source of protein for strict vegetarians. Make the panir as described on page 22. For convenience and speed substitute fresh pecorino — a white, unsalty cheese very similar to panir in flavour and texture. Ask for the variety that does not melt when subjected to heat. Frozen peas can be used instead of fresh.

Serves: 4-6

250 g (8 oz) baked ricotta or panir
  (page 22)
750 g (1½ lb) fresh peas in the pod
½ cup melted ghee or oil
2 medium onions, finely chopped
3 cloves garlic, finely chopped
2 teaspoons finely grated fresh ginger
2 teaspoons ground coriander
1 teaspoon ground cummin
1 teaspoon ground turmeric
½ teaspoon chilli powder, optional
2 firm ripe tomatoes, chopped
1 teaspoon salt
1 teaspoon garam masala (page 35)
2 tablespoons finely chopped fresh
  coriander or mint leaves

If making the panir let the curds hang in the muslin until cool, then squeeze out as much liquid as possible by twisting the muslin. Put the wrapped curds on a flat plate and put another plate or a board on top. Weigh it down and leave for about 6 hours until very firm. Remove the muslin and cut cheese into small cubes. If not using at once, cover with plastic food wrap and refrigerate.

Shell fresh peas, or defrost frozen peas. Heat the ghee or oil in a small pan and fry the cubes of cheese in one layer at a time, turning them carefully so they brown on all sides. As each batch is done, lift them out on a perforated spoon and put them on a plate. When all the cheese has been fried pour off any excess fat, leaving about a tablespoon. Fry the onions, garlic and ginger over medium low heat, stirring frequently, until they are golden. Add the ground spices and stir for a minute longer. Then add tomatoes, salt and half the garam masala. Cook and stir until tomatoes are pulpy. Add a little hot water if mixture seems too dry. Add peas and cook until they are half done, then add cheese cubes and half the coriander or mint and simmer, covered, for 10 minutes or until peas are cooked. Sprinkle with remaining garam masala and coriander and serve hot with rice or chapatis.

SAAG
PURÉE OF LEAFY GREENS

Serves: 4-6

500 g (1 lb) spinach or other greens
2 medium turnips or 1 giant white radish
1 tablespoon ghee or oil
½ teaspoon black mustard seeds or panch
  phora (page 22)
1 medium onion, finely chopped
1 teaspoon finely grated fresh ginger
½ teaspoon chilli powder
½ teaspoon ground turmeric
1½ teaspoons salt, or to taste
½ teaspoon garam masala (page 35)

Wash the greens, removing any tough stalks. Break the leaves into small pieces and put into a large pan with a sprinkling of water. Peel and dice the turnips or radish and add to the pan. Cover and cook over low heat until vegetables are soft. Drain away any liquid and chop or mash the vegetables. Heat the ghee or oil and fry the mustard seeds or panch phora for a minute, then add onion and ginger and fry on medium heat until onion is soft and golden. Add chilli, turmeric, salt and mashed vegetables. Stir and cook for 5 minutes, then sprinkle with garam masala, cover and leave on low heat for a few minutes longer until liquid evaporates. Taste and add salt or lemon juice if desired. Serve as an accompaniment to chapatis or rice and curries.

SABZI BHAJI
FRIED MIXED VEGETABLES

A colourful combination of lightly spiced vegetables. Take care not to overcook them.

Serves: 6
3 large tender carrots
250 g (8 oz) green beans
quarter of a cauliflower
half a small cabbage
3 tablespoons ghee or oil
½ teaspoon black mustard seed or 1
    teaspoon panch phora (page 22)
8 curry leaves, optional
2 cloves garlic, crushed
2 teaspoons finely grated fresh ginger
1 teaspoon ground turmeric
¼ teaspoon chilli powder or 1 fresh
    red chilli, seeded and sliced
1½ teaspoons salt, or to taste

Scrape carrots and cut into matchstick strips. String beans and slice diagonally. Cut cauliflower into slices, leaving some stem with the flowerets. Shred cabbage coarsely.

Heat ghee or oil in a large pan and fry the mustard seeds or panch phora and the curry leaves for 2 minutes, stirring. Add garlic, ginger, turmeric and chilli and stir for a minute or two, then add carrots, beans and cauliflower. Stir over medium heat until vegetables are half cooked, then add cabbage and continue to toss and cook for a further 5 minutes or until all vegetables are tender but still crisp. Sprinkle with salt, mix well, cover and cook for the last 2 minutes. Serve immediately.

TAAZI KHUMBEN ALU MATTAR KARI
CURRIED MUSHROOMS, POTATOES AND PEAS *(picture page 78)*

Serves: 6
500 g (1 lb) small white mushrooms
500 g (1 lb) small new potatoes
1 cup shelled green peas
1 tablespoon ghee or oil
1 small onion, finely sliced
1 teaspoon finely grated fresh ginger
1 clove garlic, crushed, optional
2 tablespoons finely chopped fresh
    coriander leaves
1 teaspoon ground turmeric
½ teaspoon chilli powder, optional
½ cup hot water
1½ teaspoons salt
1 teaspoon garam masala (page 35)

Wipe mushrooms with a damp paper towel. If mushrooms are large cut in halves or quarters, leaving a piece of stalk on each piece. Wash and scrub potatoes and if large cut into halves or quarters. Frozen peas can be used instead of fresh, but add them during the last 15 minutes.

Heat ghee in saucepan and fry onion over gentle heat for 3 minutes. Add ginger, garlic and coriander leaves and fry for 3 to 4 minutes longer, stirring occasionally. Add turmeric and chilli powder, fry for 1 minute, then add mushrooms, potatoes and fresh peas. Add water and salt and stir well. Cover and cook on low heat for 15 minutes. Uncover, sprinkle with garam masala and stir well. Cover and cook for a further 15 minutes or until potatoes are tender enough to be pierced with a skewer. Serve with rice or Indian bread.

PIAZ BHAJI
SPICY FRIED ONIONS OR LEEKS

Serves: 4-6
5 or 6 large leeks or 3 large onions
2 tablespoons ghee or oil
1 teaspoon panch phora (page 22) or
    cummin seeds
1 teaspoon ground turmeric
1 teaspoon finely grated fresh ginger
1 teaspoon garam masala (page 35)
1 teaspoon salt or to taste

Wash leeks well, getting rid of all grit, or peel onions. Cut leeks or onions into fairly thick slices. Heat ghee or oil in a large saucepan and fry the panch phora or cummin for a minute or two, stirring. Add turmeric and ginger and fry for a minute longer, then turn in the leeks or onions, stir well, and fry for 5 minutes. Sprinkle garam masala and salt over, cover and cook until tender, stirring occasionally.

DHINGRI KARI
MUSHROOM CURRY

Choose large, open mushrooms, because they have the strongest flavour.

Serves: 4
500 g (1 lb) mushrooms
2 leeks or 4 spring onions
2 tablespoons ghee or oil
2 cloves garlic, crushed
½ teaspoon finely grated fresh ginger
6 curry leaves
2 teaspoons curry powder
1 teaspoon salt
½ teaspoon garam masala (page 35)
½ cup thick coconut milk
2 teaspoons lemon juice

Wipe mushrooms clean and cut stems into slices, caps into quarters. Slice leeks or spring onions finely. Heat ghee and fry garlic, ginger, curry leaves and leeks until soft but not brown. Add curry powder, salt and mushrooms and continue to stir over low heat until mushrooms are soft. Cover and cook on low heat 8-10 minutes, then sprinkle with garam masala, add coconut milk and cook uncovered, stirring constantly, just until heated through. Remove from heat and stir in lemon juice. Serve with white rice or vegetable pilau.

BAIGAN DAHI
EGGPLANT WITH YOGHURT

Serves: 6
2 medium eggplants
3 tablespoons ghee or oil
2 medium onions, finely chopped
3 cloves garlic, finely chopped
2 teaspoons finely grated fresh ginger
2 teaspoons ground coriander
1 teaspoon ground cummin
½ teaspoon ground turmeric
½ teaspoon chilli powder
1½ teaspoons salt, or to taste
½ teaspoon garam masala (page 35),
   optional
sugar, optional
1 cup yoghurt

Put eggplants under a preheated griller, about 15 cm (6 inches) from the heat and grill until skins are blackened and eggplants soft throughout. Cool, then peel. Mash flesh of eggplants roughly, or chop into small pieces.

In a medium saucepan heat ghee or oil and fry onions, garlic and ginger until onion is soft and golden. Add coriander, cummin, turmeric, chilli powder and fry, stirring, for another minute. Stir in salt and add the mashed or chopped eggplant. Stir and cook for a few minutes, then sprinkle with garam masala, cover and cook for 5 minutes longer. Taste and add more salt if necessary, and, if liked, a little sugar — about 2 teaspoons. Mash the yoghurt smoothly and mix into the eggplant before serving. Serve with rice and curries and other accompaniments.

TAAZI KHUMBEN ALU MATTAR KARI (curried mushrooms, potatoes and peas) *recipe page 77.*

BRINJAL BARTHA
EGGPLANT PURÉE *(picture page 87)*

Serves: 6

2 large eggplants
2 large ripe tomatoes
3 tablespoons ghee or oil
2 medium onions, finely chopped
1½ teaspoons finely grated fresh ginger
½ teaspoon ground turmeric
½ teaspoon chilli powder
2 teaspoons salt
1 teaspoon garam masala (page 35)

Wash and dice eggplants and tomatoes. It is not necessary to peel either. Heat ghee in a saucepan and gently fry onion and ginger until they are soft and start to brown. Add turmeric, chilli powder, salt and garam masala and mix thoroughly. Add eggplant and tomato, stir well and cover. Reduce heat to low, cook until vegetables are soft, stirring occasionally to prevent vegetables sticking to pan. Cook until liquid evaporates and purée is thick and dry enough to scoop up with Indian breads. Serve hot or cold.

BHENDI BHAJI
SPICY FRIED OKRA

It is important to buy tender okra, for the mature beans are tough and stringy. Test by bending the tip of the bean. If tender, it will snap but if old it will merely bend and you will not be able to break it.

Serves: 4-6

500 g (1 lb) okra
2 tablespoons ghee or oil
½ teaspoon panch phora (page 22)
1 medium onion, finely chopped
½ teaspoon ground turmeric
½ teaspoon chilli powder, optional
½ teaspoon salt, or to taste
½ teaspoon garam masala (page 35)

Wash the okra, cut off stalk ends and slice into bite-size pieces. Heat ghee and fry the panch phora for a minute, then add onion and fry, stirring, until it starts to turn golden. Add turmeric, chilli if used, salt and garam masala. Add okra, stir well, cover and cook, stirring occasionally, until okra is tender. Serve as a vegetable accompaniment to rice or chapatis.

BHENDI KARI
OKRA CURRY

Serves: 4-6

500 g (1 lb) fresh, tender okra
1 tablespoon ghee or oil
1 large onion, thinly sliced
2 fresh green chillies, slit and seeded
1 clove garlic, finely sliced
½ teaspoon finely grated fresh ginger
½ teaspoon ground turmeric
½ teaspoon ground coriander
½ teaspoon ground cummin
1½ cups coconut milk or buttermilk
1 teaspoon salt, or to taste

Wash okra and cut off stem ends with a sharp knife. If they are large, cut into convenient lengths. Heat the ghee or oil in a saucepan and fry the onion and chillies over medium low heat, stirring occasionally, until onions are golden. Add garlic, ginger and turmeric and fry, stirring, for a minute longer, then add okra and fry for 3 or 4 minutes. Add the coriander and cummin, coconut milk or buttermilk and salt. Simmer uncovered until okra is tender, 10-12 minutes. Serve hot with rice.

GOODA BARTHA
ZUCCHINI OR MARROW PURÉE

Serves: 4
500 g (1 lb) zucchini or marrow
1 tablespoon ghee or oil
1 teaspoon cummin seed
½ teaspoon black mustard seed
2 fresh green chillies, seeded and sliced
1 medium onion, finely chopped
½ teaspoon salt
½ teaspoon chilli powder, optional

Peel and roughly chop zucchini or marrow, discarding seeds. Put into a saucepan with water to almost cover, cook until soft, then drain well and mash. Heat ghee in a saucepan and fry the cummin and mustard seeds until mustard seeds start to crackle. Add chillies and onion and cook until onion is soft. Add zucchini, salt and chilli powder and cook uncovered for 5 minutes or until liquid evaporates. Serve warm or at room temperature.

ALU CHAP
POTATO RISSOLES WITH PEAS

Serves: 4
1 kg (2 lb) potatoes
salt to taste
2 cups fresh or frozen peas
1 tablespoon ghee
1 medium onion, finely chopped
1 teaspoon finely grated fresh ginger
1 tablespoon chopped fresh coriander
    leaves
½ teaspoon ground turmeric
½ teaspoon garam masala (page 35)
¼ teaspoon chilli powder, optional
oil for deep frying
2 eggs, beaten
breadcrumbs for coating

Boil the potatoes, drain well, then mash until quite smooth, adding salt to taste. Shell the fresh peas or thaw the frozen peas. Heat the ghee in a saucepan and on low heat fry the onion, ginger and coriander leaves. When onion is soft and golden add the ground spices, about a teaspoon of salt, and the peas. Cover and cook until peas are tender and all liquid evaporated. If using fresh peas, add a little water when cooking them. Let the peas cool to lukewarm, divide the potato into 8 portions and shape each one to a flat circle. Put a spoonful of the peas in the centre and enclose with the potato, moulding it smoothly to a hamburger shape. Dip each rissole in beaten egg, then in breadcrumbs. Heat oil and fry the rissoles, two or three at a time, until golden brown all over. Drain on absorbent paper and serve hot with fresh chutney or salad.

ALU BHAJI
SAVOURY FRIED POTATOES

Serve these as an accompaniment to thosai or any of the Indian breads. Or use the same mixture mashed slightly, to fill chapatis, puris and kachoris before cooking.

Serves: 4
500 g (1 lb) potatoes
2 medium onions
1 tablespoon ghee or oil
¼ teaspoon black mustard seeds
½ teaspoon ground turmeric
½ teaspoon chilli powder
1 teaspoon salt

Boil the potatoes, peel and dice. Chop onions finely. Heat ghee in a saucepan and fry the mustard seeds until they pop. Add onions and continue frying on low heat until they are soft and golden brown. Add turmeric and chilli powder and stir, then add potatoes, sprinkle salt over and toss gently to mix well together. Serve hot or cold.

THA (1)
OTATOES (COLD)

loury potatoes
ns melted ghee
non juice
½ teaspoon salt, or to taste
hot milk as required
½ cup finely chopped fresh mint leaves
2 spring onions, finely chopped, or 1
   finely chopped small onion

Boil the potatoes in their skins and as soon as they are tender drain well, peel and mash. Add ghee, lemon juice and salt, and mix in enough hot milk to give a smooth, creamy consistency. Taste for seasoning, add more lemon juice and salt if required. It should be quite piquant. Mix in mint and spring onions. Pat into a flat shape on a plate, or pile in a bowl. Garnish with a sprig of mint. Serve cold or at room temperature.

ALU BARTHA (2)
SPICY MASHED POTATOES (HOT)

Serves: 6
500 g (1 lb) potatoes
1 tablespoon ghee or oil
½ teaspoon black mustard seeds
1 fresh green chilli, seeded and sliced
1 small onion, finely chopped
½ teaspoon ground turmeric
1 teaspoon garam masala (page 35)
1 teaspoon salt
pinch chilli powder
1-2 tablespoons lemon juice
chopped fresh mint or fresh coriander
   leaves

Boil potatoes in their skins, peel and mash. Heat ghee and fry mustard seeds until they pop, add chilli and onion and fry until onion is soft and golden. Add turmeric, garam masala, salt and chilli powder and stir for a few moments, then add lemon juice. Add potatoes and mix well, heating through. Serve sprinkled with the mint or coriander leaves.

GUJARATI KHATTAI ALU
GUJARATI POTATOES

Serves: 4-6
500 g (1 lb) floury potatoes
1 tablespoon tamarind pulp
¼ cup hot water
2 teaspoons brown sugar
1½ tablespoons ghee or oil
½ teaspoon black mustard seeds
½ teaspoon ground turmeric
½ teaspoon chilli powder
1 teaspoon ground coriander
1 teaspoon ground cummin
1 teaspoon salt, or to taste
2 fresh green chillies, seeded and sliced
2 tablespoons desiccated coconut

Peel and dice potatoes. Soak tamarind in hot water for 5 minutes, squeeze firmly to extract all the juice and strain liquid through a fine strainer to exclude seeds and fibres. Dissolve sugar in the tamarind liquid. Heat ghee and fry the mustard until the seeds pop. Add the turmeric, chilli, coriander and cummin and fry on low heat for 1 minute. Add potatoes and toss for a minute longer. Sprinkle with salt and a little water, about quarter cup, cover tightly and cook on very low heat for 15 minutes. Add tamarind juice, sliced chillies and desiccated coconut and stir. Cover and cook for a further 5-10 minutes or until potatoes are done. Serve hot with rice or chapatis.

MATTAR PANIR (peas with fresh cheese) *recipe page 76.*

ACCOMPANIMENTS

The feature that sets an Indian meal apart is the number and variety of accompaniments to the main dishes. In fact, these accompaniments are as important as the main dish.

They include dried fish or pappadams (lentil wafers) fried in deep hot oil until crisp; fresh chutneys made from herbs, coconut, acid fruits and other ingredients; bland cooling raitas based on yoghurt and featuring bananas, tomatoes and other fruit or vegetables. These raitas are called pachchadis in South India, and incorporate more spicy seasoning.

An Indian salad presupposes hot chillies as an ingredient, or a sufficient sprinkling of chilli powder to give it a 'kick'. If the raw vegetables are dressed with enough chilli, then the salad becomes a sambal.

Use your imagination and create raitas, salads and chutneys from fruit and vegetables in season. For cooked chutneys see page 89; these chutneys though popular with Westerners, are almost unknown in India.

PIAZ KA DHANIA PATTAR SALAT
ONION AND CORIANDER LEAF SALAD

Serves: 4-6
2 medium onions, thinly sliced
salt to taste
2 tablespoons lemon juice
3 tablespoons (or more) fresh coriander
  leaves, roughly chopped

Combine all ingredients, cover and chill.

KACHUMBAR
PARSI-STYLE ONION SALAD

This relish can be hot or not-so-hot. If you want the milder version, the chillies should be seeded (see handling of chillies, page 12). If even seeded chillies are likely to be too hot for your taste, substitute about half cup thinly sliced capsicum.

Serves: 4-6
2 medium onions, finely sliced
salt
tamarind pulp the size of a walnut
¼ cup hot water
2 tablespoons grated palm sugar or
  substitute
2 firm ripe tomatoes, diced
1 tablespoon fine shreds of fresh ginger
3 fresh red or green chillies, sliced
salt to taste
2 tablespoons chopped fresh coriander
  leaves

Sprinkle onions generously with salt and leave for an hour, then press out all the liquid and rinse once in cold water. Drain. Soak tamarind pulp in hot water for a minute or two, then squeeze to dissolve pulp in water. Strain, adding a little more water if pulp is too thick. Dissolve sugar in the tamarind liquid. Mix all ingredients together, chill and serve.

TAMATAR SALAT
TOMATO SALAD WITH MINT AND SPRING ONIONS

4 firm red tomatoes
6 spring onions
½ cup fresh mint leaves
3 tablespoons lemon juice
½ teaspoon salt, or to taste
2 teaspoons sugar
½ teaspoon chilli powder, optional

Peel tomatoes and cut into thin wedges. Finely slice spring onions and chop mint leaves. Mix lemon juice, salt, sugar and chilli powder together, stir until sugar dissolves, then pour over the combined ingredients and mix lightly but thoroughly. Cover and chill until serving time.

PALAK RAITA
SPINACH WITH YOGHURT AND SPICES

Serves: 4-6
500 g (1 lb) spinach
1 tablespoon ghee or oil
1 teaspoon black mustard seeds
1 teaspoon cummin seeds
1 teaspoon ground cummin
½ teaspoon fenugreek seeds
pinch chilli powder or cayenne pepper,
   optional
½ teaspoon salt, or to taste
1 cup yoghurt

Wash spinach well and remove any tough stems. Pull the leaves into pieces and put into a saucepan with the moisture on the leaves or add 1 tablespoon water. Cover and steam over low heat until spinach is tender. Drain and chop finely. Heat ghee or oil in a small saucepan and fry the mustard seeds until they start to pop. Add cummin seeds, ground cummin and fenugreek seeds and continue to fry, stirring with a wooden spoon, until the fenugreek seeds are golden brown, but do not allow to burn. Remove from heat, stir in chilli or cayenne and salt and allow to cool. Mix in the yoghurt, then stir this mixture into the spinach. Serve cold or at room temperature as an accompaniment to a meal.

KHIRA RAITA
CUCUMBER WITH YOGHURT *(picture page 87)*

Serves: 6
2 large green cucumbers
2 teaspoons salt
1 small clove garlic, crushed
¼ teaspoon finely grated fresh ginger
1 cup yoghurt
lemon juice to taste

Peel and slice cucumbers very thinly. Put in a bowl, sprinkle with salt and chill about 1 hour. Pour off the liquid, pressing out as much as possible. Mix garlic and ginger into yoghurt, then stir in the cucumbers and combine thoroughly. Taste and add more salt if necessary, add lemon juice to taste. Serve chilled.

Cucumbers in sour cream: For a richer version of cucumber raita, substitute 1 cup sour cream for yoghurt, or half cup thick cream mixed with half cup yoghurt.

BAIGAN PACHCHADI
SPICED EGGPLANT WITH YOGHURT

Serves: 4-6

3 tablespoons oil
1 teaspoon black mustard seeds
1 medium onion, finely chopped
2 fresh green chillies, seeded and sliced
1 medium eggplant, peeled and diced
1 small ripe tomato, diced
1 teaspoon salt
1 teaspoon garam masala (page 35)
½ teaspoon chilli powder, optional
¼ cup water
1 cup yoghurt
2 tablespoons chopped fresh coriander
  leaves

In a saucepan heat oil and fry mustard seeds until they pop. Add onion and chillies and fry until onion is soft. Add eggplant and fry for a few minutes, stirring, then add tomato, salt, garam masala and chilli powder. Stir well, add water, cover and cook until eggplant and tomato can be mashed to a purée. Cool, stir in yoghurt and half the coriander leaves. Serve garnished with remaining leaves.

KHIRA PACHCHADI
CUCUMBERS IN SPICED YOGHURT

2 medium cucumbers
¼ cup desiccated coconut
3 tablespoons hot water
2 fresh green chillies, seeded and chopped
1 teaspoon salt
1½ cups yoghurt
1 teaspoon ghee or oil
1 teaspoon black mustard seeds
½ teaspoon black cummin seeds, optional

Peel and seed cucumbers, and grate coarsely. Sprinkle coconut with hot water and toss lightly with fingers, until all the coconut is moistened. Mix cucumbers, coconut, chillies and salt into yoghurt.

Heat ghee in a small pan and fry seeds until the mustard seeds pop, then remove from heat and stir into yoghurt mixture. Serve cold.

KELA PACHCHADI
BANANAS IN SPICED YOGHURT

Serves: 6

3 large ripe bananas
3 tablespoons freshly grated or desiccated
  coconut
1 cup yoghurt
2 tablespoons lemon juice
2 teaspoons sugar
½ teaspoon salt
⅛ teaspoon chilli powder, optional
1 teaspoon ghee or oil
1 teaspoon cummin seeds
1 teaspoon black mustard seeds

Peel and slice bananas. There should be approximately 2 cups of sliced banana. If using desiccated coconut, sprinkle 1 tablespoon hot water over and mix until coconut is evenly moistened. Season the yoghurt with lemon juice, sugar, salt and chilli powder, and stir in the bananas and coconut.

In a small saucepan heat the ghee and fry the cummin and mustard seeds until the mustard seeds pop. Pour over the yoghurt mixture and fold in. Serve as an accompaniment to a curry meal.

DHAL (lentil puree, *top*) *recipe page 72;* BRINJAL BARTHA (eggplant purée, *top right*) *recipe page 80;* KHIRA RAITA (cucumber with yoghurt, *centre*) *recipe page 85;* PODINA CHATNI (mint chutney, *lower right*) *recipe page 88;* ELOLU KIRI HODHI (vegetable curry, *lower left*) *recipe page 142;* PARATHA (flaky wholemeal bread, *lower left corner*) *recipe page 32.*

IMLI CHATNI
TAMARIND CHUTNEY

3 tablespoons dried tamarind pulp
1 cup hot water
1 teaspoon salt
2 teaspoons black or brown sugar
1 teaspoon ground cummin
½ teaspoon ground fennel
2 teaspoons finely grated fresh ginger
lemon juice to taste
pinch chilli powder, optional

Put tamarind pulp in a bowl with hot water and allow to soak until water is cool. Knead and squeeze pulp away from the seeds until it is dissolved in the water, then strain through a fine nylon sieve, pushing all the pulp through. If necessary, add a little more water to assist in getting all the pulp from the seeds. Add salt, sugar and other ingredients to the tamarind and stir to mix well. Taste and add more salt if necessary, lemon juice to sharpen the flavour and if liked, a small pinch of chilli powder.

PODINA CHATNI
MINT CHUTNEY *(picture page 87)*

1 cup firmly packed mint leaves
6 spring onions
2 fresh green chillies
1 clove garlic, optional
1 teaspoon salt
2 teaspoons sugar
1 teaspoon garam masala (page 35)
⅓ cup lemon juice
2 tablespoons water

The easy way to make this fresh chutney is in an electric blender. Everything is put in blender container (the spring onions cut in short lengths and the chillies seeded and stalks removed), then blended to a smooth paste. If a blender is not available finely chop mint, onions and chillies. Pound in mortar and pestle a little at a time, until ground to a paste. Mix in remaining ingredients. Pack into a small dish, smooth the surface, cover and chill until serving time.

DHANIA CHATNI
FRESH CORIANDER CHUTNEY

Proceed as for podina chatni (preceding recipe), but replace mint with an equal quantity of fresh coriander. A teaspoonful of chopped fresh ginger may also be added if desired.

PIAZ SAMBAL
ONION SAMBAL

2 medium onions, finely sliced
2 tablespoons lemon juice
½ teaspoon chilli powder, or to taste
½ teaspoon salt

Sprinkle onion with lemon juice, chilli powder and salt and toss together lightly until well mixed. Serve as an accompaniment to a meal of rice and curries, or with lamb kebabs (page 63) and parathas (page 32).

NARIYAL CHATNI
GREEN COCONUT CHUTNEY

Traditionally, this chutney is served as an accompaniment to thosai, South Indian pancakes, but it is equally acceptable as an accompaniment to any other kind of Indian meal.

Serves: 6
1 lemon
1 or 2 fresh green chillies
½ cup fresh mint or fresh coriander leaves
2 spring onions, roughly chopped
1 teaspoon salt
1 cup desiccated coconut
1 teaspoon ghee or oil
2 teaspoons black mustard seeds
2 teaspoons cummin seeds

Peel lemon so that no white pith remains. Cut into pieces and remove seeds. Put lemon in container of electric blender with seeded and roughly chopped chillies, mint or coriander leaves, spring onions and salt. Blend until puréed.

Add coconut and continue blending to a smooth paste, scraping down sides of blender and adding a little more liquid if necessary.

Heat ghee in small pan and fry the seeds, stirring frequently, until mustard seeds start to pop. Mix with blended mixture. Shape into a flat cake. Serve with thosai (page 101) or rice.

AM CHATNI
SWEET MANGO CHUTNEY

This is not one of the fresh chutneys, which are the genuine chutneys of India. It is more like a Major Grey type which, though not originally Indian, has come to be expremely popular and which goes very well with Indian food.

8-10 large unripe mangoes
3 teaspoons salt
8 large dried chillies
3 cups malt vinegar
5 cloves garlic
½ cup peeled, chopped fresh ginger
1 teaspoon garam masala (page 35)
500 g (1 lb) sugar
1 cup sultanas or seedless raisins

Peel mangoes and slice thickly, discarding seeds. Put the mango slices in a large bowl and sprinkle with the salt. Remove stalks and seeds from chillies, soak them in a little vinegar for 10 minutes, then put into container of electric blender with garlic and ginger and blend. It does not matter if pieces of chilli remain. If blender is not available pound the soaked chillies with mortar and pestle and grate the cloves of garlic and the peeled ginger on fine grater.

Put remaining vinegar into an enamel or stainless steel pan with blended mixture, garam masala and sugar and bring to the boil. Simmer, uncovered, for 15 minutes. Add mangoes and sultanas and simmer until thick and syrupy. Cool and put into sterile bottles. Seal airtight.

Note: 1.5 kg (3 lb) green apples, apricots or other suitable fruit may be used in place of mangoes.

TAMATAR KASAUNDI
TOMATO OIL PICKLE

1½ tablespoons black mustard seeds
1½ cups malt vinegar
¾ cup chopped fresh ginger
20 cloves garlic
20 fresh green chillies
2 kg (4 lb) firm ripe tomatoes
1¼ cups vegetable oil
1½ tablespoons ground turmeric
4 tablespoons ground cummin
1-2 tablespoons chilli powder, to taste
1 cup sugar
1 tablespoon salt

Soak mustard seeds in vinegar overnight and grind in electric blender. Peel ginger and garlic, chop roughly and add to mustard and vinegar. Blend on high speed until puréed.

Cut chillies in halves lengthways and remove seeds. Peel and chop the tomatoes.

Heat oil in a large, heavy saucepan until smoking hot. Allow to cool slightly, then add the ground turmeric, cummin and chilli powder and fry, stirring, for a few minutes. Add tomatoes, chillies, blended vinegar mixture, sugar and salt. Simmer until tomatoes are reduced to a pulp and the oil starts to float on top. Taste and add more salt if required. Bottle and seal when cold. Leave the pickle to mature for a week before using.

AM KA ACHAR
GREEN MANGO PICKLE

My husband, Reuben, is positively inspired when it comes to making pickles. All the pickle recipes that follow come from his recipe file — which probably would not exist had I not given it to him inscribed. 'To the best cook in the world from his assistant and typist', a cunning ploy to make him record his recipes. But half the time I follow him around the kitchen, noting his every move and writing busily between complying with his demands for spices, vinegar, salt and just about everything else he needs. Oh well, genius must be pandered to, I suppose.

12 green mangoes
50 red or green chillies
kitchen salt
2½ cups malt vinegar
2 teaspoons fenugreek seeds
½ cup peeled cloves of garlic
½ cup chopped fresh ginger
½ cup ground cummin
½ cup ground coriander
5 cups oil, preferably mustard oil
2 tablespoons black mustard seeds
2 tablespoons curry leaves
1½ tablespoons fennel seeds
1 tablespoon black cummin seeds
1 tablespoon ground turmeric
1 tablespoon chilli powder, or to taste
2½ tablespoons salt, or to taste

Wash mangoes well and cut into 8 sections each. The mangoes for this pickle should be so unripe that it is possible to cut through the seed and kernel without too much effort. Split chillies in halves almost up to the stem end. Sprinkle mangoes and chillies with salt and dry for 3 days in the sun.

In a small amount of vinegar soak the fenugreek seeds overnight. Next day put the soaked seeds, garlic, ginger, cummin and coriander in container of electric blender, add enough vinegar to facilitate blending and blend on high speed until a smooth purée results.

In an enamel or stainless steel pan heat the oil. Remove from heat and add the mustard seeds, curry leaves, fennel and black cummin seeds, turmeric and chilli powder, then the blended mixture. Return to heat and fry, stirring constantly with wooden spoon, for 2 minutes. Add salted mangoes, chillies and any remaining vinegar. Bring to the boil, then reduce heat and simmer, uncovered, for 30 minutes or longer until oil rises to the top and the spices smell cooked. Add salt to taste, cool and bottle in sterilised jars. Oil should cover the top of the pickle. If it does not, heat more oil and top up the jars.

Always use a dry spoon when taking pickle from the jar and it should keep for years.

Note: Strips of salted, dried mango are available in some Asian shops. Substitute 500 g (1 lb) salted dried mango for the fresh mangoes in this recipe and omit the salting and drying process.

NIMBOO KA ACHAR
LIME OR LEMON OIL PICKLE

Proceed as for mango oil pickle, but use 12-15 lemons that have been quartered, salted and dried in the sun for 3 days.

ANANAS ACHAR
PINEAPPLE OIL PICKLE

This pickle is based on the spice combination for mango pickle. Instead of mangoes, use 2 large pineapples that are ripe but not in any way over-ripe. Skin pineapples and remove 'eyes', then cut into wedges lengthways and remove hard core. Chop the flesh and squeeze out as much juice as possible. Proceed with recipe, adding a half cup of sugar at the simmering stage if a slightly sweet pickle is desired. Continue to cook until the oil separates and floats on top. Cool, bottle and seal.

JHINGA ACHAR
DRIED PRAWN PICKLE

This is a particularly delicious and popular Indian pickle which keeps well.

Follow recipe for mango pickle, substituting 1 kg (2 lb) dried shrimps or small prawns for the mangoes. Soak prawns in salad vinegar for 2 hours, then drain vinegar and use in recipe. If possible use bird's eye chillies, which are very hot. It is not necessary to split or salt them. Increase cooking time to 45 minutes.

ACCOMPANIMENTS

Besides the fresh chutneys, sambals and salads for which recipes are given, here are some more accompaniments to serve with rice and curry:

BOMBAY DUCK:

Not a bird, as the name would suggest, but a fish. It is sold dried in packets and should be cut into pieces and deep fried for a minute or so in hot oil until light golden brown. Crisp and salty, eat it in little bites with mouthfuls of rice.

DRIED SPRATS:

Tiny dried fish sold in packets, the flavour is salty and the texture crisp when fried in oil like Bombay Duck. Sometimes labelled 'Silver Fish' or 'Ikan Bilis'.

FRESH FRUITS:

Ripe bananas are served, sliced and sprinkled with lemon juice, as a foil to a very hot curry. They may be served raw or cut into chunks and fried, and take the place of a sweet chutney.

Unripe mangoes, stoned, peeled and sliced, sprinkled with salt and chilli powder, are also served as an accompaniment, like a fresh chutney. (Or substitute tart apples.) Ripe mangoes are never served with a curry meal, but may follow as dessert.

Pineapple is another favourite fruit accompaniment. Remove 'eyes' and cut into cubes, then sprinkle with salt and chilli powder. Serve chilled.

FRIED NUTS:

Cashew nuts or almonds fried lightly in oil, drained and sprinkled with salt are sometimes served before or with a meal.

GRATED COCONUT:

Moist, freshly grated coconut makes a delightful accompaniment to curry and rice.

PAPPADAMS:

Spicy lentil wafers sold dried in packets. Deep fry one pappadam at a time for 3 or 4 seconds in hot oil. They will swell and turn pale golden. Drain well on absorbent paper. Best fried just before serving, but they may be cooled and stored in an air-tight container if prepared a few hours beforehand.

RASAM
PEPPER WATER

These thin soups are served as an aid to digestion and are part of every meal in South India. They may be used to moisten the rice, or are sipped with the meal or as a second course.

Serves: 6

1 tablespoon dried tamarind pulp
1 cup hot water
2 cloves garlic, sliced
1 peppercorn-size grain of asafoetida
¾ teaspoon ground black pepper
1 teaspoon ground cummin
4 cups cold water
2 teaspoons salt
2 tablespoons chopped fresh coriander
   leaves
2 teaspoons oil
1 teaspoon black mustard seeds
8 curry leaves

Soak tamarind in hot water for 10 minutes, squeeze to dissolve pulp in the water and strain, discarding seeds and fibres. Put tamarind liquid, garlic, asafoetida, pepper, cummin, water, salt and coriander into a saucepan and bring to the boil. Turn heat down immediately and simmer for 10 minutes. In another pan heat the oil and fry mustard seeds and curry leaves until leaves are brown. Add to the simmering liquid and serve.

DHAL RASAM
PEPPER WATER WITH LENTILS

Serves: 6
½ cup toor dhal or red lentils
small stick cinnamon
3 whole cloves
10 black peppercorns
2 small onions
4 cups water
2 teaspoons salt
2 teaspoons ghee or oil
lemon juice to taste
1 cup (or more) coconut milk, optional

Wash lentils well and put into a saucepan with the whole spices, 1 onion, the water and salt. Bring to the boil and simmer until lentils are very soft. Push lentils and onion through a sieve, discarding the whole spices. Slice remaining onion thinly and fry in the ghee until quite brown. Add the strained lentil liquid, salt and lemon juice. If a richer rasam is preferred, add a cup or more of coconut milk at end of cooking and adjust seasoning.

YAKHNI
BASIC STOCK

Many recipes require a rich, spicy stock for cooking rice for pilaus and birianis. This can be made using lamb, chicken or beef. For economy, the lamb stock is made with bones taken from leg or loin, plus 2 or 3 lamb shanks. Chicken backs and necks are often sold separately, and are much cheaper than other joints.

500 g (1 lb) chicken, lamb or beef
6 whole cardamom pods, bruised
1 large onion
6 whole cloves
1 teaspoon whole peppercorns
8-10 cups water

Put all ingredients into a large saucepan, bring slowly to the boil, then reduce heat and simmer, skimming surface for the first few minutes. Cover and simmer for 1½-2 hours. Cool, then chill, and remove fat from the surface. Freeze stock until needed.

SAMBAR
LENTIL AND VEGETABLE SOUP

Serves: 6
1 cup yellow split peas or red lentils
6 cups water
1 tablespoon tamarind pulp
1 cup hot water
500 g (1 lb) mixed vegetables such as eggplant, carrot, marrow or beans
2 tablespoons ghee or oil
1 tablespoon ground coriander
2 teaspoons ground cummin
½ teaspoon ground black pepper
½ teaspoon ground turmeric
1 peppercorn-size grain of asafoetida
2 green chillies, seeded and sliced
2½ teaspoons salt
½ teaspoon black mustard seeds or panch phora (page 22)
1 small onion, finely sliced

Wash and soak lentils overnight or for 2 hours. Drain and put in a saucepan with measured water and cook until soft. Meanwhile soak tamarind in hot water and when cool squeeze to dissolve pulp. Strain and discard seeds and fibres. Add tamarind liquid to lentils. Chop the vegetables into small pieces.

Heat 1 tablespoon of the oil and on low heat fry the ground spices and asafoetida for a minute or two, then add to the lentils with chillies, salt and vegetables. Continue cooking until the vegetables are soft, about 30 minutes.

In remaining tablespoon of oil fry the mustard seeds or panch phora and the sliced onion until onion is brown. Add to the lentil mixture. Simmer a minute or two longer, remove from heat and serve.

Note: If tamarind is not available, use lemon juice to taste, adding it at the end of cooking time.

PANI PURI (semolina wafers) *recipe pages 97-99.*

MULLIGATAWNY

*This curry-flavoured soup derives its name
from the Indian 'mulegoothani' or pepper
water. Mulligatawny as we know it is the
Anglo-Indian version, made with beef,
chicken or fish stock. This recipe includes
coconut milk, which gives it richness and
delicious flavour.*

Serves: 8-10
1 kg (2 lb) gravy beef
1 kg (2 lb) soup bones
6 cardamom pods
1 tablespoon curry leaves
2 tablespoons coriander seeds
1 tablespoon cummin seeds
3 cloves garlic
12 black peppercorns
2 teaspoons salt
1 tablespoon tamarind pulp or
   2 tablespoons lemon juice
1 onion
3 whole cloves

For finishing:
1 tablespoon ghee
2 onions, finely sliced
½ teaspoon black mustard seed
8 curry leaves
3 cups coconut milk (page *11*)
salt to taste

Put beef and bones in a large saucepan with sufficient water to cover. Add cardamom pods, curry leaves, coriander and cummin seeds, garlic, peppercorns, salt, tamarind pulp, and whole onion studded with cloves.

Bring to the boil, reduce heat and simmer gently for 1½-2 hours or until beef is tender and stock is reduced. Cool slightly. Remove beef and bones from stock, discard bones. Cut beef into small dice and reserve. Pour stock through a fine strainer; there should be approximately 6 cups of stock.

To finish: Heat ghee and fry onion until dark brown. Add mustard seed and curry leaves and stir a minute or two. Pour hot stock into pan. (It will hiss and spit, so be careful.)

Simmer for 5 minutes. Just before serving, add coconut milk. Season to taste with salt. If tamarind pulp is not used, add lemon juice. Return diced beef to pan. Heat but do not boil. Serve hot.

CHANNA KI DHAL
SAVOURY SPLIT PEAS

*Serve these as a tasty nibble with drinks, or
store them airtight for a snack at any time.*

500 g (1 lb) yellow split peas
1 tablespoon bicarbonate of soda
oil for deep frying
1 teaspoon garam masala (page 35)
½ teaspoon chilli powder, optional
2 teaspoons salt
½ teaspoon amchur (dried mango)
   powder, optional

Wash the split peas in two or three changes of water and soak overnight or at least 12 hours in cold water to cover in which the bicarbonate of soda has been dissolved. Drain, rinse in fresh water and drain again, first in a colander and then on paper towels, until the split peas are dry.

Heat oil in a deep pan and fry about half cup of the peas at a time. The oil should not be so hot that it burns the peas, nor should it be too cool or they will be very oily. Fry on medium heat until peas are golden.

Lift out peas on a perforated spoon, drain on absorbent paper. When all peas are cooked and drained, make a mixture of the spices and salt and toss the peas in it. Leave until quite cold, then store in an airtight container.

CHANNA
SAVOURY CHICK PEAS

250 g (8 oz) dried chick peas
salt
1 teaspoon ground turmeric
1 teaspoon ground cummin
½ teaspoon chilli powder
lemon juice to taste

Soak chick peas overnight in plenty of water. Next day cover with fresh water, add 2 teaspoons salt and the turmeric, bring to the boil, cover and simmer until peas are tender, 35-45 minutes, or cook in a pressure cooker if preferred. Drain while hot. Sprinkle with cummin, chilli powder and lemon juice to taste. Salt may also be needed. Toss well to distribute seasonings. Serve the peas as a snack by themselves, or as part of the pani puri accompaniments (pages 97-99).

SEV or MURUKKU
DEEP-FRIED LENTIL SAVOURY

1½ cups besan (chick pea flour)
¾ cup ground rice
1½ teaspoons garam masala (page 35)
½ teaspoon chilli powder, optional
½ teaspoon ajowan seeds, optional
½ teaspoon cummin seeds
1½ teaspoons salt, or to taste
3 tablespoons ghee, melted
about ⅔ cup water
oil for deep frying

Sift chick pea flour into a large bowl, stir through the ground rice, ground spices, aromatic seeds and salt. Rub in ghee until evenly distributed. Add water and knead to a stiff dough, about the consistency of a piped biscuit dough. Heat oil in a deep pan until smoking hot, then put some dough into a potato ricer or mouli shredder and push through into the hot oil. Fry on medium heat until golden brown. Lift out with slotted spoon and drain on absorbent paper. Repeat until all the dough is used up. Cool, then store airtight. If liked, more spice and salt can be sprinkled on the sev after cooking.

MASALA KAJU BADAM
SPICY FRIED NUTS

250 g (8 oz) raw cashews
250 g (8 oz) blanched almonds
500 g (1 lb) raw peanuts
oil for frying
1 tablespoon salt
2 teaspoons garam masala (page 35)
2 teaspoons chilli powder, or to taste
1 teaspoon amchur, optional

Heat oil in a deep frying pan and fry the nuts on medium heat, a handful at a time, keeping each variety separate. As they are fried to a pale golden colour, remove them from the oil with a slotted spoon and drain on absorbent paper. Do not leave them in the oil until they darken because they go on cooking in their own heat. When all have been fried and drained sprinkle with combined spices and salt. If an acid flavour is liked, add amchur (dried green mango) to the mix. Cool completely and store in an airtight container.

PANI PURI

If you met these delicious little savouries in Maharashtra State, you probably know them as pani puri; in the Punjab they are called gol gappa; and if you spent time in Calcutta you may recognise them under the name of pushka. They are typical of the Indian savoury snacks for between-meal nibbling. The crisp wafers, puffed up like Lilliputian balloons, are filled to individual taste.

The snack consists of fried wafers so thin and crisp that a finger pushed through one side makes a neat little hole into which you drop 2 or 3 cooked and spiced chick peas, a couple of cubes of potato and a teaspoonful of piquant tamarind juice. There are variations on the theme, with some versions favouring crisp fried lentils, chips of fresh coconut and fresh chutneys.

PANI PURI
SEMOLINA WAFERS *(picture page 95)*

Makes about 80
½ cup medium fine semolina
½ cup roti flour or plain flour
2 teaspoons besan (chick pea flour),
    optional
½ teaspoon salt
scant ½ cup lukewarm water
oil and ghee for deep frying

Accompaniments:
channa (savoury chick peas)
    recipe page 97
channa ki dhal (savoury split peas)
    recipe page 96
zeera pani (cummin and tamarind water)
    recipe page 102
imli chatni (tamarind chatni)
    recipe page 88
alu bhaji (savoury fried potatoes)
    recipe page 81
podina chatni (mint chutney)
    recipe page 88

Put dry ingredients into a bowl, add the water all at once and mix to a dough. Knead hard for 10 minutes, adding very little more flour if mixture is too soft, or a few drops of water if it is too stiff. (Flours vary in absorbency and it is difficult to give an exact measure of water, but the dough should be the consistency of bread dough.) Cover dough with a small bowl or with plastic food wrap and let it rest for 30 minutes at least.

Pinch off small pieces of dough and roll into balls the size of a hazelnut without its shell. On a floured board, using a floured rolling pin, roll each one to a thin circle no more than 5 cm (2 inches) in diameter. Put on a tray and cover with a damp tea towel to prevent drying out. Let the pastry rest for 10-15 minutes before starting to fry.

When all the circles are rolled out, heat the oil and ghee in a karahi or wok or frying pan to a depth of at least 5 cm (2 inches). Use at least 3 tablespoons ghee to flavour the oil and wait until it is smoking hot before adding 2 or 3 pastry circles at a time. As soon as they are put into the oil, spash the hot oil over them with a frying spoon to make them puff up. Do not add too many at a time, for this brings down the temperature of the oil and results in greasy wafers. Also, it is difficult to splash oil on too many at once, and the splashing with oil is important.

As they are fried to a golden colour lift them out on a slotted spoon and drain on absorbent paper laid over a cake cooler or wire rack. This helps to keep them crisp when they cool. If not serving at once, cool completely and store in an airtight tin. Fillings and wafers should be allowed to cool before serving (see page 97).

PAKORHAS
SAVOURY VEGETABLE FRITTERS

Served in India at tea time as a savoury. Try them as an accompaniment to a meal instead of plain cooked vegetables, or serve as a party savoury.

Use small pieces of raw potato, onion, cauliflower, eggplant, zucchini and green capsicum or a combination of your own choice.

Makes: 24-36
1½ cups besan (chick pea flour)
1 teaspoon garam masala (page 35)
2 teaspoons salt
½ teaspoon ground turmeric
½ teaspoon chilli powder, optional
scant 1 cup water
1 clove garlic, crushed
4 cups mixed chopped vegetables
oil for deep frying

Sieve besan, garam masala, salt, turmeric, chilli powder (if used) into a bowl. Add water gradually, mixing to a thick batter. Stir in garlic and beat well. Allow batter to stand for 30 minutes, then beat again.

Add vegetables to batter and mix thoroughly.

Heat oil in a deep pan. Drop teaspoons of mixture into oil and fry over moderate heat until pale golden on both sides. Lift out with a slotted spoon and drain on absorbent paper.

Just before serving, heat oil again. When almost smoking hot, return pakorhas to pan, a few at a time, for about 30 seconds or until golden brown on both sides. (the second frying makes them very crisp.) Drain on paper and serve immediately.

Note: If you prefer to lighten the batter and lessen the strong chick pea flavour, use half besan and half self-raising flour — a little liberty that results in puffier pakorhas, and won't topple the Taj Mahal.

Preparing SAMOOSA and SINGARA (savoury pastries). Recipes page 100.

SAMOOSA
SMALL SAVOURY PASTRIES *(picture page 98)*

These are a savoury served for afternoon tea in India, but they are equally suitable served with pre-dinner drinks.

Makes: 32-36
Pastry:
1½ cups plain flour
¾ teaspoon salt
1 tablespoon oil or ghee
½ cup warm water

Filling:
1 tablespoon oil or ghee
1 clove garlic, finely chopped
1 teaspoon finely chopped fresh ginger
2 medium onions, finely chopped
2 teaspoons curry powder
½ teaspoon salt
1 tablespoon vinegar or lemon juice
250 g (8 oz) minced steak or lamb
½ cup hot water
1 teaspoon garam masala (page 35)
2 tablespoons chopped fresh mint or
   coriander leaves
oil for frying

Pastry: Sift flour and salt into a bowl, add oil and warm water and mix thoroughly, until ingredients are combined. (Add a little more water if necessary to combine ingredients.) Knead for about 10 minutes or until dough is elastic. Cover with plastic wrap and set aside while preparing filling.

Filling: Heat ghee in a saucepan and fry garlic, ginger and half the onion until onion is soft. Add curry powder, salt and vinegar, mix well. Add minced steak and fry over a high heat, stirring constantly until meat changes colour. Turn heat down and add hot water. Cover pan and cook until meat is tender and all the liquid has been absorbed.

Towards end of cooking, stir frequently to prevent meat from sticking to base of pan. Sprinkle with garam masala and chopped mint or coriander, remove from heat and allow to cool. Mix in reserved chopped onion.

Take small pieces of dough, shape into balls and on a lightly floured board roll each one thinly to a circle, the size of a saucer. Cut each circle in half. Put a teaspoon of filling on one side of each half circle and brush edges with water. Fold dough over and press edges together firmly. You will now have triangular-shaped samoosas.

When they are all made, heat oil in a deep pan and deep fry a few at a time until golden brown on both sides. Drain on absorbent paper and serve hot.

Note: Both samoosa and singara can be made using spring roll wrappers. Cut into 6 cm (2½ inch) strips the length of the pastry. Put a teaspoon of filling at one end and fold the pastry over diagonally, then fold again and again, still keeping a triangular shape. Moisten end of strip with water or beaten egg and press lightly. See step-by-step picture on page 98.

SINGARA
SAVOURY PASTRIES *(picture page 98)*

These are similar to samoosas, but use a filling of spiced potatoes.

Boil, peel and dice 2 large potatoes. Cool and then sprinkle with half teaspoon chilli powder, half teaspoon panch phora, 1 teaspoon ground cummin and 1 teaspoon salt. Add 2 tablespoons lemon juice and mix well.

ALU LACHCHE
POTATO STRAWS

4 large potatoes
ice-cold water
oil for frying
1 teaspoon salt
½ teaspoon chilli powder
½ teaspoon ground cummin
½ teaspoon garam masala (page 35)

Peel potatoes and cut into thin slices, then cut slices into matchstick strips. Soak in ice-cold water, then drain and dry well on paper towels. Heat oil until very hot and fry the potato straws, a handful at a time, until they are crisp and golden. Lift out of oil with a perforated spoon and drain well on absorbent paper. When they are all fried sprinkle with the salt and spices mixed together.

SOOJEE VADAI
DEEP-FRIED SEMOLINA SAVOURIES

Makes about 10
1 cup semolina
1 cup boiling water
1 small onion, finely chopped
1 fresh green chilli, finely chopped
½ teaspoon finely grated fresh ginger
¾ teaspoon salt
½ teaspoon ground cummin
1 teaspoon finely chopped fresh coriander
    leaves
oil for deep frying

Put semolina in a bowl and pour on the boiling water, stirring with a wooden spoon. Add all the seasonings and mix. Dough should be stiff but not dry. Take a tablespoon of dough and pat to a circle about 7.5 cm (3 inches) across and push a finger through to make a hole in the centre (like doughnuts). Fry in hot oil until golden, turning to fry both sides. Serve warm with fresh chutney.

THOSAI
SOUTH INDIAN PANCAKES

Makes: 10-12
1 cup uncooked rice
½ cup urad dhal (blackgram dhal)
1½ teaspoons dried yeast
½ cup warm water
1 teaspoon sugar
1½ teaspoons salt
2 teaspoons ghee or oil
¼ teaspoon mustard seeds
1 small onion, finely chopped
1 fresh green chilli, finely chopped

Wash rice and dhal and soak each separately in cold water overnight or at least 8 hours. Drain and grind rice in a blender, adding just enough water to facilitate blending. Strain through a fine sieve. Remove black skins if you are using unhusked dhal, and drain. Grind in blender, adding fresh water. When dhal has been ground to a very smooth batter, add it to the rice and mix well.

Sprinkle yeast over warm water and leave for 5 minutes to soften. Stir to dissolve, add sugar and salt, then stir into ground rice and dhal. Leave for 1 hour in a warm place, and mixture will rise and double in bulk.

Heat ghee or oil in a small saucepan and fry the mustard seeds until they pop. Add chopped onion and chilli and continue frying, stirring occasionally, until onions are golden brown. Allow to cool, then stir into batter. Batter should be of a thick pouring consistency. If too thick, add a little water or coconut milk.

Heat a pancake pan or heavy frying pan and grease base with very little ghee or oil. Pour in just enough batter to cover base of pan. Pancakes should be about the size of a small plate. Cook until golden brown on underside, turn and cook other side. Serve with fresh chutneys and potato bhaji (page 81).

THOSAI
RICE PANCAKES

Makes about 10
1½ cups rice flour
1½ cups plain white flour
2 tablespoons yoghurt
2½ cups water
1 teaspoon salt, or to taste

Sift both kinds of flour into a bowl. Add yoghurt mixed with water and salt and beat with a wooden spoon to make a thick, smooth batter. Leave in a warm place overnight or until mixture ferments. Cook as for thosai (preceding recipe). Serve hot with dry vegetable preparations, fresh chutneys and sambals.

ALU CHAT
POTATO SLICES

6-8 small potatoes
1 teaspoon salt
1 teaspoon ground cummin
½ teaspoon chilli powder
½ teaspoon garam masala (page 35)
1 tablespoon lemon juice

Wash potatoes and cook them in their skins. Do not overcook. Drain, cool, peel, and cut into slices. Sprinkle with mixed salt and ground spices, then with the lemon juice. Toss lightly to mix. Serve as a snack.

ZEERA PANI
CUMMIN AND TAMARIND WATER

Cummin is reputed to be a digestive, and this refreshingly sour drink is served as an appetiser, much as tomato juice is in other countries. It is also served with festive — and therefore very rich — meals. Serve it chilled, with crushed ice, a sprig of mint and slice of lemon to garnish.

½ cup dried tamarind pulp
2 cups hot water
3 teaspoons finely grated fresh ginger
2 teaspoons ground cummin
pinch chilli powder, optional
½ teaspoon garam masala (page 35)
3 teaspoons sugar, or to taste
salt to taste
iced water and crushed ice for serving
mint sprigs, lemon slices to garnish

Soak tamarind pulp in the hot water and leave for 2 hours or overnight. Squeeze to dissolve the pulp and separate the seeds. Strain through nylon sieve. Add remaining ingredients, stir well, then strain again through very fine sieve or muslin. Chill. Dilute with iced water at serving time, add ice and garnish.

SHARBAT GULAB
ROSE-FLAVOURED COLD DRINK *(picture opposite)*

3 cups white sugar
2 cups water
20 drops rose essence
1 teaspoon liquid red food colouring
1 teaspoon tulsi seeds (see Glossary)
iced water and crushed ice for serving

Put sugar and water in a saucepan and cook over gentle heat until sugar dissolves. Cool. Add rose flavouring and red colouring. It should be a strong colour, for it will be mixed with a large proportion of water.

Soak the tulsi seeds in a cup of cold water. After a few minutes they will develop a jelly-like coating. (The seeds can be kept soaking in the refrigerator for a week. They are supposed to have a very cooling effect, and are used in almost every type of sharbat drink.)

At serving time put 2 tablespoons of syrup in each glass and fill up with iced water and crushed ice. Syrup can be increased or decreased according to taste. Add a spoonful of soaked tulsi seeds.

SHARBAT GULAB *(left)*, LASSI *(right)* and FALOODA *(centre)*. *Recipes above and page 104.*

FALOODA

(picture page 103)

There are many versions of falooda — this one is a favourite. It is a sweet drink ideal for serving with curry meals. It gets its name from the particles of cornflour vermicelli that float in it but these, which are difficult to make without special equipment, are often replaced with tiny pieces of jelly or cooked tapioca. Another easy substitute is cellophane noodles (bean starch noodles) soaked and boiled until soft and transparent, then cut into short lengths.

Falooda can be served as a dessert or as a refreshing drink. In this version a rose-flavoured syrup is mixed with ice-cold milk, crushed ice and jewel-like squares of sparkling red and green agar-agar jelly in tall glasses.

Agar-agar can be bought in powder form by the gram or ounce from chemists, or in packets from Chinese grocery stores, either powdered or in strands. It is popular in Asia for making jellies and sweetmeats because it sets without refrigeration.

agar-agar jelly, diced
rose syrup as in sharbat gulab (page 102)
ice cold milk as required, about 1 cup for
  each serving
crushed iced
soaked tulsi seeds, optional

Jelly:
3 cups water
4 teaspoons agar-agar powder or 1 cup
  soaked agar-agar strands
6 tablespoons sugar
12 drops rose essence
1 teaspoon liquid red food colouring
1 teaspoon liquid green food colouring

Put about 2 tablespoons each of diced jelly and rose syrup into each tall glass, fill up with ice-cold milk and crushed ice. If liked, some soaked tulsi seeds can be floated on top.

Jelly: Measure water into a saucepan and sprinkle agar-agar powder over. If agar-agar strands are used, soak at least 2 hours in cold water, then drain and measure 1 cup loosely packed. Bring to the boil and simmer gently, stirring, until agar-agar dissolves. Powder takes about 10 minutes and the strands take longer, about 25-30 minutes. Add sugar and dissolve, remove from heat, cool slightly and add rose flavouring. Divide mixture between two large shallow dishes and colour one red and the other green. Leave to set. When quite cold and firm, cut with a sharp knife first into fine strips, then across into small dice.

LASSI

YOGHURT DRINK *(picture page 103)*

½ cup yoghurt
2½ cups iced water
pepper and salt to taste
ice cubes

Put yoghurt into a deep jug and beat with a spoon to take any lumps out of it. Add the water, gradually at first, mixing well. Season to taste with salt and pepper and serve with ice cubes in each glass.

A more popular drink, especially with children, is a sweetened version. For each serving, beat 2 tablespoons yoghurt with 2 teaspoons or more of sugar in a tall glass. Gradually add iced soda water. This will froth and look like a milk shake, and is generally acceptable even to those who do not like yoghurt by itself.

SEVIYAN
SWEET VERMICELLI

This traditional Muslim dish is served during the Id Festival and would, on occasions like this, be garnished with edible silver leaf and pistachio nuts.

Serves: 4-6
1½ tablespoons ghee
125 g (4 oz) fine vermicelli
1½ cups hot water
¼ teaspoon saffron strands
½ cup sugar
2 tablespoons sultanas, optional
2 tablespoons slivered blanched almonds
⅛ teaspoon ground cardamom

Break the vermicelli into small pieces less than 2.5 cm (1 inch) in length. They need not be uniform, but longer pieces make stirring difficult.

Heat ghee in a heavy saucepan and fry the vermicelli until golden brown, stirring so it colours evenly. Add hot water and saffron and bring to the boil, then turn heat low, cover and simmer gently until vermicelli is cooked. Add sugar and sultanas and cook uncovered until liquid is absorbed. Stir in the almonds and cardamom, stir well and serve warm with cream.

KHEER
RICE PUDDING

Serves: 4-6
½ cup short or medium grain rice
8 cups milk
4 cardamom pods
1¼ cups sugar
2 tablespoons slivered blanched almonds, optional
¼ teaspoon ground cardamom
¼ teaspoon freshly grated nutmeg
1 tablespoon rose water or few drops rose essence

Wash the rice and boil for 5 minutes in water. Drain well. Bring milk to the boil with the cardamoms in a large saucepan, add rice and simmer, stirring occasionally, for 1 hour or until rice is very soft and milk quite thick. As milk thickens it will be necessary to stir frequently with a wooden spoon, scraping thickened milk from bottom and sides of pan. Add sugar and almonds and continue cooking until the consistency is like that of porridge. Remove from heat, pick out the cardamom pods. If you think the flavour needs intensifying, add ground cardamom. When half cool stir in the rose water. Serve warm or chilled, in a large bowl or individual sweet dishes, the top sprinkled with a little grated nutmeg.

SOOJEE HALWA
SEMOLINA PUDDING

Serves: 6
¾ cup sugar
1¼ cups water
¼ cup milk
good pinch powdered Spanish saffron
125 g (4 oz) ghee
¾ cup fine semolina
2 tablespoons sultanas
2 tablespoons slivered almonds
1 teaspoon ground cardamom
extra slivered almonds to decorate

Put sugar, water, milk and saffron into a saucepan and bring to the boil, stirring to dissolve sugar. Set aside. In a large saucepan melt the ghee, add semolina and fry over low heat, stirring constantly, until mixture is golden. Add the syrup, sultanas, almonds and cardamom and cook over medium heat, stirring with a wooden spoon, until mixture thickens and leaves sides of pan. Pour into buttered dish and when it is cold cut into diamond shapes and decorate with almonds. This halwa can be served warm or cold, with or without cream, as a dessert. A popular way of serving it in India is with puris (deep-fried Indian bread) and, surprising though it may seem to Westerners, at the beginning of a meal instead of at the end.

PERHAS
MILK SWEETMEAT

Makes: 10-12
5 cups milk
1 teaspoon ghee
½ cup caster sugar
¼ teaspoon ground cardamom
   or grated nutmeg
few slivered almonds or pistachios,
   optional

Put the milk into a large, heavy-based frying pan and make khoa (page 22). In a small aluminium saucepan heat the ghee. Add the cooled khoa, which has been crumbled into small pieces, and stir over low heat until khoa is heated through.

Add sugar and stir constantly with wooden spoon until sugar is incorporated and mixture is hot. Remove from heat and add spices. Beat until mixture is smooth. Shape into small balls by rolling between palms, then flatten slightly to a disc. Put on a buttered dish to cool and firm. The discs will not get hard, and are not supposed to — a soft fudge-like texture is correct. If liked, decorate each disc as it is made with a few slices of almond or pistachio.

NAN KHATAI
CRISP SEMOLINA SHORTBREAD *(picture opposite)*

These little shortbread biscuits made with ghee have a delightful melting texture.

Makes about 24
Cooking time: about 30 minutes
Oven temperature: 150-160ºC (300-325ºF)
125 g (4 oz) ghee
½ cup sugar
1 cup fine semolina
¼ cup plain flour
1 teaspoon ground cardamom

Cream ghee and sugar together until light. Add the sieved semolina, flour and cardamom and mix well. Allow mixture to stand for 30 minutes.

Take a scant tablespoon of the mixture, roll into a ball, then flatten slightly and put on an ungreased baking tray. Repeat process with remaining mixture, leaving a little space between biscuits.

Bake in a slow oven until biscuits are pale golden, approximately 30 minutes. Cool on a wire cooling tray. Store in an airtight container.

MYSORE PAK
CHICK PEA FLOUR SWEETMEAT

Makes 12-15 pieces
⅔ cup sugar
¼ cup water
60 g (2 oz) besan (chick pea flour)
185 g (6 oz) ghee
½ teaspoon almond essence
½ teaspoon ground cardamom

Put sugar and water into a pan and dissolve over low heat, then boil for 5 minutes. Set aside. Sift the besan. Put two thirds of the ghee into a heavy-based saucepan and heat. Add the besan gradually to the ghee and fry, stirring over low heat for 5 minutes. Add the syrup, stirring constantly and continue to cook and stir for a further 5 minutes. Add remaining ghee gradually (this can be melted and poured in or, if softened to room temperature, added by spoonfuls), stirring all the time. After adding ghee the mixture should be cooked for a further 7-10 minutes, but it should not be allowed to brown. Pour into a greased plate and cut into diamond shapes before it hardens.

At the top a plate of **SINGARA** *(recipe page 100)*, **PAKORHA** *(recipe page 99)* and **SAMOOSA** *(recipe page 100)*; the drink is **FALOODA** *(recipe page 104)*; the shortbreads are **NAN KHATAI** *(recipe above)*; the glass bowl at top holds **RAS GULA** *(recipe page 111)*.

BARFI BADAM
ALMOND CREAM SWEETMEAT

Makes about 16 pieces
4 cups milk
¾ cup sugar
125 g (4 oz) blanched almonds pulverised
  in blender, or 1 cup ground almonds
pinch of ground cardamom
2 tablespoons blanched pistachio nuts
edible silver leaf, optional

In a heavy-based saucepan or large frying pan boil the milk over fairly high heat, stirring all the time, until it is reduced and very thick. Add sugar and stir for 10 minutes on low heat. Add the ground almonds and continue to cook and stir until the mixture comes away from sides and base of pan in one mass. Remove from heat, sprinkle cardamom over and mix well. Turn on to a greased plate. Smooth top with back of buttered spoon. Cool slightly, mark in diamond shapes with knife and decorate with halved pistachio nuts and silver leaf.

Before it is quite firm cut with sharp knife along the markings, then leave to get quite cold before separating into pieces.

BARFI PISTA
PISTACHIO CREAM SWEETMEAT

Proceed as for barfi badam (above), substituting raw (not roasted) pistachio kernels. Blanch the pistachios in boiling water for 2 minutes and remove the skins, then pound to a paste with mortar and pestle, chop very finely or pass through a nut mill.

JALEBI
DEEP-FRIED BATTER SWEETMEAT

Jalebis are coils of crisply fried batter about the size of a saucer with a rose-scented syrup inside the coil. How the syrup gets inside is a mystery unless you do some research on the subject. In the bazaars and sweet shops, pyramids of brilliant orange jalebis up to a metre high testify to the popularity of this sweet, and are quickly demolished.

Makes about 25
Batter:
2 cups plain flour
½ cup ground rice or rice flour
7 g (¼ oz) fresh compressed yeast or scant
  ½ teaspoon dried yeast
½ cup lukewarm water
¼ teaspoon saffron strands
2 tablespoons boiling water
1 tablespoon yoghurt
vegetable oil for frying

Syrup:
3 cups sugar
3 cups water
1 tablespoon light corn syrup or pinch
  cream of tartar
rose essence to flavour
1½ teaspoons liquid orange food
  colouring

Sift the flour and ground rice into a large bowl. Sprinkle yeast on the warm water in a small bowl, leave to soften for 5 minutes and stir to dissolve. Put saffron strands in a cup and pour the boiling water over. Leave to soak for 10 minutes.

Pour dissolved yeast and saffron with its soaking water into a measuring jug. Add tepid water to make up 2¼ cups. Stirring with a wooden spoon, add the measured liquid to the flour and beat well until batter is very smooth. Add yoghurt and beat again. Leave to rest for 1 hour. Batter will start to become frothy. Beat vigorously again before starting to fry jalebis. (While batter stands make syrup and leave it to become just warm.)

Heat vegetable oil in a deep frying pan and when hot use a funnel to pour in the batter, making circles or figures of eight. Fry, turning once, until crisp and golden on both sides. Lift out on a slotted spoon, let the oil drain for a few seconds, then drop the hot jalebi into the syrup and soak it for a minute or two. Lift out of the syrup (using another slotted spoon) and put on a plate to drain.

Transfer jalebis to a clean plate, and serve as soon as possible after making (though they should not be served hot) because their crispness diminishes after some time.

Syrup: Heat sugar and water over low heat, stirring until sugar dissolves. Raise heat and boil hard for 8 minutes; syrup should be just thick enough to spin a thread. Remove from heat, allow to cool until lukewarm, flavour with rose (about half teaspoon of good quality essence is enough) and colour a bright orange with food colouring.

GULAB JAMUN
ROSE-FLAVOURED SWEETMEATS IN SYRUP

Makes about 20
8 tablespoons full cream milk powder
3 tablespoons self-raising flour
¼ teaspoon bicarbonate of soda
¼ teaspoon ground cardamom
1 tablespoon soft butter or ghee
approximately 3 tablespoons water
ghee or oil for frying

Syrup:
2 cups white sugar
4 cups water
5 bruised cardamom pods
2 tablespoons rose water or few drops rose
  essence

Sift milk powder, flour, bicarbonate of soda and ground cardamom into a large bowl. Rub in butter or ghee, then add enough water to give a firm but pliable dough which can be moulded into balls the size of large marbles, or into small sausage shapes.

Fry slowly in hot ghee (or oil flavoured with ghee) until they turn the colour of unblanched almonds. The frying must be done over gentle heat. Drain on absorbent paper.

Have ready the syrup, made by combining, sugar, water and cardamom pods and heating until sugar is dissolved. Put the fried gulab jamun into the syrup and soak until they are almost double in size, and soft and spongy. Add rose water when they have cooled slightly. Allow to cool completely and serve at room temperature or slightly chilled.

GAJJAR KHEER
CARROT PUDDING

Serves: 4
250 g (8 oz) carrots
4 cups milk
pinch saffron strands
½ cup sugar
2 tablespoons ground almonds, optional
⅛ teaspoon ground cardamom

Wash and scrape the carrots and grate them coarsely. In a large heavy saucepan bring milk to the boil, then take out 2 tablespoons of the boiling milk and soak the saffron strands in it. Add the grated carrots to boiling milk and cook until carrots are soft and the mixture has thickened. This takes about 30 minutes or longer. Add sugar, almonds, cardamom and the saffron soaking in the milk. Stir until sugar dissolves, then cook, stirring occasionally until the mixture is the consistency of a creamy rice pudding. Serve warm or cold.

GAJJAR HALWA
CARROT SWEETMEAT

Makes about 20 pieces
60 g (2 oz) ghee
500 g (1 lb) carrots
¼ teaspoon ground cardamom
1¼ cups sugar
½ cup hot water
1 cup cream
4 tablespoons dried milk powder or khoa
  (page 22)
2 tablespoons slivered blanched almonds
  or pistachios
edible silver leaf to garnish, optional

Heat ghee in heavy saucepan, add washed and grated carrots and cook uncovered over medium heat, stirring. Cover and turn heat very low. Cook until carrots are soft and almost all the liquid has evaporated. While carrots are cooking, make a syrup with the sugar and water. Add syrup to carrots along with cream and khoa or milk powder. Stir vigorously to blend all the ingredients and cook, stirring constantly, until mixture is dry and comes away from the pan in one mass. Turn on to a greased dish, allow to cool. Decorate top with slivered almonds and pistachios and, if liked, silver leaf. Cut in diamond shapes or squares to serve.

BOONDI

This popular sweet consists of hundreds of tiny balls of batter fried until crisp, then soaked in a saffron-flavoured syrup scented with cardamom and enriched with pistachio nuts. The syrup dries and crystallises around the fragments of batter so it may be eaten like sugar-coated peanuts, but with an infinitely more exotic flavour. It is for between meal nibbling or a tea-time treat, and is not a dessert.

Batter:
1 cup besan (chick pea flour) or plain flour and rice flour mixed
just over ¼ cup milk
¼ cup water
½ teaspoon saffron strands
1 tablespoon hot water
vegetable oil for frying
3 tablespoons ghee for flavouring the oil

Syrup:
1½ cups water
1½ cups sugar

Flavourings:
¼ teaspoon ground cardamom
1 tablespoon shelled pistachios, blanched and sliced finely

Batter: Sift besan (or equal parts of plain flour and rice flour) into a bowl. Combine milk and water and heat until just lukewarm. There should be 150 ml (5 fluid oz) of liquid. Grind saffron strands with a mortar and pestle, dissolve in the tablespoon of hot water and add half to the milk and water. Pour combined liquids into the flour and beat well with a wooden spoon to form a thick smooth batter. Let batter stand for 15 minutes. Meanwhile, make the syrup.

Syrup: Put sugar and water into a wide saucepan and bring to the boil. Boil steadily until of one-thread consistency (104°C or 220°F on a sugar thermometer). This should take about 8 minutes hard boiling. Turn heat as low as possible or remove from heat and keep syrup hot but not simmering. Add the remaining saffron liquid and the ground cardamom for flavouring.

To cook the boondi: Heat oil and ghee together in a small, deep frying pan and when smoking hot start frying the batter. Take a frying spoon or ladle with small round perforations and put it over the frying pan, then pour a spoonful of the batter on to it. Tap the frying spoon with the handle of wooden spoon so that the batter falls in small drops into the hot fat. Fry a few minutes until the drops of batter are golden, then drain on another frying spoon and put them into the syrup. Continue frying the batter in batches and adding the boondi to the syrup. When all the batter has been fried, drained and added to the syrup, stir in the pistachios and mix together well.

Allow to get quite cold, stirring occasionally to separate the balls of batter. Another way of serving these is to make laddu boondi. In this case the mixture is not allowed to get quite cold, but is pressed to form large balls while still warm and sticky, then left on a greased plate to dry and harden.

FIRNI
RICE BLANCMANGE

Serves: 4
3 cups milk
3 tablespoons ground rice
3 tablespoons sugar
½ teaspoon ground cardamom
1 tablespoon rose water or 2-3 drops rose essence
2 tablespoons blanched pistachios or almonds

Take some of the cold milk and mix with the ground rice to a smooth cream. Bring the rest of milk to the boil with sugar, stirring with a wooden spoon. Remove from heat and stir in creamed ground rice, then return pan to heat and stir constantly until mixture boils and thickens. Boil, stirring, for 3 minutes. Sprinkle over the cardamom, rose water or essence and half the pistachios, chopped. Stir well. Pour into individual dessert dishes. Decorate tops with remaining pistachios or almonds, slivered. Serve warm or chilled.

RAS GULA
CREAM CHEESE BALLS IN SYRUP

One of the most popular Indian sweetmeats, ras gula means, literally, balls of juice. Walnut-size balls of home-made cream cheese are simmered in sugar syrup with added intriguing flavours.

Serves: 5-6

3 pints milk
3-4 tablespoons lemon juice, strained
2 teaspoons fine semolina
10-12 sugar cubes
2 cups sugar
4 cups water
8 cardamom pods, bruised
2 tablespoons rose water or few drops rose essence

Pour milk into a large saucepan and bring almost to boiling point. As milk starts to rise in the pan, remove from heat, add slightly warmed lemon juice and stir once. Allow to stand for 5 minutes, when solid lumps will have formed. If milk does not curdle (lemons vary in acid content) reheat milk and add more lemon juice. Pour into a large colander lined with a large square of muslin. Drain for 30 minutes or until all the whey has dripped out, or put muslin-wrapped curds on a plate and press out as much liquid as possible with another plate on top.

Turn curds out on marble slab or laminated surface. Knead for 5 minutes, using heel of hand. Add semolina and knead again until the cream cheese is smooth. When the palm of the hand becomes greasy the cheese is ready for moulding. Shape into 10-12 walnut-size balls, moulding each one around a cube of sugar.

In a large saucepan heat sugar and water together until sugar dissolves, then bring to the boil and simmer 5 minutes. Pour half the syrup into a jug and set aside. Put ras gulas and bruised cardamom pods into syrup in the saucepan and bring to the boil. Simmer on very low heat, uncovered, until the balls swell and become spongy, approximately 1 hour. Occasionally add a little reserved sugar syrup to prevent syrup in pan from becoming too thick.

Allow to cool until lukewarm, then add rose water or essence. Serve warm or at room temperature, 1 or 2 ras gulas to a serving.

Note: Do not serve chilled, for chilling makes ras gulas firm and it is essential they should retain their spongy texture.

RAS MALAI
FRESH CREAM CHEESE BALLS IN CREAM

Ras malai is regarded as the richest and most delicious of Indian desserts. It is actually a combination of two other sweet dishes, ras gula and rabri. This version makes enough for 6 servings.

To make ras malai, proceed with ras gulas recipe above, but instead of making 10 walnut-size balls, divide mixture into 18 equal-size balls and mould them without a piece of sugar inside. Simmer in the syrup as before, keeping the syrup from becoming too thick. When they are cooked and spongy, drain them from the syrup and immerse them in 8 cups of fresh milk. Leave to become quite cool. Remove the balls of cream cheese from the milk and set aside.

Now use this milk to make rabri (page 113), but instead of reducing it to a third of its original volume, reduce it to only half so that it is thinner and not so concentrated. Remove from heat. Add half cup caster sugar, a few drops of kewra or rose essence and about half teaspoon almond essence. Stir to dissolve sugar. Return cream cheese balls to this mixture, cover and refrigerate. Sprinkle 2 tablespoons finely chopped pistachio nuts over and serve chilled.

SHAHI TUKRI
TOAST OF THE SHAH

Serves: 6

6 slices of bread, cut thick as for toasting
4-6 tablespoons ghee
1½ cups milk
1 cup cream
¼ teaspoon saffron strands
1 cup sugar
¼ teaspoon ground cardamom
1 tablespoon rosewater
1 tablespoon each slivered blanched
   pistachios and almonds

Trim crusts off the bread and if slices are large, cut in halves. Heat the ghee in a large, heavy frying pan and fry the bread until golden on both sides. It may be necessary to add more ghee. Remove slices of fried bread to a plate.

Reserve 2 tablespoons milk and add remaining milk and cream to the pan in which the bread was fried. Bring to the boil and add the sugar. In the meantime, crush saffron strands with mortar and pestle, heat reserved milk and dissolve the saffron in it. Add to simmering milk in pan and boil hard, stirring constantly, for 10 minutes.

Put in the slices of fried bread in one layer and simmer over low heat until milk is absorbed, carefully turning slices of bread over once.

Transfer bread to a heated serving dish, sprinkle with cardamom and rosewater and decorate with slivered nuts. Serve hot.

KOULFI
FROZEN DESSERT

There is no ice-cream quite like koulfi, with its cold smoothness punctuated by little lumps of cream and pieces of pistachio and almond. If one memory persists, it is of the itinerant vendor with the tin cones packed in crushed ice, shaking out a serving of the delicious rich, very cold ice-cream, watching it slide from the mould onto the plate I held. It is not mere childhood memory — koulfi is colder than commercial ice-cream. Having no gelatine content, and not being beaten up and aerated, it freezes quite solid and must be eaten before it melts. The pieces of thick cream are a delight to come upon, and even if it is not made in the traditional tin cones, koulfi out of a freezer tray is well worth experiencing.

6 cups milk
2 tablespoons arrowroot or cornflour
¾ cup sugar
khoa made from 2 cups milk (page 22)
1 cup thick cream
2 tablespoons blanched, chopped
   pistachios
2 tablespoons finely chopped blanched
   almonds
few drops rose or kewra essence to
   flavour

Mix a little of the milk with the arrowroot or cornflour. Bring remaining milk to the boil and allow to boil, stirring with a wooden spoon, for 10 minutes. Remove from heat, stir in the cornflour, giving it another good stir first to make sure it is smoothly mixed with the milk. Return the pan to low heat and stir constantly while returning to the boil. When it boils and thickens add the sugar and stir until completely dissolved. Allow to cool, stirring occasionally to prevent a skin forming on top.

The khoa used for this need not be dried completely. Cook the milk, stirring, until it is like a thick batter. Cool then stir this into the milk mixture. Add the cream. The best kind of cream to use is that skimmed from the top of the milk during boiling. In some Lebanese shops this is sold as 'ashtar'. Failing this, use commercial dairy cream. Flavour the custard with rose or kewra essence, a drop or two at a time, taking care not to add too much. Stir in the almonds and pistachios. Pour into freezer trays and freeze until firm, stirring once or twice during the freezing process to keep the nuts and cream spread through the mixture. Serve cut into small squares, topped by a spoonful each of rose syrup (page 102) and agar-agar jelly (page 104).

RABRI
CONDENSED MILK DESSERT

This condensed milk doesn't come from a can — it is made by boiling down pure fresh milk until most of the water content has evaporated. It may sound like a lot of trouble, but the end result is so vastly different from any short-cut method that it is worth trying at least once.

Serves: 4

6 cups fresh milk
⅓ cup caster sugar
2 drops kewra essence or rose essence
1 tablespoon slivered blanched almonds
1 tablespoon slivered blanched pistachios

Put milk into a heavy-based saucepan and bring to the boil, stirring constantly. Keep it cooking steadily and continue stirring until it is reduced to about 2 cups and is thick. Reduce heat, add sugar and stir until dissolved. Remove from heat and stir well, scraping in particles of dried milk from side of pan and mixing them in. Add flavouring when it is lukewarm. Pour into a pretty bowl and sprinkle top with nuts. Chill before serving

Note: Use unsalted, untoasted pistachios and boil them for 1 minute to bring out their green colour and make it easy to slip off their skins.

KELA HALWA
BANANA SWEETMEAT

Makes about 24 pieces
5 large ripe bananas
2½ tablespoons ghee
1¼ cups water
¾ cup sugar
¼ teaspoon rose essence
½ teaspoon ground cardamom

Peel bananas and cut them into small pieces. Heat ghee in a heavy frying pan and fry the bananas for 5 minutes or until they are soft, stirring frequently so they do not brown. Move pan away from heat and mash the bananas.

Add quarter cup water to bananas and cook over low heat, stirring, for 3 minutes. Add remaining water and the sugar and stir constantly over medium heat until sugar melts, then continue cooking and stirring for 15-20 minutes until mixture is quite thick.

When mixture comes away from sides of pan in one mass, remove from heat and sprinkle in the flavouring and spice. Stir well, turn into a buttered dish. If any ghee separates from the mixture, pour it off.

When halwa is cool, cut into small squares. This halwa can also be served warm.

Note: Because this makes only a small quantity, I use an oblong dish 20 x 7.5 cm (8 x 3 inches) to get the correct thickness of halwa.

SRI LANKA

I was born and lived most of my life in this small, beautiful tropical island, shaped like a tear-drop and situated at the southernmost tip of the Indian subcontinent so that it has been romantically called 'the pearl in the ear of India'.

It has been known by many names at different times, for it is an ancient land and its recorded history goes back to 483 BC, when Vijaya, a prince of the lion race (Sinhalas) set foot on the island. Some of the names by which it has been called during its 2,500 years of recorded history are Taprobane, Simundu, Salike, Sila-diva, Serendib, Zeilan and Ceylon.

Roloff Beny, in his delightful book, *Island: Ceylon*, writes, 'In Sinhala, the language of the majority of the inhabitants, it is reverently known as Sri Lanka, or ''Resplendent Island'', but I myself prefer the name given to it by the first travellers from China, which in translation is, ''The Land Without Sorrow''.'

A selection of ingredients for Asian cooking.

I had been away for a number of years and when I visited it recently it was with a small shock that I realised all over again just how beautiful a land it is. Driving along the coast road one is surrounded by greens and blues and golden hues; languid, swaying coconut palms, the Indian Ocean incredibly blue and green and even purple in patches; sandy beaches that go on for mile after smooth, golden mile. Both sea and air are so warm that there is no chill either entering the water or leaving it. And there are no sharks because the island is surrounded by protective coral reefs, so it is a skin-diver's paradise.

Within less than a hundred miles you can travel from the coast to the central hills where 2,000 metres (6,000 feet) above sea level, the air is cool and crisp and the natural vegetation includes conifers and pines; here, English and Scottish planters grew the best tea in the world and felt at home in the cold, misty climate. On the coastal plains there is a year-round temperature of 32°C (90°F) and city dwellers seek the comfort of air-conditioned buildings.

In spite of its tiny size, Sri Lanka boasts an amazing variety of food and styles of cooking. The island has a rich heritage of indigenous dishes and its regional cooking is strongly individual and varied. For example, Kandyan Sinhalese cooking, with its emphasis on hill country vegetables and fruits; coastal cooking, making the best of the abundant seafood with which the land is blessed; Tamil cooking, closely linked to that of southern India, which is especially prevalent in Jaffna, in the north.

In Sri Lanka, as in any other country, the most typical food is cooked in the villages — getting precise recipes is almost impossible. They don't cook by a book. A pinch of this, a handful of that, a good swirl of salty water; taste, consider, adjust seasoning. That's the way Sinhalese women cook, and no two women cook exactly alike. Even using the same ingredients, the interpretation of a recipe is completely individual. Ask a cook how much of a certain ingredient she uses and she'll say, 'This much,' showing you with her hand. Spoon measures would be looked upon as an affectation. You watch, make notes and try to achieve the same results by trial and error. And when you arrive at the correct formula, write it down for posterity.

In addition to regional characteristics, some of the most popular dishes reflect influences from other lands. After a hundred years or so it does not matter that this or that style of cooking was introduced by foreigners who came and and stayed, either as traders or conquerors — Indians, Arabs, Malays, Moors, Portuguese, Dutch and British. The dishes they contributed have been adapted to local ingredients, but retain their original character. They are not presented as Sinhalese dishes but accepted and enjoyed as part of the richly varied cuisine.

The influence of the Muslims and Malays is responsible for the use of certain flavourings such as saffron and rose water and the spicy *korma, pilau* and *biriani* which are Sri Lankan only by adoption.

When the Portuguese ruled Sri Lanka for 150 years in the sixteenth and seventeenth centuries, they left behind words which have worked into the language and customs which are very much a part of rural and urban life. Many recipes end with an instruction to 'temper' the dish. This comes from the Portuguese word, *temperado,* which means to fry and season. The Portuguese also contributed a number of sweetmeats which are popular to this day. These are served at celebrations (Sri Lankans are enthusiastic about celebrating every happy occasion) and people take enormous pride in old family recipes, which they guard with jealous care.

Then came the Dutch, and though their rule ended after a mere 138 years, their descendants stayed on in this prosperous land. They too brought with them recipes laden with butter and eggs in true Dutch tradition, but in the spice-rich land of their adoption they took on new flavour with the addition of cardamom, cinnamon, cloves, nutmeg and mace. The traditional Ceylon Christmas cake is a fine example of this, a fruit cake which stands above all others for flavour and richness.

My father's family trace their ancestry back to the Dutch settlers, and I have never seen anyone so meticulous about cooking. One early memory is of my paternal grandmother — regal, silver-haired, supreme ruler of her domain — making preserves in an enormous brass pan that shone like gold. She was famous for her preserves, chutneys and jellies, and regularly won gold medals at the annual show.

Then I remember preparations for Christmas, always a time of much cooking and tasting. Eggs were bought by the hundred, not the dozen. And why not? The Christmas cake would require fifty egg yolks and a *breudher* (Dutch yeast cake) twenty more. When the egg vendor appeared it was the signal for the servants of the household to bring large basins of water to the verandah where grandmother sat to make her purchases. Into these the egg seller would put the eggs. Any that floated or bobbed about uncertainly were disqualified and only those that sank sedately to the bottom, signifying freshness, were considered worthy. The cooking of traditional foods was a family affair, and everyone had their part. For instance, my youngest uncle was delegated to the task of beating the *breudher*, for this had to be done with a degree of energy that was beyond the scope of a lady. So the large marble slab was brought out, he rolled up his sleeves and, under the watchful eye of his sister, he hurled that dough on to the slab for what seemed an eternity while she added one egg yolk at a time until all twenty yolks were incorporated.

No, I do not make *breudher* this way. I was determined to find an easier way and I have, with the help of an electric mixer. And twenty egg yolks in these days of cholesterol consciousness? Indeed not. Instead, I evolved a recipe using five eggs which yields two very large, light and delicious yeast cakes. Grandmother might not have approved the new-fangled method, but I'm sure she would have liked the result.

SERVING AND EATING A SRI LANKAN MEAL

Rice is the staple food of the people of Sri Lanka and has been adopted by all the communities (except, perhaps, the die-hard British). When enquiring whether one has had a meal, the literal translation of the question as asked in the Sinhalese language is, 'Have you eaten rice?' And all over the island the midday meal is rice and curry, Sinhalese style.

For such a meal everything is put on the table at once — rice, fish and meat curries, soup, vegetables and accompaniments. It is perfectly correct to have a serving of everything on your plate at one time. Soup may be ladled over the rice or sipped from a cup between mouthfuls, but it is not the first course. While the best way to enjoy such a meal is to eat with the fingers as the people of the country do, dessertspoon and fork are widely accepted now except on special occasions such as the Sinhalese New Year, when everybody goes traditional and eats with their fingers.

Desserts are unknown except on festive occasions, and the meal usually ends with some of the luscious fruit so plentiful on the island: mangoes of at least a dozen different varieties; pawpaws so sweet they seem to have been macerated in honey; bananas in even greater variety than mangoes; mangosteens and *rambutan* in season; avocados which are served with cream and sugar, never in a salad as they are served in the West; and the huge, ungainly jak fruit, spiky green outside and the size of a large watermelon, which has large, golden, fleshy seed pods of overwhelming sweetness and distinctive flavour.

Curries, which are inevitably part of every meal, are not necessarily classified according to the main ingredients, but according to the type of spicing, the method of cooking, or the colour which, to the initiate, conveys a whole lot more than just whether a curry is white, red or black. White curries are based on coconut milk and are usually mild and have a lot of liquid so they double as soups. Red curries are based on few spices and a large amount of chilli powder or ground chillies that give the curry its vivid colour and red hot flavour. (In Sri Lanka it is quite commonplace to have as many as thirty large dried red chillies to spice a dish for 6-8 people. Unless you are accustomed to spices on a grand scale, tread warily. Use some chilli for flavour and paprika to achieve the desired colour. Discretion is by far the better part of valour!) Black curries are the most typical curries in Sri Lanka. They get their dark colour because the coriander, cummin and fennel are roasted until a rich coffee brown. This dark-roasting brings out nuances of flavour in a subtle and wholly pleasant way, making the cooking of this little island strongly individual. If buying curry powder for use in Sri Lankan recipes, look for a label that says 'Ceylon Curry Powder' and if this is not obtainable, use the recipe on page 125 if you wish to duplicate the true flavour. Or, if using individual spices, always toast the coriander, cummin and fennel in a dry pan until dark brown before adding to the recipe.

UTENSILS

Cooking in true native style is always done on stone or brick hearths over wood fires. I remember Josie, a genial, round-faced, motherly woman who was the family cook for so many years that she addressed me as 'baby' (as the youngest member of the family is called) even when I was married and with babies of my own. Josie presided over the 'big kitchen' with its huge fireplaces, blowing through a piece of hollow metal tubing to get more heat out of the fire, stirring her clay *chatties* (cooking pots) with coconut shell spoons, and producing some of the best meals I have eaten. She had no time for the 'small kitchen' where the mistress of the house cooked on a gas range or baked cakes in the oven. Everything Josie wanted to cook could be made to her satisfaction in the time honoured way, using the most primitive equipment.

Like every other cook in the land she awoke before dawn to make the breakfast specialities, and each day, before she started to cook, she would grind her spices. This is done on an oblong grinding stone the size of a pillow, using another stone shaped like a bolster. Primitive, but standard equipment in most Asian countries. In Western kitchens, a powerful electric blender does this job.

There is something about food cooked in clay *chatties*, especially curries, that is rather special though really indefinable. It is as though the clay absorbs and then gives out again the character of the food cooked in it. So though a *chatty* costs a mere few cents, when a cook gets used to a certain pot she is not easily parted from it. Most cooks keep special *chatties* for meat, others for fish, and yet others for vegetables. However, a set of heavy-based aluminium saucepans is very suitable for curry cooking, and one with a well-fitting lid for cooking rice. In place of the coconut shell spoons used for stirring, use wooden spoons. In curry cooking, metal spoons are not recommended. And keep these special curry spoons only for curries, or they may transmit the strong flavours they absorb to other dishes.

There is no special equipment you need for the recipes in this chapter, except if you wish to try the *appé* (Hoppers) and even then you can make do with a cast iron omelette pan if you cannot find the proper curved iron pan used to make these rice pancakes. A *wok* is not suitable, as the metal is too thin and gets too hot.

YOUR SRI LANKAN SHELF

aromatic ginger, ground
coriander, ground
cummin, ground
fennel, ground
fenugreek, seeds
cinnamon sticks
cardamom pods and ground
chilli powder and whole dried chillies
curry leaves, dried
cloves, whole and ground
peppercorns, whole
turmeric, ground
creamed coconut, optional
desiccated coconut
paprika
dried *rampé* (pandanus) leaf, optional
dried lemon grass, optional
black mustard seeds
dried tamarind pulp
ghee
vegetable oil (coconut oil if available)

GHEE RICE

Serves: 4-5
2 cups Basmati or other long grain rice
2½ tablespoons ghee
1 large onion, finely sliced
4 whole cloves
6 cardamom pods, bruised
1 cinnamon stick
3½ cups beef, chicken or mutton stock, or
    water and stock cubes
2½ teaspoons salt

Wash rice well and drain for at least 30 minutes. Heat ghee in a saucepan and fry onion until golden, add spices and drained rice. Fry, stirring with slotted metal spoon, for 5 minutes over a moderate heat. Add hot stock and salt and bring to the boil.

Reduce heat to very low, cover pan tightly with lid and cook for 15-20 minutes without lifting lid. At end of cooking time, uncover and allow steam to escape for 5 minutes. Gently fluff up rice with a fork, removing whole spices.

When transferring rice to a serving dish, again use a slotted metal spoon to avoid crushing grains of rice. Serve hot, accompanied by curries of meat and vegetables, pickles and sambols.

From the top: YELLOW RICE *recipe page 120;* CASHEW NUT CURRY *recipe page 145;* CUCUMBER SAMBOL *recipe page 155;* COCONUT SAMBOL *recipe page 156;* PAPPADAMS *recipe page 95;* FRIED EGGPLANT SAMBOL *recipe page 155;* and BEEF CURRY *recipe page 136.*

KAHA BATH
YELLOW RICE (*picture page 119*)

A special occasion dish in which the rice is cooked in coconut milk and delicately flavoured with spices.

Serves: 6-8
3 cups long grain rice
4 tablespoons ghee
2 medium onions, finely sliced
6 cloves
20 black peppercorns
12 cardamom pods, bruised
1½ teaspoons ground turmeric
3½ teaspoons salt
12 curry leaves
1 stalk dried lemon grass, optional
4 pieces daun pandan or rampé leaf,
  optional
about 5 cups coconut milk

Wash rice and drain thoroughly. Heat ghee in a large saucepan, add onion and fry until it begins to turn golden brown. Add cloves, peppercorns, cardamom pods, turmeric, salt, curry leaves, lemon grass and pandan or rampé leaf. Add rice and fry, stirring constantly, for 2-3 minutes, until rice is well coated with ghee and turmeric. Add coconut milk and bring to the boil. Reduce heat, cover and cook for 20-25 minutes without lifting lid.

When rice is cooked, the spices will have come to the top. Remove spices and leaves used for flavouring and fluff up the rice lightly with a fork. Serve hot, accompanied by pork badun (page 138) or other curries and accompaniments.

KOPPÉ BATH
CUP RICE

Serves: 8
yellow rice (above)
coconut sambol (page 156)
4 hard-boiled eggs, optional

Basically, this is yellow rice moulded in a cup, with a layer of coconut sambol in the centre. If liked, put a halved hard-boiled egg in the base of the cup before half filling with the warm rice. Press firmly. Cover this with a tablespoon of coconut sambol, then cover with more yellow rice. Again press down firmly, then turn out on a serving dish. Repeat until all the rice is used up. Serve with curries and accompaniments.

KIRI BATH
MILK RICE

A simple preparation of rice cooked in coconut milk, kiri bath is part of the traditions of the Sinhalese people. It is a 'must' on New Year's Day, and on the first day of each month it is the accepted breakfast dish. It is usually served with hot sambols, but some prefer it with grated palm sugar (jaggery). If you find it difficult to buy palm sugar, use unrefined black sugar (from health stores) as a substitute.

Serves: 4-5
2 cups short grain white rice
3 cups water
2 cups thick coconut milk
2 teaspoons salt
1 stick cinnamon, optional

Put rice and water into a pan and bring to the boil. Cover and cook 15 minutes. Add coconut milk, salt and cinnamon, stir well with handle of wooden spoon, cover pan and cook on low heat for further 10-15 minutes, when all the milk should be absorbed. Remove cinnamon, cool slightly, then turn out on to a flat plate. Mark off in diamond shapes and serve with coconut sambol.

LAMPRIES

Just as biriani is the ultimate in festive meals in India, lampries is the 'special occasion' dish in Sri Lanka. If you are invited to a meal in a Sri Lankan home and lampries are served, you are being honoured.

The name comes from the Dutch word, lomprijst, and it is a fascinating combination of rice cooked in stock, Dutch-style forcemeat balls, Sinhalese curries and sambols, all wrapped in banana leaves and baked.

Serves: 16-18
Cooking time: approximately 20-25 minutes
Oven temperature: 170-190°C (350-375°F)

Use large, wide banana leaves, strip them from the centre rib and cut into pieces, approximately 30-38 cm (12-15 inches) long. Wash and dry with a clean cloth and heat over a gas flame for a few seconds on each side. This makes them pliable and they will fold without splitting. If you cook by electricity, put banana leaves in a large basin or sink and pour boiling water over. If no banana leaves are available, use 38 cm (15 inch) squares of aluminium foil.

Prepare ghee rice (page 118), making three times the quantity. For 6 cups rice use 9½ cups stock. On each piece of leaf or aluminium foil, put 1 cup firmly packed ghee rice. Around rice arrange 2 tablespoons lampries curry (page 138), 2 frikkadels (page 148), 2 teaspoons vambotu pahi (page 151), 1 teaspoon chilli sambol (page 154) and 1 heaped teaspoon prawn blachan (page 153). Pour 2 tablespoons thick coconut milk (page 11) over rice.

Fold leaf over and fasten with bamboo skewers (obtainable from barbecue departments of large stores) or fold aluminium foil over to make a neat oblong package. Some people prefer to enclose leaf parcels in aluminium foil. (This is a good idea in case leaf splits while heating or serving). Heat lampries in a moderate oven for approximately 20-25 minutes. Arrange on a large tray.

When guests open the lampries, the fragrance of the food is unbelievably appetising. Allow one to two lampries for each guest. A bowl of chilled cucumber sambol (page 155) is served as an accompaniment.

Note: It is practical to make a large number of lampries, for they are ideal for parties. They freeze well and can be kept frozen for two months. Heat in a moderate oven from frozen state for 40 minutes, or 20 minutes if first thawed to room temperature.

ROTIS

Similar to the Indian flat breads, but this Sri Lankan version contains fresh grated coconut or, in its absence, desiccated coconut. Serve with curries and sambols. It is a popular breakfast in Sri Lanka.

Serves: 6-8
2 cups roti flour, self-raising flour or rice
    flour
½ cup desiccated coconut
1 teaspoon salt
scant 1 cup water
ghee or oil for cooking

Mix flour, coconut and salt in a mixing bowl. Add enough water to form a soft dough. Knead dough until it forms a ball and does not stick to sides of the bowl. Rest dough for approximately 30 minutes.

Shape dough into balls, approximately the size of a golf ball. Pat each one out to a circle the size of a saucer. Cook on a hot griddle or in a heavy frying pan very lightly greased with ghee or oil. Serve hot.

LEILA'S ROTIS

Makes about 12
4 cups rice flour, roti flour or plain flour
1 teaspoon baking powder
1 cup freshly grated or desiccated coconut
2 teaspoons salt
2 teaspoons butter or margarine
1 tablespoon finely chopped onion
2 teaspoons finely chopped fresh red or
   green chilli
1 egg, beaten
scant 2 cups water, approximately
little ghee or oil for cooking

Mix flour, baking powder, coconut and salt in a large bowl. Rub in butter until evenly distributed, stir onion and chilli through the flour, then add the egg and sufficient water to bind the mixture to a stiff dough. Knead until it forms a ball and doesn't stick to the bowl. Rest dough for 30 minutes. Take a lemon-size lump of dough and pat between floured hands to a circle the size of a bread and butter plate. Cook on a hot griddle or heavy frying pan greased very lightly. Serve hot with sambols or curries.

APPÉ
HOPPERS

The name doesn't really tell you anything unless you've been in this part of the world and eaten appé, appam or hoppers as they are variously called. They are bowl-shaped pancakes made from a batter of rice flour, yeast and coconut milk, swirled in a hemispherical pan (rather like a smaller, more acutely curved wok) and baked over hot coals with more coals heaped on the lid. They can be cooked with equal success on gas or electric stoves, and the pans are sold in shops that specialise in utensils from India and Sri Lanka. I have also made them in a small omelette pan — the shape is unorthodox but the taste is perfect. In Sri Lanka, hoppers are served for breakfast, but are equally good at any time.

Makes about 20
15 g (½ oz) fresh compressed yeast or 1
   teaspoon dried yeast
½ cup warm water
1½ teaspoons sugar
1½ cups ground rice
1½ cups rice flour or plain white flour
2 teaspoons salt
2 cups desiccated coconut
2½ cups hot milk
2 cups hot water

Sprinkle yeast over warm water, stir to dissolve, add sugar and leave for 10 minutes or so. If yeast starts to froth it is active and you can proceed with the recipe. If it has no reaction, start again with a fresh batch of yeast, or the hoppers will not be a success.

Put ground rice, rice flour and salt into a large bowl. Make coconut milk as described on page 11, using milk instead of water. When the first milk has been extracted, use the same coconut and repeat the procedure with the water. Keep the two extracts separate.

Add yeast mixture to the first extract of coconut milk and stir into the dry ingredients to form a smooth, thick batter. Allow to stand overnight, or put in a warm (turned off) oven for 1 hour until mixture rises and doubles in bulk. The batter should be of a thick pouring consistency, but thin enough to cover the sides of the pan with an almost transparent coating when the batter is swirled. It will be necessary to add some of the second extract of coconut. A little practice will tell you when you have achieved the perfect consistency, and so much depends on the absorbency of the flour that it is not possible to give an accurate measurement.

Heat the pan over low heat, rub the inside surface with a piece of folded kitchen paper dipped in oil, and pour in a small ladle of the batter. Immediately pick up the pan by both handles, using pot holders, and swirl it around so that the batter coats the pan for two thirds of the way up. Cover pan (any saucepan cover that fits just inside the top edge will do) and cook on very low heat for about 5 minutes. Lift lid and peep. When upper edges begin to turn a pale toasty colour, the hopper is ready. Where the batter has run down the sides to the centre there will be a little circle of spongy mixture, rather like a crumpet, while the curved edge is very thin, crisp and wafer-like. With a curved slotted utensil or flexible metal spatula slip the hopper from the pan on to a wire rack. Wipe pan again with oiled paper and repeat. Serve the hoppers warm, accompanied by lunu miris sambol (page 155) or any kind of meat, fish or chicken curry.

KUKUL MAS CURRY (chicken curry) *recipe page 133*

BITHTHARA APPÉ
EGG HOPPERS

Proceed as for hoppers, but as soon as the pan is coated with batter, break a fresh egg into the centre. Cover and cook as before — the egg will cook to just the right stage while the hopper bakes, and looks prettier than an egg cooked any other way. Serve with salt and pepper for seasoning.

MITI KIRI APPÉ
COCONUT CREAM HOPPERS

If preferred, hoppers can be served with sweet accompaniments such as fresh grated coconut and grated palm sugar. If to be served sweet, an extra richness is given the hopper by spooning a small amount of rich coconut milk into the centre before putting on the lid.

IDDI APPÉ
STRINGHOPPERS

Stringhoppers get their name because they are composed of fine 'strings' of dough, finer even than vermicelli, forced through a perforated mould to form lacy circles about the size of a saucer. These are steamed on woven rounds piled one on top of the other. The texture is light, fluffy, dry to the touch. An average serving is 6 or 8 stringhoppers for breakfast, served with a simple coconut milk soup (see kiri hodhi, page 149) and coconut sambol. But stringhoppers are also a favourite at festive lunches or dinners and in this setting are shredded finely and cooked as a pilau, accompanied by mulligatawny (page 149), egg ruloung (page 147), frikkadels (page 148), meat or chicken curry and chilli sambol (page 154).

I mention them because they are so typical of Sri Lankan food, but since making them is an arduous task, the recipe that follows is a substitute using Chinese rice vermicelli. I have called it 'mock stringhopper pilau'.

Serves: 8-10
500 g (1 lb) rice vermicelli
5 tablespoons ghee
3 large onions, finely sliced
10 curry leaves
1 packet powdered saffron or ½ teaspoon
   saffron strands
1 teaspoon ground turmeric
1 teaspoon ground cardamom
salt and pepper to taste
4-5 hard-boiled eggs
1 cup cooked peas
¼ cup cashew nuts or almonds, fried in
   oil until golden brown

Cook rice vermicelli in large quantity of lightly salted boiling water for 2 minutes only. Drain immediately in a large colander.

Heat ghee in a large saucepan and fry onion and curry leaves until onion is golden. Add saffron, turmeric and cardamom and stir well. Add rice vermicelli and toss ingredients together until well mixed and evenly coloured. Season to taste with salt and pepper. Serve garnished with eggs cut into slices or quarters, peas and nuts.

Note: If liked, the hard-boiled eggs can be rubbed with ground turmeric and fried in a little hot oil until golden.

PITTU

Pittu is a combination of flour and freshly grated coconut steamed in a bamboo cylinder. The resulting roll, looking something like a white suet pudding but infinitely lighter in texture, is served with fresh coconut milk and hot sambols and curries, and is especially popular as a breakfast dish. To improvise a steamer take a tall, narrow can such as a coffee can, cut away the base, make a dozen or so small holes in the lid and invert the can so the lid is now the base. Fill the can with the coconut mixture. If a steamer is not available put in a large pot with a trivet in it to hold the can above water level.

2 cups grated fresh coconut or 2 cups
   desiccated coconut and 1 cup water
1 cup plain flour or rice flour
1 cup medium fine semolina
1½ teaspoons salt

If using desiccated coconut put in a large bowl and sprinkle with the water. Work gently with the fingertips until all the coconut is moistened evenly. Fresh coconut does not need water. Add sifted flour, semolina and salt to coconut in bowl and rub gently with the fingertips as for making pastry. The mixture should be like fine crumbs. Fill bamboo or metal cylinders with this and press down lightly. Steam in a large pot over boiling water for 10-15 minutes. Allow to cool slightly, then unmould and serve with coconut milk for moistening, lunu miris sambol (page 155) or a hot curry such as tripe curry (page 141), which is traditional with pittu.

Pittu can also be served with sweet accompaniments such as coconut milk, grated palm sugar or white sugar.

CEYLON CURRY POWDER

In Sri Lankan (Ceylonese) cooking, one of the main characteristics is that the spices are dark roasted. This gives them an aroma completely different from Indian curries, so be sure to use curry powder that is labelled 'Ceylon Curry Powder'. If you cannot buy it ready-made, here is a simple recipe.

1 cup coriander seeds
½ cup cummin seeds
1 tablespoon fennel seeds
1 teaspoon fenugreek seeds
1 cinnamon stick, about 5 cm (2 inches)
1 teaspoon whole cloves
1 teaspoon cardamom seeds
2 tablespoons dried curry leaves
2 teaspoons chilli powder, optional
2 tablespoons ground rice, optional

In a dry pan over low heat roast *separately* the coriander, cummin, fennel and fenugreek, stirring constantly until each one becomes a fairly dark brown. Do not let them burn. Put into blender container together with cinnamon stick broken in pieces, the cloves, cardamom and curry leaves. Blend on high speed until finely powdered. Combine with chilli powder and ground rice if used. Store in an airtight jar.

MALU CURRY
FISH CURRY

Serves: 4-6

4 large fish steaks (Spanish mackerel,
    jewfish, kingfish or cod)
1 teaspoon ground black pepper
1 teaspoon salt
1 teaspoon ground turmeric
oil for frying
2 medium onions, finely chopped
½ teaspoon fenugreek seeds
2 cloves garlic, finely sliced
1 teaspoon finely chopped fresh ginger
1 small stick cinnamon
few pieces dried daun pandan or rampé
    leaf
8 curry leaves
1½ tablespoons Ceylon curry powder
    (page 125)
¼ cup tamarind liquid
2 cups coconut milk

Wash fish steaks, dry on kitchen paper and rub each steak well with a mixture of pepper, salt and turmeric. Heat about 1.75 cm (½ in) oil in a large frying pan and fry fish quickly to a golden colour. Drain on paper while preparing the gravy.

Heat 2 tablespoons oil in a large saucepan and gently fry onions, fenugreek, garlic and ginger until onions are soft and golden. Add cinnamon, pandan or rampé, curry leaves and curry powder and fry for two minutes, stirring. Add tamarind liquid and coconut milk and simmer, uncovered, until gravy is thickened and slightly reduced. Put in the fish steaks. If they are very large, divide into serving pieces. Spoon gravy over the fish and simmer for about 10 minutes. Serve hot with boiled rice and vegetable curries.

AMBUL THIYAL
SOUR CURRY OF FISH

In Sri Lanka, the acid used for this special preparation is called 'goraka', a bright orange fruit that is divided into segments and dried. The dried segments are almost black. If you can obtain this ingredient, use 4 segments and grind them to a pulp. I have used tamarind as a substitute because it is readily available.

Serves: 6

500 g (1 lb) firm fish fillets or steaks
1 rounded tablespoon tamarind pulp
¼ cup vinegar
1 medium onion, finely chopped
3 cloves garlic, finely chopped
1 teaspoon finely grated fresh ginger
1 teaspoon salt
6-8 curry leaves
1 stalk lemon grass or 2 strips lemon rind
2.5 cm (1 inch) piece cinnamon stick
¼ teaspoon fenugreek seeds
¼ teaspoon ground black pepper
¼ teaspoon chilli powder, optional
1½ cups water
2 tablespoons oil

Wash and dry fish, cut into serving pieces. Soak the tamarind in the vinegar until it is soft. If tamarind is very dry, heat the vinegar and tamarind in an enamel saucepan for a few minutes, adding some of the water. When cool enough to handle, squeeze the tamarind in the liquid to dissolve pulp, strain through a fine nylon sieve and discard seeds and fibres. Put all ingredients into a pan (preferably an enamel or stainless steel pan) and bring to the boil. Reduce heat and simmer uncovered until fish is cooked and gravy is thick. Shake pan or turn fish pieces carefully once or twice during cooking. Serve with white rice.

THAKKALI MALU
FISH CURRY WITH TOMATO

Serves: 4-5

500 g (1 lb) fish steaks (kingfish, tuna,
   Spanish mackerel, mullet)
1 teaspoon ground turmeric
1 teaspoon salt
oil for frying
1 large onion, roughly chopped
3 cloves garlic
2 teaspoons finely chopped fresh ginger
1 medium size ripe tomato, chopped
2 tablespoons oil
1 tablespoon Ceylon curry powder
   (page 125)
1 teaspoon chilli powder
salt to taste
2 cups coconut milk

Wash and dry fish well and rub all over with turmeric and salt. Cut each steak into serving pieces. Heat oil in a frying pan and fry the fish until golden brown on both sides. Drain.

Put onion, garlic, ginger and tomato in container of electric blender and blend to a smooth paste. Heat oil in a saucepan and fry the blended ingredients for a few minutes, until oil begins to separate from mixture. Add the curry and chilli powders and about a teaspoonful of salt, the coconut milk, and bring to the boil, stirring. Simmer for a few minutes, then add the fish and simmer for 10 minutes. Serve with rice and accompaniments.

KIRI MALU
FISH WHITE CURRY

Serves: 6

500 g (1 lb) firm white fish steaks or
   fillets
½ teaspoon ground turmeric
1 teaspoon salt
1 teaspoon fenugreek seeds
1 medium onion, finely sliced
2 cloves garlic, finely chopped
8 curry leaves
1½ cups thin coconut milk
½ cup thick coconut milk
lemon juice to taste

Wash fish and dry on kitchen paper. Rub with turmeric and half teaspoon salt. Soak fenugreek seeds in water for 30 minutes. Put fenugreek seeds into a saucepan with onion, garlic, curry leaves and thin coconut milk and half teaspoon salt. Simmer gently until onions are soft. Stir well, add fish and simmer for further 10 minutes. Add thick coconut milk and cook for a few minutes longer, remove from heat and add lemon juice to taste. Serve with rice and sambols.

SIYAMBALA MALU CURRY
FISH CURRY WITH TAMARIND

Serves: 6

500 g (1 lb) firm fish steaks or fillets
1 rounded tablespoon tamarind pulp
½ cup hot water
1½ tablespoons Ceylon curry powder
   (page 125)
1 teaspoon salt
¼ teaspoon ground turmeric
1 teaspoon chilli powder
3 tablespoons oil
6 curry leaves
¼ teaspoon fenugreek seeds
1 medium onion, finely chopped
2 cloves garlic, finely chopped

Wash and dry fish and cut into serving pieces. Soak tamarind pulp in hot water, allow to cool, squeeze to dissolve pulp. Strain through fine nylon sieve and discard seeds and fibres. Combine tamarind liquid with curry powder, salt, turmeric, chilli powder and marinate fish for 20 minutes.

Heat oil and fry the curry leaves and fenugreek seeds for 2 minutes, then add onion and garlic and continue to fry on medium heat until onion is golden, stirring occasionally. Add fish and marinade, cover and cook over low heat for 10 minutes. Uncover and cook for a further 10 minutes. Serve with white rice and vegetable curries.

MALU BOLA CUTLIS
FISH KOFTAS

Makes about 60
1 x 425 g (15 oz) can mackerel or snoek
500 g (1 lb) floury potatoes
1 large onion, very finely chopped
1 large or two small eggs, beaten
3 slices white sandwich bread
2 teaspoons salt
½ teaspoon ground black pepper
1 teaspoon Ceylon curry powder
  (page 125)
1 teaspoon dried dill weed or snipped
  fresh dill
2 teaspoons finely chopped fresh red or
  green chillies, seeded
dry breadcrumbs or cornflake crumbs for
  coating
oil for deep frying

Drain fish very thoroughly in a sieve, pressing with a spoon to get rid of as much liquid as possible. Boil potatoes, mash while hot and take same weight as that of the drained fish. Mix together in a bowl with the onion, egg, the white bread trimmed of crusts and crumbed finely, the seasoning, dill and chillies. Mix thoroughly and shape into 60 small balls. Roll in the dry breadcrumbs and fry a few at a time in deep hot oil over medium heat. Do not have oil too hot or crumb coating will float off and koftas will brown before they are cooked through. When nicely brown lift out on slotted spoon and drain on absorbent paper. These fish koftas can be made ahead, frozen in a plastic bag when cool, and reheated in a moderate oven before serving.

MALU ROAST
SPICY BARBECUED FISH

Serves: 4
4 small tailor or mullet, whole
2 tablespoons lemon juice
1½ teaspoons salt
1 teaspoon ground turmeric
¼ teaspoon ground black pepper
1 small onion, sliced
2 cloves garlic, peeled
2 slices fresh ginger
¼ teaspoon each ground cinnamon
  and cloves
½ teaspoon dried crushed curry leaves,
  optional
1 tablespoon ground coriander
1 teaspoon ground cummin
1 teaspoon chilli powder, or to taste
1 tablespoon oil
banana leaves or foil for wrapping

Clean and scale fish, leaving head on. Wipe inside fish with kitchen paper dipped in coarse salt, leaving body cavities clean. Snip out gills with kitchen scissors and trim any long spines or fins neatly. Wash fish well, cut diagonal slashes in flesh with sharp knife, about 2.5 cm (1 inch) apart, and rub fish with a little lemon juice, salt, turmeric and pepper. Put remaining ingredients into container of electric blender and blend to a smooth paste (or use a mortar and pestle). Apply to fish, rubbing well into slashes and body cavity. Spoon remaining mixture over fish. Wrap in leaves or heavy-duty foil and make a neat parcel. Put over glowing coals or under a heated griller 10 minutes on each side. Open parcel for last few minutes to allow excess moisture to evaporate. Serve hot with steamed rice.

RATHU ISSO CURRY
RED PRAWN CURRY

Serves: 6
750 g (1½ lb) small raw prawns
1 medium onion, finely chopped
3 cloves garlic, finely chopped
1 teaspoon finely grated fresh ginger
small stick cinnamon
¼ teaspoon fenugreek seeds
few curry leaves
small stem lemon grass, bruised, or
   2 strips lemon rind
1 strip daun pandan or rampé leaf
½ teaspoon ground turmeric
1½ teaspoons chilli powder
2 teaspoons paprika
1 teaspoon salt
2 cups coconut milk
good squeeze lemon juice

Wash prawns and remove heads, but leave shells on. (In Sri Lanka prawns are often cooked in their shells, for better flavour). Put all ingredients, except lemon juice, into a saucepan and bring slowly to simmering point. Simmer uncovered for 20 minutes or until onions are soft. Add lemon juice and stir. Taste and add more salt or lemon if required.

ISSO THEL DHALA
DRY-FRIED PRAWNS

Once again, paprika comes to the rescue and makes this spicy prawn preparation as enticingly red as it should be. If you are inclined to try it the real Sri Lankan way, increase the amount of chilli powder . . . but don't say I didn't warn you!

Serves: 6
1 kg (2 lb) raw prawns
3 tablespoons oil
2 large onions, finely chopped
2 cloves garlic, finely chopped
2 teaspoons salt
½ teaspoon chilli powder, or to taste
2 teaspoons paprika
¼ teaspoon ground turmeric
2 teaspoons pounded Maldive fish or dried
   prawn powder
½ cup water
2 teaspoons sugar
1 tablespoon tomato paste or sauce

Shell and de-vein prawns. Heat oil in a heavy frying pan and cook onions and garlic over low heat until soft and golden brown. When oil begins to appear around edges add chilli powder, salt, paprika and turmeric and fry for 1 minute, then add Maldive fish and prawns, stir and fry for 3 minutes. Add water, cover and simmer for 5 minutes. Stir in sugar and tomato paste and cook uncovered for a few minutes longer until gravy is dark reddish brown, thick and dry enough to coat the prawns. Serve with rice. As an appetiser these devilled prawns are delicious on small squares of fried bread.

KAKULUWO CURRY
CRAB CURRY *(picture opposite)*

A favourite in Sri Lanka where crabs are plentiful and cheap and are always sold live. Cooked crabs can be used, and are a lot easier — and safer — to handle.

Serves: 4-6
2 large crabs
3 medium onions, finely chopped
6 cloves garlic, finely chopped
2 teaspoons finely grated fresh ginger
½ teaspoon fenugreek seeds
10 curry leaves
8 cm (3 inch) stick cinnamon
1-2 teaspoons chilli powder
1 teaspoon ground turmeric
3 teaspoons salt
4 cups thin coconut milk
2 tablespoons desiccated coconut
1 tablespoon ground rice
2 cups thick coconut milk
3 tablespoons lemon juice

Remove large shells of crabs and discard fibrous tissue found under the shell. Divide each crab into 4 portions, breaking each body in half and separating large claws from body. Leave legs attached to body.

Put onion, garlic, ginger, fenugreek, curry leaves, cinnamon, chilli, turmeric, salt and thin coconut milk into a large saucepan. Cover and simmer gently 30 minutes. Add crabs and cook for 20 minutes if using raw crabs. Cook for only 5-7 minutes if cooked crabs are used. If pan is not large enough, simmer half the pieces of crab at a time. Crab should be submerged in sauce while cooking.

Heat desiccated coconut and ground rice separately in a dry frying pan over moderate heat, stirring constantly to prevent burning, until each is golden brown. Put in an electric blender container, add half the thick coconut milk, cover and blend on high speed 1 minute. Add to curry with lemon juice. Wash out blender with remaining coconut milk and add. Simmer uncovered a further 10 minutes. Serve with boiled rice.

Note: Onions vary greatly in different countries and even from one season to the next. If they are inclined to be large and tough, first soften by cooking gently in 2-3 tablespoons oil about 20 minutes before including in recipe.

DHALLO BADUN
FRIED SQUID CURRY

Serves: 4-6
about 1 kg (2 lb) squid
2 medium onions, finely sliced
4 cloves garlic, finely sliced
2 teaspoons finely grated fresh ginger
1 teaspoon ground turmeric
1 teaspoon chilli powder, optional
2 tablespoons Ceylon curry powder
  (page 125)
½ teaspoon whole fenugreek seeds
1 cinnamon stick
1 stalk lemon grass or 2 strips lemon rind
10 curry leaves
3 tablespoons vinegar
3 cups coconut milk
1½ teaspoons ghee or oil for frying

Clean squid, removing ink sac and discarding head. Cut into rings. Put into a deep saucepan with all the ingredients except ghee. Bring to the boil, then simmer for about 1 hour or until squid is tender and the gravy reduced to a small quantity. Drain pieces of squid from the gravy and, in another pan, heat the ghee and fry the squid. Pour the gravy into the pan in which the squid are fried, simmer for a minute or two longer and serve with white rice and sambols.

KAKULUWO OMLET CURRY
CRAB OMELETTE CURRY

A simple omelette when served in curry sauce is no longer commonplace, and when it is a crab omelette the result is something to remember . . . and I do. My father was not what you would call a domesticated man, but he had one culinary accomplishment: he could make a crab omelette better than any other crab omelette I ever tasted. I don't know whether it stemmed from his own inventiveness or whether the recipe was given him by one of his good friends, a Chinese dentist-turned-restaurateur who discovered it was more rewarding filling people's stomachs than filling their teeth.

Dad would go to the market and choose himself the biggest, heaviest, freshest crab he could find and bring it home, still alive and bent on escape. I seem to recall that at this point he did a quick fade out, leaving the crab to the none-too-tender ministrations of our cook. But when it had been steamed to flavoursome succulence and the meat carefully extracted from shell and claws, Dad took over once more and combined eggs, crab, spring onions and fresh chilli into a masterpiece. He never did write down his recipe, but I have managed to reconstruct something very like it. Do try to use fresh crab meat — it is a vast improvement on the frozen or canned variety. Serve as an omelette or in curry sauce.

Serves: 2-4
4 eggs
salt and pepper
1 cup flaked crab meat
lemon juice to taste
1 tablespoon butter
3 spring onions, finely sliced
1 fresh green or red chilli, seeded and
   finely chopped
1 teaspoon finely snipped fresh dill,
   optional
1 quantity gravy as for vegetable curry
   (page 142)

Beat eggs slightly, as for a French omelette. Season with half teaspoon salt and a good grinding of black pepper. Season crab meat with salt and pepper to taste and a squeeze of lemon juice.

Heat butter in a large, heavy omelette pan and gently fry the spring onions and chilli until soft, stirring frequently. Pour in the beaten eggs and stir in dill. Cook, pulling in set portion from sides of pan and letting the uncooked egg run out to the edges. When set and golden on the bottom, creamy on top, spoon heated crab meat down the centre of the omelette and fold over once. Spoon hot gravy over. Serve with rice.

Note: The omelette curry can also be made without the crab.

KUKUL MAS CURRY
CHICKEN CURRY

Serves: 4-5

1.5 kg (3 lb) chicken or chicken pieces
3 tablespoons ghee or oil
¼ teaspoon fenugreek seeds, optional
10 curry leaves
2 large onions, finely chopped
4-5 cloves garlic, finely chopped
2 teaspoons finely grated fresh ginger
1 teaspoon ground turmeric
1 teaspoon chilli powder
1 tablespoon ground coriander
1 teaspoon ground cummin
½ teaspoon ground fennel
2 teaspoons paprika
2 teaspoons salt
2 tablespoons vinegar
2 tomatoes, peeled and chopped
6 cardamom pods, bruised
1 stick cinnamon
1 stalk lemon grass or 2 strips lemon rind
1 cup thick coconut milk

Joint chicken. Cut breast and thighs in halves, leave wings and drumsticks whole. Heat ghee and fry fenugreek and curry leaves until they start to brown. Add onions, garlic and ginger and fry gently until onions are quite soft and golden. Add turmeric, chilli, coriander, cummin, fennel, paprika, salt and vinegar. Stir well. Add chicken and stir over medium heat until chicken is thoroughly coated with spices. Add tomatoes, whole spices and lemon grass and cook, covered, over low heat 40-50 minutes. Add coconut milk, taste and add more salt and a squeeze of lemon juice if desired. Do not cover after adding coconut milk. Serve with rice and accompaniments.

Note: Paprika is used to give the required red colour — in Sri Lanka the colour is achieved by using about 30 red chillies!

THARA PADRÉ CURRY
DUCK PADRÉ CURRY

The name of this curry has always fascinated me. Why it is called 'padre' curry is not clear. It contains a substantial amount of arrack or whisky and one explanation offered is that it was a favourite with the padre because it was his only opportunity to imbibe!

Serves: 6-8

2 ducks cut into joints
2 large onions, chopped
6 cloves garlic, chopped
1½ tablespoons finely chopped ginger
2 tablespoons Ceylon curry powder
  (page 125)
1 stick cinnamon
8 pieces dried daun pandan or rampé leaf
1 stalk lemon grass or 2 strips lemon rind
3 cups coconut milk
2 teaspoons salt
¼ cup vinegar
¼ cup arrack or whisky
1 tablespoon brown sugar
2 tablespoons ghee or oil

Cut ducks into joints and put into a large heavy saucepan with all the ingredients except arrack, sugar and ghee. Bring to the boil, then cover and simmer until duck is tender. Heat ghee in another pan and fry the pieces of duck, then pour in the gravy, add arrack and sugar and simmer a further 10 minutes. Serve with plain boiled rice or ghee rice, fried onion sambol, cucumber sambol. For another version of this dish, garnish the top of the curry with slices of potato, fried until brown.

KUKUL GUJURA CURRY
CHICKEN GIZZARD CURRY

Serves: 6
750 g (1½ lb) chicken gizzards
1½ tablespoons ground coriander
3 teaspoons ground cummin
4 tablespoons oil or ghee
2 medium onions, finely chopped
5 cloves garlic, finely chopped
1 tablespoon finely chopped fresh ginger
1 teaspoon chilli powder
½ teaspoon ground turmeric
½ teaspoon ground fenugreek, optional
2 ripe tomatoes, chopped
1½ teaspoons salt
2 tablespoons chopped fresh coriander
    leaves

Wash and clean the gizzards well, leave to drain in colander. Put the ground coriander in a small dry pan and stir over low heat for a few minutes until roasted to a fairly dark brown and giving out a pleasant aroma. Turn the coriander on to a plate. Roast the cummin in the same way.

Heat the oil in a large heavy saucepan. When hot, put in onions, garlic and ginger. Fry, stirring, until onions are soft and start to turn golden brown. Add the chilli powder, turmeric, fenugreek and the previously roasted coriander and cummin. Cook, stirring, for 1 minute, then add the tomatoes and salt and stir well. Add the chicken gizzards and stir until they are well coated with spice mixture. Add hot water to cover and simmer for 1 hour or until gizzards are tender. Sprinkle with coriander leaves, stir and cook for 5 minutes longer. Serve hot with rice.

MAS ISMORU
BEEF SMOORE (picture opposite)

A large piece of beef, cooked in a spicy coconut milk mixture, cut in slices like roast beef and served with plenty of rich thick gravy spooned over. Accompany with boiled rice or rotis (page 121) and onion sambol (page 155).

Serves: 6-8
1.5 kg (3 lb) stewing steak, in one piece
2 medium onions, finely chopped
6 cloves garlic, finely chopped
1 tablespoon finely chopped fresh ginger
1 stick cinnamon
10 curry leaves
1 stalk lemon grass or 2 strips lemon rind
3 tablespoons Ceylon curry powder
    (page 125)
½ teaspoon fenugreek seeds
½ cup vinegar
½ pickled lime or lemon (page 152) or
    ½ cup tamarind liquid
2 cups thin coconut milk
1 teaspoon ground turmeric
2 teaspoons chilli powder, or to taste
2 teaspoons salt, or to taste
1 cup thick coconut milk
2½ tablespoons ghee

Pierce the meat well with a skewer and put in a large saucepan with all the ingredients except the thick coconut milk and ghee. Cover and simmer gently until meat is tender, approximately 1½-2 hours. Add thick coconut milk and cook, uncovered, 15 minutes longer.

Lift meat out on to a serving dish and if gravy is too thin, reduce by boiling rapidly uncovered. Transfer gravy to a bowl. Rinse pan to remove any gravy, return to stove and heat ghee in it. Fry meat on all sides, pour gravy over meat and heat through.

JAGGERY SATAY
MEAT WITH PALM SUGAR

Sweet, sour, salty, hot, this meat preparation is all of these, but does not use any of the curry spices. A spicy sauce may be served with it if liked, but is not strictly necessary. Of course, without jaggery (palm sugar), which is not easy to obtain in Western countries, the flavour will not be exactly right, but black or brown sugar can be substituted.

Serves: 6
750 g (1½ lb) round, blade or other lean steak
2 tablespoons tamarind pulp
1 cup hot water
2 teaspoons chilli powder, or to taste
½ teaspoon ground black pepper
½ teaspoon salt or to taste
¼ cup chopped jaggery or 2 tablespoons black or brown sugar
⅓ cup oil

Cut meat into 2 cm (¾ inch) cubes. Soak the tamarind pulp in hot water for 10 minutes, then squeeze to release all the pulp from the seeds. Strain. If more pulp is left on the seeds, add a little more water and dissolve this too. Strain again, preferably through a fine nylon sieve. Add chilli powder, pepper, salt and sugar and stir to dissolve sugar.

In a small frying pan heat the oil until very hot and fry a small portion of the meat at a time (divide meat into 5 or 6 portions) until the cubes are lightly browned. This generally takes only 1 minute if the oil is hot enough and not too much is put in at one time. Lift out with slotted spoon and put into a saucepan. Wait until oil stops spitting, then add and fry next batch. Repeat until all the meat has been fried, putting each batch into a saucepan.

Pour the tamarind mixture over the beef, bring to the boil, then allow to simmer, covered, until meat is tender and the gravy very much reduced. Thread on skewers and serve with white rice.

HARAK MAS CURRY
BEEF CURRY *(picture page 119)*

Serves: 8-10
1.5 kg (3 lb) stewing beef steak
3 tablespoons ghee or oil
2 large onions, finely chopped
1 tablespoon finely chopped fresh ginger
3-4 cloves garlic, finely chopped
4 tablespoons Ceylon curry powder (page 125)
1 teaspoon ground turmeric
2 teaspoons black mustard seeds
2 teaspoons salt
1 tablespoon vinegar
2 fresh red chillies, seeded and chopped
3 ripe tomatoes, peeled and chopped

Cut steak into 5 cm (2 inch) squares. Heat ghee in saucepan and gently fry onions, ginger and garlic until just beginning to turn golden. Add curry powder, turmeric, mustard seeds and fry over low heat for 2-3 minutes. Add salt and vinegar and stir well. Add steak and fry, stirring to coat meat well. Add chillies and tomatoes, cover pan and simmer on very low heat for about 2 hours. Serve with rice and other accompaniments. If gravy is too thin when meat is tender, cook over high heat, uncovered, until reduced.

SATAY CURRY
SKEWERED BEEF CURRY

The ground coriander, cummin and fennel
should be dry roasted first (as described on
page 135) to bring out the flavour.

Serves: 6
750 g (1½ lb) rump steak
½ teaspoon ground turmeric
½ teaspoon ground black pepper
½ teaspoon salt
thin slices fresh ginger root
thin slices of garlic
3 tablespoons ghee or oil
¼ teaspoon fenugreek seeds
8 curry leaves
2 medium onions, finely chopped
3 cloves garlic, finely chopped
1 teaspoon finely grated fresh ginger
1 tablespoon ground coriander
2 teaspoons ground cummin
½ teaspoon chilli powder
½ teaspoon ground fennel
½ teaspoon ground aromatic ginger
  (inguru piyali)
¼ teaspoon ground cardamom
pinch ground cloves
1 teaspoon salt
2½ cups coconut milk

Cut steak into bite-size pieces and leave some of the fat on the meat. Sprinkle with turmeric, pepper and salt and mix well with the hands, then thread pieces of meat on small bamboo skewers alternately with slices of ginger and garlic, about 3 or 4 pieces of meat to each skewer (cut skewers with secateurs to about 10 cm or 4 inches). Heat ghee in heavy pan and fry meat in two or three batches on high heat to brown and seal. Remove to a plate. To ghee in pan add fenugreek seeds and curry leaves and fry for 1 minute, then add onions, garlic and ginger and fry on low heat until onions are soft and golden, stirring frequently.

This takes quite a long time but don't hurry the process because this thorough frying is what makes a good curry. When ghee starts to separate again from the frying mass add the ground coriander, cummin, chilli and fennel and fry for a minute or two longer, stirring. Then add remaining ingredients mixed with the coconut milk and simmer, uncovered, until thick and smooth. If necessary add more water or coconut milk.

Return skewered beef to gravy, spoon the gravy over and simmer a further 20 minutes or until meat is tender. Serve with white rice or ghee rice and other accompaniments.

KURUMA IRAICHCHI
BEEF PEPPER CURRY

Serves: 8
1 kg (2 lb) lean stewing steak
2 teaspoons salt
2-4 teaspoons ground black pepper
1 tablespoon ground coriander
2 teaspoons ground cummin
1 teaspoon ground fennel
½ teaspoon ground turmeric
2 medium onions, finely chopped
3 cloves garlic, finely chopped
1½ teaspoons finely grated fresh ginger
2 fresh red chillies, seeded and sliced
8 curry leaves
2 strips daun pandan or rampé leaf
1 stem lemon grass or 2 strips lemon rind
2 tablespoons vinegar
2 cups thin coconut milk
1 tablespoon ghee or oil
1 cup thick coconut milk

Cut the meat into 5 cm (2 inch) squares and beat lightly with a meat mallet. Season with salt and pepper and mix well. Roast separately in a dry pan the coriander, cummin and fennel. Add coriander to meat and set aside the cummin and fennel. Put meat into a saucepan with spices and all other ingredients except roasted cummin and fennel, ghee and the thick coconut milk. Bring slowly to the boil, reduce heat and simmer covered, until meat is tender. If gravy thickens too quickly add a little water. Pour gravy into another pan, and to the meat left in the pan add the ghee or oil and let the meat fry in it for a few minutes, stirring. Add the cummin and fennel to the thick coconut milk and mix with the cooked gravy, then return everything to pan with the meat and continue to simmer uncovered over a very low heat until the gravy is thick and flavours well blended. Serve with rice and other accompaniments.

LAMPRIES CURRY

This curry, traditionally included in lampries (page 121) is made with four different meats and is delicious.
Serves: 16-18

500 g (1 lb) chuck steak
500 g (1 lb) mutton
5 teaspoons salt
8 cardamom pods
20 black peppercorns
500 g (1 lb) chicken breasts or thighs
500 g (1 lb) pork
1 tablespoon ghee
2 tablespoons oil
4 medium onions, finely chopped
8 cloves garlic, finely chopped
1 tablespoon finely chopped fresh ginger
2 teaspoons ground curry leaves
¼ teaspoon fenugreek seeds, optional
4 tablespoons Ceylon curry powder (page 125)
1 teaspoon ground turmeric
2 teaspoons chilli powder
1 cinnamon stick
1 teaspoon ground cardamom
6-8 pieces daun pandan or rampé leaf, optional
2 stalks lemon grass, or 4 strips lemon rind
2 tablespoons lemon juice
2½ cups thin coconut milk
2½ cups thick coconut milk
extra salt to taste

Put steak and mutton in large saucepan. Cover with cold water, add 2 teaspoons of the salt, and all cardamom pods and peppercorns. Cover pan and simmer for 30 minutes. Add chicken and simmer a further 15 minutes. Allow to cool slightly, strain, and reserve stock for boiling rice. Cut pork and parboiled meats into very small dice.

Heat ghee and oil in a large saucepan and gently fry onion, garlic, ginger and curry leaves until onion is soft and starts to turn golden. Add fenugreek seeds if used and fry 1 minute longer. Add curry powder, turmeric, chilli powder, cinnamon stick, cardamom, pandan or rampé leaf and lemon grass or rind. Add remaining 3 teaspoons salt, lemon juice, diced pork and half the coconut milk. Stir well. Cover and cook over a low heat for 30 minutes, stirring occasionally. Add parboiled meats and remaining coconut milk, and simmer uncovered for approximately 1½ hours, or until meat is tender and gravy very thick. Add extra salt to taste if necessary. Remove cinnamon stick, pandan or rampé leaf and lemon grass before serving.

OOROOMAS BADUN
FRIED PORK CURRY *(picture opposite)*

Serves: 6-8

1 kg (2 lb) pork
3 tablespoons oil
10 curry leaves
¼ teaspoon fenugreek seeds, optional
2 medium onions, finely chopped
4 cloves garlic, finely chopped
1½ teaspoons finely grated fresh ginger
3 tablespoons Ceylon curry powder (page 125)
1-2 teaspoons chilli powder
2 teaspoons salt
1 tablespoon vinegar
1 tablespoon tamarind pulp
1½ cups hot water
5 cm (2 inch) cinnamon stick
4 cardamom pods
1 cup thick coconut milk

Cut pork into large cubes. Heat oil in a large saucepan and fry curry leaves and fenugreek, if used, until they start to brown. Add onion and garlic and fry over a low heat until onion is soft and golden. Add ginger, curry powder, chilli powder, salt, vinegar and pork. Fry on high heat, stirring thoroughly until meat is well coated with the spice mixture. Squeeze tamarind pulp into hot water, strain and discard seeds. Add tamarind liquid, cinnamon and cardamom, cover and cook on low heat until pork is tender, about 1 hour. Add coconut milk and cook 10 minutes or more, uncovered.

Pour gravy into another saucepan, return pork to heat and allow to fry in its own fat. (If pork is not fat enough, add 1 tablespoon of ghee or oil to pan.) When pork is nicely brown, return gravy to pan and cook, uncovered, until gravy is thick. Serve hot with boiled rice.

OOROOMAS RATHU CURRY
PORK RED CURRY

Serves: 8

1 kg (2 lb) pork belly
8-10 large dried chillies
1½ cups hot water
1 tablespoon tamarind pulp
½ teaspoon ground turmeric
1 medium onion, roughly chopped
5 cloves garlic
1½ teaspoons chopped fresh ginger
5 cm (2 inch) cinnamon stick
2 teaspoons salt
1 stem lemon grass or 2 strips lemon rind
10 curry leaves
¼ teaspoon fenugreek seeds
1 strip daun pandan or rampé leaf,
    optional
½ cup thick coconut milk
1 tablespoon oil or melted ghee
1 small onion, finely sliced
2 tablespoons lemon juice

Cut the pork into 5 cm (2 inch) pieces and put into a saucepan. Remove stalks and seeds from dry chillies and soak them in half the hot water for 10 minutes. Soak and dissolve tamarind pulp in remaining hot water. Put chillies and soaking water into container of electric blender with the turmeric, roughly chopped onion, garlic and ginger and blend until smooth. Pour over pork in pan, add cinnamon and strained tamarind water. Add salt, half each of the lemon grass, curry leaves, fenugreek seeds and pandan or rampé leaf. Bring to the boil, then turn heat low, cover and simmer until pork is tender. Add coconut milk and simmer, uncovered, for 10 minutes longer. In another pan heat the oil or ghee and fry the sliced onion and the remaining lemon grass, curry leaves, fenugreek seeds and pandan or rampé. When onion is golden brown, turn in the cooked pork mixture and add the lemon juice, stir and simmer on very low heat for about 5 minutes. Serve with rice and accompaniments.

PEEGODU CURRY
DICED LIVER CURRY

Serves: 4

500g (1 lb) calves' liver, sliced
10 black peppercorns
1 teaspoon salt
1 tablespoon ghee or oil
1 medium onion, finely chopped
3 cloves garlic, finely chopped
1 teaspoon finely chopped fresh ginger
1 stalk lemon grass or 2 strips lemon rind
¼ teaspoon ground cloves
½ teaspoon ground black pepper
½ teaspoon ground cinnamon
8 curry leaves
3 tablespoons vinegar
2 cups coconut milk
2 tablespoons chopped fresh dill or
    ½ teaspoon dried dill weed

Wash liver, put into small saucepan with water to cover, add peppercorns and salt and cook until liver is firm, about 15 minutes. Cool. Cut liver into very small dice. Heat ghee or oil and fry onion, garlic and ginger until soft. Add all ingredients, including liver, and cook uncovered over a low heat until gravy is thick.

BABATH CURRY
TRIPE CURRY

Serves: 6
1 kg (2 lb) tripe
8 large dried chillies
½ cup hot water
2 teaspoons ground cummin
½ teaspoon ground turmeric
½ teaspoon fenugreek seeds
½ teaspoon aromatic ginger
  (inguru piyali)
8 curry leaves
1 stem lemon grass or 2 strips lemon rind
1 strip dried daun pandan or rampé
8 whole cardamom pods
4 whole cloves
1 small stick cinnamon
2 medium onions, finely chopped
4 cloves garlic, finely chopped
1½ teaspoons finely grated fresh ginger
2 cups thin coconut milk
1½ teaspoons salt
1 cup thick coconut milk
2 tablespoons lemon juice

Wash tripe well and cut into 5 cm (2 inch) squares. Soak chillies (stalks and seeds removed) in the hot water for 10 minutes, then blend in electric blender until pulverised. Alternatively, use 2 teaspoons chilli powder. Put tripe and all other ingredients except thick coconut milk and lemon juice into a large saucepan and bring to the boil. Cover and simmer for 1½ hours or until tripe is tender and gravy smooth and thickened. Add thick coconut milk and simmer, uncovered, stirring for 10 minutes. Remove from heat, add lemon juice and serve with rice or pittu (page 125).

KARAVADU VAMBOTU CURRY
SALT FISH AND EGGPLANT CURRY

Serves: 6
250 g (8 oz) dried salted fish
2 medium eggplants, about 500 g (1 lb)
1 teaspoon ground turmeric
1 teaspoon salt
12 large fresh sweet chillies
oil for frying
10 cloves garlic, peeled and left whole
1 large onion, finely sliced
3 cups coconut milk
3 tablespoons Ceylon curry powder
  (page 125)
small stick cinnamon
walnut size piece of tamarind pulp
¼ cup malt vinegar
½ teaspoon salt, or to taste
1-2 teaspoons sugar

Wash the dried fish, drain, then cut into 5 cm (2 inch) pieces. Slice the eggplants thickly, rub each slice with turmeric and salt and set aside for 30 minutes. Wash chillies, slit and remove seeds. Drain liquid given off from eggplant slices and dry each slice on kitchen paper.

Heat about quarter cup oil in a frying pan and fry separately the dried fish, chillies, garlic, onion and eggplant, removing each to a dish as fried. It may be necessary to replenish the oil as it is used up, for the eggplant absorbs quite a lot.

Put the coconut milk into a saucepan with the ground and whole spices, tamarind dissolved in vinegar, and salt. Stir until it comes to the boil, add fried ingredients and keep stirring frequently as the mixture cooks, uncovered. When it is thick, add sugar and stir to dissolve before serving

Note: Sweet chillies are slightly wider in shape and milder in flavour than hot chillies. They are the variety popular with Italian and Yugoslavian cooks.

ELOLU KIRI HODHI
VEGETABLE CURRY *(picture page 87)*

Here is the basic white curry. In it you can cook beans, pumpkin, okra, capsicum, potatoes, zucchini, asparagus or other vegetables of your choice.

Serves: 4-6
3 cups thin coconut milk
1 medium onion, finely sliced
2 fresh green chillies seeded and split
½ teaspoon ground turmeric
2 cloves garlic, finely sliced
½ teaspoon finely grated fresh ginger
5 cm (2 inch) cinnamon stick
4 pieces dried daun pandan or rampé leaf
1 stalk lemon grass or 2 strips lemon rind,
  optional
8 curry leaves
750 g (1½ lb) vegetables, sliced
salt to taste
1 cup thick coconut milk

Put all ingredients, except sliced vegetables, salt and thick coconut milk, in a large saucepan and simmer gently, uncovered, for approximately 10 minutes. Add sliced vegetables and salt and cook gently until vegetables are just tender. Add thick coconut milk and simmer about 5 minutes longer. Serve with boiled rice, other curries and accompaniments.

VATAKOLU CURRY
RIDGED GOURD CURRY

These ridged gourds have a very sweet and delicate flavour and are sometimes sold by market gardeners and in Chinese general stores. They are generally around 45 cm (18 in) long and should not be confused with the short-ridged bitter gourd.

Serves: 6
500 g (1 lb) ridged gourd
2 tablespoons oil
8 curry leaves
1 medium onion, finely chopped
2 fresh green chillies, sliced
1 teaspoon ground coriander
½ teaspoon ground cummin
¼ teaspoon ground turmeric
¼ teaspoon ground chilli powder,
  optional
1½ cups coconut milk
1 teaspoon salt

Peel the gourd. A potato peeler is useful for removing the sharp ridges. Cut into slices crossways.

Heat oil in a saucepan and fry the curry leaves, onion and chillies until the onions are golden brown. Add the ground spices and stir for a few seconds, then add the gourd, stir and fry for a few minutes. Add the coconut milk and salt and let it come to the boil, stirring occasionally. Simmer until tender, not covering the pan for this might cause the coconut milk to curdle.

VATAKKA CURRY
YELLOW PUMPKIN CURRY

Serves: 6
500 g (1 lb) pumpkin
1 small onion, finely chopped
2 cloves garlic, finely chopped
3 fresh green chillies, seeded and chopped
8-10 curry leaves
½ teaspoon fenugreek seeds
½ teaspoon ground turmeric
2 teaspoons pounded Maldive fish or dried
   prawns
1½ cups thin coconut milk
1 teaspoon salt
½ cup thick coconut milk
1 teaspoon black mustard seeds

Peel pumpkin and cut into large chunks. Put into a pan with all the ingredients except the thick coconut milk and mustard seeds. Bring slowly to simmering point and cook gently, uncovered, until pumpkin is almost tender. Meanwhile, grind the mustard seeds in mortar and pestle and mix with the thick coconut milk. Add to the simmering pot and cook for 5 minutes longer on very gentle heat.

BANDAKKA CURRY
OKRA BEAN CURRY

Serves: 4
250 g (8 oz) tender okra beans
½ teaspoon ground turmeric
oil for frying
1 small onion, finely chopped
2 fresh green chillies, seeded and sliced
6 curry leaves
1 teaspoon roasted ground coriander
½ teaspoon roasted ground cummin
1 teaspoon pounded Maldive fish or dried
   prawns
small piece cinnamon stick
½ teaspoon salt
¼ teaspoon chilli powder, optional
1½ cups coconut milk

Wash okra, cut off tops, then slice diagonally into bite-size lengths. Rub with ground turmeric. Heat oil in a small frying pan and deep fry the beans until lightly browned. Drain.

Put all the other ingredients into a saucepan and simmer. uncovered, until onions are cooked, about 10 minutes. Add the fried okra, simmer until tender and remove from heat. Serve with rice.

SAPATTU MAL CURRY
HIBISCUS CURRY

The single red hibiscus is used in sambols, curries and as a refreshing drink, and is said to have the effect of purifying the blood.

Serves: 6
12 single red hibiscus flowers
   (Hibiscus rosa sinensis)
1 cup flour
pinch salt
1 egg, beaten
water
oil for frying

Curry Gravy:
1 small onion, finely chopped
2 fresh green chillies, seeded and sliced
¼ teaspoon ground turmeric
2 teaspoons pounded Maldive fish or dried
   prawns
small stick cinnamon
2 cups thin coconut milk
salt to taste
½ cup thick coconut milk
2 teaspoons vinegar or lemon juice

Wash the flowers, shake off all the water or blot with paper towels. Pick off the calyx and the stamen. Sift flour and salt together and make a batter with the flour, beaten egg and water. Heat oil in a small deep pan and when hot dip each flower in the batter and fry in oil. Fry until golden , drain on absorbent paper.

Prepare the curry gravy. Heat a tablespoon of oil in a saucepan and gently fry the onion and chillies until golden brown. Add turmeric and stir for a minute longer, then add Maldive fish, cinnamon and thin coconut milk. Add salt to taste. Bring to the boil and add the hibiscus and simmer on low heat for 5 minutes. Add thick coconut milk and simmer, stirring, for 5 minutes longer, then remove from heat and stir in vinegar or lemon juice.

ALU KEHEL CURRY
GREEN BANANA CURRY

The green bananas used for this curry must be really unripe, otherwise the texture will not be suitable for cooking in this way.

Serves: 6
4 or 5 unripe bananas
1 teaspoon salt
1 teaspoon ground turmeric
¼ cup oil
2 cups coconut milk
1 small onion, finely sliced
2 fresh green chillies, sliced
2 teaspoons pounded Maldive fish or dried
   prawns
¼ teaspoon fenugreek seeds
8 curry leaves
small stick cinnamon

Rub hands with oil before starting to handle unripe bananas, for this prevents staining. Or wear rubber gloves. Peel the bananas, cut them in halves crossways and then into slices or quarters lengthways. Rub them with salt and turmeric.

Heat oil in small frying pan and fry the banana slices a few at a time, until they are golden brown all over. Set aside. Put all the remaining ingredients into a saucepan and simmer, uncovered, until onion is soft. Add fried bananas and simmer until gravy is thick.

CADJU CURRY
CASHEW NUT CURRY *(picture page 119)*

A curry of fresh cashew nuts is one of the delights of Sinhalese cooking. Fresh cashew nuts are not obtainable except in the country in which they are grown, but raw cashews, from health food shops and Chinese grocery stores, make a very good substitute if soaked overnight in cold water.

Proceed as for vegetable curry (page 142), but substitute 250 g (8 oz) raw cashew nuts for sliced vegetables. Simmer for approximately 30 minutes, or until cashews are tender. Serve with boiled rice and other accompaniments.

PARIPOO
LENTILS, SRI LANKAN STYLE

Serves: 6
2 cups red lentils
2 cups thin coconut milk
1 dried red chilli, broken into pieces
2 teaspoons pounded Maldive fish
1 teaspoon ground turmeric
1 tablespoon ghee or oil
6 curry leaves
2 medium onions, finely sliced
5 cm (2 inch) strip daun pandan or rampé leaf
5 cm (2 inch) stick of cinnamon
small stalk lemon grass or strip of lemon rind
½ cup thick coconut milk
salt to taste

Wash lentils well until water is clean. Remove and discard lentils that float on the surface of the water or any that are discoloured. Put drained lentils in a saucepan with the thin coconut milk, chilli, Maldive fish and turmeric. Bring to the boil, then cover and cook slowly until lentils are soft.

In another saucepan heat the oil and fry the curry leaves, onions, rampé, cinnamon and lemon grass until onions are brown. Reserve half the onions for garnishing the dish and turn the lentil mixture into the saucepan. Add thick coconut milk and salt to taste, and simmer uncovered until lentils are very soft and the consistency of runny porridge. Serve with rice and curries.

LEEKS MIRISATA
LEEKS FRIED WITH CHILLI

Serves: 6
4 medium size leeks
¼ cup oil
½ teaspoon ground turmeric
1 teaspoon chilli powder, or to taste
2 tablespoons pounded Maldive fish or dried prawns
1 teaspoon salt

Wash leeks very well, taking care to remove all sand and grit. Discard any tough or withered leaves but use the green portions as well. With a sharp knife slice very thinly. When slicing the leaves make a tight bundle and hold firmly.

Heat oil in a large saucepan and add the leeks. Fry, stirring, for 5 minutes, then add the remaining ingredients and stir well. Cover and cook over low heat for 30 minutes, stirring occasionally. The leeks will reduce considerably in volume. Uncover and cook until liquid evaporates and leeks have an oily appearance. Serve as an accompaniment to a rice meal.

MALLUNG
SHREDDED GREEN LEAVES WITH COCONUT

A mallung is very much part of the Sri Lankan diet. It can best be described as a dry accompaniment, very tasty, to be eaten with rice. One or two different mallungs are served with every meal and play an important part in nutrition because this is how the people of Sri Lanka get their vitamins.

The leaves of many common plants are used; some of them grow in Western countries too — for instance, the yellow-flowered cassia. The flowers are dried to make an infusion for medicinal purposes, and the leaves are stripped from the stems and used for mallung. They have a pleasant sour flavour. Tender passionfruit leaves also make delicious mallung. One of the most popular is 'gotukolle', which looks like violet leaves but is a type of cress which grows near water; as a substitute, use the common curly parsley so readily available.

Serves: 6
2 cups finely shredded green leaves
1 medium onion, finely chopped
2 green chillies, seeded and chopped, optional
½ teaspoon ground turmeric
2 teaspoons pounded Maldive fish or dried prawn powder
2 tablespoons lemon juice
1 teaspoon salt
2-3 tablespoons freshly grated or desiccated coconut

Put leaves into a saucepan with all the ingredients except coconut. If there is not much water clinging to leaves after washing, add a sprinkling of water. Stir well, cover and cook over medium heat, about 6 minutes. Uncover, add coconut and toss over low heat until coconut absorbs all the liquid. Remove from heat. Serve hot or cold as an accompaniment to rice.

GOVA MALLUNG
SHREDDED CABBAGE

Serves: 6
250 g (8 oz) cabbage
1 medium onion, finely chopped
2 fresh green chillies, seeded and chopped
¼ teaspoon ground turmeric
¼ teaspoon ground black pepper
½ teaspoon ground black mustard
1 teaspoon salt
2 teaspoons pounded Maldive fish or dried prawn powder, optional
½ cup desiccated or freshly grated coconut

Shred cabbage very finely. Wash well, drain and put into a large saucepan with the water that clings to the cabbage. Add all other ingredients except the coconut. Cover and cook gently until cabbage is tender but not overcooked, stirring from time to time. Uncover and add coconut. Stir well, and when any liquid in the pan has been absorbed by the coconut, the mallung is ready.

RABU KOLLÉ MALLUNG
SHREDDED RADISH LEAF

Serves: 4
leaves from 1 bunch small red radishes
1 medium onion, finely chopped
½ teaspoon ground turmeric
2 teaspoons Maldive fish or dried
 prawn powder
1 tablespoon lemon juice
½ teaspoon salt
¼ teaspoon chilli powder
2 tablespoons desiccated coconut

Wash the leaves well, discarding any that are yellow or withered. Chop finely and put into a saucepan with the water that clings to the leaves and all ingredients except coconut. Cover and cook over medium heat. The leaves will give off moisture. When this moisture is almost evaporated add the coconut and stir over low heat for about 3 minutes, when the coconut will have absorbed all the liquid. A mallung must be fairly dry in consistency. Serve with rice and curries.

ABBA
COUNTRY MUSTARD

This must be made with the tiny black or brown mustard seeds. It is used in Sri Lanka for serving as an accompaniment to meats, for spreading on sandwiches, or for adding to certain stews or curries. Leftover turkey is made into a rich stew and a good spoonful of this mustard is added, with perhaps some chilli thrown in for good measure, and it is then very aptly called 'turkey devil'! It is amazingly similar to the French mustard sold in stone pots.

½ cup black mustard seed
vinegar
1 clove garlic, optional
1 tablespoon finely chopped fresh ginger
2 teaspoons sugar
salt to taste

Put mustard seed into a glass or earthenware bowl and pour over enough vinegar to cover. Use white or malt vinegar, or red wine vinegar. Herbed vinegar can be used for extra flavour. Let stand.

Next day, put the mustard and vinegar into container of electric blender together with garlic and ginger and blend on high speed until seeds are pulverised. Add sugar and salt to taste. Store in a clean, dry jar.

OGU RULOUNG
SCRAMBLED EGGS WITH FLAVOURINGS

This is part of the traditional range of stringhopper accompaniments. Try it with the mock stringhopper pilau (page 124).

Serves: 6
8 large eggs
1 teaspoon finely chopped fresh dill or
 ½ teaspoon dried dill weed
1 teaspoon salt
½ teaspoon ground black pepper
6 spring onions
2 tablespoons ghee or oil
1 teaspoon ground dried curry leaves

Beat eggs as for an omelette and add 2 tablespoons cold water. Stir in the dill weed, salt and pepper. Finely slice the spring onions and fry gently in the ghee until pale golden, then put in the ground curry leaves and fry for 1 minute longer. Stir in egg mixture and cook on low heat, stirring, until mixture begins to set. Do not cook until too set or dry; the eggs should be moist and creamy.

BOMBILI MIRISATA
BOMBAY DUCK CHILLI FRY

Serves: 4
6 Bombay ducks (see Glossary)
½ cup oil
2 medium onions, finely sliced
2 cloves garlic, finely chopped
3 dried chillies, seeded and broken
   into pieces
lemon juice and salt to taste

Cut Bombay ducks into 5 cm (2 inch) lengths. Heat oil in a small pan and deep fry the pieces, take them out and drain them. Pour off oil, leaving about half the original amount. In it fry the onions and garlic until onion is soft and golden. Add chillies and fry for 2 or 3 minutes longer, return the Bombay duck pieces and stir fry for a minute. Add lemon juice and salt to taste. Serve hot or at room temperature.

FRIKKADELS
DUTCH FORCEMEAT BALLS

Makes about 40
1 tablespoon butter
1 small onion, finely chopped
500 g (1 lb) minced steak
½ cup soft white breadcrumbs
1½ teaspoons salt
½ teaspoon ground black pepper
2 teaspoons chopped fresh dill or
   ½ teaspoon dried dill weed
¼ teaspoon ground cinnamon
¼ teaspoon ground cloves
1 clove garlic, crushed
½ teaspoon finely grated fresh ginger
2 teaspoons Worcestershire sauce or
   lemon juice
1 egg, beaten
dry breadcrumbs for coating
oil or ghee for deep frying

Heat butter in a small frying pan and gently fry onion until soft. Combine with minced steak, breadcrumbs, salt, pepper, chopped dill, cinnamon, cloves, garlic, ginger and Worcestershire sauce. Mix thoroughly and shape into small balls about 2.5 cm (1 inch) in diameter. Dip into beaten egg and coat with dry breadcrumbs. Deep fry in hot oil until golden brown. Drain on absorbent paper before serving.

THAMBUNG HODHI
SOUR SOUP

Serves: 4
2 tablespoons ground coriander
1 tablespoon ground cummin
1 dried chilli, optional
¼ teaspoon whole black peppercorns
8 curry leaves
5 cups hot water
1 tablespoon tamarind pulp
1 medium onion, finely sliced
4 cloves garlic

Put coriander, cummin, chilli, peppercorns and curry leaves into a saucepan and dry roast over medium heat, shaking the pan or stirring constantly, until the spices smell aromatic. Add the water, tamarind, onion and garlic and bring to the boil, then simmer for 20 minutes or until onions and garlic are soft. Serve for sipping between mouthfuls of rice.

CHICKEN MULLIGATAWNY

Serves: 6-8
1 steaming chicken
8-10 cups water
2 teaspoons salt
½ teaspoon whole black peppercorns
few celery leaves
2 medium onions
4 whole cloves
1 tablespoon ground coriander
1 teaspoon ground cummin
1 teaspoon ground fennel
½ teaspoon ground turmeric
2 cloves garlic, chopped
1 teaspoon finely grated fresh ginger
1 x 5 cm (2 inch) stick cinnamon
500 g (1 lb) ripe tomatoes, diced
2 teaspoons ghee or dripping
10 curry leaves
1 cup thick coconut milk
lemon juice to taste

Cut chicken into joints and put into a large saucepan with sufficient water to cover. Add salt, peppercorns, celery leaves and 1 onion peeled and stuck with the whole cloves. Bring to the boil on high heat, then turn heat low, cover and simmer for 30 minutes. Add coriander, cummin, fennel, turmeric, garlic, ginger, cinnamon and tomatoes and simmer for a further hour or until the chicken is tender.

Strain stock into a large bowl. When chicken is cool enough to handle, cut half the flesh into dice and return to the stock (remaining chicken can be used for sandwiches).

Slice the remaining onion. Wash out pan in which chicken cooked, dry it well and in it heat the ghee or dripping. Fry the curry leaves and sliced onion until the onion is well browned, then pour stock into pan and let it come to the boil. Reduce heat, stir in coconut milk and when soup returns to simmering point again remove from heat. Taste and add lemon juice to sharpen the flavour. If necessary add more salt. Serve hot, either as a first course or to be sipped throughout the meal. This soup is also suitable for pouring over rice or stringhoppers when they are served with dry accompaniments.

KIRI HODHI
COCONUT MILK GRAVY

Serve as an accompaniment to be spooned over rice or to be sipped between mouthfuls of rice and curry. If a less rich soup is required, substitute skimmed milk for part of the coconut milk.

Serves: 6
1 tablespoon fenugreek seeds
1 large onion, finely chopped
12 curry leaves
1 small stick cinnamon
2 fresh green chillies, slit and seeded
¼ teaspoon ground turmeric
½ teaspoon salt
2 teaspoons pounded Maldive fish or dried
  prawn powder, optional
2½ cups thin coconut milk
2 cups thick coconut milk
lemon juice to taste

Wash the fenugreek seeds and soak in cold water for at least 30 minutes. Put into a saucepan with all the ingredients except thick coconut milk and lemon juice. Simmer on very low heat until onions are reduced to a pulp and the milk has been thickened by the fenugreek seeds. Stir well, add thick coconut milk and heat without boiling, then stir in lemon juice and add more salt if required.

If a thicker soup is preferred, add a few slices of potato at the start.

THORA MALU MOJU
FISH PICKLE

Serves: 8-10

500g (1 lb) fish slices (Spanish mackerel)
salt and turmeric
oil for frying
1 tablespoon finely chopped garlic
1 tablespoon finely chopped ginger
2 teaspoons black mustard seeds
1 cup vinegar
½ cup oil
10 curry leaves
3 strips dried daun pandan or rampé,
   optional
2 tablespoons ground coriander
1 tablespoon ground cummin
1 teaspoon ground fennel, optional
½ teaspoon fenugreek seeds
2 teaspoons chilli powder
1 teaspoon turmeric
1 teaspoon salt
1 tablespoon sugar

Wash fish slices, dry and rub with salt and turmeric and shallow fry in hot oil until brown and crisp. Set aside on plate. In container of electric blender combine garlic, ginger, mustard seeds and some of the vinegar and grind to a purée. Heat oil and fry curry leaves and pandan or rampé. Add coriander, cummin, fennel, fenugreek seeds and fry, stirring until spices are dark brown but do not allow to burn. Add chilli powder and turmeric and fry for a few seconds longer. Add the ground mustard mixture and fry for a few more minutes. Wash out blender container with remaining vinegar, add to pan with salt and sugar, bring to the boil and add the fish. Turn heat low and simmer for 30 minutes. Cool and store in an earthenware vessel, or bottle airtight. To serve, heat 2 tablespoons ghee or oil and fry the required amount of the fish pickle to heat through.

THORA MALU SIYAMBALA ACHCHARU
SEER FISH PICKLE WITH TAMARIND

The popular seer fish of Sri Lanka and India is called Spanish mackerel in Australia. Any firm, dark-fleshed fish will be suitable.

Serves: 10-12

500 g (1 lb) fish steaks
1 teaspoon salt
½ teaspoon ground turmeric
¼ cup oil
½ cup tamarind pulp
¾ cup vinegar
3 tablespoons ground coriander
1½ tablespoons ground cummin
3 teaspoons ground fennel
1 tablespoon chilli powder
salt and sugar to taste

Wash the fish and dry well on paper towels. Cut steaks into serving pieces, rub over with salt and turmeric and fry in hot oil until deep brown and crisp all over. Pour off oil. Dissolve tamarind pulp in vinegar, squeezing between the fingers to release all the pulp from the seeds. Push through a fine nylon sieve, adding a little extra vinegar if necessary. Discard seeds and fibres left in sieve.

In a dry pan roast the coriander, cummin and fennel separately for a few minutes until they smell aromatic and the colour darkens slightly. Combine them with the tamarind pulp and chilli powder. Pour over the fish slices in the pan and simmer for a few minutes. Add salt to taste and, if liked, a little sugar. Store in clean dry bottles. Serve as an accompaniment with rice and curries.

VAMBOTU PAHI
EGGPLANT PICKLE

2 large eggplants
2 teaspoons salt
2 teaspoons ground turmeric
oil for frying
1 tablespoon black mustard seeds
½ cup vinegar
1 medium onion, finely chopped
4 cloves garlic, sliced
1 tablespoon finely chopped fresh ginger
1 tablespoon ground coriander
2 teaspoons ground cummin
1 teaspoon ground fennel
½ cup tamarind pulp
¾ cup hot water
3 fresh green chillies, seeded and sliced
8 cm (3 inch) cinnamon stick
1 teaspoon chilli powder, optional
2 teaspoons sugar
extra salt to taste

Slice eggplant thinly, rub with salt and turmeric, put in a bowl and leave at least 1 hour. Drain off liquid and dry eggplant on paper towels. Heat about 2.5 cm (1 inch) oil in frying pan and fry eggplant slices quite slowly until brown on both sides. Lift out with slotted spoon and put in a dry bowl. Reserve oil.

Put mustard seed and vinegar in blender container, cover and blend on high speed until mustard is ground. Add onion, garlic, and ginger, cover and blend again until a smooth paste. Set aside.

Put coriander, cummin and fennel in small dry pan and heat gently, shaking pan or stirring, until medium brown in colour. (If preferred, substitute 1½ tablespoons Ceylon curry powder for these ingredients.)

Squeeze tamarind pulp in hot water, strain and discard seeds, reserve liquid.

Heat half cup reserved oil and fry blended mixture for 5 minutes. Add coriander mixture or curry powder, chillies, cinnamon, chilli powder if used and tamarind liquid. Add fried eggplant and any oil that has collected in the bowl, stir well, cover and simmer for 15 minutes. Remove from heat, stir in sugar. Add extra salt if necessary. Cool thoroughly and store in clean dry jars. Keeps for weeks in the refrigerator.

ABBA ACHCHARU
MUSTARD PICKLE

½ cup black mustard seed
3 cups vinegar
2 teaspoons salt
1 teaspoon ground turmeric
1 cup peeled shallots or tiny pickling
   onions
12 fresh red or green chillies
1 cup sliced unripe pawpaw, optional
1 cup green beans, sliced
1 cup cauliflower sprigs
1 cup carrot strips
1 bitter melon, seeded and cut in strips
6 cloves garlic
1 tablespoon grated fresh ginger
3 teaspoons sugar

Soak mustard seed in vinegar to cover overnight. Next day bring remaining vinegar to the boil with salt and turmeric in a medium-size enamel saucepan. Put onions in, bring to the boil and boil for 1 minute. Lift out on slotted spoon and put into a nylon strainer to drain and cool. Do the same with all the other vegetables. Allow extra time for the beans, carrots and cauliflower which should be tender but still crisp to bite. When all vegetables are drained and cooled, put them into a clean, dry bottle or earthenware jar.

In electric blender blend the soaked mustard with all the other ingredients. Mix in vinegar remaining in pan and pour over the vegetables in the bottle, adding more vinegar if necessary to cover vegetables. Use a jar with a cork stopper if possible. If jar has metal lid, cover with two thicknesses of greaseproof paper first. This pickle will keep for months.

DEHI ACHCHARU
PICKLED LEMONS

thin-skinned lemons
coarse cooking salt
malt vinegar

Put whole lemons in pan with cold water, bring to the boil and boil for 10 minutes or until each lemon splits slightly. Remove from heat, drain off water and when cool enough to handle, stuff the slit in each lemon with salt, pressing it in well. Arrange lemons in a wide-mouthed earthenware jar or glass bottle, pour over vinegar to cover, seal tightly and leave for 6 months before using. The lemons will keep indefinitely and are an ingredient in beef smoore (page 135), lime and date chutney (below), and pickled lemon sambol (page 153).

DEHI LUNU
SALTED LIMES OR LEMONS

At my grandmother's house there were always large stoneware jars of salted limes, steeped so long that the fruit were a translucent brown and the juice around them turned to clear amber jelly. When limes or lemons are in season it is a good idea to put down a couple of bottles of these salt-preserved fruit. They will keep indefinitely, and can be made into chutneys, pickles or simple curry accompaniments.

25 to 30 thin-skinned lemons or limes
rock salt

Wash and dry the fruit well. Starting at the bottom cut each one into quarters almost to the stem end but do not separate the pieces. Open the slits slightly and stuff each with about a tablespoon of salt. Put into a clean dry jar as it is done. If possible use stone jars, or glass jars with plastic, not metal lids. Cover tightly and leave jars in the sun every day for three weeks, then store in cellar or cupboard for six months, or longer.

DEHI RATA INDI CHUTNEY
LIME AND DATE CHUTNEY

500 g (1 lb) whole dates
6-8 salted or pickled limes or lemons
20 large dried red chillies, or less for a mild
  chutney
1 tablespoon black mustard seed
2 cups vinegar
20 cloves garlic, peeled
2 tablespoons finely grated fresh ginger
3 cups white sugar
1 cup sultanas

Halve the dates and remove seeds. Cut the limes into eighths, then cut each piece across into fine strips.

Soak the dry chillies (stalks and seeds removed) and the mustard seeds in vinegar overnight. Next day grind in the blender together with garlic and ginger. Put the blended ingredients and sugar into a large pan and bring to the boil. Cook until thick as tomato sauce. Add the dates, lemons and sultanas and bring back to the boil, then turn heat low and simmer, stirring, for a further 15-20 minutes. Store in sterilised bottles.

DEHI ACHCHARU TEMPERADO
LIME OIL PICKLE

8 salted limes or lemons
6 fresh red chillies
6 fresh green chillies
2 tablespoons black mustard seed
1 tablespoon cummin seed
2 teaspoons fennel seed
2 teaspoons black cummin seed
2 teaspoons fenugreek seed
½ cup mustard oil or peanut oil
2 tablespoons sesame oil
small piece asafoetida the size of a
   peppercorn
6 cloves garlic, sliced
1 tablespoon finely grated fresh ginger
1 stem lemon grass or 2 strips lemon rind
1 stick cinnamon
½ cup vinegar
1 teaspoon chilli powder

Separate limes into quarters and cut each quarter into 3 or 4 pieces. Remove stems and seeds of chillies and cut into halves or quarters depending on size.

In a dry pan roast the various seeds separately over medium heat, stirring constantly to prevent burning. When they smell aromatic turn them out of the pan onto a plate to cool. Heat both kinds of oil in a large pan and fry the asafoetida, then lift it out and discard. Fry garlic and ginger over low heat until golden, then add the remaining ingredients, bring to the boil and let simmer for about 10 minutes, stirring constantly. Remove cinnamon stick and lemon grass. Cool and bottle.

DEHI LUNU SAMBOLA
SALTED LIME SAMBOL

1 salted or pickled lime or lemon
2 tablespoons finely sliced shallots or
   onions
2 fresh red or green chillies, seeded and
   sliced

Cut the lemon into small pieces and mix with sliced shallots and chillies. Put into a small bowl and serve with a rice and curry meal. A teaspoon of this is sufficient for a serving, as it is meant to be only a taste accent.

PRAWN BLACHAN

This is an essential accompaniment to lampries (page 121), the festive meal wrapped in banana leaves.

Serves: 18-20
1 cup dried prawn powder
½ cup desiccated coconut
2 teaspoons chilli powder or to taste
2 medium onions, chopped
5 cloves garlic, sliced
1 tablespoon finely chopped fresh ginger
⅔ cup lemon juice
1 teaspoon salt, or to taste

Put prawn powder in a dry frying pan and heat for a few minutes, stirring. Turn on to a large plate. Put desiccated coconut in the same pan and heat, stirring, until a rich brown colour. Turn on to a plate to cool. Put remaining ingredients into blender container, cover and blend until smooth. Add prawn powder and desiccated coconut, cover and blend again, adding a little water if necessary to bind ingredients. Scrape down sides of container occasionally with a spatula. Turn on to a plate and shape into a round, flat cake. Serve with rice and curries.

KOONEE SAMBOLA
SHRIMP SAMBOL

The dried shrimps (koonee) used in this delicious sambol are really minute — no thicker than a piece of twine. They are sold in Japanese shops, neatly packaged in cellophane.

1 small onion, finely chopped
3 fresh red chillies, finely chopped
1 teaspoon fenugreek seeds
1 tablespoon lemon juice
1½ teaspoons salt
½ teaspoon ground turmeric
3 tablespoons dried shrimps
½ cup water
1½ cups freshly grated or desiccated
   coconut

Put all ingredients except coconut into a saucepan and cook, covered, until onions are soft. Add coconut and toss, uncovered, until coconut absorbs all liquid. Taste for seasoning and add extra salt and lemon if necessary. Serve with rice and curries.

SEENI SAMBOLA
CHILLI SAMBOL

Chilli sambol is a popular accompaniment to rice and curry. Thanks to convenient canned 'prawns in spices' (sold in Chinese food stores) this simplified version can be prepared in a fraction of the time it takes to make the original recipe, but it tastes as good.

½ cup oil
4 medium onions, finely sliced
2 teaspoons chilli powder
1 x 170 g (6 oz) can 'prawns in spices'
2 tablespoons vinegar
salt to taste
2 teaspoons sugar

Heat oil in a large frying pan and fry onions very slowly, stirring occasionally until soft and transparent. It is important to fry onions slowly — all the liquid in the onion must evaporate if the sambol is to have good keeping qualities.

When the onion is golden brown, add chilli powder, 'prawns in spices' and vinegar. Stir thoroughly, cover and simmer for 10 minutes. Uncover pan and continue simmering, stirring occasionally, until liquid evaporates and oil starts to separate from other ingredients. Season to taste with salt. Remove from heat, stir in sugar and allow to cool before putting in a clean dry jar. Use in small quantities.

Note: If a hotter sambol is preferred, increase quantity of chilli powder.

MOONG ATA SAMBOLA
BEAN SPROUT SAMBOL

125 g (4 oz) fresh bean sprouts
3 fresh green chillies, seeded and sliced
1 small onion, finely sliced
3 tablespoons grated fresh coconut or
   desiccated coconut
1 teaspoon salt
1 tablespoon lemon juice, or to taste

Wash bean sprouts thoroughly, removing as many of the green skins as possible. Drain well. Mix all ingredients well together and serve as an accompaniment to rice and curries.

LUNU MIRIS SAMBOLA
GROUND ONION AND CHILLI SAMBOL

This simple sambol is as basic to the food of Sri Lanka as salt and pepper are to Western food. Very hot, very acid and distinctly salty, it is often the only accompaniment to serve with rice, boiled yams, manioc or sweet potato, or any of the starches that are the staple of the native diet.

10 dried chillies
1 tablespoon pounded Maldive fish or
   dried prawns
1 small onion, chopped
lemon juice and salt to taste

Remove stalks from chillies and, if a less hot result is preferred, shake out the seeds. Pound all together in a mortar and pestle. In Sri Lanka this would be either pounded or ground on the grinding stone. It can be done in a blender, but a wet result is not desirable. It should be a paste. Serve with rice or pittu (page 125).

BADHAPU LUNU SAMBOLA
FRIED ONION SAMBOL

½ cup oil
2 large onions, finely sliced
6 dried chillies, broken into pieces
2 tablespoons Maldive fish or
   prawn powder
1 teaspoon salt, or to taste
2 tablespoons lemon juice

Heat oil in a frying pan and fry onion slowly until soft and transparent. Add chillies and Maldive fish, cover and cook for 10-15 minutes, or until oil separates from other ingredients. Stir occasionally while cooking. Add salt and lemon juice and cook a few minutes longer. Serve with boiled rice and curries.

BADHAPU VAMBOTU SAMBOLA
FRIED EGGPLANT SAMBOL *(picture page 119)*

2 eggplants
2 teaspoons salt
2 teaspoons ground turmeric
oil for frying
3 fresh red or green chillies
2 small onions
lemon juice
3 tablespoons thick coconut milk

Prepare eggplant slices as for vambotu pahi (page 151). Fry in hot oil and drain on absorbent paper. Mix with seeded and chopped chillies, finely sliced onion, lemon juice to taste and 3 tablespoons thick coconut milk.

PIPINJA SAMBOLA
CUCUMBER SAMBOL *(picture page 119)*

1 large or 2 small green cucumbers
2 teaspoons salt
½ cup thick coconut milk
1 fresh red chilli, seeded and sliced
1 fresh green chilli, seeded and sliced
1 small onion, cut in paper-thin slices
2 tablespoons lemon juice

Peel cucumber and slice very thinly. Put in a bowl, sprinkle with salt and let stand for at least 30 minutes. Press out all liquid and if too salty, rinse with cold water. Drain well. Mix with remaining ingredients and serve as an accompaniment to a curry meal.

KARAVILA SAMBOLA
BITTER GOURD SAMBOL

Serves: 4-6
3 bitter gourds
½ teaspoon ground turmeric
½ teaspoon salt
oil for shallow frying
1 medium onion, sliced very thinly
2 fresh green chillies, seeded and sliced
lemon juice to taste

Wash bitter gourds and cut crossways into fairly thin slices. Rub with turmeric and salt and fry in oil until golden brown on both sides. Drain on paper, then mix with the onion and chillies, and season with lemon juice and more salt if necessary.

POL SAMBOLA
COCONUT SAMBOL *(picture page 119)*

1 cup desiccated coconut
1 teaspoon salt
1 teaspoon chilli powder, or to taste
2 teaspoons paprika
2 teaspoons Maldive fish or
   prawn powder, optional
2 tablespoons lemon juice, or to taste
1 medium onion, finely chopped
2-3 tablespoons hot milk

Combine coconut, salt, chilli powder, paprika and Maldive fish if used, in a bowl. Sprinkle with lemon juice, onion and milk. Mix well with the hands, rubbing ingredients together so that the coconut is evenly moistened. Pile into small bowl.

Note: If liked, add 1-2 fresh red or green chillies, seeded and finely chopped.

KALUPOL SAMBOLA
ROASTED COCONUT SAMBOL

In Sri Lanka, this is made with fresh coconut, roasted in the ashes of the fire until dark brown, then ground on a large stone, but this adaption is a lot easier to make.

1 cup desiccated coconut
2 medium onions, finely chopped
1 teaspoon salt
2 teaspoons Maldive fish or prawn
   powder
approximately ¼ cup lemon juice

Heat desiccated coconut in a heavy-based frying pan and stir constantly until it is evenly browned. It should be a fairly deep brown, but be careful not to burn it. Spread coconut on a large plate to cool.

Combine all ingredients in an electric blender, cover and blend on high speed to a smooth paste. (It may be necessary to add a little more chopped onion or lemon juice if there is not sufficient liquid.)

Shape into a round flat cake and mark the top in a criss-cross pattern with a fork or the back of a knife. Serve with rice and curry.

AVOCADO FOOL

Serves: 4-6
3 large, fully ripe avocados
caster sugar to taste
1 cup cream
dash of rum, optional

Cut avocados in halves lengthways, remove seeds and reserve. Scoop pulp from shells and mash smoothly with a fork. Add sugar to taste and stir in the cream. Put into serving bowl, return seeds to the pulp, cover closely with plastic wrap and chill before serving.

The presence of the seeds in the purée is said to keep the avocado from discolouring, but make sure that the surface is protected from air by putting the plastic on the surface of the mixture. If liked, extra whipped and sweetened cream can be piped over the top of the dessert and a few paper-thin slices of avocado (sliced at the last moment and sprinkled with lemon juice) used for decoration.

Note: While some favour rum for flavouring, I prefer to let the delicate avocado flavour stand alone.

ALLA ALUWA
POTATO HALVA

After a rich curry meal, serve this sweetmeat with black coffee.

Makes about 18 pieces
1½ cups sugar
1½ cups milk
1 x 410 g (14½ oz) can sweetened
   condensed milk
125 g (4 oz) ghee or butter
1 cup cooked mashed potato
1 cup finely chopped cashew nuts,
   optional
2 tablespoons rose water
1 teaspoon ground cardamom, optional

Put sugar, milk, condensed milk and ghee into a large heavy saucepan (a non-stick pan is excellent for this). Cook over medium heat, stirring constantly, until mixture reaches soft-ball stage or 116°C (240°F) on a candy thermometer. (To test for soft-ball stage, drop a little into a cup of ice-cold water. If it firms enough to be moulded into a soft ball, it has reached the required temperature.)

Remove from heat, add smoothly mashed potato and beat with a rotary beater until all lumps are beaten out. If using a pan with non-stick lining, pour mixture into a bowl before doing this or the metal beaters will scratch the non-stick surface. Return to heat and cook to soft ball stage or 116°C (240°F) once more. Remove from heat, stir in nuts, rose water and cardamom and mix well.

Pour into a well-buttered shallow dish or baking tin. Press lightly with a piece of buttered banana leaf or aluminium foil to smooth and flatten the surface. Allow to cool and set, then cut into diamond shapes.

PATTIES

At every birthday party (birthdays are celebrated with much enthusiasm in Sri Lanka) these popular savoury pastries are served — love cake (page 164) and patties are 'musts' for parties. The traditional pastry used for patties is a rather unusual one that uses coconut milk. I am giving the recipe in case you wish to try it; but also give a very good shortcrust pastry which may be easier to handle. However, the original pastry does taste delicious.

Makes about 75 patties
Patty Pastry:
2 cups plain flour
½ teaspoon salt
3 tablespoons dripping or butter
¼ cup thick coconut milk
2 yolks of eggs, beaten
oil for frying

Filling:
500 g (1 lb) chicken
500 g (1 lb) beef or lamb
250 g (8 oz) pork
125 g (4 oz) bacon or ham
1 tablespoon ghee
1 medium onion, finely chopped
8 curry leaves
2 teaspoons Ceylon curry powder (page 125)
1 teaspoon ground turmeric
¼ teaspoon each ground cloves and cinnamon
½ teaspoon ground black pepper
2 teaspoons salt
1 stalk lemon grass or 2 strips lemon rind
½ cup thick coconut milk
2 teaspoons finely chopped fresh dill
4-6 hard-boiled eggs

Shortcrust pastry:
2 cups plain flour
pinch baking powder
½ teaspoon salt
1 teaspoon caster sugar
60 g (2 oz) dripping
60 g (2 oz) butter or margarine
2 tablespoons lemon juice
4-5 tablespoons iced water

Pastry: Sift flour and salt into a bowl and rub in the shortening with your fingertips. Add the coconut milk and egg yolks mixed together and knead lightly to a smooth dough. If necessary add a little extra milk or flour — flour varies in absorbency and it is difficult to be absolutely precise. Wrap dough in greaseproof paper and chill for 30 minutes. Take one quarter of the dough at a time and roll out very thinly on lightly floured board. Cut into circles using a large scone cutter 8 cm (3¼ inches) in diameter.

Put a teaspoonful of the filling and a piece of hard-boiled egg on the pastry rounds. Wet the edges of the pastry with egg white, fold over to make half circle and press edges firmly together to seal. In Sri Lanka the edge is always ornamented by pressing with a key or the tines of a fork.

When all the patties are made, fry a few at a time in deep hot oil. Coconut oil is used in Sri Lanka but any good vegetable oil such as peanut oil can be substituted. Drain on absorbent paper and serve warm.

Filling: Put chicken, beef and pork into a saucepan with just enough water to cover, bring to the boil, cover and simmer for 20 minutes. Cool. Remove the parboiled chicken meat from the bones and cut into small dice. Do the same with the beef and pork. Remove rind from bacon and cut into small squares. Heat ghee in a saucepan and fry the onion and curry leaves until onion is soft and starts to turn brown. Add the curry powder, turmeric, cloves, cinnamon, pepper and salt and stir well. Add about 1½ cups of the stock left from cooking the meats. Add lemon grass and the diced meat. Mix well, cover and simmer gently until meats are tender and liquid almost evaporated. Add the coconut milk and dill, stir and cook uncovered until coconut milk is absorbed.

Remove from heat. When cool, pick out the lemon grass or lemon rind and the curry leaves. Cut the hard-boiled eggs in pieces and gently mix in. Make sure each patty has a piece of hard-boiled egg in it. If preferred, the eggs can be kept separate and a piece or two put on top of the curried filling before sealing the pastry.

Shortcrust pastry: Sift flour, baking powder, salt and sugar into a bowl and rub in the shortening. Mix lemon juice and iced water and add to flour, mixing to a smooth dough. Add a little more water if needed. Wrap in greaseproof paper and chill for 30 minutes before rolling out.

BASIC DOUGH

Especially suitable for adding ingredients like butter, sugar and eggs. The extra gluten helps it to rise and hold its shape.

½ cup milk
3 teaspoons sugar
2 teaspoons salt
90 g (3 oz) butter
1½ cups warm water
30 g (1 oz) compressed yeast or
 1 packet active dry yeast
5½-6 cups unsifted plain flour
1 tablespoon gluten flour

Scald milk, stir in sugar, salt and butter and allow to cool to lukewarm. Measure warm water into a large warm bowl. Sprinkle yeast over water, stir until dissolved. Add lukewarm milk mixture and 3 cups of the flour sifted with the gluten. Beat with a wooden spoon until smooth. Add enough additional flour to make a soft dough. Turn on to a lightly floured board, knead until smooth and elastic, about 10 minutes. Shape into a smooth ball. Put in a greased bowl, turn dough to grease top. Cover with a cloth and allow to prove in a warm place, free from draughts, until doubled in bulk, about 1 hour. Now make into breudher (page 163) or mas paan (page 161).

BOLO DE COCO
COCONUT CAKE

In Sri Lanka, the moist, rich flesh of coconuts fresh from the tree is grated, then ground finely on a stone slab. The resulting texture is much like finely ground almonds but much wetter, due to the presence of the rich coconut milk. If you live in a country where fresh coconuts are available, use 2 medium-size nuts. If, however, you can obtain only the desiccated variety, treat it in the way described below and you will still have a delicious coconut cake.

Cooking time: 1¼-1½ hours
Oven temperature: 160°C (325°F)
*Makes: 1 x 25 cm (10 inch) square cake or
 two loaves*
3 cups desiccated coconut
3 cups water
4 eggs, separated
2 cups white sugar
2 cups rice flour
1 cup self-raising flour
2 teaspoons baking powder
½ teaspoon ground cardamom
¼ teaspoon ground cloves
¼ teaspoon ground cinnamon
1 tablespoon rose water or
 ½ teaspoon rose essence
125 g (4 oz) raw cashew nuts or
 blanched almonds, finely chopped
extra ¼ cup sugar

Preheat oven to moderately slow. Line a deep 25 cm (10 inch) square cake tin with buttered greaseproof paper, or use two loaf pans.

Put 1½ cups each of desiccated coconut and water into container of electric blender and blend on high speed until coconut is finely ground, about 1 minute. Empty blender container, repeat with remaining coconut and water.

In large bowl of electric mixer, beat yolks of eggs and 2 tablespoons of the coconut mixture with the sugar until light and creamy. Add remaining coconut and beat well. Sift the flour with baking powder and ground spices and stir into the mixture with the rose water or essence and nuts. Beat eggwhites until stiff peaks form, add extra sugar and beat again until thick and glossy. Fold into coconut mixture. Pour into prepared tin or tins and bake in a moderately slow oven for 1¼ to 1½ hours or until risen and golden brown on top. A fine skewer inserted in centre of cake should come out clean. Half cool cake in tin, then lift out and let cake cool completely on a wire rack. Cut into squares to serve.

FOGUETE
DEEP-FRIED PASTRY WITH SWEET FILLING

The name is Portuguese, and this is one of the recipes left by the one time conquerors of Sri Lanka. The translation is 'rocket' because they look like miniature fireworks. Little hollow tubes of pastry are fried, cooled and filled with a sweet mixture. Very often they are dipped in a crystallising syrup to coat the pastry. This keeps them crisp for a few days, but also makes the overall effect very sweet. I prefer to fill them on the day they are to be served and omit the crystallising process.

Pastry:
2 cups plain flour
pinch salt
60 g (2 oz) butter
2 whole eggs
2 egg yolks
1 tablespoon icing sugar
1 teaspoon vanilla essence
cold water if necessary
oil for frying
short lengths of 2 cm (¾ inch) dowelling

Fillings:
pineapple or melon jam
1 cup chopped raw cashews and
   1 cup chopped raisins, mixed together

Have ready about twelve x 7.5 cm (3 inch) lengths of 2 cm (¾ inch) diameter round wooden dowelling, rough edges smoothed with sand paper. Grease them with butter.

Pastry: Sift flour and salt into a large bowl, rub in butter with fingertips until mixture resembles fine crumbs. Beat eggs and egg yolks together, add icing sugar and vanilla and approximately 2 tablespoons of cold water. If eggs are very large the water may not be necessary. Make a well in centre of flour, pour in egg mixture and mix well to a dough. Knead lightly for 10 minutes or until dough is smooth and shiny. Wrap in foil or plastic wrap and chill for 1 hour.

Roll out small portions of dough on a lightly floured board, as thinly as possible. Dough should be fine and even, and almost parchment-thin. Cut into strips a little narrower than the lengths of dowelling, about 6.25 cm (2½ inches), and long enough to fit rather loosely round the rods. Wet a thin strip on one end with egg white and pinch both ends together, giving a fluted effect. Pinch and flute on opposite side of tube of dough, then in between the two fluted lines. This should make the dough fit more closely around the rod, but it should not be tight.

Heat oil or ghee (or mixture of both) in a frying pan, making it deep enough to submerge the tubes. When oil is hot drop in a few at a time, fry on medium heat until pale golden, then lift out of oil and cool for a minute or until cool enough to handle. Gently slip the rod from the centre and return tubes to oil to finish frying. When golden brown, lift out on slotted spoon and drain on absorbent paper. Repeat until all the dough is used up. Cool completely on paper lined wire rack, then store in airtight tin until required for filling.

Filling: With tiny teaspoon or coffee spoon fill tubes with filling of your choice. Dust with icing sugar and serve. If preferred, use bolo folhado filling (page 165) in the foguete.

MAS PAAN
MEAT BUNS

Popular as a snack at any time of day, yeast buns filled with curried meat are sold piping hot from the oven at almost every tea boutique.

Makes about 30
1 quantity beef curry (page 136)
500 g (1 lb) potatoes
1 quantity basic dough (page 159)
  or 2 loaves frozen dough
1 egg yolk beaten with 1 tablespoon water

Prepare curry and add peeled, diced potatoes 30 minutes before end of cooking. Cook curry until it is very dry. Allow to cool. Prepare dough and after it has proved the first time punch down and divide into 30 equal portions. Flatten each portion to a circle, put a spoonful of meat and potato curry in the centre and bring edges together, pressing and moulding to seal. Buns should be nicely rounded on top and not too bready at the bottom. To achieve this keep dough thicker in centre of rounds and thin at the edges.

Put buns join downwards on greased baking trays, well apart to allow for rising and spreading. Cover with a dry cloth and leave in a warm place for 30-40 minutes or until nearly doubled in bulk. Brush with egg glaze and bake in a hot oven 200°C (400°F) until golden brown. Serve hot or cold.

VATTALAPPAM
SPICY COCONUT CUSTARD

This rich custard, Malayan in origin, is very popular in Ceylon. If jaggery (palm sugar) is not available, substitute with half cup firmly packed black sugar and half cup maple syrup.

Cooking time: approximately 1¼ hours
Oven temperature: 150-160°C (300-325°F)
Serves: 6-8
4 eggs
175 g (5 oz) palm sugar (jaggery)
½ cup water
1½ cups thick coconut milk (see below)
¾ cup evaporated milk
½ teaspoon ground cardamom
¼ teaspoon ground mace
pinch ground cloves
1 tablespoon rose water

Beat eggs slightly (they should not be frothy). Dissolve palm sugar in water over a low heat, cool slightly. Add palm sugar syrup, or black sugar and maple syrup, to beaten eggs, add the coconut milk and stir to dissolve sugar.

Strain through a fine strainer into a large jug, add evaporated milk, spices and rose water. Pour into individual custard cups. Put custard cups in a baking dish with water to come halfway up sides of cups and bake in a slow oven to set, approximately 1¼ hours.

Alternatively put the same depth of water into an electric frypan. Set temperature at 120°C (260°F), put custard cups in, cover and cook until set, approximately 1¼ hours. Cool and chill custards before serving.

Coconut milk: For this custard, the coconut milk is made with milk instead of water. Put 2 cups desiccated coconut in a saucepan, pour over 2½ cups milk and bring slowly to the boil. Cool to lukewarm, then extract coconut milk (page 11). Use only the first extract in this recipe.

BREUDHER
(picture opposite)

A Dutch recipe, this rich yeast cake is traditionally served at Christmas and New Year.

Oven temperature: moderate 170°C (350°F)
Cooking time: 30-35 minutes
Makes: 2 large cakes
1 quantity basic bread dough (page 159)
315 g (10 oz) unsalted butter
315 g (10 oz) caster sugar
5 eggs
2 teaspoons vanilla
250 g (8 oz) sultanas

After proving dough (see page 159), cream butter and sugar until light and creamy. Add dough in small pieces, beating well, until all the dough has been incorporated. An electric mixer is essential unless you have a strong beating arm. Add the eggs, one at a time, beating well after each. Stir in vanilla and sultanas. Divide dough between two well-buttered 10-cup tube pans and leave in a warm place, protected from draughts, for 30 minutes or until almost double in bulk. Bake in a moderate oven for 30-35 minutes or until well risen and golden brown on top. If top starts to brown too soon, cover with foil or paper and cook until a thin skewer comes out clean. Cool in pan for 10 minutes, then turn out on to a wire rack and cool completely before cutting. Serve spread with unsalted butter and sprinkled with caster sugar or, if preferred, with thin slices of Dutch Edam cheese.

TRADITIONAL CHRISTMAS CAKE
(picture opposite)

Oven temperature: slow 130°C (275°F)
Cooking time: 2¼-2½ hours
250 g (8 oz) seedless raisins
375 g (12 oz) sultanas
250 g (8 oz) mixed glacé fruit
250 g (8 oz) preserved ginger
2 small cans chow chow preserves or
   500 g (1 lb) melon and ginger jam
125 g (4 oz) mixed peel
250 g (8 oz) glacé cherries
250 g (8 oz) raw cashews or
   blanched almonds
¼ cup brandy
375 g (12 oz) butter
500 g (1 lb) caster sugar
12 egg yolks
2 teaspoons grated lemon rind
1½ teaspoons ground cardamom
1 teaspoon ground cinnamon
1 teaspoon grated nutmeg
¾ teaspoon ground cloves
2 tablespoons vanilla essence
1 tablespoon almond essence
2 teaspoons rose essence
1 tablespoon honey
250 g (8 oz) fine semolina
6 egg whites
almond paste (page 164)

Line a 25 cm (10 inch) round or square cake tin with three thicknesses each of newspaper and brown paper, then two layers of greaseproof paper liberally brushed with melted butter.

Chop raisins and sultanas. Cut glacé fruit into small pieces (use a mixture of pineapple, apricot and quince — avoid figs). Drain syrup from preserved ginger and chow chow preserves and chop finely. Chop mixed peel. Cut cherries in halves. Chop nuts very finely or put through a nut mill. Combine fruits and nuts in large bowl, sprinkle with brandy, cover and leave while mixing cake. This can be done the day before, allowing the fruit more time to soak in the brandy.

Cream butter and sugar until light. Add yolks of eggs one at a time, beating well after each addition. Add grated rind, spices, flavourings and honey and mix well. Add semolina and beat until well combined, then mix in fruit. Use biggest bowl or pan you have and mix in fruit with both hands (it's much easier than a spoon and professional pastry cooks do it this way). When fruit is thoroughly mixed in, whip egg whites until stiff and fold through mixture.

Turn into prepared cake tin and bake in slow oven for 2¼-2½ hours, covering cake with paper after first hour to prevent over-browning. The result will be very rich and moist. If you prefer a darker and drier result, bake for 4½-5 hours. It will not be dry, but certainly firmer than if you use shorter baking time.

Cool completely, preferably overnight, then remove paper and wrap cake in foil. A tablespoon or two of brandy may be sprinkled over cake after it is cold, just before wrapping. If liked, ice with almond paste and fondant icing. Cut in small pieces and wrap in foil and coloured cellophane. This cake can be kept in an airtight tin for a year or longer.

Note: Chow chow preserves can be purchased at Chinese groceries or specialty food stores. The nearest equivalent is melon and ginger jam.

TRADITIONAL CHRISTMAS CAKE and BREUDHER *recipes above,* and LOVE CAKE (cut in squares in foreground), *recipe page 164.*

LOVE CAKE (1)

A very popular cake in Sri Lanka, though no one knows why it is called by this name. There are many recipes, some using butter while others do not, some insisting that only egg yolks should be used and other including the egg whites as well. Here is my favourite recipe.

Oven temperature: 150°C (300°F)
Baking time: about 1 hour
7 eggs, separated
500 g (1 lb) caster sugar
250 g (8 oz) semolina
375 g (12 oz) raw cashews, finely chopped
2 tablespoons rose water
2 tablespoons honey
½ teaspoon finely grated lemon rind
½ teaspoon ground mace or nutmeg
½ teaspoon ground cardamom
½ teaspoon almond essence, optional

Grease and line a 20 cm (8 inch) square tin with 2 thicknesses of greaseproof paper. Brush inner paper with melted butter.

Beat the egg yolks and caster sugar until light and creamy. Stir in the semolina, cashews, rose water, honey, lemon rind, spices and almond essence. Beat egg whites until they hold firm peaks and fold into the mixture, turn into prepared tin and bake in moderately slow oven until cake is evenly golden brown on top and feels firm to the touch. If cake starts to brown too quickly, cover top with paper or foil.

When cooked the centre of the cake should still be somewhat moist so the skewer test is not recommended.

Remove from oven and leave in the tin to get quite cold before cutting. Do not attempt to turn out this cake. Cut into small squares and lift each one separately on to serving plate.

LOVE CAKE (2)

Oven temperature: 150°C (300°F)
125 g (4 oz) butter
250 g (8 oz) semolina
10 egg yolks
500 g (1 lb) caster sugar
185 g (6 oz) raw cashew nuts,
   finely chopped
2 tablespoons each rose water and honey
¼ teaspoon each grated nutmeg,
   lemon rind and ground cinnamon

Soften butter and mix with semolina. Beat egg yolks and sugar until thick and creamy. Add semolina and butter mixture and beat until well mixed. Add chopped nuts, rose water, honey, nutmeg, lemon rind and cinnamon and mix well together. Pour mixture into a flat cake tin lined with greased paper and bake in a moderately slow oven until top is nicely browned and cake cooked through.

ALMOND PASTE

250 g (8 oz) ground almonds
500 g (1 lb) pure icing sugar, sifted
1 small egg, beaten
1 tablespoon brandy
1 tablespoon sherry
½ teaspoon almond essence, optional
beaten egg white

Mix ground almonds and icing sugar in a large bowl, add egg mixed with brandy, sherry and almond essence, then knead until it holds together. If too moist knead in a little extra sifted icing sugar. Roll out half the almond paste on pastry board dusted with icing sugar and cut to fit top of cake. Brush cake with beaten egg white, place almond paste on top and press lightly with rolling pin. Roll remaining almond paste into a strip and fit around side of cake. In Sri Lanka it is traditional for the cake to be cut into pieces and each piece individually wrapped.

BOLO FOLHADO
MANY-LAYERED CAKE

Curiously like a large, rich Danish pastry, this is one of the most popular sweets handed down from the time the Portuguese ruled Sri Lanka. It is not made among the Sinhalese, but is much prized by the descendants of the Dutch and Portuguese, the Burghers. Only a thin layer of filling is necessary between the layers of pastry.

Cooking time : 50-55 minutes
Oven temperature : 200°C (400°F)
Makes about 20 serves

Pastry :
3 cups plain flour
pinch salt
125 g (4 oz) butter
1 teaspoon fresh compressed yeast
    or ½ teaspoon dried yeast
¼ cup lukewarm water
¾ cup lukewarm milk
1 teaspoon sugar
2 egg yolks
1 egg, beaten

Filling :
2 cups sugar
1 cup water
375 g (12 oz) raw cashews,
    very finely chopped
1 tablespoon rosewater

Pastry: Sift flour and salt into a bowl. Add a quarter of the butter and rub in with fingertips until mixture resembles breadcrumbs. Dissolve yeast in the water, add milk, sugar and beaten egg yolks. Make a well in the centre of the flour and add liquid. Mix in flour to make a soft dough, turn on to a floured board and knead lightly until free from cracks. It may be necessary to add a little more flour if dough is too soft. Wrap dough in plastic or greaseproof paper and chill for 30 minutes. Roll the dough to a 60 x 20cm (24 x 8 inch) rectangle and spread two thirds of the surface with the remainder of the butter, leaving edges free. Fold the unbuttered third to the centre and fold the last third over it. Turn the dough so the folds are to right and left, press with the rolling pin to seal the open ends and roll out again. Fold as before, wrap in plastic and chill. Repeat rolling and folding twice more.

Divide dough into four parts, one just slightly larger than the other three. Roll out dough into three 28 cm (11 inch) rounds and one 30 cm (12 inch) round. Grease and flour a baking tray or tart tin, put the largest circle of pastry on it. Spread to within 2.5 cm (1 inch) of the edge with a third of the cooled filling. Cover with a second circle of pastry and another layer of filling. Continue until filling and pastry are used up. Brush edge of bottom layer of pastry with egg white, then fold it over the upper layers and flute around the edge, or press with a fork to seal. Decorate top with leaves or other shapes cut from pastry trimmings. Brush over with beaten egg and bake in a hot oven for 15 minutes, then reduce heat to moderate 170°C (350°F) and continue baking for 35 to 40 minutes or until nicely browned. Cool, cut into thin wedges to serve.

Filling: Put sugar and water into a heavy saucepan and bring to the boil. Boil for 5 minutes or until heavy syrup forms. Stir in the cashews and cook over low heat until thick but not stiff. Cool slightly, add rose water, allow to cool completely.

THALA GULI
SESAME SEED AND PALM SUGAR BALLS

One of Sri Lanka's best-known local candies. They are sold on the road to Kandy, the ancient hill capital and favourite tourist resort, by village belles who also offer young coconuts for drinking.

2 cups sesame seeds
500 g (1 lb) palm sugar or substitute
generous pinch of salt

In a mortar and pestle pound the sesame, a little at a time, until the seeds are crushed and oily. As each batch is done, turn it into a bowl. Grate the palm sugar and add to the sesame with the salt. Mix well with hands. The heat of the hands and vigorous kneading slightly melts the palm sugar, and after a while the mixture will hold together. Make balls the size of a large marble. These are wrapped in rectangular pieces of wax or greaseproof paper fringed at the ends. The paper is twisted on either side of the thala guli so each one looks like a miniature Christmas cracker. Serve at the end of a curry meal, or as a between-meal treat.

INDONESIA

From the air, the Indonesian archipelago is like a beautiful necklace of aquamarine and sapphire and emerald hues, strung between Australia and mainland Southeast Asia. Of its more than 13,000 islands, only half are large enough to have names and less than a thousand are populated, yet it includes some of the world's largest islands and is home to more than 120 million people, making it the fifth most populous nation on earth.

On the ground it is green, green, green. The steamy heat of the lowlands and the lush growth on every hand suggest that one is in a giant greenhouse, a notion that holds true for all but the chilly mountain peaks and high volcanic craters that are the backbones of most of the major islands.

Indonesia has, at various times, been in the thrall of animism, Buddhism, Hinduism and Islam. It has been influenced or conquered by the Chinese, the Indians, the Portuguese, the Dutch and the English. It had huge and magnificent temples centuries before

Europe's great gothic cathedrals were dreamed of. Its handcrafts and theatre — *batik* and the famed *wayang kulit* or 'shadow plays' — are as alive today as they were a thousand years ago.

This rich and varied history, coupled with many different traditions and languages, has inevitably produced a cuisine that is also rich and varied — and which offers much to the adventurous eater.

Indonesian food is, unquestionably, some of the most delicious in the world. There isn't much subtlety about it, but what a great awakening for your taste buds! This doesn't mean that every dish is hot or pungent, but there's always a combination of sweet and sour and salty tastes; unexpectedly gentle coconut-milk sauces fragrant with lemon grass or other herbs; crisp textured accompaniments; hot *sambal* to be tasted in tiny quantities; all of which create an awareness that what you are eating is not just body fuel but an expression of culinary artistry.

One of the simplest, most unsophisticated Indonesian meals I have eaten was at an open air restaurant in Jakarta. Near the entrance were tables laden with enormous piles of tender coconuts and spiky, strong-smelling *durian*; from beams in the little thatched shelter hung strings of purple mangosteens; mangoes, *rambutan* and other exotic fruit were there in profusion.

At this restaurant the speciality was fish. And fish there were, all around. Paths wound between ponds well stocked with varieties of fish considered delicacies in Indonesia. The water was recirculated by means of fountains in the ponds. Pavilions open on all sides dotted the grounds and here one sat at bare tables. Before sitting down we chose our fish, pointing them out to the men who waded in, net in hand, to capture our dinner.

The meal, when it came, was extremely simple. There was a whole fish to each person; some had been deep fried, others barbecued. To accompany the fish was a basket filled with steaming white rice. Each diner had a bowl of soup, very light and clear, but full of unusual flavour. Acid with tamarind, sweet with the natural sweetness of vegetables like corn and pumpkin, this was for sipping between mouthfuls of food, not for downing as a first course. There was a salad of cucumber spears and other vegetables and fresh green leaves far more intriguing than lettuce; even tender *papaya* leaves were included. Each of us had a small stone dish of freshly ground chilli *sambal* with a stone pestle-like spoon resting in it. This was the dynamite that set the whole meal apart and assured us that we were dining in Indonesia.

The fish was delightful. Fried or barbecued, the flesh was moist and delicate, the small bones so crisply cooked that they crunched and melted. To take care of the big bones there were numerous friendly and well-fed cats (it was considered quite in order to throw the bones to the feline clientele.)

To drink, we had young coconuts with the top cut off, a dash of orange-flavoured syrup and crushed ice added to the water inside. For dessert we were deluged with fresh green-skinned citrus fruits of amazing sweetness and a whole string of mangosteens — gentle pressure between the palms cracks open the thick purple shell to disclose a number of milky white segments like those in a mandarin, but with no covering membrane or little seeds. Their sweet-sour, slightly astringent, refreshing flavour makes you eat another and yet another until there is a tell-tale heap of purple shells before you.

Indonesian sweets are mostly made from glutinous rice, but don't shrug them off with thoughts of rice pudding — there's not the slightest resemblance. The rice might be steamed in tiny baskets woven of fresh leaves, sweetened with palm sugar, flavoured with fragrant leaves and flowers; or it might be ground and cooked with coconut milk to a smooth paste, flavoured and coloured and poured in unbelievably fine alternate layers of white and green or pink or yellow or chocolate. I particularly liked the green and white layered sweet flavoured with fresh *pandan* leaves.

SERVING AN INDONESIAN MEAL

Whatever else is served, rice is always the foundation of an Indonesian meal. Cook your rice by the absorption method or by steaming; it has so much more flavour than rice cooked in water and drained, and it also has the correct texture and pearly appearance.

With rice it is customary to serve a fish curry and a poultry or meat curry, or both; two or more vegetable dishes, one a *sayur* with lots of gravy, and at least one other vegetable, stir fried, boiled or as a salad; accompaniments such as *krupuk* and chilli-based condiments are an integral part of the meal.

The word 'sambal' implies something fried with lots of chillies. It doesn't only include high-powered condiments such as *sambal ulek* or *sambal bajak*, which are basically pastes of ground chilli and other seasonings; it can also mean one or more of several main dishes known as *sambal sambalan* — there are prawn sambals, chicken sambals, beef sambals — so you could accompany your rice with a generous helping of *sambal cumi-cumi pedis* (recipe, page 181) and a tiny accent of *sambal bajak* (recipe, page 206).

Most popular Indonesian *sambal* pastes or condiments are available in Western countries. Making them involves handling large quantities of fresh chillies and this can be an unforgettable experience if one is in the least bit careless. I recommend buying these sambals in bottles. They are eaten or used in recipes in such tiny quantities that it is hardly worth the trouble to make them. Store bottles in the refrigerator after opening and use a dry spoon, and they'll keep well. There are some recipes for those who find it impossible to buy the sambals.

Because Indonesian cookery never gets very far without fresh chillies, have disposable gloves ready and use them when handling any kind of chilli. If you do forget and touch the chillies, keep your hands away from your eyes, your face and especially your baby. Wash well with soap and water, but don't be surprised if the more pungent chillies cause a tingling and burning sensation that goes on for hours.

When planning an Indonesian meal the curries can be prepared a day or two before and refrigerated. They usually develop more flavour with keeping. Accompaniments can also be made earlier in the day and chilled, or heated up at the last minute if they are to be served hot. Soups and *sayur* can be made ahead too, but short-cook the dish so that the final reheating will not result in the vegetables being overcooked.

For a rice meal set the table with a plate, dessertspoon, fork and a bowl for soup. Everything is put on the table at the same time except sweets or fruits. Rice is taken first and should be surrounded by small helpings of curries and other accompaniments, which are mixed with the rice either singly or in combination.

It is quite polite to eat an Indonesian meal with one's fingers, as most Indonesians do, but practise in private first. There's quite an art to doing it properly. Only the tips of the fingers of the right hand are used. When soups and *sayur* are part of the meal a spoon proves more convenient.

Fingerbowls are provided, with slices of lemon or lime floating in hot water.

UTENSILS

The range of saucepans, knives and spoons already in the kitchen will do very well for cooking Indonesian food, but there is one pan that will make things a lot easier. This is the curved metal pan with a shallow bowl-like shape called a *kuali* or *wajan* in Indonesia but much better known by its Chinese name, *wok*. Woks are readily available in most Western cities and are not expensive. See information on the wok on page 369.

In most Indonesian kitchens, grinding stones are part of the essential equipment, as is a stone mortar and pestle. You can buy a mortar and pestle from your chemist for pounding small amounts of spices, but to substitute for the grinding stone you need a powerful blender. I would stress that some blenders do a better job than others. If you don't already own one, look for a model that has a glass goblet, a powerful motor and a shape that will effectively blend small quantities as well as large. I use my blender all the time for grinding spices, pulverising onions, chillies, garlic and ginger, making coconut milk and a number of other tasks.

In Asian kitchens you will find a special implement for grating fresh coconut (see illustration on page 16), but rather than try to grate the coconut with an ordinary grater, peel away the dark brown outer skin and pulverise the coconut in the blender.

On the subject of graters, I have often recommended using grated ginger or garlic. This is because it is the nearest you can come to the ground ingredient and because most blenders need more than a couple of cloves of garlic or a fragment of ginger to work on. But please choose the right grater surface — not the one for grating cheese or the larger shredder, but the small version of the shredder. This gives a very satisfactory result.

YOUR INDONESIAN SHELF

This is a list of spices, herbs, sauces, sambals and other flavourings which keep well. Fresh ingredients are not included.

coriander, ground
creamed coconut
cummin, ground
desiccated coconut
daun pandan (dried pandan leaves)
daun salam
gula jawa (palm sugar), or substitute black or
    brown sugar
laos powder
kencur powder
kemiri nuts (candle nuts)
peanut oil
petis or shrimp sauce
sambal ulek
sesame oil
soy sauce
sweet soy sauce *(kecap manis)*
tamarind, dried or instant
sereh powder (dried lemon grass)
trasi (dried shrimp paste)
turmeric, ground

NASI PUTIH
WHITE RICE

Serves: 6
500 g (1 lb) short grain rice
2½ cups water
2 teaspoons salt, optional

Put rice into a saucepan with a well-fitting lid, add water and salt and bring to the boil. As soon as it comes to the boil, turn heat very low, cover tightly and allow to steam for 15 minutes. This gives a very firm rice, which can be eaten hot or allowed to get cold and used for nasi goreng. Though firm, rice will be cooked through if lid is put on immediately rice comes to the boil, and if lid fits well enough to hold steam in. It is also possible to bring water and salt to the boil, add the rice and when it returns to the boil, cover and steam as before.

If a slightly softer result is preferred (but with each grain separate and not mushy) increase water to 3 cups.

For long grain rice, use 4 cups water to 500 g (1 lb) rice, for the absorption rate is almost double that of short or medium grain rice. Use the same method of cooking, bringing rice and water to the boil and then lowering heat so that it cooks very gently, covered with a well-fitting lid. Increase time to 20 minutes after rice comes to the boil.

A most important point when cooking rice is that the lid should not be lifted during cooking time, for valuable steam is lost and can affect the result. Also, rice is *never* stirred during this first 15-20 minutes.

NASI UDUK
RICE COOKED IN COCONUT MILK WITH SPICES

Serves: 6
500 g (1 lb) long grain rice
4½ cups coconut milk
2½ teaspoons salt
1 onion, finely chopped
2 cloves garlic, chopped
1 teaspoon ground turmeric
1 teaspoon ground cummin
2 teaspoons ground coriander
½ teaspoon dried shrimp paste (trasi)
¼ teaspoon kencur powder
1 teaspoon finely chopped lemon rind, or
   1 stem of lemon grass

If rice needs washing, wash and drain well. Put all ingredients except rice into a saucepan with a well-fitting lid, and bring slowly to the boil, uncovered, stirring frequently. Add the rice, stir and bring back to the boil. Turn heat as low as possible, cover pan tightly and steam for 20 minutes. Uncover, fork rice lightly from around sides of pan, mixing in any coconut milk that has not been absorbed, replace lid and steam for 5 minutes longer. Serve hot with ayam goreng jawa (page 184) and sambals.

NASI GURIH
FRAGRANT RICE

Serves: 6
4½ cups coconut milk
½ teaspoon ground black pepper
1 teaspoon finely grated lemon rind or 1
   stalk fresh lemon grass
½ teaspoon ground nutmeg or mace
¼ teaspoon ground cloves
1 daun salam or 3 curry leaves
2½ teaspoons salt
500 g (1 lb) long grain rice

Put the coconut milk with all the flavourings and spices and salt into a large saucepan with a well-fitting lid, and bring slowly to the boil, uncovered. Stir in the rice and return to the boil, then turn heat very low, cover and steam for 20 minutes. Uncover, fork the rice lightly from around sides of pan, mixing in any coconut milk that has not been absorbed, and replace lid for 5 minutes. Serve hot with fried chicken or curries and hot sambals.

NASI KUNING LENGKAP
FESTIVE YELLOW RICE *(picture page 166)*

Serves 8-10

1 kg (2 lb) long grain rice
4 tablespoons oil
2 large onions, finely sliced
3 cloves garlic, finely chopped
8 cups coconut milk
4 teaspoons salt
2 teaspoons ground turmeric
3 daun salam or 6 curry leaves
2 strips pandanus leaf, optional
banana leaves or bamboo leaves, for
    serving

Garnish:
marbled eggs (page 211)
2 green cucumbers
3 fresh red chillies
3 fresh green chillies

If rice needs washing, wash well beforehand and allow to drain at least 1 hour.

Heat oil in a large saucepan with a well-fitting lid. Fry onions and garlic until onions are soft and golden, stirring frequently to prevent burning. Add rice and fry for a minute or two, then add coconut milk, salt, turmeric, and leaves for flavouring. Bring to the boil, stirring with a long spoon. As soon as liquid comes to the boil turn heat very low, cover tightly with lid and allow to steam for 20 minutes. Uncover, quickly stir in with a fork any coconut milk that remains unabsorbed around edge of pan, replace lid and leave on same low heat for a further 3 minutes. Turn off heat, uncover and allow steam to escape and rice to cool slightly. Remove leaves used for flavouring and gently fork rice on to a large platter or a tray lined with well-washed banana leaves or bamboo leaves. Shape into a cone, pressing firmly. Use pieces of greased banana leaf or foil to do this. Surround with all the accompaniments, which should be made beforehand, then garnish.

Garnish: Shell the marbled eggs and cut each in halves lengthways. Score the skin of the cucumbers with a fork and cut in very thin slices. Make a flower with one of the red chillies, and cut all other chillies into thin diagonal slices. Flip out seeds with point of small knife. To make the chilli flower, cut off stem end of chilli and slit several times with point of sharp knife from 2.5 cm (1 inch) above the tip to the cut end at the stem. Drop into iced water and the strips will curl. Put this on top of the cone, scatter the sliced chillies around the side of the cone, and put sliced cucumbers and marbled eggs around base of cone.

Accompaniments to this festive rice meal can be as few or as many as you wish. Here are some that provide contrasts in flavour and texture and may be prepared in advance: ayam ungkap (fried chicken), or ayam goreng jawa (Javanese-style fried chicken); sambal goreng udang (fried prawn sambal); rempah-rempah (meat and coconut patties); serundeng (crisp spiced coconut); acar kuning (vegetable pickle); krupuk udang (prawn crisps); rempeyek kacang (peanut wafers).

NASI GORENG
FRIED RICE

Serves: 6-8
3 eggs
salt and pepper
oil for frying
250 g (8 oz) raw prawns
500 g (1 lb) pork or lean beef steak
2 medium onions
2 cloves garlic
½ teaspoon dried shrimp paste (trasi)
4 cups cold cooked rice
6 spring onions, thinly sliced
2 tablespoons light soy sauce
3 tablespoons onion flakes (page 206)
1 green cucumber, thinly sliced

Beat eggs with salt and pepper to taste. Heat very little oil in a frying pan and make an omelette with half the beaten eggs. Turn on to a plate to cool (do not fold omelette). Repeat process with remaining beaten eggs. When cool, put one omelette on top of the other, roll up and cut into thin strips.

Shell and de-vein prawns, cut beef or pork into fine strips. Chop onions roughly and put in blender container with garlic and trasi. Cover and blend to a paste. (If blender is not available, finely chop onions and crush garlic. Dissolve trasi in a little hot water. Combine these three ingredients.)

Heat 3 tablespoons of oil in a large frying pan or wok and fry the blended ingredients until cooked. Add prawns and meat to pan and fry, stirring constantly, until they are cooked. Add 2 tablespoons more oil and when hot stir in the rice and spring onions, tossing and mixing thoroughly until very hot. Sprinkle with soy sauce and mix evenly.

Serve the fried rice garnished with strips of omelette, fried onion flakes and cucumber.

MIE GORENG
FRIED NOODLES

Serves: 4
250 g (8 oz) fine egg noodles
1 large pork chop
250 g (8 oz) prawns, raw or cooked
4 tablespoons peanut oil
1 onion, finely chopped
3 cloves garlic, finely chopped
1 fresh red chilli, seeded and sliced
½ teaspoon dried shrimp paste (trasi)
2 stalks celery, finely sliced
small wedge of cabbage, finely shredded
1 teaspoon salt
½ teaspoon pepper
1-2 tablespoons light soy sauce

Garnish:
fried onion flakes (page 206), optional
4 spring onions
thinly sliced cucumber

Soak noodles in hot water, while bringing large saucepan of water to the boil. Drain noodles and drop into the boiling water, allow to return to the boil and boil from 1-3 minutes, depending on the noodles. Some are cooked in the shorter time, while others take a little longer. Keep testing one strand every half minute or so, because they must not overcook; like good spaghetti they must be tender but still firm to bite. As soon as they reach this stage, drain in colander and run cold water through them until cool or they will continue to cook in their own heat. Drain well.

Cut away rind and bone from pork chop and cut into small dice. Shell and de-vein prawns. Heat peanut oil in a wok or large deep frying pan and fry onion, garlic and chilli until onion is soft and starts to turn golden. Add trasi. Add the pork and prawns and stir fry until cooked through. Add celery, cabbage, salt and pepper and fry for a further minute or just until tender. Vegetables should retain their crispness. Add noodles and keep turning the mixture so that every part of it gets heated through. Season with soy sauce to taste. Pile into a serving dish and sprinkle onion flakes over the top. Chop the spring onions, green leaves and all, and sprinkle over. Arrange cucumber slices around edge of dish. Serve hot.

SAMBALAN
BASIC SAMBAL SEASONING

A quick, convenient way to accomplish the myriad dishes that go to make up an Indonesian meal. If you like hot food you will find it useful to make up a quantity of this base, which you can cook and keep bottled in the refrigerator ready to add to such varied ingredients as boiled or fried potatoes, breadfruit, yams or other starchy vegetables; hard-boiled eggs; bean curd cut in dice or strips and fried; fresh or dried fish, fried; fried prawns and other shell fish; crisp-fried strips of meat or liver. There is no end to the variations on this theme.

15-20 large dried chillies
3 large onions, roughly chopped
8 cloves garlic
2 teaspoons dried shrimp paste (trasi)
½ cup peanut oil, or more as required
1 cup tamarind liquid
3 teaspoons salt
2 tablespoons palm sugar or substitute

Soak chillies in hot water for 20 minutes. In container of electric blender grind the chillies, onions, garlic and trasi, with enough oil to help the blades draw down the solid ingredients. It may be necessary to use more than half the oil, depending on the size and shape of the blender. When blended to a smooth paste, heat remaining oil in a wok or frying pan and when hot put in the blended ingredients. Fry over medium heat, stirring constantly, until mixture is cooked and dark in colour and oil separates and shows around edges. Wash out blender container with the tamarind liquid, add to pan with salt and sugar and simmer for a few minutes longer, stirring. Cool completely and bottle. Store in refrigerator. (If mixture had been cooked in a wok, turn it into a glass or earthenware bowl to cool).

To use: Heat the required amount (approximately 1 tablespoon to 250 g or 8 oz of the main ingredient) and stir fry the already cooked main ingredient in it briefly. If a gravy is required, add ½-1 cup thick coconut milk and heat to simmering point, stirring constantly.

TAUCO IKAN
FISH IN BROWN BEAN SAUCE WITH STIR-FRIED VEGETABLES

Serves: 6
750 g (1½ lb) fish steaks (tuna, mackerel, jewfish or any other firm fish)
salt
2 small onions
6 sweet chilli peppers or 1 red capsicum
125 g (4 oz) fresh green beans
1 cup sliced canned bamboo shoot
2 cloves garlic, finely chopped
1½ teaspoons finely grated fresh ginger
2 tablespoons bean sauce (tauco)
4 tablespoons peanut oil
1 teaspoon dried shrimp paste (trasi), optional
1 tablespoon light soy sauce
⅔ cup water

Cut fish into serving pieces, sprinkle with salt and leave while preparing other ingredients.

Peel onions. Cut one in eighths lengthways, then cut each section in half crossways. Separate layers of onion. Remove seeds and membranes from sweet peppers or capsicum and cut in strips lengthways, then cut the strips in half crossways. Thinly slice beans diagonally. Slice bamboo shoot in pieces of similar size. Set each vegetable aside separately. Chop remaining onion very finely and combine it with garlic, ginger, and bean sauce.

Wipe fish with paper towels to remove excess moisture. Heat peanut oil in a wok or frying pan and fry fish on high heat until pieces are browned on both sides. Remove from pan. Pour off all but 2 tablespoons oil. Add onion, ginger, garlic, and bean sauce and fry, stirring constantly, over medium heat until onions are soft. If using trasi, add it now. Add beans and stir fry for 2 minutes. Add peppers and onion and stir fry 1 minute. Add bamboo shoot, soy sauce and water, stir well, cover and simmer for 3 minutes. Add fish and heat through. Serve with white rice.

Note: There is another method in which fish is not fried in oil. The serving pieces are added after adding water, brought to simmering point, covered and simmered until fish is cooked, 6-8 minutes depending on thickness of fish. In this case, only 2 tablespoons of oil will be necessary.

IKAN PANGGANG (1)
FISH GRILLED IN BANANA LEAVES *(picture opposite)*

Serves: 4
4 small whole fish or 4 fish steaks
2 cloves garlic, crushed
3 teaspoons palm sugar or substitute
2 fresh red chillies, seeded and chopped
½ cup dark soy sauce
3 tablespoons lemon juice
¼ teaspoon kencur powder
½ teaspoon sereh powder
banana leaves and foil for wrapping
2 lemons, sliced thinly

Buy fish cleaned and scaled with head left on. Rub body cavity with damp kitchen paper dipped in coarse salt until free of blood. Wash fish, make diagonal cuts on each side. If using fish steaks, wash and dry well.

Crush garlic with some of the measured sugar. Combine garlic, sugar, chillies, soy sauce, lemon juice, kencur and sereh, pour over fish in a shallow dish and marinate for 30 minutes. Drain from marinade and place each fish (or each fish steak) on a square of washed banana leaf backed with a large square of heavy-duty aluminium foil. Pour one spoonful of marinade inside fish and over top. Put a few lemon slices on fish, overlapping them slightly. Make a neat parcel, keeping the seam on top so you will know which side to open.

Grill fish over glowing coals or under a preheated griller for 10 minutes on each side. Simmer marinade for 2 or 3 minutes, adding more soy sauce and water if necessary. Serve fish in its parcel and use marinade separately as a sauce. Serve with rice, vegetables and sambals.

IKAN PANGGANG (2)
GRILLED FISH WITH SPICES

Serves: 6
500 g (1 lb) fish steaks (fresh tuna or
    other firm fish)
1 onion, roughly chopped
1 fresh red chilli or ½ teaspoon sambal
    ulek
1 clove garlic
½ teaspoon dried shrimp paste (trasi)
½ teaspoon kencur powder
1 teaspoon salt
1½ cups thick coconut milk
1 stalk lemon grass or 2 strips lemon rind
2 tablespoons chopped fresh basil
vegetable oil
lemon juice and salt to taste

Wash and dry fish steaks and put in a single layer in glass dish. In container of electric blender put onion, chilli, garlic, trasi, kencur and salt with half cup of the coconut milk. Blend until smooth. If blender is not available, grate onion and garlic finely and use sambal or chilli powder in place of fresh chilli. Crush trasi and combine all these ingredients with the coconut milk.

Marinate fish in the spice mixture for about 1 hour, turning slices once. Preheat griller until hot and line tray with foil. Spoon off marinade, leaving only what clings to the fish. Put marinade into a small saucepan with the remaining coconut milk, the lemon grass or lemon rind and the chopped basil and put on low heat to simmer, stirring frequently to prevent curdling. Do not cover.

Brush fish with oil and put under griller about 10 cm (4 inches) from heat until fish is cooked and touched with brown on one side. Turn fish steaks, brush with more oil and grill other side as before. If steaks are large, divide into serving pieces, removing large centre bone. Arrange fish on serving platter. Taste sauce and add more salt if necessary and lemon juice to taste. Spoon over fish and serve.

Ingredients for **IKAN PANGGANG** (fish grilled in banana leaves) *recipe above.*

IKAN BALI
BALINESE-STYLE FISH

Serves: 6

1 kg (2 lb) fish steaks
2 medium onions, finely chopped
2 cloves garlic, finely chopped
1½ teaspoons finely grated fresh ginger
1½ teaspoons sambal ulek (page 206)
1 teaspoon finely grated lemon rind
1 teaspoon laos powder
2 tablespoons lemon juice
2 tablespoons palm sugar or substitute
2 tablespoons dark soy sauce
½ teaspoon salt
peanut oil for frying

Wash fish, dry on absorbent paper towels and cut into serving portions. Heat about 2 tablespoons oil in a small saucepan and fry the onions until soft. Add garlic and ginger and stir over medium heat until golden brown. Add sambal ulek, lemon rind, laos, lemon juice, sugar, soy sauce and salt and simmer for 2 or 3 minutes. Set aside. Heat peanut oil for deep frying and fry the fish until golden brown on both sides. Drain, put on serving plate and spoon the sauce over.

GULAI IKAN
FISH IN COCONUT MILK AND SPICES

Serves: 6

1½ lb firm dark fish steaks (tuna,
    mackerel, kingfish)
salt to taste
juice of half a lemon
2 onions, finely chopped
3 cloves garlic, crushed
2 teaspoons finely grated fresh ginger
1 teaspoon ground turmeric
½ teaspoon dried shrimp paste (trasi)
1 teaspoon sambal ulek or chilli powder
1 stalk lemon grass or 2 strips lemon rind
1 teaspoon salt
1½ cups thin coconut milk
2 tablespoons chopped fresh basil
¼ cup tamarind liquid
1 cup thick coconut milk

Wash fish, rub with a little salt and lemon juice and set aside. Combine onions, garlic, ginger, turmeric, trasi, sambal ulek, lemon grass and salt in a saucepan with thin coconut milk. Bring to simmering point and simmer uncovered until onions are soft and liquid thickened. Add fish, basil and tamarind liquid and simmer until fish is cooked. Stir in the thick coconut milk and heat through but do not boil, stirring so that coconut milk does not curdle. Serve with white rice, vegetables and sambals.

IKAN PANGGANG PEDIS
GRILLED FISH WITH CHILLIES

This very simple recipe was told to me by an Indonesian fish seller. If you like hot chillies as an accompaniment to fish, you will enjoy this dish.

Serves: 4-6

1.5 kg (3 lb) tuna or Spanish mackerel in
    one piece
sambal ulek or fresh red chillies, ground
salt and lemon juice, optional

Buy the portion of fish just above the tail if possible, so that you avoid the stomach cavity. Put it a good distance above glowing coals or under a preheated griller and cook fairly slowly until skin is very brown and fish is cooked through to the centre bone. Serve accompanied by sambal ulek or fresh chillies pounded to a pulp in a mortar and pestle. If you do not want too much fire in the sauce, remove the seeds. Add a little salt and lemon juice to the chillies and take tiny dabs with the fish. To serve the fish, cut into wedges lengthways, following the natural divisions made by the centre bone.

IKAN BANDENG
BAKED FISH

If you can get some large banana leaves to wrap the fish in, do so. They give a subtle and appetising fragrance and look exotic when the dish is served at the table.

Serves: 4-6
Cooking time: 35-40 minutes
Oven temperature: 170-190°C (350-375°F)

1 medium-size snapper or jewfish, about 1.5 kg (3-4 lb)
1 medium onion, chopped
2 cloves garlic
1 teaspoon finely chopped fresh ginger
2 tablespoons tamarind liquid
1 tablespoon dark soy sauce
1 tablespoon oil
1 teaspoon sambal ulek, optional
1 teaspoon salt
1 teaspoon ground turmeric
3 tablespoons finely chopped fresh coriander leaves
banana leaves or foil for wrapping

Wash fish and dry well with paper towels. Score the flesh diagonally on each side.

Put onion, garlic, ginger, tamarind liquid, soy sauce, oil, sambal ulek, if used, salt and turmeric into blender container, cover and blend until smooth. Rub blended mixture well into the fish on both sides and put remaining mixture inside body cavity. Put fish on 2 or 3 large pieces of banana leaf in a baking dish, sprinkle with chopped coriander leaves and fold banana leaves over to enclose fish. Secure with bamboo skewers.

Bake in a moderate oven for 35-40 minutes or until fish is cooked. When ready to serve, the flesh will look milky white and flake easily when tested with a fork. Replace banana leaves after testing, lift fish on to a serving plate and open banana leaves at the table.

IKAN BUMBU SANTAN
FRIED FISH WITH SPICY COCONUT MILK

Serves: 4-6

2 whole fish, about 500 g (1 lb) each (mullet, mackerel or other oily fish)
oil for frying
2 medium onions, finely chopped
2 cloves garlic, crushed
1½ teaspoons finely grated fresh ginger
3 or 4 fresh red chillies, ground or 1 teaspoon sambal ulek
2 tablespoons canned salted yellow beans or bean sauce
1 teaspoon palm sugar or substitute
1 cup coconut milk
1 fresh red chilli to garnish, optional
few sprigs fresh sweet basil

Ask fishmonger to clean fish and remove head, then to split each fish along backbone and open out flat, without dividing it in two. If you're very persuasive and he is not very busy, he might even remove the backbone for you, leaving you with a 'butterflied' fish. At home, use kitchen scissors to trim off fins and spines. Lift out the long bones that form the rib cage of the fish. Wash fish, cleaning away any black membrane with kitchen paper dipped in coarse salt. Dry fish thoroughly on paper towels.

Heat 2 tablespoons oil in a small saucepan and fry onions, garlic, ginger and chillies over medium heat, stirring frequently, until onions are soft and translucent. As they start to brown add the yellow beans (rinsed in a small sieve under the cold tap, then drained and mashed roughly with a fork). Stir 2 minutes. Add sugar and coconut milk and keep stirring while mixture simmers until thickened. Keep warm while frying fish.

Heat enough oil in a large frying pan to cover the base of pan to 12 mm (½ inch) depth and when oil is hot fry fish skin side down until brown, then turn and fry until other side is brown. Drain on absorbent paper. Fry other fish in the same way. Arrange both fish, skin side down, in serving dish. Pour sauce over, garnish with seeded and sliced red chilli and roughly chopped basil leaves. Serve at once with rice.

IKAN KECAP
FISH IN SOY SAUCE

Serves: 4
500 g (1 lb) fish steaks
2 tablespoons peanut oil
1 medium onion, finely chopped
2 or 3 fresh hot chillies, seeded and
   chopped, or 1 teaspoon sambal ulek
2 cloves garlic, finely chopped
1 teaspoon finely grated fresh ginger
½ teaspoon ground black pepper
½ teaspoon kencur powder
1 teaspoon laos powder
½ teaspoon ground nutmeg
3 tablespoons tamarind liquid
2 tablespoons dark soy sauce
2 teaspoons palm sugar or substitute

Wash the fish steaks and dry on paper towel. If large cut into halves or quarters.

Heat oil in a frying pan and fry onion, chillies, garlic and ginger on low heat for 5 minutes or until the onion is soft and starts to colour, stirring occasionally. Add the pepper, kencur, laos and nutmeg and stir, then add the fish and fry for 2 or 3 minutes on each side. Add the tamarind liquid, soy sauce and sugar, cover and simmer gently for 6-10 minutes depending on thickness of fish steaks. Fish must be cooked but not overcooked. Check after 5 minutes and if liquid is drying up add 2 or 3 tablespoons hot water. Liquid should thicken but it should not cook away completely. Serve fish with the remaining spicy soy liquid. White rice, vegetable dishes, a sayur and sambal would round off the meal.

IKAN KACANG
FISH WITH PEANUT SAUCE

Serves: 4-6
2 large fish steaks
lemon juice
salt
black pepper
oil for frying
2 tablespoons light soy sauce
2 tablespoons peanut sauce (page 207)
½ cup thick coconut milk
1 tablespoon tamarind liquid or vinegar
1 tablespoon chopped fresh coriander
   leaves

Wash fish, rub all over with lemon juice and season generously with salt and pepper. Let stand 15 minutes. Heat oil and fry fish steaks (well dried on paper towels) until brown on both sides. Pour off all but a tablespoon of the oil, add remaining ingredients mixed together, except the fresh coriander. Spoon over the fish. Sprinkle with coriander, cover and simmer 5 minutes. Serve with rice.

SAMBAL GORENG UDANG ASAM
PIQUANT FRIED PRAWN SAMBAL (picture page 214)

Serves: 6
500 g (1 lb) shelled raw prawns
2 tablespoons peanut oil
1 onion, finely chopped
3 cloves garlic, finely chopped
½ teaspoon finely grated fresh ginger
2 teaspoons sambal ulek or 4 fresh red
   chillies
½ teaspoon laos powder
2 strips thinly peeled lemon rind
⅓ cup tamarind liquid
1 teaspoon salt
1 teaspoon palm sugar or substitute

Chop prawns into pieces the size of a peanut. Heat oil in a frying pan and fry onion, garlic and ginger until onion is soft and starts to turn golden. Add sambal ulek, laos powder and lemon rind, then add chopped prawns and fry, stirring constantly, until prawns change colour. Add tamarind liquid and simmer on low heat until gravy is thick and oil starts to separate. Remove lemon rind. Stir in salt and sugar. Taste and correct seasoning if necessary. Serve as a side dish with rice and curries.

REMPEYEK KACANG (peanut wafers) recipe page 216

SAMBAL KEPALA UDANG
HOT-SOUR PRAWN HEAD SAMBAL

This is one of the by-products using the tastiest part of the prawn — the head. It contains most of the fat and therefore most of the flavour. While it may not be the easiest thing to swallow, it is worth chewing on (and politely discarding) just to savour the combination of flavours.

Serves: 4

heads from 500 g (1 lb) raw prawns
2 tablespoons peanut oil
5 or 6 curry leaves
1 onion, finely chopped
1 large clove garlic, crushed
½ teaspoon finely grated fresh ginger
1 teaspoon sambal ulek or 2 fresh red
    chillies, seeded and chopped
1 teaspoon dried shrimp paste (trasi)
1 teaspoon ground coriander
½ teaspoon ground cummin
3 tablespoons tamarind liquid
½ teaspoon salt

Wash prawn heads well and remove the hard, armour-like shell, the long thin feelers and the eyes. Drain well in a colander and then on absorbent paper.

Heat oil in a small pan or wok and fry the curry leaves for a few seconds. Add the onion, garlic and ginger and fry on medium low heat, stirring occasionally, until the onion is soft and starts to brown. Add the sambal ulek or fresh chillies. Add the trasi and crush it against the side of the pan. Fry, stirring, for 3 minutes then add coriander and cummin and fry for 1 minute longer. Add prawn heads and fry, turning them frequently, for 2 or 3 minutes. Add tamarind liquid and salt, turn heat very low and simmer uncovered until the liquid evaporates completely and the prawn heads start to sizzle in the oil. This takes about 10-15 minutes. Serve as a tasty side dish with rice and curries.

SAMBAL GORENG UDANG
FRIED PRAWNS WITH COCONUT MILK

Serves: 4

500 g (1 lb) raw prawns
2 tablespoons peanut oil
6 curry leaves or 1 daun salam
1 onion, finely chopped
2 fresh red chillies, seeded and chopped
3 cloves garlic, finely chopped
½-1 teaspoon sambal ulek
½ teaspoon laos powder
½ cup prawn stock
30 g (1 oz) creamed coconut, grated
¾ teaspoon salt
½ teaspoon palm sugar or substitute

Shell and de-vein prawns, saving heads and shells for making stock. Heat oil in a frying pan and fry the curry leaves, onion, chillies and garlic on low heat for 5 minutes or until onions are soft and golden. Stir occasionally. Add sambal ulek and laos powder and fry for a few seconds, then add prawns and stir fry until they change colour. Stir in the stock, creamed coconut, salt and sugar. Simmer uncovered on low heat until liquid thickens and oil starts to separate. Serve as an accompaniment to rice and curries.

To make stock: Wash and well drain the prawn heads and shells. Heat a tablespoon of oil in a saucepan and when very hot throw in the shells and heads. Stir fry until they turn bright pink, then add 2 cups hot water and simmer until liquid is reduced to less than a cup. Strain before using.

Note: If prawns are bought already shelled, use half a cup milk instead of prawn stock. Alternatively, omit creamed coconut and use instead two thirds of a cup thick coconut milk.

SATÉ UDANG
SKEWERED GRILLED PRAWNS

Serves: 4

750 g (1½ lb) raw prawns
3 tablespoons lemon juice
½ cup thick coconut milk
½ teaspoon sambal ulek
½ teaspoon dried shrimp paste (trasi)
1 tablespoon dark soy sauce
1 teaspoon palm sugar or substitute
finely grated rind of 1 lemon
2 small cloves garlic
1 teaspoon salt
vegetable oil

Shell and de-vein prawns. Put lemon juice, coconut milk, sambal ulek, trasi, soy, sugar, lemon rind and garlic crushed with the salt into a bowl and stir well until sugar dissolves. Add prawns, stir and marinate for 15 minutes or longer. If leaving for longer than 1 hour, cover and refrigerate. Thread 3 or 4 prawns on bamboo skewers which have been soaked in water for a few hours. Brush lightly with oil and grill over hot coals or under pre-heated griller until prawns are lightly browned. Meanwhile simmer left-over marinade briefly, stirring constantly. Add more coconut milk or soy sauce to taste if necessary and serve as a sauce.

GULAI CUMI-CUMI
SQUID CURRY

Serves: 6

500 g (1 lb) fresh squid
1 medium onion, finely chopped
2 cloves garlic, crushed
1 teaspoon finely grated fresh ginger
1 teaspoon salt
1 teaspoon chilli powder
½ teaspoon dried shrimp paste (trasi)
1¾ cups coconut milk
4 kemiri nuts or brazil nuts, grated
1 stalk lemon grass, finely sliced or 1
    teaspoon grated lemon rind
1 teaspoon palm sugar or substitute
4 tablespoons tamarind liquid or lemon
    juice to taste

Clean squid, removing head and ink sac. Wash well inside and out and rub away spotted skin from body. Cut each squid in halves lengthways, then into bite-size pieces. Put all other ingredients except sugar and tamarind or lemon into a saucepan and bring to simmering point, stirring. Allow to simmer, uncovered, until thickened. Stir occasionally. Add squid, simmer for 5 to 6 minutes. Add sugar and tamarind or lemon juice, taste and add more salt if necessary. Serve hot with rice and vegetables.

SAMBAL CUMI-CUMI PEDIS
SQUID FRIED WITH CHILLIES

Serves: 6

250 g (8 oz) fresh squid
4 large dried chillies
1 small onion, roughly chopped
3 cloves garlic
½ teaspoon dried shrimp paste (trasi)
½ teaspoon salt
4 tablespoons peanut oil
¼ cup tamarind liquid
12 red bird's-eye chillies
2 teaspoons palm sugar or substitute

Clean squid, removing head and ink sac, and wash well. Cut off tentacles and reserve. With a sharp knife cut squid into narrow rings. Soak chillies in hot water 20 minutes. Put chillies, onion, garlic, trasi and salt into container of electric blender and blend until smooth, adding a little of the liquid in which the chillies soaked if necessary. Heat oil and fry blended mixture over medium heat, stirring constantly, until colour changes to a dark brownish red. Add squid, tamarind liquid and bird's-eye chillies and simmer uncovered, stirring occasionally, for 4 or 5 minutes. Stir in sugar. Serve with rice and curries.

Note: Bird's-eye chillies are the hottest of hot! Unless you know what to expect, don't eat them. Do not crush them before cooking. Remember to warn your guests *before* they bite into a bird's-eye chilli.

OPOR AYAM
CHICKEN IN COCONUT MILK *(picture opposite)*

Serves: 4-6

1.5 kg (3 lb) roasting chicken or chicken
    pieces
3 cloves garlic, crushed
1 teaspoon salt
½ teaspoon ground black pepper
1½ teaspoons finely grated fresh ginger
3 kemiri nuts or brazil nuts, finely grated
3 teaspoons ground coriander
1 teaspoon ground cummin
½ teaspoon ground fennel
½ teaspoon laos powder, optional
4 tablespoons oil
2 medium onions, finely sliced
2 cups thin coconut milk
2 daun salam or 6 curry leaves
1 stem lemon grass or 3 strips thinly
    peeled lemon rind
5 cm (2 inch) piece cinnamon stick
1½ cups thick coconut milk
1 tablespoon lemon juice or tamarind
    liquid
extra salt to taste

Divide chicken into serving pieces. In a small bowl, combine garlic, salt, pepper, ginger, nuts, coriander, cummin, fennel and laos if used. Mix to a paste, adding a little of the oil if necessary. Rub paste well into the pieces of chicken and leave for 1 hour.

Heat 2 tablespoons of the oil in a frying pan and fry sliced onion slowly until golden brown. Drain from oil and set aside. Add remaining oil to pan and fry the spiced chicken pieces gently, just until they start to colour. Add thin coconut milk, daun salam, lemon grass or rind and cinnamon stick. Stir until it comes to the boil, then cook uncovered for 30 minutes or until chicken is tender. Add thick coconut milk, stir thoroughly and cook for a further 15 minutes, uncovered. Remove from heat, add lemon juice and season to taste with extra salt. Remove whole spices. Garnish with fried onions and serve the chicken with white rice, vegetables and sambals.

AYAM PANGGANG
ROAST SPICED CHICKEN

Grilling over glowing coals is the best way to finish cooking this dish, but it can be roasted in the oven.

Serves: 4

1 x 1.5 kg (3 lb) roasting chicken
2 tablespoons dark soy sauce
1 tablespoon lemon juice
1 medium onion, roughly chopped
2 cloves garlic
½ teaspoon sambal ulek
½ teaspoon ground black pepper
½ teaspoon dried shrimp paste (trasi)
½ cup water or coconut milk

Cut chicken in half lengthways, or split it open down the breast and open it out flat. Wash chicken and dry well with paper towels. Put soy sauce, lemon juice, onion and garlic into container of electric blender and blend until smooth. If blender is not available grate onion and garlic finely and mix with the sauce and lemon juice. Add sambal ulek, pepper and crushed trasi to the onion mixture and rub all over the chicken. Leave for 30 minutes or longer. If blender is used, wash out container with the water or coconut milk.

Put the liquid into a large frying pan or wok and cook the chicken, skin side upwards, for 10 minutes over medium heat. Turn and cook for 10 minutes over low heat. Do not cover during cooking, and baste with the marinade and juices in the pan. Meanwhile, preheat oven to 190°C (375°F) or moderately hot. Put chicken, skin side upwards, on a rack in a roasting pan with 12 mm (½ inch) of water in it. Spoon marinade over chicken. Roast for 30 minutes or until skin is crisp and brown. Turn and cook other side 20-25 minutes. Serve hot.

If finishing chicken over coals, position rack 10-13 cm (4-5 inches) away from heat so that the chicken can cook through before skin gets too brown.

OPOR AYAM (chicken in coconut milk, *top*) *recipe above;* and
SAMBAL GORENG TELUR (eggs in chilli sauce) *recipe page 187*

SINGGANG AYAM
SPICED GRILLED CHICKEN

For this recipe the chicken is split down the breast and flattened, then marinated and simmered in coconut milk and finally barbecued or cooked under the griller. If you do not have a pan large enough to accommodate a spreadeagled chicken, cut the bird in half.

Serves: 6-8
1 x 1.5 kg (3 lb) roasting chicken
1 large onion, roughly chopped
3 cloves garlic
3 fresh red chillies or 1½ teaspoons sambal ulek
2 teaspoons chopped fresh ginger
2 strips lemon rind or 1 stalk lemon grass
½ teaspoon ground turmeric
1 teaspoon ground black pepper
2 teaspoons ground coriander
1½ teaspoons salt
2 daun salam or 4 curry leaves
2 lime or lemon leaves, optional
3 cups coconut milk

Split chicken and spread out flat. Put onion, garlic, chillies, ginger and lemon rind into container of electric blender with 2 or 3 tablespoons of the coconut milk and blend to a smooth paste. Add turmeric, pepper, coriander and salt and a spoonful more milk if necessary and blend again for a few seconds.

Spread some of this spice paste over the chicken inside and out and let it marinate for half an hour or longer. Put the remaining spice mixture in a wok or large pan with the leaves and the coconut milk (wash out the blender container with some of the coconut milk) and bring slowly to simmering point, stirring constantly. Lower the chicken into this gravy and continue simmering, stirring and ladling the gravy over the chicken occasionally. Turn chicken after 10 minutes and continue cooking until chicken is done. Lift chicken from pan and grill over coals or under a preheated griller, a good distance away from the heat source, until chicken is touched with brown. In the meantime continue simmering gravy, stirring occasionally, until it is thick. When chicken has been grilled on both sides transfer to a serving plate and spoon a little of the gravy over. Serve the rest of the gravy separately.

AYAM GORENG JAWA
JAVANESE-STYLE FRIED CHICKEN

Serves: 4-6
1 x 1.5 kg (3 lb) roasting chicken
1 medium onion, chopped
2 cloves garlic, crushed
1 teaspoon chopped fresh ginger
3 fresh red chillies or 1 teaspoon sambal ulek
2 kemiri or brazil nuts
¾ cup coconut milk
1 tablespoon desiccated or fresh grated coconut
2 teaspoons ground coriander
1 teaspoon laos powder, optional
½ teaspoon ground turmeric
1½ teaspoons salt
1 stem lemon grass, or 3 strips thinly peeled lemon rind
2 daun salam or 6 curry leaves
oil for deep frying

Cut chicken into joints — separate drumsticks from thighs, wings from breast and cut breast in half lengthways. Cut back into three pieces. Chicken pieces can be used for this dish if preferred, wings and breasts being most suitable. If large, cut breasts into quarters and wings into halves.

Put onion, garlic, ginger, chillies and nuts in blender container with half the coconut milk and the desiccated coconut. Cover and blend on high speed for approximately 30 seconds or until smooth. Put blended mixture in a saucepan with the chicken pieces. Wash out blender container with remaining coconut milk and add to pan. Add all remaining ingredients, bring slowly to the boil, stirring. Cook, uncovered, until chicken is tender and gravy thick and almost dry.

Lift out chicken pieces and deep fry in hot oil until brown, turning occasionally (a wok or deep frying pan is ideal). Serve with white rice or nasi goreng and a sayur or a curry with plenty of gravy.

AYAM BALI
BALINESE-STYLE FRIED CHICKEN

Serves: 4

1 onion, roughly chopped
2 cloves garlic
1 teaspoon chopped fresh ginger
3 fresh red chillies, seeded and roughly
  chopped
4 kemiri nuts
1 tablespoon dark soy sauce
1 x 1.25 kg (2½ lb) frying chicken
peanut oil
2 teaspoons palm sugar or substitute
2 tablespoons lemon juice
½ teaspoon salt
1 cup coconut milk

Put onion, garlic, ginger, chillies, kemiri nuts and soy sauce into container of electric blender and blend to a smooth paste. Cut chicken in quarters. Dry well on paper towels. Heat half a cup peanut oil in wok or frying pan and fry the chicken pieces quickly until brown. Remove chicken and drain on absorbent paper. Pour off oil, leaving only 1 tablespoon, and fry the blended mixture for a few minutes, stirring constantly. Add sugar, lemon juice, salt and coconut milk and keep stirring while mixture comes to the boil. Return chicken and simmer uncovered for 25 minutes or until chicken is tender and gravy thick. Serve with plain white rice or nasi gurih, vegetable dishes and other accompaniments.

AYAM GORENG ASAM
PIQUANT FRIED CHICKEN

Serves: 6-8

1 x 1.5 kg (3 lb) roasting chicken
3 cloves garlic
1½ teaspoons salt
1 teaspoon ground black pepper
1 teaspoon palm sugar or substitute
2 teaspoons ground coriander
1 teaspoon ground cummin
½ teaspoon ground turmeric
⅓ cup tamarind liquid
oil for frying

Cut chicken into small serving pieces, as for curry. Crush garlic with salt to a smooth paste and combine with pepper, sugar, coriander, cummin, turmeric and tamarind liquid. Rub over the chicken pieces and leave for 1 hour, or cover and marinate in refrigerator overnight. Heat enough oil in a large heavy frying pan to cover base of pan. Take chicken pieces from marinade and drain on paper towels to get rid of excess moisture. Put pieces into the frying pan and cook over medium heat for 2 minutes on each side, turning with tongs until golden brown. Reduce heat, cover pan and cook for 10-12 minutes longer, turning pieces half-way through. Drain on absorbent paper and serve warm.

AYAM PANGGANG PEDIS
GRILLED CHICKEN WITH HOT SPICES

Serves: 6

1 x 1.5 kg (3 lb) roasting chicken
2 teaspoons salt
3 teaspoons ground black pepper
3 teaspoons sambal ulek or ground fresh
  red chilli
2 tablespoons finely grated onion
2 cloves garlic, crushed
2 tablespoons dark soy sauce
2 teaspoons palm sugar or substitute
2 tablespoons lemon juice
2 tablespoons peanut oil

Cut the chicken into serving pieces and score the skin and flesh to allow flavours to penetrate. Combine all the other ingredients and rub the chicken well with this marinade, cover and leave for 1 hour or refrigerate and leave for longer. Preheat a griller or prepare a barbecue and have the coals glowing hot. Cook chicken at a good distance from the source of heat so that the chicken is cooked right through before skin gets too brown. Brush with marinade or extra oil and keep turning chicken pieces. Test for doneness by piercing thigh joint with a sharp knife. Juice that runs out should be clear, not pink.

SATÉ AYAM
CHICKEN GRILLED ON SKEWERS

Serves: 6

750 g (1½ lb) chicken breast
2 red chillies or ½ teaspoon sambal ulek
2 medium onions, roughly chopped
3 teaspoons finely chopped fresh ginger
2 tablespoons lemon juice
1½ teaspoons salt
2 tablespoons light soy sauce
2 tablespoons dark soy sauce
2 tablespoons sesame oil
2 tablespoons palm sugar or substitute
½ cup thick coconut milk

Bone chicken and remove skin. Cut into small squares. In container of electric blender put seeded and roughly chopped chillies, onions, ginger, lemon juice, salt and soy sauce. Blend until smooth, pour into a bowl and stir in oil and sugar. Add chicken and stir until each piece is well coated with the marinade. Cover and marinate for 1 hour. Chicken can be marinated overnight in the refrigerator. There will be a generous amount of marinade, because this is used as the base for a sauce to serve with the satay.

Thread pieces of chicken on bamboo skewers which have been soaked for 1-2 hours in cold water, leaving at least half the skewer free at the blunt end. Grill over glowing coals or under a preheated griller, about 5 cm (2 inches) from heat source, for 5-8 minutes or until chicken is crisp and brown. Brush with extra oil during grilling, once on each side.

Pour remaining marinade into a small saucepan, add thick coconut milk and simmer over low heat until smooth and thickened, stirring constantly. Pour into a small bowl and serve with the satay.

AYAM PETIS
CHICKEN WITH SHRIMP SAUCE

Serves: 6

1 x 1.5 kg (3 lb) chicken
3 tablespoons peanut oil
1 large onion, finely chopped
3-4 gloves garlic, finely chopped
1 teaspoon finely chopped fresh ginger
3 fresh red chillies, seeded and chopped
1 teaspoon ground turmeric
1 teaspoon ground black pepper
½ teaspoon dried shrimp paste (trasi)
½ teaspoon laos
1 stalk lemon grass or 2 thinly peeled
    strips lemon rind
2 teaspoons petis or Chinese shrimp sauce
1½ teaspoons salt
1½ cups coconut milk
1 tablespoon palm sugar or substitute
2 tablespoons lemon juice

Cut chicken into curry pieces. Heat peanut oil and fry the onion, garlic and ginger until onion is soft. Add the chillies, turmeric, pepper, trasi and laos and fry, stirring, for 1 minute longer. Add the lemon grass or rind, petis, salt and chicken pieces and stir fry over medium heat until chicken is well coated with the mixture. Add coconut milk and sugar and bring to simmering point on low heat, uncovered, stirring frequently. Turn heat low, and simmer 30 minutes or until chicken is tender and the gravy has thickened. If necessary cook 15 minutes longer, stirring occasionally. If gravy is still not thick enough, remove chicken pieces to serving dish and reduce gravy over high heat, stirring constantly. Add lemon juice, pour gravy over chicken and serve with rice and sambals.

PINDANG TELUR
EGGS IN SOY SAUCE

Serves: 4-6
2 tablespoons peanut oil
1 small onion, finely sliced
1 fresh red chilli, seeded and sliced
1 clove garlic, crushed
½ teaspoon finely grated fresh ginger
½ teaspoon dried shrimp paste (trasi)
1 large ripe tomato, diced
1 tablespoon vinegar
½ teaspoon salt
1 tablespoon palm sugar or substitute
3 tablespoons light soy sauce
½ cup water
4-6 eggs, hard-boiled and shelled

Heat peanut oil in a saucepan and over gentle heat fry the onion, chilli, garlic and ginger until onion is soft and starts to turn golden. Add trasi and fry, mashing with back of spoon. Add tomato and cook, stirring, until tomato is pulped. Add vinegar, salt, sugar, soy sauce and water. Cover and simmer until sauce is thickened and smooth. Put in halved eggs and heat through.

SAMBAL GORENG TELUR
EGGS IN CHILLI SAUCE *(picture page 183)*

This is a very hot dish, intended as a sambal or accompaniment and therefore half a hard-boiled egg per serving is sufficient.

Serves: 6
3 eggs
3 tablespoons peanut oil
1 medium onion, finely chopped
1 clove garlic, crushed
½ teaspoon dried shrimp paste (trasi)
3 teaspoons sambal ulek or chilli powder
½ teaspoon laos powder
3 kemiri or brazil kernels, finely grated
½ teaspoon salt
2 teaspoons palm sugar or substitute
½ cup coconut milk
lemon juice to taste

Hard-boil the eggs, stirring them gently for the first 3 or 4 minutes of cooking so that the yolks are centred. Heat oil and fry onion and garlic until onion is soft and golden. Add trasi, sambal ulek, laos and grated nuts and fry for a few seconds, crushing the trasi with the spoon. Add salt, sugar, coconut milk and lemon juice and simmer gently, stirring constantly, until thick and oily in appearance. Put in the shelled and halved eggs, spooning the sauce over them. Serve hot or at room temperature.

TAHU TELUR
BEAN CURD OMELETTES

Serves: 4

3 squares fresh bean curd
3 eggs, beaten
½ teaspoon salt
¼ teaspoon ground black pepper
6 spring onions, finely chopped
peanut oil for frying

Sauce:
1 tablespoon oil
1 small onion, very finely chopped
2 cloves garlic, finely chopped
1 firm ripe tomato, finely chopped
2 tablespoons dark soy sauce
2 tablespoons water
1 tablespoon sugar

Chop bean curd into small pieces or mash roughly with a fork. Stir into the eggs, season with salt and pepper and add spring onions. Heat a large flat frying pan, grease the base lightly with oil and fry the egg mixture in small round omelettes no larger than saucer size. Make several and keep warm on a hot plate until all the mixture is cooked. Pour over them the sauce (which can be made well ahead) and serve immediately. Garnish if liked with thin diagonal slices of the green part of a spring onion.

Sauce: In a small saucepan heat the oil and fry onion and garlic on a low heat, stirring frequently, until onion is soft, about 5 minutes. Add tomato and fry, stirring, for 3 or 4 minutes, or until tomato is cooked to a pulp. Add soy sauce, water and sugar, bring to the boil. If made ahead, reheat before using.

SINGGANG DAGING
SPARERIBS SPECIAL (using beef ribs)

Serves: 4-6

1.5 kg (3 lb) beef spareribs
3 cloves garlic, finely chopped
1 teaspoon finely grated fresh ginger
1 teaspoon salt
3 tablespoons peanut oil
¼ cup dark soy sauce
½ cup water
2 tablespoons dry sherry
½ teaspoon five spice powder
¼ teaspoon ground black pepper
1 tablespoon palm sugar (or substitute) or
  honey

Have spareribs cut into individual ribs and short lengths. They are easier both to cook and eat this way. Rub them with garlic, ginger and salt. Heat oil in a wok and stir fry for 5 or 6 minutes over high heat until ribs are browned. Combine all the other ingredients and pour over the ribs. Bring to the boil, then reduce heat to simmer, cover pan and cook until meat on ribs is very tender and liquid reduced. Uncover, stir in honey or sugar until dissolved. Serve hot. Ribs can be roasted in a preheated moderately hot oven for a few minutes until further glazed and browned.

LAPIS DAGING SEMARANG
SEMARANG-STYLE SLICED BEEF

Serves: 4

500 g (1 lb) lean steak
1 onion, roughly chopped
4 cloves garlic
1 teaspoon coarsely ground black pepper
3 tablespoons dark soy sauce
2 tablespoons palm sugar or substitute
2 tablespoons peanut oil
2 ripe tomatoes, chopped

Use Scotch fillet, topside, rump or round steak for this dish, but buy it in one piece so that you can cut it into thin round slices. Beat out thinly with meat mallet, taking care not to break through the slices. Put onion, garlic, pepper, soy sauce and sugar into container of electric blender and blend until smooth. Marinate the meat in this mixture for 1 hour (longer in the refrigerator).

Heat oil in a wok or large frying pan, add meat slices drained of the marinade and fry over high heat until brown on both sides. Add remaining marinade and tomatoes and cook on medium heat, stirring frequently, until gravy is thick and smooth and the meat tender, about 12 minutes.

ABON DAGING
SHREDDED CRISP-FRIED MEAT

This will be a curious preparation to those not familiar with Asian foods, but is typical of the strongly flavoured dishes referred to colloquially as 'rice pullers'. The chief ingredient might be fish, prawns or, as in this case, meat. Thoroughly cooked and then fried until crisp, it can be bottled and kept for weeks to sprinkle over the bland rice and make a meal appetising. The first time I made abon I had spent the better part of an hour shredding the meat with a mallet when my eye fell on the electric blender, and I decided to try an easier way. I found that using slow speed, adding only 2 tablespoons of meat at a time, and blending for no more than 4 or 5 seconds, I was able to shred the meat effortlessly. If blended for longer the shreds will turn into meat paste, so be careful.

750 g (1½ lb) round or topside steak
2½ teaspoons salt
3 cloves garlic
1 teaspoon petis or Chinese shrimp paste
2 tablespoons tamarind liquid or lemon juice
½ teaspoon ground black pepper
1 teaspoon chilli powder, optional
2 teaspoons ground coriander
1 teaspoon ground cummin
½ cup peanut oil
4 dried chillies
4 tablespoons dried onion flakes
2 teaspoons dried minced garlic

Put meat in a large pan with enough water to cover, add 2 teaspoons salt and bring to the boil. Cover and simmer for 1½-2 hours or until meat is so tender it will pull apart with a spoon. Lift meat from stock (save stock for soup or sayur) and drain in a colander until dry and cool. Break up meat into small pieces and use a meat mallet to pound it to very fine shreds or use electric blender as described in lefthand column.

Crush garlic with remaining half teaspoon salt, dissolve the petis in the tamarind liquid, mix with pepper, chilli, coriander and cummin. Add to the meat and mix.

Heat peanut oil in a wok or frying pan and fry the whole chillies for a few seconds, drain on absorbent paper and cool. Put the onion flakes in a wire strainer and lower into the oil for a few seconds, just until they turn golden. Lift out and drain on absorbent paper. In the same wire strainer fry the dried garlic for 2 or 3 seconds. Turn on to paper to drain and cool.

Now add meat to the oil and fry, stirring constantly, until it is a rich brown, but do not overcook (over medium heat this should take 3 or 4 minutes). Drain and cool on absorbent paper.

Remove stems and seeds from chillies and crumble or chop the crisp pods. When meat is quite cold sprinkle with a little extra salt to taste and mix in chillies, onion and garlic. If liked, a teaspoon of sugar can be mixed in. Store in an airtight jar.

DAGING MASAK BALI
BALINESE-STYLE BEEF STRIPS

Serves: 6
750 g (1½ lb) blade steak
1 medium onion, roughly chopped
3 cloves garlic
1 tablespoon chopped fresh ginger
4-6 fresh red chillies, seeded
½ teaspoon dried shrimp paste (trasi)
3 tablespoons peanut oil
1 cup water
2 tablespoons tamarind liquid
2 tablespoons dark soy sauce
2 teaspoons palm sugar or substitute
salt to taste

Cut beef into thin strips. Put onion, garlic, ginger, chillies and trasi in blender container, cover and blend until smooth. Heat oil in a wok or saucepan and fry mixture, stirring constantly, for about 5 minutes or until it no longer sticks to the pan and the oil separates from the blended ingredients. Add beef strips and continue to stir and fry until they change colour. Add water, tamarind liquid and soy sauce, cover and simmer gently until beef is tender. Uncover and cook until liquid has almost evaporated. Stir in sugar and season to taste with salt. Serve with boiled rice, vegetables and sambals.

RENDANG
DRY MEAT CURRY

Serves: 8

1 kg (2 lb) beef or mutton
2 medium onions
2 cloves garlic
1 tablespoon chopped fresh ginger
3 tablespoons peanut oil
1 small stick cinnamon
4 or 5 whole cloves
3 teaspoons ground coriander
1 teaspoon ground cummin
1 teaspoon ground black pepper
1 teaspoon chilli powder, or to taste
½ teaspoon ground fennel
½ teaspoon ground kencur (aromatic ginger)
3 tablespoons desiccated coconut, toasted
4 cups thin coconut milk
2 teaspoons salt
¼ cup tamarind liquid
1 cup thick coconut milk

Cut meat into large cubes. Finely slice one onion and set aside. Roughly chop the other onion and put into container of electric blender with garlic and ginger. (If blender is not available, finely grate the onion, garlic and ginger). Blend to a smooth purée, adding 2 tablespoons of thin coconut milk if necessary. Put meat into a bowl, mix well with ground ingredients and set aside.

In a large saucepan heat the oil and fry sliced onion and whole spices, stirring occasionally, until onion is soft and starts to turn golden. Add meat and fry until meat changes colour. Add ground spices, coconut, thin coconut milk and salt. Stir while bringing to the boil and continue stirring for about 10 minutes. Simmer uncovered until meat is almost tender. Add tamarind liquid, stir well and simmer until liquid is almost dry. Add thick coconut milk, stirring constantly, and allow to simmer again until oil separates from gravy and curry is very dry.

RENDANG DAGING
DRY-FRIED BEEF CURRY *(picture opposite)*

It is worth making a large quantity of this because it keeps so well, developing more flavour each day.

Serves: 8

1.5 kg (3 lb) chuck, blade or round steak
2 medium onions, roughly chopped
6 cloves garlic
1 tablespoon chopped fresh ginger
6 fresh red chillies, seeded
2 cups thick coconut milk
1½ teaspoons salt
1 teaspoon ground turmeric
3 teaspoons chilli powder, optional
2 teaspoons ground coriander
2 daun salam or 6 curry leaves
1 stem fresh lemon grass
   or 3 strips thinly peeled lemon rind
1 teaspoon laos powder
½ cup tamarind liquid
2 teaspoons sugar

Cut beef into strips about 2.5 cm (1 inch) wide and 5 cm (2 inches) long.

Put onion, garlic, ginger and chillies in blender container with half cup of coconut milk. Cover and blend until smooth. Pour into a large saucepan and wash out blender with remaining coconut milk. Add to saucepan with all remaining ingredients except tamarind liquid and sugar. Mix well, add meat and bring quickly to the boil.

Reduce heat to moderate, add tamarind liquid and cook uncovered, until gravy is thick, stirring occasionally. Turn heat to low and continue cooking until gravy is almost dry, stirring frequently to ensure mixture does not stick to pan. At end of cooking time, approximately 2½ hours, when oil separates from the gravy, add sugar and stir constantly. Allow meat to fry in the oily gravy until it is dark brown. Serve with white rice, one or two vegetable dishes, sambals and prawn crisps.

Clockwise from top: **RENDANG DAGING** *recipe above.* **SAYUR LODEH** (vegetables in coconut gravy), *page 198,* **KRUPUK UDANG** (shrimp wafers) *page 209,* **SAMBAL BAJAK** (fried chilli sambal), *page 206.* **SAMBAL BUNCIS** (green bean sambal) *page 205.*

DENDENG RAGI
DRY-FRIED MEAT AND COCONUT

Serves: 6
500 g (1 lb) topside or round steak
1 cup desiccated coconut
1 onion, grated
2 cloves garlic, crushed
1½ teaspoons salt
1 teaspoon ground black pepper
3 teaspoons ground coriander
1 teaspoon ground cummin
1 teaspoon sambal ulek or 2 fresh red
    chillies, finely chopped
½ cup tamarind liquid
¼ cup water
2 teaspoons palm sugar or substitute
⅓ cup peanut oil

Trim meat of all fat and slice into very thin strips. Combine remaining ingredients, except oil, in a medium saucepan. Add meat and mix. Cook slowly over low heat with lid on pan until meat changes colour. Uncover and stir occasionally. As mixture dries, cook uncovered, stirring until all liquid is absorbed. Take care that coconut does not stick to pan.

Heat oil in a wok or frying pan and fry the mixture, stirring, until dark brown and crisp. Drain on absorbent paper if very oily, but in most cases at end of cooking there is no excess oil. Serve as an accompaniment with rice and vegetable dishes.

DENDENG
DRIED SPICED MEAT

Prepared this way, meat can be kept for a long while without spoiling. Use raw meat or remember this recipe when you've roasted a big piece of meat and it has been disappointing and tough. This is a good way to use it up. Dendeng may be served as an accompaniment to a meal of rice, vegetables and sambal.

1 kg (2 lb) round or topside steak
5 tablespoons peanut oil
2 cloves garlic, crushed
½ teaspoon finely grated ginger
2 teaspoons ground coriander
1 teaspoon ground cummin
1 teaspoon petis or dried shrimp paste
    (trasi)
1½ teaspoons salt
1 teaspoon sambal ulek
6 tablespoons dark soy sauce
2 tablespoons tamarind liquid
3 teaspoons palm sugar or substitute

Cut steak into slices about 5 cm (2 inches). Heat oil in a large saucepan and fry the garlic, ginger, coriander, cummin and petis or trasi for a minute or two, then add salt, sambal ulek, soy sauce and tamarind liquid. Add meat and fry, stirring, until meat is coated with spice mixture. Reduce heat, cover pan and let cook over very low heat for 30-35 minutes. Stir occasionally. At the end of this time the liquid should be almost dry. Uncover, add sugar and stir to dissolve. Turn the meat in this mixture over medium heat until liquid in pan has evaporated, but do not let it burn. Remove pan from heat and spread the meat in an oven dish in a single layer. Put into a low oven 125°C (250°F) for 30 minutes. Turn pieces of meat and continue cooking in the oven for a further 20-30 minutes. Meat should be very dark brown but not burnt, and the oil should come out from the meat and be visible at the edge of the pan. Cool and store airtight.

RENDANG GINJAL
DRY-FRIED KIDNEY CURRY

Serves: 6
750 g (1½ lb) ox kidney
1 teaspoon finely grated fresh ginger
2 cloves garlic, crushed
1 teaspoon salt
3 tablespoons peanut oil
2 onions, finely chopped or sliced
1 teaspoon ground turmeric
2 teaspoons ground coriander
1 teaspoon ground cummin
½ teaspoon ground fennel
½ teaspoon ground black pepper
1 teaspoon chilli powder or 2 fresh red
    chillies, seeded and chopped
3 kemiri nuts, finely grated
2 cups coconut milk
1 small stick cinnamon
2 tablespoons tamarind liquid
2 teaspoons palm sugar or substitute

Wash kidneys, remove and discard core. Cut kidneys into small dice. Rub with ginger and garlic crushed with salt and set aside.

Heat oil and fry onions until they are soft and start to colour, stirring frequently. Add turmeric, coriander, cummin, fennel and pepper and stir fry for 1 minute. Add chillies, kemiri nuts and kidneys, continue to fry, stirring constantly, until kidneys change colour. Add coconut milk and cinnamon and simmer gently, uncovered, until gravy is thick and reduced. This will take almost 2 hours of gentle simmering. Stir occasionally during simmering period. As mixture thickens it will be necessary to stir more frequently. Add tamarind liquid and sugar, stir and cook for a few minutes longer. Serve hot.

PERGEDEL GORENG JAWA
JAVANESE-STYLE FRIED MEATBALLS

*Freely adapted from Dutch frikkadels, with
hot chillies and spices giving a local flavour.
Serve hot as a snack or cold as picnic fare.*

Makes about 60-70 meatballs
500 g (1 lb) finely minced lean beef
2 medium onions, finely chopped
2 cloves garlic
1 teaspoon salt
2 fresh red chillies or 1 teaspoon sambal
    ulek
500 g (1 lb) floury potatoes
1 tablespoon dark soy sauce
1 tablespoon lemon juice
2 teaspoons palm sugar or substitute
½ teaspoon dried shrimp paste (trasi)
3 teaspoons ground coriander
2 teaspoons ground cummin
1 teaspoon ground nutmeg or mace
1 egg, beaten
peanut oil for frying

Put minced beef into a large bowl. Add onions, garlic crushed with salt, and the chillies, which have been seeded and chopped very finely or, preferably, pounded to a paste with mortar and pestle. Boil the potatoes, drain well, and dry them off in the pan before mashing until smooth. Add to the bowl. In the soy and lemon juice dissolve the brown sugar and trasi and mix in the coriander, cummin and nutmeg. Pour over the ingredients in bowl together with the beaten egg. Mix very thoroughly with the hand and shape into small meatballs. Allow to stand for an hour.

Heat sufficient oil in a wok or frying pan to deep fry the balls. Add no more than 6-8 at a time to the hot oil and fry on medium heat until brown. This should take only 3 or 4 minutes. Drain on absorbent paper.

REMPAH-REMPAH
MEAT AND COCONUT PATTIES *(picture opposite)*

Yields 30 flat hamburger shapes or 60 small balls

250 g (8 oz) desiccated coconut
6-7 tablespoons hot water
500 g (1 lb) finely minced beef
½ teaspoon dried shrimp paste (trasi)
2 cloves garlic
1½ teaspoons salt
½ teaspoon ground black pepper
1½ teaspoons ground coriander
1 teaspoon ground cummin
½ teaspoon ground kencur (aromatic ginger)
2 eggs, beaten
peanut oil for deep frying

Put coconut into a bowl and sprinkle hot water over. Mix well until all the coconut is moistened. Put into a large bowl with the minced beef. Crush trasi with back of spoon and dissolve in a tablespoon of hot water. Crush garlic and salt to a smooth paste. Add all the spices, the garlic and trasi to the beaten eggs and mix well. Pour over the meat and coconut in the bowl. Mix and knead well with the hands so that spices are evenly distributed and mixture becomes smooth. Shape into small hamburger shapes or into small balls. Shallow fry the hamburger shapes, or deep fry the balls, until they are crisp and golden brown all over. Drain on paper and serve as an accompaniment to a rice dish or as a snack by themselves. Serve cold at picnics. The balls, made small enough, are ideal to serve with drinks.

SEMUR DAGING
BEEF COOKED IN SOY SAUCE

Spicy, sweet and salty all at the same time, this simple recipe will be a favourite with children as well as adults.

Serves: 4-6

500 g (1 lb) chuck or round steak
2 tablespoons peanut oil
1 large onion, finely chopped
2 cloves garlic, crushed
½ teaspoon salt
1 teaspoon finely grated fresh ginger
½ teaspoon coarsely ground black pepper
¼ teaspoon each ground cardamom, cinnamon and nutmeg
⅛ teaspoon ground cloves
3 tablespoons dark soy sauce
1 tablespoon palm sugar or substitute
2 tablespoons tamarind liquid
1 cup hot water

Cut meat into small cubes. Heat oil in a saucepan and fry onion until soft and transparent. Add garlic, crushed with salt, and ginger and fry again, stirring until onions start to colour. Add meat and fry, stirring, until it loses its redness. Add spices, soy sauce, sugar, tamarind liquid and water. Bring to the boil, lower heat, cover and simmer until meat is tender and gravy reduced. Uncover after 1¼ hours to help reduce the liquid. Serve with white rice and vegetables.

EMPAL JAWA
BEEF IN SOY SAUCE AND CHILLIES

Serves: 6
500 g (1 lb) topside, round or rump steak
3 tablespoons peanut oil
1 onion, finely chopped
3 cloves garlic, crushed
1 ½ teaspoons sambal ulek or 2 fresh red
   chillies, seeded and finely chopped
½ teaspoon dried shrimp paste (trasi)
½ teaspoon laos powder
1 teaspoon finely chopped lemon rind or
   ½ teaspoon sereh powder
2 tablespoons dark soy sauce
¼ cup stock
1 teaspoon palm sugar or substitute

Put the meat, trimmed of all fat, into a medium saucepan with just enough water to cover. Bring to the boil, then simmer for 15 minutes. Allow meat to cool to lukewarm in the stock. When cool enough to handle, slice meat into thin strips. Heat peanut oil in a wok or frying pan and fry onions over low heat until soft and transparent. When starting to turn golden add garlic, chillies, trasi, laos and lemon rind. Crush trasi in the pan with the back of a wooden spoon and stir fry for a minute. Add beef and stir fry for about 3 or 4 minutes on medium heat. Add soy sauce, stock and sugar, stir and continue to cook on low heat until liquid has almost evaporated and oil separates from the rest of the gravy. The oil should have a reddish colour from the chillies. Serve hot with boiled rice and vegetable dishes.

ASAM BABI GORENG
FRIED TAMARIND PORK (BALI)

Serves: 4-6
500 g (1 lb) pork spareribs
1 onion, roughly chopped
2 cloves garlic
2 teaspoons chopped fresh ginger
2 tablespoons dark soy sauce
1 teaspoon sambal ulek or 2 fresh red
   chillies, seeded
1 tablespoon oil
4 tablespoons tamarind liquid
½ teaspoon salt
2 teaspoons palm sugar or substitute

Chop spareribs into short lengths, about 5 cm (2 inches). Put onion, garlic, ginger, soy sauce, and sambal or chillies into container of electric blender and blend for a few seconds until smooth. Heat oil in wok or frying pan and stir fry pork over high heat until brown all over. Pour off excess fat. Add blended mixture, stir fry for 4 or 5 minutes over medium heat. Add tamarind liquid, salt and about quarter cup hot water, reduce heat, cover and simmer 25-30 minutes. Add sugar and cook uncovered, stirring, until gravy is dark and almost dry. Serve hot.

SATÉ KAMBING MADURA
MADURESE-STYLE LAMB SATAY

Serves: 4-6
500 g (1 lb) boneless lamb from leg
1 small onion, grated
2 cloves garlic, crushed
½ teaspoon salt
1 teaspoon sambal ulek, or 2 fresh red
   chillies, seeded and crushed
½ teaspoon dried shrimp paste (trasi)
1 tablespoon tamarind liquid
1 tablespoon dark soy sauce
2 tablespoons fresh grated or desiccated
   coconut

Cut lamb into small cubes. Combine grated onion with all other ingredients. If using desiccated coconut, moisten with a tablespoon of hot water. Mix marinade well into the meat, cover and leave at room temperature for 2 hours or longer in refrigerator. Thread on bamboo skewers. Grill, turning frequently and taking care that the coconut does not burn. Serve with rice and satay sauce (page 197).

SATÉ MANIS
SWEET SATAY

Serves: 4-6

750 g (1½ lb) fillet or rump steak, or
    pork fillet
1 tablespoon palm sugar or substitute
1 clove garlic, crushed
½ teaspoon salt
2 tablespoons dark soy sauce
1 tablespoon oil
1 teaspoon ground cummin

Satay Sauce:
½ cup peanut sauce (page 207)
2 tablespoons tamarind liquid or lemon
    juice
2 teaspoons sambal bajak (page 206)
3-4 tablespoons water

Cut beef or pork into 2 cm (¾ inch) cubes. Thread 4-5 cubes on each bamboo skewer, not pushing them too close together. If skewers have been soaked in cold water for an hour or so beforehand, it prevents them burning when satay is cooked. Combine sugar with garlic, salt, soy sauce, oil and cummin. Stir until sugar dissolves. Pour into a long shallow dish and put satay in the marinade, turning each one so the marinade coats the meat. Cover and refrigerate for a few hours.

Cook over glowing coals or under a hot grill for approximately 15 minutes, not too close to the source of heat for pork must be well done; even beef is always well cooked, never rare, in satay. Turn skewers every 5 minutes, and brush with marinade. Serve hot accompanied with satay sauce.

Satay Sauce: Combine all ingredients and serve in a bowl. The sauce is spooned over the satay before eating.

SATÉ BUMBU
SPICY SATAY

Serves: 4-5

500 g (1 lb) lean steak, topside, round or
    blade
2 tablespoons dark soy sauce
2 tablespoons tamarind liquid
1 medium onion, roughly chopped
2 cloves garlic
½ teaspoon laos powder
½ teaspoon sambal ulek
½ teaspoon ground black pepper
½ teaspoon dried shrimp paste (trasi)
2 tablespoons peanut oil
½ cup coconut milk
1 daun salam or 3 curry leaves
1 stalk lemon grass or 2 strips lemon rind
2 teaspoons palm sugar or substitute

Trim meat and cut into long strips 2-2.5 cm (¾-1 inch) wide and about 6 mm (¼ inch) in thickness. Put soy sauce, tamarind liquid, onion and garlic into container of electric blender and blend to a smooth paste. (If blender is not available, finely grate onion and garlic, then mix with the liquid.) Mix in laos, sambal ulek, pepper, and crushed trasi. Heat peanut oil in a wok or frying pan and fry the blended mixture, stirring constantly until it turns brown and comes away from sides of pan. Add meat and fry, stirring, for a minute or so, until meat changes colour. Add coconut milk, curry leaves, lemon grass and sugar. Stir, reduce heat and simmer uncovered until sauce is very thick and almost dry.

Thread the meat on bamboo skewers, one strip to each skewer, looping it like a ruffled ribbon. Keep meat at pointed end of skewer, leaving the rest of the skewer for holding. It may be wise to wrap strips of foil around exposed end of skewer. Grill over hot coals or under preheated griller until lightly touched with brown. If there is any leftover sauce in pan, spoon it over the satay to serve.

SATÉ BABI
PORK SATAY

Soak bamboo skewers in water for a few hours before threading meat on them for grilling. This helps prevent the ends of the skewers burning.

Serves: 6

1 kg (2 lb) pork fillet or boned pork loin
1 medium onion, roughly chopped
1 clove garlic
1 teaspoon chopped fresh ginger
3 tablespoons tamarind liquid or lemon juice
2 tablespoons dark soy sauce
1 teaspoon sambal ulek or 2 fresh red chillies, seeded and chopped
½ teaspoon salt
1 teaspoon palm sugar or substitute
2 tablespoons peanut oil

Ask butcher to remove rind from pork loin. Cut pork into small cubes about 2 cm (¾ inch) square. Put onion, garlic, ginger, tamarind liquid, soy sauce, sambal ulek or chillies, salt and sugar into blender container and blend until smooth. Pour into a bowl, stir in oil, then add cubed pork and stir until all the pieces are well coated with marinade. Leave for at least 1 hour or longer in the refrigerator. Thread on skewers 5 or 6 pieces, not pushed too close together and leaving a few inches on end of skewer for holding. Leaving space between pieces enables them to cook more evenly, and pork *must* be well cooked. Grill over glowing coals or under preheated griller for 6 or 7 minutes on each side, or until pork is well cooked through and brown on all sides. Do not put too close to source of heat or outside will be brown before pork is cooked through.

SAYUR LODEH
VEGETABLES IN COCONUT GRAVY *(picture opposite)*

Any vegetables in season can be used. French beans, cabbage, cauliflower, broccoli, zucchini, pumpkin and winter bamboo shoots are an excellent combination.

Serves: 6
500-750 g (1-1½ lb) vegetables
2 tablespoons peanut oil
1 onion, finely chopped
2 cloves garlic, crushed
1 teaspoon sambal ulek, or 1 fresh red chilli, seeded and chopped
1 teaspoon trasi (dried shrimp paste)
1 stalk lemon grass, or 2 strips lemon rind, or ½ teaspoon sereh powder
1 large ripe tomato
2 cups vegetable, chicken or beef stock
1½ cups coconut milk
3 teaspoons peanut sauce or peanut butter
2 teaspoons salt, or to taste

Slice vegetables into small pieces: cauliflower or broccoli should be broken or cut into flowerets; beans sliced very thinly; cabbage shredded coarsely and the shreds cut across once or twice — if they are too long it makes the dish awkward to eat; zucchini or pumpkin can be sliced thinly or diced; winter bamboo shoots, much more tender than the ordinary variety, are cut into short strips, or can be halved and sliced for a half-moon shape.

Heat oil in a medium saucepan and fry the onion until soft and starting to colour, then add garlic, sambal and trasi and fry over low heat for 2 minutes, crushing the trasi with the back of the spoon and stirring the mixture. Add lemon grass or substitute and the tomato which has been peeled, seeded and chopped. Stir and cook to a pulp.

Add stock and coconut milk and bring to simmering point with lid off. Add vegetables according to the time they take to cook. They should be tender but still crisp. In the selection suggested you would add the beans, simmer for 4 minutes, then add the cauliflower and broccoli, simmer for a further 3 minutes, then add the cabbage, zucchini, pumpkin and bamboo shoots and cook for 3 minutes longer. Stir in the peanut sauce and add salt to taste. A squeeze of lemon juice may be added if a sharper flavour is preferred.

Ingredients for SAYUR LODEH (vegetables in coconut gravy) *recipe above*

GULAI MANIS KANGKUNG
WATERCRESS IN SWEET GRAVY

Kangkung is a dark green leaf used in Asian countries and highly prized for its vitamin value. Substitute watercress, spinach or chicory. Although chicory is bitter, this preparation contains sugar, and the resulting bitter-sweet combination is fascinating.

Serves: 6
500 g (1 lb) kangkung or substitute
4 tablespoons dehydrated shrimps
1½ cups coconut milk
1 large onion, finely chopped
1 small clove garlic, crushed
1 teaspoon salt
1 teaspoon finely grated fresh ginger
1 fresh red chilli, seeded and sliced
2 tablespoons palm sugar or substitute
½ teaspoon laos powder

Wash the greens very well in several changes of cold water and drain. Slice coarsely. Pour half cup hot water over shrimps and soak 5 minutes. If using the brownish dried shrimps instead of the white dehydrated shrimps, they will need longer soaking, about 25 minutes. Put coconut milk and all other ingredients into a large saucepan and bring to the boil, uncovered. Add soaked shrimps, the water in which they soaked, and the green vegetable. Cover and simmer on low heat for 20 minutes or until tender. Serve hot with rice and other dishes.

PECAL TERUNG
EGGPLANT PETJAL

Serves: 6
2 large firm eggplants
1½ tablespoons peanut oil
5 kemiri nuts
1 teaspoon dried shrimp paste (trasi)
½ teaspoon laos powder
½ teaspoon sambal ulek
1 tablespoon tamarind liquid
1 tablespoon dark soy sauce
1 teaspoon palm sugar or substitute
½ cup thick coconut milk

Peel the eggplant and cut into cubes. Drop into lightly salted boiling water or cook over steam until tender. Drain well. Heat oil in a wok or small frying pan and fry the kemiri nuts and trasi over low heat, stirring constantly and crushing the trasi into the oil. Add laos, sambal ulek, tamarind liquid, soy sauce, sugar and coconut milk. Simmer gently, pour over eggplant before serving.

SAYUR KOL
SPICY CABBAGE IN COCONUT MILK

500 g (1 lb) cabbage
2 onions, chopped
2 cloves garlic
2 fresh red chillies, seeded and chopped,
   or 1 teaspoon chilli powder
1 teaspoon dried shrimp paste (trasi)
1 daun salam or 3 curry leaves
2 tablespoons peanut oil
2 strips lemon rind
1½ cups thick coconut milk
1 teaspoon salt
3 tablespoons tamarind liquid

Wash and coarsely shred the cabbage. Put chopped onions, garlic, and chillies into container of electric blender and blend to a purée. Or grate onions and garlic, and chop chillies finely or substitute chilli powder. Wrap the trasi in a piece of foil and roast under the griller for 5 minutes, turning halfway through. In a wok or large saucepan fry the leaves in hot oil for 1 minute, turn in the blended mixture and the trasi and fry, stirring, until the mixture turns a darker colour. Stir constantly or mixture might stick to base of pan. Add lemon rind, coconut milk and salt, stir well while bringing to simmering point. Add the cabbage and simmer, uncovered, for a few minutes until the cabbage is cooked but still crisp. Stir in the tamarind liquid and serve.

SAYUR TUMIS
STIR-FRIED VEGETABLES

Use any kind of vegetable, or a mixture of different vegetables — coarsely shredded cabbage, watercress broken into bite-size lengths, chokos peeled and sliced, beans sliced diagonally, bean sprouts, sliced celery, and so on.

3 cups prepared vegetable
2 tablespoons vegetable oil
1 clove garlic, crushed
1 small onion, finely chopped
2 daun salam or curry leaves
¼ teaspoon dried shrimp paste (trasi)
½ teaspoon salt, or to taste
1 tablespoon light soy sauce, or to taste

Vegetables should be washed and well drained. Heat oil in a wok or large frying pan and fry the garlic, onion, curry leaves and trasi over medium heat, stirring constantly, until onion is soft. Crush trasi with spoon. Add vegetables and stir fry until lightly cooked but still crisp. If using a mixture of vegetables, add first those that take longest to cook. Add salt and soy sauce to taste and serve immediately.

SAYUR BUNCIS
BEAN SAYUR

Serves: 6
2 tablespoons peanut oil
1 onion, finely chopped
2 cloves garlic, crushed
2 fresh red chillies, seeded and chopped
1 teaspoon dried shrimp paste (trasi)
1 teaspoon finely grated lemon rind
2 teaspoons ground coriander
1 teaspoon ground cummin
½ teaspoon laos powder
1 teaspoon salt
2 tablespoons tamarind liquid or lemon
   juice
1 daun salam or 3 curry leaves
3 cups chicken stock
500 g (1 lb) fresh green beans, sliced
1 cooked chicken breast, skinned, boned
   and diced
1½ cups coconut milk

Heat oil, fry onion, garlic, chillies and trasi for 5 minutes over medium heat, stirring and crushing trasi with back of spoon. Add lemon rind and ground spices, fry 1 minute. Add salt, tamarind liquid, daun salam or curry leaves, stock and beans. Bring to the boil, simmer for 8 minutes. Add chicken and coconut milk. Simmer 5 minutes and serve.
Note: Rice vermicelli can be added to this sayur when it is the main dish. Soak 125 g (4 oz) of rice vermicelli in very hot water for 10 minutes, and drain well. Add to sayur and cook for further 2 minutes.

SAYUR KARI
VEGETABLE COOKED IN COCONUT MILK WITH CURRY SPICES *(picture opposite)*

Serves: 6

2 tablespoons peanut oil
2 medium onions, finely chopped
2 fresh red chillies, seeded and sliced
4 cloves garlic, finely chopped
2 teaspoons finely grated fresh ginger
2 teaspoons ground coriander
1 teaspoon ground cummin
1 teaspoon ground turmeric
1 teaspoon ground black pepper
½ teaspoon laos powder
2 stalks lemon grass or 1 teaspoon finely
　chopped lemon rind
½ teaspoon dried shrimp paste (trasi)
125 g (4 oz) finely diced beef
4 cups beef stock
2 cups thick coconut milk
2½ teaspoons salt
2 daun salam, optional
2 large potatoes, peeled and diced
250 g (8 oz) green beans, finely sliced
500 g (1 lb) cabbage, coarsely shredded
125 g (4 oz) rice vermicelli, soaked in hot
　water
lemon juice to taste

Heat peanut oil in a large saucepan and fry the onions and chillies, stirring occasionally, over medium heat until onions are soft and start to colour, about 4 or 5 minutes. Add the garlic and ginger and fry for 1 minute, stirring, then add all the ground spices, the lemon grass and trasi and fry for a further minute, stirring constantly. Add the diced beef and fry, stirring for 3 or 4 minutes or until the beef changes colour. Add stock and coconut milk, salt and daun salam and bring slowly to the boil, stirring occasionally. Add potatoes and simmer 10 minutes, uncovered, then add beans and simmer 5 minutes. At no stage must the sayur be covered. Add cabbage, return to the boil, then add soaked and drained vermicelli and simmer 2 or 3 minutes. Turn off heat, add lemon juice to taste and serve immediately.

GADO-GADO
VEGETABLES WITH PEANUT SAUCE

Serves: 6-8

3 large potatoes, boiled
250 g (8 oz) fresh bean sprouts
500 g (1 lb) green beans
3 carrots
½ small cabbage
1 green cucumber
small bunch watercress
3 hard-boiled eggs
peanut sauce (page 207)

Peel potatoes and cut in slices. Wash bean sprouts, pinching off any brown 'tails'. Pour boiling water over bean sprouts, then rinse under cold tap. Drain. String beans and cut in diagonal slices or bite-size lengths and cook in lightly salted boiling water until just tender. Beans should still be crisp to bite. Scrub carrots and cut into thin strips, cook until tender. Drain. Slice cabbage, discarding tough centre stem. Blanch in boiling salted water for a minute or two, until tender but not limp. Drain and refresh under cold water. Score skin of cucumber with a fork and cut into very thin slices. Wash watercress and break into sprigs, discarding tough stalks. Chill until crisp.

　Put watercress on a large platter and arrange the various vegetables in separate sections on top. Surround with slices of cucumber and put wedges of hard-boiled egg in centre. Serve cold, accompanied by peanut sauce, which is spooned over individual servings.

TAHU GORENG KACANG
FRIED BEAN CURD WITH PEANUTS

Serves: 4

5 cakes hard yellow bean curd

peanut oil for frying

½ cup raw peanuts

1 large clove garlic, crushed

½ teaspoon dried shrimp paste (trasi)

½ cup crushed roasted peanuts, or crunchy
   peanut butter

2 tablespoons dark soy sauce

3 tablespoons tamarind liquid

½ teaspoon sambal ulek

1 teaspoon palm sugar or substitute

½ cup coconut milk

1 cup shredded cabbage

1 cup fresh bean sprouts

4 spring onions, finely sliced, to garnish

Wipe bean curd thoroughly on paper towels. Cut squares of bean curd into 9 dice each. Heat peanut oil in a wok or frying pan and fry the bean curd, taking care not to stir or break the dice, until they are golden brown on all sides. Drain on absorbent paper. In the same oil fry peanuts for 3 or 4 minutes, drain, rub off skins. Set aside.

Make the sauce by pouring off all but a tablespoon of oil and frying the garlic and trasi over low heat, stirring constantly and crushing the trasi with back of spoon. Add crushed peanuts, soy sauce, tamarind liquid, sambal and sugar. Stir until well mixed. Remove from heat. Gradually add the coconut milk until sauce is of a thick pouring consistency.

Put bean curd on a dish, cover with the shredded cabbage and then with the bean sprouts. Spoon sauce over and garnish with spring onions and fried peanuts.

TAHU GORENG KECAP
FRIED BEAN CURD WITH SOY SAUCE

Serves: 6

4 cakes hard yellow bean curd

oil for deep frying

125 g (4 oz) fresh bean sprouts

4 spring onions, finely sliced

¼ cup dark soy sauce

1 tablespoon palm sugar or substitute

1 onion, roughly chopped

1 teaspoon sambal ulek, or 1 fresh chilli,
   seeded and chopped

1 clove garlic

Wipe bean curd thoroughly on paper towels. Cut each cake of bean curd into 9 dice and deep fry in hot oil, taking care not to break the curd, until browned on all sides. Drain on paper, then arrange on dish. Spread washed and drained bean sprouts over, then garnish with the spring onions. Spoon over the sauce and serve.

Sauce: In container of electric blender put the soy sauce, sugar, onion, chilli or sambal and garlic. Blend until smooth. If a less pungent sauce is preferred, make one as in the recipe for bean curd omelettes (page 188).

PACARI
PINEAPPLE COCONUT CURRY

Serves: 6

1 small pineapple, not too ripe
1 tablespoon oil
1 small onion, finely chopped
1 clove garlic, finely chopped
small stick cinnamon
3 whole cloves
3 cardamom pods, bruised
3 teaspoons ground coriander
1½ teaspoons ground cummin
½ teaspoon chilli powder, or 1 fresh
    chilli, seeded and sliced
1 teaspoon salt
1 cup thick coconut milk
1 teaspoon palm sugar or substitute

Peel pineapple with a sharp knife and remove the eyes as shown on page 14. Cut pineapple in quarters lengthways and remove the hard core. Now cut each quarter in two lengthways, then into thick slices crossways. Heat oil in a saucepan and fry onion, garlic and whole spices over medium heat, stirring frequently, until onion is soft. Add coriander, cummin, chilli and salt and stir for a few minutes until spices are browned. Add pineapple and stir well to coat with the spice mixture. Add coconut milk and sugar and bring to simmering point, stirring constantly. Do not cover pan. Simmer for 3 or 4 minutes, or until pineapple is just tender. Fruit should not be too soft.

URAP
COOKED VEGETABLES WITH COCONUT

Serves: 4-6

250 g (8 oz) fresh green beans
4 carrots
250 g (8 oz) bean sprouts
½ small cabbage
1 canned bamboo shoot
1 cup fresh grated or desiccated coconut
2 tablespoons hot milk or water (if using
    desiccated coconut)
1 small onion, finely chopped
½ teaspoon sambal ulek or chilli powder
1 teaspoon salt
2 tablespoons lemon juice
½ teaspoon dried shrimp paste (trasi)

Prepare beans, carrots, bean sprouts and cabbage as for gado-gado (page 202). Cut bamboo shoot into strips the same size as the beans. Put the coconut into a bowl (if using desiccated coconut, sprinkle hot milk or water over and mix with the fingertips to moisten evenly). Add onion, sambal or chilli powder, salt, lemon juice and the trasi which has been wrapped in foil and grilled for 5 minutes, or heated in a dry frying pan. Mix thoroughly together. Sprinkle coconut mixture over vegetables, reserving some to garnish the dish when served. Put vegetables in a steamer and steam for 5-8 minutes. Turn on to serving dish and sprinkle with reserved coconut. Use as an accompaniment to a meal, or as a salad by itself.

SAMBAL BUNCIS
GREEN BEAN SAMBAL *(picture page 214)*

Serves: 6

250 g (8 oz) fresh green beans
1 tablespoon peanut oil
½ teaspoon instant minced garlic
½ teaspoon sambal ulek
½ teaspoon salt to taste
1 small onion, finely sliced

String beans and cut in very fine diagonal slices. Heat oil in a wok or frying pan and toss beans on high heat 2 minutes, add garlic and fry 1 minute more. Add sambal and salt and fry 1 minute longer. Beans should be tender but still crunchy crisp. Remove from heat, mix in the onion slices and serve as an accompaniment or 'side dish' to a rice and curry meal.

SAMBAL ULEK
HOT CHILLI PASTE

25 fresh red chillies
vinegar or tamarind liquid
2 teaspoons salt

Put the chillies, seeds and all, into container of electric blender. Add enough vinegar or tamarind liquid to keep the mass moving and blend to a paste. Add salt. Put into a sterilised bottle and store in the refrigerator.

SAMBAL BAJAK
FRIED CHILLI SAMBAL

Cooled, then stored in an airtight bottle, this sambal will keep for weeks in the refrigerator. When serving, use a teaspoon for portions and warn guests it should be eaten in tiny quantities with rice, not by itself. As a taste for this torrid sambal is acquired, however, it is enjoyed on crisp crackers, in sandwiches, on steaks — in fact there is no limit to the ways a sambal addict will use it.

Yields about 1 cup
6 large fresh red chillies, roughly chopped
1 large onion
6 cloves garlic
8 kemiri nuts, finely grated
3 tablespoons peanut oil
½ teaspoon laos powder
1 tablespoon dried shrimp paste (trasi)
1 teaspoon salt
5 tablespoons tamarind liquid
2 tablespoons palm sugar or substitute

Put chillies, onion and garlic in container of electric blender and blend to a pulp. If blender is small, blend in small portions. It might be necessary to stop and start the motor several times to draw the onions and chillies down on to the blades. When everything has been blended smoothly, heat the oil in a small frying pan or a saucepan and fry the blended mixture over low heat, stirring, for 5 minutes or until well cooked but not brown. Add kemiri nuts, laos, trasi and salt. Crush the trasi against the side of the pan and fry, stirring, until mixture is well blended. Add tamarind liquid and sugar, stir and simmer until well fried and reddish-brown in colour and the oil separates from the mixture. Cool. This sambal is not served hot from the fire.

Note: If electric blender is not available, seed the chillies and chop very finely. Peel and chop onion finely, crush garlic with salt, then proceed as above.

Sambal Bajak and Sambal Ulek (above) may be purchased ready made in some shops selling Asian ingredients.

BAWANG GORENG
FRIED ONION FLAKES

An important garnish as well as a flavouring for many Indonesian dishes.

The easiest way to make these is to use the dried onion flakes readily available. These cook in seconds, so put them on a wire strainer and lower them into deep oil that is hot but not too hot. They will take a few seconds to turn golden brown. Lift them out immediately and drain on absorbent paper. When cool, bottle airtight.

Using fresh onions it takes much longer. Slice the onions very thinly, making sure not only that the slices are paper-thin, but also that they are all the same thinness, otherwise some will burn while others are uncooked. Fry in deep hot oil until deep brown, but not black. Lift out, drain and bottle when cool. They must be cooked slowly so that all the moisture is cooked out.

SAUS KACANG (1)
CRUNCHY PEANUT SAUCE

There are many recipes for peanut sauce, but this is my favourite. Without the addition of liquid, it keeps for weeks in a bottle. When required, add 3 parts coconut milk (see page 11) or water to 1 part sauce and reheat. Try it without additional liquid as a sandwich spread, a relish with cold meats or grills, a savoury dip, or a topping for cocktail canapes.

7 tablespoons peanut oil
1 teaspoon dried garlic flakes or instant
    minced garlic
2 tablespoons dried onion flakes
2 large dried chillies
1 teaspoon dried shrimp paste (trasi)
1 tablespoon lemon juice
1 tablespoon dark soy sauce
375 g (12 oz) crunchy peanut butter
1½ tablespoons palm sugar or substitute

Heat oil in a small wok or frying pan and fry garlic flakes for a few seconds until golden (put them in a fine mesh wire strainer and lower them into oil that is not too hot, for they burn easily; the strainer enables them to be lifted out as soon as they change colour). Drain on absorbent paper. Fry onion flakes in the same way, again taking care that they do not burn. Drain and cool. Fry whole chillies until they are puffed and crisp, which should take less than a minute. Remove chillies from pan, drain and cool. Discard stalks and seeds and crumble or chop chillies into small pieces. Set aside with onion and garlic.

In oil remaining in pan, fry the trasi, crushing it with the back of the spoon. Add lemon juice and soy sauce. Remove from heat, add peanut butter and stir until well blended. Cool. When quite cold add crisp garlic and onion flakes, crumbled chillies and sugar. Mix thoroughly and put in a screw-top jar to store.

Use as is, or mix in enough coconut milk or water to make more liquid consistency. Add salt as required.

Note: Fresh garlic and onion can be used instead of dried garlic and onion flakes. Peel 6 garlic cloves and cut into thin slices. Peel and finely slice 1 medium-size onion. Fry separately over low heat, removing from heat as soon as they turn golden brown. Drain on absorbent paper and cool. Crumble the crisp garlic slices before adding to sauce.

SAUS KACANG (2)
MILD PEANUT SAUCE

Ideal for when you're in a hurry, this sauce can be mixed up in a few minutes. It is also good to serve when you're not sure of the spice tolerance of your guests.

6 tablespoons peanut butter (smooth or
    crunchy)
1 cup water
¾ teaspoon garlic salt
2 teaspoons palm sugar or substitute
2 tablespoons dark soy sauce
lemon juice to taste
½ teaspoon shrimp paste or anchovy
    essence, optional
coconut milk or water for thinning

Put peanut butter and water in a saucepan and stir over gentle heat until mixed. Remove from heat and add all other ingredients. It will be necessary to add some coconut milk or water to make the paste a thick, pouring consistency. After doing so, check seasonings and add more salt and lemon juice if needed.

SAUS KACANG PEDIS
HOT PEANUT SAUCE (QUICK METHOD)

¼ cup peanut oil
1 tablespoon dried onion flakes
1 clove garlic, crushed
¼ teaspoon dried shrimp paste (trasi)
4 fresh red chillies, seeded and chopped,
    or 2 teaspoons sambal ulek
4 tablespoons peanut butter
¾ cup water
½ teaspoon salt
1 tablespoon dark soy sauce
2 teaspoons palm sugar or substitute
1 tablespoon tamarind liquid or lemon juice

Heat oil in a wok or small frying pan and fry onion flakes briefly until they turn golden, remove from oil and drain on absorbent paper. Leave about 2 tablespoons oil in pan, fry the garlic, trasi and chillies for a minute on low heat, crushing the trasi with back of spoon. Add peanut butter and water and stir until blended. Remove from heat and add salt, soy sauce, sugar and tamarind. If necessary add more water to make it a thick pouring consistency. When cool stir in crumbled onion flakes. Serve at room temperature.

SERUNDENG (1)
CRISP SPICED COCONUT WITH PEANUTS *(picture page 214)*

1 cup desiccated coconut
1 small onion, very finely chopped
1 clove garlic, crushed
1 teaspoon finely grated fresh ginger
½ teaspoon dried shrimp paste (trasi)
2 tablespoons peanut oil
1 teaspoon ground coriander
1 teaspoon ground cummin
1 teaspoon salt
1 tablespoon tamarind liquid or lemon
    juice
1 cup roasted unsalted peanuts

In a bowl mix the coconut, onion, garlic and ginger. Heat peanut oil in a wok or frying pan and fry the trasi, crushing it with the frying spoon, for a minute or two on low heat. Add coconut mixture and fry on medium low heat, stirring constantly, until coconut is golden brown. Add coriander, cummin, salt, tamarind liquid or lemon juice and continue stirring and frying on very low heat until coconut is dry and crisp. This takes quite a while and cannot be hurried by raising the heat. Allow to cool, then mix in peanuts. Serve as an accompaniment to a rice meal, or use as a garnish to sprinkle over dishes.

SERUNDENG (2)
CRISP SPICED COCONUT WITH PEANUTS (QUICK METHOD)

½ cup desiccated coconut
½ teaspoon instant minced garlic
2 tablespoons dried onion flakes
½ teaspoon ground coriander
½ teaspoon ground cummin
½ teaspoon salt
½ cup roasted unsalted peanuts

In a dry frying pan stir the coconut over medium low heat until golden. Add dried garlic and onion flakes, crushing the onion flakes into small pieces first. Continue stirring the mixture over heat until the coconut is deep golden and the garlic and onion flakes are toasted too. Add coriander, cummin and salt, stir well, then remove from heat. Allow to cool and mix in the peanuts. This can be stored in a bottle for weeks.

PISANG GORENG
FRIED BANANAS *(picture page 214)*

These fried bananas are served as an accompaniment to rice and curries.

Serves: 6
6 medium or 3 large bananas, ripe but
  quite firm
oil for frying

Peel bananas. If large, cut in half crossways. Smaller bananas need only to be cut down the centre lengthways. Heat a little oil in a frying pan, put in the bananas and fry over medium high heat until brown all over. Turn bananas carefully, for they break easily when hot. Lift on to a small plate to serve, and sprinkle lightly with salt.

RUJAK BUAH-BUAH PEDIS
SPICY FRUIT SALAD *(picture page 210)*

Serves: 6-8
1 grapefruit or pomelo
1 orange or mandarin
2 tart green apples
1 cucumber
1 small pineapple
½ teaspoon dried shrimp paste (trasi)
½ teaspoon sambal ulek
1 tablespoon palm sugar or substitute
1 tablespoon dark soy sauce
2 tablespoons lemon juice

Peel grapefruit and orange with a sharp knife, removing peel and white pith. Cut in between membranes to release segments. Do this over a bowl, saving juices from fruit. Remove seeds. Peel and slice apples thinly. Peel and dice cucumber. Peel pineapple, remove core and dice flesh. Wrap the trasi in a piece of foil and roast for 5 minutes under griller, turning once. Dissolve trasi, sambal ulek and sugar in soy sauce and lemon juice, pour over fruit and mix well. Allow to stand for a few minutes before serving.

KRUPUK UDANG
PRAWN CRISPS or SHRIMP WAFERS *(picture page 214)*

These come in various shapes, sizes and colours, but the most flavoursome are the large, salmon-pink variety roughly as long as an average hand and half as wide. They cost more than other types, but more than compensate because of the distinct shrimp flavour.

Another popular variety comes in multi-colours and these are delightful for adding interest to a table and are a great favourite with children. Made from a starch base and ground shrimps, they need to be fried in deep hot oil to become light, crisp, crunchy and swell to more than double their original size.

Sometimes they become damp due to climatic conditions, and do not puff as they should when fried. It is a good precaution to dry them out in a low oven for 10-15 minutes, spread out in a single layer on a baking sheet. Let them cool, then store them really airtight. Or dry them out in the oven as required just before cooking.

Heat oil in a wok or deep frying pan and fry the larger wafers one at a time, spooning oil over them as they cook. The oil should be hot enough to make them swell within 2 or 3 seconds of being dropped in. Test with a small piece first. If oil is not the right temperature they will be tough and leathery, not crisp and melting. On the other hand if the oil is too hot they will brown too fast. A little practice will tell how hot the oil should be. Lift out with tongs or a slotted spoon and drain on absorbent paper. Cool thoroughly before storing airtight. The smaller wafers can be fried a few at a time, in the same way as the large ones.

KRUPUK EMPING
FRIED MELINJO NUT WAFERS

These flattened-out kernels of the melinjo nut are sold in packets, and need only a few seconds frying in deep hot oil.

Make sure the oil is hot but not too hot. If they brown they will taste bitter. Drop only a few into the oil at a time, spooning the oil over them as they cook, which should take less than a minute. Lift them out quickly on a slotted spoon and drain on absorbent paper. Sprinkle lightly with salt before serving as an accompaniment to a meal or as a nibble with drinks.

TELUR BERWARNA
MARBLED EGGS

The Southeast Asian love of bright colours is reflected in this favourite garnish for a festive meal. Employing the method used by the Chinese in their marbled tea eggs or soya sauce eggs, Indonesians give hard-boiled eggs a marbling of bright red, green or yellow.

6 eggs
water
salt
red, green and yellow food colouring

If eggs have been refrigerated, allow them to come to room temperature. Put them gently in a saucepan with enough cold, salted water to cover, and put them over gentle heat. Bring to simmering point, stirring gently during first 5 minutes with the handle of a wooden spoon. This is to ensure that the yolks are centred. When water bubbles gently cook eggs for about 7 minutes, then cool them under cold tap. Meanwhile, put water in 3 small saucepans and colour each either a deep red, green or yellow with food colouring. Bring to the boil.

On a hard surface gently tap the eggs to crack the shells all over, but do not remove any part of the shell. Put 2 eggs into each pan and simmer for a further 5 minutes, then turn off heat and allow eggs to stand in coloured water for at least 2 hours.

When shell is removed, there will be a bright marbling of colour on the whites of the eggs. Halve lengthways, and use as garnish for nasi kuning or other festive dishes.

TERUNG LODEH
PRAWN AND EGGPLANT SOUP

Serves: 4

1 tablespoon dried prawns or 125 g (4 oz) fresh prawns
2 tablespoons peanut oil
1 onion, finely chopped
2 cloves garlic, finely chopped
2 fresh red chillies, seeded and chopped
1 ripe tomato, peeled and chopped
2 daun salam
2 cups chicken stock (made with cubes)
1 medium eggplant
1 cup coconut milk
½ teaspoon brown sugar, optional
1 teaspoon salt, or to taste

Soak dried prawns in half cup hot water for 10 minutes. If using fresh prawns, shell and de-vein, then chop into small pieces.

Heat oil in a large saucepan and fry onion, garlic and chillies until onions are soft and start to turn golden. Add tomato and daun salam leaves and fry for 5 minutes, mashing the tomato to a pulp. Add stock, bring to the boil and simmer gently while peeling and dicing the eggplant. Add eggplant to pan and simmer for 10-15 minutes or until just tender. Add coconut milk, sugar and salt and stir while heating through. Taste and add more salt if necessary. Serve with rice and curries.

RUJAK BUAH-BUAH PEDIS (spicy fruit salad) *recipe page 209*

SOTO AYAM (1)
CHICKEN SOUP (DELICATE)

Serves: 6

1 chicken, about 1.5 kg (3 lb)
2 teaspoons salt
few whole peppercorns
1 stalk celery or few celery tops
1 small onion
2 slices fresh ginger, bruised
2 cloves garlic, bruised
60 g (2 oz) cellophane noodles
1½ cups fresh bean sprouts

Garnish:
2 hard-boiled eggs, chopped
2 or 3 spring onions, finely chopped

Joint chicken, put into a large saucepan with enough cold water to cover and add salt, peppercorns, celery, onion, ginger and garlic. Bring to the boil, then reduce heat, cover and simmer gently 35-45 minutes. Cool to lukewarm, strain. Remove skin and bones of chicken and cut flesh into small pieces.

While chicken is cooking soak cellophane noodles in hot water, drain and drop into boiling water for 8-10 minutes. Drain in colander and cut into short lengths. Add to strained broth together with chicken pieces. Taste and adjust seasoning.

Put bean sprouts into soup tureen and pour the boiling broth over. Garnish top with chopped eggs and spring onions and serve at once.

SOTO AYAM (2)
CHICKEN SOUP (VERY SPICY)

Serves: 6

1 chicken, about 1.5 kg (3 lb)
8 cups of cold water
3 teaspoons salt
½ teaspoon whole black peppercorns
few celery tops
2 onions
2 tablespoons peanut oil
2 fresh red chillies, seeded and chopped
2 daun salam or 6 curry leaves
2 cloves garlic, crushed
1 teaspoon finely grated fresh ginger
1 teaspoon dried shrimp paste (trasi)
1 teaspoon ground turmeric
1½ tablespoons ground coriander
2 teaspoons ground cummin
½ teaspoon ground fennel
½ teaspoon ground black pepper
½ teaspoon ground nutmeg
lemon juice to taste
2 small bundles egg noodles

Garnish:
3 hard boiled eggs, chopped
6 cloves garlic, sliced and fried
8 spring onions sliced
fried onion flakes
fried dried chillies
crumbled potato crisps
sambal bajak or sambal ulek

Cut chicken into joints and put into large saucepan with cold water. Water should be sufficient to cover chicken. Add salt, peppercorns, celery tops and one onion. Bring quickly to the boil, then reduce heat, cover and simmer for 35-40 minutes or until chicken is tender. Cool to lukewarm, then strain stock into a bowl.

Remove all bones and skin and cut chicken into small pieces. Set aside. Slice remaining onion finely. Heat peanut oil in large saucepan and fry the onion, chillies and daun salam until onion is soft and starts to turn brown. Add garlic, ginger, trasi and fry, crushing trasi with spoon. Add the ground spices and fry, stirring, for a few seconds longer. Add the strained stock and bring to the boil, then reduce heat, cover and simmer for 10 minutes. Add lemon juice.

Soak egg noodles in hot water and bring about 5 cups water to the boil in another saucepan. Drain the noodles and drop into the boiling water. Boil for 3 minutes, drain and add to soup, together with chicken meat. Ladle into soup tureen. Garnish with the chopped eggs, fried garlic, spring onions, fried onion flakes. Serve the dried chillies, potato crisps and sambal in separate bowls to be added to individual servings according to taste. Sambals should be added in very small amounts, no more than a quarter of a teaspoon at first, and only by those who know what to expect and like their soto fiery hot.

Note: To fry garlic, peel cloves and cut into slices of equal thickness. Fry in deep oil over low heat just until garlic turns pale golden. Remove from oil immediately and drain on absorbent paper. Do not let colour darken in oil or the garlic will have a bitter taste. If using dried onion flakes, they should be immersed in the oil for only a few seconds on a wire strainer, then lifted out and drained. Dry chillies too take only a few seconds to fry.

SUP KEMBANG KOL
CAULIFLOWER SOUP

Serves: 6
8 cups strong beef stock
¼ teaspoon ground black pepper
¼ teaspoon ground mace
2 teaspoons ground coriander
1 teaspoon ground cummin
1 onion, finely chopped
1 clove garlic, crushed
500 g (1 lb) cauliflower, coarsely chopped
2 small bundles fine egg noodles

If making the beef stock for the soup, add 3 or 4 whole cloves, 10 peppercorns, few blades of mace, a tablespoon of coriander seeds and half that amount of cummin seeds. This will eliminate the need for the ground spices. If, however, the stock is a by-product of something else and has not been cooked with whole spices, add all the *ground* spices listed above, the onion and garlic, and simmer for 10 minutes. Add the cauliflower and bring to the boil again. Simmer for 4 minutes. In the meantime soak the noodles in hot water for a few minutes, until the strands separate. Drain and add to the boiling soup. Return to the boil and cook for 3 minutes. Serve at once so that cauliflower and noodles do not overcook. Garnish with fried onion flakes if liked.

PERGEDEL JAGUNG
CORN FRITTERS

Makes: 12-14
375 g (12 oz) whole kernel corn (fresh, frozen or canned)
½ cup plain flour
½ cup ground rice
¼ teaspoon baking powder
½ teaspoon salt
1 teaspoon ground coriander
½ teaspoon ground cummin
¼ teaspoon laos powder, optional
½ teaspoon chilli powder, optional
1 medium onion
1 clove garlic
pinch salt
1 stalk celery
scant ½ cup water
1 egg, beaten
½ teaspoon dried shrimp paste (trasi), optional
squeeze of lemon juice
oil for frying

Cut corn from cobs with a sharp knife, drain canned corn or thaw frozen corn.

Sift into a bowl the flour, ground rice, baking powder, salt, coriander, cummin, laos and chilli powder.

Quarter the onion and cut into very thin slices. Crush the garlic to a smooth paste with a little salt. Chop celery into fine dice.

Mix together the water, beaten egg, trasi and lemon juice and add to the flour mixture, beating until smooth. Stir in the corn, onion, garlic and celery. Heat vegetable oil in a frying pan to a depth of 12 mm (half inch). When oil is hot drop mixture by large tablespoons into the oil, spreading it with the back of the spoon to make a circle about 7.5 cm (3 inches) across. Fry until underside of fritter is golden brown, then turn with tongs and fry other side. Lift out and drain on absorbent paper placed on a wire rack. This keeps the fritters crisp.

Note: Without the chilli powder and shrimp paste the fritters are milder in flavour, but if you like a little excitement in the flavouring, add them. If ground rice is difficult to obtain use plain flour, but ground rice adds crispness.

LEMPER
RICE ROLLS WITH SPICY FILLING

Wrapping food in banana leaves is a very popular method of cooking and serving in Southeast Asia. Where banana leaves are available, prepare them by stripping the leaves from the thick middle rib with a sharp knife. Leaves will be inclined to split, but this doesn't matter, for they will have to be cut into suitably sized pieces anyway. Wash the leaves to remove any dust, then pour boiling water over them. This makes them pliable enough to fold without splitting. Ti leaves or bamboo leaves (from Chinese stores) can be used instead of banana leaves, but heavy-duty aluminium foil does the job as efficiently even if not in so picturesque a manner. Ideal for picnics or buffet parties.

500 g (1 lb) ketan (glutinous rice)
2 cups water
1 cup thick coconut milk
250 g (8 oz) pork mince or finely chopped
    chicken
½ teaspoon salt
½ teaspoon ground black pepper
2 tablespoons oil
2 cloves garlic, crushed
2 daun salam or curry leaves
2 teaspoons ground coriander
1 teaspoon ground cummin
½ teaspoon ground turmeric
½ teaspoon dried shrimp paste (trasi)
squeeze of lemon juice
squares of banana leaf or aluminium foil

Wash rice and drain. Put into saucepan with water and bring to the boil, then turn heat very low, cover pan tightly and steam for 15 minutes. Mix three-quarter cup of the coconut milk with half cup water in a small saucepan and heat without boiling. Add to rice, stir gently with a fork, cover and steam for 5-10 minutes, until coconut milk has been absorbed. Leave to cool.

Season pork or chicken with salt and pepper. Heat oil in a wok or medium-size saucepan and fry the garlic and daun salam for 1 minute. Add ground spices and trasi and fry, stirring, for a minute longer, crushing the trasi with the spoon. Add pork or chicken and fry until the colour changes and it no longer looks raw. Add reserved quarter cup coconut milk and simmer, uncovered, on low heat until well cooked and quite dry. Add lemon juice to taste, check seasoning and add more salt and pepper if necessary. Cool.

To make lemper: Take a large tablespoonful of rice and flatten on a piece of banana leaf till 12 mm (half inch) thick. Put a good teaspoonful of the filling in the middle and mould the rice around it to a cylindrical shape. Roll up in the banana leaf and secure with wooden toothpicks, or roll in the foil to make a neat parcel. These parcels can be heated over a barbecue or steamed for 15 minutes, then allowed to cool once again. They are served at room temperature as a snack.

Accompaniments *(clockwise from top)*: PISANG GORENG (fried bananas) *recipe page 209* and SAMBAL BUNCIS (green bean sambal) *recipe page 205;* SERUNDENG (crisp spiced coconut with peanuts) *recipe page 208;* KRUPUK UDANG (prawn crisps) *recipe page 209;* and SAMBAL GORENG UDANG ASAM (piquant fried prawn sambal) *recipe page 179*

REMPEYEK KACANG
PEANUT WAFERS *(picture page 178)*

An accompaniment to rice and curries on festive occasions, these crisp and crunchy wafers are also delicious served by themselves as a snack or as an accompaniment to drinks. In this case, make them rather small.

½ cup rice flour
2 tablespoons ground rice
1 teaspoon ground coriander
½ teaspoon ground cummin
¼ teaspoon ground turmeric
⅛ teaspoon kencur powder (aromatic ginger), optional
¾ teaspoon salt
1 cup coconut milk
1 clove garlic, crushed
1 small onion, finely chopped
125 g (4 oz) roasted, unsalted peanuts
oil for frying

Sift all the dry ingredients into a bowl. Add the coconut milk and beat to a smooth thin batter, then stir in garlic, onion and peanuts. Make sure garlic is crushed to a paste and stir to distribute it well through the batter.

Heat enough oil in a frying pan to cover base of pan to a depth of 12 mm (half inch). Oil must be hot, but not to the point of smoking. Drop tablespoons of the batter into the oil. The batter should be thin enough to spread into a lacy wafer. If it holds together and has to be spread with the spoon, it is too thick, and must be thinned by adding a spoonful of coconut milk at a time until the correct consistency is obtained. Fry until golden brown on underside, then turn wafers and fry until golden on other side. Drain on absorbent paper over a wire rack to allow air to circulate. This will help them retain their crispness for a few hours. Cool and store in an airtight container.

Note: Raw peanuts are also used in this recipe, but I find that by the time the batter has fried to a golden crispness, the peanuts are still somewhat underdone for my taste. If raw peanuts are roasted in a moderate oven 30-35 minutes, and the skins rubbed off, they are suitable for use in this recipe. Roast a larger quantity than the amount called for here, and store them in an airtight tin for future use. Alternatively, buy just the small amount required.

REMPEYEK UDANG
PRAWN FRITTERS

Makes: 18-22
250 g (8 oz) shelled raw prawns
2 eggs, beaten
1 tablespoon water
1 tablespoon rice flour
2 tablespoons ground rice
1 small clove garlic, crushed
¾ teaspoon salt
¼ teaspoon ground black pepper
¼ teaspoon kencur powder (aromatic ginger)
¼ teaspoon sereh powder
1 fresh red chilli, seeded and sliced
1 small onion, quartered and sliced
peanut oil for deep frying

De-vein prawns and chop roughly. Combine eggs, water, rice flour, ground rice, garlic, seasonings and spices. Fold in the chilli, onion and prawns. Heat peanut oil and when very hot drop batter by half-tablespoons into the oil, 3 or 4 at a time. Fry over medium heat until golden on both sides, drain on absorbent paper and serve hot.

REMPEYEK KELAPA
COCONUT WAFERS

Proceed as for peanut wafers (above), but omit nuts and add instead three-quarter cup freshly grated or desiccated coconut.

PILUS
FRIED SWEET POTATO BALLS

500 g (1 lb) sweet potatoes
1 tablespoon palm sugar or substitute
1-2 tablespoons ground rice
oil for frying

Peel sweet potatoes, dropping them into cold water immediately to prevent discolouring. Cut into even-size pieces and boil until tender but not mushy. Drain well, dry off in the pan and mash until free of lumps. Mix in the sugar and enough ground rice to make the mixture firm enough to mould. Roll into small balls, the size of a large marble. Deep fry in hot oil over medium heat until deep golden brown all over. Serve plain or with sugar syrup and fresh grated coconut.

SPEKKOEK KUEH LAPIS
MANY-LAYERED SPICE CAKE

This fascinating cake is not difficult to make, but you do need patience for the special cooking method.

The layers, each hardly thicker than a wafer biscuit, are baked and then grilled one at a time. Be prepared to hover over the oven for a couple of hours—preferably when the weather is cold enough to make this a comfortable occupation!

Some people prefer a light textured cake, while others prefer a pudding-like texture which is richer and sweeter. If the former is to your taste use the recipe as printed. But if you prefer the sweeter, moist cake that most Indonesians consider the acme of their sweetmeats, then use only half a cup of flour and four egg whites instead of eight. The cake is served in very small, thin slices since it is so rich.

Makes: 1 x 20 cm (8 inch) round or square cake

10 egg yolks
1½ cups caster sugar
250 g (8 oz) butter
2 teaspoons vanilla
8 egg whites
1½ cups plain flour, sifted
1 teaspoon ground cinnamon
1 teaspoon ground nutmeg
1 teaspoon ground cardamom
½ teaspoon ground cloves
extra melted butter, optional

In electric mixer whisk the egg yolks with ½ cup sugar until thick and light. Cream butter with ¾ cup sugar and the vanilla essence until light and smooth. In a clean, dry bowl whisk the egg whites until stiff, add the remaining ¼ cup sugar and whisk again until glossy.

Mix egg yolk and butter mixtures together well. Fold in the flour, then the egg whites. Divide mixture into two almost equal portions and mix the ground spices into the slightly larger portion.

Preheat oven to moderately slow, 160°C (325°F). Generously butter a 20 cm (8 inch) springform cake tin with softened butter and line the base with buttered greaseproof paper. Dust with flour and tip out excess.

Put a measured amount of spice batter into the tin, about a third of a cup. Use a ladle of this capacity for simplicity, and spread the batter thinly with a spatula. Then tap the tin very firmly on the bench top to help the batter spread thinly and evenly. Bake in the centre of the oven until firm, about 10 minutes. Meanwhile, preheat griller and place the tin under the griller for 30-40 seconds, about 15 cm (6 inches) from heat, until top is evenly browned. Watch carefully so it does not burn, but a really dark coffee colour is what you should aim for.

Now spread the same amount of plain batter over the spicy layer. Return to oven and cook 10 minutes, then grill as before. Continue until all the batter has been used, putting spice and plain layers alternately and spreading the batter as thin as possible.

The extra melted butter is for those who like a really buttery cake, and is used to brush lightly over each layer after it has been grilled and before the next layer of batter is spread over.

When the last layer has been baked, insert a skewer in the centre. It should emerge slightly buttery, but not with uncooked batter clinging to it. Bake for a few minutes longer if necessary. Cool on a wire rack, remove the side of the springform and cut the cake in thin, small slices to serve.

MALAYSIA

Malaysia is a lush, green country typical of the monsoon lands of Southeast Asia. Because of its local produce and the various styles of cooking that come together it has much to offer in adventurous eating. The cooking styles include Malay, Indonesian, Indian, Chinese and Ceylonese, for people from all these countries have settled in Malaysia. The Malay style of cooking is very similar to some Indonesian dishes, and in both countries the languages are almost identical.

In predominantly Muslim Malaysia the food is rich and spicy. Many kinds of meat and fish are used, but never pork — it is considered unclean, and it would be a serious *faux pas* to offer it to anyone of the Muslim faith. Among the Chinese it is used, and is one of their favourite meats. The Hindus do not eat beef, for cattle are sacred to them. Apart from these restrictions, the nation is fairly free-eating.

One of the most fascinating meals I had in Malaysia was in Kuala Lumpur, at a *makan malam* or night food stall. These indoor/outdoor eating places come to life when the sun goes down. Perambulating food shops are set up, each one specialising in a particular dish. I was the guest of two charming Malaysian girls, and together we sampled chicken satay, small pieces of chicken threaded on bamboo skewers and hot from the coal fire they had been cooked on a few paces away. They tasted of spices and fresh lemon grass, and were served with a peanut sauce and *ketupat*, pressed rice cakes cooked in small woven baskets of coconut palm fronds. The sauce was surprisingly mild, being quite heavily sweetened to balance the spices.

Then we ordered *kari laksa kerang*, a spicy noodle soup with cockles; *sotong kangkong*, a rich, red sauce with squid (*sotong*) and the greens so popular in Southeast Asia, *kangkong* being a type of water convolvulus that grows throughout the area; next on the menu was *poh pia,* a sort of unfried spring roll (page 256 in the Singapore chapter). In this version there was no pork in the filling, but a combination of crabmeat and bean sprouts, finely shredded Chinese cabbage, green beans and fried garlic. *Sambal kacang*, a hot peanut preparation, gave the hot, spicy accent to the meal.

All this was followed by a couple of unusual sweets. Ice *kacang* came in a tall glass packed half full with shaved ice doused in a sweet red syrup with cooked and sweetened corn kernels and red beans added. Milk was poured over, turning pink as it mixed with the coloured syrup and making a drink rather than a sweet. It needed a spoon, however, for scooping up the corn and beans. The other exotic

dessert was *lengchee kang*, served in a bowl, which was mostly a sugar syrup flavoured with fresh *daun pandan* and including ingredients such as sweetened lotus nuts, various cooked fruits and a tiny, hard-cooked plover's egg.

Just as intriguing as the food we ate was the method of ordering. As soon as we sat at the table we were surrounded by half a dozen young boys who acted as waiters for the numerous stalls surrounding the dining area. Each represented a different chef. There was no printed menu, but they chanted the names of the dishes available from the chef they worked for in a sing-song vocal menu. It is decidedly different from anything a Western city has to offer, but adds greatly to the charm of this friendly land.

Another meal I enjoyed in Malaysia was at a restaurant that specialised in ethnic dishes, but which was run in a more formal and Westernised fashion. The food was set out on many tables like a smorgasbord. Again there was no menu but patrons could eat as many dishes as they wished and return for further helpings too, all for a set price.

The variety was so great that, to my disappointment, I could not taste as many dishes as I would have liked to, but what I did eat was altogether enjoyable — *rendang*, *biriani*, bean curd cakes filled with fresh bean sprouts, numerous curries and *sambal*, followed by *cendol* (bean flour blancmange shaped in tiny droplets and floating in sweetened coconut milk flavoured with pandanus leaf); green mung beans boiled and sweetened with palm sugar; and the famous *gula melaka* pudding, sago and palm sugar served with rich, thick coconut milk.

Another experience I will not forget was an early morning visit to an open air market. Oh, the baskets piled high with fresh, shiny chillies of all shapes and sizes and ranging from bright green through yellow and orange to vivid scarlet; the bundles of green and white lemon grass and other herbs; the dark green edible fern fronds in bundles; the eggplants in amazing variety — green, purple, white, large, small, round or long, and one variety only as large as a pea. Everything looked so good, so fresh, so tempting that I had to restrain myself from a mad buying spree. I did succumb, however, to large bunches of fresh *rambutan* — those bright red, oval fruit the size of a pullet's egg and covered with fleshy hairs which give them a bizarre appearance. When the skin is removed (it is thin and soft enough to be peeled by a thumb nail) there is a translucent white kernel looking very much like a *lychee*. The flavour is refreshingly sweet-sour, and *rambutan* are a great favourite with local people and visitors alike.

It was in Malaysia too that I ate the best star fruit I

ever tasted. Star fruit is a long, deeply ridged waxy fruit that is star-shaped in cross section and is usually rather watery with only a faint acid and sweet flavour. But one afternoon at the hairdressing salon a friendly girl on the staff offered me a piece of star fruit which was so deeply golden and full of flavour that it quite changed my opinion of star fruit as being only a thirst quencher or table decoration.

SERVING AND EATING
A MALAYSIAN MEAL

To save space, I would like to refer you to the Indonesian chapter, for what has been written about Indonesian food applies to true Malay food. In addition, Malaysian cooks take pride in their rich *korma* and *biriani*, which the Indian settlers brought with them and which have become part of the culinary scene.

Food is traditionally eaten with the fingers, but nowadays spoon and fork is considered more refined. However, on family and ceremonial occasions people revert to the old ways.

Unlike many Asian countries where desserts are not often served, Malays love rich, sweet desserts

and these are based on sago, mung beans, bean flour or glutinous rice. Palm sugar is added for sweetness, coconut milk for richness and pandanus leaf, the Asian equivalent of the vanilla bean, for flavour. In some recipes the sweet spices such as cardamom, cinnamon and clove are used.

UTENSILS

The Malayan version of the *wok* is the *kuali* — shaped the same, but generally thicker and heavier. Wood fires are gradually giving way to gas or electric stoves. In the absence of the clay pots (*blangah*) which are favourites for curry cooking, aluminium or enamel saucepans are recommended, especially for dishes using a large proportion of coconut milk, which discolours in an iron *kuali*. Coconut shell spoons can be replaced with wooden spoons. A deep frying pan is useful, and while the grinding stone (*batu giling*) features largely in preparing Malaysian spices, the electric blender will do this job in a Western kitchen.

YOUR MALAYSIAN SHELF

Please refer to Indonesian ingredients (page 165).

NASI KUNYIT
GLUTINOUS YELLOW RICE

Serves: 6
500 g (1 lb) pulot (glutinous rice)
2 cups water
2 teaspoons salt
1 clove garlic, crushed
1 teaspoon ground turmeric
½ teaspoon ground black pepper
1 daun pandan
2 cups hot coconut milk
crisp fried onion flakes

Wash rice and drain. Put into a saucepan with water, salt, garlic, turmeric, pepper and pandanus leaf for flavouring. Bring to the boil, reduce heat, cover tightly and steam for 10 minutes. Uncover, add coconut milk (which should be very hot), and with a long-pronged fork stir gently so that the rice is mixed with the coconut milk. Cover and cook 10 minutes longer. Serve garnished with onion flakes and accompanied by other dishes.

KETUPAT
COMPRESSED RICE CAKES

These firm rice cakes are usually cooked in individual baskets of woven coconut leaves so that the rice swells until it fills the basket and becomes firmly compressed. Here is a simple and more practical way of producing similar results in Western kitchens.

Serves: 6
500 g (1 lb) short or medium grain rice
4 cups water
banana leaf or aluminium foil

Bring the water and rice to the boil, cover tightly with lid, turn heat very low and cook for 35-40 minutes until all water is absorbed. Stir vigorously with a wooden spoon, then press rice into a cake tin or pie plate to a depth of about 2.5 cm (1 inch). Use a piece of washed and greased banana leaf or greased aluminium foil to cover the surface of the rice and put another plate on top, then press down very firmly. Put a weight on top and leave at room temperature for a few hours, until very firm. Remove weight, plate and banana leaf and use a wet knife to cut rice into 5 cm (2 inch) squares.

IKAN BRIANI
LAYERED SPICED FISH AND RICE

Serves: 6
Fish Savoury:
750 g (1½ lb) firm white fish fillets or
    steaks
lemon juice
salt, pepper, ground turmeric
oil for frying
2 onions, finely chopped
3 cloves garlic, crushed
1 teaspoon finely grated fresh ginger
3 teaspoons ground coriander
2 teaspoons ground cummin
1 large ripe tomato, peeled and chopped
½ cup water
¼ cup thick coconut milk

Spiced Rice:
2 tablespoons ghee
1 onion, finely sliced
5 whole cardamom pods, bruised
4 whole cloves
small piece cinnamon stick
500 g (1 lb) long grain rice
4 cups hot stock or water
2 teaspoons salt

Wash fish fillets and cut each into 2 or 3 pieces. Sprinkle lightly with lemon juice and turmeric, season with pepper and salt. Leave for 15 minutes. Drain fish on paper towels and fry in about 12 mm (½ inch) of hot oil on medium heat until lightly browned on both sides. Remove fish pieces to a plate as they are done. Pour off excess oil and leave about 2 tablespoons in pan. In it fry the onions, garlic and ginger until onion is soft and transparent, stirring frequently. Add coriander, cummin, half teaspoon turmeric and stir for a minute longer. Add the tomato and stir, add water and about three-quarter teaspoon salt, cover and simmer until tomato is pulpy. Uncover, add coconut milk and simmer again, uncovered, until mixture is smooth and very thick. Add fish, spoon sauce over, simmer further 3 or 4 minutes. Turn off heat and leave while preparing rice.

Spiced Rice: Heat all but a teaspoonful of the ghee and fry sliced onion until golden. Add whole spices and rice and fry, stirring constantly, until rice is coated with ghee. Add the hot stock and bring to the boil. Add salt, stir, turn heat very low, cover and cook for 15 minutes. Remove from heat and leave covered for 5 minutes. Uncover and lift out whole spices. Grease a baking dish with the remaining teaspoon of ghee and put in a layer of rice, about a third of the whole amount. On this spread a layer of half the fish savoury, another layer of rice, then the remaining fish savoury, and finally the rest of the rice on top. Cover and cook in a moderately slow oven (160°C or 325°F) for 25 minutes, then serve hot.

If liked, this dish can be prepared a day ahead and refrigerated without baking, then heated in the oven before serving. Allow to come to room temperature and bake 35-40 minutes. Sprinkle top with a little milk or water to prevent rice grains drying out during baking, then cover with lid or foil. Garnish with cucumber and tomato slices or serve with a salad.

CHAR KWAY TEOW
FRIED RICE NOODLES *(picture page 218)*

Serves: 6-8

1 kg (2 lb) kway teow (fresh rice noodles)
125 g (4 oz) barbecued pork
250 g (8 oz) small raw prawns
250 g (8 oz) small squid, optional
2 lap cheong (Chinese sausage)
1 cup fresh bean sprouts
4 tablespoons lard or oil
2 cloves garlic, finely chopped
4 small onions, sliced
4 fresh red chillies, seeded and chopped
2 tablespoons dark soy sauce
2 tablespoons light soy sauce
1 tablespoon oyster sauce
3 eggs, beaten
4 spring onions, chopped
pepper and salt to taste

Cut kway teow into strips about a pencil's width. Cut barbecued pork into thin slices. Shell and de-vein prawns. Clean squid thoroughly and slice thinly. Steam the lap cheong and cut into very thin diagonal slices. Pinch straggly tails off bean sprouts.

Heat 2 tablespoons of the lard or oil in a wok and fry the garlic, onions and chillies over medium heat, stirring, until they are soft. Add pork, prawns, squid and lap cheong and fry for 2-3 minutes or until all the seafood is cooked. Add bean sprouts and toss once or twice, then remove mixture from the wok. Heat remaining lard or oil, and when very hot add the kway teow and stir fry until it is heated through. Add all the seasonings and toss well to mix. Pour in the beaten egg and stir constantly until it is set. Return fried mixture to wok, toss to mix well and serve hot, garnished with spring onions.

Note: Fresh rice noodles are sold at Chinese grocery stores as 'sa hor fun'.

IKAN KUKUS (NONYA)
STEAMED FISH (STRAITS CHINESE STYLE)

Serves: 4

4 dried Chinese mushrooms
1 whole fish, about 750 g (1½ lb), or
    500 g (1 lb) fish fillets
salt and ground black pepper
few drops sesame oil
3 tablespoons finely shredded Chinese
    preserved vegetables
1 fresh red chilli, finely sliced
2 teaspoons light soy sauce
1 or 2 spring onions, finely sliced
2 tablespoons fresh coriander leaves
1 leaf shredded lettuce

Soak dried mushrooms in hot water for 30 minutes, then remove stalks and slice caps finely. While mushrooms are soaking prepare the fish. If using a whole fish, clean well, scale, wash, trim fins and tail; if using fillets wash and dry well on paper towels. Season with salt and pepper. Put fish in dish lightly greased with sesame oil, sprinkle with sliced mushrooms, preserved vegetable and chilli. Sprinkle soy sauce over, cover with another plate or with foil and steam for 20 minutes. Garnish top with spring onions and fresh coriander leaves and arrange lettuce around edge. Serve with white rice.

IKAN KELAPA
SPICED COCONUT FISH

Serves: 4
500 g (1 lb) fish fillets
½ cup desiccated coconut
¾ cup hot water
1 clove garlic
12 mm (½ inch) fresh ginger
¼ teaspoon ground kencur (aromatic ginger)
1 teaspoon ground cummin
1 teaspoon ground coriander
1 teaspoon garam masala (page 35)
1 teaspoon salt
1½ tablespoons lemon juice
1 tablespoon chopped fresh coriander leaves
banana leaves, foil

Wash, clean and scale fillets and cut into approximately 10 cm (4 inch) lengths. Blend together, at high speed, the coconut, hot water, garlic, ginger, kencur, cummin, coriander, garam masala and salt, until coconut is very finely ground. Mix in lemon juice and coriander leaves. Put equivalent of 1 fillet of fish on each piece of banana leaf placed on square of foil. Spoon 2-3 teaspoons of coconut mixture on fish. Wrap leaf over, make a parcel of foil, steam for 15 minutes. Serve hot.

GULAI IKAN
FISH CURRY

Serves: 4-6
500 g (1 lb) firm fish steaks
2 medium onions, roughly chopped
2 cloves garlic
2 teaspoons chopped fresh ginger
1 teaspoon sambal ulek or chilli powder
1 cup thin coconut milk
1 tablespoon ground coriander
1 teaspoon ground cummin
½ teaspoon ground fennel
½ teaspoon ground turmeric
2 strips thinly peeled lemon rind
6 curry leaves
2 tablespoons lemon juice
1 teaspoon salt
½ cup thick coconut milk

Cut fish steaks into serving pieces. Put onions, garlic, ginger and sambal ulek into blender container and blend to a smooth paste, adding a tablespoon of thin coconut milk if necessary. Scrape the blended mixture into a saucepan, wash out blender with the thin coconut milk and add to saucepan together with the ground spices, lemon rind and curry leaves. Bring to the boil, reduce heat and simmer for about 8 minutes, then add the fish, tamarind liquid and salt and simmer for 5 minutes. Add thick coconut milk and stir until curry reaches simmering point once more. Serve with rice.

IKAN GORENG TAUCEO
FRIED FISH WITH SALTED SOYA BEANS

Serves: 4
500 g (1 lb) fish steaks
oil for frying
2 onions, finely sliced
2 cloves garlic, finely chopped
1 teaspoon finely grated fresh ginger
2 teaspoons salted soya bean paste (tauceo)
3 fresh red chillies, sliced
1 teaspoon light soy sauce
¾ cup water
lemon juice to taste

Wash and wipe fish steaks. Fry in enough oil to cover base of pan until golden brown on one side, then turn and fry other side. Drain on absorbent paper. Pour off all but 2 tablespoons oil from pan and fry onions until soft and transparent. Add garlic and ginger and fry until golden brown. Add salted soya bean paste and fry for 1 minute, then add chillies, soy sauce and water. Allow to simmer until gravy thickens slightly, then add fish and cook for 5 minutes, turning slices halfway through. Add lemon juice to taste and serve with white rice.

Note: Tauceo is sold at Chinese grocery stores in bottles labelled 'Bean Sauce'.

ACAR IKAN
VINEGARED FISH

Serves: 6

500 g (1 lb) fish steaks (tuna, kingfish,
    Spanish mackerel)
juice of half a lemon
salt
1 small onion, roughly chopped
2 cloves garlic
1 teaspoon chopped fresh ginger
3 candlenuts (buah keras)
2 fresh red chillies or 1 teaspoon sambal
    ulek
½ cup water
3 tablespoons peanut oil
1 medium onion, thinly sliced
½ teaspoon salt
2 tablespoons vinegar

Cut the fish steaks into serving pieces, rub with the lemon juice and a little salt. Let stand while preparing other ingredients. Put the chopped onion, garlic, ginger, candlenuts and seeded chillies into container of electric blender with 2 tablespoons of the water and blend to a smooth purée. Heat the peanut oil in a wok or frying pan and fry the fish (wiped with paper towels to remove excess moisture) over medium heat until brown on both sides. Lift fish on to a plate. Fry sliced onion in oil remaining in pan until golden brown. Add blended ingredients and fry, stirring, until colour darkens and it is cooked, about 3 or 4 minutes. Wash out blender with measured water and add to pan. Add salt. Allow to simmer for 5 minutes, then add vinegar, return to the boil, add fish and heat through. Serve with white rice, vegetable dishes and sambals.

SAMBAL GORENG IKAN
FRIED FISH SAMBAL

Serves: 6

500 g (1 lb) fresh sprats, 5-7.5 cm
    (2-2½ inches) long
1 onion, roughly chopped
2 candlenuts (buah keras)
2 strips lemon rind
2 teaspoons chilli powder
1 teaspoon laos powder
½ teaspoon dried shrimp paste (blacan)
3 tablespoons tamarind liquid
    (see Glossary)
peanut oil for deep frying
½ cup thick coconut milk
2 daun salam or curry leaves
¾ teaspoon salt, or to taste
plain flour

Wash fish well, removing heads and stomach bags. Rinse again in cold water and drain in a colander, then on absorbent paper. Start making the hot sauce.

Put onion, candlenuts, lemon rind, chilli, laos and blacan into container of electric blender and blend to a smooth paste. It may be necessary to add a tablespoon or two or the tamarind liquid to enable the mixture to be drawn down on to the blades. Heat 3 tablespoons peanut oil in a saucepan and fry the blended mixture, stirring constantly, until it is thick, dark in colour and does not stick to pan. Add remaining tamarind liquid, the coconut milk, daun salam leaves and salt and simmer, uncovered, until it is thick and looks oily on top. Remove from heat and leave aside until fish is fried.

Roll the fish in plain flour to coat thinly, dust off excess flour. Heat enough peanut oil in a wok or small frying pan to deep fry the fish. When oil is very hot put in the fish, a handful at a time. Fry over medium heat until brown and crisp, 4 or 5 minutes. Drain on absorbent paper. When all the fish have been fried turn them on to the spice mixture and mix gently but thoroughly. Serve at once, while the fish is still crisp. If this dish has to be made ahead, do not combine fish and spices until the last minute.

Note: If you do not like sambals to be too hot, reduce chilli powder and use paprika instead to impart a good colour without the pungent taste.

SAMBAL GORENG SOTONG
SQUID SAMBAL (*picture opposite*)

Serves: 4-6
500 g (1 lb) small squid
2 onions, roughly chopped
2 cloves garlic
½ teaspoon dried shrimp paste (blacan)
2 strips lemon rind
5 fresh red chillies or 3 teaspoons sambal
   ulek
3 tablespoons peanut oil
¼ cup tamarind liquid (see Glossary)
2 teaspoons palm sugar or substitute
1-2 teaspoons paprika

Clean squid, discarding head, transparent spine and everything in body cavity. Reserve flower-like tentacles, cutting them off with a sharp knife just below the 'beak'. With kitchen paper rub off spotted skin of squid. Wash squid well, drain, then cut across into slices. Put onion, garlic, blacan, lemon rind and chillies into container of electric blender and blend until smooth, adding some of the peanut oil to help the mixture down onto the blades. In a wok or frying pan heat remaining oil and add the blended mixture. Stir and cook over medium heat until it is dark in colour and the oil shows around the edges. Add tamarind liquid, sugar and paprika (for good colour) and stir in the squid. Cook uncovered, stirring until squid is cooked and mixture is thick and oily. Serve with rice.

   Note: In Malaysia, a higher proportion of red chillies would be used to give colour to the dish, making use of paprika unnecessary.

KARI AYAM KELAPA
CHICKEN CURRY WITH TOASTED COCONUT

Serves: 6
1 x 1.5 kg (3 lb) roasting chicken
4-6 fresh red chillies
½ cup desiccated coconut
2 cups thick coconut milk
2 onions, roughly chopped
3 cloves garlic
1 teaspoon dried shrimp paste (blacan)
1 teaspoon ground turmeric
1 tablespoon ground coriander
2 teaspoons ground cummin
1 stalk fresh lemon grass or 2 strips lemon
   rind
3 tablespoons peanut oil
2 teaspoons salt
4 daun salam or 6 curry leaves
2 teaspoons laos powder

Cut chicken into joints. Boil whole chillies in a small amount of water for 2 minutes. Drain. Remove seeds if you don't want a very hot curry.

   Put desiccated coconut into a heavy frying pan and fry on medium heat, stirring constantly, until it becomes a rich, dark brown. Immediately turn it on to a plate, for it will burn if left in the pan. When coconut has cooled slightly put it into the container of an electric blender, grind finely, then add about half cup of the coconut milk and blend again on high speed for 1 minute (in Asia fresh coconut would be roasted over coals and the nut meat then ground to a paste on a grinding stone, but in Western kitchens other means must be found). Set the coconut mixture aside in a bowl and, without washing blender container, put in the chillies, onions, garlic, blacan, turmeric, coriander, cummin and sliced lemon grass or lemon rind. Blend to a purée. The water content of the onions should be enough to turn the mixture to a purée but if necessary add a tablespoon of the peanut oil.

   Heat remaining oil in a large saucepan and fry the onion mixture on low heat, stirring constantly, until moisture evaporates and oil shows around edge. Add ground coconut, coconut milk, salt, daun salam and laos powder and stir well. Add chicken and stir gently as mixture comes to simmering point. Simmer, uncovered, for 1 hour or until chicken is tender, stirring occasionally. Serve with rice and other accompaniments.

RENDANG AYAM
CHICKEN IN COCONUT MILK

Serves: 6

1 x 1.5 kg (3 lb) roasting chicken
2 medium onions, roughly chopped
4 cloves garlic, sliced
2 teaspoons chopped fresh ginger
2 stalks fresh lemon grass, sliced, or
   4 strips lemon rind
4 fresh red chillies
2 cups coconut milk
1 teaspoon laos powder
1 teaspoon ground coriander
1 teaspoon ground turmeric
2 daun salam or 6 curry leaves
½ teaspoon ground black pepper
1½ teaspoons salt

Joint chicken and cut any large pieces, such as thighs and breasts, into halves. Put into container of electric blender the onions, garlic, ginger, sliced lemon grass and chillies. Add about half cup of the coconut milk and blend to a smooth purée. Put into a saucepan. Wash out the blender container with the rest of the milk, and add to the pan. Add the laos, coriander, turmeric, daun salam or curry leaves, pepper and salt. Bring slowly to the boil, stirring occasionally. Do not cover pan, or coconut milk will curdle. Add chicken, return to the boil and simmer gently, uncovered, until chicken is tender. Serve with white rice.

Note: This dish should continue cooking until gravy is almost all absorbed — but for this try to get an older and slightly tougher bird, or by the time the gravy is reduced the flesh will be falling off the bones. The more readily available roasting chicken can be served when it is cooked through and impregnated with the flavours of the gravy even though the gravy is not absorbed.

AYAM LEMAK
CHICKEN WITH SPICY COCONUT MILK GRAVY

Serves: 6

1 x 1.5 kg (3 lb) roasting chicken
2½ teaspoons finely grated fresh ginger
2 medium onions, chopped
3 stalks lemon grass or rind of 1 lemon
6 fresh red chillies, seeded, or 2 teaspoons
   sambal ulek
1 teaspoon ground turmeric
3 tablespoons oil
3 cups thick coconut milk
3 strips (finger length) daun pandan
   or few leaves fresh basil
2 teaspoons salt

Cut chicken into curry pieces. Pound the ginger, onions, lemon grass or rind and the chillies with a mortar and pestle, or grind in electric blender with a little oil until they form a paste. Rub chicken pieces with turmeric until they are coated all over. Heat oil in a heavy saucepan and fry the ground ingredients over a low heat, stirring constantly, for 15 minutes or until soft and golden. Add chicken and fry for further 10 minutes. Add coconut milk, pandan or basil leaves and salt and simmer uncovered until chicken is tender. Serve with white rice or nasi lemak.

GULAI AYAM REBONG
CHICKEN AND BAMBOO SHOOT CURRY

Serves: 6-8

1 x 1.5 kg (3 lb) roasting fowl
1 can bamboo shoots
2 medium onions
4 tablespoons coconut or peanut oil
1½ tablespoons ground coriander
1 teaspoon dried shrimp paste (blacan)
1 teaspoon laos powder
1 teaspoon chilli powder
2 teaspoons salt
2 cups thin coconut milk
1 cup thick coconut milk

Cut chicken into curry pieces. Drain bamboo shoots and cut into quarters, then into slices. Chop onions finely. Heat the oil in a large saucepan and fry onions over medium heat, stirring, until soft and golden. Add coriander, blacan, laos, chilli and salt and fry, stirring constantly, for a few minutes until spices are brown. Add chicken pieces and stir until well mixed with the spices, then add thin coconut milk and bring to simmering point. Simmer for 20-25 minutes. Add bamboo shoot, stir, and simmer for a further 20 minutes or until chicken is tender. Add thick coconut milk and simmer, uncovered, stirring gently. Taste and add salt if necessary. Continue simmering until oil rises to the surface. Serve with rice, vegetables and sambal.

GULAI AYAM
WHOLE CHICKEN CURRY

You really need a tough boiling fowl for this recipe, because the longer the cooking time, the better the flavour. If using a roasting chicken, shorten the cooking time so that the chicken stays whole, and reduce the gravy as described at the end of the recipe.

Serves: 6-8

1 boiling fowl, about 2 kg (4 lb)
3-4 cups coconut milk
3 teaspoons chilli powder, or to taste
2 teaspoons ground cummin
½ teaspoon ground turmeric
¼ teaspoon fenugreek seeds
2 teaspoons salt
1 onion, finely sliced
3 cloves garlic, finely chopped
2 teaspoons finely chopped fresh ginger
1 stalk lemon grass or 2 strips lemon rind
1 small stick cinnamon
1 strip daun pandan, optional
1½ teaspoons ground fennel
2 tablespoons lemon juice
1 tablespoon ghee

Truss fowl as for roasting and put it into a large saucepan with enough coconut milk to come two thirds of the way up the bird. Add all the ingredients except the fennel, lemon juice and ghee. Bring to the boil, then simmer 30 minutes. Add fennel and lemon juice, turn the bird over and continue simmering until the fowl is tender. It may be necessary to add more hot water or coconut milk if the liquid cooks away.

Pour gravy into a bowl, leaving the bird in the pan. Add ghee to pan and fry the bird, turning it on all sides, until golden brown all over. Pour the gravy back into the pan and simmer until thick.

If using a roasting chicken, remove it from pan after browning, pour gravy back and cook until thick, then return chicken to heat through. Taste and add more salt and lemon juice if necessary. Serve with rice and other curries and accompaniments.

SEMUR ATI
SPICED BRAISED LIVER

Serves: 4

500 g (1 lb) calves' liver or chicken livers
3 tablespoons oil
1 medium onion, finely sliced
2 cloves garlic, finely chopped
1 teaspoon finely grated fresh ginger
1½ teaspoons ground coriander
½ teaspoon ground cummin
½ teaspoon salt
¼ teaspoon ground black pepper
2 tablespoons dark soy sauce
⅓ cup water

Slice liver very thinly, wash, drain on kitchen paper and set aside. If using chicken livers remove tubes and any discoloured spots and divide each one in half.

Heat the oil in a large, heavy frying pan and fry onion, garlic and ginger over medium heat, stirring frequently, for 5 minutes or until golden. Add the slices of liver in a single layer and sprinkle over them the coriander, cummin, salt and pepper. Turn them and fry other side for 2 minutes, then add soy sauce and water, cover and simmer about 5 minutes, depending on the thickness of the slices. Do not overcook. Liver should lose its pinkness inside but not be allowed to get hard and dry. Serve immediately.

SATAY DAGING
MALAY BEEF SATAY *(picture opposite)*

Serves: 6
750 g (1½ lb) rump steak
2 teaspoons ground turmeric
2 teaspoons ground cummin
2 teaspoons ground fennel
finely grated rind of half lemon
1½ teaspoons salt
1 tablespoon sugar
4 tablespoons thick coconut milk

Cut beef into small cubes, about 2 cm (¾ inch) thick each way. Trim off excess fat, leaving a thin layer of fat on some of the cubes. Cut the trimmed-off fat into thin squares.

Combine turmeric, cummin, fennel, lemon rind, salt, sugar and coconut milk in a bowl and stir to dissolve sugar. Add beef and mix well, cover and leave to marinate for 1 hour or longer. The longer it is left, the more the flavours will penetrate the meat. Thread on bamboo skewers that have been soaked in cold water for a few hours, putting about 5 pieces on the end of each skewer and leaving at least half the skewer uncovered. Use the squares of fat where necessary, for they keep the meat tender. Grill over hot coals or under a preheated griller until beef is well done and crisp and brown on all sides. Serve immediately with ketupat (page 222) and chilli and peanut sauce (page 234).

GULAI KAMBING
SPICY MUTTON CURRY

Serves: 6
750 g (1½ lb) mutton
4 tablespoons desiccated coconut
¼ cup tamarind liquid
2 large onions, roughly chopped
4 cloves garlic
1 tablespoon roughly chopped fresh ginger
2 teaspoons ground coriander
1 teaspoon each ground cummin and
  turmeric
½ teaspoon each ground cinnamon,
  fennel, nutmeg and black pepper
¼ teaspoon each ground cloves and
  cardamom
4 candlenuts (buah keras)
4-8 dried red chillies, or to taste
1 stalk lemon grass or 1 teaspoon finely
  chopped lemon rind
2 tablespoons peanut oil
2 ripe tomatoes, chopped
1½ cups coconut milk
1½ teaspoons salt

Cut mutton into small cubes. Brown the coconut in a dry frying pan, stirring constantly over medium low heat for 4 or 5 minutes or until it is a rich golden brown colour. Set aside. Pour quarter cup very hot water over a walnut-size piece of dried tamarind pulp and leave for 5 minutes. Squeeze the tamarind in the water to dissolve. Strain through a fine sieve.

In container of electric blender put the tamarind liquid and onions and blend to a smooth, thick liquid. Add garlic and ginger and blend again. Add the spices, candlenuts, dried chillies and, last of all, the toasted coconut. Blend until smooth and well combined. If lemon rind is being used it can be blended too, but if lemon grass is available add it later on.

Heat the oil in a large saucepan and fry the blended mixture for 5 minutes, stirring frequently at the beginning and constantly at the end. Add meat and fry for 3 minutes, stirring well so that each piece is coated with spices. Add tomato and fry for a further 3 minutes. Add coconut milk, salt and lemon grass and bring slowly to the boil. Reduce heat to very low and simmer, uncovered, until meat is tender, stirring now and then. This may take from 1½ to 2 hours. Serve with white rice.

SHAMI KEBAB
MUTTON AND LENTIL RISSOLES

Serves: 4

250 g (8 oz) lean meat
125 g (4 oz) red lentils or yellow split peas
2 medium onions, finely chopped
¼ teaspoon ground cinnamon
¼ teaspoon ground cardamom
⅛ teaspoon ground cloves
1 teaspoon salt
½ teaspoon ground black pepper
1 egg, beaten
2 tablespoons finely chopped mint
oil for frying

Use lean mutton or lamb, or topside beef. Ask butcher to mince it for you, or mince it at home, using fine screen. Wash the red lentils or split peas well and put into a saucepan with 2 cups water. Bring to the boil, add meat and onions, cook on medium low heat stirring occasionally until lentils are cooked. Stir as mixture becomes dry and continue cooking until liquid is completely absorbed. Turn into a bowl and when cool enough to handle mix in the spices and seasonings, egg and mint. Mix thoroughly, then shape into flat round patties. Fry in shallow hot oil until golden brown on both sides. Drain and serve hot.

SAYUR MASAK LEMAK
VEGETABLE CURRY

Serves: 6 as an accompaniment

1 onion, finely sliced
1 clove garlic, finely chopped
2 fresh red or green chillies, seeded and
  sliced
½ teaspoon dried shrimp paste (blacan)
½ teaspoon ground turmeric
1 cup thin coconut milk
1 large potato, peeled and diced
3 cups coarsely shredded cabbage
1 teaspoon salt
1 cup thick coconut milk
lemon juice to taste

Put the onion, garlic, chillies, blacan, turmeric and thin coconut milk into a saucepan and bring to simmering point. Add potato and cook for 10 minutes or until potato is half cooked. Add cabbage and salt, cook for 3 minutes, then add the thick coconut milk and stir gently until cabbage is cooked. Remove from heat and add lemon juice to taste.

SAMBAL GORENG KEMBANG
CHILLI-FRIED CAULIFLOWER

Serves: 6

3 tablespoons peanut oil
4 fresh red chillies, finely chopped or
  2 teaspoons sambal ulek
1 large onion, finely chopped
2 cloves garlic, finely chopped
1 teaspoon dried shrimp paste (blacan)
1 teaspoon salt
500 g (1 lb) cauliflower, sliced
2 tablespoons hot water

Heat oil in wok or frying pan and fry the chillies, onion and garlic over low heat, stirring frequently, until onion is soft and golden. Add blacan and crush with back of spoon. Fry for a minute longer. Add salt, then turn in the cauliflower and toss and stir constantly until cauliflower is thoroughly mixed with the fried chilli and onion mixture. Sprinkle with the hot water, cover and cook for 10 minutes. Serve hot.

TAUKWA TAUCEO
BEAN CURD IN SALTED SOYA BEAN PASTE

Serves: 6

3 squares yellow bean curd (taukwa)
2 cloves garlic
3 fresh red chillies
2 teaspoons salted soya bean paste (tauceo)
250 g (8 oz) raw prawns or ½ cup crab meat
2 tablespoons peanut oil
¼ cup water
1 tablespoon light soy sauce
salt to taste
2 tablespoons chopped celery leaves
2 tablespoons chopped spring onions

Cut bean curd into dice, grate garlic finely, seed and shred chillies. Mash salted soya beans. Chop prawns or flake crab meat. Heat oil and fry garlic and chillies until garlic starts to turn brown, then add salted soya beans and fry for 1 minute, stirring. Add crab meat or prawns and stir until cooked, add bean curd and fry, stirring. Add water and soy sauce and cook until liquid dries up. Taste and add salt if necessary. Remove from heat, mix in celery and spring onions and serve.

TAUKWA DAN TAUGEH
BEAN CURD AND BEAN SPROUTS

Serves: 6

2 squares yellow bean curd (taukwa)
250 g (8 oz) fresh bean sprouts (taugeh)
2 cloves garlic, crushed
2 tablespoons oil
salt and pepper to taste
soy sauce to taste

Cut the bean curd in slices. Wash and drain the bean sprouts, pinching off any brown 'tails'.

Fry garlic in oil until turning golden, add bean curd and bean sprouts and stir fry for 3 to 4 minutes. Add seasonings to taste and serve immediately.

ACAR KUNING
VEGETABLE PICKLE

1 cup carrot sticks
1 cup green beans
10 fresh red and green chillies
1 green cucumber
2 tablespoons peanut oil
2 cloves garlic, finely grated
2 teaspoons finely grated fresh ginger
3 candlenuts or brazil kernels, grated
1 teaspoon ground turmeric
½ cup white vinegar
½ cup water
2 teaspoons sugar
1 teaspoon salt
1 cup cauliflower sprigs

Cut carrots into julienne strips. Cut beans into pieces of the same length, then slice each piece in two lengthways. If beans are very young and slender it will not be necessary to slice them. Leave the chillies whole, but remove stems. Peel cucumber and cut in half lengthways, remove seeds and slice into pieces the same size as the carrots and beans.

Heat oil in a saucepan and fry garlic and ginger on low heat for 1 minute, then add grated nuts and turmeric and fry for a few seconds longer. Add vinegar, water, sugar and salt and bring to the boil. Add carrots and beans, chillies and cauliflower sprigs, return to the boil and boil for 3 minutes. Add cucumber and boil for 1 minute longer.

Turn into an earthenware or glass bowl and allow to cool. Use immediately or bottle and store in refrigerator for a week or two.

SAMBAL KELAPA
COCONUT SAMBAL

1 cup fresh grated coconut or desiccated
  coconut
1 teaspoon salt
½-1 teaspoon chilli powder or 1 fresh red
  chilli, seeded and chopped
¼ teaspoon dried shrimp paste (blacan)
2 tablespoons finely chopped onion
1 small clove garlic, crushed
juice of half a lemon

If desiccated coconut is being used, sprinkle with 2 tablespoons hot water or milk and mix thoroughly to moisten. Add all other ingredients, first wrapping the blacan in foil and grilling or heating it in a dry frying pan for 5 minutes. Mix well by hand. Serve as an accompaniment to rice and curries.

SAUS KACANG
CHILLI AND PEANUT SAUCE

oil for deep frying
1 cup raw peanuts
10 large dried red chillies
1 medium onion, roughly chopped
6 cloves garlic, peeled
½ teaspoon dried shrimp paste (blacan)
3 tablespoons coconut or peanut oil
3 tablespoons tamarind liquid
  (see Glossary)
1 teaspoon salt
1 cup thick coconut milk
1 tablespoon palm sugar or substitute

Heat oil in a wok or frying pan and fry the raw peanuts over medium heat, stirring constantly and lifting them out as soon as they show signs of turning golden. They will continue to cook in their own heat, so don't leave them in the oil until they are brown or they will be overdone and bitter. Drain on absorbent paper and allow to cool, then rub off skins and pound, crush or work in blender until they are coarsely ground. They should be crisp and have lots of crunchy bits, not worked to a smooth paste.

Put dry chillies in a bowl and pour very hot water over them to cover. Soak for 20 minutes at least.

In the container of an electric blender put the soaked chillies and about 2 tablespoons of the soaking water, the onion, garlic and blacan and blend until a smooth paste. Heat 3 tablespoons oil in a wok or frying pan and fry the blended mixture over medium heat, stirring constantly, until it darkens in colour and the onions and garlic smell cooked. Remove from heat. Stir in the tamarind liquid, salt, coconut milk and sugar and transfer to a bowl to cool. When sauce has cooled stir in the peanuts so they retain their crunchiness. Serve this hot sauce with Malay beef satay (page 231) and ketupat (page 222). Garnish the ketupat with sliced cucumber, not only for appearance but also because it is the ideal thing to cool a tongue startled by the heat of the sauce. For novices, reduce the number of chillies to 3 or 4.

SOTO AYAM
CHICKEN SOUP (SPICY)

Serves: 6

1 chicken, about 1.5 kg (3 lb)
8 cups cold water
3 teaspoons salt
½ teaspoon whole black peppercorns
few celery tops
1 large brown onion, sliced
2 tablespoons peanut oil
2 daun salam or 6 curry leaves
2 cloves garlic, finely grated
½ teaspoon finely grated fresh ginger
½ teaspoon dried shrimp paste (blacan)
½ teaspoon ground turmeric
2 teaspoons ground coriander
1 teaspoon ground cummin
4 candlenuts (buah keras), finely grated
125 g (4 oz) rice vermicelli
2 large potatoes, cooked and diced
lemon juice to taste

Garnish:

8 spring onions, finely sliced
2 hardboiled eggs, finely chopped
crumbled potato crisps

Cut chicken into joints and put into a large saucepan with cold water. Water should cover the chicken. Add salt, peppercorns, celery tops and half the onion. Bring quickly to the boil, then lower heat, cover and simmer for 30 minutes or until chicken is tender. Allow to cool to lukewarm (if chicken is taken out while it is hot, the flesh will be dry) then strain stock into a bowl.

Remove skin and bones from chicken. With a sharp knife cut flesh into dice or strips. Set aside. Heat peanut oil in the saucepan and when very hot fry the daun salam and onion until onion is golden brown. Add the garlic, ginger, blacan and stir over medium heat, crushing the blacan with back of spoon. Add the turmeric, coriander, cummin and candlenuts and fry, stirring, for a few seconds longer. Add the strained stock and bring to the boil, then reduce heat, cover and simmer for 10 minutes. Meanwhile soak the rice vermicelli in hot water for 10 minutes, drain and cut into short lengths. Add it to the simmering soup, return to the boil and cook for 1 minute. Add chicken meat, potatoes and lemon juice and heat through. Pour into a large soup tureen and garnish with the spring onions and egg. Serve the potato crisps in a separate bowl for sprinkling on individual servings.

SAYUR UDANG BAYAM
PRAWN AND SPINACH SOUP

Serves: 6

250 g (8 oz) raw prawns
3 tablespoons peanut oil
1 small bunch spinach or silver beet
1 onion, finely sliced
1 or 2 fresh red chillies, seeded and sliced
1 clove garlic, crushed
½ teaspoon ground turmeric
1 teaspoon salt
2 cups prawn stock (see method)
2 cups thin coconut milk
½ cup thick coconut milk

Wash, shell and de-vein the prawns. Drain the heads and shells and use for making stock. To make stock, heat 1 tablespoon of the oil in a saucepan and when very hot throw in the heads and shells. Fry, stirring, until they change colour. Add 4 cups hot water and 1 teaspoon salt, bring to the boil and simmer for 20-30 minutes or until liquid is reduced by half. Set aside.

Wash spinach or silver beet thoroughly. Separate leaves from stems and chop both roughly. Heat remaining 2 tablespoons oil in a large saucepan and fry onion and chillies until onion is soft and golden. Add the garlic and turmeric and fry for 1 minute longer. Add spinach stems and fry, stirring, for a few minutes then add salt, strained prawn stock, and thin coconut milk. Bring to the boil, lower heat and simmer 5 minutes. Add spinach leaves and simmer for 3 minutes, then add the prawns, finely chopped, and the thick coconut milk. Let mixture return slowly to the boil and simmer for no more than 2 or 3 minutes longer or prawns will toughen. Serve immediately.

SOTHI
COCONUT MILK SOUP

This soup is spooned over boiled rice, not served as a first course by itself.

Serves: 6
2 cups thin coconut milk
2 medium onions, sliced
6 curry leaves
2 fresh red or green chillies, seeded
½ teaspoon ground turmeric
1½ teaspoons salt
2 tablespoons prawn powder
1½ cups thick coconut milk
2 tablespoons lemon juice

Put thin coconut milk in saucepan with all other ingredients except thick coconut milk and lemon juice. Bring to boil and simmer 15 minutes. Add thick coconut milk and heat gently, stirring to prevent soup from curdling. Remove from heat, add lemon juice and stir.

Serve as an accompaniment to boiled rice and a dry curry.

ROTI JALA
LACY PANCAKES

These pancakes are served with gulai kambing or other rich, dry curries and form a substantial snack that is almost a meal.

Makes about 12 pancakes
2 eggs
2¾ cups coconut milk or fresh milk
2 cups plain flour, sifted
½ teaspoon salt
2 tablespoons oil for frying

Beat eggs thoroughly, add milk and mix. Put flour and salt into a large bowl and add the liquid steadily, pouring it into the middle of the flour while mixing with a wooden spoon. Do not add liquid too slowly at first or it will be difficult to get rid of the lumps. When all the liquid has been added, beat until batter is smooth.

Heat a heavy omelette pan or pancake pan and grease lightly with a piece of kitchen paper dipped in oil. Pour batter into pan, moving the ladle back and forth so that the pancake will have a perforated appearance. Cook until set and pale golden underneath, then turn and cook other side. Continue until all the batter is used up. If batter thickens on standing, add a little water and stir well.

SERIKAYA DENGAN AGAR-AGAR
COCONUT MILK JELLY

Serves: 6-8
7 g (¼ oz) agar-agar strands or
  5 teaspoons agar-agar powder
6 cups water
3 pods cardamom, bruised
1 small stick cinnamon
2½ cups palm sugar or substitute
2 cups thick coconut milk
pinch of salt

Soak agar-agar strands in cold water overnight. Drain. When drained, they should measure approximately 1½ cups loosely packed. Put agar-agar strands into a saucepan with 6 cups fresh cold water, cardamom and cinnamon. Bring to the boil and simmer gently 30 minutes or until agar-agar strands are dissolved. Stir occasionally, add sugar and stir until dissolved. Add coconut milk and salt and stir constantly while bringing just to simmering point. If agar-agar powder is used simmer only 5-10 minutes before adding other ingredients. Strain through fine nylon sieve, pour into a wetted mould and cool to room temperature, then chill until serving time.

Note: If using agar-agar powder, sprinkle evenly on surface of water or it might turn lumpy.

GULA MELAKA
SAGO PUDDING

'Gula melaka' means palm sugar, but it is so integral a part of the recipe that this popular dessert has become known by the same name. Sago pudding takes on a new dimension when prepared this way—no wonder it is popular throughout South East Asia.

Palm sugar is sometimes sold under the named of Coconut Preserves in a solid cylinder of concentrated sweetness derived from the sap of coconut or other varieties of palm. If you find it difficult to buy, substitute an equivalent amount of black or brown sugar. For each cup of sugar add ½ cup maple syrup.

Serves: 6-8

2 cups sago
8-10 cups water
1 small stick cinnamon, optional
2 tablespoons coconut milk
pinch of salt

For serving:
250 g (8 oz) palm sugar or substitute
½ cup water
2 strips pandan leaves, fresh or dried
1¼ cups coconut milk
pinch salt

Slowly dribble the sago into the water which you have brought to a fast boil in a large saucepan with the cinnamon stick if used. Let it boil for 5-7 minutes. Turn off heat, cover the pan with a well fitting lid and leave for 10 minutes. The sago will finish cooking in the stored heat and the grains will be clear. Run cold water into the pan, stir, then drain in a sieve, shaking the sieve so the water runs off. Discard the cinnamon.

Turn the sago into a bowl, stir in the 2 tablespoons of coconut milk and pinch of salt. This quantity of milk is just enough to give it a pearly white appearance instead of that unattractive grey look. Divide between individual dessert dishes or moulds, or pour into one large mould. Chill until set.

Unmould and serve the sago chilled, accompanied by gula melaka syrup and coconut milk. A little syrup may be poured around the mould when it is turned out on the serving dish, but it is more usual to serve the syrup and coconut milk in small jugs or bowls with spoons so each person may help themselves.

To make the syrup, chop the gula melaka into small pieces or shave with a sharp knife. Put into a small saucepan with the water and pandan leaves and heat gently until the sugar is melted. Strain through a fine sieve to remove any small impurities. Cool and chill.

Either extract coconut milk from grated fresh coconut (see page 12) or use a good brand of canned coconut milk. Canned coconut milk may need diluting with a little water if very thick. Stir in a good pinch of salt as this accentuates the flavour. Coconut milk should be freshly made and served at room temperature, as chilling will solidify the fat content.

SINGAPORE

Singapore is a gourmet's dream come true. Any kind of food you wish to eat, Eastern or Western, is available at its best in this cosmopolitan city. I have eaten some of the best Chinese meals of my life in Singapore, at exclusive restaurants and at street stalls, not to mention Malay and Indian and Japanese food that made me look forward with eagerness to future visits.

But the most interesting food, because it is peculiar to Singapore, is the Nonya style of food — a mixture of Chinese ingredients and Malay spices, cooked in a way that is a perfect mingling of the two cultures. This came about quite naturally, because when Chinese labour was recruited in the last century, it was only men who were allowed to leave China and come to the Straits Settlements of Penang,

Malacca and Singapore. They married Malay wives and these alliances resulted in a singular and quite distinctive style of cooking, a cuisine that the Nonyas are proud of and cannot live without.

Nonyas are Straits-born Chinese. The women are 'Nonyas', the men 'Babas' and together they are known as 'Peranakan'.

I had the chance to meet and speak with Mrs Lee Chin Koon, author of the most comprehensive volume available on Nonya cooking and a keen practical cook. Her aim in teaching cooking and writing her recipes is to ensure that Nonya cooking is kept alive, because she sees the younger generation not as interested in the domestic arts with the changing emphasis as women become more career conscious. Their entertaining is done in restaurants and with the increased tempo of life and the new freedom Eastern women enjoy, young wives no longer spend hours in the kitchen with the older women of the household, watching, helping and learning.

Apart from her accomplishments in the culinary field, this alert and energetic seventy-year-old lady is the mother of Singapore's popular and powerful Prime Minister, Lee Kuan Yew, and is affectionately referred to as 'Mama Lee'.

'To us, our Nonya food is very special and we prefer to eat it to any other type of food. It is totally different from Chinese food, though we do use some Chinese ingredients, like pork, which the Malays, who are Muslims, are forbidden to touch or eat,' writes Mrs Lee. 'Ingredients found in Malay, Indonesian and Chinese kitchens can be found in our kitchens, however not all of our ingredients can be found in other typical Chinese kitchens.'

Nonya recipes are usually hot and spicy. They use herbs and spices that are never used in Chinese food. Most recipes are based on a *rempah* — a paste of various spices including hot chillies, spring onions, lemon grass, candlenuts, *lengkuas*, turmeric and *blacan* pounded to just the right degree with a stone mortar and pestle. The pounding itself is an art that must be mastered. Too little and the paste will not be smooth enough, too much and it will become too liquid.

I understood perfectly what Mama Lee meant when she said the recipes in her book are six generations old but that the book itself represents seven years of work, merely to translate the 'agak' or estimated measures into cups and spoons, precise weights and measures. In writing down Asian recipes I have had this problem myself.

Even with recipes that have been in the family for years, one finds they are done by instinct and learned almost by a process of osmosis. Young cooks learn from their mothers, grandmothers, aunts and after marriage from the all-powerful mother in law. There are no written recipes or precise measures. Experienced cooks know just how much of this or that ingredient to use and the amount can vary depending on how strong or fresh the ginger or garlic is, how hot the chillies, how large or how small the spring onions or stems of lemon grass. When it comes to passing on the recipes, especially to cooks who may be making a dish for the first time and do not know how hot or sour or salty it should be, it requires the utmost discipline to do every recipe over again, measuring by standard cups and spoons, trying to even out all the variables and write down the method in painstaking detail.

Mrs Lee's attitude towards sharing recipes is a refreshing change from the unwillingness to give recipes which characterises most Asian women who have built themselves a reputation as good cooks and who guard their secrets jealously. A request to divulge a recipe may be met with a firm refusal; or a vital ingredient or step in preparation may be left out so that attempts to duplicate a dish will not be successful. Mrs Lee decries this attitude and wants only that good Nonya cooking should survive. 'A good recipe is meant to be shared,' she states firmly, and I could not agree more.

I cannot remember every meal I have eaten in the garden city of Singapore, but some are outstanding and cannot be forgotten. There was the Kashmiri-style food at the Omar Khayyam, owned and run by Mr Wadhu Sakhrani, a gracious and most knowledgeable host. The exquisite decor, the original paintings done by an Indian artist (which are enlargements of very old miniatures), the small alcoves in the walls, each one holding a simple oil lamp, set the mood for the meal to come. And when it comes it is perfect in every detail. I have never eaten better Indian food, in or out of India. Typical of Kashmiri food, there are no mind-blowing hot tastes. Instead, there are exquisite fragrance and delicate spicing.

As Mr Sakhrani's guest I was invited to sample a much larger variety of dishes than could normally be consumed at a single meal. *Tandoori* chicken rubbed with a spice marinade and cooked in a fiercely hot clay oven buried in the earth comes tender, golden brown and crisp, with a flavour that defies description; Kashmiri prawn curry, richly red but not hot; *kofta* of finely minced tender lamb, spiced and sauced; chicken livers cooked in spices, onions, herbs and ginger; chicken simmered in butter with herbs and tomatoes. Then a *raita* that was smooth, rich and creamy, given a special, extravagant touch with pistachio nuts; Persian *pilau*, fine long grains of rice cooked with saffron, orange peel and almonds; *biriani nentara*, a vegetable and rice preparation; *Khayyam naan*, one of the large flat breads so popular in India; *tandoor roti*, another kind of bread cooked in the *tandoor*. And, to finish the feast, *koulfi* — the ice-cream of Kashmir that bears no resemblance to the fluffy, gelatine-boosted ice-creams of the West (page 112) — and *ras malai*, queen of Indian desserts, featuring home-made cream cheese, rose and cardamom flavourings and rich clotted cream (page 111).

Another meal to remember was a superb Szechwan-style banquet at the Golden Phoenix restaurant in the Hotel Equatorial, which is reputedly the best place to eat Szechwanese food. Cold hors d'oeuvre including marinated duck and strips of jellyfish; deep-fried prawns and chillies; stir-fried chicken with vegetables; Szechwan soup — sour, slightly hot, laden with shredded pork, shrimps, bean curd and Chinese mushrooms so that a small bowl of it was rich and filling. The Szechwan pancake served for dessert was a totally new experience — a very thin *crêpe* filled with sweet bean paste and folded over to enclose it, then fried until golden and crisp on the outside. Toasted sesame seeds clung to the batter and even when folded it filled a large Chinese dish, so I could not help but wonder at how large the pancake must have been at first. It was brought to the table neatly cut into bite-size strips but left in the original shape.

While these meals were superbly presented and cooked by experts, there was an element of fun and informality added when we dined at the Orchard Road Car Park. By day it *is* a car park, but at night it turns into one of those outdoor eating places for which Singapore is famous. No snowy white cloths or elegant decor here. Instead, you wander around watching each chef cooking his speciality and decide which to order. You can partake of a dozen different noodle dishes; curries and *roti* in Indian or Malay style; fried rice, *chap chye*, chilli crabs, *satay* and sauces, *poh pia* (egg rolls with a selection of fillings) — in fact just about any Chinese, Indian, Indonesian or Malay food you care to name.

And you top it off with one of the local sweets or with a glass of freshly pressed juice. Orange and sugar cane vie for top place and it was sugar cane juice, frothy and pale green and just pressed, that I chose. It is one of the most refreshing drinks — not too sweet, very clean tasting. While it lacks the tang of lime or orange it has a delicacy of flavour I have not met in any other drink. Canned sugar cane juice is a poor substitute. It has none of the fresh flavour or refreshing quality, and if not for the label on the can it would be hard to identify with the fresh product, so wait until you can taste the real thing or pass it up.

SERVING AND EATING A NONYA MEAL

While Singapore is predominantly Chinese, I am choosing Nonya-style cooking, for this originated here and is synonymous with Singapore. It is, as with most Asian meals, all served at one time. Rice or noodles, curries, *sambal*, soup, vegetable dishes are placed on the table and each person makes their own choice.

Dinner plates are used for eating. While the traditional way is to mix and eat the spicy food with the fingers, modern manners favour the use of spoon and fork. This type of food is called *lauk pering*, or food served on a plate. When soup dishes such as *laksa* or *meehoon* are on the menu they are served in Chinese-style bowls.

To finish the meal, sweets made of glutinous rice and coconut milk are popular. Wine is not served with this kind of food, and instead of Chinese tea most Nonyas prefer to drink Malay coffee.

UTENSILS

The traditional kitchen with its wood fire is almost a thing of the past. In the modern high-rise housing developments that have taken the place of the *kampung* (clusters of little shacks huddled together in a common garden) modern gas stoves are used. Even where *kampung* persist, the tin or thatched roof shacks have been replaced with neat wooden houses and the kitchens too have been modernised.

For curry cooking the traditional vessel is the clay *chatty* so popular in Southeast Asia. Discerning cooks treasure their special clay pots much as a French cook holds sacred her omelette pan.

For Chinese or Nonya-style cooking a *wok* or *kuali* is best; you'll also need a sharp Chinese chopper and heavy wooden chopping board. A heavy mortar and pestle is invaluable for pounding spices and most cooks cherish their grinding stones, but a powerful electric blender can replace these two essentials in a Western kitchen. A coconut grater is also essential in an Asian kitchen, but nowadays cooks buy fresh grated coconut at the market. Again, an electric blender can be used for making coconut milk (page 11).

Good quality saucepans, a deep frying pan, wooden spoons and the usual frying spoons found in any reasonably well-equipped kitchen will cope with the recipes in this chapter.

YOUR SINGAPORE SHELF

black beans, canned
black pepper, ground
candlenuts (*buah keras*)
chillies, dried
chilli powder
chilli sauce
Chinese bean sauce
Chinese mushrooms, dried
Chinese wine or dry sherry
cinnamon, ground
creamed coconut or desiccated coconut
coriander, ground
cummin, ground

dried shrimp paste (*blacan*)
egg noodles
fennel, ground
five spice powder
laos powder
oyster sauce
peanuts, unsalted
peanut oil
rice vermicelli
sesame oil
soy sauce
tamarind pulp or instant tamarind
turmeric, ground
wood fungus, dried

Besides these ingredients, which have a long shelf life, fresh ginger root and garlic, spring onions, lemon grass or lemon rind and fresh coriander herb are the heart of the flavouring of many Southeast Asian dishes.

NASI LEMAK
COCONUT RICE

Serves: 4-5
500 g (1 lb) medium or long grain rice
1¼ cups coconut milk
2½ teaspoons salt

Soak rice in cold water overnight. Drain rice, spread in top part of a steamer and steam over rapidly boiling water for 30 minutes. Halfway through steaming, stir rice and turn it so that the rice on the bottom comes to the top and vice versa. Gently heat the coconut milk with the salt in a large saucepan, stirring. Do not boil. Add the steamed rice, stir well, cover tightly and let stand for a further 30 minutes, by which time the milk should be completely absorbed. Once more spread the rice in top of steamer, bring water back to the boil and steam for 30 minutes, starting on high heat and gradually turning heat lower until in the end the water merely simmers. Serve hot with meat, poultry, fish or vegetable dishes, both mild and hot.

CHEE CHEONG FUN
FRESH RICE NOODLE SNACK

Serves: 2-3
1 packet (500 g) twin rice noodles
  (chee cheong fun)
1 tablespoon Chinese barbecue sauce
1 tablespoon light soy sauce
1 teaspoon sesame oil
1 teaspoon sweet chilli sauce
1 tablespoon toasted sesame seeds

Cut rice noodles into thin strips, put into a bowl and pour boiling water over them. Cover and leave 5 minutes, drain. Alternatively, put sliced noodles in a colander and steam for a few minutes until heated through. Put noodles in a bowl, add all other ingredients and toss lightly until well mixed.

FRIED NOODLES, SINGAPORE STYLE

(picture page 255)

This recipe can be prepared using fresh rice noodles (kway teow) or fresh yellow wheat noodles (Hokkien mee).

Serves: 8-10
1 kg (2 lb) fresh noodles
500 g (1 lb) boiled pork
500 g (1 lb) small raw prawns
250 g (8 oz) fresh bean sprouts
6 cloves garlic
1 tablespoon canned salted black beans
 or bean sauce
¼ cup water or stock
1 teaspoon salt, or to taste
½ cup oil
3 stalks celery, finely chopped

Garnish:
4 eggs
pepper and salt to taste
8 spring onions
3 or 4 fresh red chillies
few stalks fresh coriander leaves
10 cloves garlic

If using fresh rice noodles, cut into 5 mm (¼ inch) strips and pour boiling water over to soften and separate the layers. Drain in a colander. If using Hokkien mee (thick yellow noodles), rinse in hot water and drain.

Slice the pork finely, then cut into narrow strips. Shell and de-vein the prawns; if small prawns are not available, cut large prawns into pieces. Wash bean sprouts, rinsing away any skins, then pinch off straggly 'tails'. Crush garlic, rinse salted beans and mash with a fork or chop finely. Bean sauce can be used straight from the jar.

At serving time heat a wok, pour in oil and when oil has heated stir fry the garlic on low heat until just starting to change colour. Add beans or bean sauce and stir fry for 30 seconds. Turn heat to high, add pork and fry for 1 minute, then add prawns and continue to stir fry for 2 minutes. Add water or stock, bring to the boil and add salt. Cook quickly, uncovered for 1 minute, then add celery and bean sprouts and toss for a further minute. Add the noodles and keep tossing until all the ingredients are thoroughly mixed and noodles heated through.

Dish on to a large flat platter and sprinkle the top of the noodles with all of the prepared garnishes. Serve immediately. If liked, put a bowl of rojak alongside. Rojak is a salad that usually accompanies the fried noodles (page 252).

Garnish: Beat eggs and season with pepper and salt. Heat a frying pan and grease lightly with oil. Fry the mixture, a little at a time, into thin round omelettes. Do not fold but turn them on to a plate as they are cooked. When cool, roll up and cut into thin strips.

Cut spring onions, including green leaves, into 5 cm (2 inch) lengths. Seed the chillies, then slice finely. Wash the fresh coriander, then chop leaves and stalks. Finely chop or pound garlic, rinse in cold water, squeeze dry in kitchen paper and fry over low heat until pale golden. Drain and crumble into small pieces.

FRESH NOODLES, FRIED

Serves: 4-6
500 g (1 lb) fresh wheat noodles
3 rashers bacon or slices of cooked pork
250 g (8 oz) lean steak
250 g (8 oz) small prawns
3 tablespoons oil
2 teaspoons salted soya bean paste
 (tauceo)
2 cloves garlic, crushed
½ teaspoon finely grated fresh ginger
2 cups shredded white Chinese cabbage
4 spring onions, cut into 5 cm (2 inch)
 lengths
¾-1 cup hot water
2 tablespoons light soy sauce

Put noodles in colander and steam over boiling water for 15 minutes. Meanwhile, remove rind and cut bacon or pork into fine strips. Cut steak into paper-thin slices and then into shreds. Shell and de-vein prawns. Heat a wok, add the oil and when hot fry the bacon for 1 minute. Add the beef, prawns, tauceo, garlic and ginger and stir fry until beef changes colour. Add cabbage and spring onions and stir fry 1 minute, then add noodles, hot water and soy sauce.

Cover and simmer on very low heat for 5-8 minutes, uncovering and turning noodles over every few minutes so they do not stick on bottom of pan. When noodles have absorbed all the liquid and are soft (but not too soft) the dish is ready. Serve hot.

FISH WITH CRAB SAUCE

Serves: 5-6
1 kg (2 lb) white fish fillets
½ teaspoon finely grated fresh ginger
1 teaspoon salt
2 teaspoons cornflour
oil for deep frying

Sauce:
2 tablespoons peanut oil
6 spring onions, chopped
½ teaspoon finely grated fresh ginger
8 tablespoons chicken or fish stock
185 g (6 oz) crab meat
pinch pepper
2½ teaspoons cornflour
1 tablespoon cold water

With a sharp knife, remove skin from fish. Wash fish and pat dry. Lay the fillets on a chopping board and rub with grated ginger. Cut fillets into halves lengthways, then into bite-size pieces. Toss in a mixture of salt and cornflour.

Heat peanut oil in a small deep pan or wok and quickly fry the fish, not too many pieces at a time, for 1 minute over medium heat. Drain on absorbent paper and keep warm while preparing sauce. Arrange fish on a dish, spoon sauce over and serve immediately.

Sauce: Heat oil and gently fry spring onions and ginger for a few seconds, stirring, then add stock, cover and simmer for 3-4 minutes. Add crab meat, heat through for not longer than a minute. Season with pepper. Mix cornflour smoothly with the cold water and stir into sauce. Continue stirring over medium heat until sauce boils. Taste and add salt if necessary.

DEEP-FRIED FISH WITH VEGETABLES

Serves: 4-6
750 g (1½ lb) white fish fillets
1 tablespoon egg white
1 teaspoon salt
½ teaspoon five spice powder
1 tablespoon cornflour
6 tablespoons oil
1 clove garlic, crushed
½ teaspoon finely grated fresh ginger
2 cups sliced white Chinese cabbage
6 spring onions, cut in 5 cm (2 inch) lengths
1 tablespoon light soy sauce
1 tablespoon oyster sauce
½ cup water
1 teaspoon cornflour, extra

Cut fish fillets into finger pieces, dip in egg white and then in a mixture of the salt, spice and cornflour. Dust off excess flour. Heat oil in a wok and fry fish on high heat, one quarter of the quantity at a time, for just long enough to cook it through. This should take less than 2 minutes and as little as 1 minute, depending on the thickness of the fish. Drain on absorbent paper and keep warm. Pour off all but a tablespoon of the oil, add garlic, ginger and cabbage and stir fry for 1 minute. Add spring onions and stir fry 1 minute more. Add sauces and water, bring liquid to a boil, stir in extra cornflour mixed with very little cold water and stir until sauce boils and thickens. Arrange on a dish with fish pieces on top and serve immediately with rice or noodles.

STIR-FRIED SHRIMP WITH BEAN SPROUTS AND SNOW PEAS

Serves: 4-6

2 tablespoons dried wood fungus
250 g (8 oz) shrimps or small raw prawns
250 g (8 oz) fresh bean sprouts
12-18 snow peas
2 celery stalks
2 tablespoons oil
1 clove garlic, crushed
½ teaspoon finely grated fresh ginger
2 teaspoons cornflour
1 teaspoon sugar
1 tablespoon light soy sauce
1 tablespoon Chinese wine or dry sherry

Soak wood fungus in hot water for 10 minutes. It will swell and soften. Trim off any gritty pieces. Shell and de-vein the prawns. Wash bean sprouts and drain. If 'tails' are long and straggly, pinch them off. Remove stems and strings from snow peas. Slice celery thinly in diagonal slices.

Heat oil in a wok. Add garlic and ginger and stir for 10 seconds, then add the sliced celery and stir fry on high heat for 2 minutes. Add bean sprouts and fry for 1 minute longer or until vegetables are tender but still crisp. Remove from pan. Add very little more oil to wok and stir fry the shrimps until they turn pink. Add snow peas and stir fry for 30-40 seconds. Return other vegetables, heat through, then move food to side of pan, thicken liquid with the cornflour mixed with the sugar, soy sauce and wine, and serve immediately.

FRIED PRAWNS SWEET AND SOUR

Serves: 4

500 g (1 lb) medium-size raw prawns
3 cups cold water
salt
½ teaspoon finely grated fresh ginger
2 egg whites
2½ tablespoons cornflour
peanut oil for deep frying
1 small green cucumber, finely sliced
5 spring onion curls

Sauce:
¼ cup white vinegar
¾ cup pineapple or orange juice
3 tablespoons sugar
½ teaspoon salt
pinch red colouring powder
1 tablespoon arrowroot
1 tablespoon cold water

Shell and de-vein the prawns, leaving only the last segment of the shell and the tail on. Wash the prawns, then soak them in cold water with half teaspoon salt for 30 minutes. Drain well in a colander and then blot on kitchen paper. Put prawns into a dry bowl and sprinkle with another half teaspoon of salt. Add the ginger and mix well with the hand. Add egg whites and cornflour and mix again until prawns are thoroughly coated. Cover and refrigerate for 4 hours or leave overnight.

At serving time make the sauce and have it ready, then heat oil for deep frying (at least 3 cups of oil in a wok). When oil is hot add half the prawns and fry for 1 minute or less — just until prawns turn opaque and pink. Do not overcook or they will lose their succulence and become tough. Lift out on wire spoon and drain on absorbent paper. Let oil get hot again and fry remaining prawns. After draining, put the prawns on serving plate and pour sauce over. Garnish with slices of cucumber and spring onion curls and serve at once.

Sauce: Combine vinegar, fruit juice, sugar, salt and sufficient colouring to give a bright pink colour. Bring to the boil, remove from heat and stir in arrowroot mixed smoothly with cold water. Return to heat and stir until sauce boils and thickens.

Note: To make spring onion curls, cut 10 cm (4 inch) lengths of spring onion, using green leaves as well as white portion. With a sharp, pointed knife cut one end into fine strips. Soak in iced water and the strips will curl outwards.

PRAWNS IN CHILLI BEAN SAUCE

Serves: 2-3
12 large raw prawns
1 clove garlic, crushed
½ teaspoon salt
½ teaspoon finely grated fresh ginger
2 teaspoons Chinese wine or dry sherry
1 red capsicum
1 green capsicum
1 tablespoon canned salted black beans
1-2 teaspoons Chinese chilli sauce
2 teaspoons hoi sin sauce
2 tablespoons peanut oil
spring onion brushes and chilli flowers to
    garnish

Shell and de-vein prawns, then put in a bowl and mix in garlic crushed with the salt. Add ginger and wine and leave to marinate while preparing other ingredients.

Cut capsicums in small squares. Rinse black beans and drain, then crush or chop finely and mix with chilli sauce and hoi sin sauce. Pour oil into a heated wok, stir fry capsicums for 2 minutes, then remove them to the side of the wok and add prawns to the oil. Fry over high heat until they turn pink, about 2 minutes. Move prawns to one side and add a little more oil, about half a tablespoon. Add black bean and sauce mixture to oil and stir over heat for 30 seconds, then mix the prawns and capsicum into the sauce and fry for a few seconds until coated with the black bean mixture. Garnish and serve at once.

DEEP-FRIED PRAWNS WITH CHILLI

Serves: 4
500 g (1 lb) raw prawns
3 fresh red chillies
1 clove garlic
2 teaspoons finely grated fresh ginger
1 tablespoon sugar
1 tablespoon light soy sauce
1 tablespoon Chinese wine or dry sherry
oil for deep frying

Shell and de-vein the prawns, rinse and dry well on paper towels. Slit the chillies and remove seeds, then chop them finely. Crush garlic with a little of the measured sugar and mix with the chillies and ginger.

Heat about half cup oil in a wok until very hot and deep fry the prawns a few at a time for 2 or 3 minutes or just until the colour changes. Do not fry too long. Remove from pan and drain on absorbent paper. Pour off most of oil from pan, leaving only about a tablespoon. Add the chillies, garlic and ginger and fry on low heat, stirring. Add the remaining sugar, soy sauce and wine, then add prawns and stir only until reheated. Serve immediately with rice or noodles.

FRIED CHILLI CRABS
(picture opposite)

Serves: 4
2 medium size raw crabs
½ cup peanut oil
2 teaspoons finely grated fresh ginger
3 cloves garlic, finely chopped
3 fresh red chillies, seeded and chopped
¼ cup tomato sauce
¼ cup chilli sauce
1 tablespoon sugar
1 tablespoon light soy sauce
1 teaspoon salt

Wash crabs well, scrubbing away any mossy patches on the shell. Remove hard top shell, stomach bag and fibrous tissue and with cleaver chop each crab into 4 pieces, or 6 pieces if they are large.

Heat a wok, add oil and when oil is very hot fry the crab pieces until they change colour, turning them so they cook on all sides. Remove to a plate. Turn heat to low and fry the ginger, garlic and red chillies, stirring constantly, until they are cooked but not brown. Add the sauces, sugar, soy sauce and salt, bring to the boil, then return crabs to the wok and allow to simmer in the sauce for 3 minutes, adding very little water if sauce reduces too much. Serve with white rice.

FRIED CHILLI CRABS *recipe above*

ABALONE IN OYSTER SAUCE

Serves: 4-5
1 x 454 g (1 lb) can abalone
4 dried Chinese mushrooms
12 snow peas or 4 Chinese mustard
   cabbage leaves
4 spring onions

Sauce:
1 tablespoon oyster sauce
1 teaspoon light soy sauce
1 tablespoon Chinese wine or dry sherry
¾ cup water
2 teaspoons cornflour

Drain liquid from can of abalone. Slice abalone in paper-thin slices. Soak mushrooms in hot water for 30 minutes, then cut off and discard stalks and slice each mushroom into 4. String snow peas or cut cabbage into bite-size pieces. Cut spring onions into similar lengths.

Sauce: Combine oyster sauce, soy sauce and wine, add a little to the cornflour and mix until smooth, then combine with water. Bring to the boil in a small pan, stirring constantly. Add mushrooms, peas or cabbage and spring onions. Cook, stirring until the vegetables are tender but still crisp, about 2 minutes. Add abalone and just heat through. Do not cook abalone on high heat or for longer than is necessary to just heat it or it will toughen.

COUNTRY CAPTAIN

Serves: 6
1.5 kg (3 lb) chicken or chicken pieces
2 cloves garlic, crushed
2 teaspoons salt
1 teaspoon ground turmeric
½ teaspoon ground black pepper
4 tablespoons oil
4 large onions, thinly sliced
2 fresh red chillies, seeded and sliced
½ cup water

Cut chicken into serving pieces. Combine garlic, salt, turmeric, pepper and rub well into chicken. Heat oil in a large saucepan and gently fry half the sliced onion until brown. Remove onion from pan and set aside.
   Fry remaining onion and chillies until just starting to colour, then add chicken to pan and fry until golden all over. Add water, cover and simmer gently until chicken is tender. Uncover and continue to simmer, allowing any liquid remaining in pan to evaporate. Serve hot, garnished with the reserved fried onion and accompanied by fried potatoes or ghee rice (page 118).

SATAY-FLAVOURED ROAST CHICKEN

Serves: 4-5
Cooking time: 1½-1¾ hours
Oven temperature: 170-190°C (350-375°F)
1 x 1.5 kg (3 lb) roasting chicken
1 medium onion, roughly chopped
1 clove garlic
2 fresh red chillies, seeded and chopped
2 cups coconut milk
2 teaspoons ground coriander
1½ teaspoons ground cummin
½ teaspoon ground fennel
½ teaspoon ground turmeric
½ teaspoon laos powder, optional
½ teaspoon finely grated lemon rind
2 candlenuts or brazil kernels, finely grated
1½ teaspoons salt
1 tablespoon lemon juice
2 tablespoons oil or ghee

Wash chicken well and dry inside and out with kitchen towels. Put onion, garlic and chillies into container of electric blender and blend to a smooth paste, adding 2 tablespoons of the coconut milk if necessary. Mix in the ground spices, lemon rind and grated nuts.
   Heat oil or ghee in pan and fry the mixed ingredients, stirring constantly, until colour darkens and oil separates from the mixture. It should smell cooked and come away cleanly from the pan. Remove from heat and mix in salt and lemon juice. Rub the mixture inside and outside the chicken, truss it and put it in a roasting pan breast upwards. Pour the coconut milk around the chicken. Roast in preheated moderate oven, basting after 15 minutes. After a further 15 minutes, turn the chicken breast downwards, baste again and continue cooking until tender in this position, basting every 20 minutes. If coconut milk shows signs of drying up, add about ½-1 cup more. Turn chicken breast upwards for 15 minutes longer or until a nice golden brown and cooked through. Carve chicken and serve with the thick coconut milk gravy spooned over. Serve with rice and accompaniments.

CRISP-SKIN CHICKEN

A recipe which I have pursued for years, but never been entirely happy with until now. There are many versions and I wouldn't be surprised if I've tried them all in my search for perfection! When you have a few hours to spare between planning your meal and eating it, you may care to try this method . . . I'm sure the results will please you as they did me.

Serves: 4
1 small frying chicken, about 1 kg (2 lb)
salt
five spice powder
1 teaspoon cayenne pepper
2 teaspoons ground cinnamon
1 tablespoon honey
1 lemon

Wash chicken and remove neck and giblets. Wipe with kitchen paper towels inside and out, and rub inside the chicken with 1 teaspoon salt mixed with quarter teaspoon five spice powder.

In a saucepan bring to the boil 6 cups of water with the cayenne pepper, cinnamon and 2 teaspoons five spice powder and pour over the chicken in a bowl. Leave chicken in this while bringing to the boil 4 more cups water and the honey. Add the lemon cut in slices. Drain chicken from the first mixture and put it in a colander. Pour the honey mixture over, making sure it comes in contact with all parts of the chicken. Put the chicken on a wire cake rack in front of a window or in some airy place to dry; in the sunlight would be ideal if you can hang it in a safe place. Leave to dry for 5 hours.

Just before serving, heat about 8 cups of oil in a wok and heat it but do not have it too hot. Tie the legs of the chicken together, leaving some string to hold it with, and lower the bird into the oil. With a ladle, spoon oil over the chicken as it cooks, and turn it so that it is cooked and brown on all sides. On medium heat the chicken should be cooked through in about 12-15 minutes. Test by piercing with a fine skewer where the thigh joins the body. If juice that runs out is clear the chicken is done, but if it is pink return it to the pan for further cooking. Lift on to a board with slotted spoon and cut the chicken in half lengthways with a heavy chopper. Place each half cut side down on the board and chop through into 2.5 cm (1 inch) wide strips, then reassemble the bird on a serving dish. Serve with salt and five spice mix (page 432) and wedges of lemon. Garnish with fresh coriander leaves if liked and serve immediately. The pieces of chicken are sprinkled with the spice mix and lemon juice by each person before eating.

EASTERN-STYLE CROQUETTES

Makes about 18
2 tablespoons oil
1 medium onion, finely chopped
2 cloves garlic, finely chopped
½ teaspoon finely grated fresh ginger
2 fresh green chillies, seeded and chopped
2 teaspoons ground coriander
1 teaspoon ground cummin
500 g (1 lb) minced beef steak
1½ teaspoons salt
½ teaspoon ground black pepper
2 tablespoons finely chopped fresh
   coriander leaves
6 spring onions, finely chopped
1 kg (2 lb) potatoes
extra salt and pepper to taste
1 egg, beaten
fine dry breadcrumbs for coating
oil for deep frying

Heat oil and gently fry onion, garlic, ginger and chillies until soft. Add coriander, cummin and minced steak and fry, stirring, until meat changes colour. Add salt and pepper, cover and cook until meat is tender. (There should be no liquid left when meat is cooked). Stir in coriander and allow to cool. When quite cold mix in spring onion.

Cook potatoes in boiling salted water until tender. Drain well and mash until smooth. Season to taste with salt and pepper. Take 2 tablespoons of mashed potato in one hand, flatten slightly, then put 1 tablespoon of meat mixture in the centre. Mould potato around meat and form into an oval shape. Repeat process until all the meat and potato is used. Dip croquettes in beaten egg, then in breadcrumbs and deep fry in hot oil until golden brown. Drain on absorbent paper and serve hot with chilli sauce (page 253).

BEEF OR PORK SATAY

Serves: 6
500 g (1 lb) pork fillet or rump steak
1 strip lemon rind
2 medium onions, roughly chopped
1 tablespoon light soy sauce
1-2 tablespoons oil
2 teaspoons ground coriander
1 teaspoon ground cummin
1 teaspoon ground turmeric
¼ teaspoon ground cinnamon
1 teaspoon salt
1 teaspoon sugar
2 tablespoons roasted peanuts

Cut the pork or beef into small cubes, the size of the tip of your finger. Put the lemon rind, onions, soy sauce and 1 tablespoon of oil into container of electric blender and blend until smooth, then add the remaining ingredients and blend for a few seconds longer, adding remaining tablespoon of oil if necessary to draw ingredients down over blades. Pour marinade over meat, mix well and leave for at least 1 hour. Thread on bamboo skewers, about 6 pieces to a skewer and reaching less than halfway up the skewer. Grill over glowing coals or under a preheated griller just until meat is cooked. Serve with peanut sauce, white rice or nasi lemak, and a salad; or if liked serve a satay gravy (page 252) instead of the peanut sauce (page 207).

FRIED PORK WITH MEEHOON

Serves: 4
250 g (8 oz) meehoon (fine rice vermicelli)
250 g (8 oz) belly pork
4 tablespoons peanut oil
1 cup cubed raw potato
2 medium onions, sliced very finely
2-3 cloves garlic, finely chopped
2 tablespoons light soy sauce
½ cup water
ground black pepper to taste
¼ teaspoon salt
3 teaspoons sugar

Put the meehoon in a large bowl, pour warm water over and leave to soak for 5 minutes, then drain in a colander. Remove skin of pork and cut meat into very small dice. Heat a wok, add the oil and when oil is smoking hot add the cubed potato and fry over high heat for 2 minutes, then reduce heat to medium and continue frying until cubes are golden. Remove with slotted spoon. Add the onions and garlic and fry 2 minutes, stirring, on medium low heat, then add the pork, stir and fry for 5 minutes or until pork is cooked and golden brown. Add the drained meehoon, and half the soy sauce and water mixed together. Toss and stir until water is absorbed, then add remaining sauce and water. Add pepper, salt and sugar, continue stirring until liquid is almost all absorbed, taking care not to let mixture stick at base of wok. Stir in potatoes and heat through. Serve immediately.

PORK WITH SZECHWAN VEGETABLE

Serves: 3-4
125 g (4 oz) rice vermicelli
250 g (8 oz) pork
2 tablespoons oil
5 cloves garlic, finely chopped
2 teaspoons finely grated fresh ginger
1 piece canned Szechwan vegetable,
    chopped (about 3 tablespoons)
5 leaves white Chinese cabbage, sliced
1 teaspoon light soy sauce
¾ cup pork stock or water

Soak rice vermicelli in hot water for 10 minutes, then drain. Cut pork into very small dice. Heat oil in a wok or frying pan and when very hot put in the pork and stir fry until brown and crisp. Remove from pan and drain on absorbent paper. Pour off excess oil from pan, leaving 1 tablespoon. On medium low heat fry garlic, ginger and Szechwan vegetable until garlic and ginger are soft and golden. Add cabbage leaves and stir fry for 2 minutes. Add soy sauce and stock and bring to the boil, then add rice vermicelli and cook until liquid is absorbed. Serve hot.

BARBECUE-STYLE PORK WITH BLACK BEANS

Serves: 6
750 g (1 ½ lb) boneless loin of pork
3 cloves garlic
½ teaspoon salt
1 teaspoon finely grated fresh ginger
1 tablespoon honey
1 tablespoon Chinese wine or dry sherry
½ teaspoon five spice powder
1 tablespoon black beans, chopped
1 tablespoon dark soy sauce
1 tablespoon barbecue sauce (see Glossary)
1 tablespoon peanut oil

Ask butcher to remove rind from the pork. Cut pork into strips 5 cm (2 inches) long and 2.5 cm (1 inch) wide. Crush garlic with salt and combine with all the other ingredients except oil. Rub over the pork and leave for at least 15 minutes to marinate.

Heat wok, add oil and swirl to coat wok. Add the pork pieces, reserving marinade. Stir fry the pork until browned, then add reserved marinade, washing out the bowl with half cup hot water and adding that too. Reduce heat, cover and simmer for 30-40 minutes until pork is tender. Stir occasionally and add more hot water if liquid looks like drying up. Be careful that the sweet marinade does not burn. The heat should be very low throughout the cooking.

When pork is tender remove from heat and if not serving straight away it may be reheated at serving time. Serve with plain white rice.

Note: A larger quantity of pork can be cooked like this, and part of it refrigerated and used for adding to dishes that call for a small amount of barbecued pork.

SPICED SPARERIBS

A favourite recipe because it is so easy and the flavour so special — it can also be prepared a day ahead. When required, grill the spareribs a few minutes on each side, just to heat through. The best way to enjoy spareribs is to pick them up in the fingers.

Serves: 6
Cooking time: 1 hour
Oven temperature: 170-190°C (350-375°F)
1.5 kg (3 lb) pork spareribs
4 cloves garlic
1 ½ teaspoons salt
½ teaspoon ground black pepper
½ teaspoon five spice powder
1 tablespoon honey
1 tablespoon sesame oil
3 tablespoons light soy sauce
½ cup hot water
plum sauce (page 432)

Separate spareribs with a sharp knife or ask the butcher to do it for you. Crush garlic with salt, combine with pepper, five spice powder, honey, sesame oil and soy. Rub well into spareribs. Put them in a roasting pan and cook in a moderate oven. After 30 minutes, turn spareribs, add hot water to pan and continue roasting, basting with the liquid every 10 minutes, for a further 30 minutes.

Alternatively, heat 1-2 tablespoons peanut oil in a large heavy frying pan and brown spareribs. Add water, cover and simmer for 30-35 minutes or until tender.

Serve hot with boiled rice and plum sauce.

SAMBAL BABI
PORK AND HOT SPICES COOKED IN COCONUT MILK

Serves: 6-8
750 g (1½ lb) belly pork
1½ cups coconut milk
finely grated rind of 1 lemon, or 1 stalk
   lemon grass, bruised
1½ teaspoons laos powder
2 teaspoons finely grated fresh ginger
2 small onions, finely chopped
4 cloves garlic, crushed
1-2 teaspoons chilli powder
1 teaspoon dried shrimp paste (blacan)
1 teaspoon ground coriander
1 teaspoon ground cummin
1-2 teaspoons sugar to taste
1 teaspoon salt

Cut the pork, skin and all, into small cubes. Make the coconut milk as described on page 11, using only the first extract for this dish. Put pork, coconut milk and all other ingredients into a pan and bring slowly to the boil, stirring constantly. This prevents the coconut milk curdling. Turn heat low and continue to simmer until pork is tender and liquid almost absorbed, stirring frequently. This takes about 1 hour. Serve with white rice and other accompaniments such as cooling salads because these sambals are very hot. Reduce quantity of chilli if a less volcanic result is preferred.

SATAY GRAVY

Sufficient for about 750 g (1½ lb) meat or chicken.

4 tablespoons oil
1 stalk lemon grass, sliced and crushed, or
   3 strips lemon rind, finely chopped
1 medium onion, finely chopped
3 cloves garlic, finely chopped
2 teaspoons dried shrimp paste (blacan)
185 g (6 oz) roasted, skinned peanuts
1½ tablespoons dried tamarind
1 cup hot water
1 teaspoon chilli powder
1½ teaspoons laos powder
2 tablespoons sugar
1 teaspoon salt

Put 2 tablespoons oil in blender container, add lemon grass or lemon rind, onion, garlic, and blacan and blend to a paste. Scrape out blender container, add peanuts and crush finely. Set aside. Soak tamarind in hot water, squeeze to dissolve pulp, strain.

Heat remaining oil in a wok and stir fry the blended mixture over medium heat until it smells cooked, add the chilli powder, laos, tamarind liquid, sugar, salt and peanuts. Simmer, stirring until thickened, about 8 minutes.

ROJAK

Serves: 8-10
1 large or 2 small cucumbers
1 small pineapple, not too ripe
3 fresh red or green chillies

Dressing:
3 tablespoons Chinese vinegar or
   other mild vinegar
2 tablespoons sugar
2 teaspoons sambal ulek or
   crushed fresh chillies
1 teaspoon dried shrimp paste *(blacan),*
   or to taste
salt and lemon juice to taste

Peel cucumbers, cut lengthways and remove seeds, then cut into matchstick strips. Cut skin off pineapple and remove all the eyes. See illustration on page 14. Cut pineapple into wedges lengthways, slice off core, then cut flesh into dice. Seed chillies and cut into thin slices. Combine cucumbers, pineapple and chillies in a bowl and sprinkle lightly with salt.

Dressing: Wrap the blacan in foil. Put under a preheated griller or over coals for about 5 minutes on each side. Unwrap and dissolve in the vinegar. Add sugar, chilli, salt and lemon juice to taste and toss the dressing with the pineapple mixture. Alternatively, serve the dressing separately.

CHILLI SAUCE

250 g (8 oz) fresh red chillies or
  ½ cup chilli powder
3 cups sugar
1 x 750 ml (26 fl oz) bottle white vinegar
375 g (12 oz) sultanas
8 cloves garlic
3 teaspoons salt or to taste
1 tablespoon finely grated fresh ginger

Be sure to wear rubber gloves when handling chillies. Discard stems. The seeds may be removed by splitting the chillies lengthways and scraping them out. Chop the chillies roughly and put them into a blender with sufficient vinegar to facilitate grinding the chillies.

Put all the ingredients in a large enamel or stainless steel saucepan and bring to the boil. Simmer gently until the sultanas and chillies are very soft. Cool, then purée in a blender or rub through a sieve. Pour into sterilised bottles and seal.

LAKSA LEMAK
MIXED SEAFOOD SOUP

Laksa is a one-dish meal of rice noodles and seafood in a spicy soup. The Singapore version is rich with coconut milk, while Penang style Laksa omits the coconut milk and is piquant in flavour. The former, also known as Laksa Lemak, is more popular.

Serves: 6-8
500 g (1 lb) raw prawns
500 g (1 lb) prepared fish cakes
185 g (6 oz) crabmeat, optional
1 tablespoon oil
10 cups water
salt
375 g (12 oz) rice vermicelli
250 g (8 oz) fresh bean sprouts
1 green cucumber
small bunch laksa leaves *(Vietnamese mint)*
sambal ulek or sambal bajak
fresh limes, optional

For the soup:
6 large dried red chillies
2 tablespoons dried prawns or 2 teaspoons
  dried shrimp paste (blacan)
2 medium onions
2 small knobs fresh or brined laos root or
  2 teaspoons laos powder
6 candlenuts or macadamia or brazil
  kernels
2 stems lemon grass or thinly peeled rind
  of 1 lemon
4 tablespoons peanut oil
1 teaspoon ground turmeric
1 tablespoon ground coriander
6 cups coconut milk (pages 11-12) or 2
  cans coconut milk diluted with water

Wash the prawns well, remove shells and heads and reserve for making stock. De-vein the prawns, slice the fish cakes and pick over the crabmeat for any bony bits. Keep the seafood refrigerated until required.

Heat a tablespoon of oil in a saucepan, add the well-drained prawn shells and heads and fry, stirring, until they turn red. Add the water and 2 teaspoons salt and simmer, covered, for about 1 hour or until reduced by a third. Strain stock, discard shells and heads.

Pour very hot water over the rice vermicelli in a bowl and leave to soak for 10 minutes. Drain. Pinch any straggly tails off the bean sprouts, wash well and drain in a colander. Peel and seed the cucumber and cut into matchstick strips. Shred the laksa leaf finely.

To make the soup: Break off stems of dry chillies and shake out the seeds. Soak the chillies and dried prawns in hot water for at least 10 minutes. Put the chillies, prawns, onions, laos, candlenuts and finely sliced lemon grass (use only the white portion) into the container of an electric blender. Add a little of the soaking water to facilitate blending, and grind to a purée.

Heat 3 tablespoons oil in a heavy saucepan and fry the ground mixture, stirring to prevent burning, until it is brown and smells fragrant. Add the turmeric and coriander and stir fry for a minute longer. Add the strained stock and simmer for about half an hour.

Before serving, add the coconut milk, taste and correct seasoning. Add the sliced fish cakes and crabmeat and bring to simmering point. Drain the rice vermicelli and add to the soup. Heat a tablespoon of oil and stir fry the prawns for just a couple of minutes, adding a little salt to taste.

Serve the laksa in large bowls, topping each bowl with bean sprouts, cucumber strips, a few prawns and shreds of laksa leaf. Serve chilli sambal separately for intrepid chilli eaters and halved limes or lemon for those who prefer a more piquant flavour.

MAH MEE
SOUP NOODLES

Serves: 5-6
500 g (1 lb) raw prawns
1 tablespoon peanut oil
4 cups water
1½ teaspoons salt
2 cups chicken stock
250 g (8 oz) barbecued pork
250 g (8 oz) bean sprouts
1 tablespoon sesame oil
3 cloves garlic, finely grated
½ teaspoon finely grated fresh ginger
125 g (4 oz) fine egg noodles
1 teaspoon five spice powder
90 g (3¼ oz) can crab meat
½ cup finely chopped spring onions
1 small cucumber, peeled and diced

Shell and de-vein prawns. Wash prawn shells and heads thoroughly, drain. Heat peanut oil in a saucepan and fry heads and shells over a high heat until they turn pink. Add water and salt, cover and cook for 20 minutes. Strain. (If liked, the prawn heads and a little of the stock can be blended for a few seconds in an electric blender, then passed through a fine strainer and the liquid added to the prawn stock. This results in a more flavoursome soup.) Combine prawn and chicken stocks.

Cut barbecued pork into thin slices. Wash and drain bean sprouts. Heat sesame oil and gently fry garlic and ginger. When starting to brown add stock and prawns. Bring to the boil and cook for 5 minutes. Add noodles and cook for a further 5 minutes. Add pork, bean sprouts and five spice powder, simmer for 2 minutes and serve in a large bowl, garnished with crab meat, spring onions and cucumber.

HOKKIEN MEE SOUP

Serves 6 as a main dish, 8-10 as part of a meal with other dishes
500 g (1 lb) small cooked prawns
500 g (1 lb) Hokkien mee
 (thick yellow noodles)
125 g (4 oz) rice vermicelli
500 g (1 lb) fresh bean sprouts
12 spinach leaves

Garnishes:
125 g (4 oz) pork fat
4 tablespoons dried onion flakes
4 dried chillies, optional
soy sauce
oil for frying

Soup:
8 cups pork or chicken stock
2 dried chillies, seeded
1 tablespoon oil
sugar, soy sauce and salt to taste
½ cup cooked pork cut into small strips, optional

Peel the prawns. Bring a large amount of lightly salted water to the boil in a saucepan or wok, drop in the fresh noodles and parboil. Drain in colander, run cold water over to stop cooking process. Put rice vermicelli in a bowl, run hot water in to cover. leave to soak for 10 minutes, drain. Scald the fresh bean sprouts by pouring boiling water over them in a colander, then run cold water over to cool. Remove stems of spinach, cook in a little boiling water until half done, drain and cut into short strips. Have all these ingredients ready in separate bowls.

Garnishes: Put about 1 tablespoon oil in a wok, heat and add pork fat cut into tiny dice. Stir fry until crisp. Remove from pan and drain on absorbent paper. Add about 3 or 4 tablespoons oil to the wok and fry the dried onion flakes over low heat, watching very carefully for they can burn and taste bitter in a few seconds. Do not have the oil too hot. A good way to fry dried onion or garlic is to put the flakes in a fine strainer and lower them gently into the oil, let them fry in the strainer and lift them all out together. Drain on absorbent paper. Cut tops off the chillies and shake out seeds, then fry them until they turn dark. Drain. When cool crumble them into small pieces. Put each of these garnishes into a small bowl, and have a bowl of soy sauce for seasoning individual portions.

Soup: Bring the stock to the boil. In another pan heat the tablespoon of oil (oil left over from frying the garnishes can be used) and fry the 2 dry seeded chillies. When they turn dark add the hot stock, sugar, soy and salt, and simmer for 5 minutes.

To serve the soup, put a serving of Hokkien noodles, rice vermicelli, bean sprouts, prawns and spinach leaves into each large soup bowl. Pour the boiling soup over, then serve with the garnishes already on the table so each person can add according to taste.

Ingredients for FRIED NOODLES *recipe page 243*

POH PIA
(picture page 259)

This popular snack of Chinese origin is known as poh pia in Singapore and Malaysia, kau pyan in Burma and bears a strong resemblance to the lumpia of the Philippines. It is a fresh spring roll — in other words, one that is not fried. Ideal for a do-it-yourself meal where everyone assembles his or her own, adding a portion of each ingredient that goes to make up the medley of flavours within the egg roll wrapping.

The poh pia consists of three parts: (1) the wrapping; (2) the cooked filling; (3) the garnishes, which are served separately and added to the filling according to taste.

Makes about 25

Egg Roll Wrappers:
5 eggs
1½ cups cold water
½ teaspoon salt
2 tablespoons oil
1 cup plain flour

Filling:
4 tablespoons oil
2 cakes yellow bean curd, cut in strips
500 g (1 lb) belly pork, boiled and diced
6 cloves garlic, finely chopped
3 tablespoons salted soya beans, mashed, or bean sauce
250 g (8 oz) raw prawns
1 x 800 g (1 lb 12 oz) can bamboo shoots, drained and cut into matchstick strips
250 g (8 oz) Chinese sweet turnip (bangkwang), peeled and cut into matchstick strips
½ teaspoon salt, or to taste

Garnishes:
1 large lettuce
185 g (6 oz) canned or frozen crab meat
1 small cucumber
250 g (8 oz) bean sprouts
6 lap cheong (Chinese sausages)
3 eggs
10 to 15 cloves garlic
small bunch fresh coriander leaves
chilli sauce (page 253)
dark soy sauce, sweetened or kecap manis

Egg Roll Wrappers: With rotary beater beat eggs and water together until well mixed but not too frothy. Add salt, oil and flour and beat until smooth. Allow to rest for 30 minutes while preparing filling. (If liked, the batter can be made in an electric blender, putting in the liquid ingredients first then the flour. Blend for just a few seconds, stop motor and scrape down sides of blender container, then blend for a further few seconds. This batter must be allowed to rest for a longer time, and if there is still froth on top when ready to cook the wrappers, spoon it off before starting to cook.) Lightly oil a heavy frying pan or pancake pan with a piece of absorbent paper dipped in oil and rubbed over the heated pan. Pour in a small ladle of batter, swirl the pan quickly to make a very thin coating and pour any excess back into the container of batter. Cook over low heat until underside is cooked and very pale golden. Turn and cook other side for a few seconds only. These wrappers should not be allowed to brown. Pile one on top of the other on a flat plate as they are cooked.

Filling: Heat the oil in a wok and fry the strips of bean curd until they are golden brown all over. Drain on absorbent paper. Cut into small dice.

Pour off all but a tablespoon of the oil from the wok, add the diced pork and fry, stirring until the fat begins to run. Add the garlic and the mashed or pounded soya beans and fry, stirring until the garlic begins to smell cooked. Add the shelled, de-veined and chopped raw prawns and toss until the prawns change colour. Add the bamboo shoots and sweet turnip and fry, stirring and tossing, until cooked but still crisp, then add the bean curd. Sprinkle with salt and mix, then taste and add more salt if necessary. Simmer uncovered in the wok until filling is almost dry. Invert a small bowl inside a larger bowl and put the filling in this so that any liquid or oil from the filling can drain away under the little bowl.

Garnishes: Wash the lettuce well, separating the leaves. With a stainless knife remove the thick leaf rib and cut each leaf into two or three pieces lengthways. Blot lettuce gently on absorbent paper or leave to drain, then pile leaves on a plate. Flake the crab meat, removing any bits of bony tissue. Put into a small bowl. Pinch straggly 'tails' off bean sprouts, wash well, scald by pouring boiling water over, then refresh under running cold water. Drain well, pile into a bowl. Peel and seed cucumber, cut in strips.

Steam the lap cheong in a colander for 10 minutes, then cut into thin slices. Put into a bowl and keep warm. Beat the eggs, season with salt and pepper, and fry in a lightly oiled frying pan to make 4 or 5 very thin omelettes. Do not fold. Turn on to a plate as they are done. When cool roll up and cut into thin strips. Put into a bowl.

Finely chop garlic, or bruise with mortar and pestle. Rinse garlic in cold water, drain well in fine sieve, then wrap in kitchen paper and squeeze gently to remove as much moisture as possible. Heat about 4 tablespoons oil in a wok and fry the garlic over low heat, stirring constantly, until it starts to turn golden. Remove pan from the heat at once and let it finish cooking in the stored heat of the oil. When cool remove from oil and drain on kitchen paper. Put into a small bowl.

Wash fresh coriander leaves very well, dry on kitchen paper, then chop leaves fairly fine. Put into a small bowl. Put chilli sauce (either home-made [page 253] or the sweet type made in Singapore or Malaysia and available from Chinese grocery stores) into a small bowl. In another bowl mix dark soy sauce with a little sugar to sweeten.

Have all the garnishes ready before starting to cook the egg roll wrappers and the filling.

To Serve: Assembling the poh pia is half the fun and adds greatly to the enjoyment of eating this snack. Each person puts an egg roll wrapper on his or her plate. On this goes a piece of lettuce leaf, which is then spread with chilli sauce or sprinkled with the sweetened soy. A spoonful of the cooked filling is then put on the leaf and garnishes as desired are added. Roll up the egg wrapper, turning in the sides so that the filling is completely enclosed. Poh pia should be eaten immediately, not left to stand, for the wrapper will get soggy.

SPRING ROLLS

This popular snack is within the scope of any home cook now that the spring roll wrappers, or 'skins' or 'shells' as they are called, are available frozen from Chinese grocery stores, approximately 20 to a packet. Thaw before attempting to separate these delicate pastry squares.

Makes: 20
6 dried Chinese mushrooms
3 tablespoons peanut oil
1 tablespoon sesame oil
1 clove garlic, finely grated
½ teaspoon finely grated fresh ginger
250 g (8 oz) pork, chopped finely
250 g (8 oz) raw prawns, de-veined and chopped
2 cups shredded Chinese cabbage
1 cup shredded giant white radish
12 water chestnuts, chopped
1 cup chopped bamboo shoots
125 g (4 oz) bean sprouts
6 spring onions, finely chopped
1 tablespoon light soy sauce
1 tablespoon oyster sauce
1 teaspoon salt
3 teaspoons cornflour
1 packet frozen spring roll wrappers
oil for deep frying

Cover mushrooms with hot water and soak for 20 minutes. Remove stalks and chop mushrooms. Heat peanut and sesame oil in a wok and slowly fry garlic and ginger for a few seconds. Add pork, raise heat and stir fry until it changes colour. Add prawns and continue stirring and frying until they are cooked. Add prepared vegetables, soy sauce, oyster sauce and salt, combine thoroughly. Push mixture to one side and tilt wok so liquid gathers. Stir in cornflour, which has been mixed with a little cold water until smooth. Cook, stirring, until thick. Remove wok from heat and mix thickened liquid into the filling. Allow to cool completely.

Put 2 tablespoons of mixture at one end of spring roll wrapper and roll up, turning in the sides so that filling is completely enclosed. Dampen edges with water or a mixture of cornflour and water and press to seal.

Fry one or two at a time in deep hot oil until golden brown. Drain on absorbent paper and serve immediately with chilli sauce (page 253) if liked.

MURTABA
ROTIS WITH SAVOURY FILLING

This recipe is Indian in origin, but has come to be associated with Singapore and the open-air eating places. In Sri Lanka too they are very popular and the 'godamba roti' man walks suburban streets at the dinner hour tinkling a bell to attract customers (of which there is no lack) and pushing his perambulating kitchen before him. This is nothing more than a small cart with a roof under which is a large sheet of steel heated by coals. On one side, looking like a batch of large eggs, is the dough, and in a pot he carries steaming curry.

Anyone who has seen murtaba being made will never believe it can be done at home, for the men who have spent a lifetime making these parchment-thin rotis achieve this by flinging a handful of dough in ever-widening curves. An egg-size lump becomes a large sheet in about a minute. It is then cooked on a griddle and filled with savoury meat or seasoned beaten egg. At home you may not put on such a spectacular display, but it is possible to get the required thinness by soaking the balls of well-kneaded dough in oil for an hour or more, then spreading them with the hands much as if you were smoothing a linen sheet on a bed. Use a smooth surface (a laminated work bench is ideal), then carry the thin pastry to the hot griddle over a rolling pin because fingers can easily make holes. The edges will be somewhat thicker than the centre, but this does not matter.

The problem in a domestic kitchen is getting a griddle large enough to cook murtaba on, but there's no law that murtaba has to be a specific size and smaller ones taste just as good.

Makes: 10-12
3 cups roti flour or plain white flour
1 teaspoon salt
1 tablespoon ghee or oil
1 cup luke warm water
½ cup oil

Filling:
use recipe for keema mattar on page 69,
   omitting yoghurt and peas
2 beaten eggs, optional
pepper and salt
1 onion, finely sliced

Put flour and salt in a large bowl, rub in ghee or oil, then add the water all at once and mix to a fairly soft dough. Knead dough for at least 10 minutes. Divide into balls of equal size and put them in a small bowl containing the oil. If there is not quite enough oil to cover the dough add a little more. Leave for at least 1 hour.

Have the filling ready. It should be cooked until it is quite dry. Season the eggs well with pepper and salt. You can have a choice of fillings, or use some beaten egg and some meat together.

On a very smooth surface spread a little oil from the bowl and flatten one of the dough balls with a rolling pin or with the hand. Gently press with fingers, spreading the dough until it is almost as thin as strudel pastry. Have griddle preheated and ready. Grease it lightly with ghee or oil. Drape the roti over a rolling pin and carry it to the griddle, placing it on the hot surface much as you would put the top on a pie. It will cook very quickly, so spoon on some beaten egg and spread it over the middle portion of the roti with the underside of the spoon. Sprinkle some meat over and finally add a few slices of onion. Fold over the sides of the roti, envelope-fashion, to completely enclose the filling, then turn with a frying slice and cook other side, spreading a little more ghee or oil on the griddle before you put it down. When crisp and golden on both sides it is ready. Serve hot.

Sometimes the murtaba is cooked without any filling and served with a curry. It is broken, dipped and eaten in the same way as chapati or paratha.

POH PIA *recipe page* 256

SILVER FUNGUS IN SWEET SOUP

Serves: 6
3 tablespoons silver fungus (see Glossary)
2 cups water
¾ cup rock sugar or white sugar
1 can longans or lychees
12 ice cubes

Wash silver fungus and soak in hot water until it swells and softens, about 10 minutes. Drain and put into a saucepan with sugar. Bring to the boil, stirring until rock sugar dissolves. Cover and simmer 10 minutes. Cool and chill. Before serving combine with fruits and syrup in a pretty serving bowl and add the ice cubes. Serve in bowls with porcelain spoons. Alternatively, serve warm or at room temperature and omit the ice cubes.

TOFFEE APPLES

Chinese toffee apples are not the glazed red apples on sticks that Westerners associate with the name. They are thick slices of apple fried in batter, then dropped into a sugar glaze with black sesame seeds, hardened quickly in a bowl of iced water and eaten with chopsticks. Great fun to do, especially if you have two table cookers — guests can join in and take a turn at toffee-ing their own apples!

Makes 24 pieces
3 medium-size cooking apples
1 egg
⅔ cup cold water
1 cup plain flour
peanut oil for deep frying

Glaze:
1½ cups sugar
½ cup cold water
2 teaspoons black sesame seeds

Quarter the apples, peel and core the pieces, then cut each quarter into 2 thick slices, 3 if the apples are large. Set aside. Beat the egg in a medium-size bowl, add the water and beat again until combined, then tip in all the flour at once and beat vigorously with rotary beater until batter is smooth. Do not overbeat. Let batter stand while preparing glaze. As sugar cooks, start to heat oil for deep frying. Try to have oil for frying and sugar glaze ready at the same time. If oil is not put over too high a heat this should not be difficult.

When a haze begins to rise from the surface of the oil drop pieces of apple into the batter, turn to coat them completely, then take one piece at a time with chopsticks, a fondue fork, or fingers and drop into the oil. Do not cook too many at one time. Deep fry until the batter is golden, then lift out with a slotted spoon and put straight into the saucepan containing the glaze. Turn pieces of apple in the glaze to coat the entire surface, then lift out and drop into a bowl containing cold water and ice cubes. The glaze will harden and become brittle almost at once. Lift them out quickly and put on a lightly oiled serving plate. Serve as soon as possible. If left to stand too long the glaze will melt and the batter become leathery.

Glaze: Put sugar and water into a small saucepan and place over medium high heat. Do not stir at all. This is important. If you do, the sugar will crystallise and the glaze will not be clear. Let sugar mixture bubble until it starts to turn faintly golden around the edges of the pan. Stir in sesame seeds and turn heat as low as it will go. Or remove pan from heat, replacing it from time to time if sugar begins to harden before all the apples have been dipped.

ALMOND BISCUITS

Makes about 16
Cooking time : 25-30 minutes
Oven temperature : 150-160°C (300-325°F)
125 g (4 oz) lard
½ cup caster sugar
1 teaspoon almond essence
few drops yellow food colouring, optional
1½ cups plain flour
8 blanched almonds
1 egg yolk
1 tablespoon water

Soften lard to room temperature and beat lard and sugar together until soft and creamy. Add almond essence and, if liked, a little yellow colouring. Add unsifted flour gradually, stirring well to combine. After adding the last of the flour it will be necessary to work the mixture with the hand, but it will still be of a crumbly consistency.

Take level tablespoons of the dough and shape into flat round cakes about 5 cm (2 inches) in diameter. Edges of cakes will have little cracks in them. Put on a well-greased baking tray. Put almonds in a small pan with a little cold water, bring to the boil, drain. Split almonds in two. Press half an almond in the centre of each biscuit. Beat egg yolk with water and brush tops of biscuits.

Bake in a slow oven for 30 minutes or until pale golden. Cool slightly on tray, then carefully lift on to wire rack, using a spatula. When cold, store airtight.

AGAR-AGAR JELLY

Serves : 6
6 cups water
4 teaspoons agar-agar powder
1 cup sugar
few drops red food colouring
3 or 4 drops rose essence
½ teaspoon vanilla essence
few drops green food colouring
3 or 4 drops almond essence

Pour water into a saucepan, sprinkle the agar-agar powder over the surface and bring slowly to the boil. Boil until agar dissolves, 5-10 minutes. Add sugar and stir over heat until it dissolves. Remove from heat, pour 2 cups of the jelly into a bowl, colour pink with red colouring and flavour with rose essence. Pour into a glass bowl rinsed with cold water. Keep remaining jelly warm in a pan of hot water. Refrigerate pink jelly.

As soon as the first layer sets (this takes only a few minutes) pour 2 cups more agar mixture into the bowl and flavour with vanilla. Pour gently over the first layer and chill. Repeat with remaining jelly coloured a pale shade of green and flavoured with almond essence. Chill until serving time and serve from the bowl.

Although the jelly is delicious chilled, an advantage in hot countries where no refrigeration is available is that it sets at a temperature of 27°C (80°F).

BURMA

I was too young to remember my first visit to my grandmother's home in Rangoon, Burma, but the second visit, which lasted a year, has left a medley of impressions. I remember the two storey house set back in its leafy garden and kept cool by ceiling fans and wooden venetian blinds at the windows; the staircase of polished dark wood which seemed so high I never dared slide down the balustrade; the spacious rooms so typical of homes in the tropics, and the quiet orderliness of life under my grandmother's stern but loving reign.

My most vivid memories of Burma are of glittering golden pagodas and delicious food. I recall saving my pocket money to buy snacks from the vendors who streamed through the suburban streets calling their wares. In the evenings we often visited the bazaar area where the streets were lined with food stalls of every kind. Snacks, sweets, cool drinks, complete meals — each stall specialised in one particular item. What I liked best was fresh sugar cane juice, extracted from cane crushed between large, shiny steel rollers and poured on to ice clinking in tall glasses.

My mother, who was born in Mandalay, had left Burma as a young bride to live in Sri Lanka (Ceylon), so Burma was a country new and fascinating to me. It was during this second visit that I first met Aunt Connie, my mother's youngest sister. She made an impression at least as deep and lasting as those made by my favourite foods, for I was overwhelmed by her beauty and vivacity and wondered which of her many admirers would be lucky enough to marry her.

The next time we met was in England, where I had been sent to finish my education. Happily, Connie was spending a year there and I lived with her delightful family in a beautiful country house, one of the happiest times of my life.

Because she lived many years in Burma and cooks delicious Burmese food even when thousands of miles away from that country, I asked her help in making this chapter the best possible source of information on Burmese food. Thanks to my wonderful aunt, Constance Hancock, and Mrs Ida Htoon Phay I have added to the Burmese recipes learned from my mother and grandmother.

PANTHÉ KAUKSWÉ (chicken curry with noodles) *recipe page 269*
Clockwise from top: KYAZAN (cellophane noodles) *recipe page 267*, lemon wedges, chicken curry, sliced spring onions, fried garlic slices, chilli powder, roasted chick pea powder, fried dry chillies.

'Cooking should not be a chore,' writes Connie. 'The busy housewife must use her head and try to make life a little easier for herself if she wants to venture into exotic cooking. So, in order not to spend a fortune on air-fresheners every time she prepares strong-smelling foods, it is useful to know that onions, garlic and curry ingredients can be cooked in large quantities and stored in jars or in a freezer. It's the initial cooking process that makes the most lingering smells.

'When the basic curry ingredients [page 273] are cooked, I put them into margarine containers and seal them again in polythene bags and freeze them. One container [about a quarter kilo or half a pound] of curry ingredients is sufficient for a three pound [1.5 kg] chicken or a pound and a half [750 g] of beef, lamb or pork. As fish and meat curries are made from the same basic curry ingredients there is no problem. To the basic ingredients I add, as the recipe requires, other spices or herbs which make the dish taste the way it should.

'Family and friends who turn up unexpectedly are amazed that I can start from scratch and produce a whole meal in less than an hour. The dish that takes longest to cook is started first and so on. I always have a supply of crisp fried brown onions and garlic, pounded dried prawns and *balachaung*. They keep well in airtight jars. Also hot mango pickles and chutneys. And my deep freezer holds treasures like chopped coriander leaves, green and red peppers cut into pieces, so I can take out only what I require.'

SERVING AND EATING
A BURMESE MEAL

The cornerstone of a Burmese meal is, as elsewhere in Asia, a dish of perfectly cooked, steaming hot, fluffy rice. This is brought to the table just before or after guests are seated so that it will be hot. The soup too is always piping hot, but for the rest, the dishes are placed on the table beforehand and many of the accompaniments are served at room temperature.

A table set for a meal is a colourful sight. Browns, greens, red and yellows feature in curries, vegetables and accompaniments. The various dishes served should complement or contrast. Plain soups with rich, oily curries; stronger soups with mild dishes. There should always be one chilli condiment; one raw salad of leaves, fruit or vegetables; one soup; one, two or three curries of meat, fish, prawns or eggs; perhaps a bowl of lentils, a home-made pickle, and almost always that Burmese favourite, *balachaung*. There is no set rule as to which dishes should be served together, so an unlimited number of combinations is possible.

The table is set with plates for the rice, bowls and porcelain spoons for soup. It is customary to eat a Burmese meal with the fingers, but nowadays dessertspoons and forks are also used. There are some Burmese meals, though, that *must* be eaten with the fingers — read about *lethoke* on page 266. In this case a bowl of hot water, soap and a towel are placed on a side table for hand washing before one is seated.

When one does begin, it is polite to start with small portions. Not too much rice first, then one tiny helping from one of the dishes to be mixed with the rice and tasted, then something from another dish, and so on. When all the dishes have been sampled, the decision is made whether to stick to one particular dish or to combine various flavours. Second or third helpings of rice are offered. It is quite in order to ask for a dish which is out of reach. Spoonfuls of soup are taken between mouthfuls of rice and curries.

After the meal the hands are washed again — in Burma, hot water, soap and towels are brought around by a servant. Fruit or a cooling sweet and cups of steaming hot tea follow.

Doing your own thing: There are certain Burmese meals where a one-dish speciality is featured, such as *moh hin gha, kaukswe, kyazan* or *htamin lethoke*. These are do-it-yourself specials where rice or noodles is served with a myriad flavoursome accompaniments and you create your own masterpiece.

When you sit down to this kind of meal there is no guarantee that your food will taste exactly like the next person's. In fact, it's highly unlikely. You will help yourself from the same dishes, but from there on it becomes a no-holds-barred improvisation.

Do you want a gently seasoned meal? Or one so hot it brings tears to your eyes? Is it pungent herbs and garlic that send you on a taste trip? With a Burmese meal of this sort you please yourself. Add a little of this, a lot of that. There will be chopped fresh coriander leaf, garlic slices fried crisp and golden, piquant tamarind liquid, hot chilli powder or fried whole chillies, brilliant red chilli oil, rich brown fried onions, sliced spring onions, nutty-flavoured roasted chick-pea powder. Depending on the proportions in which you add these you create a taste sensation made to order — just as *you* like it.

These are fun meals. If you feel you need help, it is considered quite the thing to do to ask someone if you can taste their meal — or ask them to taste yours and advise on what is needed, or even to mix your portion for you . . . all delightfully informal.

UTENSILS

Like other Asian kitchens, that of a Burmese household is simply equipped. A brick fireplace for charcoal or wood fires, or a portable charcoal brazier; a selection of pots and pans, nothing that cannot be replaced by a Western-style utensil except the 'dare-oh', a rounded, deep pan in heavy iron with two handles, similar to the Chinese *wok*; the large flat grinding stone, a stone mortar and pestle and the usual colander, sieve, wooden and bamboo spatulas, skewers and ladles, sharp choppers and knives. Every recipe in this chapter can be prepared without any special equipment except, perhaps, a *wok*. As I have said in other chapters, the cook's best friend when handling ingredients that would, in the country of origin, be prepared on the grinding stone, is a powerful and efficient electric blender.

YOUR BURMESE SHELF

You will be surprised at how few spices you will need for Burmese cooking. Burmese curries do not use curry powder. They are based on onion, garlic, ginger and chilli, and what you do need is large amounts of these as well as the ubiquitous *ngapi* (or *blachan*, as it is most popularly called), a dried prawn paste. Without it, Burmese cooking is just not authentic and while it may take some getting used to

in its more concentrated forms (*ngapi htaung* or *ngapi chet*), a small amount added to a recipe is what characterises the food of the country.

> *besan* (chick pea flour)
> cardamom, ground
> cloves, ground
> Chinese dried mushrooms
> cellophane noodles (*kyazan*)
> creamed coconut, optional
> corn oil or peanut oil
> chilli powder
> desiccated coconut
> egg noodles
> *ngapi* (dried shrimp paste)
> *ngan pya ye* (fish sauce)
> paprika
> roasted chick peas (from Greek delicatessens)
> rice vermicelli
> sesame oil
> sesame seeds
> soy sauce
> turmeric, ground

Fresh coriander herb or Chinese parsley, as it is sometimes called, is a must if your dishes are to have true Burmese flavour. A large seed company markets the seeds in packets and I have even grown the herb from seed which has been bought for cooking. See Glossary for more information.

HTAMIN
RICE

Rice is served at all main meals except when noodle dishes are the main course. Most often it is plain boiled white rice, and no matter what other elaborate or expensive foods are on the table, it is of prime importance that the rice should be light and fluffy, well cooked but never mushy or lumpy. On special occasions other types of rice are served, such as coconut rice (page 266), golden rice (page 289), kitcheree, and dhan bauk htamin, similar to pilau rice and featuring duck, chicken or mutton combined with the rice.

BOILED RICE

Always use long grain rice for Burmese meals. Allow 1 cup raw rice for 2 or 3 people. To 1 cup of long grain rice allow 2 cups water. For each cup of rice additional to the first cup, allow 1½ cups water:

> 1 cup rice . . . 2 cups water
> 2 cups rice . . . 3½ cups water
> 3 cups rice . . . 5 cups water

. . . and so on. These measures will give perfect results.

Burmese cooks always wash the rice very well. With packaged Australian-grown rice it is not necessary to wash. Some types of rice absorb less water than others. Much depends on the variety of rice and even on the age of the grain — this year's crop may need slightly less water than last year's. The older the rice the more highly it is regarded in Asian countries, for it tends to cook drier and is more fluffy than new rice.

OHN HTAMIN
COCONUT RICE

Serves: 6
2½ cups long grain rice
5 cups coconut milk
2½ teaspoons salt

Put the rice, coconut milk and salt into a saucepan and bring to the boil. Turn heat very low, give it a good stir, then put lid on and cook for 20 minutes, not lifting lid or stirring. If all the coconut milk is not absorbed at the end of this time stir very lightly around the edges of pan with a fork, just to mix in the milk, replace lid and continue cooking on very low heat for a further 5-10 minutes. Serve hot with any of the Burmese curries, fried prawns or pork, oil pickles and ngapi htaung (page 280).

HTAMIN LETHOKE
'RICE MIXED WITH FINGERS'

The literal translation of the Burmese name suggests what to expect. Each person helps himself to one or more of the main ingredients and some of each of the accompaniments. The only way to really enjoy this type of food is to use one's fingers to mix and eat it. It is a fun thing, and though the ingredients are numerous, very little cooking is involved. If a stock of the basics is kept in the pantry, a lethoke meal can be served in next to no time.

Serves: 6
1 cup long grain rice
2 fresh red chillies or 1 teaspoon chilli powder
2 tablespoons oil
2 tablespoons water
125 g (4 oz) rice vermicelli
60 g (2 oz) cellophane noodles
125 g (4 oz) fine egg noodles
3 large potatoes
60 g (2 oz) kyauk pwint (dried seaweed), optional
250 g (8 oz) bean sprouts

Accompaniments:
3 eggs
10 medium onions
20 cloves garlic
1 cup oil
1 cup powdered dried prawns
1 cup roasted chick pea powder
2 tablespoons chilli powder
½ cup fish sauce (ngan pya ye)
½ cup dried tamarind pulp

Cook rice as on page 265. It should be dry and fluffy. Pound chillies to a paste and cook with oil and water on low heat. When chillies smell cooked, mix with rice and set aside.

Boil rice vermicelli for 2 minutes or till just tender. Drain and set aside. Boil cellophane noodles, drain and set aside. Boil egg noodles until just tender. Drain and run cold water through so that noodles will not stick together. Drain well. Boil potatoes, peel, slice. Soak seaweed in boiling water for 10 minutes. Drain. Pour boiling water over bean sprouts and leave for 10 minutes, then drain.

These are the main ingredients for lethoke and they are served cold. Arrange rice, various noodles, potatoes, seaweed and bean sprouts in separate mounds on a large tray or platter. The accompaniments in their individual bowls are placed on the table.

Accompaniments: Beat eggs, fry as for omelette. Cool, cut into fine shreds and set aside. Slice half the onions thinly, wash well in cold water, drain and put into bowl. Slice remaining onions and half the garlic and fry in oil until light brown, then transfer to serving bowl. Onions and garlic are left in the oil which is served as a component of the dish. The remaining cloves of garlic are put into a small bowl and served raw for intrepid garlic eaters. Put powdered dried prawns, chick pea powder and chilli powder, fish sauce and tamarind liquid into separate bowls.

To make tamarind liquid, soak pulp in 1½ cups hot water. When cool, squeeze to dissolve pulp and strain through a fine sieve. Discard seeds and fibres.

Note: Roasted chick peas are available from Greek or other Middle Eastern delicatessens. In place of kyauk pwint use hijiki seaweed sold at Japanese grocery stores.

SEE HTAMIN
OIL RICE

Serves: 4-6
2 cups glutinous rice
3 large onions
1½ teaspoons turmeric
6 tablespoons oil
4 cups hot water
2 teaspoons salt
4 tablespoons toasted sesame seeds

Wash rice well and leave to drain and dry. Slice onions thinly, keeping them uniform in thickness. Sprinkle turmeric over onions and mix lightly. Heat oil in a medium-size saucepan and fry onions until brown. Remove two thirds of the onions and set aside for garnish. Add rice to pan and stir until it is well mixed with the oil. Add water and salt, stir well and bring to the boil. Turn heat very low, cover tightly and cook for 20 minutes by which time the rice should be cooked and the water completely absorbed. Some people like a crust on the rice. To encourage a crust to form leave the rice on low heat for 5-10 minutes longer until a slight crackling sound is heard. Serve hot, garnished with fried onion and accompanied by the sesame seed lightly bruised and mixed with a little salt. This is generally served as a dish by itself, not with curries.

KYAZAN
CELLOPHANE NOODLES

The main ingredient in this dish (pronounced 'chah-zan') is cellophane noodles. Fine, transparent and with no flavour of their own, they are flavoured by what you eat with them. They are served with panthé kaukswé curry and appropriate accompaniments.

Serves: 6-8
375 g (12 oz) cellophane noodles

Bring a large saucepan of salted water to the boil, drop in noodles and cook for 20 minutes. Drain. Serve in a large bowl. Serving is easier if the noodles are cut into shorter lengths with a sharp knife.

Each person puts some noodles in a bowl, ladles panthé kaukswé curry or some soup over the noodles and adds whichever accompaniments he pleases. Everything is mixed together and a lemon wedge squeezed over to add piquancy. The crisp fried chillies are held by the stalk and bitten into (with caution, please, if this is your first attempt) when a hot mouthful is desired.

Accompaniments to kyazan, panthé kaukswé, moh hin gha and kaukswé kyaw include the following:
finely sliced spring onions, both green and white portions
chopped fresh coriander leaves
finely sliced white onion
roasted chick peas, finely ground in a blender or crushed with
    mortar and pestle
crisp fried noodles, broken into small pieces
fried onion flakes
thin slices garlic, fried in oil until golden
lemon wedges
dried chillies, fried in oil 3-4 seconds
chilli powder.
    Note: Roasted chick peas are sold in Greek delicatessen shops.

MOH HIN GHA
RICE VERMICELLI WITH FISH SOUP *(picture page 270)*

The national dish of Burma, moh hin gha is to the Burmese what onion soup is to the French. Bowls of moh hin gha are a popular snack sold at roadside stalls or by vendors who carry their cooking apparatus from house to house on a bamboo pole slung over one shoulder. At one end is the portable fireplace while on the other are all the makings.

This one-course meal is often used when entertaining large numbers of people. No outdoor market fair or festival is complete without the moh hin gha sellers. The rice vermicelli used is made fresh every day with slightly fermented rice flour. Few housewives make it themselves but it is bought fresh from moh sellers ('moh' is the word used for flour and everything made with wheat or rice flour). Chinese rice vermicelli or Italian fine vermicelli can be used instead.

While the base of the dish is a curried fish soup, a vital ingredient is the tender heart of a banana tree — common as grass in Burma, but rather hard to come by in Australia. My grandmother, who was born in Burma and lived most of her life there, would not let a little thing like that deter her. When she came to Australia she was in her seventies. One day she decided moh hin gha would be on the menu, went into the garden and cut down a banana tree herself. The feast she prepared

brought back memories of the land of golden pagodas.

If you have access to a spare banana tree and are determined to make this dish in true Burmese fashion, protect your hands with gloves and put on your oldest clothes, because the sap from a banana tree leaves a stain that defies the best stain removers science has to offer. Use about 30 cm (12 inches) of the tender heart of the tree. Peel off the outer layers and discard. Cut the inner portion in thin crossways slices. Soak in a large basin of salted water for several hours. The sticky juice forms strong hair-like strands. Pull these away and discard.

Realising that for most Western readers the idea of getting a banana tree to use in this dish makes the whole thing rather remote, I have suggested using finely sliced canned bamboo shoot instead. This brought the wrath of many Burmese people down on my head, but honestly, it is such a fine-flavoured dish that I feel it is better to try it with the readily obtainable ingredient than not at all. As you sit around your bowls of steaming fish soup and noodles, adding different flavours and textures from the array of accompaniments that are so much a part of moh hin gha, I feel sure your enjoyment will in no way be diminished.

Serves: 6-8

500 g (1 lb) fillets of strong-flavoured fish or 2 cans of herrings in tomato sauce
4 medium onions, roughly chopped
6 cloves garlic, peeled
2 teaspoons finely chopped fresh ginger
1 teaspoon ground turmeric
½ teaspoon chilli powder
2 tablespoons sesame oil
4 tablespoons peanut oil
2 fresh chillies, seeded and chopped
4 cups thin coconut milk
banana heart or 255 g can bamboo shoots
1 teaspoon dried shrimp paste (ngapi)
1 tablespoon fish sauce (ngan pya ye)
3 tablespoons chick pea flour (besan)
2 cups thick coconut milk
2 tablespoons lemon juice
salt to taste
500 g (1 lb) fine egg noodles or rice vermicelli
accompaniments (page 267)

If using fresh fish wash and scale the fillets and simmer for 5 minutes in just enough water to cover. Reserve the stock. Put onions, garlic, ginger, turmeric and chilli powder in container of electric blender and blend to a purée. Heat both oils in a large saucepan and fry the blended ingredients and chillies, as explained in basic curries (page 273). When it is golden brown and beginning to stick to the pan add fish stock, thin coconut milk and prepared banana heart. Bring to the boil, turn heat low and simmer until banana heart slices are tender. Dissolve dried shrimp paste in fish sauce and add to mixture. Mix the chick pea flour smoothly with a little cold water or some of the thick coconut milk and add to pan. Keep stirring as it comes to the boil. Simmer 5 minutes, add fish and, if using canned fish, the liquid from the can as well. Add thick coconut milk and lemon juice, stir as it comes to simmering point. Season to taste with salt if necessary.

Cook noodles in boiling salted water until just tender. Drain well and serve in a large bowl alongside the soup. Have small bowls with accompaniments ready on the table.

Serve moh hin gha in a tureen or other large receptacle and provide deep bowls or old-fashioned soup plates. Noodles are served first and soup ladled over the top. Moh hin gha must be served piping hot. Guests make their own choice of accompaniments.

KAUKSWÉ KYAW
MIXED FRIED NOODLES

Serves: 6
500 g (1 lb) egg noodles
½ cup oil
500 g (1 lb) chicken meat
1 chicken liver
1 chicken gizzard, parboiled
5 medium onions, chopped
5 cloves garlic, chopped
2 tablespoons soy sauce
¼ cabbage, shredded
2 stalks celery, sliced and shredded
¼ white Chinese cabbage, shredded
4 or 5 dried Chinese mushrooms,
  soaked and sliced
6 spring onions, finely sliced
4 eggs, beaten
salt and pepper to taste

Soak noodles in warm water while bringing water to the boil in a large saucepan. Add drained noodles and cook until just tender. Drain and spread on large dish or tray. Pour 2 tablespoons oil evenly on noodles and toss gently. This prevents noodles sticking to each other and gives a glossy appearance. Finely slice chicken meat, liver and gizzard. Heat oil in wok. Fry onions and garlic till soft. Add meat, liver and gizzard and fry. Add soy sauce. Cover and simmer gently till meat is tender. Add shredded vegetables and continue frying and tossing till done. Remove from wok and set aside. Put noodles in wok, toss gently for about 3 minutes and remove. In the same wok, scramble the eggs, adding a little oil if necessary. Add salt and pepper to taste. When ready to serve, spread noodles on dish first, then cover with meat and vegetables. Garnish with scrambled eggs. Serve hot or cold.

PANTHÉ KAUKSWÉ
CHICKEN CURRY WITH NOODLES *(picture page 262)*

A popular Burmese dish that particularly appeals to Westerners, this is a mild curry with lots of gravy. It is ladled over a bowl of egg noodles or kyazan (page 267) and served with a number of accompaniments with contrasting flavours.

Serves: 6-8
1.5 kg (3 lb) chicken or chicken pieces
5 cloves garlic, chopped
3 medium onions, chopped
1 tablespoon finely chopped fresh ginger
1 teaspoon dried shrimp paste (ngapi)
2 tablespoons peanut oil
1 tablespoon sesame oil
1-2 teaspoons chilli powder
2 teaspoons salt
2 cups thin coconut milk
2 cups thick coconut milk
2 tablespoons chick pea flour (besan)
500g (1 lb) thin egg noodles or
  cellophane noodles
accompaniments (page 267)

Cut chicken into serving pieces. Put garlic, onion, ginger and dried shrimp paste into blender container, cover and blend until smooth, adding 1 tablespoon of peanut oil if necessary. Heat remaining oil and fry blended ingredients for 5 minutes. Add chicken and continue to fry, stirring constantly. Add chilli powder, salt and thin coconut milk. Simmer until chicken is tender, adding a little hot water if mixture becomes too dry. Add thick coconut milk, return to heat and bring slowly to the boil, stirring constantly to prevent mixture from curdling. Mix chick pea flour with a little cold water to a smooth cream, add to curry and cook for a further 5 minutes uncovered (there should be a lot of gravy).

Just before serving, cook noodles in a large saucepan of boiling salted water until just tender, about 6 minutes. Pour cold water into pan to stop noodles cooking, then drain in colander.

Serve noodles in a large bowl and the curry in a separate bowl. Each person takes a serving of noodles, ladles on a generous amount of the curry and sprinkles various accompaniments over the top.

KYAZANGYI KAUKSWÉ
LARGE RICE NOODLES WITH CURRY

Serves: 6-8

1 x 1.5 kg (3 lb) roasting chicken
1 teaspoon ground turmeric
2 teaspoons salt
¼ cup fish sauce (ngan pya ye)
1½ cups thick coconut milk
3 large onions, finely sliced
3 cloves garlic, crushed
½ cup besan (chick pea flour)
2 cups thin coconut milk
4 eggs hard-boiled
500 g (1 lb) rice noodles, dried or 1 kg
  (2 lb) fresh rice noodles
2 teaspoons chilli oil (see Glossary)

Joint chicken and put into a saucepan with turmeric, salt, fish sauce and just enough water to almost cover. Bring to the boil then reduce heat, cover and simmer until chicken is tender. Cool, then discard bones and cut meat into small pieces.

Cook thick coconut milk in a saucepan, stirring constantly, until it becomes thick and oil rises to the top. Keep cooking until it is very oily, then add half the onions and all the garlic and fry, stirring, until they start to colour. (Set aside remaining onion to be served raw with the finished dish.)

Add chicken meat to the frying onions and cook, stirring constantly for a few minutes. Set aside.

Mix besan with cold water to form a thin cream. Add thin coconut milk to the pan and when it comes to a boil stir in the besan mixture. Cook and stir constantly until it thickens, taking care it does not become lumpy or stick at the base of the pan. Add strained chicken stock a little at a time until the gravy is as thick as that of a stew. Add the chicken and onion mixture.

If fresh rice noodles are bought as large sheets (sa hor fun, available at Chinese grocers), cut them into narrow strips and pour boiling water over them in a colander or steam gently for a few minutes to heat through.

Bring the chicken combination to simmering point, stir in chilli oil and remove from the heat. Serve in a large bowl, with noodles, sliced hard-boiled eggs and raw onions served separately.

Note: If dried rice noodles are used, they will have to be soaked 2 hours in cold water, then drained and boiled in a large amount of water until cooked through. Do not overcook. Drain well.

NGA BAUNG DOKE (1)
FISH STEAMED IN LEAVES

These leaf-wrapped parcels of fish are a popular Burmese dish and easily made, substituting aluminium foil for banana leaves.

Serves: 4

750 g (1½ lb) fillets of firm fish
1 teaspoon salt
¼ teaspoon ground black pepper
½ teaspoon ground turmeric
2 medium onions
4 cloves garlic
1 teaspoon finely grated fresh ginger
¼ teaspoon chilli powder, optional
1 tablespoon thick coconut milk
1 tablespoon ground rice
2 teaspoons sesame oil
8 leaves of Chinese mustard cabbage
large pieces of banana leaf or aluminium
  foil
few sprigs fresh coriander leaves

Cut fish into 8 pieces of equal size, wash and dry well, then sprinkle with half the salt, pepper and turmeric. Leave aside while preparing remaining ingredients. Slice one onion and set aside. Chop the other onion and put into container of electric blender with garlic and ginger, chilli powder and coconut milk. Blend to a purée. Mix purée with remaining salt, pepper and turmeric, ground rice and sesame oil. Put in the pieces of fish and mix well.

Slice the thick middle rib out of the mustard cabbage leaves and use in another dish (lettuce or spinach leaves may be used if these are not available). Cut banana leaves into pieces large enough to wrap the pieces of fish and scald them or hold over heat to make them pliable. On each piece of banana leaf put a leaf of mustard cabbage and on it a piece of fish and some of the spice mixture. Top with a few coriander leaves and some of the sliced onion. Wrap fish first in the cabbage leaf, then make a parcel with the banana leaf. Fasten with short bamboo skewers or wooden toothpicks. Alternatively wrap in foil. Put in a steamer and steam over gently boiling water for 20-25 minutes. Serve in the leaves. Guests open their parcels on their own plates. Serve a bowl of white rice alongside, and other accompaniments such as balachaung (page 280).

Ingredients for MOH HIN GHA (rice vermicelli with curried fish soup) *recipe page 268*

NGA BAUNG DOKE (2)
SESAME COCONUT FISH STEAMED IN LEAVES

Serves: 6

1 kg (2 lb) fish fillets
1 cup desiccated coconut
½ cup hot water
2 cloves garlic
1 tablespoon finely grated fresh ginger
2 tablespoons toasted sesame seeds
2 teaspoons salt
1 teaspoon ground turmeric
1 teaspoon ground black pepper
juice of half a lemon
2 tablespoons rice flour
3 tablespoons chopped fresh coriander
   leaves
banana or bamboo leaves and foil for
   wrapping

Wash and dry fish fillets. Put next four ingredients in blender container, blend until coconut is very finely ground. Turn into a bowl, mix in other seasonings. Put fish fillets (cut into serving pieces) on banana or bamboo leaves, top with 3 teaspoons of the coconut mixture, wrap first in leaves, then in foil, and steam for 15 minutes.

NGA THA LAUK PAUNG
SOUSED FISH

Hilsa, a very rich and bony fish, is used for this dish in Burma. Substitute herrings, mackerel or similar fish.

Serves: 4

500 g (1 lb) cleaned whole fish, one or
   more according to size
1 medium onion, sliced lengthways
4 cloves garlic, sliced lengthways
1 teaspoon finely shredded fresh ginger
5 whole black peppercorns
½ teaspoon salt, or to taste
1 fresh green chilli
vinegar as needed

Have fish cleaned and scaled and head, fins and tail removed. Wash well, put in a casserole dish with a lid and scatter the onion, garlic, ginger, peppercorns and salt over the fish. Put the chilli on top and add vinegar to just cover the fish. Cover the casserole with lid and seal with a thich dough of flour and water to prevent moisture escaping. Put in a very slow oven 112°C (225°F) and cook for six hours. This method of cooking helps to soften the bones.

PAZOON KYAW (1)
FRIED PRAWNS

Serves 4 as appetiser

16 large prawns, peeled
1 teaspoon each salt, ground turmeric and
   chilli powder
2 tablespoons sesame oil
2 tablespoons peanut oil
thin bamboo skewers

Dust prawns with mixed salt, turmeric and chilli powder. Bend prawns into a half circle and thread on skewer through top and tail to keep this shape. Put four prawns on each skewer. Shallow fry skewered prawns until golden. Serve immediately.

PAZOON KYAW (2)
STIR-FRIED PRAWNS WITH VEGETABLES

Serves: 4
250 g (8 oz) bean sprouts or 2 cups
  shredded cabbage
500 g (1 lb) prawns, peeled and if large,
  cut in two
1 tablespoon oil
1 medium onion, thinly sliced
salt and black pepper
2 teaspoons soy sauce, optional

Prepare vegetables and prawns. Heat oil and stir fry onion for a few seconds, add prawns and vegetables and stir fry 3 minutes on high heat. Add salt, pepper and soy sauce. Cover and remove from heat. Serve immediately.

BURMESE CURRIES

The ingredients basic to all Burmese curries never vary — onion, garlic, ginger, chilli and turmeric. The chilli can be used in powder form, or whole dried chillies can be ground with the other ingredients, but chilli is used sparingly and may be omitted if a hot curry is not desired. There will still be lots of flavour.

The more onions used, the thicker the 'gravy'. To make a curry for four people using 750 g (1½ lb) of meat, fish or poultry, here is a well-balanced mixture: one large onion, two or three cloves of garlic, one teaspoon finely grated fresh ginger, half a teaspoon ground turmeric and quarter teaspoon chilli powder, and two or three tablespoons oil for frying. Animal fat of any sort is never used. Light sesame oil is best for capturing the true Burmese flavour. If corn, peanut, sunflower or other vegetable oil is used, add a small amount of Chinese-style dark sesame oil for flavour in the proportions of a teaspoon of sesame oil to a tablespoon of vegetable oil.

PREPARATION OF BASIC INGREDIENTS
There is only one way to cook these basic ingredients in order to achieve a mellow flavour in which no single ingredient predominates.

Grind to a purée the onion, garlic and ginger. In the absence of the Asian grinding stone, this is best done in an electric blender, first chopping the ingredients roughly. It will be necessary to stop the motor frequently and scrape down the sides of the blender container. Or, if using the smaller blender jars provided with many machines, lift off and shake the jar to redistribute the contents. When puréed smoothly mix in the turmeric and chilli powder.

Heat 3 tablespoons of oil in a saucepan until smoking hot. Be careful when putting in the ground ingredients, for the hot oil splutters violently. Reduce heat and stir well to mix ingredients with the oil. Cover pan and simmer the mixture, lifting lid frequently to stir and scrape the base of pan with a wooden spoon. This initial frying takes at least 15 minutes. If mixture fries too rapidly and begins to stick before the smell has mellowed and the onions become transparent, add a small quantity of water from time to time and stir well. When the water content of the onions has evaporated and the ingredients turn a rich red-brown colour with oil showing around the edge of the mass, the first stage of cooking, and the most important one, is complete.

There is a Burmese term to describe this —'see byan', meaning 'oil returned', that is, with the water completely evaporated and the oil returned to just oil. The basic ingredients will not have the required flavour unless this procedure is followed. The meat, fish or vegetables added will release their own juices while cooking slowly in the pan with the lid on. A roasting chicken will be sufficiently cooked by the time its own juices have evaporated. Boiling fowls, duck, some cuts of beef and pork may need a little water added from time to time as cooking continues until they are tender. Fish and prawns cook very quickly but some types may need a little more liquid added — fish stock, water or coconut milk. Vegetables seldom require any added liquid, but if a wetter result is preferred add water or coconut milk.

NGA SOKE LONE HIN
FISH KOFTA CURRY

*My grandmother taught me how to make this
most delicious of all fish curries. There is no
use pretending it is a quick and easy recipe,
but it is the tastiest way of serving fish. For a
more delicate dish, poach the fish koftas in
simmering water and serve as a fish soup
accompanied by boiled rice.*

Serves: 6
Fish Koftas:
1 kg (2 lb) jewfish or cod fillets
2½ teaspoons salt
½ teaspoon pepper
1 medium onion, finely chopped
1 large clove garlic, crushed
1½ teaspoons finely grated fresh ginger
2 tablespoons lemon juice, strained
1 tablespoon finely chopped fresh
   coriander leaves or dill
2 slices white bread, soaked in hot water
   and squeezed dry
1 teaspoon anchovy paste or sauce,
   optional

Curry:
¼ cup sesame oil
3 medium onions, finely chopped
6 cloves garlic, finely chopped
1 tablespoon finely chopped fresh ginger
1 teaspoon ground turmeric
1-2 teaspoons chilli powder, optional
1 teaspoon paprika, optional
2 tomatoes, peeled and chopped
1½ teaspoons salt
1 teaspoon dried shrimp paste (ngapi)
aluminium foil
1½ cups hot water
2 tablespoons chopped fresh coriander
   leaves
2 tablespoons lemon juice

With a sharp knife remove skin from fish. Finely mince fish,
taking care to remove bones. (To do this without a mincer, cut
fillets in thin slices lengthways, then chop finely across.) Put
minced fish in a large bowl, add remaining ingredients. Mix
thoroughly with the hands. Shape the mixture into walnut-size
balls or koftas (this quantity should make 24 balls).

Curry: Heat oil in large saucepan and fry onion, garlic and
ginger until soft and golden. Add turmeric, remove from heat
and add chilli powder and paprika (if used), tomato and salt. (In
Burmese cooking the amount of chilli used would be enough to
give a red colour to the gravy, but the paprika is suggested here as
a substitute for a portion of it, with chilli used to suit individual
tastes.)

Wrap dried shrimp paste in aluminium foil and cook under hot
griller for a few minutes on each side. Unwrap, dissolve in hot
water and add to the gravy. Cook gravy until tomato is soft and
pulpy. If gravy seems too reduced, add a little hot water. There
should be enough gravy to almost cover the fish koftas. Gently
put the fish koftas in the gravy and simmer over a moderate heat
until they are cooked, about 20 minutes. Shake pan gently from
time to time. *Do not stir until fish is cooked and firm,* or the
koftas might break. Stir in the chopped coriander leaves and
lemon juice and cook 5 minutes longer. Serve with white rice
and balachaung (page 280).

NGA SEE BYAN
FISH CURRY WITHOUT GRAVY

Serves: 4-6
1 kg (2 lb) firm white fish
¼ teaspoon dried shrimp paste (ngapi) or
   2 teaspoons fish sauce (ngan pya ye)
2 medium onions
3 cloves garlic
1 teaspoon finely grated fresh ginger
1 stalk lemon grass or 2 strips lemon rind
3 tablespoons vegetable oil
1 teaspoon salt or to taste
1 teaspoon ground turmeric
1 green chilli, split and seeded, optional
fresh chopped coriander leaves to garnish

Cut fish into serving pieces. Marinate in dried shrimp paste dissolved in a tablespoon hot water, or in the fish sauce.

Prepare and cook basic ingredients, as described on page 273, using a wide-based pan. When ingredients are well cooked and still sizzling, put pieces of fish in the pan and cook 3 or 4 minutes on one side, then turn and cook the other side. Sprinkle with chopped coriander leaves. Serve warm.

PAZOON HIN
PRAWN CURRY WITH GRAVY

Serves: 4
500 g (1 lb) shelled prawns
1 large onion
3 cloves garlic
1 teaspoon finely grated fresh ginger
½ teaspoon ground turmeric
½ teaspoon chilli powder
3 tablespoons light sesame or corn oil
pinch each of ground cloves, ground
   cardamom and ground fennel
1 large potato, diced
2 ripe tomatoes, chopped
½ cup thin coconut milk
½ cup thick coconut milk
1 tablespoon chopped coriander leaves
2 tablespoons chopped spring onion leaves
salt to taste

De-vein prawns, prepare and cook basic ingredients as described on page 273. Add ground cloves, cardamom, fennel, potato and tomato and stir well. Cook for 10 minutes with lid on pan. Add thin coconut milk and gently simmer uncovered for 10 minutes, then add prawns and thick coconut milk and simmer, stirring frequently, until prawns are cooked, about 3 minutes. Add coriander leaves and cook a further 3 minutes, then remove from heat and stir in the spring onion. Taste and add more salt if required. Serve hot with white rice and accompaniments (pages 280-284).

PAZOON SEE BYAN HIN
DRY PRAWN CURRY *(picture page 279)*

Serves: 4
500 g (1 lb) shelled prawns
1 large onion
3-4 cloves garlic
1 teaspoon finely grated fresh ginger
½ teaspoon ground turmeric
¼ teaspoon chilli powder
3 tablespoons light sesame or corn oil
1 tablespoon chopped fresh coriander
   leaves
1 teaspoon salt or to taste
2 tablespoons chopped spring onion leaves

De-vein prawns, rinse and drain. Prepare and cook basic ingredients as on page 273. When well cooked and sizzling, put in the prawns and stir well. Sprinkle with the fresh coriander leaves, cover and cook 3 or 4 minutes or until prawns are done. Turn off heat, stir in the spring onion and serve hot with white rice and accompaniments, choosing from those on pages 280-284.

KYETHA SEE BYAN
CHICKEN CURRY WITHOUT GRAVY

Serves: 4-6

1 x 1.5 kg (3 lb) chicken
2 medium onions
3 cloves garlic
1 teaspoon finely grated fresh ginger
1 stalk lemon grass or 2 strips lemon rind
3 tablespoons vegetable oil
1½ teaspoons salt or to taste
1 teaspoon ground turmeric
½ teaspoon chilli powder, optional
¼ teaspoon ground cardamom
1 tablespoon chopped fresh coriander
   leaves

Cut chicken into curry pieces. Peel and roughly chop onions and put into blender container with garlic, ginger, sliced lemon grass or lemon rind. Add a little oil to facilitate blending and blend ingredients to a smooth pulp.

Heat remaining oil in a saucepan and when very hot add blended ingredients, salt, turmeric and chilli powder (if used) and fry over medium heat, stirring well with a wooden spoon. Add a few drops of water if mixture starts to stick to base of pan. Simmer on low heat until the moisture content of the onions has evaporated and the ingredients turn a rich red-brown colour. At this stage they will begin to stick to the pan so keep stirring, and add the chicken pieces, turning them well in the mixture so that they are coated. Cover and simmer for 35-45 minutes or until chicken is tender. The juices from the chicken will provide sufficient liquid for this curry, so do not add water or other liquid. As cooking is nearing completion, stir occasionally to prevent sticking. Add cardamom and coriander leaves, stir quickly and replace lid for a few seconds to hold in the aroma. Serve with white rice and other accompaniments (pages 280-284).

KYETHA HIN
CHICKEN CURRY WITH GRAVY

Serves: 4-6

1 x 1.5 kg (3 lb) chicken
2 medium onions
3 cloves garlic
1 teaspoon finely grated fresh ginger
1 stalk lemon grass or 2 strips lemon rind
3 tablespoons vegetable oil
2 teaspoons salt or to taste
1 teaspoon turmeric
1 teaspoon chilli powder, optional
1 cup water
1 large ripe tomato, chopped
2 large potatoes, peeled and cubed or
   2 cups cauliflower sprigs
1 tablespoon fish sauce (ngan pya ye)
1 tablespoon tamarind liquid or lemon
   juice
1 tablespoon chopped fresh coriander
   leaves
¼ teaspoon ground cardamom

Proceed as for kyetha see byan (preceding recipe). When chicken is half cooked, add water, tomato, potato, fish sauce, and tamarind or lemon juice. Continue cooking until potato is done, stirring occasionally. If cauliflower is used in preference to potato, add it when chicken is nearly done. Finally add coriander leaves and cardamom. Stir and serve.

WETHA SEE BYAN
DRY PORK CURRY

Serves: 4
500 g (1 lb) pork
1 large onion
3 cloves garlic
1 teaspoon finely grated fresh ginger
½ teaspoon chilli powder
½ teaspoon ground turmeric
3 tablespoons light sesame oil or corn oil
1 stalk lemon grass or 2 strips lemon rind
2 tablespoons tamarind liquid
1 tablespoon fish sauce (ngan pya ye)

Cut pork into 5 cm (2 inch) pieces. Excess fat should be removed or the curry will be too rich, but a little fat left on the meat is quite acceptable.

Purée and cook onion, garlic, ginger, chilli and turmeric as described on page 273. When well cooked, add pork and simmer gently in its own juices until tender. Add crushed or finely chopped lemon grass or rind, tamarind juice and fish sauce and stir well. Cook until all water has evaporated and the oil separates from the gravy.

The flavour of the curry can be varied by adding extra chilli powder for a hot curry, or stirring in a piece of hot Indian mango pickle. Slices of lemon, chopped fresh coriander leaves or chopped spring onions can be added at end of cooking if desired.

WETHANI KYET
FRIED PORK CURRY

You may take one look at the ingredients and feel sure there's been a mistake in the amount of garlic and ginger, but this isn't so. This favourite Burmese preparation has the most delicious flavour, and is supposed to be a way of preserving pork for months without refrigeration — in our house, however, it's eaten so quickly I haven't been able to test the theory!

Serves: 8-10
2 kg (4 lb) pork loin or leg
2 large or 4 medium onions,
　roughly chopped
20 cloves garlic
1 cup peeled, roughly chopped fresh
　ginger
2 teaspoons salt
2 tablespoons vinegar
1-2 teaspoons chilli powder
¾ cup peanut oil
¼ cup sesame oil
1 teaspoon ground turmeric

Remove any bones from pork, cut away skin and cut the meat and fat into 2.5 cm (1 inch) cubes. Put onions, garlic and ginger into container of electric blender and blend, stopping and starting motor if necessary, until onions, garlic and ginger are mushy. Turn contents of blender into a nylon strainer set over a bowl and push with the back of a spoon to extract as much liquid as possible. Pour this liquid into a large saucepan, add the pork, salt, vinegar, chilli powder and half the peanut oil. Bring to the boil, cover and simmer over low heat for 1-1½ hours or until pork is almost tender.

In another large pan with heavy base heat remaining peanut oil and the sesame oil. When very hot add the garlic, onion and ginger solids left in the strainer. Add turmeric, stir and cook over low heat as described on page 273, until mixture smells cooked and oil separates from mass. I find it necessary to add a tablespoon of water from time to time and to stir frequently to prevent sticking to pan. Because of the large quantity it takes almost 25 minutes to reach the right stage. Halfway through cooking the onion mixture, spoon off some of the oil that has risen to the top of the pork mixture and add it to the onions.

When mixture is a reddish-brown add the contents of the first pan and cook, uncovered, until the oil separates again and the liquid is almost evaporated. Stir frequently during this stage to ensure it does not stick and burn at base of pan. Serve with white rice and accompaniments.

AMÉ HNAT
VERY DRY BEEF CURRY

Serves: 4-6
750 g (1½ lb) stewing steak
2 large onions
5 large cloves garlic
2 teaspoons chopped fresh ginger
1 teaspoon ground turmeric
1 teaspoon chilli powder
6 tablespoons light sesame oil or corn oil
¼ teaspoon ground black pepper
2 tender stalks lemon grass, finely
   chopped, or 4 strips lemon rind
1 cup hot water
1½ teaspoons salt
2 large onions, finely sliced and fried
   until crisp and brown

Cut beef into 5 cm (2 inch) squares. Cook basic ingredients as described on page 273. When well cooked and sizzling, add beef, pepper and lemon grass or rind. Continue frying slowly until all juices from the beef have completely evaporated and meat is brown.

Add water and salt, cover and simmer until meat is tender, adding more water if necessary. Remove lid, raise heat and cook rapidly until the meat is oily-dry and well coated with the gravy. Garnish with fried onions and serve with white rice and accompaniments (pages 280-284).

AMÉTHA NET ALOO HIN
BEEF AND POTATO CURRY

Serves: 4-6
750 g (1½ lb) beef
375 g (12 oz) potatoes
2 large onions
5 large cloves garlic
2 teaspoons chopped fresh ginger
1 teaspoon ground turmeric
1 teaspoon chilli powder
8 tablespoons light sesame oil or corn oil
½ teaspoon ground cummin
½ teaspoon ground coriander
1½ teaspoons salt or to taste
2 cups water

Cut beef into large squares. Peel and cut potatoes into quarters. Cook basic ingredients as described on page 273. When cooked and sizzling, add cummin and coriander, then add meat and fry; stirring for a few minutes. Add salt, about 2 cups water, potatoes and simmer slowly until meat is tender and potatoes are cooked.

Note: Some cooks prefer to rub the cummin, coriander and salt into the beef before cooking.

AMÉTHA NET SHWEPHAYONE THEE HIN
BEEF AND PUMPKIN CURRY

Serves: 4-6
750 g (1½ lb) beef
500 g (1 lb) pumpkin
2 large onions
5 large garlic cloves
2 teaspoons chopped fresh ginger
1 teaspoon ground turmeric
1 teaspoon chilli powder
8 tablespoons light sesame oil or corn oil
1 cup water
1½ teaspoons salt or to taste

Cut beef into large squares. Peel and cut pumpkin into 5 cm (2 inch) squares. Cook basic ingredients as described on page 273. When cooked and sizzling, add meat and fry slowly, stirring for a few minutes. Add water and cook slowly with cover on pan until meat is nearly done. Add salt and pumpkin and continue cooking until meat is tender and pumpkin is soft.

Note: In place of pumpkin the following vegetables can be used: tomatoes, green beans, potatoes, eggplant, peas, split peas, okra, cauliflower, kohlrabi, butter beans, broad beans, white radish.

Clockwise from Top: White rice, *recipe page 265.* PAZOON SEE BYAN HIN (dry prawn curry) *recipe page 275,* HIN CHO (Mild Soup) *recipe page 285.* BALACHAUNG (dried prawn relish) *recipe page 280*

ACCOMPANIMENTS

'Tolee molee', the Burmese colloquialism meaning 'bits and pieces', includes all the different condiments that are served with every Burmese meal. This descriptive phrase covers hot or sweet pickles, thanhat or salads, crisply fried foods like beya kyaw or nga baung kyaw (split pea fritters or fried vegetables), little bowls of chopped green herbs, raw salads and so on. Of them all, I think that balachaung is the favourite and well worth trying. There are two types, one dry and crisp while the other is more oily. Both keep well in airtight bottles if carefully made with all moisture fried out of the onions.

NGA CHAUK
SALT FISH

Flat bony salt fish is usually used in hin gha soups or sour curries. Thick fleshy salt fish is cut in cubes and either fried or toasted and served with plain boiled rice and hin cho (see page 285) and other mild dishes.

NGAPI HTAUNG
POUNDED PRAWN PASTE

To be eaten in very small quantities with rice
2 tablespoons prawn powder
2 tablespoons dried shrimp paste (ngapi)
2 medium onions
4 cloves garlic
2 teaspoons chilli powder, optional
1 teaspoon salt
juice of half a lemon

Press the dried shrimp paste into a flat cake, wrap in foil and put under a hot griller for 15 minutes, turning to cook both sides. Wrap onions and garlic in foil and put under griller with the dried shrimp paste. These ingredients are pounded together in a mortar and pestle and the remaining ingredients mixed in. Alternatively, the crumbled dried shrimp paste, peeled onions and garlic can be blended in an electric blender with lemon juice and combined with other ingredients.

BALACHAUNG (1)
OILY BALACHAUNG *(picture page 279)*

Balachaung is a preparation of fried dry prawns served as an accompaniment to rice, and is perhaps the most popular of all Burmese accompaniments. It will keep for weeks.

20 cloves garlic
4 medium onions, finely sliced
2 cups peanut oil
1 x 250 g (8 oz) packet of prawn powder
2 teaspoons chilli powder, optional
2 teaspoons salt
1 teaspoon dried shrimp paste (ngapi)
½ cup vinegar

Peel garlic, cut into thin slices. Cut onions into thin slices. Heat oil and fry onion and garlic separately on low heat until golden. Lift out immediately and set aside. They will become crisp and darken as they cool.

In the same oil, fry prawn powder for 5 minutes. Add chilli powder, salt and shrimp paste mixed with vinegar, stir well and fry until crisp. Allow to cool completely. Mix in fried onion and garlic, stirring to distribute evenly. Store in an airtight jar.

BALACHAUNG (2)
DRY BALACHAUNG

Make as before (preceding recipe), but after frying onion and garlic pour off oil and reserve, leaving only about 1 cup in the pan. Add prawn powder and fry on low heat. All the prawn powder should be moistened by the oil. If there is not enough oil, add a spoonful or two from the reserved oil. Fry gently until very crisp. Cool completely before mixing in onions and garlic.

PAZOON NGABAUNG KYAW
PRAWNS FRIED IN BATTER

500 g (1 lb) small prawns or shrimp
½ cup chick pea flour (besan)
½ cup self-raising flour
1 teaspoon salt
1 clove garlic, crushed
½ teaspoon finely grated fresh ginger
¼ teaspoon ground turmeric
½ cup water
oil for deep frying

Take heads off prawns — there is no need to shell or de-vein them if they are as small as they should be. Mix remaining ingredients together to form a dipping batter, stir in the prawns, then put small spoonfuls into the hot oil and fry until golden brown and crisp. Fry only a few spoonfuls at a time, and prevent them from sticking to each other by spooning oil over them as each one is added to the oil. Drain on absorbent paper and serve warm.

WETHA, NGA, PAZOON LONE KYAW
FRIED PORK, FISH OR PRAWN BALLS

500 g (1 lb) lean pork meat or boneless
    fish fillets or shelled prawns
1-2 medium onions
1 green chilli
¼ teaspoon turmeric powder
1 tablespoon chopped fresh coriander
    leaves
plain flour
salt to taste
oil for shallow frying

Mince pork, fish or prawns through the fine blade of a mincer. Chop very finely onions, chilli and coriander and mix with all other ingredients. Shape into little balls and roll in flour to coat. Heat oil in a frying pan and shallow fry balls until golden.

BOOTHI NGABAUNG KYAW
WHITE MARROW FRIED IN BATTER

Served as a between-meal snack or as part of a meal, this is a favourite way of preparing vegetables. Try it with tender chokos too.

2-3 cups sliced marrow
oil for deep frying
batter as for pazoon ngabaung kyaw

Peel marrow and remove seeds. Cut into slices about the thickness of a finger. Heat oil in a large frying pan or wok and when a faint haze begins to rise dip marrow slices in batter and drop, one at a time, into the oil. Do not try to fry more than 6 or 8 pieces at a time. When batter is golden remove from oil, drain on absorbent paper and serve immediately. This can be accompanied by ngan pya ye chet (page 282) for dipping.

NGAPI CHET
SHRIMP PASTE SAUTÉ

½ cup vegetable oil
1 onion, chopped
6 cloves garlic, chopped
¼ teaspoon turmeric
1 tablespoon dried shrimp paste (ngapi)
3-4 tomatoes, quartered
1 cup dried prawn powder
2 green chillies, sliced
1 tablespoon tamarind liquid
½ teaspoon salt or to taste

Heat oil until very hot, reduce heat to medium and fry onion, garlic and turmeric till dark golden and nearly sticking to pan. Add dried shrimp paste, tomatoes, prawn powder, green chillies and tamarind liquid. Stir and cook until all the liquid has evaporated and oil separates from the mass. Add salt to taste.

NGAN PYA YE CHET
FISH SAUCE SAUTÉ

1 teaspoon oil
1 large onion, finely chopped
1 cup fish sauce (ngan pya ye)
1 stem lemon grass, finely sliced crossways,
   or 2 strips lemon rind, finely chopped
6 cloves garlic, finely chopped
2 spring onions, finely chopped
½ teaspoon chilli powder

Heat oil in frying pan. Put in chopped onion and fry for a few seconds, pour in fish sauce and bring to the boil. Remove from heat and immediately add lemon grass, garlic, spring onions and chilli powder. Allow to cool.

PE THEE PIN PAUK NGABAUNG KYAW
BEAN SPROUTS FRIED IN BATTER

250 g (8 oz) fresh bean sprouts
oil for deep frying
batter as for pazoon ngabaung kyaw (page
   281).

Wash bean sprouts, drain well, pinch off tails. Make batter, fold in bean sprouts. Heat oil and when very hot fry spoonfuls of mixture until golden brown and crisp. Drain on absorbent paper, serve hot.

THA HNAT
CUCUMBER PICKLE

Serves: 6
2 large green cucumbers
½ cup malt vinegar
2 cups water
1 teaspoon salt
¼ cup peanut oil
2 tablespoons sesame oil
8 cloves garlic, sliced, or 1 teaspoon
   instant minced garlic
1 medium onion, finely sliced, or 2
   tablespoons dried onion flakes
2 tablespoons sesame seeds

Peel cucumbers, halve lengthways and scoop out seeds. Cut into strips of finger thickness, then cut strips into 5 cm (2 inch) pieces. Bring vinegar, water and salt to the boil, drop in cucumbers and boil just until they look transparent. Do not over-cook. Drain immediately and leave to cool.

Heat both oils together and fry the garlic until pale golden. Drain. Fry the onion until golden brown. Toast the sesame seeds in a dry frying pan, stirring constantly, until they are evenly golden brown. Turn on to a plate to cool. When the oil is cold, dress the cucumbers with 3 tablespoons of the oil, mixing well with the fingers. Put into a small serving dish, add the onion, garlic and sesame seeds, and toss lightly.

BEYA KYAW
SPLIT PEA FRITTERS

1 cup split peas
2 medium onions, finely chopped
2 fresh red chillies, finely chopped,
    or ¼ teaspoon chilli powder
½ teaspoon ground turmeric
½ teaspoon salt
oil for deep frying
sliced onion and lemon wedges to garnish

Soak split peas overnight, or for at least 6 hours, in water to cover. Drain, grind to a paste in blender or put twice through fine screen of mincer. Mix in all other ingredients except oil. Make small balls and flatten to 12 mm (½ inch) thickness. Heat oil in deep frying pan and put the fritters one at a time into the oil. Fry until golden brown. Drain on absorbent paper. Serve garnished with sliced raw onion and lemon wedges.

Note: The Burmese name for this recipe is pronounced 'be-ah-jaw'.

HMO KYAW KYET
MUSHROOMS FRIED WITH CHICKEN

Serves: 6
500 g (1 lb) fresh mushrooms
500 g (1 lb) chicken meat
3 tablespoons oil
1 large onion, finely sliced
3 cloves garlic, finely chopped
1 tablespoon light soy sauce
salt to taste

Wipe mushrooms with damp kitchen paper. Do not wash. If large, cut in halves or quarters. Slice chicken meat into narrow strips.

Heat oil in wok and fry onion and garlic until golden brown. Add chicken and stir fry for 2 minutes, on high heat, then cover and cook for 3 minutes on medium heat. Add soy sauce and salt to taste, then the mushrooms. Cover and simmer for 3-4 minutes, then raise heat and cook uncovered until most of the liquid has evaporated. Serve hot with rice.

THANATSONE
MIXED VEGETABLE SALAD

Use any combination of the following vegetables in the required amounts — beans, cabbage, cauliflower, okra, carrots, bamboo shoots, spring onions, bean sprouts, cucumber or zucchini.

Serves: 6
3 cups sliced vegetables
salt
½ cup vegetable oil
1 tablespoon sesame oil
½ teaspoon ground turmeric
2 large onions, finely sliced
4 cloves garlic, finely sliced
3 tablespoons sesame seeds
2 tablespoons white vinegar

Cut vegetables into bite-size strips and boil for only 1 or 2 minutes in lightly salted water, just until tender but still crisp. Drain and run cold water over the vegetables in colander to prevent overcooking. Drain again.

Heat the two oils in a small deep frying pan, add turmeric, onions and garlic and fry over medium heat, stirring all the time, until onions and garlic start to brown. Remove pan from heat and continue stirring until they are brown and crisp. When cool, pour a little of this oil over the vegetables, add onions and garlic and toss lightly but thoroughly, adding extra salt and vinegar to taste.

In a dry pan roast the sesame seeds over medium heat until golden brown. Turn on to a plate to cool, then sprinkle over the vegetables. Serve as an accompaniment to rice and curry.

HIN THEE HIN YWET
VEGETABLES

The Burmese name embraces all vegetables, fruits and edible leaves, and these are an essential part of Burmese food. They go into soups, curries and fries, or are served as crisp and crunchy raw salads. Both tropical and temperate vegetables grow in various parts of Burma according to the climatic conditions of the region or the season of the year.

Aunt Connie tells me that 'the Burmese housewife knows her onions in every sense of that useful cliché. For instance, onions are not just chopped up any old how. They are sliced lengthways for certain dishes, in rings for others and ground on a stone or pounded to a pulp for curries. Cabbage is shredded lengthways for fries and crossways for soups, but greens that cook very quickly such as spinach and Chinese cabbage are shredded crossways. The vegetables have to *look* right when they are served.

Except in soups and gravy-curries, water is hardly ever used in cooking vegetables. Like the Chinese, the Burmese prefer to cook vegetables by stir frying.

AKYAW

2 teaspoons sesame or corn oil
1 or 2 onions, finely sliced lengthways
2 cloves garlic, sliced lengthways
salt and pepper
fish sauce (ngan pya ye) optional

Heat oil until a haze rises, add onions and garlic and reduce heat immediately. Add 3 to 4 cups washed and prepared vegetables. Stir fry until vegetables are tender but still crisp to the bite. Add salt and pepper to taste and a sprinkling of fish sauce if liked. Do not prepare vegetables this way until just before serving, for if left to stand they will go limp.

Other Vegetables: Prepare vegetables for 'stir fry' in the following ways:
Okra or 'ladies' fingers': top and tail, slice thinly
Eggplant: slice thinly or dice small
Marrow, squash: peel, seed and cut into strips
Zucchini: cut in thin slices
Giant white radish: cut in strips
Bitter melon: slice thinly, sprinkle with salt, then rinse
Green beans, butter beans, runner beans or snake beans: cut in bite-size lengths
Snow peas: remove strings and leave whole
Carrots: scrape and slice very thinly
Cucumbers: halve lengthways, seed and slice thickly
Cabbage: shred lengthways
Spinach: tear into pieces
Bean sprouts: use whole, pinch off 'tails' if necessary
Bamboo shoot: fresh bamboo shoot must first be boiled until tender, then sliced or cut in matchstick pieces
Celery: slice diagonally
Onions: slice lengthways
Spring onions: cut into bite-size lengths

HIN
BURMESE SOUPS

A light-bodied piping hot soup is served at both main meals of the day. It can be a clear mild soup or a sour peppery hot soup depending on the weather or the other items on the menu.

Pork bones, fish heads or prawn heads are boiled and the stock used in the soups, but prepared stock is not absolutely necessary and sufficient flavour is obtained by using water and adding dry prawns or ngapi (a paste made from salted prawns and shrimps).

There are also substantial soup-curries, such as moh hin gha and panthe kaukswe, which are served with noodles. They are one-dish meals, but those that follow are for everyday meals — not as a first course, but for sipping through the meal.

HIN CHO
MILD SOUP *(picture page 279)*

Any of the following vegetables may be used in this recipe: marrow, peeled and cut in thin strips; zucchini, cut thinly in discs; pumpkin, diced; okra, topped and tailed and sliced diagonally; cauliflower, each floweret sliced lengthways; cabbage, shredded finely; chinese cabbage or other leaves, shredded crossways.

Serves: 4-6
4 to 6 cups stock or water
2 medium onions, peeled and sliced finely
1 tablespoon powdered dried prawns or 3 whole fresh prawns
3 peppercorns
¼ teaspoon dried shrimp paste (ngapi), optional
2 to 3 cups vegetables

Bring stock or water to the boil. Add onions, prawn powder, peppercorns and dried shrimp paste and boil for a further 5 minutes. Last of all add half cup of the vegetable chosen to each cup of water or stock. Pumpkin and cauliflower may take about 5 minutes to cook sufficiently, but the other vegetables should be done in about 3 minutes. Add salt if necessary.

HIN GHA
STRONG SOUP

Follow preceding recipe, but add 4 cloves garlic, sliced, and quarter teaspoon ground black pepper together with onions and other ingredients.

CHIN HIN
SOUR SOUP

Sour greens such as tender young tamarind leaves are used to make the stock for this soup (or substitute green tomatoes or rhubarb stalks). If rhubarb stalks are used, cut them into short lengths and boil, then strain and use the liquid combined with spinach or other green leaves.

Serves: 4-6
2 teaspoons sesame oil or corn oil
1 onion, finely sliced lengthways
2 cloves garlic, crushed
¼ teaspoon ground turmeric
2 or 3 green tomatoes, chopped
1 cup torn spinach or other greens
4-6 cups rhubarb stock, fish stock or boiling water
¼ teaspoon dried shrimp paste (ngapi)
salt to taste

Heat oil in a saucepan and when very hot fry the onion, garlic and turmeric, stirring for 30 seconds. Add the tomatoes and spinach, stir well, then add the stock or water and bring to the boil. Add shrimp paste, cover and simmer until vegetables are tender. Taste and add salt as necessary. Serve with rice.

KYAZAN HIN CHO
MILD SOUP WITH CELLOPHANE NOODLES

It is difficult to measure a small amount of cellophane noodles by weight as they are so light, or by volume as they are so unwieldy. Collaborator on this chapter, my aunt Constance Hancock, tells me to use 'a four-inch [10 cm] bunch of the strands which fits in the crook of your finger'.

Serves: 4
small bunch cellophane noodles (as above)
5 cups chicken or pork bone stock
1 onion, finely sliced
2 cloves garlic, finely sliced
6 button mushrooms, sliced
1 tablespoon light soy sauce
125 g (4 oz) fresh shrimps or prawns
1 zucchini, finely sliced in discs
salt and pepper to taste

Soak noodles in hot water and when softened cut into short lengths. Bring stock to the boil, add onion and garlic. Add the drained noodles and cook until they are swollen and soft. Add the mushrooms, soy sauce, prawns and zucchini and cook just until prawns are done. Taste and add salt and pepper as required. Serve hot.

KYAZAN HIN GHA
CELLOPHANE NOODLE SOUP WITH PEPPER

Serves: 4-6
small bunch cellophane noodles as for kyazan hin cho (above)
½ small chicken
1 tablespoon fish sauce (ngan pya ye)
6 dried Chinese mushrooms
1 tablespoon oil
2 medium onions, sliced lengthways
6 cloves garlic, sliced lengthways
½ teaspoon ground black pepper
salt to taste
3 tablespoons chopped fresh coriander leaves
3 spring onions, finely sliced
chilli powder for serving
lemon wedges for serving

Soak noodles in hot water and when softened cut into short lengths. Joint chicken, put into saucepan with plenty of water to cover. Add fish sauce and simmer until chicken is tender.

Cool to lukewarm, remove bones, cut flesh into small pieces and shred with fingers. Reserve stock. Soak mushrooms in hot water for 20-30 minutes, cut off stems and discard. Slice mushroom caps finely.

Heat oil in a saucepan and cook onions and garlic until onions are slightly soft. Add pepper, stock in which chicken was simmered, noodles and mushrooms. Bring to the boil, then simmer on low heat for 10 minutes. Add chicken meat and heat through, then add salt or extra fish sauce to taste. Remove from heat, sprinkle with coriander leaves and spring onions and serve hot, with a small bowl of chilli powder and the lemon wedges served separately for seasoning individual portions.

GOORAKATHEE KYAWJET HIN
CHOKO SOUP

Serves: 4-6
2 chokos
1 tablespoon oil
1 large onion, sliced lengthways
2 cloves garlic, sliced lengthways
1 tablespoon dried prawns
½ teaspoon dried shrimp paste (ngapi)
¼ teaspoon ground turmeric
4-6 cups water

Peel chokos, halve them lengthways and cut into thin slices. Heat oil in a saucepan and add onion, garlic, chokos, dried prawns, shrimp paste and turmeric. Toss together over medium heat for a few minutes, then cover and cook over low heat for 10 minutes. Add water and allow to simmer for 10 minutes. Add salt if necessary and serve hot with rice and curries.

WET CHE DAUK HINCHO
PIG TROTTER SOUP

Serves: 4

1 pig's trotter (front preferable)
2 tablespoons light soy sauce
3 medium onions
6 cloves garlic
4 tablespoons finely chopped fresh
   coriander leaves or celery leaves
salt to taste
pepper to taste

Wash and clean trotter. Chop into four pieces. Rub with soy sauce. Put into saucepan with 4 cups water or more if necessary and bring to boil. Remove any scum that may rise to surface while boiling. When meat is tender, remove and discard bones. Add onions and garlic and continue cooking for further 10 minutes. For flavour sprinkle with chopped coriander or celery leaves. Add salt and pepper to taste. Serve hot with rice.

SET HNIT MYO HINCHO
TWELVE VARIETIES SOUP

Serves: 6

125 g (4 oz) chicken, duck, or pork meat
2 tablespoons oil
2 onions, sliced
2 cloves garlic, sliced
6 slices boiled pork liver
1 tablespoon soy sauce
1 small choko
¼ cup bean sprouts
¼ cup shredded cabbage
¼ cup shredded cauliflower
¼ cup sliced green beans
¼ cup dried mushrooms, soaked
¼ cup dried wood fungus, soaked
1 sprig tender celery leaves
2 spring onions
2 eggs
salt to taste
pepper to taste

Slice poultry or pork meat thinly. Heat oil in wok and fry onions and garlic. Add sliced meat and pork liver. Stir well. Add soy sauce. Cover and cook gently for 5 minutes. Add all the vegetables and again cook briefly with lid on. When vegetables are slightly wilted, transfer contents into a large saucepan. Add 4 cups water and bring to boil rapidly. Just before serving add unbeaten eggs to the rapidly boiling soup and stir. Add salt and pepper to taste just before serving.

BURMESE SWEETS

Burmese meals do not include desserts, but fresh fruits in season are served after a meal. Between meals, however, sweets are eaten to satisfy a sweet tooth, or taken in the form of a cooling drink such as moh let saung (say 'molosaung'), page 291. Then there is durian preserve — just as strong smelling as the fruit, and arousing as much passionate for and against discussion as the fruit itself; mango preserve; wild plums cooked in jaggery treacle; and jaggery toffee.

Agar-agar is the base of many jelly preparations. They are generally much firmer than jellies served in Western countries. I remember my grandmother making huge cauldrons of seaweed jelly and letting it drip through a jelly cloth all night (hurrying it at this stage would cloud the jelly). When finished it was cut into large diamond-shaped pieces as clear and golden as topaz. I have never tasted anything of quite the same flavour since — and its texture was not melting and soft like gelatine jellies, but firm and crunchy.

There are also a number of cakes, fritters, doughnuts and steamed sponges made from finely ground rice flour and sweetened with jaggery. They may be served with jaggery treacle, freshly grated coconut, toasted sesame seeds, and quite often a pinch of salt. The contrast is surprisingly pleasant. Unlike Indian sweetmeats, the Burmese specialties are only slightly sweet.

Most of them are prepared and sold by professional sweetmakers, and each sweetmaker specialises in only one variety. They are not made at home, for they require special equipment and hours of preparation. The very mention of moh sein boung (steamed sponge cake) is enough to make an expatriate Burmese go misty eyed. This is a beautiful light textured rice flour sponge steamed in a tall mould in two layers of white and brown. The brown portion gets its colour from jaggery (palm sugar). Hawked through the streets at breakfast time, it is eaten off banana leaves with a sprinkle of grated coconut and mixture of crushed toasted sesame seeds and salt. Not very sweet or rich, but very satisfying.

MOH LOUNG YE BAW
TEETHING CAKE

This is the famous cake that is prepared and sent around to neighbours and friends, or fed to the poor, in celebration of a baby's first tooth. They are little dumplings cooked in coconut milk.

1 cup plain white flour
1 cup rice flour
pinch salt
½ teaspoon bicarbonate of soda
1 tablespoon light sesame or corn oil
scant ⅔ cup water
1 cup fresh grated coconut
½ cup grated palm sugar or
    substitute
4 cups coconut milk for simmering
1 tablespoon or more sugar

Sift the flours, salt and bicarbonate of soda into a bowl. Mix thoroughly, and rub in the oil. Add enough water to make a firm paste, knead well to a smooth dough. Mix together the grated coconut and palm sugar. Take little lumps of dough, roll into balls, then flatten to a circle and put very little of the coconut and palm sugar mixture on each. Close the opening and mould the dough together to seal. Roll again to a perfect globe.

Boil the coconut milk and sugar in a large saucepan and when boiling fast, drop in the balls. They will sink at first but rise slowly to the top as they cook. Stir gently in case some stick to the bottom. When cooked the balls will float on the surface. Simmer for at least 10 minutes after they start to float. Serve hot or cold with a little of the liquid.

KYAUK KYAW (1)
SEAWEED JELLY *(picture page 290)*

This jelly is made from transparent strands of refined seaweed that look like crinkled strips of cellophane. This is sold in Chinese groceries as refined agar-agar. Agar-agar powder is also sold in packets at Chinese stores and pharmacies. The name of the recipe is pronounced 'chow chaw'.

Makes about 18 pieces
7 g (¼ oz) agar-agar strands or 4
    teaspoons agar-agar powder
4 cups coconut milk
½ cup sugar
few drops rose flavouring

Soak the strands of agar-agar in cold water overnight or at least 1 hour. Drain and measure. There should be 1½ cups, loosely packed. Put the strands and coconut milk into a saucepan and stir constantly while bringing to the boil. Add sugar and keep stirring and simmering for 15-20 minutes, or until all the strands are completely dissolved. If using agar-agar powder, sprinkle on top of the milk and bring to the boil, then simmer and stir for 10 minutes. Flavour to taste, pour into a dish rinsed out with cold water, and allow to set. Cut into squares. This is a very firm jelly and can be picked up with the fingers.

KYAUK KYAW (2)
ICED JELLY DRINK

The agar-agar or seaweed jelly also gives its name to a drink served in Burma and so popular that it is sold on every street corner.

syrup made from palm sugar or slab sugar
  sold in Chinese stores
rose concentrate
iced water
crushed ice
1 can grass jelly (see Glossary)

Make a syrup from the sugar and water, and when cool flavour lightly with rose concentrate. Chop grass jelly into thin slivers. Put a tablespoon of jelly into each glass. Add a couple of spoonfuls of the syrup, then fill up with iced water and crushed ice. Stir well and serve. Another version of this uses coconut milk instead of water, and is also delicious and cooling on a hot day.

Note: Chopped agar-agar jelly can be used in place of canned grass jelly.

SHWÉ HTAMIN
GOLDEN RICE

Serves: 2-3
1 cup long grain rice
1 tablespoon oil
2 cups coconut milk
¼ teaspoon ground turmeric
¼ teaspoon salt
2 tablespoons sugar
1 cup grated fresh coconut
2 tablespoons toasted sesame seeds

If rice needs washing, wash and drain thoroughly. Heat oil in a medium-sized saucepan and fry the rice for 3 minutes, stirring and turning rice with a metal spoon. Add coconut milk, turmeric, salt and sugar and bring to the boil. When the liquid looks thick (which should take only a minute or two) turn heat very low, cover and cook 15 minutes or until all liquid has evaporated. While still hot, fluff up with a fork and mix in the grated coconut, then transfer rice to a greased ovenproof dish and smooth top. Press down firmly. Sprinkle with sesame seeds and bake in a slow oven for 20 minutes. Cut in diamond shapes and serve with more grated fresh coconut and toasted sesame seeds which have been slightly crushed and mixed with a little salt.

SANWIN MAKIN
SEMOLINA PUDDING

This dish (pronounced 'sinamakin') is rich with coconut milk, ghee and sesame seeds. It is cut and served like a cake.

1 cup medium fine semolina
3 cups thick coconut milk
1 cup sugar
125 g (4 oz) ghee or butter
pinch of salt
¼ teaspoon ground cardamom
3 eggs, separated
2-3 tablespoons sesame seeds

Put the semolina in a large, heavy saucepan and stir in the coconut milk gradually, keeping the mixture free from lumps. Add the sugar, put over medium heat and bring to the boil, stirring all the time. When the mixture boils and thickens add a small amount of ghee or butter at a time and continue cooking until mixture becomes very thick and leaves the sides of the pan. Add salt and ground cardamom and mix well.

Beat in the egg yolks, one at a time, then stiffly beat the egg whites and fold in. Turn the mixture into a buttered 22 cm (9 inch) cake pan or ovenproof dish and smooth the top. Toast the sesame seeds in a dry pan over medium heat, stirring constantly, until they are golden. Sprinkle liberally over semolina mixture.

Bake in a moderately slow oven 160°C (325°F) for 45 minutes to 1 hour or until well risen and golden brown. Cool in the dish, then cut into large diamond-shaped pieces. Serve as a sweet snack or as dessert.

MOH-LET-SAUNG
ICED COCONUT MILK WITH SAGO

A cooling drink of sago, coconut milk, and palm sugar which can be served as a dessert.

1 cup sago
4 cups water
¾ cup chopped palm sugar
ice cubes
4 cups coconut milk

Wash and soak sago for approximately 1 hour, drain and put in a large saucepan with 3 cups of the water. Bring to the boil and simmer over a moderate heat until sago grains are clear. Cool and chill.

Put palm sugar in a small saucepan with remaining water and heat gently until the cakes of sugar dissolve. Cool and strain the syrup.

For each serving, put approximately 4 tablespoons of chilled sago into a tall glass, add 3 tablespoons syrup (or more according to taste) and mix well. Add 2-3 ice cubes and fill up with coconut milk. Stir and serve immediately.

GIN THOKE
GINGER MIX

This after-meal digestive tid-bit is pronounced 'jintho'. The Burmese, a very relaxed people, sit around talking for a long time after meals and eat snacks like this instead of sweet desserts. Offer individual portions in very tiny bowls, and eat with the fingers.

125 g (4 oz) very tender fresh ginger
4-6 tablespoons lemon juice
2 tablespoons peanut oil
1 tablespoon sesame oil
12 cloves garlic, sliced
2-3 tablespoons sesame seeds
salt to taste

Ideally, the ginger root should be so young that the skin is almost transparent and the roots tipped with pink. If the ginger you buy is more mature, use the small knobs growing off the main root. (The rest of the ginger can be peeled and preserved in a jar by covering with dry sherry. Use in cooking.) Scrape skin off ginger with a sharp knife and cut ginger into very thin slices, then cut the slices into fine slivers. Marinate in lemon juice for at least 1 hour and the ginger will turn pink.

Meanwhile, heat peanut and sesame oil in a small frying pan and fry the sliced garlic slowly until pale golden. Remove from heat immediately (it burns easily) and drain on absorbent paper. Allow to cool and become crisp. Put sesame seeds in a dry frying pan and stir constantly over moderate heat until golden brown. Turn immediately on to a plate to cool.

When ready to serve, drain ginger from lemon juice and put in a bowl. Add salt to taste and sprinkle with garlic and sesame seeds. Toss together lightly.

NGAPYAW KYAW
BANANA SNACKS

Long green bananas, short yellow bananas, three-cornered bananas, large red bananas, small sour bananas, sweet and butter-smooth bananas — they all grow in Burma and are available all year round.

Sweet, delicately flavoured varieties are eaten as they are, but others are the starting point for all sorts of sweet snacks. They can be sliced, rolled in flour and fried; boiled in coconut milk; mashed with egg and a little plain flour to make a thick batter and shallow fried. These snacks are often served with a syrup made from palm sugar.

KYAUK KYAW (seaweed jelly) *recipe page 288*

THAILAND

Thai cooking, like that of the whole of Southeast Asia, is very much a taste-and-add affair. While the results are splendid, it is very difficult to obtain exact recipes because most Thai cooks don't use them. It is best to watch the cook closely, noting every move and taking careful and copious notes.

During a most enjoyable stay in Thailand I was fortunate to meet and speak with some outstandingly good Thai cooks and learn some of their recipes. One was Mom Luang Terb Xoomsai, a charming and worldly member of the Thai nobility who is famous for her good cooking. Between trips abroad to represent Thailand at food festivals and exhibitions she runs a catering firm and the SEATO canteen.

I lunched at the canteen as her guest, and chose to taste the Thai dishes rather than the European style food that was also provided. After lunch we sat and talked, then she took me into the kitchen to show me how various things were done. All in all, I have seldom spent so edifying an afternoon.

She pointed out that, like every country, Thailand has a classic cuisine and a peasant cuisine. She uses both, depending on the occasion. The meals in the canteen are, she said, of the peasant style (but delicious, just delicious) and when she catered for parties something grander was usually required. An example of this, being prepared then for a special party the next day, was *lug chup*, which translates as 'small magic' — and that's exactly what it was.

Tiny moulded fruits looking like marzipan fruit, but more delicate, they shone with a glaze that could have been a thin sugar coating at the brilliantly clear hard-crack stage. However, the fruits were not marzipan but mung bean paste, sweetened with sugar and coloured and flavoured with fresh fruits and vegetables. 'I would not touch them if they had artificial colouring and flavouring,' vowed Terb Xoomsai. Nor was the glaze sugar (which would melt in Thailand's humid climate); the fruits had been dipped in an agar-agar solution to give them a clear and completely non-sticky coating. Tiny natural calyxes from fruits were attached and the whole effect was one of delicacy and beauty.

I also met chef Miki Pichit, chef de cuisine at the Oriental Hotel, one of Bangkok's oldest and most famous hotels. I had been overwhelmed by his presentation of Thai food at the lavish banquet held to mark the Loy Krathong festival, the biggest celebration of the year. It takes place on the full of the twelfth moon and symbolises the passing of the old and the coming of the new lunar year. Lotus-shaped *krathongs* or floats made from flowers, leaves, coloured paper and (a modern touch) polystyrene foam to keep them afloat, are sent down the Chao Phraya river, each with lighted candles and incense sticks in them. The lights flickering on the water are a pretty sight, but not many survive more than a few yards downstream where scores of little boys wait in boats to snatch them from the water and profit from the *baht* coins tucked into them by devotees hoping to propitiate the gods.

Because the hotel is right on the river, there is a spectacular celebration held there each year attended by tourists and local society alike. Tableaux presented on an open-air stage tell stories of the grandeur of ancient Siam. Beautiful girls in breathtaking costumes dance traditional dances. There are music and singing, and an interpreter with a microphone translates for the benefit of *farangs* or foreigners.

To turn to the banquet . . . there was every conceivable dish displayed, both Western and Thai style. Smoked salmon and ham vied for attention with *kaeng* of every kind and such a selection of *krueng kieng* that discretion and diets were cast to the winds. Among the most delicious and curious dishes I tasted was a finely pounded paste of fresh fish seasoned with the ever-present Thai flavouring combination of coriander roots, peppercorns and garlic ground together. This was steamed in banana leaves cut and curved to look like a flower. I met this combination again at a very exclusive Thai restaurant, when it was steamed in the shape of tiny fish, each one no larger than a thumb, and presented on lettuce leaves as though swimming around the dish.

The sweets of every shape, flavour and hue were as dazzling to the eye as was the display of fireworks on the river. I could not help but wonder how many hours of work had gone into the making of hundreds of tiny baskets made from *bai toey* (pandanus leaves), each holding a mere mouthful of sweets made variously from glutinous rice, yams, agar-agar jelly, mung bean paste, mung bean flour and, of course, the richness of coconut milk and the sweetness of palm sugar. I particularly enjoyed the ice-cream made from fresh coconut milk. Delicately sweet, ice-cold, creamy but not too rich, it was the perfect ending to a perfect meal. A chef stood by the old-fashioned ice-cream churn, scooping out servings for guests who had still some space left to taste it.

Understandably the following day was chef Miki's day off, but a couple of days later I spoke to him about Thai food as he cooks it. His recipes will be treasured and used often.

On a tour of the hotel kitchens I met chef Silaprachai, a specialist in fruit carving. If you have not seen fruit as carved by the Thais, you cannot imagine the impact of huge pyramids of melons, pawpaws, *lamoot*, mandarins, pomelos, *champoos*, *rambutan*, all presented to look like flowers. The melons in particular, being large enough to decorate in more elaborate fashion, bore classic designs cut into the skin and in some instances were carved to look like birds, each feather separate and perfect.

It amazes the visitor to Thailand to see the care that goes into even the smallest detail. Even the *krathongs*, to be admired for a few hours and then floated down the river, were formed with such dexterity and attention to detail. Each 'petal' of the lotus shapes, approximately a handspan in length, was composed of hundreds of tiny red rose petals, each one rolled separately to form a flaring cone and arranged in perfectly symmetrical rows. These 'petals' were then edged with tight white buds of a jasmine-like flower.

COOKING AND SERVING A THAI MEAL

As in the rest of Southeast Asia, Thailand's staple food is rice. The words for rice and food are synonymous and everything else is called 'with the rice'.

Thailand is one of the greatest rice-growing countries in the world and exports of rice account for almost half of the country's export revenue. There are as many, if not more, ceremonial rituals attached to the planting and harvesting of rice in Thailand as there are in other Asian countries, where rice represents life and is revered as such.

To cook rice in the Thai manner, choose a long grain variety of polished white rice. Thai cooks wash the rice several times, but there is no need to do this if the rice is clean, for washing carries away soluble nutrients. It is then cooked by the absorption method.

Another method is to soak the rice overnight, then to drain and steam it. This takes much longer than cooking it directly in the water, but gives a very fluffy and grainy result. However, it must be served directly it is ready, because it will go hard and dry if left to stand. This method is almost always used with glutinous rice, a special variety much prized in northern Thailand, Laos and other countries in the area. Except in Laos, it is used exclusively in the making of sweets.

A Thai meal is based on rice, but the number and variety of dishes served with the rice is limited only by the cook's time, imagination, patience and budget. It is customary to have a soup, two or more *kaengs* (dishes with gravy) and as many *krueng kieng* (side dishes) as possible. These can be prepared beforehand and served at room temperature. There is not, in Thailand, the Western compulsion to have everything piping hot. Just cook the rice at the last moment so it will be steaming fresh and all will be well.

Modern Thais eat mostly with spoon and fork, though for those who can manage the old-fashioned way, with the fingers, the food does seem to taste even better. Everything is served at once and diners take this or that according to individual taste, combining or tasting separately each dish against the bland background of rice. Rice in Thailand is never cooked with salt. Seasonings and sauces added later make it inadvisable to cook rice with salt, because the sauces are so strong and salty.

Malee (meaning 'jasmine') is a petite Thai lass who spent some time in my kitchen as we cooked and exchanged recipes. From her I learnt that though a mainstay of the Thai flavouring combination is *kapi*,

Thai shrimp paste, she dislikes the flavour so she leaves it out. Her cooking was still full of flavour. So take courage. Any recipe is adaptable to your own taste.

UTENSILS

You don't need anything very special in the way of equipment to cook Thai food. But, like the cooking of many Asian countries, Thai food uses ground spices and herbs for flavouring and an electric blender helps. So does a mortar and pestle for pounding small quantities.

A *wok* is once again the classic shape for the stir-frying technique that is employed in many dishes, so if you enjoy cooking Chinese, Thai, Indonesian or other Asian food, it will be a wise investment. Read more about *woks* and their versatility on page 369.

YOUR THAI SHELF

mung bean flour
glutinous rice
long grain rice
fish sauce *(nam pla)*
dried shrimp paste *(kapi)*
palm sugar or raw or brown or black sugar
dried lemon grass or *sereh* powder
dried shrimps
dried fragrant mushrooms (Chinese mushrooms)
dry bean curd sheets, optional
laos powder
kencur powder

ground turmeric
dry chillies
chilli powder
chilli sauce
whole black peppercorns
cellophane noodles
light soy sauce
dark soy sauce
peanut or other vegetable oil
ground cummin
ground coriander
ground turmeric
paprika
whole cinnamon sticks or ground cinnamon
whole or ground cloves
whole cardamom pods
ground decorticated cardamom
creamed coconut
desiccated coconut
rice vermicelli
tamarind
raw peanuts
red ginger
tomato paste
dried wood fungus

Read about unfamiliar ingredients in the Glossary. In addition to these shelf ingredients, try to grow fresh lemon grass in your garden. Plants are available at some nurseries. Coriander herb, also called Chinese parsley, is so essential to Thai food that if you are in an area where you cannot buy it, grow some from seed. It is the soul of Thai food.

KHAO KLUK KAPI
RICE WITH KAPI

Serves: 6
1 tablespoon dried shrimps
4 or 5 large cloves garlic, finely chopped
2 fresh bird's eye chillies (very hot, tiny chillies)
2 eggs, beaten
pepper and salt to taste
1 tablespoon dried shrimp paste (kapi)
4 tablespoons lard or oil
½ cup finely diced cooked pork
4 cups hot cooked rice
2-3 tablespoons fish sauce
4 tablespoons chopped fresh coriander leaves

Soak shrimps in hot water for 10 minutes, then drain. Remove sandy vein and chop shrimps. Seed and chop the chillies. Beat eggs and season with salt and pepper. In a flat frying pan lightly greased with oil make 2 or 3 flat omelettes and cut them into thin strips. Wrap dried shrimp paste in foil and grill for 5 minutes. Heat oil in a wok and fry the garlic and chillies on low heat until golden. Do not have oil too hot when the garlic is put in or it will brown too quickly. Add the shrimps and dried shrimp paste and fry, stirring constantly, for 2 or 3 minutes. Add pork and fry for 1 minute. Add the rice and toss together with other ingredients until heated through. Season with fish sauce to taste, pile on a platter and garnish with the omelette strips and coriander leaves. More hot chillies may be used for garnish if liked.

KAI KWAM (fried eggs stuffed with pork and seafood) *recipe page 309*

KHAO SUEY
STEAMED RICE

Serves: 6-8
500 g (1 lb) long grain rice
3 cups water

If rice needs washing, wash well then allow to drain in a colander. Put rice into saucepan with the 3 cups water and bring to the boil. Lower heat to medium and cook uncovered until water is absorbed and holes appear on surface of rice mass. Remove from heat, scoop rice into a steamer or colander and steam over fast boiling water for 25-30 minutes. Grains will be firm and separate.

KHAO PHAT
THAI FRIED RICE

Serves: 4
4 cups cold steamed rice
3 tablespoons peanut oil
2 medium onions, finely chopped
1 large pork chop, finely diced
250 g (8 oz) raw prawns, shelled and de-veined
185 g (6 oz) can crab meat
3 eggs, beaten
salt and pepper to taste
2 tablespoons fish sauce
1 tablespoon chilli sauce, optional
2 tablespoons tomato paste
1 cup chopped spring onions
3 tablespoons chopped fresh coriander leaves

Cook rice by the steaming method (above). Spread out and allow to cool. Heat oil in a wok or large frying pan and fry the onions on medium low heat, stirring constantly, until soft and translucent. Increase heat to high. Add pork and fry for 3 minutes. Add prawns and crab meat and fry for a further 3 minutes or until cooked. Season beaten eggs well with salt and pepper and pour into centre of wok. Stir until just beginning to set, then add rice and stir well. Continue tossing and stirring until rice is heated through. Sprinkle fish sauce over and mix well, then add chilli sauce and tomato paste and toss thoroughly so the rice has a reddish colour. Remove from heat, stir the spring onions through, and transfer to serving platter. Sprinkle with chopped coriander leaves and serve.

KHAO PHAT PRIK
CHILLI FRIED RICE *(picture page 299)*

Serves: 4
4 cups cold steamed rice
3 tablespoons peanut oil
1 large onion, finely chopped
1 fresh red chilli and 1 fresh green chilli, seeded and sliced
1 tablespoon red curry paste (page 300)
1 pork chop, finely diced
500 g (1 lb) raw prawns, shelled and de-veined
2 eggs, beaten
pepper and salt to taste
3 tablespoons fish sauce or light soy sauce
1 cup chopped spring onions including green tops
½ cup chopped fresh coriander leaves
chilli flowers for garnish

Cook rice by steaming method (above). Allow to cool. Heat oil in wok and fry onion and sliced chillies until soft. Add the curry paste and fry until the oil separates from the mixture. Add pork and fry until cooked, then add prawns (chopped into pieces if they are large). Fry for a minute or two longer, until prawns turn pink, then add rice and toss thoroughly until coated with the curry mixture and heated through. Push rice to side of wok and pour the beaten eggs, seasoned with salt and pepper, into the centre. Stir until eggs start to set, then mix through the rice, tossing on high heat until eggs are cooked. Sprinkle fish sauce evenly over the rice and mix well, then remove from heat. Stir the spring onions through. Gernish with coriander leaves and chilli flowers and serve.

PHAT WUN SEN
MIXED FRIED VERMICELLI

Serves: 4
250 g (8 oz) rice vermicelli
10 dried Chinese mushrooms
185 g (6 oz) pork fillet
250 g (8 oz) raw prawns
2 leeks or 6 spring onions
1 canned bamboo shoot
2 tender carrots
3 large cloves garlic
2 fresh red chillies, optional
2 tablespoons peanut oil
2 tablespoons fish sauce
1 tablespoon white vinegar
1 teaspoon salt
2 teaspoons sugar
½ teaspoon black pepper
fried onion flakes, optional
3 tablespoons chopped fresh coriander
  leaves

Soak vermicelli in hot, not boiling, water for 10 minutes, then drain in a colander. Soak mushrooms in hot water for 20 minutes, squeeze out water, slice mushroom caps thinly and discard stems. Cut the pork into very thin shreds. Shell and devein the prawns and cut into pieces if large. Wash leeks well, making sure there is no sand left among leaves. Use the white portion and about 5 cm (2 inches) of the green leaves. Slice very finely. If spring onions are used, cut into short lengths. Cut bamboo shoot and carrots into julienne strips. Chop garlic finely and slice the chillies diagonally, flipping out the seeds with point of knife.

Heat oil in wok or large frying pan and fry the garlic and chillies on gentle heat until soft. Move to side of pan, raise heat to medium and add the pork. Stir fry for 3 or 4 minutes, until cooked. Add prawns, leeks, bamboo shoots and carrots and stir fry for a further 3 minutes. Add all the seasonings mixed together and simmer for 1 minute, then add the vermicelli and toss until well mixed and heated through. Serve on a long dish and garnish with finely chopped coriander leaves and, if liked, crisp-fried onion flakes (page 206).

MEE KROB
CRISPY NOODLES

The noodles in this dish are fine rice noodles, also known as rice vermicelli. On a recent visit to Thailand I attended the Bussaracum cookery school where the lady who taught young Thai housewives the secrets of good Thai cooking demonstrated how to make perfect Mee Krob. The essential feature of this dish is that the noodles should be crisp and crunchy, therefore please ensure it is served at once, on its own. The salty, hot, sweet and sour flavours need no accompaniment.

Serves: 6
200 g (7 oz) rice vermicelli
3 cups peanut oil for deep frying
125 g (4 oz) minced pork or chicken
125 g (4 oz) shelled prawns, chopped
1 cup finely diced firm bean curd
⅓ cup white vinegar
⅓ cup sugar
⅓ cup fish sauce
3 eggs, beaten
½ teaspoon ground black pepper
2 whole heads pickled garlic, finely sliced
3 red chillies, seeded and sliced
¾ cup chopped fresh coriander
¼ cup chopped garlic chives

Dip the rice noodles briefly in cold water, or run the cold tap over them. Shake off excess water and leave in a breezy place about 30 minutes. (When these noodles are fried, they will not puff up as spectacularly as when fried straight from the packet, but will hold their crispness longer.) Heat the oil in a wok and when a light haze rises from the surface, test the heat of the oil with a few strands of the vermicelli. It should puff and swell immediately. If it sinks to the bottom it means the oil is not hot enough, and the vermicelli will be tough and oily instead of light and crisp.

Fry the vermicelli in small handfuls, and remove from the oil as soon as it puffs and becomes pale golden in colour. Drain on absorbent paper and allow to cool completely. May be stored airtight and kept for a few hours.

Pour off the oil into a metal bowl, leaving a small amount in the wok, about ¼ cup. Reheat this oil and fry the minced pork on high heat, stirring and pressing it against the hot wok, until it has lots its pinkness. Add the prawns and fry for 1 minute, add bean curd and toss until heated through.

Stir vinegar, sugar and fish sauce in a bowl until sugar dissolves, pour into the wok and bring to the boil. Pour in the beaten eggs seasoned with pepper, stirring until the eggs are set and firm. Prepare ahead up to this stage if convenient, but do not leave the mixture in an iron wok or it will develop unpleasant flavours because of the acid.

Just before serving, heat the cooked mixture, add the fried noodles, the sliced pickled garlic and most of the sliced chillies and chopped herbs. Mix well. Serve in individual bowls or a serving dish and sprinkle with chopped coriander, garlic chives and chillies. Urge your guests to eat Mee Krob without delay.

KRÜNG KAENG KHIEU WAN
GREEN CURRY PASTE

4 large fresh green chillies
1 teaspoon black peppercorns
1 small brown onion, chopped
1 tablespoon chopped garlic
2 tablespoons chopped fresh coriander
   plant, including root
2 teaspoons chopped lemon rind
1 teaspoon salt
2 teaspoons ground coriander
1 teaspoon ground cummin
1 teaspoon serai powder
1 teaspoon laos powder
2 teaspoons dried shrimp paste (kapi)
1 teaspoon ground turmeric
1 tablespoon oil

Remove stems of chillies, and leave the seeds in if you want the curry paste to be hot. Roughly chop the chillies and put into container of electric blender together with all other ingredients. Blend to a smooth paste, turning off motor and scraping down sides of blender with a spatula and adding a little extra oil or a tablespoon of water if necessary.

KRÜNG KAENG MASAMAN
MUSLIM CURRY PASTE

You can make this curry paste two ways — either using the whole spices, roasting and grinding them (you will need a stout mortar and pestle for this) or by using the ground spices. In some areas it is easier to buy whole spices while in others one can only obtain ground spices, so I have tested this recipe using both forms. One is just as successful as the other, and the ground spices certainly require less effort.

7-10 dried chillies or 2 teaspoons chilli
   powder
2 tablespoons coriander seeds or ground
   coriander
1 teaspoon cummin or fennel seeds or
   ground fennel
2 teaspoons laos powder, optional
1 teaspoon shredded lemon grass or finely
   peeled lemon rind
5 whole cloves or ¼ teaspoon ground
   cloves
1 stick cinnamon or 1 teaspoon ground
   cinnamon
5 cardamom pods or ½ teaspoon ground
   cardamom
1 blade mace or ½ teaspoon ground mace
2 tablespoons oil
2 medium sized onions, finely sliced
5 cloves garlic, peeled and sliced
½ teaspoon dried shrimp paste (kapi)

Break the chillies, shake out the seeds, and roast them lightly in a dry pan. Pound in a mortar and pestle. Roast the coriander seeds until aromatic and dark brown, shaking pan frequently or stirring. Pound in a mortar until seeds are reduced to fine powder (if spices are pounded while hot they are easily pulverised). Roast cummin seeds until they crackle and start to pop, then grind to a powder. I have not suggested grinding them in a blender because the quantities are so small there is not enough for the blades to work on. Add laos and lemon rind to the ground spices. Parch the cloves, cinnamon stick, cardamom pods and mace in a dry pan over low heat, shaking the pan. Separate the cinnamon into layers, it will roast more quickly. Grind all the spices in mortar and pestle to a fine powder and combine with the previously roasted and ground ingredients. Set aside.

Heat oil in a frying pan and on low heat fry sliced onions and garlic until soft and golden brown, stirring occasionally. Add dried shrimp paste and fry for a minute longer, crushing it in the oil with back of spoon. Put this fried mixture, when it has cooled slightly, into container of electric blender with lemon rind and blend to a paste. If necessary, add a little coconut milk or water to assist action of blender. Turn into a bowl and combine with dry ground spices. The curry paste is now ready to use.

If using ground spices, dry-roast the ground coriander and fennel over low heat, stirring constantly and taking care they do not burn. Roast until they turn a rich brown and have an aromatic smell. It is not necessary to roast the chilli powder or the other ground spices.

If a blender is not available, crush the onions and garlic as much as possible after they are cooked, combine with the spices and use in the same way.

KHAO PHAT PRIK (chilli-fried rice) *recipe page 296*

KRÜNG KAENG PHED
RED CURRY PASTE

4-6 dried red chillies
2 small brown onions, chopped
1 teaspoon black peppercorns
2 teaspoons ground cummin
1 tablespoon ground coriander
2 tablespoons chopped fresh coriander
   plant, including root
1 teaspoon salt
2 teaspoons chopped lemon rind
1 teaspoon serai powder
1 teaspoon laos powder
1 tablespoon chopped garlic
2 teaspoon dried shrimp paste (kapi)
1 tablespoon oil
1 teaspoon turmeric
2 teaspoons paprika

Remove stems from chillies, but keep the seeds in if you want the curry paste to be as hot as it is in Thailand. Break the chillies into pieces and put into container of an electric blender together with all the other ingredients. Blend to a smooth paste, stopping motor frequently and pushing ingredients on to blades. It may be necessary to add a tablespoon of water or extra oil.

KAENG PHET KUNG
PRAWN RED CURRY

Serves: 4
500 g (1 lb) raw prawns
2 cups coconut milk
2 tablespoons red curry paste (above)
1-2 tablespoons fish sauce or 1 teaspoon
   salt
1 fresh red chilli, seeded

Shell and de-vein prawns, but reserve heads. Wash prawn heads well, discarding only the hard top shell. Put the coconut milk into a pan with the curry paste, fish sauce or salt and the fresh chilli. Bring slowly to simmering point, stirring. Add prawns and prawn heads and cook uncovered, stirring frequently, on low heat until prawns are cooked and flavours mellow, about 15 minutes. This curry is even better prepared ahead and re-heated when required. Serve hot with white rice and other accompaniments. The prawn heads have a wonderful flavour and may be served as part of the curry.

KAENG KHIEU WAN PLA
GREEN CURRY OF FISH

Serves: 4
500 g (1 lb) fish steaks
2½ cups coconut milk
2 tablespoons green curry paste (page 298)
2 sprigs citrus leaves
1 teaspoon salt
1 tablespoon fish sauce
1 or 2 small green chillies, seeded and
   chopped
2 tablespoons finely chopped fresh basil

Wash fish well and trim any spines with kitchen scissors. Bring coconut milk to the boil with the curry paste, stirring constantly. Add fish, reduce heat and simmer with citrus leaves, salt and fish sauce until the fish is cooked through, about 15 minutes. Add chillies and fresh basil and simmer a few minutes longer, then serve with white rice.

KAENG KHIEU WAN KAI
GREEN CURRY OF CHICKEN

The green colour is imparted by the finely chopped chillies and fresh herbs added during the last few minutes of cooking. These two ingredients not only give colour, but also a distinctive flavour that distinguishes Thai dishes from other spiced preparations with a coconut milk gravy, all called 'kaeng' for want of a more definitive word.

Serves: 6
1 roasting chicken, 1.5 kg (3 lb)
3½-4 cups coconut milk
3 tablespoons green curry paste (page 298)
2 sprigs tender citrus leaves
1 teaspoon salt
2 tablespoons fish sauce
2 tablespoons finely chopped fresh green chillies, seeds removed
4 tablespoons finely chopped fresh basil or coriander leaves

Divide chicken into joints. Make coconut milk as instructed on page 11 and put the first extract or thick milk in the refrigerator or in a cool place for an hour or so until the cream rises to the top. Spoon off the cream or richest part of the milk into a cup. Heat this cupful of coconut cream in a large heavy saucepan, stirring constantly until it comes to the boil. Lower heat and continue cooking, stirring occasionally, until the cream thickens and oil bubbles around it. By this time it should be reduced to a quarter of the original amount. Add the curry paste and fry the rich oily cream for about 5 minutes, stirring constantly. The curry paste will smell cooked and oil will separate from it when it is ready.

When this happens add the pieces of chicken and cook over medium low heat stirring frequently and turning them, for about 15 minutes. The chicken will change colour and have a cooked appearance. Add the remaining coconut milk, citrus leaves, salt and fish sauce and stir while the coconut milk comes to the boil. Then turn heat low and allow to simmer uncovered for 35-45 minutes or until the chicken is well cooked and tender and the gravy rich and oily. (In Thai curries the aim is *not* to reduce the liquid to a small amount of thick, almost dry gravy.) Stir in the chopped fresh chillies and herbs, simmer for 5 minutes longer, then turn into serving dish. Serve with white rice.

KAENG KHIEU WAN PET
GREEN CURRY OF DUCK *(picture page 306)*

Using one medium-size roasting duck, proceed as for green curry of chicken (previous recipe).

KAENG MASAMAN
MUSLIM CURRY

Chicken or beef may be used in this very spicy curry.

Serves 6-8
1 kg (2 lb) beef or 1 roasting chicken about 1.75 kg (3½ lb)
4 cups coconut milk
1 cup roasted, unsalted peanuts
2 tablespoons fish sauce
15 cardamon pods
1 stick cinnamon, about 5 cm (2 inches)
1 quantity masaman curry paste (page 298)
3 tablespoons tamarind liquid
2 tablespoons lime or lemon juice
1-2 tablespoons palm sugar or substitute
extra fish sauce if necessary

Cut chicken into curry pieces, or beef into large cubes. Put into a 3½ litre (6 pint) saucepan with the coconut milk, peanuts, fish sauce, cardamom pods and cinnamon. Bring slowly to simmering point, stirring frequently with a wooden spoon. Turn heat low and allow to simmer, uncovered, until meat is tender. This should take about an hour for beef, 35-40 minutes for a roasting chicken. (A boiling fowl is excellent for this curry, but increase the coconut milk to 5 or 6 cups because it will need to simmer for about 2 hours.) Do not cover at any stage or the coconut milk will curdle. Stir occasionally during this initial cooking.

Meanwhile, make the curry paste. When the meat is just tender lift it out and simmer the coconut milk a little longer, until it is reduced by about a third. If it has already reduced considerably, do not give it this further cooking. Stir in the curry paste, tamarind liquid, lemon juice, sugar. Return beef or chicken to pan and continue simmering until the gravy is thickened slightly. Taste and add more fish sauce if necessary. Serve with white rice.

KAENG PHED NUER
RED CURRY OF BEEF *(picture page 306)*

Serves: 6

1 kg (2 lb) stewing steak
2 cups thick coconut milk
3 tablespoons red curry paste (page 300)
2 cups thin coconut milk
2 sprigs tender citrus leaves
1 teaspoon salt
2 tablespoons fish sauce
2 fresh red chillies, seeded and sliced

Trim the meat and cut into cubes. Make coconut milk (page 11) and leave the first extract or thick milk in the refrigerator long enough for the cream to rise to the top, then spoon it off until you have a cup of the top of the coconut milk. Simmer this in a large saucepan, stirring constantly, until it comes to the boil, then cook over a low heat until the cream thickens and the oil starts to show around the edges. Add the curry paste and fry for 5 minutes or so, stirring constantly.

When done the curry paste will smell cooked and oil will start to separate from the mass again. Add beef and stir well, then add remaining coconut milk, both first and second extracts. Add all remaining ingredients. Stir while bringing to the boil, then lower heat and simmer until beef is tender. If the beef has not become tender and the gravy seems to be cooking away, add a little more coconut milk or hot water and stir. The gravy should be rich and red, and there should be quite a lot of it. Serve with white rice and krueng kieng.

TOM KHA KAI
CHICKEN WITH COCONUT MILK AND LAOS

If you live in a country where you can get fresh laos (kha) and lemon grass by all means use them, substituting a knob of laos sliced, and 2 stalks lemon grass, for the dried or powdered laos and the lemon rind.

Serves: 5

6 pieces dried laos or 4 teaspoons laos
   powder
1 roasting chicken, about 1.25 kg (2½ lb)
2½ cups thin coconut milk
1 cup thick coconut milk
½ teaspoon black pepper
2-3 fresh coriander roots, crushed
6 strips thinly peeled lemon rind
3 fresh green chillies
1½ teaspoons salt
3 fresh leaves from lemon or other citrus
   tree
1 tablespoon fish sauce
lemon juice to taste
3 tablespoons finely chopped fresh
   coriander leaves

Soak the dried laos in hot water for 30 minutes. Cut chicken into serving pieces and put into saucepan with thin coconut milk, laos, pepper, coriander roots, lemon rind, chillies (whole), salt and citrus leaves. Bring slowly to the boil and simmer, uncovered, until chicken is tender, stirring occasionally. Add thick coconut milk and stir constantly until it returns to the boil. Remove from heat and stir in the fish sauce and lemon juice. Serve in a deep dish or bowl with chopped coriander leaves on top. Accompany with white rice.

Ingredients for curry pastes *recipes pages 298-300.*

KUNG TOM YAM
PRAWN SOUP *(picture page 315)*

Serves: 6

1 kg (2 lb) raw prawns
1 tablespoon oil
8 cups hot water
1½ teaspoons salt
2 stalks lemon grass or 4 strips lemon rind, thinly peeled
4 lemon or other citrus leaves
2 or 3 fresh whole chillies
1 tablespoon fish sauce
2 tablespoons lemon juice, or to taste
1 fresh red chilli, seeded and sliced
2 tablespoons chopped coriander leaves
4 spring onions (with green tops), chopped

Shell and de-vein prawns. Wash prawn heads well, drain thoroughly. Heat oil in a saucepan and fry heads and shells of prawns until they turn pink. Add hot water, salt, lemon grass or lemon rind, citrus leaves and whole chillies. Bring to the boil, cover and simmer for 20 minutes. Strain stock, return to the boil, add prawns and simmer for 3-4 minutes or until prawns are cooked. Add fish sauce and lemon juice to taste. This soup should have a pronounced acid flavour, so add sufficient lemon juice to achieve this. Serve in a large tureen or in soup plates, sprinkled with sliced chilli, coriander leaves and spring onions.

KAENG CHÜD DOK MAI CHIN
PRAWN SOUP WITH LILY BUDS *(picture page 315)*

One of the most delicious soups you can imagine, robustly flavoured with garlic and fresh coriander.

Serves: 6-8

90 g (3 oz) cellophane noodles
30 dried lily buds
8 dried Chinese mushrooms
4 or 5 cloves garlic
3 whole fresh coriander plants, including roots
500 g (1 lb) small raw prawns
3 tablespoons peanut oil
1 medium onion, sliced finely
8 cups water
6 spring onions, sliced diagonally
4 tablespoons fish sauce
1 tablespoon light soy sauce
1 teaspoon sugar
2 eggs

Put the cellophane noodles into a bowl and cover with warm water. In another bowl soak the lily buds and the dried mushrooms in hot water for 30 minutes. Pinch off the hard ends of the lily buds and if you have the time and patience, tie a knot in each one (this is what the Thais and Chinese do). However, if you haven't the time, cut the buds in two so they are bite-size. Cut off and discard the tough stems of the mushrooms and slice the caps thinly. Cut the cellophane noodles in short lengths no more than 5 cm (2 inches).

Peel garlic. Wash coriander plants very well and reserve leaves of one plant for garnish. Roughly chop remaining plants including roots and put into container of electric blender with garlic. Add 2 tablespoons water and blend to a purée. If blender is not available pound garlic and coriander with mortar and pestle to a smooth paste.

Shell and de-vein the prawns. Do not discard shells and heads, but wash and drain well, then use for making stock. Heat 1 tablespoon of the oil in a large saucepan, add the well-drained shells and heads and fry over high heat for a few minutes until the shells turn bright pink. Add the 8 cups water, cover and simmer for 20 minutes, then strain stock and discard shells.

Wash and dry the saucepan and heat remaining 2 tablespoons oil. Fry the onion until soft and translucent, stirring occasionally. Add the garlic and coriander purée and stir constantly over medium heat until oil separates from the mixture. Add prawns and fry until they change colour, about 3 minutes. Add hot stock, lily buds, mushrooms and cellophane noodles and bring soup to the boil. Lower heat and simmer gently for 5 minutes. Add spring onions, fish sauce, soy sauce and sugar. Taste and if necessary add a little extra salt. Beat the eggs slightly and pour into the boiling soup, stirring constantly. Remove from heat at once. Serve garnished with finely chopped fresh coriander leaves.

KAENG CHUD MU KAI
PORK AND CHICKEN SOUP

Serves: 6
500 g (1 lb) pork loin
6 cups water
½ cup fish sauce
½ cup palm sugar or substitute
half a small chicken or 2 chicken legs
1 teaspoon peppercorns
1 whole coriander plant, including root
½ teaspoon salt
5 dried Chinese mushrooms
90 g (3 oz) cellophane noodles
3 tablespoons chopped spring onion,
    including green leaves
3 tablespoons chopped fresh coriander
    leaves
1 red chilli, seeded and sliced, optional

Cook pork as in sweet pork recipe (page 309). Cool and chill, then remove fat from surface of stock.

Put chicken into a saucepan with 6 cups water, peppercorns, well-washed coriander plant, and salt. Bring to the boil then cover and simmer until chicken is tender. Soak mushrooms in hot water for 20 minutes, cut off stems and add stems to simmering chicken for extra flavour. Slice the caps finely and set aside. Soak cellophane noodles in hot water for 15 minutes, drain and cut into short 5 cm (2 inch) lengths.

When chicken is ready, remove from heat and allow to cool in the stock, then lift out, remove skin and bones and cut chicken into small dice. Strain the stock. There should be about 4 cups. Cut half the pork into dice, reserving remaining pork for use in another dish, or simply serve as sweet pork. Measure pork stock and use 2 cups to combine with chicken stock. Bring to a boil, add cellophane noodles and mushrooms and simmer for 10 minutes. Add diced chicken and pork, chopped spring onion and coriander and turn off heat immediately. Serve at once, and garnish if liked with the chilli slices.

PLA TOD
FRIED FISH WITH TAMARIND

Serves: 4-6
1 whole fish, about 1 kg (2 lb)
lard for frying
3 cloves garlic, crushed
3 tablespoons soy sauce
1 tablespoon palm sugar or substitute
2 tablespoons fish sauce
4 tablespoons tamarind liquid
1 tablespoon finely shredded fresh ginger
3 spring onions, cut into bite-size pieces
3 tablespoons chopped fresh coriander
    leaves
3 fresh red chillies, sliced

Buy fish cleaned and scaled, complete with head. Trim fins and tail, wipe out cavity with kitchen paper dipped in salt, wash and dry well. Fry the fish in hot lard until brown on both sides, but do not over-cook. Drain on absorbent paper, cover fish with foil and keep warm.

Pour off all but a tablespoon of the lard and on low heat fry the garlic until starting to brown. Immediately add the soy sauce, sugar, fish sauce and tamarind liquid and bring to the boil. Add ginger and spring onions and cook for 1 minute. Spoon the sauce over the fish and serve garnished with coriander leaves and chillies, as an accompaniment to white rice.

PLA NAM
FISH IN RED SAUCE

Serves: 4-6
750 g (1½ lb) fish fillets
4 tablespoons oil
2 onions, finely chopped
4 ripe tomatoes, peeled and chopped
2 tablespoons vinegar
salt and pepper
2 or 3 fresh chillies, seeded and chopped
3-4 tablespoons chopped fresh coriander
    leaves

Heat oil and fry onions over moderate heat until soft and golden brown. Add tomatoes, vinegar, salt and pepper to taste, and the chillies. Cover and simmer for 20 minutes or until tomatoes are pulpy and sauce thick. Add fish, cover and cook until fish is done. Serve hot, sprinkled with chopped coriander leaves.

PLA CIAN
THAI-STYLE FRIED FISH

1 x 1 kg (2 lb) whole snapper or bream or
   750 g (1½ lb) fish fillets
¼ cup peanut oil
6 spring onions, cut into 2.5 cm (1 inch)
   pieces
4 cloves garlic, crushed
3 teaspoons finely grated fresh ginger
2 tablespoons light soy sauce
1 tablespoon palm sugar or substitute
1 tablespoon tamarind liquid or lemon
   juice
1 tablespoon fish sauce
¼ teaspoon ground black pepper
2 tablespoons chopped fresh coriander
   leaves
1 fresh red chilli, seeded and sliced

Wash and wipe fish well. Fry in hot oil first on one side and then on the other until lightly browned and cooked through. Remove fish to serving platter and keep warm. Let oil cool slightly, then fry the spring onions until soft, add garlic and ginger and cook on low heat, stirring until soft and golden. Add soy sauce, sugar, tamarind liquid, fish sauce and pepper and simmer for 1 minute. Pour over the fish, garnish with coriander leaves and chilli and serve at once with white rice.

PLA PRIO WAN
WHOLE FRIED FISH WITH GINGER SAUCE *(picture page 311)*

A simple and delicious way of serving fish. Prepare ingredients for sauce before starting to cook the fish. Sauce can simmer while the fish is being fried and the dish served immediately the fish is cooked, while at its best.

Serves 2-3 as a main dish, more if other dishes are served

1 whole fish, about 1 kg (2 lb) (snapper,
   bream, jewfish)
flour, seasoned with salt to taste
oil for frying

Ginger Sauce:
8 dried Chinese mushrooms
6 tablespoons vinegar
6 tablespoons sugar
¾ cup water
2 tablespoons soy sauce
2 tablespoons finely chopped spring onion
1 tablespoon cornflour
1 tablespoon cold water
4 tablespoons chopped red ginger (see
   Glossary)

Buy fish cleaned and scaled, but with head left on. Trim fins and tail with kitchen scissors, and wipe out cavity with kitchen paper dipped in coarse salt. Wash well and dry thoroughly. With a sharp knife slash the fish diagonally on each side almost to the centre bone, forming diamond shapes in the flesh. Dip fish in seasoned flour, then dust off excess flour. Deep fry in hot oil until golden brown, drain on absorbent paper, then transfer fish carefully to serving dish, spoon sauce over and serve immediately.

Ginger Sauce: Soak mushrooms in hot water for 30 minutes. Slice mushroom caps finely, discarding tough stems. Put mushrooms, vinegar, sugar, water and soy sauce into a small saucepan and boil for 5 minutes. Add spring onion, using most of the green portion as well. Blend cornflour smoothly with cold water and stir into the sauce. Cook, stirring, until clear and thickened. Remove from heat, stir in ginger and pour over fish. Garnish with a sprig of fresh coriander leaves if desired.

KAENG KHIEU WAN PET (green curry of duck, *top*) *recipe page 301;*
YAM MA MUANG (green mango or apple salad, *right*) *recipe page 313;*
and KAENG PHED NUER (red curry of beef, *bottom*) *recipe page 303*

PLA NERNG
STEAMED FISH

Serves: 6
500 g (1 lb) fish fillets
2 dried chillies
1 teaspoon salt
1 small onion, chopped
3 cloves garlic, chopped
½ teaspoon chopped lemon rind
½ teaspoon ground turmeric
¼ teaspoon ground black pepper
2 tablespoons fish sauce
1 cup thick coconut milk
1 egg, beaten
1 teaspoon rice flour, optional
3 tablespoons finely chopped spring
   onions, green leaves included
2 tablespoons chopped fresh coriander
   leaves

Remove all skin and bones from fish and cut into thin slices. Put chillies, salt, onion, garlic, lemon rind, turmeric, pepper and fish sauce into container of electric blender and blend to a smooth paste. Add a tablespoon of the coconut milk if more liquid is required.

Put the blended mixture in a large bowl, add the sliced fish and half the coconut milk and the egg. Mix well until most of the liquid has been absorbed by the fish. Line a heatproof dish with a large cabbage leaf and turn the fish into this. Mix rice flour with remaining ½ cup coconut milk and spoon over the fish. Sprinkle with the spring onions and coriander leaves. Cover and steam for 30 minutes. Allow to cool slightly and firm before serving. Serve as an accompaniment to rice.

KAI TOD TAUCHEO
DEEP-FRIED CHICKEN WITH YELLOW BEAN SAUCE

Serves: 3
1 large chicken breast
1 tablespoon egg white
2 teaspoons water chestnut flour or
   cornflour
oil for deep frying
1 tablespoon lard
1 tablespoon yellow bean paste
1 teaspoon sugar
2 tablespoons Chinese wine or sherry
½ teaspoon sesame oil

Skin and bone the chicken breast and cut flesh into small dice. Slightly beat the egg white and mix into chicken meat together with water chestnut flour. Heat oil and deep fry chicken, a few pieces at a time, for a few seconds, until colour changes. Drain on absorbent paper.

Heat lard, add bean paste and fry for a few seconds. Add sugar, wine or sherry and sesame oil and mix well, then add chicken and heat through. Serve immediately with white rice.

KAI YANG
GARLIC CHICKEN

This may sound like a lot of garlic and pepper, but the result is so unusual and delicious that I hesitate to modify the recipe. The coarsely crushed peppercorns are not as hot as the same amount of finely ground pepper.

Serves: 4-5
1 x 1.5 kg (3 lb) roasting chicken or 1 kg
   (2 lb) chicken breasts
6 cloves garlic
2 teaspoons salt
2 tablespoons black peppercorns
4 whole plants fresh coriander,
   including roots
2 tablespoons lemon juice

Cut chicken into serving pieces, or cut breasts in halves. Crush garlic with the salt. Coarsely crush peppercorns with a mortar and pestle or in a blender. Finely chop the well-washed coriander — roots, stems and leaves. Mix all the seasonings together and rub well into the chicken pieces. Cover and stand for 1 hour at least, or in refrigerator overnight.

Put pieces of chicken on a grill tray and put under a hot grill approximately 15 cm (6 inches) from heat. Cook, turning every 5 minutes, until chicken is tender and skin is crisp. (If possible, cook on a barbecue over glowing coals.)

Serve with boiled rice, fresh tomatoes sliced and seasoned with a pinch of chilli powder, salt and lemon juice to taste, or thinly sliced onion.

KAI PHAT KHING
CHICKEN WITH GINGER SHREDS

Serves 2 as a main dish, 4-5 with other dishes
1 large chicken breast
½ cup dried wood fungus
2 tablespoons finely shredded fresh ginger
1 small onion, thinly sliced
1 tablespoon lard or oil
3 cloves garlic, finely chopped
1 tablespoon light soy sauce
1 tablespoon fish sauce
1 tablespoon vinegar
1-2 teaspoons sugar
3 spring onions, finely chopped
2 tablespoons chopped, fresh, coriander
  leaves

Remove skin and bones from chicken breast and cut the meat into small dice. Soak wood fungus in hot water for 10 minutes, wash well, remove any gritty portions and cut into bite-size pieces. Soak ginger in lightly salted water for 10 minutes, then squeeze out moisture. This makes the ginger less pungent. (To shred ginger, thinly peel off brown skin, cut into very thin slices, then cut slices into long, thread-like strips.)

Heat lard or oil and on medium low heat fry the onion until soft and translucent, add garlic and stir until garlic starts to turn golden. Add chicken and ginger and stir fry until chicken changes colour, then add the sauces, vinegar and sugar. When liquid boils reduce heat, cover and simmer 3 minutes. Do not overcook. Stir in spring onions and coriander leaves and serve immediately.

KAI KWAM
FRIED EGGS STUFFED WITH PORK AND SEAFOOD *(picture page 294)*

Serves: 8
4 large eggs
½ cup chopped raw prawns
½ cup cooked crab meat
½ cup chopped cooked pork
1 teaspoon chopped fresh coriander leaves
⅛ teaspoon ground black pepper
½ teaspoon salt
1 tablespoon fish sauce
1-2 tablespoons thick coconut milk

Batter:
½ cup plain flour
½ cup tepid water
2 teaspoons oil
¼ teaspoon salt

Put eggs in a pan of cold water and bring slowly to the boil, stirring frequently with a wooden spoon, and being careful not to crack the shells. Keep stirring until the eggs have been simmering for 3 minutes. This helps centre the yolks, leaving an even layer of white all around and making the eggs easy to fill. Simmer for 12 minutes or until hard boiled, then run cold water into the pan to cool the eggs quickly. Shell and cut in halves lengthways.

Scoop out the yolks into a medium-size bowl and mash thoroughly with a fork. Add prawns, crab meat and pork, coriander leaves, pepper, salt and fish sauce. Mix well, then add as much of the coconut milk as the mixture will take without getting too moist.

Divide the yolk mixture into 8 equal portions and fill the egg whites, shaping filling to a rounded shape so that it looks like a whole egg. Dip in batter and fry in deep hot oil for 3 minutes or until golden brown. Keep filling downwards in the oil when frying. Drain on absorbent paper and serve warm or cold.

Batter: Mix together flour, water, oil and salt, beating with a wooden spoon until smooth.

MU WAN
SWEET PORK

Pork cooked in this way is mainly used as an ingredient in other dishes, but is also delicious eaten with a hot chilli sauce as an accompaniment to rice.

500 g (1 lb) or more, loin of pork
½ cup palm sugar or substitute
½ cup fish sauce

Remove rind and cut pork into thin slices. Put pork and rind into a saucepan with about 3 cups water, the sugar and fish sauce. Bring to the boil, skim top, reduce heat and cook for 30-40 minutes. Uncover and cook until pork is tender and fat transparent. The skin too should be very soft. Allow to cool in the sauce.

TOD MAN NUER
FRIED MEAT BALLS

Yields: about 30 small balls
125 g (4 oz) minced beef
125 g (4 oz) minced pork
¼ teaspoon ground black pepper
scant ½ teaspoon ground nutmeg
2 tablespoons finely chopped fresh
   coriander leaves
4 cloves garlic, crushed
½ teaspoon salt
1 spring onion, finely chopped
2 teaspoons fish sauce
1 tablespoon beaten egg
plain flour
lard for frying

Mix the beef and pork mince together. If the pork is very lean add a tablespoon of finely diced pork fat. Combine with all other ingredients except flour and lard. Make small balls the size of a hazelnut in its shell. Roll in plain flour and fry in hot lard over medium low heat for 5 minutes or until cooked through and golden brown. Drain on absorbent paper.

SI-KLOK
PORK AND CRAB SAUSAGE

Stop and think before embarking on this recipe. You've got to have one of two things — lots of patience or an efficient sausage-making machine. I don't have either, but was well into it before I realised I needed them. The sausage is delicious and will spoil you for ordinary sausages for a long time to come, but it does take time and perseverance to fill the sausage skin. (When patience ran out I used the remaining mixture to make tiny balls, fried them in a small amount of oil until very well done and they tasted great.)

Serves: 4-6
185 g (6 oz) finely minced pork
125 g (4 oz) crab meat
2 tablespoons finely chopped onion
2 tablespoons finely chopped fresh
   coriander leaves
2 tablespoons roasted peanuts, coarsely
   ground
2 teaspoons red curry paste (page 300)
½ teaspoon salt
2 teaspoons fish sauce
2 tablespoons thick coconut milk
sausage skin

Put all the ingredients for filling into a bowl and mix thoroughly with the hand, adding the coconut milk last of all and kneading until it is absorbed by the other ingredients. (To help even distribution of seasoning, dissolve curry paste and salt in the coconut milk first.)

Using a funnel, pack the mixture into the sausage skin and fasten both ends firmly with a knot. Prick sausage in several places with a fine bamboo skewer. Curl the sausage into a flat coil.

Grill under a pre-heated griller as far away from the heat as possible so that the sausage cooks thoroughly. Cooking time should be at least 25 minutes. Turn once during grilling.

The authentic method of cooking is to grill the sausage over glowing coals and when cooking is nearly done to sprinkle some of the coconut from which the milk was squeezed, over the coals. This will make smoke which will give more flavour to the sausage. Serve warm or cold.

Note: Sausage skin can be bought from your butcher. Run cold water through skin before filling with the mixture.

PLA PRIO WAN (whole fried fish with ginger sauce) *recipe page 307*

YAM NANG MU
PORK SKIN SALAD

½ cup finely sliced boiled pork skin
½ cup finely chopped boiled lean pork
1 cup fresh mint leaves
½ teaspoon grated lemon rind
3 tablespoons dried prawn powder
1 tablespoon chopped fresh coriander
   leaves
1 tablespoon chopped spring onions
2-3 tablespoons coconut cream (page 11)
1 tablespoon nam prik (page 313)
1 tablespoon lime juice
1 tablespoon fish sauce
1-2 teaspoons sugar

The pork for this yam should be boiled, and if cooked as for sweet pork (page 309) will have lots of flavour. Slice fat away from skin and use only the jelly-like skin.

Mix all ingredients just before serving and serve sprinkled with chopped coriander leaves and spring onions.

YAM TANG KWA
CUCUMBER SALAD

2 green cucumbers
1 small onion
2 tablespoons dried prawn powder
1 or 2 fresh red chillies, seeded and
   chopped
2 tablespoons fish sauce
lemon juice to taste

Peel, seed and coarsely grate the cucumbers. Peel and grate the onion. Mix all ingredients together and serve.

YAM KRACHUP
WATER CHESTNUT SALAD

*Use fresh water chestnuts if possible,
otherwise canned ones make a suitable
substitute.*

250g (8 oz) fresh water chestnuts or 1
   small can, drained
1 small onion, finely chopped
2 teaspoons chopped garlic
1 tablespoon lard or oil
2 tablespoons fish sauce
2 tablespoons lemon juice
1 tablespoon sugar
¼ cup diced cooked pork
¼ cup chopped cooked prawns
¼ cup flaked crab meat
2 tablespoons chopped fresh
   coriander leaves
3 or 4 very tender citrus leaves, chopped
2 fresh red chillies, seeded and chopped

Wash and peel fresh water chestnuts and cut into slices, then into strips; if using canned chestnuts, drain and cut in similar fashion. Fry the onion and garlic in hot fat on medium heat, taking care not to let them burn. Combine fish sauce, lemon juice and sugar in a dressing with the onions and garlic. Combine chestnuts, pork, prawns and crab meat in a bowl and pour the dressing over. Toss to mix, arrange in serving dish and garnish with the chopped leaves and chillies.

YAM MA MUANG
GREEN MANGO OR APPLE SALAD *(picture page 306)*

In Thailand this would be made with green mangoes. If green mangoes are not readily available, substitute tart green apples.

Serves: 6
3 green cooking apples or green mangoes
1 teaspoon salt
1 tablespoon peanut oil
4 cloves garlic, thinly sliced
6 spring onions, sliced
250 g (8 oz) pork fillet, shredded
1 tablespoon dried prawn powder
1 tablespoon fish sauce
2 tablespoons roasted peanuts, crushed
1 teaspoon palm sugar or substitute
pepper to taste
finely chopped red chillies, optional

Peel and slice apples thinly, put into a large bowl and sprinkle with salt. Heat oil and fry garlic and spring onions separately and set aside. In the same pan quickly fry the pork until cooked, add the prawn powder, fish sauce, peanuts and sugar. Remove from heat. Just before serving mix everything together, add pepper to taste and, if liked, sprinkle finely chopped red chillies over the top.

NAM PRIK
THAI SHRIMP SAUCE

Favourite sauce of a sauce-loving people, nam prik in its various versions is what Thais use to season almost everything they eat. Try it as a dip for raw or lightly cooked vegetables, cooked shrimps or prawns, fried fish pieces, wedges of hard-boiled egg. Use white rice to provide a neutral background to the pungency of the sauce.

2 tablespoons dried shrimps
1 teaspoon dried shrimp paste (kapi)
4 cloves garlic
2 teaspoons ground chillies (sambal
     ulek) or 2 fresh red chillies
2 teaspoons palm sugar or substitute
2 tablespoons lemon juice
1½ tablespoons soy sauce
3 tablespoons water

Wash shrimps and soak in hot water for 20 minutes. Rinse the shrimps thoroughly. Wrap dried shrimp paste in aluminium foil and put under a hot grill for 3 minutes on each side. Put drained shrimps and dried shrimp paste in blender container with garlic, chillies, sugar, lemon juice, soy sauce and water. Cover and blend until smooth. Pour into a bowl and serve with other ingredients arranged around the sauce.

If blender is not available, use a mortar and pestle to pound the shrimps and garlic. Use sambal ulek instead of chillies. After grilling dried shrimp paste, dissolve in the liquid ingredients, then combine everything.

NAM SOM KRATIEM
GARLIC AND VINEGAR SAUCE

2 or 3 fresh red chillies
3 cloves garlic
2 tablespoons sugar
4 tablespoons vinegar
salt to taste

Pound together the chillies and garlic. Add sugar, vinegar and salt and mix well. This may be done in a blender, putting all the ingredients in together, but because blending makes the sauce frothy, it should be made a few hours before and left to stand. Alternatively, use sambal ulek instead of chillies, crush the garlic and mix everything together.

KAPI PLA
SHRIMP PASTE SAMBAL

This is about as pungent as an accompaniment can get, and is popular in Burmese and Thai menus. An acquired taste, perhaps, but if you want to know the true taste of these countries, it is a must.

3 tablespoons dried shrimp paste (kapi)
2 tablespoons finely chopped onion
1 tablespoon finely chopped garlic
2 tablespoons dried prawn powder
¼ cup lime or lemon juice
1 tablespoon palm sugar or substitute
fish sauce to taste
1 teaspoon finely shredded lime or lemon
  rind
chopped fresh red chillies to garnish

Form dried shrimp paste into a flat cake and wrap completely in foil. Roast under a hot griller for 4 or 5 minutes on each side. Allow to cool. In mortar and pestle pound the onion and garlic, the dried shrimp paste, prawn powder, and add lime juice gradually to work into a paste. Add sugar and fish sauce, mixing well. Press into a small bowl or form into a mound and garnish with shreds of citrus rind and chillies.

HAE KÜN
PRAWN ROLLS

Serves: 4
2 large sheets dried bean curd skin
250 g (8 oz) raw prawns
1 tablespoon cornflour
2 tablespoons pork fat, finely diced
1 clove garlic, crushed
½ teaspoon salt
½ teaspoon finely grated fresh ginger
¼ teaspoon ground black pepper

Soak the bean curd skin in warm water and leave until soft. Shell and de-vein prawns and chop finely. Mix the prawns, cornflour, pork fat, crushed garlic, salt, ginger and pepper well together. Divide in two equal portions and shape each into a roll. Place each one on a sheet of bean curd skin and roll up. Steam for 10 minutes. Allow to get quite cold, then cut into diagonal slices and fry in hot oil until brown. If liked, the slices may be dipped in batter before frying. Serve with sweet and sour sauce (page 432).

MA UON
FAT HORSES

Somewhat reminiscent of a dim sum filling, but seasoned differently, this combination of pork, chicken, and crab meat is steamed in tiny cups instead of pastry. Sake or Chinese wine cups are a suitable size — or borrow the cups from a little girl's tea set.

Makes 12-16 depending on size of cups
125 g (4 oz) pork, both lean and fat
125 g (4 oz) chicken meat without bones
125 g (4 oz) cooked crab meat
2 tablespoons chopped whole coriander
  plant, including roots
¼ teaspoon ground black pepper
5 cloves garlic, crushed
1 tablespoon finely chopped spring onion
2 tablespoons fish sauce
2 tablespoons coconut cream
½ teaspoon palm sugar or substitute
1 large egg or 2 small eggs

Remove any bones and skin from the pork and chop very finely. Do the same with the chicken. Flake the crab, discarding any bony tissue, chop it finely and mix together all the meats with the coriander, pepper, garlic, spring onion, fish sauce, coconut cream and sugar.

Separate egg white from yolk, leaving the yolk in the egg shell. With a small spoon or end of a chopstick break up the yolk, add half of it to the white and beat until foamy. Add to pork mixture and mix well. Fill the tiny cups, pressing mixture down firmly, and brush over the top of each with the remaining egg yolk. Steam for 20 minutes. Allow to cool, then remove from cups.

KUNG TOM YAM (prawn soup, *top*) *recipe page 304*; and KAENG CHÜD DOK MAI CHIN (prawn soup with lily buds, *bottom*) *recipe page 304*

MA IIO
GALLOPING HORSES *(picture page 318)*

A savoury pork mixture used as a filling or topping for fresh fruit. The contrasting flavours are deliciously tantalising.

250 g (8 oz) pork, lean and fat mixed, or pork mince
5 cloves garlic
4 roots fresh coriander
2 tablespoons lard or oil
3 tablespoons roasted peanuts, coarsely ground
1½ tablespoons fish sauce
⅛ teaspoon ground black pepper
4 tablespoons palm sugar or substitute
1 fresh chilli, seeded and chopped
2 tablespoons chopped fresh coriander leaves
mandarins, pineapple slices or rambutans

Chop the pork very finely, removing any skin or bone. Crush garlic and coriander roots and fry on low heat in the lard or oil. When garlic turns golden add the pork, peanuts, fish sauce, pepper, sugar, chilli and coriander leaves and continue to stir fry until the mixture is well cooked, dark brown in colour and quite dry.

Prepare fruit. Peel mandarins and remove all white pith. Separate into segments and cut each segment open down the back. Lay them flat on a serving dish, skin downward. Pineapple slices may be cut into mouth-size pieces. Rambutans must be peeled, and the seeds removed. The nearest substitute is canned lychees, which must be well drained.

Pile the pork mixture on top of the mandarin segments or pineapple pieces, or into the hollow of the rambutans or lychees. Serve with the rice, or as an unusual hors d'oeuvre.

PRATAD LOM
PORK AND CRAB BALLS

Yields: 12-14
250 g (8 oz) pork fillet
60 g (2 oz) pork fat
185 g (6 oz) crab meat
2 tablespoons finely chopped fresh coriander leaves
1 teaspoon salt
¼ teaspoon ground black pepper
2 tablespoons beaten egg
1 tablespoon cornflour
6 sheets dried bean curd skin
lard for frying

Soak the bean curd skin in slightly warm water to soften. Chop pork fillet and pork fat finely and mix together with crab meat (flaked and picked over for any bony tissue). Add coriander leaves, salt, pepper, egg and cornflour and mix thoroughly.

Cut the softened bean curd skin in 10 cm (4 inch) squares. Put a scant tablespoon of the pork and crab filling on each square, and gather up the edges and tie in the middle to form a pratad lom (cracker ball) — a plastic covered wire twist tie is ideal for holding the bean curd together during steaming. Steam the balls for 10-12 minutes, then deep fry in hot lard until crisp and golden brown. Drain on absorbent paper. Serve with a dip made from 2 tablespoons fish sauce, 4 tablespoons white vinegar, 2 cloves crushed garlic, ¼ teaspoon salt and 2 finely chopped fresh chillies or ¼ teaspoon sambal ulek.

Note: Wonton pastry can be used instead of bean curd.

TAUHU SOD SAI
STUFFED SOY BEAN CAKE

Makes: 12
oil for frying
125 g (4 oz) minced pork
3 cloves garlic, crushed
¼ teaspoon salt
⅛ teaspoon pepper
1 tablespoon chopped fresh coriander leaves
2 teaspoons fish sauce
12 cubes fried bean curd (see Glossary)

Heat 1 tablespoon oil and fry pork with garlic, salt and pepper until well cooked. Add coriander leaves and fish sauce and mix. Make a small hole in each of the squares of bean curd (the end of a chopstick is useful for this) and stuff some of the pork mixture into the opening. Heat enough oil to deep fry the bean curd and just before serving re-fry the stuffed bean cakes briefly. Drain on absorbent paper and serve with garlic and vinegar sauce (page 313).

KHAO NIEO KAEO
SWEET COCONUT RICE

Serves: 6-8
500 g (1 lb) glutinous rice
water
2½ cups coconut milk
⅔ cup sugar

Soak rice overnight in water. Drain and steam rice for 45 minutes or until grains may be pressed in the fingers and there is no hard core. Put the rice into a saucepan, add coconut milk and sugar and simmer on very low heat, stirring occasionally, until all the milk is absorbed. Turn on to a plate and flatten with a greased banana leaf or the back of a spoon. Allow to cool and set, then cut into diamond shapes. Serve as a dessert or snack with sliced ripe bananas or na kachik (page 319).

KHANOM TALAI
STEAMED COCONUT MILK PUDDING

Very reminiscent of a Sri Lankan sweet called seenakku, this steamed pudding made from coconut milk and rice flour sweetened with palm sugar is about as simple a dessert as any. Yet, when made in Thailand the coconut milk is extracted using scented water . . . water infused with jasmine or other sweet-smelling blossoms, a romantic and fanciful notion the Thais use often.

Makes 10 tiny cupfuls
1¼ cups thick coconut milk (page 11)
2½ tablespoons rice flour
pinch salt
4 tablespoons palm sugar or substitute

Make coconut milk and leave for 30 minutes so that the richest part rises to the surface. Spoon off half cup of this rich milk, and add it gradually to 1 tablespoon of the rice flour, mixing until smooth.

In remaining coconut milk dissolve the palm sugar and add salt. In another bowl combine the remaining 1½ tablespoons rice flour with the milk, adding liquid gradually and stirring until smooth.

Strain this through a fine sieve. Pour the sweetened mixture into small cups — sake or Chinese wine cups are an ideal size — two thirds filling them. Set the cups carefully in a steamer and steam for 15 minutes or until set. With a spoon pour the white mixture over to almost fill the cups, cover and steam for a further 20-25 minutes. Serve at room temperature.

SANKHAYA
STEAMED CUSTARD IN PUMPKIN SHELL

This custard may also be steamed in young coconuts, husks removed and the shell cut straight across the top. This quantity fills a medium butternut pumpkin. For a large pumpkin, double the quantities.

Serves: 4-6
¾ cup thick coconut milk
½ cup palm sugar or substitute
3 eggs
few drops rose water
1 medium-size pumpkin

If possible, extract the coconut milk (page 11) using freshly grated coconut and scented water, which is how this custard would be made in Thailand. Otherwise use the normal method of extracting milk from desiccated coconut, using milk instead of water since it should be very rich. Beat eggs slightly, add sugar. Mix with coconut milk and stir until sugar dissolves, then flavour with rose water.

Wash the pumpkin well, and if it is a large round one cut a hole in the top and remove all seeds and spongy tissue, scraping well with a spoon to leave the pumpkin smooth. If it is a long straight pumpkin or squash, cut off the top and then cut a round hole into the centre to remove seeds and spongy tissue, leaving a shell of pumpkin about 2.5 cm (1 inch) thick.

Strain the custard and pour into the pumpkin to come just to the top. Put the pumpkin in a dish that just fits it and put the dish and pumpkin in a steamer. Steam for 1 hour or until a knife inserted in the centre of the custard comes out clean. Cool, chill and serve cut into slices so that there is a portion of custard surrounded by pumpkin. Run a knife around the edge of each slice and remove skin. If liked, serve with sweetened coconut milk to pour over.

Note: See description of how to make scented water in introduction to narayana bantom sindhu, page 319.

KHANOM BUALOI
GOLDEN BEAN CAKES

250 g (8 oz) mung beans
1 cup white sugar
½ cup water
caster sugar

Sugar Syrup:
⅓ cup sugar
1 tablespoon water

Soak beans in cold water 24 hours, then change water several times and wash beans so that all the green skins float away. Put into a saucepan with sufficient water to come just to the level of the beans and bring to the boil. Cook until beans are very soft. Drain thoroughly and while beans are still hot, mash to a smooth paste.

Put sugar and water in a heavy-based saucepan and stir over medium heat until sugar dissolves. Add bean paste and cook, stirring occasionally at the start and more frequently as mixture thickens. When the bean mixture is thick and starts to come away from side of pan, it is ready. Allow to cool until it can be handled, and make small balls of the paste. Dip in sugar syrup then in caster sugar and leave to dry. Put in small paper cases.

Sugar Syrup: Dissolve sugar in water and cook over gentle heat until syrup spins a thread.

NA KACHIK
COCONUT AND PALM SUGAR SWEET

Use as a filling or topping for sweet coconut rice (page 317) or simply serve with the rice.

250 g (8 oz) freshly grated coconut or 1 cup desiccated coconut
½ cup crushed palm sugar or substitute
3 tablespoons water
pinch of salt

If using desiccated coconut, sprinkle over it quarter cup hot milk and mix lightly. Fresh grated coconut will not need this.

Put sugar and water into a small saucepan. If black sugar is used, add 2 tablespoons maple syrup, which makes the flavour resemble palm sugar. Stir over gentle heat until it forms a syrup. Add coconut and salt and stir until mixture thickens. If the Na Kachik is to be used as a filling it must be stiff enough to hold its shape in a spoon.

NARAYANA BANTOM SINDHU
VISHNU IN THE SEA OF MILK

A sweet ice-cold drink most refreshing in Thailand's hot climate. Use scented water, as the Thais do, by soaking jasmine or roses in water overnight (or substitute pure rose water or rose concentrate) for flavouring the cooked mixture and for scenting the water used to extract the coconut milk. This is popularly known as sa rim.

2 tablespoons mung bean flour (see Glossary)
2 cups water
rosewater to taste
green food colouring
4 cups coconut milk
4 tablespoons white sugar
crushed ice

Blend together bean flour and water and stir over low heat until it boils, thickens and becomes clear. Remove from heat, stir in 2 or 3 teaspoons rosewater (available from chemists) or a few drops of rose concentrate to give it a faint but definite flavour. Tint it a delicate shade of green. Push through a colander into a bowl of cold water. Leave until firm, drain and chill. Dissolve sugar in the coconut milk, add a little rose flavouring and chill separately. At serving time put a large spoonful of the bean flour mixture into a tall glass, fill with coconut milk and crushed ice.

MA HO ('galloping horses') *recipe page 316*

CAMBODIA
& LAOS

CAMBODIA (KHMER)

'Cambodian food is very much like Thai or Lao food with a touch of Chinese influence,' I was told by John Lee Kha and Miss Lyna, recent arrivals from Cambodia.

Rice is the staff of life and is served boiled with fish or a little poultry or buffalo meat for breakfast, lunch and dinner. Sometimes a bowl of noodle soup may take its place at breakfast, but for the two main meals of the day it is rice (cooked without salt) that is the central dish. It is accompanied by fried fish, *kari*, vegetables and a soup. All the dishes are served at once, and diners make their own choice.

As we talked over lunch, I noticed that John's cup was filled with what seemed to be water, yet it steamed like hot tea. When I asked him what was generally drunk with meals in Cambodia, he told me that tea or coffee are seldom served and when tea is served, Chinese tea is preferred, but it is usual for a cup of warm water (gesturing towards his cup) to be sipped along with the meal. In very hot weather the evening meal might consist only of plain boiled rice to give the digestion a rest.

Cambodian cooking is full of flavour, but many of the herbs used are not widely available outside

Southeast Asia, so I have chosen dishes using the better-known flavourings. As in most other Asian countries, cooking in Cambodia is not an exact science, but everything is cooked 'to taste' and the cook is expected to use originality and initiative to improve the flavour of a dish, so feel free to season to taste.

The principal diet of the people is rice and fish. Fish and shellfish are plentiful, from both the Mekong River and the sea. Vegetables grow easily in this lush green land and are also a principal part of the diet.

Buffalo meat, pork, chicken, duck, pigeons and tiny paddy birds (even smaller than sparrows), which come to the rice fields and are captured in nets, are eaten with enjoyment, but in much smaller quantities than in the West. Meat and poultry are never the main dish, but always the accompaniment. Mutton is not eaten at all.

In common with the people of Laos, Vietnam, Burma and other neighbours, Cambodians consider their fish sauce, *nguoc mam*, next to rice in importance. It would be unthinkable to them to have to do without it.

A very popular Cambodian dish is *trei aing*, fish grilled over charcoal and served with a dish of raw vegetables such as cucumber slices and fresh bean sprouts, salad greens and herbs (mint, dill, fresh coriander). But this is incomplete until the pungent sauce is served. The sauce is based on fish sauce with garlic, fresh chillies, lemon juice, sugar and vinegar, up to which point it is strikingly similar to Vietnam's *nuoc cham*. But the Cambodian version also includes roasted ground peanuts, which ingredient it shares with Lao and Thai sauces. Small pieces of the grilled fish are wrapped in a salad leaf with cucumber, bean sprouts and a sprig or two of fresh herbs and the whole parcel is dipped in the hot sauce before being eaten with rice.

Kitchens in Cambodia are very simple and may, to the Western woman, seem impossibly ill-equipped. Most cooking is done in a *wok*, called *chhnang khteak* in Cambodia.

LAOS

The most unusual feature about Laotian food is that it gives prominence to sticky rice. In other Asian countries, sticky (or glutinous) rice, sometimes called 'sweet rice', is used exclusively for sweets or little snacks, but Laotians prefer this rice for all kinds of dishes and serve it at meals.

Mrs Vatsana Souvannavong of Vientiane told me that rice is served three times a day. For breakfast, glutinous rice is soaked 8-10 hours, steamed until soft and eaten with mango, coconut or *padek*, a fish product made at home in which chunks of fish are preserved in brine in large earthenware jars. The liquid in which the fish is steeped is also used and is known as *nam padek*. The rice is also sometimes combined with black beans or yams and steamed together with these.

Cities in Cambodia and Laos do not have restaurants serving local food. When people eat out, they eat excellent Chinese or French food, although the French influence on the food of these countries has not mingled with the local dishes. It has remained separate and became very popular.

'When you are in Vientiane you might like to go to a restaurant for a Lao meal,' said Mrs Souvannavong. 'Well, I am sorry to say that you won't find one. This is not because the Lao people do not like to eat out but because it is not very easy to run a Lao restaurant. If you really want to try Lao dishes, you have to be invited to a Lao house.' I was fortunate to be invited to eat with the Souvannavongs and some of their Laotian friends.

Lao dishes take a long time to prepare and all the ingredients have to be fresh. Meals are not planned in advance and the menu depends on whatever is available when meal time comes.

They don't believe in frozen food. Lao people enjoy eating fresh meat, fresh vegetables and fresh fruit. Not many people have refrigerators in which to store their food, and even if they had they would not like to store food for too long.

Every typical Lao house has a small garden in front or at the back to grow vegetables and the myriad herbs that are used in Laotian food — different types of mint, lemon grass (citronella), lao ginger, lao eggplant, chillies of various kinds and banana trees are the most common. The banana tree is put to many uses. The fruit is eaten both fresh and ripe, or cooked when it is unripe. The large, heavy flower is used as a vegetable. The leaves are invaluable for wrapping food before steaming or grilling over coals and even the inside of the tree trunk is used — the tender, honeycombed part (for an example of this, see recipe for *moh hin ga* on page 268). Some ingredients — onions, garlic, chillies, tamarind, among others — are also stored dried for when they are out of season.

The daily income is far from sufficient for most families, so some of the men hunt for food and are rewarded with deer or other game. Others go fishing, for there are plenty of fish in the many tributaries of

the Mekong River. Chickens, ducks, pigs and turkeys are commonly grown for food.

The meals eaten in Laos are simple. For breakfast, sticky rice is served with black or white coffee. Sometimes tasty morsels of dried meat, fried chicken, beef, fish or pork may be served with the rice and accompanied by chilli paste.

Lunch is again rice, accompanied by soup, a fish dish, meat or chicken, some fresh or cooked vegetables and, of course, the hot sauce. The evening meal is on the same lines as lunch, but do not imagine that this makes the food repetitive or dull. An imaginative cook, in Laos as elsewhere, can vary the same main ingredients with a hundred different combinations of flavours. On Sundays, for a special lunch, the traditional dish called *lap* or *koy* is prepared.

After Sunday breakfast one visits the local market for a leg of fresh venison and some of the deer's liver as well as one or two kinds of vegetables. Back home, the preparation begins. All the best meat is cut into thin slices or minced. The scraps and the bone are used to make a strong, tasty stock, which is simmered on low heat. Meanwhile, the liver is cut into thin slices like the meat; dried red chillies are fried and then ground; glutinous rice is roasted until dark brown, then pounded finely; lao ginger (fresh laos root) is scraped and cut into shreds; spring onions are sliced; three kinds of mint are chopped; fish paste is cooked and mixed to a sauce which is served with the *lap*, and some wild vegetables and bitter greens are picked from the garden or from a neighbour's garden. (Like many Asian people, Laotians are very willing to share, and when the food is cooked a dish of it is often sent to friends and neighbours.)

When the meal is about to be served, fish sauce, lime juice and chopped spring onions are added to the stock to 'sharpen the taste'. The raw meat and liver are mixed with lime juice, ground chilli and ground rice, lao ginger and herbs. Steamed sticky rice, which is kept warm in woven bamboo baskets, is served along with the *lap*. *Lap* also means 'luck', and this dish is traditionally served at weddings, house-warming ceremonies and other important occasions. Instead of venison one may substitute fresh fish, chicken or half-cooked pork. Rice wine is usually served.

SERVING AND EATING A LAOTIAN MEAL
Though dining tables are sometimes used, most people prefer to sit on the floor mat around a large rattan tray. Each tray is big enough to accommodate six people and stands about 40-50 cm (15-20 inches) high. All the dishes are placed on the tray and the rice baskets are put between the diners. Forks and spoons might be used, but 'we have to use our fingers to eat sticky rice.'

A tray of fresh bananas, pawpaws or other fruit is placed on one side so that people can help themselves after the meal.

UTENSILS
Of prime importance in a Lao kitchen is a mortar and pestle. So is a sharp chopper and stout chopping board. Cooking is done in a *wok*, and steaming takes place over earthen pots of water in baskets woven of bamboo.

'We do not have small modern kitchens but simple large ones,' I was told. 'We do the cooking with charcoal or wood fires. Some people in the cities use gas and electricity. The kitchen is large because we need a lot of help when we cook.'

For the recipes that follow, a *wok* plus the equipment in a Western kitchen will suffice.

YOUR CAMBODIAN AND LAOTIAN SHELF
A patch of garden in which mint, lemon grass and fresh coriander grow is just as important to the flavours of these countries as the ingredients on your shelf. Garlic, fresh ginger and spring onions are also essentials.

bamboo shoot, canned
black pepper, ground
cellophane noodles
chillies, dried
chilli powder
creamed coconut or desiccated coconut
coriander, ground
cummin, ground
fennel, ground
fish sauce *(nuoc mam)*
laos powder
mushrooms, Chinese dried variety
peanut oil
peanuts, raw or roasted (unsalted)
rice wine or dry sherry
shrimps, dried
sesame seed
soy sauce
turmeric, ground
water chestnuts, canned

NOEUNG BONGKORNG (lobster salad) *recipe page 324*

BAY POUN
MOULDED RICE

Serves: 4
½ cup chopped pork fat
½ cup chopped lean pork
½ cup chopped chicken meat
3 cloves garlic, finely chopped
3 spring onions, finely sliced
4 cups hot cooked rice
fish sauce to taste
¼ teaspoon ground black pepper

In a wok heat the pork fat until it fries crisp and golden and the fat is melted. Add the pork, chicken, garlic and onions and stir fry until the meats are well cooked. Add rice and toss well to mix, then add sauce and pepper. Remove from heat, press firmly into a greased mould, cover with a piece of greased paper or foil and keep warm. Turn out and serve with extra fish sauce.

PHU KHOUA KAI NOR MAY
LONG RICE WITH CHICKEN AND BAMBOO SHOOTS

Serves: 6
500 g (1 lb) chicken pieces or half a
    roasting chicken
1 clove garlic, crushed
250 g (8 oz) cellophane noodles (long rice)
1 tablespoon peanut oil
1 medium onion, cut into wedges
2 canned bamboo shoots, cut into strips
1 tablespoon fish sauce
¼ teaspoon black pepper
½ cup stock or water

Cut chicken meat from bones, reserving bones for stock. Cut meat, together with skin, into bite-size pieces. Mix with the crushed garlic.

Soak noodles in hot water 15 minutes, then drop into lightly salted boiling water and cook 5-8 minutes. Drain and cut in short lengths.

Heat peanut oil in wok and when very hot throw in the chicken and stir fry over high heat until flesh turns white. Push to side of wok. Add onion (separated into layers) and bamboo shoots and fry for 1 minute, then combine with chicken in centre of wok and add the fish sauce, pepper and stock. Cook 2 minutes longer, then add drained noodles and stir to combine thoroughly. Serve hot with rice and nuoc mam sauce (page 341).

NOEUNG BONGKORNG
LOBSTER SALAD *picture page 322*

Serves: 6
1 cooked lobster
250 g (8 oz) cellophane noodles
1 or 2 pieces dried wood fungus
3 cups shredded white Chinese cabbage
3 seedless cucumbers, sliced
2 tablespoons peanut oil
1 tablespoon dried garlic flakes
125 g (¼ lb) pork mince
3 tablespoons dried shrimp floss*
3 tablespoons fish sauce
3 tablespoons sugar
4 tablespoons lime juice
⅓ cup chopped toasted peanuts
⅓ cup desiccated coconut, toasted

Garnish:
3 pickled garlics, finely sliced*
3 mandarins or oranges, segmented
salad greens
springs of mint of polygonum*

Remove lobster tail, slit underside, remove meat in one piece and cut into medallions. Shred remaining meat in head. Reserve the shell for garnish.

Boil cellophane noodles for 10 minutes, drain and cut into short lengths. Soak the wood fungus in hot water for 20 minutes. Drain and cut into fine shreds, discarding any woody parts.

Heat the peanut oil in a wok and gently fry the dried garlic flakes until pale golden, remove immediately to absorbent paper. Do not let them brown or they will be bitter. In the same oil stir-fry the minced pork on high heat until browned, add the shrimp floss, 1 tablespoon each of fish sauce and sugar and fry until dry. Remove from wok and cool.

Combine remaining fish sauce and sugar with lime juice, stirring until sugar dissolves. Combine with all the ingredients and toss well, arrange on a platter lined with salad greens. Place medallions of lobster meat in a row and garnish with the lobster shell, segments of mandarin or orange, pickled garlic and mint sprigs. Serve at room temperature.

* **Note:** Dried shrimps may be reduced to a floss in electric blender or food processor. Whole heads of garlic, pickled, are available in Asian food stores. Polygonum is commonly known as Vietnamese or Cambodian mint.

PA KHING
STEAMED FISH WITH YOUNG GINGER

Serves: 3-4
750 g (1½ lb) fresh fish fillets or steaks
about 125 g (4 oz) fresh young ginger root
juice of 1 lemon
2 tablespoons peanut oil
1 tablespoon sesame oil
6 cloves garlic, finely sliced
3 tablespoons sesame seeds
2 tablespoons shrimp soy or dark soy sauce
banana leaves or aluminium foil

Wash and scale fish. Scrape skin off ginger and slice very thinly, then cut slices into very fine slivers (almost threads). Marinate ginger in strained lemon juice while preparing remaining ingredients.

Heat oils in a small pan and fry sliced garlic slowly, taking care not to let it burn. Slices should be pale golden. Pour oil and garlic over the ginger. In same pan dry fry the sesame seeds until golden brown. Add to ginger/garlic mixture. Add soy and mix well, then sprinkle over fish fillets and steam in individual leaf or foil packages for 15 minutes.

SOUSI PA
FISH WITH COCONUT CREAM

Serves: 4
500 g (1 lb) fish fillets
2 large dried chillies
15 cloves garlic
3 tender lemon leaves
1 slice fresh laos or 1 teaspoon laos
   powder
2 stalks lemon grass, finely sliced, or 2
   strips lemon rind
1 cup thick coconut milk
3 cups thin coconut milk
1 tablespoon fish sauce
2 tablespoons chopped roasted peanuts
sprigs of fresh basil
5 or 6 small dried chillies
oil for frying

Wash fillets and cut into serving pieces. Remove stalks and seeds from large dried chillies and soak in hot water for 10 minutes. With mortar and pestle pound the chillies, garlic, lemon leaves, laos, lemon grass or lemon rind to a paste. (An electric blender can be used, but it may be necessary to add a tablespoon or so of thick coconut milk to facilitate blending to a paste.)

Heat the thick coconut milk in a saucepan until you see the oil floating on top. This takes about 10-15 minutes on low heat. Add pounded or blended mixture and fry until cooked, stirring constantly. Add pieces of fish and turn them in the mixture, then add thin coconut milk and fish sauce and simmer for 10 minutes. Add peanuts just before end of cooking. Serve garnished with basil and small whole dried chillies that have been fried for a few seconds in hot oil.

KOY PA
RAW FISH SALAD

Serves: 4-6
500 g (1 lb) white fish fillets
½ cup lemon juice
6 tender raw green beans, thinly sliced
4 spring onions, thinly sliced
2 cloves garlic, crushed
1 fresh red chilli, seeded and sliced
1 tablespoon fish sauce

For serving:
lettuce leaves
mint leaves
coriander leaves

Remove all skin and bones from the fish and chop it rather fine. Put it into a glass or earthenware bowl and pour the lemon juice over. Mix and leave for 3 hours, or overnight in the refrigerator, then combine with the other ingredients.

To serve: Put some of the fish mixture in the centre of a lettuce leaf, add a sprig of mint or a few leaves of coriander. Fold over and eat.

TREI CHORM HOY
STEAMED WHOLE FISH

Serves: 4

1 x 750 g (1½ lb) fresh snapper or other
   whole white fish
2 teaspoons salt
2 tablespoons light soy sauce
2 tablespoons peanut oil
2 teaspoons sesame oil
1 teaspoon finely grated fresh ginger
8 spring onions, finely chopped

Scale, clean and wash fish and trim spines and fins but leave head and tail on. Steam over boiling water for 15 minutes or until cooked through. Meanwhile, prepare the sauce.

Heat peanut oil in a small saucepan and fry the ginger and spring onions very gently until soft but not brown. Remove from heat, add sesame oil and soy sauce. Put fish on a serving dish (on a bed of braised lettuce if liked) and spoon the sauce over. Serve immediately.

TREI CHEAN NOEUNG SPEI
DEEP-FRIED FISH WITH VEGETABLES

Serves: 4-6

750 g (1½ lb) white fish fillets
1 tablespoon egg white
1 teaspoon salt
1 tablespoon cornflour
6 tablespoons oil
1 clove garlic, crushed
½ teaspoon finely grated fresh ginger
2 cups sliced white Chinese cabbage
6 spring onions, cut in 5 cm (2 inch)
   lengths
2 tablespoons fish sauce
½ cup water
1 teaspoon extra cornflour

Cut fish fillets into finger pieces, dip in egg white and then in a mixture of salt and cornflour. Dust off excess flour. Heat oil in a wok and fry fish on high heat, one quarter of the quantity at a time, for just long enough to cook it through (this should take from 1-2 minutes depending on the thickness of the fish). Drain on absorbent paper and keep warm. Pour off all but a tablespoon of the oil, add garlic, ginger, cabbage, and stir fry for 1 minute. Add spring onions and stir fry 1 minute more. Add fish sauce, water. Bring liquid to the boil, then stir in extra cornflour mixed with very little cold water. Stir until sauce boils and thickens. Arrange on a dish with fish pieces on top and serve immediately with rice or noodles.

KARI BONKONG TRASAK
PRAWN AND SWEET GOURD CURRY

Serves: 6

500 g (1 lb) large raw prawns
1 sweet gourd, tender marrow or 2 green
   cucumbers
5 cloves garlic
1 small onion, roughly chopped
2 teaspoons finely chopped fresh ginger
½ teaspoon chilli powder
½ teaspoon ground fennel
2 teaspoons ground coriander
¼ teaspoon ground turmeric
4 tablespoons oil
2 cups coconut milk
1 stalk lemon grass, bruised
2 tablespoons lemon juice
1 teaspoon sugar, optional
1 tablespoon fish sauce

Shell and de-vein prawns. Peel gourd or cucumbers, cut in halves lengthways, scoop out seeds and cut in thick slices. Put garlic, onion and ginger into container of electric blender and blend to a purée. Mix in the ground spices.

Heat oil in a pan and fry the blended ingredients until they are well cooked and the oil starts to show around the edges, much as described in the basic method for Burmese curries (page 273). Add the prawns and stir fry for 3 minutes, then add coconut milk and bring to simmering point. Add sliced gourd or cucumber, remaining seasonings, and stir gently until gourds or cucumbers are cooked and tender but not too soft. Serve with rice.

MOAN CHUA NOEUNG PHSET KREAM
STIR-FRIED CHICKEN WITH MUSHROOMS

Serves: 4-6
6 dried Chinese mushrooms
1 small roasting chicken
4 cloves garlic, crushed
½ teaspoon finely grated fresh ginger
2 tablespoons lard or oil
1 cup water
2 tablespoons fish sauce
2 teaspoons sugar
2 tablespoons chopped fresh coriander leaves

Soak mushrooms in hot water for 30 minutes. Squeeze dry, cut off and discard stems, cut caps into quarters if they are large. Cut chicken into small pieces with cleaver, chopping through bones as well. Fry garlic and ginger in the hot lard or oil for a few seconds, then add chicken and stir fry until colour changes. Add mushrooms, water, fish sauce and sugar, cover and simmer until chicken is cooked. Sprinkle with chopped coriander and serve with rice.

KAI LAO
LAOTIAN CHICKEN

Serves: 6
1 x 1.5 kg (3 lb) roasting chicken
1½ teaspoons salt
2 cloves garlic, crushed
1 tablespoon oil
2 medium onions, finely chopped
250 g (8 oz) pork mince
½ teaspoon salt
½ teaspoon ground black pepper
1 fresh red chilli, finely chopped
1 tablespoon chopped fresh coriander leaf
½ cup uncooked rice
1 cup thick coconut milk
2 cups thin coconut milk
1 tablespoon fish sauce

Wash and dry chicken well, then rub it inside and out with salt and half the crushed garlic. Heat oil in frying pan, fry remaining garlic and onions with the pork mince. Season with salt, pepper and chilli. When pork has been fried well, add coriander, rice and thick coconut milk. Bring to simmering point, then reduce heat, cover and cook for 10 minutes or until liquid is absorbed. Remove from heat and leave until cool enough to handle. Stuff chicken with pork mixture. Put chicken in a large saucepan with thin coconut milk and fish sauce, cover and simmer for 1 hour or until chicken is tender.

KHAO POUN
LONG RICE SOUP

Serves: 4-6
¾ cup soaked cellophane noodles
½ teaspoon salt
5 cups boiling water or chicken stock
125 g (4 oz) finely minced pork
⅓ cup finely chopped smoked ham
1 tablespoon chopped water chestnuts
½ teaspoon cornflour
2 teaspoons light soy sauce
1 teaspoon finely chopped spring onions

Soak noodles in cold water for 30 minutes. Drain and cut into 15 cm (6 inch) lengths. Add to boiling water with salt and boil for 20 minutes. Mix pork, ham, water chestnuts, cornflour and soy sauce, shape into small balls and drop into the soup. Return to the boil for 10 minutes. Do not stir. Add spring onions and serve immediately.

KANG SOM PA
LAOTIAN FISH SOUP

Serves: 4-6

500 g (1 lb) freshwater fish
4 cups water
1 stalk lemon grass, bruised, or 2 strips
  lemon rind
½ teaspoon salt
2 tablespoons fish sauce
2 medium tomatoes, quartered
4 spring onions, finely sliced
1 tablespoon chopped fresh coriander
  leaves
lemon juice to taste

Buy the fish cleaned and scaled, then cut it into slices. Bring water to the boil with lemon grass and salt and let it simmer for 10 minutes. Then add the fish and the fish sauce and return it to the boil. Add tomatoes and simmer gently, uncovered, for 10 minutes. Remove from heat, discard lemon grass or lemon rind and add the spring onions and coriander. Add lemon juice. Taste and add more fish sauce or salt if necessary. Serve hot.

SAMLOR CHHROOK
PORK SOUP

Serves: 4

500 g (1 lb) pork chops
1 tablespoon lard or oil
5 cloves garlic, finely chopped
5 cups stock or water
1 tablespoon fish sauce
1 tablespoon lemon juice
2 teaspoons sugar
1 tablespoon finely shredded tender
  ginger
2 tablespoons chopped fresh coriander
  leaves

Cut pork from the bones and chop into small pieces. Use the bones to make stock. Heat the lard or oil and gently fry garlic until soft, add pork pieces and fry for 1 minute, then add stock and all other ingredients except coriander. Cover and simmer for 30 minutes. Serve, sprinkled with coriander.

KANG KUNG
MELON AND DRIED SHRIMP SOUP

Serves: 6

½ cup dried shrimps
6 dried Chinese mushrooms
500 g (1 lb) soup melon (any variety) or
  cucumbers
8 cups chicken stock
1-2 tablespoons fish sauce
6 thin slices fresh ginger
2 tablespoons Chinese wine or dry sherry

Soak dried shrimps in water overnight. Soak mushrooms in hot water for 30 minutes, cut off and discard stems, slice mushroom caps finely. Peel melon and discard centre spongy portion with seeds. Cut melon flesh into bite-size pieces. Put stock, fish sauce, ginger, mushrooms and dried shrimps into a saucepan, bring to the boil and simmer for at least 30 minutes. Discard ginger slices. Add melon or cucumber and simmer for 5 minutes longer. Serve hot.

KANG HED SAY HOM POM
MUSHROOM SOUP WITH CORIANDER

Serves: 8
500 g (1 lb) fresh mushrooms
1 small white onion, finely chopped
1 tablespoon butter or ghee
1 tablespoon vegetable oil
1 teaspoon ground coriander
½ teaspoon ground cummin
1 teaspoon salt
¼ teaspoon ground black pepper
2½ cups hot water
3 chicken stock cubes, optional
3½ cups milk or coconut milk
3 teaspoons cornflour
1 tablespoon cold water
2 tablespoons chopped fresh coriander leaves

Chop mushroom stems finely. Cut caps into thin slices, then cut across twice or three times, depending on size of mushrooms. Chop the onion finely. Melt butter or ghee and oil in saucepan large enough to hold the amount of liquid. Add onion and fry gently for 5 minutes, stirring frequently. Add mushrooms, coriander and cummin and continue to stir for a few minutes. Add salt and pepper, then cover saucepan, turn heat very low and allow to cook for 10 minutes, lifting lid and stirring two or three times. Add hot water and stock cubes and bring to the boil. Simmer 10 minutes. Add milk and allow to come to the boil once more, stirring occasionally. Mix cornflour with cold water and add to the soup off the heat, then return to heat and stir constantly until it boils and thickens. Serve immediately, sprinkled with coriander leaves.

KUAY NAMUAN
BANANAS COOKED IN COCONUT MILK

Serves: 6
6-8 large ripe bananas
2 cups thick coconut milk
2 tablespoons sugar

Peel and cut each banana into 3 or 4 pieces. Make coconut milk as on page 11 or from the creamed coconut available in packets or tubs. Simmer coconut milk and sugar until thick and creamy. Add bananas and cook gently until bananas are soft but not mushy. Serve warm.

VIETNAM

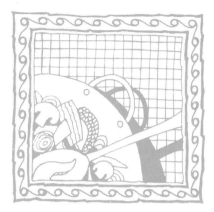

While the food of Vietnam has been influenced to a certain extent by the cooking of China, it would not be mistaken for Chinese food, for true Vietnamese food has a character and flavour all its own.

Instead of soy sauce there is the universal use of fish sauce, *nuoc mam,* which is added during cooking. *Nuoc mam* is more pungent than other Southeast Asian fish sauces; if it is not available, add a little dried shrimp paste to Chinese fish sauce for a good substitute. But *nuoc mam* **sauce** (or *nuoc cham),* which is served as an accompaniment with practically everything, is based on *nuoc mam* with the addition of fresh chillies, garlic, sugar, lime or lemon and vinegar. The flavour is sharper and more pungent than anything the Chinese cuisine has to offer.

When I served this sauce to homesick Vietnamese students they were delighted, but suggested I increase the amount of garlic. I leave to you, the cook, the responsibility of how much garlic you will add. It is one thing when you live in a country where everyone else has eaten heartily of the same food, but when you are likely to be at a business meeting the next day and your associates have dined sedately on Anglo-Saxon fare, you may find yourself slightly unpopular! However, if you are getting together with other enthusiasts for a weekend feast of Asian food, be daring and find out what the real tastes of Southeast Asia are.

Another way of doing this is to visit a Vietnamese restaurant, but make sure they serve authentic Vietnamese food — when you see Vietnamese themselves visiting a restaurant regularly, you can be sure that the food will have the true flavours of Vietnam.

While the best Vietnamese restaurants are said to be in Paris and Noumea, there is one in Sydney of which I had heard good reports. I visited it to find a young and enthusiastic staff of Vietnamese students under the leadership of Le Thang Tien, who is studying engineering in Australia. Tien is a self-taught cook. When he left his home years ago he missed the food so much that he attempted to reconstruct from memory the tastes and textures that meant home to him. His persistence has paid off, for now he runs the restaurant. There is a constant stream of customers and no sooner is a table vacated than it is taken by newcomers. The food is Vietnamese in character, but mercifully toned down as to chilli content. However, if you wish, you have only to ask and the smiling young waitresses (also Vietnamese students) will bring you a sauce dish of fresh ground chillies.

Tien and his knowledgeable cousin and assistant, Hien, were happy to discuss Vietnamese food and very kindly translated the titles of recipes for this chapter.

Rice and noodles are the staple starches in the Vietnamese diet, but they have also cultivated a taste for French bread over the years and combine it with beef, cooked Vietnamese style, to make delicious, if somewhat unorthodox sandwiches.

Breakfast in Vietnam is usually noodle soup. It is rather overpowering by Western standards, for it is redolent of fresh coriander herb (called Vietnamese parsley), garlic and *nuoc mam.* Rice, accompanied by dishes of meat, poultry or fish, is the basis of the other meals.

BÒ XÀO MĂNG (beef with bamboo shoots) *recipe page 338*   331

SERVING & EATING A VIETNAMESE MEAL

Together with rice, soup is a basic item in a Vietnamese meal. Sometimes the meal is only a soup — but a soup with the addition of a number of substantial ingredients. Like the Burmese with their national soup dish, *moh hin gha,* the Vietnamese will stop at any time of day or night to partake of a bowl of *pho* (pronounced 'far'), a delicate beef soup that Westerners will enjoy. See recipe on page 344. The long simmering gives a strong, nourishing stock and is served together with cooked noodles and raw vegetables, and your choice of raw or slightly cooked slices of beef. Thousands of Vietnamese enjoy it every day. There are sellers of *pho* on streets and in small food shops, but particularly in the market place.

Rice is cooked by the absorption method, without salt. It is meant to be firm and separate, the grains having just enough cling so they can be picked up easily with chopsticks. Pot-roasted rice, a simple variation, has a flavour all its own and is considered a delicacy. It is easy to prepare and this method of cooking rice results in a drier and fluffier consistency. Tien tells me that rice of a fluffy consistency is considered desirable in Vietnamese cooking.

Chicken, fish, poultry and beef are all used in Vietnam, but mutton is not used. Beef too is something of a luxury, for cattle are working animals. Pork is the commonest meat. Chickens and ducks are reared and considered good investments because they produce eggs and provide meat. Fish and shellfish are common and cheap, for they are found in great abundance, and even in the flooded rice paddies. They are used in many ways, but the most important use for them is in the making of *nuoc mam* or fish sauce, for which a tiny fish called 'rice fish' is used. They are so small that they are likened to grains of rice.

Salads are popular in Vietnam. Simple combinations such as cooked chicken and shredded cabbage are given an exotic touch by the addition of chopped mint and fresh coriander leaves and the inevitable *nuoc mam* sauce *(nuoc cham),* used as a dressing.

Vietnamese food includes a lot of fresh, uncooked vegetables and fruit, and food is cooked in water rather than oil — two reasons why a Vietnamese meal does not bring on a feeling of surfeit.

Bowls and chopsticks are used to set the table and all the food is served at one time.

Desserts are not served at the end of a Vietnamese meal, but sweets and cakes are served as between-meal snacks, and offered to guests. Vietnamese people are adept at preserving fruits and make a deliciously crisp preserve of winter melon, a recipe that takes three days to prepare.

UTENSILS

To cook Vietnamese-style, a *wok* would be most useful, so would a heavy stone mortar and pestle, but for most grinding an electric blender prepares ingredients with much less time and effort. The one recipe I feel really needs a mortar and pestle is *nuoc cham.* The liquid becomes too frothy when a blender is used, so depending on how enthusiastic you are and how authentic you want the food to be, choose your method of pulverising the chillies and garlic.

Bottled gas and kerosene are modern innovations that have been welcomed in most Vietnamese kitchens, but some traditionalists still prefer to cook over charcoal fires in an open fireplace with a built-up hearth of stones. There are three prominent stones on which the pot rests. This method also prevails in rural and poor areas.

While much of the food is steamed or boiled, stir frying is popular and a *wok* (known as *chao*) is used. Wooden chopsticks are used for stirring and mixing. A large, heavy frying pan, a steamer and a large pot will cope with any of these recipes.

YOUR VIETNAMESE SHELF

bamboo shoot, canned
dried shrimp paste (blachan) or Chinese shrimp sauce
black peppercorns, whole
black pepper, ground
cellophane noodles
fish sauce
lily flowers, dried
lotus root, dried
mushrooms, Chinese dried
peanuts, unsalted
peanut oil
rice, medium grain
rice, roasted ground
rice wine or dry sherry
sesame oil
sesame seeds
sesame sauce or paste

Just as important are the fresh herbs and other flavourings such as coriander leaf, mint, spring onions, garlic and ginger, and lemon grass. See Glossary for descriptions of ingredients and possible substitutes.

CỎM CHÌÊN
POT ROASTED RICE

With short or medium grain rice, the amount of water in this recipe gives a dry, fluffy result, with firm grains. If using long grain rice, increase hot water to 2½ cups for the same result because the long grain variety has a greater absorbency.

2 cups medium grain rice
2 tablespoons peanut oil or lard
1¾ cups hot water

If rice needs washing, wash well and drain for 30 minutes or until dry. Melt lard or heat oil in a heavy saucepan with a well-fitting lid. Fry rice, stirring gently with a metal spoon, for 10-15 minutes or until rice becomes opaque and turns golden. Add hot water, bring to boil, then reduce heat to very low. Cover tightly and cook for 20 minutes. Serve with nuoc cham and other dishes.

CÁ HẤP
STEAMED FISH

Serves: 6
1 x 1kg (2lb) whole fish or 750 g (1½ lb) firm white fish fillets
90 g (3oz) cellophane noodles
8 dried Chinese mushrooms
1 carrot
3 thin slices fresh ginger
1 large clove garlic
½ cup finely sliced cooked pork
2 tablespoons light soy sauce
¼ teaspoon salt
¼ teaspoon black pepper
2 tablespoons fish sauce
6 tablespoons coconut milk
2 tablespoons chopped fresh coriander leaves
2 tablespoons finely sliced spring onion

Wash fish and clean cavity with kitchen paper dipped in coarse salt. Rinse well again, dry with paper towels and trim fins and tail. Slash the flesh diagonally to allow the seasonings to penetrate. Put in a heatproof dish.

Soak noodles in hot water for 30 minutes. Soak mushrooms in hot water 30 minutes. Drain and cut the noodles into short lengths, squeeze out water from mushrooms, cut off and discard stems and slice caps thinly. Scrape carrot and cut into matchstick strips. Cut ginger into thin shreds and finely grate the garlic. Combine all these ingredients in a bowl together with the pork, soy sauce, salt, pepper and fish sauce. Spread this over the fish, put in a steamer and steam for 30 minutes or until fish is cooked through and milky white right to the bone when flaked with a knife or fork. Fillets should take only 15-20 minutes. Pour the coconut milk over, garnish with coriander and spring onion and serve at once with white rice.

CÁ VÒ VIÊN XÀO CẢI BẸ TRẮNG
FISH CAKES WITH CHINESE CABBAGE

Serves: 4
3 Chinese-style fish cakes (see Glossary)
1 tablespoon oil
1 clove garlic, crushed
½ teaspoon grated fresh ginger
½ medium-size white Chinese cabbage
1 tablespoon light soy sauce
½ teaspoon salt
2 teaspoons oyster sauce
¼ cup stock or water
½ teaspoon cornflour

Slice the fish cakes thinly. Wash Chinese cabbage, drain well and cut into slices 2.5 cm (1 inch) wide. Heat oil in a wok and fry garlic and ginger on low heat for a few seconds, then add cabbage and stir fry for 1 minute. Add soy, salt, oyster sauce and stir well. Add stock or water and bring to the boil, then turn in the sliced fish cakes and heat through. Push ingredients to side of wok, add cornflour mixed with a little cold water to the liquid in the centre and stir constantly until it boils and thickens. Stir all the ingredients together and serve at once with white rice.

TRỨNG CHIÊN VỞI CUA
CRAB OMELETTE

Serves: 3-4
4 eggs
½ teaspoon salt
¼ teaspoon black pepper
125 g (4 oz) crab meat, fresh, frozen or canned
2 spring onions, chopped
1 teaspoon fish sauce
1 fresh red chilli, sliced, optional
oil for frying

Beat eggs slightly and season with salt and pepper. Pick over crabmeat and discard any bits of bony tissue. Heat 1 tablespoon oil in a frying pan and saute the spring onions and chilli for 1 minute, add crab and continue to fry for a further minute or two. Sprinkle fish sauce over. Remove mixture to a small plate and allow to cool. Heat a teaspoonful of oil in the frying pan, pour in beaten eggs and cook, drawing egg mixture in from sides of pan, until set on the bottom, creamy on top. Spoon crab mixture down centre of omelette and fold in half. Serve on a warm plate. This may be accompanied by nuoc cham.

MỰC DỒN THỊT
SQUID STUFFED WITH PORK *(picture opposite)*

Serves: 6-8
6 dried Chinese mushrooms
10 dried lily flowers
250 g (8 oz) minced pork
½ cup cellophane noodles
1 clove garlic, crushed
3 spring onions, chopped
½ teaspoon salt
1 tablespoon fish sauce
¼ teaspoon black pepper
500 g (1 lb) fresh squid
peanut oil for frying

Soak mushrooms and lily flowers in hot water for 30 minutes. Discard mushroom stems and any tough portions of the flowers and chop the rest finely. Add to the pork. Soak cellophane noodles in hot water 20 minutes, chop and add half cup to pork. Season pork mixture with crushed garlic, spring onions, salt, pepper and fish sauce. Mix well with the hands.

Clean squid thoroughly, discarding head and 'beak' and everything inside the body. Reserve tentacles. Wash inside of squid under cold tap, rub off spotted skin. Chop tentacles finely and mix with minced pork.

Stuff pork mixture into squid, packing firmly. Sew the opening shut with a coarse needle and thread. Heat 3-4 tablespoons peanut oil in a wok or frying pan and sauté squid on medium heat for 5 minutes. Prick squid with a fine skewer and continue to cook on medium heat for further 10 minutes, or longer if squid is large and pork mixture needs extra time for cooking through. Cut in thin slices and arrange on a bed of shredded lettuce.

GÀ HẤP CÀ
STEAMED CHICKEN WITH TOMATOES

Serves: 4
750 g (1½ lb) chicken pieces (breast and thighs)
3 ripe tomatoes
3 spring onions
3 thin slices fresh ginger
2 tablespoons fish sauce
½ teaspoon salt
½ teaspoon sugar
ground black pepper to taste
2 teaspoons sesame or other vegetable oil

Bone the chicken and cut flesh into bite-size pieces. Reserve bones for stock. Put chicken into a heatproof bowl or other deep dish. Add tomatoes cut into thin wedges, spring onions finely sliced and ginger cut into thin strips. Add seasonings and oil and mix thoroughly. Put the dish in a pan with water to come almost halfway up the dish. Cover and steam for 25-35 minutes or until chicken is tender. Serve with rice and nuoc cham.

NẤM ĐÔNG CÔ TIỀM GÀ
STEAMED CHICKEN WITH MUSHROOMS

Serves: 4

6 dried Chinese mushrooms
1 small roasting chicken, about 1 kg (2 lb)
1 tablespoon finely shredded fresh ginger
3 spring onions, sliced diagonally
good grinding of black pepper
2 teaspoons fish sauce
1 small glove garlic, crushed
¼ teaspoon salt
1 teaspoon sesame oil

Pour hot water over mushrooms and leave to soak at least 20 minutes. Cut off and discard stems, cut mushroom caps into thin slices. Divide chicken into two parts. (Depending on what you want to do with the remaining flesh, cut the bird into halves lengthways, or reserve the breast and wings for another dish). With a sharp knife bone the chicken. Use the bones for stock, and cut the flesh (together with skin) into bite-size pieces. Put these into a heatproof bowl with the mushroom slices, ginger, spring onions, pepper, fish sauce, garlic, salt and sesame oil. Mix well.

Bring water to the boil in a large saucepan or deep frying pan or wok. Put the bowl in the pan — water should come a third of the way up the bowl. Cover and steam for 25-30 minutes or until chicken is cooked. Check periodically to ensure that water has not boiled away, and add more boiling water if it is getting low. Serve with rice, noodles or cellophane noodles.

GÀ XÀO XẢ ỚT
CHICKEN WITH LEMON GRASS

If you cannot get fresh lemon grass, this is one recipe where dried lemon grass will not do. Instead, use the finely peeled rind of a large lemon to get a close approximation of the original recipe.

Serves: 4-6

1 small roasting chicken, about 1 kg (2 lb)
3 or 4 stalks lemon grass or rind of 1
   large lemon
3 spring onions
1 teaspoon salt
¼ teaspoon ground black pepper
2 tablespoons oil
1 or 2 fresh red chillies, seeded and
   chopped
2 teaspoons sugar
extra black pepper to taste
½ cup roasted peanuts, finely chopped
2 tablespoons fish sauce

Cut chicken into small serving pieces, Chinese style, chopping through the bones with a sharp cleaver. Remove outer leaves of the lemon grass and finely slice the tender white part at the base of the stalks. Bruise with mortar and pestle or handle of cleaver. Finely slice the spring onions, including the green leaves. Mix the chicken with the salt, pepper, lemon grass and spring onions and set aside for 30 minutes. If lemon rind is used instead of lemon grass, shred the thinly peeled rind very finely with a sharp knife.

Heat a wok, add oil and when oil is hot add the chicken mixture and stir fry for 3 minutes. Add chillies and stir fry on medium heat for a further 10 minutes or until chicken no longer looks pink. Season with sugar and pepper and add peanuts. Stir well. Add fish sauce and toss to distribute evenly, then serve with rice or noodles.

GÀ XÀO BÚN TÀU
CHICKEN WITH CELLOPHANE NOODLES

Serves: 4-6
500 g (1 lb) chicken meat or 750 g (1½ lb) thighs and breasts
125 g (4 oz) cellophane noodles
2 spring onions
1 tablespoon oil
2 tablespoons fish sauce
1 tablespoon light soy sauce
¼ teaspoon ground black pepper
½ cup water
2 firm ripe tomatoes
2 white onions
sugar, vinegar, salt, pepper

Remove skin and bone from chicken thighs or breasts and cut the flesh into large bite-size chunks. Reserve bones for soup. Put noodles in a large bowl, pour boiling water over and allow to stand for 10 minutes, then drain and cut noodles into bite-size lengths. Cut spring onions into thin slices.

Heat a wok, add oil and swirl to coat inside of wok. Add chicken and onions, stir fry for 2-3 minutes. Add fish sauce, soy sauce, pepper and water, bring to boil and simmer for 3 minutes. Add noodles, return to the boil, stirring constantly and cook for 3 minutes longer. Serve hot, accompanied by a salad of sliced tomatoes and white onions, dressed with a dash of white vinegar, a sprinkling of sugar, salt and pepper to taste.

TRỨNG HẤP
STEAMED EGG WITH MUSHROOMS

Serves: 3-4
4 dried Chinese mushrooms
½ cup soaked cellophane noodles
125 g (4 oz) crab or prawn meat
125 g (4 oz) cooked pork
5 eggs
2 spring onions, finely chopped
2 teaspoons finely chopped fresh coriander leaves
½ teaspoon salt
⅛ teaspoon black pepper

Soak mushrooms in hot water 30 minutes. Discard stems, squeeze excess water from caps and slice finely. Soak a small amount of cellophane noodles in hot water for about 10 minutes, then measure half cup. Flake crab meat and discard any bony bits, or chop the shelled and de-veined prawns into small pieces. Chop pork finely.

Beat eggs until yolks and whites are well mixed but not frothy. Stir in the chopped spring onions, coriander, salt and pepper and the prepared mushrooms, noodles, seafood and pork. Put into a heatproof dish and steam until firm, exact time depending on the depth of the mixture in the dish. Serve with rice and nuoc cham.

BÒ XÀO DẦU MÈ
BEEF WITH SESAME SAUCE

Serves: 3-4
250 g (8 oz) round steak
½ teaspoon salt
¼ teaspoon bicarbonate of soda
2 tablespoons hot water
1 tablespoon soy sauce
1 clove garlic, crushed
3 tablespoons peanut oil
½ cup beef stock
3 teaspoons cornflour
2 tablespoons cold water
2 teaspoons sesame paste
1-2 teaspoons Chinese chilli sauce

Shred beef into very thin strips. Mix salt, bicarbonate of soda, hot water and soy sauce together. Pour over meat, beat with chopsticks or knead with hand until liquid is absorbed, then leave for 2 hours or refrigerate overnight. (If rump or other tender steak is used, this step may be omitted.)

Heat peanut oil in a wok, add garlic and meat and stir fry over high heat until meat has changed colour, about 2 minutes. Add stock and bring to the boil, then stir in cornflour mixed smoothly with cold water, stirring until it boils and thickens. Turn off heat, stir in sesame paste and chilli sauce. Serve with white rice.

If liked this can become a meat and vegetable combination dish by adding such vegetables as bamboo shoots, bean sprouts, Chinese cabbage.

BÒ XÀO MĂNG
BEEF WITH BAMBOO SHOOTS *(picture page 330)*

Serves: 3-4

375 g (12 oz) rump or fillet steak
2 tablespoons peanut oil
extra 2 tablespoons of peanut oil
1 large can bamboo shoots, sliced
6 spring onions, sliced
1 tablespoon fish sauce
½ teaspoon salt
1 clove garlic, crushed
4 tablespoons sesame seed, toasted and
  crushed

Cut beef into very thin slices about 5 cm (2 inches) long. Heat peanut oil in wok, stir fry beef quickly for only about 1 minute. Remove from wok while meat is still pink. In same wok heat extra oil and fry well-drained sliced bamboo shoots and spring onions for about 2 minutes. Add fish sauce and salt and fry for a further 5 minutes. Add crushed garlic, stir and fry for a further minute, then return beef to wok and stir fry for a minute. Add sesame seeds and mix well. Serve hot with rice.

Note: Do not double this recipe. If a larger quantity is needed, make two lots.

THỊT HEO KHO TIÊU
PORK STRIPS, DRY-COOKED

Serves: 6-8

750 g (1½ lb) lean pork chops
2 tablespoons water
2 tablespoons fish sauce
1 tablespoon sugar
3 spring onions, thinly sliced
¼ teaspoon ground black pepper

Remove skin and bones from pork chops, and cut meat into thin strips. Put into a small, deep saucepan — a large saucepan will not do for this dish, as the little liquid there is must suffice for cooking the pork and not be allowed to evaporate over a large surface area. Add all other ingredients and bring to a boil over high heat. Stir, cook for 2 minutes on high heat, then reduce heat to medium and boil for 20 minutes or until liquid is completely absorbed. Stir towards end of cooking time so that meat does not burn. It will turn brown. Serve with white rice and a green vegetable or salad.

THỊT HEO KHO KHÔ
PORK COOKED WITH SUGAR

Serves: 6-8

1-1.25 kg (2-2½ lb) pork belly or loin
2 tablespoons oil
3 spring onions, finely chopped
good pinch ground black pepper
2 teaspoons sugar
½ teaspoon salt
4 cups water
2 tablespoons fish sauce

Cut pork into large cubes. Do not discard fat, for this is a delicious way of cooking it. Heat oil in a large saucepan and fry the spring onions gently until golden. Add pork and fry, stirring, until pork loses its pinkness, then add sugar, salt and pepper, and continue stirring until meat is browned. Add water and simmer without covering pan for 1 hour. Add fish sauce and continue to simmer until the pork is almost dry, taking care to stir frequently as liquid reduces or the pork may burn. Serve with plain white rice.

NEM NƯỚNG
SKEWERED PORK, BARBECUED

The pork for this recipe is pounded, not minced. If the thought exhausts you, take the easy way out, but the results will not be the same.

Serves: 6
500 g (1 lb) pork fillet
2 cloves garlic
½ teaspoon salt
½ teaspoon sugar
3 teaspoons rice wine or dry sherry
1 tablespoon roasted ground rice (see Glossary)
3 teaspoons fish sauce
2 tablespoons melted pork fat or lard

For serving:
500 g (1 lb) fresh rice noodles or 125 g (4 oz) dried rice noodles
1 medium lettuce
sprigs of fresh coriander or mint
nuoc leo sauce (page 341)

Cut the pork fillet into very thin slices, then cut in small squares. Crush garlic finely with salt and sugar, then mix with wine or sherry. Pour over the pork, mix well and leave for 30 minutes.

With mortar and pestle pound a small portion of the meat at a time until it has a paste-like consistency. As each lot is done, remove it to a bowl or plate. Add melted pork fat, ground rice and fish sauce. Knead mixture well, then form small sausage shapes and mould them onto bamboo skewers, squeezing them on very firmly. Barbecue over glowing coals or under a griller, at a good distance from the source of heat so they are well done before the outside is browned. Turn the skewers to ensure the meat cooks on all sides.

To serve: Slice fresh rice noodles and steam them, or soak dried rice noodles in warm water for 2 hours, then drop into boiling water and cook until tender. Do not overcook. Drain. Serve skewers of pork with well-washed and dried lettuce separated into leaves, the noodles, and a small bunch of fresh coriander or mint.

Each person assembles his own snack. A leaf of lettuce is topped with a few rice noodles, some of the barbecued pork, a sprig of fresh coriander or mint, a spoonful of sauce, then rolled up to form a neat roll. This takes some practice. If preferred, the sauce may be served as a dipping sauce.

ĐÙI HEO KHO NỒI ĐẤT
POT-ROASTED PORK

This is not eaten as a one-sitting meal, but prepared and then used in a number of dishes requiring cooked pork, just as barbecued pork fillet is used in Chinese cooking.

1.5-2 kg (3-4 lb) leg of pork
5 cloves garlic
2 teaspoons salt
½ teaspoon ground black pepper
1 tablespoon fish sauce
1 tablespoon oil
1 cup water

Slice four of the garlic cloves. Make small deep incisions in the pork with tip of a small knife and insert slices of garlic in each. Crush remaining garlic clove with salt, mix with pepper and fish sauce and rub well all over the pork. Heat oil in a large deep fireproof casserole or heavy saucepan and brown the pork all over on medium heat. Add water, allow it to come to the boil, then turn heat low, cover tightly and cook for 1½ hours or until pork is well cooked. Turn the piece of pork 3 or 4 times during cooking so that all sides come into contact with the base of the pot.

Allow it to cool, then slice and serve with salad, or use in other dishes requiring pork.

CHẢ ĐÙM
PORK LOAF

Serves: 4-6
8-10 dried Chinese mushrooms
750 g (1½ lb) minced pork
6 spring onions, finely chopped
4 eggs, beaten
1 tablespoon fish sauce
½ teaspoon salt
¼ teaspoon ground black pepper

Soak mushrooms in hot water for at least 30 minutes. Squeeze out moisture, cut off and discard stems and chop the caps very finely. Add to pork in mixing bowl with spring onions. Mix beaten eggs with fish sauce, salt and pepper, add to pork and mix everything well together. Grease a loaf tin and pack the mixture firmly into it, cover with a double thickness of greaseproof paper or foil and steam over high heat for 1 hour or longer, according to height of loaf. The pork must be well cooked. Let it cool slightly in the tin until firm, then turn out, slice and serve with lettuce salad and nuoc cham.

CƠM CHAY
STIR-FRIED MIXED VEGETABLES

Serves: 4
6 dried Chinese mushrooms
½ cup water
1 tablespoon dark soy sauce
1 teaspoon sesame oil
2 teaspoons sugar
3 stalks celery
¼ medium cabbage or white Chinese cabbage
few leaves mustard cabbage
1 small lettuce
3 spring onions
1 clove garlic, finely grated
½ teaspoon finely grated fresh ginger
1 tablespoon oil
1½ tablespoons light soy sauce
¼ cup water
1 teaspoon cornflour

Soak dried mushrooms in hot water for 30 minutes. Remove and discard stems, slice tops thinly, then simmer in a small saucepan with half cup water, soy sauce, sesame oil, and sugar until liquid is almost all absorbed. Slice celery diagonally into bite-size pieces, cut white cabbage, mustard cabbage and lettuce into bite-size squares and spring onion into short lengths. Fry garlic and ginger in oil over medium low heat for a few seconds only. Add stems of vegetables and stir fry over high heat for 2 minutes, then add leafy parts and fry 30 seconds. Add sauce and prepared mushrooms and mix together. Add water, bring to the boil, thicken with cornflour blended with a little cold water and stir until it boils and thickens. Serve at once with rice.

TÔM VÓ VIÊN CHIÊN
FRIED SHRIMP CAKES

Serves: 4-6 as a meal with rice and soup
1 quantity shrimp paste (opposite)
1 spring onion, finely chopped
pinch of ground black pepper
oil for frying

Mix shrimp paste with onion and pepper and form into small flat cakes with lightly oiled hands. Heat about 2.5 cm (1 inch) vegetable oil in a frying pan and fry on medium heat until golden, about 3 minutes. Drain on absorbent paper and serve hot with rice, soup and nuoc cham.

These cakes are also suitable for serving as appetisers with lettuce leaves and chopped fresh coriander or mint. Wrap in lettuce, adding a sprinkling of herbs and dip in nuoc cham. Eat immediately.

NƯỚC CHẤM
GARLIC, CHILLI AND FISH SAUCE *(picture page 343)*

No meal is considered complete without this sauce which is used as freely as salt and pepper. It is also known as nuoc mam sauce.

2 ripe red chillies
1 clove garlic
1 teaspoon sugar
1 lemon
1 tablespoon vinegar
1 tablespoon water
4 tablespoons fish sauce

Wearing gloves, cut off stalks from chillies, split down the centre and remove seeds and centre membrane. Cut into pieces, and pound in mortar and pestle together with peeled clove of garlic. Add sugar. Peel lemon, removing all the white pith. Slice and remove seeds. Add a small piece at a time to the chillies and pound to a pulp. Stir in the vinegar, water and fish sauce. Serve in a small bowl and use in small quantities

Note: A blender may be used instead of mortar and pestle, but this makes a frothy sauce. However, the flavour will be correct.

NƯỚC LÈO
GLUTINOUS RICE AND SOYBEAN SAUCE

½ cup glutinous rice
4 cups water
4 or 5 cloves garlic
1 tablespoon oil
250 g (8 oz) minced pork
½ teaspoon ground black pepper
3 tablespoons Chinese bean sauce
2 cups chicken or pork stock
2 tablespoons sugar
1 tablespoon fish sauce
2 teaspoons Chinese chilli sauce
1 cup roasted peanuts, pounded

Put rice and water in a heavy-based saucepan and bring to the boil. Cover, reduce heat and cook for 20 minutes, then uncover and allow to cook, stirring occasionally, until all the water has been absorbed.

Crush garlic with a little of the measured sugar. Heat oil in a wok, fry garlic on low heat until it starts to change colour. Add pork and stir fry on medium heat until it loses its pink colour. Add pepper and bean sauce, stir well. Simmer for a minute, then add stock, sugar and fish sauce, stir well and simmer a further minute or two. Add cooked rice, continue simmering for 5 minutes, stirring frequently. Remove from heat. Stir in chilli sauce and peanuts ground in a blender or pounded with mortar and pestle. Serve warm or at room temperature.

TÔM BẦM
SHRIMP OR PRAWN PASTE

500 g (1 lb) raw shrimp or prawns
1 egg white
60 g (2 oz) pork fat, finely chopped,
1 tablespoon oil
1 tablespoon fish sauce
½ teaspoon salt
¼ teaspoon sugar
⅛ teaspoon ground black pepper

Shell and de-vein the prawns, wash well and drain thoroughly. Put prawns twice through mincer using fine blade, or chop very finely, then whiz in electric blender or pound until it is a soft paste. If using blender add oil and fish sauce to facilitate blending and stop motor every now and then to scrape down sides of goblet. Add all other ingredients and mix thoroughly. Use in shrimp soup (page 342), fried shrimp cakes (page 340), or shrimp toast (page 345).

CANH GÀ BÍ ĐAO
CHICKEN AND WINTER MELON SOUP

Serves: 6

500 g (1 lb) chicken wings or half a
   chicken
1 kg (2 lb) Chinese winter melon
6 spring onions
5 cups water
1 teaspoon salt
1 tablespoon fish sauce
black pepper to taste

Cut chicken wings or half chicken into joints. Peel melon, discard skin and spongy centre with seeds. Cut melon into bite-sized pieces. Slice spring onions. Put chicken into saucepan with spring onions, water and salt. Bring to the boil, then cover and simmer for 1 hour or until liquid is reduced and well flavoured. Add winter melon, bring to the boil for one minute only. Add fish sauce and pepper to taste. Serve immediately, with rice if desired.

   Note: Peeled, sliced and seeded cucumber can be used as a substitute for winter melon.

CANH ĐẬU HỦ
SOUP WITH BEAN CURD

Serves: 2

2 cups strong chicken stock
2 squares fresh bean curd
½ cup chopped cooked chicken
1 tablespoon chopped fresh coriander
   leaves

Chill stock and remove all fat from surface. Bring stock to the boil, add bean curd and chicken and heat through. Sprinkle with fresh coriander and serve immediately.

CANH CỦ SEN
PORK AND LOTUS ROOT SOUP

Serves: 4

500 g (1 lb) lean pork ribs
500 g (1 lb) fresh lotus root or 8 slices
   canned lotus root
3 spring onions
½ teaspoon salt
6 cups water
1-2 tablespoons fish sauce

Ask butcher to cut the pork ribs into short lengths. Peel lotus root thinly and cut into slices. Slice spring onions, using both green and white parts. Put these ingredients into a saucepan with the salt and water, bring to the boil, then cover and simmer for 1½ hours or until well cooked and the liquid reduced to 4 cups. Add fish sauce to taste. Serve with white rice.

CANH TÔM VÒ VIÊN
SHRIMP DROP SOUP

Serves: 4

4 cups fish or chicken stock
1 tablespoon fish sauce
½ quantity shrimp paste (page 341)
2 cups finely shredded white Chinese
   cabbage
salt to taste
3 spring onions, finely sliced

Bring the stock to the boil and add fish sauce. Take half teaspoons of the shrimp paste, using an oiled teaspoon, and drop them into simmering stock. When cooked they will turn opaque and rise to the top. Add cabbage, bring back to the boil, cover and leave for a minute, or until cabbage is tender. Sprinkle spring onions on top and remove from heat at once. Cover and leave for 1 minute, then serve.

NƯỚC CHẤM *(nuoc mam sauce or garlic, chilli and fish sauce) recipe page 341*

PHỞ
BEEF SOUP WITH SALAD

You may well think a soup and a salad are an odd combination when served together, but don't miss out on this national dish by being too cautious. Rather like the moh hin gha of Burma, the strong stock is combined with other ingredients to make a meal in a bowl. Serve it right at the table, keeping the stock hot in an electric utensil and adding other components to each bowl.

Serves: 6-8

3 kg (6 lb) beef rib bones
500 g (1 lb) gravy beef
2 onions, sliced
thumb-size piece of fresh ginger
stick of cinnamon
1 teaspoon whole black peppercorns
salt to taste
500 g (1 lb) fresh rice noodles or 250g
   (8 oz) dried rice noodles
500 g (1 lb) fresh bean sprouts
6 spring onions
4 firm ripe tomatoes
2 white onions
500 g (1 lb) rump steak
fish sauce
lemon wedges
fresh red or green chillies, chopped
chopped fresh coriander leaves

Put bones and gravy beef in a very large pan, add cold water to cover, sliced onions, scraped and sliced ginger, cinnamon stick, whole peppercorns. Bring to the boil, turn heat very low, cover and simmer for at least 6 hours. Add salt to taste.

If using fresh rice noodles (look fun, chee chong fun), slice them into 1 cm (½ inch) strips and pour boiling water over, then drain, or steam in a colander for 5 minutes. If using dried rice noodles, they have to be soaked in warm water for at least 2 hours, then drained and cooked in boiling water until just tender. Drain well.

Prepare salad ingredients. Scald bean sprouts by pouring boiling water over them in a colander. Run cold water over. If necessary pinch off any straggly brown tails. Slice spring onions thinly. Cut tomatoes in half lengthways, then slice each half. Peel and slice onions thinly. Slice steak paper thin in bite-size pieces. Arrange all on a serving plate.

To serve: Put a ladle of noodles and a ladle of bean sprouts in each large soup bowl. Put a few slices of beef, tomato and onion in a large ladle, immerse in the boiling stock until beef begins to lose its redness. Beef should be pale pink. Pour contents of the ladle over the noodles and bean sprouts. Guests add fish sauce, lemon juice, chillies and fresh coriander to taste.

CANH BÚN TÀU
FISH AND CELLOPHANE NOODLE SOUP

Serves: 6-8

500 g (1 lb) white fish fillets
1 teaspoon finely grated fresh ginger
3 tablespoons fish sauce
1 teaspoon salt
½ teaspoon ground black pepper
60 g (2 oz) cellophane noodles
1½ tablespoons peanut oil
1 medium onion, thinly sliced
2 cloves garlic, crushed
2 daun salam or few curry leaves
1 teaspoon turmeric
1 teaspoon dried shrimp paste
1 teaspoon finely grated lemon rind
6 cups hot water
3 tablespoons finely sliced spring onions

Remove skin and bones from fish and chop flesh coarsely. Mix fish with ginger, 1 tablespoon of fish sauce and half the salt and pepper. Set aside. Soak noodles in warm water 15 minutes. In a large saucepan heat oil and fry onion, garlic, daun salam, until onion is soft. Stir frequently while frying. Add turmeric and dried shrimp paste and fry for another minute, crushing paste against side of pan. Add lemon rind, water and cellophane noodles and remaining fish sauce, salt and pepper. Boil 5 minutes, then add fish and simmer for 5 minutes longer. Remove from heat, pour into soup tureen or serving bowl, sprinkle with spring onions and serve hot.

CHẢ GIÒ
FRIED PORK AND CRAB ROLLS

One of the most popular snacks in Vietnam. The Vietnamese rice papers are very difficult to buy, but it is worth trying the recipe using Chinese spring roll wrappers which are sold in many Oriental stores

Makes about 24
½ cup soaked cellophane noodles
1 small onion, finely chopped
6 spring onions, finely chopped
250 g (8 oz) pork mince
185 g (6 oz) crab meat, frozen or canned
½ teaspoon salt
1 tablespoon fish sauce
¼ teaspoon ground black pepper
half packet Chinese spring roll wrappers
oil for deep frying
lettuce leaves
fresh mint or parsley or fresh coriander
  leaves
strips of cucumber
nuoc cham (page 341)

Soak a small amount of cellophane noodles in hot water for 10 minutes, then drain and measure ½ cup. Cut into 2.5 cm (1 inch) lengths with a sharp knife. Put into a bowl with the onion, spring onion, pork, flaked crab meat (pick out any bits of bony tissue), salt, fish sauce and pepper. Mix well.

Cut each spring roll wrapper in halves and put 2 teaspoons of filling on one end, shaping it into a neat roll. Roll up, turning in the sides so that the filling is completely enclosed. Moisten edge of wrapper with a little water or egg white to stick. When all the rolls are made, heat oil in a wok and fry a few at a time on medium heat until they are crisp and golden. Do not have oil too hot or the filling will not cook through. Drain on absorbent paper.

To serve: Wrap each roll in a lettuce leaf including a small sprig of mint, coriander or parsley and a strip of cucumber. Dip in nuoc cham and eat right away.

BÁNH MÌ CHIÊN TÔM
SHRIMP TOAST

Serve as hors d'oeuvre or a snack

Makes 24 pieces
12 slices stale bread
1 quantity shrimp paste (page 341)
oil for deep frying
lettuce leaves
fresh coriander leaves or mint
cucumber slices
nuoc cham (page 341)

Bread that is two days old is better than fresh bread for this recipe. Trim off crusts and cut each slice into halves lengthwise. Spread shrimp paste on the bread. Heat oil for deep frying and put in a few pieces of bread at a time, shrimp side down. Fry until golden, drain on absorbent paper. Serve hot, with lettuce leaves for wrapping, nuoc cham for dipping and coriander or mint sprigs and cucumber slices as accompaniments.

CHUỐI NƯỚNG
BANANA CAKE WITH CASHEWS

Cooking time: 1 hour:
Oven temperature: moderate (170-190°C or
* 350-375°F)*
3 eggs
1 cup sugar
¾ cup cream
1½ cups flour
2 kg (4 lb) very ripe bananas
1 cup coarsely chopped fresh cashews
1 cup grated fresh coconut

Beat eggs and sugar together in electric mixer until mixture is thick and pale. Use a fairly low speed. Pour cream into bowl and beat for a few seconds longer, just to mix. Sift flour, add to bowl and stir with a wooden spoon. Peel bananas and smash with the flat side of a chopper, but do not mash. Add to batter with nuts and coconut. Stir only until all ingredients are combined. Grease two 20 cm (8 inch) pans and dust with flour, shaking out any excess. Bake in a preheated moderate oven for 1 hour or until top is golden brown. Serve warm or cold. This is a very solid, pudding-like but flavoursome cake.

THE
PHILIPPINES

A mixture of Malay, Chinese and Spanish, with just a touch of American influence, is the combination that makes the food of the Philippines and the people themselves the exotic blend of East and West that they are.

Originally the islands were inhabited by Negritos, a negroid race in the Malayo-Polynesian region. Then came traders from Malaya, Indonesia and China who settled and intermarried. In the sixteenth century came the Spanish conquerors, who stayed four hundred years. The Spanish made a lasting impact on the way of life in the Philippines. They brought Catholicism, which was wholeheartedly embraced by the Filipinos, making the Philippines the only Christian country in Asia. They also introduced many of their foods and special festive dishes, so that now the cuisine of the Philippines is as much influenced by Spanish tastes as it is by the Malay and Chinese way of cooking.

In the Philippines, as in the rest of Asia, rice is the staple food of the people. Rice and fish comprise the native breakfast, but more popular is a breakfast of spicy native sausages, called *longaniza*, made of lean and fat pork well flavoured with pepper, garlic and other ingredients and briefly cured. These are fried and kept warm while leftover cooked rice is fried in the pork fat that remains. Fried eggs too are popular at breakfast. Sometimes Continental types of bread, such as *pan de sal*, are served in place of rice. The Filipinos drink coffee and chocolate, not tea. Hot chocolate and *ensaimadas* is a favourite mid-morning snack. *Ensaimadas* are made from a dough like that used for *brioche*, rich with butter, sugar and eggs; the unusual feature is that they have a filling and sometimes a topping of finely grated mature cheese, but the sweet/savoury combination is delicious (see recipe on page 364.)

Lunch and dinner are both big meals in the Philippines, and among the well-to-do may include four or five courses — soup, fish, meat, fresh fruit and finally a rich, sweet dessert so beloved of the Filipinos. This is eating Spanish style. If the meal is served Filipino style, then everything is put on the table at once but will still include Spanish-influenced dishes, for this is the type of cooking considered 'upper class'.

Between lunch and dinner there is yet another meal, *merienda*, which can best be compared to an English high tea. It consists not only of sandwiches and cakes and tea, but also on the table will be *lumpia* (a type of spring roll), a dish of *pancit* (fried noodles with vegetables, shrimp, pork, chicken or ham), and at least a couple of local sweets made from grated coconut, coconut milk, glutinous rice or pineapple and other tropical fruits.

In spite of the Spanish influence, many truly native dishes are very popular. One of these is *suman*, of which there are many kinds. One is made of glutinous rice steamed in a hollow bamboo and served with fresh grated coconut and sugar. Other types of *suman* are made with *cassava* or *saba* bananas (plantains). In some cases, instead of being steamed in a hollow bamboo, the mixture is tied tightly in banana leaves and simmered in water.

Adobo is the most popular and best known dish of the Philippines. It is a method of cooking, not one precise and unalterable recipe, and thus you may find chicken *adobo*, pork *adobo*, or a combination of both. It is typical of the flavours Filipinos find pleasing — vinegar, garlic and pepper. Fish or shellfish are also made into *adobo*. Sometimes coconut milk is one of the ingredients, sometimes not. But the garlic, vinegar and pepper remain constant. It is a way of tenderising and giving flavour to the meat to pre-soak it in the vinegar mixture for an hour or more before starting to cook.

Other traditional dishes of the Philippines are *guinataan*, in which food is cooked in coconut milk; *pesa*, indicating a dish of plain boiled fish with a large amount of fresh root ginger and ground black pepper for seasoning; *diniguan*, a dish using the internal organs and blood of a chicken or pig; *sinigang*, a sour soup of fish or meat, most refreshing in hot weather and in its own country always including the flowers and fruit of the tamarind tree.

Then there is *kilawin*, a raw fish salad similar to Mexican *ceviche*, which makes a delightful first course and wins requests for the recipe every time I serve it; *pipian*, chicken or meat in a sauce bright with *annatto* seeds and thickened with ground peanuts; *kari-kari*, a popular stew using economical cuts of meat like oxtail and shin, which are very juicy and flavourful. *Kari-kari* is similar to *pipian* in that it also includes *annatto* seeds and is thickened with peanuts and roasted ground rice.

Among the iced desserts that Filipinos love is iced *buko*, a simple coconut ice. The clear water in the centre of the young coconut is mixed with the tender flesh lining the shell, sweetened with sugar and frozen. Scraped into individual glasses like sherbet, it is the most delicately flavoured, refreshing dessert. It *must* be made with young coconuts at the stage where the meat is transparent and jelly-like.

Some of the most popular festive dishes of the Philippines are decidedly Spanish and of these I have included *arroz a la paella, menudo, pochero, morcon, fritada, cardillo, leche flan, capuchinos* and *membrillo*, because the people of the Philippines have adopted these and many more as their own and at most meals you are certain to be served as many Spanish-influenced dishes as native ones.

The Chinese influence is strongly evident in *pancit* and other noodle dishes. *Pancit guisado* is a fried noodle dish, *pancit luglog* is a noodle soup and *pancit molo* is the Philippine version of Chinese short soup or *won ton* soup, a legacy from the Visayan Islands where it is cooked to perfection.

Some helpful hints for cooking Filipino style in foreign countries were given to me by Mr C. Quevos of the Philippines, who cooks the food of his country at a restaurant in Sydney and who caters for special parties when the Consul General for the Philippines entertains. 'You cannot buy *annatto* (achuete) seeds in Australia,' he said, 'so we substitute paprika but have to be careful not to overdo it because the colour is much redder (*annatto* seeds give an orange colour). The vinegar we use in the Philippines is palm vinegar, much milder than wine vinegar, so I usually dilute strong vinegar with two parts water, mild vinegar with one part water.'

If *annatto* seeds are not available as a colouring agent, the same effect can be gained by using a quarter teaspoon of paprika powder and an eighth teaspoon of ground turmeric for each recommended teaspoon of *annatto* seeds. The resulting colour should be bright orange. Be careful not to fry the paprika and turmeric mixture — add it with the onion and garlic when they are added to the frying oil.

SERVING AND EATING A FILIPINO MEAL

Tables often have a raised circular turntable on which the dishes of food are placed to make it easy to present the food to everyone sitting at the table without having to pass dishes to and fro. Flat dinner plates, spoons, knives and forks are used, with bowls for soup. In outlying islands or rural areas the old custom of eating with the fingers still persists, but it is very outmoded in the cities.

Wine is seldom served with a meal, water being the popular drink, as in most Asian countries. However, the food of the Philippines is more suited to being served with wine than are the hot spicy foods of neighbouring countries. Coffee is the preferred beverage among Filipinos. Tea is considered the proper drink for old people and invalids and is served with lemon as a cure for colds and fever.

UTENSILS

The traditional way of cooking rice in the Philippines is to wash it several times, then cook it in earthenware pots lined with banana leaves to prevent it from sticking to the bottom of the pot.

While the occasional traditional cook may still use a clay *palayok* and cook in the old-fashioned way, modern city dwellers hardly ever use earthen pots. In the Philippines the rounded pan shaped like a *wok* is called a *carajay* (pronounced 'cara-hai') and most likely was introduced by the Chinese. It is useful for sitr-fried noodle dishes, but nowadays it is considered fashionable to cook in Western saucepans, frying pans and casseroles, so it is no problem at all to cook the food of this Asian country using the modern equipment of a Western kitchen.

YOUR PHILIPPINES SHELF

annatto seeds, optional
bagoong (shrimp sauce)
bay leaves·
black pepper, ground
creamed coconut
cellophane noodles
desiccated coconut
dried Chinese mushrooms
dried tamarind pulp
misu (salted bean curd)
olive oil
paprika
patis (fish sauce)
Spanish saffron
soy sauce
turmeric, ground
vinegar

Besides these ingredients with a long shelf life, fresh garlic, ginger and coriander herb are important.

ARROZ A LA PAELLA
RICE WITH CHICKEN AND SEAFOOD *(picture page 350)*

Among the many dishes with Spanish flavour found in the Philippines is this delicious combination, a favourite for feast days.

Serves: 6-8
1 x 1.5 kg (3 lb) roasting chicken
salt and pepper to taste
500 g (1 lb) pork chops
2 chorizos (hot Spanish sausages)
1 raw lobster tail, optional
500 g (1 lb) raw prawns
500 g (1 lb) fresh mussels
olive oil for frying

Sofrito:
3 tablespoons olive oil
2 large onions, finely chopped
½ teaspoon saffron strands
5 cloves garlic, finely chopped
2 large ripe tomatoes or 1 cup canned
   tomatoes
3 teaspoons salt
3 teaspoons paprika
2½ cups long grain rice
4½ cups chicken or fish stock
1 cup green peas
1 red capsicum, seeded and cut in strips

Cut chicken into serving pieces, dry on kitchen paper and season well with salt and pepper. Cut pork chops into dice, discarding skin and bones. Pierce chorizos in a few places with a sharp knife, put into a saucepan with water to cover and bring to the boil. Reduce heat and simmer for 5 minutes, drain and slice into rounds.

Chop lobster tail into large slices, shell and all. Wash prawns but do not remove shells. Scrub mussels with a stiff brush, beard them, and discard any that are not tightly closed.

Heat enough olive oil in a large, heavy frying pan to cover base of pan and brown the pieces of chicken on all sides. Remove to a plate. Add lobster and cook for a minute or two until shell turns pink. Transfer to plate. Brown chorizo slices, drain on absorbent paper. Brown the pork quickly, drain. Discard oil in pan.

Sofrito: In a large frying pan or heavy saucepan heat olive oil and fry onions over medium heat until soft and golden. While onions are cooking pour 2 tablespoons boiling water over saffron and leave to soak. Add garlic, soaked saffron, peeled and chopped tomatoes and fry, stirring, until tomatoes are soft and pulpy. Add salt and paprika and stir well. Add rice and stir over medium heat for 3 or 4 minutes, then add hot stock and stir well.

When stock comes to the boil add chicken, pork, chorizo and lobster, cover and cook on very low heat for 15 minutes. Add prawns and mussels, pushing mussels into the mass of rice so they will cook in the steam. Do not stir. Scatter peas over top. Cover and cook for a further 15 minutes, when rice should be cooked through and liquid absorbed. Decorate top of paella with strips of red capsicum and serve.

ARROZ CALDO
RICE WITH CHICKEN

Serves: 6
1 x 1 kg (2 lb) roasting chicken
2 tablespoons oil
10 cloves garlic, finely chopped
1 onion, finely sliced
1 teaspoon finely chopped fresh ginger
2½ cups rice
4 cups water
3 tablespoons fish sauce
4 spring onions, finely sliced

Cut chicken into serving pieces. Heat oil in a large frying pan and fry the garlic until pale golden. Remove and reserve. Add onion and ginger to pan and fry until soft, then add chicken and fry, turning, until chicken is golden and half cooked. Add rice and stir fry for a few minutes, then return half the fried garlic to pan, add water and fish sauce. Bring to the boil, then turn heat low, cover tightly and cook 20 minutes without lifting lid. Serve garnished with reserved fried garlic and spring onions.

PANCIT GUISADO
FRIED NOODLES WITH MIXED MEATS

Serves: 6-8
500 g (1 lb) raw prawns
500 g (1 lb) thin egg noodles
3-4 tablespoons lard or oil
5 cloves garlic, crushed
2 onions, finely sliced
1 cup flaked cooked chicken
1 cup cooked pork, cut in thin strips
½ cup ham, cut in thin strips
1 cup shredded cabbage
3 tablespoons light soy sauce
salt and pepper to taste
lemon wedges for garnish

Cook prawns in a little lightly salted water, cool, then shell and de-vein. Cut into pieces if large. Reserve 1 cup of the prawn stock. Soak noodles in warm water while bringing a large pan of water to the boil. Drain noodles and drop them into the fast-boiling water, bring back to the boil and cook for 2 minutes or until just tender. Do not overcook. Drain immediately, spread on a large baking tray lined with kitchen paper and allow to dry for at least 30 minutes, sprinkling a little oil over to prevent sticking.

Heat a tablespoon of lard in a large wok and when very hot fry noodles, a handful at a time, until golden on both sides, adding more lard to the wok as necessary. Remove noodles from wok. Heat a little more lard or oil and fry separately the garlic, onion, prawns, chicken, pork and ham. Set aside some of each for garnishing the dish and return the rest to the pan together with cabbage, soy sauce, prawn stock, salt and pepper. Cook uncovered until almost dry, then return noodles and heat through, tossing well to mix. Arrange on serving platter and garnish with the reserved ingredients and wedges of lemon.

PESA
FISH WITH GINGER

Serves: 4
2 x 500 g (1 lb) flathead or other delicate
   white fish
3 tablespoons oil
3 tablespoons finely chopped fresh ginger
1 teaspoon ground black pepper
rice washings (see note)
salt to taste
4 spring onions
1 sprig coriander leaves (kinchay)

Clean and scale fish and rub cavity with kitchen paper dipped in coarse salt. Rinse. Heat oil and fry ginger until soft and golden. Add pepper and stir, then put fish into the pan and add enough rice washings to almost cover. Add half teaspoon salt, lay a spring onion on each fish, cover and simmer until fish is cooked. Transfer fish carefully to serving dish, replace cooked spring onions with remaining uncooked onions and garnish with celery leaves. Pour cooking liquid around fish and serve with white rice and misu tomato sauce (following recipe).

Note: 'Rice washings' is the water in which rice has been washed prior to cooking.

MISU TOMATO SAUCE

Serve as sauce for pesa (above)
2 tablespoons chopped pork fat
2 cloves garlic, crushed
1 medium onion, finely chopped
2 tomatoes, peeled and chopped
2 tablespoons red misu (salted bean curd
   paste)
1 tablespoon vinegar
¼ teaspoon ground black pepper

Heat pork fat and fry garlic and onion until soft and golden. Add tomatoes, stir and cook to a pulp. Add all other ingredients, stir and simmer for a few minutes.

ARROZ A LA PAELLA (rice with chicken and seafood) *recipe page 349*

CARDILLO
FRIED FISH WITH TOMATOES AND EGG

Serves: 4
500 g (1 lb) firm white fish fillets
salt
2 tablespoons lard or olive oil
1 clove garlic, crushed
1 medium onion, sliced
2 tomatoes, sliced
½ cup water
2 eggs, beaten

Clean fish, removing any skin and scales. Cut into fingers. Rub a little salt onto fish. Heat lard in frying pan and fry fish pieces until golden brown. Remove and set aside. Fry garlic in lard remaining in pan and when golden add onion and tomatoes and salt to taste. Cook until tomato is soft and pulpy, then add water and simmer 3-5 minutes. Put fried fish into sauce, remove from heat and add the well-beaten eggs. Stir to heat through and serve immediately.

KILAW
MARINATED FISH SALAD *(picture page 346)*

Fish is marinated in lime or lemon juice and the acid turns the fish white and opaque so that it looks like cooked fish. This technique is also used in Mexico and Tahiti. I have used this recipe with many kinds of fish and found that the best results were with snapper, redfish and flathead, but any fish with delicate flavour is suitable.

Serves: 8
1 kg (2 lb) firm white fish fillets
lemon juice
1 teaspoon salt
2 medium onions, very thinly sliced
1 large red capsicum, diced
1 large green capsicum, diced
6 spring onions, finely sliced
3 or 4 firm red tomatoes, peeled and diced
1 large lettuce, washed and crisped
185 g (6 oz) creamed coconut
¾ cup hot milk
1 clove garlic
1 teaspoon finely grated fresh ginger
½ teaspoon ground black pepper
¼ teaspoon ground turmeric
salt to taste
finely chopped parsley or fresh coriander
   leaves

Remove all traces of skin and any bones from fish. Cut into bite-size pieces. Put fish into a glass or pottery bowl and add enough strained lemon juice to cover. Add salt and onions and mix well with a wooden spoon. Do not use metal utensils. Cover and refrigerate at least 8 hours, stirring once or twice while marinating.

Prepare vegetables and chill. Grate the creamed coconut coarsely and put it into the container of an electric blender with milk, garlic, ginger, pepper, turmeric. Blend until smooth. Cool.

Drain lemon juice from fish, add coconut dressing and mix well. Toss with prepared vegetables and serve on a dish lined with lettuce leaves.

Note: If creamed coconut is not available, make coconut cream by extracting coconut milk as described on page 11 , using milk instead of water. When the first extract has been obtained, chill it for about an hour, then spoon off the rich, creamy portion that rises.

GUINATAAN HIPON
PRAWNS IN COCONUT MILK

Serves: 6
750 g (1½ lb) raw prawns
2 cups thick coconut milk (page 11   )
1 tablespoon finely chopped garlic
1 teaspoon finely chopped fresh ginger
1 teaspoon salt
¼ teaspoon black pepper

Wash prawns well but do not shell them. Put into a saucepan with coconut milk, garlic, ginger, salt and pepper and bring to the boil, stirring. Reduce heat and simmer uncovered for 15 minutes, stirring frequently. Serve with hot white rice.

CHICKEN FRITADA

Serves: 4-6
1 x 1.5 kg (3 lb) chicken
2 tablespoons lard
5 cloves garlic, peeled and crushed
1 large onion, finely sliced
2 ripe tomatoes, diced
1½ teaspoons salt
½ teaspoon black pepper
1½ cups hot chicken stock
500 g (1 lb) new potatoes, scrubbed
1 red capsicum
1 green capsicum

Cut chicken into serving pieces. Use neck, back and wing tips for making stock. Heat lard in large frying pan and fry garlic and onion until onion is soft. Add chicken pieces and brown on both sides. Add tomatoes, salt, pepper and stock, cover and cook on medium heat until chicken is half done. Add potatoes (if they are large, halve or quarter) and capsicums cut into strips. Cook until potatoes are tender. Serve hot with white rice.

ADOBONG MANOK
CHICKEN ADOBO WITH COCONUT SAUCE

Serves: 6
1 x 1.5 kg (3 lb) roasting chicken
1 tablespoon finely chopped garlic
¾ cup white vinegar
1-1½ cups water
1 teaspoon salt
1 bay leaf
½ teaspoon whole peppercorns
few annatto seeds for colouring (see Glossary)
2 tablespoons light soy sauce
oil for frying
½ cup thick coconut milk

Cut chicken into serving pieces, separating drumsticks from thighs and cutting breast into four. Put into a medium saucepan. Add garlic to pan with vinegar, water, salt, bay leaf, peppercorns and annatto seeds. Liquid should be enough to almost cover the chicken. Bring to the boil, then reduce heat and simmer very gently 25-30 minutes. Uncover and simmer about 10 minutes longer. Chicken should be tender but not falling off the bones. Remove chicken pieces from pan, raise heat, and boil quickly until liquid is thickened and reduced to about 1½ cups. Strain into a small bowl and refrigerate briefly. Take as much fat as possible off sauce and heat in a frying pan, adding enough oil to cover base of pan. Add chicken pieces in one layer and fry on high heat to brown, then turn and brown other side. Remove pieces of chicken to a heated serving platter as they are done. Heat sauce with coconut milk and pour over. Serve with plain boiled rice.

PIPI-AN
CHICKEN AND PORK IN PEANUT SAUCE

Serves: 6-8
1 x 1.5 kg (3 lb) chicken
500 g (1 lb) pork
125 g (4 oz) raw ham
salt and pepper

Sauce:
½ cup uncooked rice
4 tablespoons lard
1 teaspoon annatto seeds (see Glossary)
1 clove garlic, crushed
2 onions, finely chopped
2 tablespoons pork fat, diced
½ cup peanut butter
salt to taste

Remove skin and bone from chicken and excess fat from pork. Cut both meats into large squares. Dice ham. Put meats into a saucepan with just enough water to cover and season with salt and pepper. Bring to the boil, reduce heat and simmer until meat is tender.

Sauce: Toast rice in a dry pan over low heat until golden, then grind to a powder in electric blender or pound with mortar and pestle. Heat lard in frying pan and fry annatto seeds over low heat for 1 minute. Cover pan as seeds tend to spatter and jump. Lift out seeds with a slotted spoon and discard. In the coloured oil fry the garlic, onions and pork fat until soft and golden brown.

Mix ground rice with enough stock from chicken and pork to make a smooth cream and add to frying pan with peanut butter. Cook until sauce boils, adding more liquid as necessary, heat meats through in this sauce and serve with rice.

CHICKEN WITH SOTANGHON

Serves: 4-6
1 x 1.5 kg (3 lb) chicken
2 tablespoons lard
1 onion, sliced
2 cloves garlic, crushed
1 tablespoon fish sauce
2 teaspoons annatto seeds (see Glossary)
250 g (8 oz) cellophane noodles
   (sotanghon) soaked and cut in 5 cm (2 inch) lengths
6 large dried Chinese mushrooms, soaked
   in hot water, de-stemmed and chopped
12 spring onions, finely sliced
pepper and salt

Put whole chicken in a saucepan, cover with water and bring to the boil. Simmer on low heat, covered, until chicken is almost tender. Lift out chicken and let cool a little, strain stock and reserve. Remove all bones from the chicken and cut meat into large pieces.

Heat lard in frying pan and fry onion and garlic until soft and golden. Add chicken meat and fish sauce and allow to simmer for a few minutes. Pour 2 tablespoons hot water over annatto seeds, stir until water is bright orange, then strain off water and add to pan with strained chicken broth. Bring to the boil, add noodles and chopped mushrooms and simmer 15 minutes. Add spring onions and pepper and salt to taste.

CHICKEN TINOLA

Serves: 4-6
1 x 1.5 kg (3 lb) chicken
1 onion, sliced
2 cloves garlic, crushed
1 tablespoon finely grated fresh ginger
1 tablespoon lard
2 cups water
1 green papaya (pawpaw)
fish sauce to taste
pepper

Cut chicken into serving pieces. In a large heavy-based saucepan fry onion, garlic and ginger in lard until soft. Add chicken pieces and stir fry until chicken is well browned. Pour in water, cover pan and reduce heat. Simmer gently until chicken is just tender. Peel and slice papaya, add to pan and continue to simmer until papaya is just tender. Add fish sauce and pepper to taste, and serve.

MECHADO
BEEF POT ROAST

Serves: 6-8
1.5 kg (3 lb) beef topside in one piece
strips of pork fat, optional
4 large onions, quartered
4 large tomatoes, halved
1 bay leaf
½ cup vinegar
1 tablespoon light soy sauce
6 potatoes, peeled and quartered
½ teaspoon ground black pepper
2 tablespoons lard

Insert strips of pork fat into beef at regular intervals if desired. This keeps the beef moist, but this step may be omitted. Put the meat in a deep, heavy saucepan with onions, tomatoes, bay leaf, vinegar, soy sauce and water to cover. Bring to the boil, then reduce heat, cover pan and simmer until meat is almost tender. Add potatoes and pepper and simmer uncovered until potatoes are cooked and liquid almost evaporated. Transfer sauce to serving plate, add lard to pan and fry beef on high heat until brown all over. Slice the meat and serve with potatoes and sauce.

MORCON
STUFFED ROLLED BEEF

Serves: 6-8
1.5 kg (3 lb) thick skirt or flank steak in
  one piece
1½ teaspoons salt
½ teaspoon ground black pepper
2 tablespoons lemon juice
2 cloves garlic, crushed
2 sweet gherkin pickles
2 chorizo sausages
2 thick slices cooked ham
2 hard-boiled eggs
2 tablespoons lard
2 tablespoons vinegar
3 ripe tomatoes, peeled and chopped
2 cups water

With a sharp knife cut steak through the middle, starting at the thickest edge and being careful not to cut through. This should give you a very flat piece of steak almost double the size it was originally. Sprinkle with salt, pepper, lemon juice and smear with crushed garlic.

Cut pickles and chorizos into slices lengthways, and the slices of ham into strips. Quarter the hard-boiled eggs. Arrange all ingredients in rows starting at one end of the beef. Roll up carefully and tie with string, not making it too tight.

Heat lard in a large frying pan and brown meat on all its outer surfaces, turning it gently with wooden spoons or tongs. Drain off excess fat. And vinegar, tomatoes and water and bring to the boil, reduce heat and simmer gently, with lid on pan, for 1¼ hours or until meat is tender when tested with a thin metal skewer. Lift out meat, thicken sauce by rapid boiling, remove string holding meat roll and cut into slices. Serve with the sauce.

SINIGANG NA CARNE
SOUR SOUP OF BEEF

Serves: 6-8
500 g (1 lb) shin beef
500 g (1 lb) soup bones
250 g (8 oz) pork chop, with fat removed
1 medium onion, sliced
2 under-ripe tomatoes, sliced
2 teaspoons salt
1 tablespoon dried tamarind pulp
1 cup boiling water
1 large sweet potato, peeled and diced
1 giant white radish, sliced
2 cups shredded greens (such as spinach)
fish sauce to taste
lime or lemon wedges

Put beef, bones and pork into a large saucepan with water to cover. Add onion, tomatoes and salt. Bring to the boil then reduce heat and simmer, covered, until meat is tender. Remove meat to cool. Meanwhile soak tamarind pulp in boiling water until water cools, then squeeze to dissolve all the tamarind pulp and strain into simmering soup, discarding seeds and fibres of tamarind.

Cut pork into thin slices, beef into dice. Discard bones. Return meat to soup. Add sweet potato and radish to soup and simmer until almost soft, add greens and season to taste with fish sauce. As soon as leaves are cooked, serve hot with lime or lemon wedges for extra seasoning.

355

KARI-KARI
BEEF AND VEGETABLE STEW

Serves: 6-8
2 kg (4 lb) oxtail, jointed
1 kg (2 lb) shin of beef on bone, sliced
3 teaspoons salt
3 tablespoons vegetable oil
2 teaspoons annatto seeds (see Glossary)
2 large onions, very finely sliced
4 large cloves garlic, finely chopped
8 cups water
¼ teaspoon ground black pepper
½ cup uncooked rice
½ cup roasted skinned peanuts
375 g (12 oz) tender green beans
2 medium eggplants
2 tablespoons sliced spring onion
2 tablespoons chopped celery leaves
2 tablespoons fish sauce, or to taste

Put oxtail and shin of beef into pressure cooker with just enough water to cover and 2 teaspoons salt. Cook under pressure for 1 hour. Allow to cool to lukewarm and strain. Chill stock in refrigerator so fat may be lifted from surface. If no pressure cooker is available, simmer meat until almost tender.

Wipe pieces of meat on absorbent paper so no moisture remains. Heat 1 tablespoon oil in a large, deep saucepan or fireproof casserole and brown pieces of meat, putting in a few at a time and turning with tongs to ensure even browning. Remove each batch from pan to a plate. Pour off fat from pan and heat remaining oil, not making it too hot. Add annatto seeds, cover pan because they are inclined to pop and spatter, and warm on very low heat for 1 minute. Remove from heat, lift out seeds with a perforated spoon. Fry onions and garlic on medium heat in the annatto oil until soft, about 10 minutes. Return meat to pan, remove fat from stock and reheat it, then make up to 8 cups with hot water. Pour into pan, add pepper, bring to the boil then turn heat low and simmer, with lid on pan, but allowing a little steam to escape, until meat is tender.

While meat is simmering, put uncooked rice into a heavy frying pan and roast over medium heat, stirring frequently and shaking pan so grains colour evenly. When they are deep golden allow to cool slightly, then grind to a powder in electric blender. Tip ground rice into a bowl and blend peanuts until they too are reduced to powder. If some particles are large, sift and use only the fine ground nuts. Test tenderness of meat. Meat should be easily pierced with a fork, but not falling off the bone, and there should be sufficient liquid in pan to cover the meat. If necessary add more hot water. Stir in rice and peanut powder with a wooden spoon, stirring until smooth. String and cut beans into large bite-size lengths. Wash eggplants, remove stems and cut in 8 lengthways wedges, then cut wedges into 3, crossways. Stir into the stew and cook, uncovered, for 10 minutes or until vegetables are tender but not mushy. Add 1 tablespoon fish sauce, or more if liked. Serve from casserole or ladle into a large soup tureen. Sprinkle spring onions (green portion and all) and celery leaves over and serve hot with white rice. If liked, accompany this dish with extra fish sauce, soy sauce, a hot sambal sauce, or (for real Filipino eating) a sauce made from equal quantities of bagoong and lime juice; Chinese shrimp sauce is the equivalent of bagoong.

PICADILLO

Serves: 6
1 tablespoon lard
4 cloves garlic, finely chopped
1 medium onion, finely chopped
500 g (1 lb) lean minced beef
2 tomatoes, peeled and chopped
2 cups beef stock
1 teaspoon salt
¼ teaspoon ground black pepper
500 g (1 lb) potatoes, peeled and cubed

Heat lard and cook garlic and onion over gentle heat until soft and golden. Add beef and stir until meat has changed colour. Add tomatoes and cook until they are soft. Add stock, salt and pepper and bring to the boil. Cook, covered, on medium heat for 20 minutes, then add potatoes and cook 25 minutes longer or until potatoes are done. Serve hot.

ALMONDIGAS (1)
BEEF AND PORK BALLS SIMMERED IN STOCK

Serves: 4
250 g (8 oz) pork mince
250 g (8 oz) minced beef
1 teaspoon salt
¼ teaspoon pepper
1 small egg
1½ tablespoons oil
2 cloves garlic, finely chopped
1 medium onion, finely chopped
2 ripe tomatoes, diced
4 cups broth or rice water
2 teaspoons soy sauce

Combine pork, beef, salt, pepper and egg thoroughly and form into balls. Heat oil and fry garlic and onion until golden brown, then add tomatoes and fry, stirring, until soft. Add broth or water from washing rice, bring to the boil, then add meat balls one by one and let them simmer slowly until well cooked. Serve hot.

ALMONDIGAS (2)
PORK AND PRAWN BALLS

Serves: 4
250 g (8 oz) raw prawns
250 g (8 oz) pork mince
1 spring onion, finely chopped
½ teaspoon salt
1 tablespoon oil
1 medium onion, finely chopped
2 cloves garlic, crushed
½ teaspoon bagoong or Chinese shrimp
  sauce
3 cups hot water
salt and pepper to taste
½ cup meesua (fine wheat noodles)

Shell and de-vein prawns and chop very finely. Combine prawns, pork, spring onion and salt, mix well and form into balls the size of a large marble. Heat oil and fry onion and garlic gently until golden brown. Add shrimp sauce and water, bring to the boil and drop in the balls a few at a time, keeping the water boiling. Simmer 8 minutes or until balls are cooked, drop in the meesua and remove from heat. Cover and stand 5 minutes, then add pepper and salt to taste and serve hot.

Note: If meesua are not available, use rice vermicelli but allow to cook for 1 minute before removing from heat.

MENUDO

Serves: 6
500 g (1 lb) pork
2 teaspoons annatto seeds (see Glossary)
1 tablespoon oil
1 tablespoon crushed garlic
1 onion, finely chopped
2 tomatoes, sliced
3 potatoes, diced
250 g (8 oz) pork liver
2 teaspoons salt
½ teaspoon ground black pepper

Cut pork into cubes about 5 cm (2 inches). Fry annatto seeds in oil over low heat for 1 minute, then lift out seeds with a slotted spoon and discard. In the red oil fry the garlic and onion until soft and golden, add tomatoes and cook until soft and pulpy. Add pork to pan, cover and bring to the boil. Reduce heat and simmer until pork is tender. Add potatoes and a little water or stock if there is very little liquid in the pan. Simmer until potatoes are cooked. Meanwhile cut liver very finely. Add to pan when potatoes are cooked, season and bring back to the boil. Serve hot.

UMBA
SIMMERED PORK

Serves: 6
1 kg (2 lb) pork shoulder
2 cloves garlic, finely chopped
1 cup water
2 tablespoons soy sauce
2 tablespoons brown sugar
1 teaspoon salt
½ cup vinegar
½ bay leaf

Cut pork into large cubes and put into a heavy saucepan with the rest of the ingredients. Bring to the boil, then lower heat, cover and simmer until pork is tender. Serve with rice.

ADOBONG BABOY
PORK ADOBO

Serves: 6
6 pork loin chops or leg chops, about 1 kg (2 lb)
8-10 cloves garlic
1 cup white vinegar
1 cup water
1½ teaspoons salt
2 bay leaves
½ teaspoon ground black pepper
lard or oil for frying

Cut skin from pork and discard. If chops are large, cut into serving pieces. Put pork and all other ingredients except oil or lard into a heavy saucepan, and marinate for 1 hour. Bring to the boil, then reduce heat and simmer for 40 minutes or until pork is tender. Remove pork from pan, boil liquid over high heat until reduced and thickened. Strain into small bowl and spoon fat from top into frying pan. Add lard or oil so that base of pan is covered with 5 mm (¼ inch) fat and fry the pork pieces until evenly brown and crisp all over. Arrange on a heated serving plate and pour the sauce over. Serve very hot accompanied by white rice.

CHICKEN AND PORK ADOBO

Serves: 6-8

Follow previous recipe, reducing pork to 500 g (1 lb) and adding a roasting chicken weighing about 1.25 kg (2½ lb) cut into serving pieces. Reduce cooking time to 30 minutes in the vinegar and garlic liquid. Continue as before. Serve garnished with pimiento strips or tomato wedges, and accompanied by white rice.

POCHERO

A two course meal from one pot, rather like the French pot au feu, but featuring mixed meats.

Serves: 6
1 cup dried chick peas
1 x 1.5 kg (3 lb) chicken
500 g (1 lb) pork
2 chorizo sausages
1 large onion, sliced
4 teaspoons salt
1 teaspoon whole black peppercorns
4 tablespoons oil
10 cloves garlic, finely chopped
1 medium onion, finely chopped
2 ripe tomatoes, peeled and diced or 1
   small can whole tomatoes
500 g (1 lb) sweet potatoes, peeled and cut
   into chunks
1 white Chinese cabbage cut across in 5
   cm (2 inch) sections
8 spring onions, cut in 5 cm (2 inch)
   lengths

Wash chick peas and soak overnight in plenty of water. Cut chicken into serving pieces. Cut pork into large cubes. Slice chorizos into 2.5 cm (1 inch) pieces. Put all these ingredients into a large pan, add water to cover, put in sliced onion, salt and peppercorns and bring to the boil. Reduce heat, cover and simmer until meat and chick peas are almost tender.

In another pan heat oil and fry garlic and chopped onion on low heat, stirring frequently, until golden brown. Add tomatoes and cook to a pulp, then add to meat and stock together with sweet potatoes. Simmer until potatoes are half cooked, then add cabbage and spring onions for the last few minutes. Serve broth as soup and the meat and vegetables separately.

RELLENONG TALONG
STUFFED EGGPLANT

Serves: 4
2 medium eggplants
1 tablespoon oil
3 cloves garlic, finely chopped
1 medium onion, finely chopped
250 g (8 oz) minced pork
1 large ripe tomato, chopped
1 teaspoon salt
¾ teaspoon ground black pepper
1 cup soft fresh breadcrumbs
1 egg, beaten
dry breadcrumbs for coating
oil for frying

Cut eggplants in halves lengthways, parboil in lightly salted water, but do not let them become too soft. Remove from water and drain, cut side downwards. Scoop out some pulp, leaving a firm shell.

Heat oil and fry garlic and onion until golden, add pork and fry until all pinkness disappears. Add tomato, salt and pepper and cook for 15 minutes. Add chopped eggplant pulp and continue cooking until mixture is not too moist. Remove from heat, mix in soft breadcrumbs, taste and add more seasoning if necessary. Divide mixture among eggplant halves and fill them, then brush tops with beaten egg and coat with breadcrumbs. Heat oil for shallow frying and fry eggplants first on one side, then on the other, until golden. Serve hot.

AMPALAYA
BITTER MELON WITH PRAWNS

Serves: 6
500 g (1 lb) bitter melons
250 g (8 oz) prawns
250 g (8 oz) pork
lard or oil for frying
2 medium onions, chopped
5 cloves garlic, chopped
1 kg (2 lb) ripe tomatoes, peeled and
   chopped
½ cup vinegar
salt and pepper to taste

Cut the bitter melons in halves lengthways. Scoop out seeds and discard. Cut green portion crossways into thin slices. Boil prawns, shell and de-vein them, reserving stock. Cut pork into thin slices. Heat lard or oil and fry onion and garlic until golden brown. Add pork and fry, then add tomatoes. Cook until tomatoes are reduced to a pulp, then add prawns and cup of reserved stock. Stir until mixture returns to the boil, add vinegar and simmer for a few minutes, add bitter melon. Cook until bitter melon is tender. Season to taste and serve with rice.

AMARGOSO SALAD
BITTER MELON SALAD

Serves: 4
1 tender bitter melon, thinly sliced
250 g (8 oz) cooked prawns
2 firm red tomatoes, peeled and diced
2 hard-boiled eggs, chopped

Dressing:
3 tablespoons vinegar
½ teaspoon salt
2 teaspoons sugar
¼ teaspoon ground black pepper

Drop bitter melon into boiling water, bring back to the boil for 1 minute, then drain immediately. Shell and de-vein prawns, and if large, cut into small pieces. Put all salad ingredients into a bowl. Stir dressing ingredients together, pour over salad and toss to mix. Cover and chill.

PAPAYA SALAD

Serves: 6
1 medium, firm papaya (pawpaw)
1 small ripe pineapple, peeled and diced
2 spring onions, finely sliced
1 cooking apple, peeled and diced
½ cup thinly sliced celery
½ cup salad dressing or mayonnaise
salt and pepper to taste

Peel papaya, cut in halves and scoop out seeds. Cut flesh into dice. Combine with all the other ingredients, cover and chill before serving.

LUMPIA

Lumpia, a popular snack, may be 'fresh' or fried. Fresh lumpia means that the filling is enclosed in a lettuce leaf and egg roll wrapper and eaten without further cooking, while fried lumpia is similar to a spring roll. There are many versions of lumpia, each featuring a main ingredient — for example, lumpia labong (with bamboo shoot), lumpia with peanuts, and the most sought after, lumpia with ubod. Ubod is the heart of the coconut palm and has justly earned its reputation for being food for millionaires, because a whole tree has to be sacrificed to obtain the tender, nutty, creamy-white heart-of-palm.

Here is a basic recipe for lumpia. To this you may add chopped bamboo shoots or crushed roasted peanuts for variation. If you yearn to taste the heart-of-palm filling, cut canned hearts of palm into matchstick strips and mix only with an equal quantity of diced cooked shrimp or lobster and season to taste with salt and pepper.

Makes about 24 lumpia.

1 chicken breast or half a small chicken, cooked
250 g (8 oz) cooked pork
250 g (8 oz) cooked prawns
125 g (4 oz) fresh bean sprouts
250 g (8 oz) cabbage
125 g (4 oz) green beans
2 tablespoons peanut oil
4 cloves garlic, finely chopped
1 cup finely diced celery
½ cup finely chopped spring onions
2 teaspoons salt
½ teaspoon ground black pepper
2 tablespoons light soy sauce
1 packet spring roll wrappers or 1 quantity egg roll wrappers (page 256)

Bone, skin and dice chicken breast. Dice pork finely. Shell, devein and roughly chop the prawns. Wash bean sprouts and drain, pinch off straggly brown tails and chop roughly. Shred cabbage finely, discarding tough stems and outer leaves. String beans and cut into very thin diagonal slices.

Heat oil and fry garlic over low heat for 1 minute, then add chicken, pork and prawns and stir fry for 1 minute before adding beans. Stir fry for 2 minutes, then add bean sprouts, cabbage, celery, and spring onions. Toss and cook until tender but still crunchy. Add seasoning, mix well, then drain away excess moisture.

For fresh lumpia, put a leaf of romaine or cos lettuce, washed and dried, on an egg roll wrapper. Put 2 tablespoons of filling on the leaf, roll up so that one end is enclosed and the leaf shows at the other end. Serve at room temperature accompanied by dipping sauce (following recipe).

For fried lumpia do not use the lettuce but put filling on spring roll wrapper or egg roll wrapper and roll as for spring rolls (page 257) so that filling is completely enclosed. If not serving immediately refrigerate, covered with foil or plastic wrap, until needed. Fry in deep oil heated to 190°C (375°F) for 2 minutes or until golden brown and crisp. Drain on absorbent paper and serve with sauce.

SAUCE FOR LUMPIA

4 tablespoons sugar
¼ cup light soy sauce
1 cup clear chicken stock or water
2 tablespoons cornflour
¼ cup cold water
1 clove garlic, crushed
¼ teaspoon salt

Combine sugar, soy, and stock. Bring to the boil. Add cornflour mixed smoothly with the cold water and stir until mixture thickens. Simmer, stirring for 1 minute. Stir in garlic crushed with salt.

EMPANADAS
MEAT-FILLED PASTRIES

Makes about 2 dozen
Pastry:
2 cups plain flour
½ teaspoon salt
½ cup water
1 tablespoon sugar
1 egg yolk, beaten
¼ cup melted butter or margarine
1 egg white, lightly beaten
lard or oil for deep frying

Filling:
3 rashers bacon
1 tablespoon lard or oil
2 cloves garlic, finely chopped
1 medium onion, finely chopped
250 g (8 oz) pork and veal mince, or
  Spanish sausage, finely chopped
125 g (4 oz) finely chopped raw chicken
¾ teaspoon salt
¼ teaspoon ground black pepper
2 tablespoons tomato sauce
3 hard-boiled eggs, chopped
2 tablespoons chopped pickled gherkins

Pastry: Sift flour and salt into a bowl. Mix together water, sugar and egg yolk. Make a well in the centre of the flour and pour in the mixture, then blend and knead until smooth. Leave to rest for 15 minutes. Roll out half the pastry very thinly on a lightly floured board and brush with half the melted butter. Roll up pastry to a long, thin roll, making sure it is rolled tightly and firmly. Cut into slices about 2.5 cm (1 inch) thick and roll each slice out again to a circle about the size of a small saucer.

Put a spoonful of filling on each, brush edges of pastry with lightly beaten egg white, fold to a half circle shape and press edges firmly together to seal. Decorate with tines of a fork. Repeat with remaining pastry and filling.

Heat lard or oil in a deep frying pan and when moderately hot fry the empanadas, a few at a time, until golden brown. Drain well on absorbent paper and serve warm.

Filling: Remove rind, chop bacon into small pieces and fry until fat runs. Remove bacon from pan, add lard or oil and fry garlic and onion over low heat until soft and golden. Increase heat, add meats and fry, stirring, until they change colour. Add salt, pepper and tomato sauce, stir well. Lower heat, cover and cook for 15 minutes. Stir in hard-boiled eggs and pickled gherkins and allow to cool before filling pastry. Taste, and add more seasoning if necessary.

CAPUCHINOS
SMALL BRANDIED CAKES

Makes 12
¼ cup melted butter
½ cup plain flour
½ teaspoon baking powder
pinch salt
2 large eggs
½ cup sugar
1 tablespoon brandy

Syrup:
½ cup sugar
½ cup water
1 tablespoon brandy

Make syrup and set aside to cool. Preheat oven to hot, 200°C (400°F). Grease muffin tins. Melt butter and allow it to cool. Sift flour, baking powder and salt together.

Beat eggs with rotary beater until frothy, add sugar gradually and continue beating until thick and light. Mix in melted butter and brandy, then fold in the dry ingredients.

Half fill muffin tins with batter and bake in a hot oven for 10-12 minutes or until cakes are golden brown. Remove from tins, dip briefly into syrup for no more than a second and put on a cake cooler to dry.

Syrup: Put sugar and water into a small saucepan and dissolve sugar over low heat. Boil hard for 2 minutes, then allow to cool and stir in brandy.

UKOY
PRAWN AND SWEET POTATO FRITTERS

Makes about 20
250 g (8 oz) small red prawns
1 cup water
1½ teaspoons salt
1 cup plain flour
½ cup ground rice
¼ cup cornflour
2 eggs
¼ teaspoon ground black pepper
1 medium-size sweet potato
1 cup fresh bean sprouts
4 spring onions, finely sliced
oil for deep frying

Wash prawns well, bring water and salt to the boil and drop in the prawns. When water returns to the boil, cover and cook for 3-4 minutes or until prawns are pink. Drain prawns, reserving the liquid they cooked in. Remove heads of prawns. In the Philippines the prawns are left in their shells and this may be done if they are very tiny prawns. If they are not very small the shells are somewhat tough and I prefer to shell them, leaving only the tails on.

Put flour, ground rice and cornflour into a large bowl. Beat eggs and stir in 1 cup of the liquid the prawns were cooked in, making up the amount with water if necessary. Add pepper.

Pour the liquid into the dry ingredients and beat well with a rotary beater for a minute or two, until batter is smooth.

Peel the sweet potato and grate coarsely. Measure 1 cup. Wash bean sprouts, pinch off straggly brown tails and pour boiling water over the sprouts in a colander, then run cold water over. Drain well. Stir grated sweet potato, bean sprouts and half the spring onions into the batter.

Heat oil in a deep frying pan or wok and when a haze starts to form slip in about a tablespoon of the batter at a time, placing 2 or 3 prawns and a sprinkling of spring onions on top of the spoonful before sliding it into the oil. Do not fry too many fritters at a time. Spoon the oil over them as they cook and when underside is golden brown turn and fry other side. The oil should not be too hot or they will darken before they are cooked and crisp. Drain on kitchen paper towels and serve hot accompanied by garlic and vinegar dipping sauce. To make the sauce crush a clove of garlic with 1 teaspoon salt and stir into quarter cup mild vinegar.

MANGO ICE CREAM

Ice creams made from fruit, coconut and purple yam are popular in the Philippines.

Serves: 6
2 cups milk
2 eggs
½ cup caster sugar
1½-2 cups mango pulp, fresh or canned
1 teaspoon unflavoured gelatine
2 tablespoons water
1 cup cream

Turn freezer to its coldest setting. Put milk in a saucepan and bring slowly to the boil. Meanwhile separate eggs and beat the yolks with half the sugar in a bowl until thick and light. Pour a little of the hot milk on to the yolks, stirring constantly, then return yolk mixture to saucepan and cook over hot water or on very low heat. Stir all the time and do not allow to reach simmering point or the custard will curdle. As soon as it is thick enough to lightly coat back of spoon, remove from heat and keep stirring until it cools somewhat. Pour into freezer tray and freeze until mushy.

Sprinkle gelatine over cold water in a cup and stand the cup in a small saucepan of water. Bring water to the boil so gelatine dissolves. Stir this into the mango pulp. Whip the cream until it holds soft peaks. Do not overbeat or ice cream will have a buttery texture. Beat egg whites until soft peaks form, add remaining sugar and beat until soft and glossy.

Scrape half-frozen custard into a bowl and beat with rotary beater until it is smooth, but do not let it melt. Chilling bowl and beater helps in hot weather. Fold in the mango pulp, egg whites and whipped cream and return to freezer trays. Freeze until firm.

BOMBONES DE ARROZ
RICE FRITTERS

Makes about 24
2 cups cooked rice
2 large eggs, beaten until frothy
½ cup sugar
½ teaspoon vanilla
½ teaspoon grated nutmeg
6 tablespoons plain flour
3 teaspoons baking powder
oil for deep frying
icing sugar for sprinkling

In a large bowl mix rice, eggs, sugar, vanilla and nutmeg. Sift flour and baking powder together and stir into rice mixture until thoroughly combined. Heat oil in a deep frying pan and when moderately hot drop mixture in spoonfuls into the oil and fry on medium heat until golden brown and nicely puffed, turning them to brown all over. Lift out with slotted spoon and drain on absorbent paper. Sprinkle with icing sugar and serve warm.

ENSAIMADA
SWEET BREAD ROLLS

Oven temperature: 170°C (350°F)
Baking time: 10-12 minutes
Makes: 18
30 g (1 oz) compressed yeast
¼ cup lukewarm water
3 teaspoons sugar
4 cups plain flour
185 g (6 oz) butter or margarine
½ cup caster sugar
6 egg yolks
½ cup milk
extra ½ cup melted butter
125 g (4 oz) finely grated mature cheese,
    preferably Dutch Edam
2-3 tablespoons extra caster sugar

Crumble yeast into warm water in a small bowl. Stir in 3 teaspoons sugar until dissolved. Sprinkle with a spoonful of flour and set aside in a warm place.

Beat butter or margarine until soft, add caster sugar and continue beating until light. Add egg yolks, one at a time, beating well after each. Stir in flour and milk alternately, then the yeast mixture. Beat well until smooth. (Depending on the absorbency of flour, which varies, it may be necessary to add a tablespoon or two more of flour. The dough should be soft but not so soft that it sticks to the sides of the bowl.) Form dough into a ball and leave on a floured board for 10 minutes. Wash bowl in hot water, dry well, grease lightly and put dough in the warm bowl. Cover with a cloth and leave in a warm place until double in volume, about 1 hour.

Divide dough into 2 equal portions and roll each on lightly floured board to a rectangle 45 cm x 38 cm (18 x 15 inches) in size. Brush with some of the melted butter and sprinkle with half the grated cheese. Cut rectangle into 3 equal strips lengthways and roll up each strip like a Swiss roll, starting at the long end. Cut each long roll into 3 pieces, so you have 9 pieces in all.

Roll each piece with hands on the board until as thin as a pencil, then form into snail-like coils or twists. Put on a greased baking sheet, leaving spaces in between, cover with a dry cloth and leave in a warm place 30-40 minutes or until dough once more almost doubles in bulk.

Preheat oven to moderate, 170°C (350°F) and bake 10-12 minutes or until golden brown. Remove from oven and while hot brush with melted butter and sprinkle with caster sugar. Serve ensaimadas warm or at room temperature.

LECHE FLAN
CARAMEL CUSTARD

Serves: 6-8
½ cup sugar
¼ cup water
3 large eggs
2 egg yolks
½ cup caster sugar
2½ cups hot milk
2 teaspoons vanilla

Put sugar and water into a small saucepan and heat without stirring until a deep golden brown. Remove from heat and pour at once into a 6-cup ovenproof mould. Rotate mould to coat base and sides with caramel.

In a large bowl beat the whole eggs and egg yolks until foamy. Gradually add the caster sugar, beating until thick and light. Heat milk and add very gradually, beating constantly. Stir in vanilla, then strain custard into the caramel-lined mould. Put mould into a baking tin and pour boiling water around to come half way up mould. Bake in a slow oven, 150°C (300°F) for 35-45 minutes or until a knife inserted in centre of custard comes out clean. Remove from oven and cool. When cold, cover and chill in refrigerator overnight at least, preferably for two days. Run a knife around edge, invert a chilled serving plate over the mould, then grasping both together turn them over so that the custard slips on to the serving plate. Serve chilled.

GUAVA JELLY

2 kg (4 lb) slightly under-ripe guavas
4 green cooking apples
sugar
lemon juice

Wash fruit and cut into quarters. Put into a large saucepan with just enough cold water to cover. Cook, uncovered, until fruit is soft and loses its colour, at least 1 hour. Strain through 2 or 3 layers of muslin or a jelly bag. Do not squeeze or the jelly will not be sparkling and clear. Wet the cloth and wring it out before pouring fruit into it, or a lot of juice will be absorbed by the cloth.

Measure the strained juice and cook no more than 4 or 5 cups at a time. Allow ¾ cup sugar to each cup of juice. Bring juice to the boil, add warmed sugar and about 2 tablespoons strained lemon juice and stir until sugar dissolves. Now cook jelly without stirring, skimming off any froth that rises to the top, until jelly will set. To test, take a spoonful of the liquid, cool slightly and pour back into pan from the side of the spoon. When it no longer runs off in a steady stream but thickens and 'sheets' as it falls, it is ready. Pour jelly into sterile jars and cover with a thin layer of melted paraffin.

MEMBRILLO
GUAVA PASTE

After straining off the juice for jelly (previous recipe), the pulp of the fruit may be used to make this sweetmeat.

Push pulp through a fine nylon sieve, discarding seeds and skins. Weigh pulp and allow three quarters of its weight in sugar. Heat pulp and sugar with the juice of 1 lemon and stir constantly until very thick. Use a long-handled wooden spoon and cook over very low heat. Take care because as the mixture thickens it spatters. Cook and stir until mixture is stiff and comes away from the pan in one mass. Turn into a buttered dish, flatten with a buttered spoon or a piece of buttered banana leaf, and leave until quite cold and firm. Cut into thin slices to serve.

CHINA

Imagine a visit to Hong Kong just to sample Chinese specialities and learn from some of the best Chinese chefs in the business. I consider myself very lucky indeed to have had the chance to do just that. It was an education to see specialist chefs in action. For instance, chef Chan Wong, the man behind the best of Hong Kong's famous *dim sum* breakfasts, prepared *dim sum* of many kinds with such speed and nimbleness of fingers that it was obvious that not just knowledge but constant practice contributed to the results.

Then there was chef Wong Hon Ming, a noodle specialist whose technique was more like that of a magician performing sleight of hand than a chef making noodles. In seconds he transformed a lump of well-kneaded dough into dozens of incredibly fine strands, stretching it to arm's length, folding the ends together and stretching it again so that first there was one thick rope of dough, then two, four, eight, sixteen and so on, ending in a veritable curtain of noodles which he dropped into a bubbling cauldron.

Peking duck with mandarin pancakes was another of the famous dishes I watched being prepared, and chef Chan Shun took pride in his position as a renowned expert in this justly acclaimed preparation with its perfectly crisp, deep reddish-brown skin. The secret is in blowing air between the skin and the flesh of the duck until it inflates like a balloon, then tying tightly around the neck and hanging it in a special drying chamber before cooking so that the skin cannot fail to achieve the right crackling crispness.

Chef Lai Tai, smiling, amiable, in perfect control of a busy kitchen and numerous chefs, invited me behind the scenes and let me help cook some of the dishes we were to have for lunch, among them deep-fried fish pieces in a batter of extreme lightness; lemon chicken; stir-fried prawns with walnuts. He insisted that I try some of each dish then and there rather than wait until they reached the table.

A visit to the central market in Hong Kong was enough to make my head spin, there was such variety. One can purchase anything there, from dozens of different vegetables and fruits to all sorts of meat and seafood including enormous tiger prawns, eels, snakes and live turtles.

But this fairly recent experience was not my first introduction to Chinese food. It has always been a part of my life.

I grew up in Eastern countries with sizable Chinese populations and the opportunity to know good Chinese food. To help matters along, the man I married is really keen on Chinese food — not just eating it, but cooking it. He would pursue recipes with the singlemindedness of a bloodhound and so it came about that between us we learned a great deal about a cuisine neither of us was born into.

There are many regional varieties of cooking in a country as vast as China, but there are five major styles. The Peking or Shantung style of cooking emphasises delicacy of flavour; Szechwan food is hot and spicy; Honan cooking is spicy, sweet and sour; the Fukien school of cooking is famous for its clear soups, seafood dishes and subtlety of flavouring; Cantonese cooking, best known in Western countries, is a combination of many styles, with an emphasis on stir-fried dishes and subtle flavours, and is light and digestible because less fat is used than in other styles of cooking. It is Cantonese cooking that excels in the steamed dumplings of various kinds that are known as *dim sum.*

The reason Cantonese food is best known abroad is because in the nineteenth century it was from Canton, in the south of China, that large numbers of Chinese emigrated to America, Europe and Southeast Asia and introduced their cooking to these regions. It became immensely popular and has remained so to this day.

A feature of Chinese food is the variety of ingredients used. This is not because the Chinese were in search of exotic foods (though in the palaces this may have been their primary aim), but because they had to be resourceful and use everything edible in order to survive. So they made use of ingredients like dried wood fungus and lily buds, lotus seed and lotus root, fish's maw and all kinds of meat, seafood and vegetables. Bird's nest soup is perhaps the most widely known preparation featuring an unusual ingredient. These nests are not made from twigs but from the saliva of tiny swifts and have the reputation of being very nourishing. Because the nests have to be gathered from sheer, almost inaccessible cliffs and require soaking and a lot of careful cleaning, the soup is served as a prestige course at banquets. Its presence on the menu proclaims that the host and his cooks have gone to a lot of trouble. When a special banquet is held it would not be a compliment to the guests if the menu did not include rare and expensive treats.

By contrast, everyday Chinese cooking is easy and the recipes in this chapter are within the scope of the housewife who does not have all day to spend in the kitchen.

Once the basic methods of cutting, chopping and seasoning are learned, anyone can turn out excellent Chinese food. There are no complex sauces, no tricky techniques, no mysterious procedures that will need the skill of a master chef. Anyone really interested can learn from simply expressed recipes the cooking methods and distinctive seasonings, and turn out delicious Oriental dishes in a Western kitchen.

COOKING A CHINESE MEAL

The cooking methods employed by the Chinese are those that are familiar in the West: boiling, braising, deep frying, steaming and roasting. In addition, there is stir frying, which means stirring and tossing ingredients in very little oil over high heat. It does mean that all the preparation must be done before the cooking starts, and all ingredients are cut into pieces of even size and shape. The method was evolved to conserve fuel, and because of the small size of the pieces of food, the cooking time is often only 5 minutes from start to finish, but everything must be ready before cooking is started, the seasonings measured out and put within easy reach, because a delay while ingredients are cooking could mean a disappointing result. Ingredients are added in a certain order, those which take longest to cook being put in first. With a little practice, this split-second timing becomes second nature. This type of cooking is not for doing ahead. It is better to let guests wait for such a dish, rather than the other way around, because if the food has to wait it will continue cooking in its own heat and the effect will be spoilt. A great deal depends on texture in Chinese food and the vegetables must be crisp, the meat or fish just cooked and juicy, never overdone or dry.

SERVING AND EATING A CHINESE MEAL

A Chinese meal does not feature one main dish, but a number of dishes of equal importance. A formal banquet is served as a succession of courses with pauses in between for drinking, conversation and playing games, which explains how diners can partake of ten or more courses. At family meals, or informal entertaining, all the dishes are placed on the table at once. This makes it unnecessary for the hostess to leave the table once the meal has started.

Rice, of course, is always the basis of the meal — plain white steamed rice of the short or medium grained varieties, cooked without salt. Fried rice is not usually served with meals, but is a snack in itself, composed of cold cooked rice and other ingredients. Leftover rice is ideal.

Each place-setting includes a bowl, chopsticks and porcelain spoon, cups for wine or tea and a small plate which doubles as a saucer under the eating bowl and also acts as a bone plate. It is considered quite polite to extricate bones from the mouth, using chopsticks, and put them on a bone plate. A small sauce dish is also part of the individual setting for meals that require a dipping sauce.

Table decorations are not part of the setting, even at banquets. It is the food that takes pride of place and commands attention.

When first choosing a menu for a Chinese meal, do not attempt more than one stir-fried dish. Instead, choose a braised dish, perhaps a cold hors d'oeuvre to start, a roasted dish, soup and a cold dish such as chicken with oyster sauce.

Desserts are not a part of Chinese meals for everyday eating, but a special meal finishes with a sweet such as almond jelly or fresh fruit.

UTENSILS

A Chinese kitchen usually has a 'bench' fireplace along one wall, with holes in the bench top to hold the *woks* above the direct heat, most often supplied by wood fires. In restaurants they use fierce gas jets to provide the quick and flexible heat required in many Chinese cooking methods.

Almost every Chinese dish can be prepared in a Western kitchen using Western equipment, but here I would urge that you acquire a *wok*, rather than make do with a frying pan or saucepan, because it is really a remarkably versatile utensil.

THE WOK: If I had to choose one cooking pan to be marooned on a desert island with, I'd choose a *wok!* It would cope with any kind of food that happened to be available. In it you can boil, braise, fry, boil and steam, and while you can do all these things in pans you already possess, the *wok* is almost indispensable for the stir-frying technique that many Chinese dishes call for.

You can use a large, deep frying pan, but I have cooked stir-fried dishes in a deep frypan side by side with a *wok* and I would say without hesitation that the *wok* is a winner every time. Because of its rounded shape and high, flaring sides you can toss with abandon and stir fry ingredients without their leaping over the sides; and because the *wok* is made of thin iron you get the quick, high heat so necessary in Chinese cooking.

Though a *wok* is best used with gas, it is possible to get good results from electricity. Because quick, high heat is required in stir frying, turn the hot-plate being used on to the highest heat and place the *wok* directly on it; it is possible to buy *woks* with a flat base for more contact, or, invest in an electric *wok* where the heating element is built right into the pan. The 30-35 cm (12-14 inch) *wok* is most useful. You can cook small quantities in a large *wok,* but not vice versa.

The *wok* made of stainless steel is a modern innovation, but a modestly priced iron *wok* heats up quickly and evenly and, if you remember to dry it well after washing, it will not rust. The handles get rather hot, but I've found that winding two or three layers of insulating tape around them keeps the handles comfortable to hold and is a wise precaution if, like me, you are forgetful enough to grab hot handles without grabbing a pot holder first.

Before use, an iron *wok* must be seasoned. Prepare it by washing thoroughly in hot water and detergent. Some *woks,* when new, have a lacquer-like coating, which must be removed by almost filling the *wok* with water, adding about 2 tablespoons bicarbonate of soda and boiling for about 15 minutes. This softens the coating and it can be scrubbed off with a fine scourer. If some of the coating still remains, repeat the process until the *wok* is free from any lacquer on the inside. To season the new *wok*, dry it well, put over gentle heat and, when the metal heats up, wipe over the entire inner surface with a wad of absorbent kitchen paper dipped in peanut oil. Repeat a number of times with more oil-soaked paper until paper remains clean. Allow to cool. Your *wok* is now ready for use.

After cooking in it, do not scrub the *wok* with steel wool or abrasives of any kind. Soak in hot water

to soften any remaining food, then rub gently with a sponge or dish mop, using hot water and detergent. This preserves the surface. Make sure the *wok* is quite dry, because if moisture is left in the pan it will rust. Heat the *wok* gently to ensure complete dryness, then rub over the inside surface with a lightly oiled paper. A well-used *wok* will soon turn black, but this is normal — and the more a *wok* is used, the better it is to cook in.

CHOPPING KNIVES AND BOARDS: You may use a good kitchen knife, but once you have become accustomed to a razor-sharp Chinese chopper, you'll never want to use anything else. Choppers may look clumsy with their wide blade, but the corner of the blade can do anything the point of a knife can do. A chopper is the best thing for slicing, shredding, chopping or dicing. As an extra bonus, its big blade can be used to carry cut ingredients from chopping block to cooking pan. It is wise to have both a chopper and a cleaver, the cleaver being thicker and heavier and intended for chopping through bones, a technique used widely in Chinese cooking, while the chopper with its thin blade does the more delicate jobs with ease and precision.

Use the chopper and cleaver on a wooden block or board. I do not recommend laminated chopping boards, whatever kind of knife you use. Young homemakers often succumb to their attractive appearance, but when you get down to serious cooking there's nothing to take the place of a solid wooden chopping board. Wood is safer too because the surface is not smooth and slippery.

OTHER UTENSILS: The Chinese use steamers of bamboo and aluminium, but these are not strictly essential because it is easy enough to improvise a steamer. Steaming can be done in any covered pot large enough to accommodate a plate placed on a rack or a bowl to hold it well above the level of the boiling water. The plate should be of a size that will allow free circulation of steam around and above it. The food to be cooked is put on the plate, the pot covered with a well-fitting lid, and there you have a perfectly adequate steamer.

Chinese bamboo steamers are particularly suitable for steaming buns or dumplings, for the natural perforations of the lid allow excess steam to escape and not gather inside (as they do on a metal lid) and drop back on to the buns, making them wet and spoiling their appearance. Overcome this problem by putting buns and *dim sum* on a perforated rack over boiling water, cover the pan with a clean cloth folded double and then a lid. The cloth prevents steam gathering on the lid and falling back on to the buns.

Chinese ladles and frying spoons *(wok chan)* are useful but not strictly neccessary if you have other utensils that will do the job. Any kind of ladle can be used for dipping out stock, and I have found that the curved, slotted spatula available so cheaply from hardware departments or chain stores is ideal for tossing and stir frying and for lifting food from deep oil.

Chinese frying spoons of finely twisted wire mesh are useful. So too is a large wire spoon that can cope with a whole fish, lifting it out of the oil with ease — a consideration if you like cooking whole fish.

Long wooden cooking chopsticks are also useful, especially for separating noodles as they cook, and for a variety of other purposes from beating eggs to stirring ingredients.

YOUR CHINESE SHELF

agar-agar, strands or powder
bamboo shoot, canned
barbecue sauce (optional)
black beans, salted and canned
chilli oil
chilli sauce
Chinese mushrooms, dried
chow chow preserves
five-spice powder
hoi sin sauce
lily buds, dried
lotus nut paste, canned
lotus root, canned
oyster sauce
plum sauce
preserved melon shreds
red colouring powder
sesame oil
sesame paste
soy sauce, dark and light
star anise
straw mushrooms, canned
walnuts, peeled
water chestnuts, canned
wood fungus, dried

In addition to these ingredients, which have a long shelf life, there are the essential fresh ingredients that give flavour to Chinese food — fresh ginger root, garlic, Chinese parsley (fresh coriander herb) and spring onions. When required for special dishes, fresh bean sprouts and snow peas can be bought and stored in the refrigerator for one week. Chinese sausages are also useful. Spring roll wrappers and *wonton* pastry keep well in the freezer.

Chinese vegetables

FAN
WHITE RICE

Serves 4-6
500 g (1 lb) short or medium grain rice
3 cups water

If you buy rice in bulk, measure out 2½ cups, which is equivalent to the above. Wash rice if it needs washing and drain well, then put measured water (hot or cold, it does not matter) in saucepan, add rice and bring to the boil over high heat. Let it boil rapidly for a minute or two, then turn heat to medium and cook until holes appear in the rice mass and the surface looks dimpled. Cover pot with a well-fitting lid, turn heat as low as it will go and cook over low heat for a further 10 minutes. Without removing lid turn off heat and let rice sit undisturbed for a further 10 minutes.

CHING CHOONG CHOW FAN
SPRING ONION AND SOY FRIED RICE

Very simple, very good.

Serves: 3-4
2 tablespoons peanut oil
3-4 cups cold cooked rice
1 tablespoon light soy sauce
1 tablespoon mushroom soy sauce
6 spring onions, sliced diagonally

Heat oil in wok until very hot. Add rice and stir fry until grains are all separate and lightly coloured. Sprinkle with sauces and toss to mix evenly. Add sliced spring onions and toss over heat for 1 minute longer. Serve hot.

Note: Vary this recipe to make fried rice as elaborate as you wish so it can be a meal on its own. Add one or more of the following ingredients, which should be fried before combining with the rice: chopped ham or bacon; chopped cooked pork; sliced lap cheong (Chinese sausages); small cooked prawns, shelled; beaten eggs, seasoned; cooked green peas.

CHAI CHOW FAN
VEGETARIAN FRIED RICE

Serves: 6
2 cups short grain rice
2½ cups water
12 dried Chinese mushrooms
2 leeks
4 stalks celery
250 g (8 oz) green beans
125 g (4 oz) bean sprouts, optional
1 cup coarsely grated carrot
1 cup sliced bamboo shoot, optional
3 tablespoons peanut oil
1 tablespoon sesame oil
1 teaspoon finely grated fresh ginger
2 cloves garlic, finely grated
1 cup chopped spring onions
½ cup mushroom liquid
2 tablespoons light soy sauce
salt to taste

Cook rice in water the day before required, or cook some hours ahead (see above) and allow to cool. With the fingers, separate grains and spread out rice so grains dry. Refrigerate.

Soak mushrooms in hot water for 30 minutes, then squeeze out as much liquid as possible and reserve liquid. With a sharp knife cut off and discard stems, cut mushroom caps into thin slices. Wash leeks very well in cold water, making sure all grit is washed away, then cut into thin slices. Use the white portion and only 5-7 cm (2-3 inches) of the green leaves. String celery and green beans and cut into very thin diagonal slices. Wash and drain bean sprouts and pick off any brown tails.

Heat peanut oil and sesame oil in a large wok or very large frying pan, add ginger and garlic and fry, stirring well, for 30 seconds. Add mushrooms, leeks, celery, beans and carrots and stir fry over high heat for 3 minutes. Add bean sprouts and bamboo shoot and fry 1 minute longer. Add rice, toss and fry over high heat until heated through. Add spring onion. Mix mushroom liquid and soy sauce together, and sprinkle evenly over the rice. Continue stirring to mix well together and season to taste with salt. Serve hot.

GAI SEE FUN GUEN
STEAMED RICE BUNDLES WITH CHICKEN AND MUSHROOMS

Serves: 8-10
500 g (1 lb) medium grain rice
4 cups water
2 tablespoons light soy sauce
3 teaspoons sesame oil
6 dried Chinese mushrooms
1 tablespoon dark soy sauce
2 teaspoons sugar
2 chicken breasts
250 g (8 oz) barbecued pork
1 clove garlic, crushed
½ teaspoon finely grated fresh ginger
1 teaspoon salt
½ cup mushroom water
2 teaspoons cornflour
dried bamboo, corn or lotus leaves

Put rice into saucepan with water, light soy sauce and 1 teaspoon of sesame oil. Bring to the boil quickly, then turn heat very low, cover and cook for 15 minutes.

While rice cooks soak mushrooms in hot water for 30 minutes. Reserve soaking liquid. Cut off and discard stems, slice the caps and put them into a saucepan with ¾ cup of the soaking water, the dark soy sauce, remaining 2 teaspoons sesame oil and the sugar. Cover and simmer for 10 minutes.

Bone chicken breasts and cut flesh into small dice. Dice pork. Add chicken and pork to saucepan with garlic, ginger and salt and about half a cup more of the soaking water and mix with the mushrooms. Cover and simmer 5 minutes longer. Thicken gravy with cornflour mixed with a little cold mushroom liquid, then remove from heat and allow to cool to lukewarm. Mix gently through the rice. Take ¾ cup portions and put on 4 overlapping bamboo leaves, or 1 lotus leaf which has been soaked in cold water to soften. Wrap securely and tie with string. Steam for 25 minutes and serve warm, cold or reheated.

Note: If leaves are not available, form into parcels with foil.

DAHN MIN
EGG NOODLES

Perhaps the most popular noodles, these are made of wheat flour and are sold in 450-500 g (1 lb) packets, each packet consisting of seven or eight bundles. An important point about cooking them is that the bundles of noodles must be soaked in hot water for about 10 minutes first. This is not mentioned in the cooking instructions, yet it does make cooking them so much easier. As the bundles soften the strands spread and separate and the noodles cook more evenly than when they are dropped straight into boiling water.

A spoonful of oil in the water prevents boiling over. When water returns to the boil, cook fine noodles for 2-3 minutes, wide noodles for 3-4 minutes. Do not overcook. Drain immediately in a large colander, then run cold water through the noodles to rinse off excess starch and cool the noodles so they don't continue to cook in their own heat. Drain thoroughly. To reheat, pour boiling water through noodles in colander. Serve with stir-fried dishes or use in soups and braised noodle dishes.

HO FUN
RICE NOODLES

There are various kinds of rice noodles. Depending on the type of noodle and thickness of the strands, they have to be soaked in cold water for 30 minutes to 1 hour or longer. Drain, drop into fast boiling water and boil 6-10 minutes, testing every minute after the first 6 minutes so you will know when they are done. As soon as they are tender, drain in a colander and rinse well in cold running water. Drain once more. If well rinsed so that no excess starch remains on the noodles, they can be prepared beforehand, then fried or heated in soup before serving.

MI FUN
RICE VERMICELLI

Rice vermicelli has very fine strands and cooks very quickly. Drop into boiling water and cook for 2 or 3 minutes only. Drain well. Serve in soups or with dishes that have a good amount of sauce. Or, if a crisp garnish is required (for example, a base for presenting prawn fritters or other hot hors d'oeuvres) use rice vermicelli straight from the pack and fry small amounts at a time in deep hot oil for just a few seconds. It will puff and become white as soon as it is immersed in oil, but make sure the oil is hot enough. Lift out quickly on a slotted spoon or wire strainer, drain on absorbent paper.

FUN SEE
CELLOPHANE OR BEAN STARCH NOODLES

Also known as transparent noodles, bean threads, silver threads, spring rain noodles, harusame or fenszu. For a crisp garnish fry in the same way as rice vermicelli, straight from the packet. For use in soups or braised dishes, soak 20 minutes in hot water, drain, then cook in boiling water 15 minutes or until tender.

E MIN
SOFT FRIED NOODLES

Boil and drain noodles as described for dahn min (egg noodles, page 373). When noodles are well drained, spread them on a large baking tray lined with kitchen paper and allow them to dry in the air for at least 30 minutes. A little peanut oil may be sprinkled over them to prevent sticking.

Heat 2 tablespoons each of peanut oil and sesame oil in a wok or frying pan and when very hot add a handful of noodles. When golden on one side, turn and fry other side. Repeat with remaining noodles. It may be necessary to add more oil to the pan if a large quantity of noodles is being fried, but make sure the fresh oil is very hot before adding noodles.

Serve with beef, pork, poultry or vegetable dishes, or combine with stir-fried ingredients for chow mein.

CHOW MIN
CRISP FRIED NOODLES

Rice vermicelli and cellophane noodles can be fried in deep hot oil straight from the packet. Egg noodles need to be cooked first, then well drained and spread on a large baking tray lined with paper towels to dry for at least 30 minutes. A little peanut oil can be sprinkled over them to prevent sticking.

Heat peanut oil in a wok and deep fry noodles in handfuls until crisp and golden brown. These crisp noodles are used mainly as a garnish.

YOOK NUP FUN SEE
CELLOPHANE NOODLES WITH PORK

In Szechwan tradition, this dish is seasoned with hot bean sauce. If this is not available make your own substitute by using an equal amount of canned salted yellow beans, rinsing them briefly in a fine strainer, then mashing with a fork and stirring in 1 teaspoon Chinese chilli sauce to each tablespoon of beans.

Serves: 4-6
125 g (4 oz) cellophane noodles
4 dried Chinese mushrooms
185 g (6 oz) pork
1 tablespoon Chinese wine or dry sherry
1 tablespoon light soy sauce
1 teaspoon salt
¾ cup light stock (page 416) or water
1 teaspoon cornflour
3 tablespoons oil for frying
4 spring onions, finely chopped
2 teaspoons finely grated fresh ginger
2 tablespoons hot bean sauce (see Glossary)
1 large fresh red chilli or red capsicum, seeded and finely chopped
2 tablespoons chopped fresh coriander leaves

Put the noodles in a large bowl, pour over boiling water to cover, then leave 10 minutes or until soft and transparent. Strain and cut into short lengths with a sharp knife. Soak mushrooms in hot water for 30 minutes, squeeze dry, discard stems, dice finely. Cut pork into small dice. Mix all sauce and seasoning ingredients together in a small bowl.

Heat a wok over high heat, add oil and swirl around wok. When oil is hot add the pork and mushrooms and stir fry until cooked and brown. Add spring onions and ginger, stir for a few seconds, then add bean sauce and red chilli and cook over medium heat for a minute or until the mixture looks and smells cooked.

Add the seasonings and sauce mixture and stir until it comes to the boil, then add noodles and simmer, stirring until all the liquid has cooked down. Stir in coriander leaves and serve at once. If liked, garnish with a chilli flower and extra coriander leaves.

NGAU YOOK DAU KOK CHOW MI FUN
RICE VERMICELLI WITH BEEF AND LONG BEANS

Serves: 4-5
250 g (8 oz) rice vermicelli
375 g (12 oz) lean steak
375 g (12 oz) long beans
3 tablespoons peanut oil
1 clove garlic, crushed
½ teaspoon finely grated fresh ginger
1 cup beef stock (page 417)
1 teaspoon salt
2 tablespoons light soy sauce
few drops chilli oil, optional

Soak rice vermicelli in a large bowl of cold water for 10 minutes. Slice beef very thinly, cut beans into 5 cm (2 inch) lengths. Heat oil in wok, stir fry beans for 2 minutes, remove from wok. Add garlic, ginger and beef, stir fry until beef changes colour, then add stock, salt and soy sauce. Add well-drained rice vermicelli and toss until heated through. Cover and cook on fairly low heat for 3 minutes. Return beans to wok, toss with other ingredients for 1 minute and serve at once. Chilli oil can be served separately for sprinkling on individual servings.

JAHP WUI CHOW MIN
COMBINATION CHOW MEIN

Chow mein, a popular dish in Western countries, is sometimes made with crisp-fried noodles to pander to Western preference, but the authentic recipe calls for soft-fried noodles combined with other ingredients. A delicious way of using leftovers. The quantities are only a guide — use what you have on hand.

Serves: 6
6 bundles (about 500 g or 1 lb) fine egg
  noodles
peanut oil for frying
1 clove garlic, crushed
½ teaspoon finely grated fresh ginger
1 cup sliced barbecued pork (page 403)
1 cup diced cooked chicken
½ cup sliced abalone
1 cup sliced white Chinese cabbage or
  mustard cabbage
1 cup bean sprouts, washed and drained
8 spring onions, cut in 5 cm (2 inch)
  lengths
1 cup sliced bamboo shoot
½ cup light stock (page 416) or water
2 tablespoons light soy sauce
2 teaspoons cornflour
2 tablespoons cold water

Cook noodles and soft fry as described on page 374. Remove from wok and keep warm. Heat 2 tablespoons peanut oil in a wok and fry the garlic and ginger for a few seconds. Add pork, chicken, abalone, cabbage, bean sprouts, spring onions and bamboo shoot. Stir fry for a minute or two until heated through. Push ingredients to side of wok.

Add stock and soy sauce, bring to the boil, then stir in cornflour mixed smoothly with cold water. Stir until it boils and thickens, mix in the meat and vegetables and serve immediately over the fried noodles.

CHOY YUEN HAR KAU CHOW MI FUN
RICE VERMICELLI WITH PRAWNS AND CHINESE CABBAGE

Serves: 3-4
250 g (8 oz) rice vermicelli
6 leaves white Chinese cabbage or
   mustard cabbage (wong bok or gai choy)
250 g (8 oz) shelled raw prawns
3 tablespoons peanut oil
1 clove garlic, crushed
1 teaspoon finely grated fresh ginger
1 tablespoon Chinese wine or dry sherry
1 teaspoon salt
1 tablespoon light soy sauce
½ cup fish or chicken stock (page 416)

Soak vermicelli 10 minutes in hot water. Drain in colander. Wash cabbage leaves and slice into thin strips. De-vein prawns and, if they are large, cut in two lengthways. Mix together the garlic, ginger, wine, salt, soy and stock.

Heat a wok, sprinkle oil around side of pan and when it reaches the centre and is thoroughly hot add the prawns, stir fry until they change colour, then transfer to a bowl. Let the oil regain its heat, add the sliced cabbage and stir fry for 1 minute. Add the mixed liquids and cook for a further 2 minutes. Add rice vermicelli to pan and toss until heated through. Return prawns, toss to mix well, then serve at once.

YAU PAO YIU GOR YUE KOW
QUICK BOILED FISH WITH FRIED CASHEWS

Serves: 4-6
1 whole snapper or other white fish
   about 1.5 kg (3 lb)
salt

For cooking fish:
1 large onion, sliced
2 stalks celery with leafy tops
1 large carrot, quartered
6 thin slices fresh ginger
½ cup Chinese wine or dry sherry
½ teaspoon whole black peppercorns
1 large chicken stock tablet

For dressing fish:
¼ cup oil for frying
½ cup raw cashews, divided into halves
60 g (2 oz) fat barbecued pork
1 tablespoon dark soy sauce
2 teaspoons sesame oil
2 spring onions, cut in thin diagonal slices

Clean and scale fish, but leave head and tail on. Dip a piece of dampened paper towel in coarse salt and clean out the cavity of the fish carefully, washing away all traces of blood. Trim sharp spines with kitchen scissors.

Into a large wok pour enough water to cover the fish, but don't add the fish yet. Add onion, celery, carrot, ginger, wine or sherry, peppercorns and stock tablet. Bring slowly to the boil and allow to simmer for 5 minutes to develop flavour, then bring to a fast boil and add the fish. After water comes to the boil again, lower heat and poach gently for 8-10 minutes or until fish is cooked (test by flaking at thickest part — fish should be milky white and opaque when done). Turn off heat, carefully lift fish out with two large frying slices, allow excess liquid to drain for a few seconds, then put fish on a warm platter.

Dressing and garnish: Heat oil in a wok and fry cashews over medium heat until pale golden. Lift out and drain on absorbent paper. Pour remaining oil into a heatproof bowl and set aside. In same wok fry the fatty barbecued pork cut into small pieces, stirring frequently until they are crisp. Pour off fat that has collected in wok, return 3 tablespoons of oil in which cashews were fried and heat gently. Combine soy sauce and sesame oil and spoon over fish. Quickly pour over the hot oil from the wok. Garnish with sliced spring onions, crisp pork and cashew nuts and serve immediately accompanied by white rice.

Note: The stock from cooking the fish can be strained and served as a soup with the addition of some winter melon or fuzzy melon pieces, cooked until tender but still crisp, or 2 squares of bean curd cut into tiny dice and heated through.

HO YAU CHANG DAU DEW PIN (squid with green peas in oyster sauce) *recipe page 388*

HO NAN JUM CHOA YUE
BOILED WHOLE SNAPPER, HONAN STYLE

Serves: 4

1 x 750 g (1½ lb) fresh snapper or other
   whole white fish
2 teaspoons salt
2 tablespoons peanut oil
1 teaspoon finely grated fresh ginger
8 spring onions, finely chopped
2 teaspoons sesame oil
2 tablespoons light soy sauce

Scale, clean and wash fish and trim spines and fins but leave head and tail on. Put enough water into a wok or frying pan to cover the fish (but do not add fish yet), bring to the boil with the salt and when boiling lower the fish into it, cover and return to the boil. Reduce heat and cook 5-7 minutes. Remove from liquid and drain well.

Heat peanut oil in a small saucepan and fry ginger and spring onions very gently until soft but not brown. Remove from heat. Add sesame oil and soy sauce. Put fish on a serving dish (on a bed of braised lettuce if liked — see page 412). Spoon the sauce over and serve at once.

HUNG SHIU YUE HAR GUEN
BRAISED FISH AND PRAWN ROLLS

Serves: 4-6

18 raw prawns
750 g (1½ lb) firm white fish fillets
2 tablespoons peanut oil
3 thin slices fresh ginger
¾ cup hot water
1½ tablespoons light soy sauce
2 tablespoons Chinese wine or dry sherry
½ teaspoon sugar
3 spring onions, sliced finely
1 teaspoon arrowroot or cornflour
1 tablespoon cold water

Shell and de-vein prawns. Remove skin and any bones from fish fillets and cut into 18 strips, each large enough to roll round a prawn. Fasten with wooden toothpicks.

Heat peanut oil in wok, add slices of ginger and fry until they turn golden. Add fish rolls and fry for 2 minutes, turning them carefully with chopsticks or tongs. Add hot water, soy sauce, wine and sugar. Cover and simmer for 5 minutes. Remove fish rolls to serving dish, add spring onions and arrowroot mixed with cold water and stir until sauce boils and thickens. Remove slices of ginger and pour sauce over fish. Garnish as desired and serve at once with rice or noodles.

HOI SEEN JEUNG BOON YUE LAU
FISH FILLETS WITH HOI SIN SAUCE

Serves: 3-4

375 g (12 oz) fresh white fish fillets
2 tablespoons oil
1 clove garlic, bruised
1 tablespoon light soy sauce
½ teaspoon finely grated fresh ginger
1 teaspoon hoi sin sauce
spring onions for garnish

Remove skins from fish fillets, wash and dry well on paper towels. Heat oil in wok, fry garlic until golden, remove and discard. Put in the fillets, one at a time, turning after a few seconds and moving to side of wok to make room for the next. When all the fish has been added to the wok sprinkle with soy sauce, cover with lid and simmer for 1 minute. Add ginger to liquid in pan, cover and simmer 1 minute more. Remove from heat, stir hoi sin sauce into gravy. Arrange fish on serving platter, spoon gravy over, garnish with spring onion strips and serve with white rice.

SUEN LAHT CHEUNG BOON YUE
DEEP-FRIED FISH WITH HOT SOUR SAUCE

Serves: 4
500 g (1 lb) firm white fish fillets
½ teaspoon salt
½ teaspoon finely grated fresh ginger
1 egg white, very slightly beaten
oil for frying
cornflour for dusting

Sauce:
1 fresh red chilli
1 fresh green chilli
½ cup canned Chinese pickles
½ cup pickle juice from can
½ cup water
1 tablespoon sugar
½ teaspoon salt
1 tablespoon cornflour

Remove all skin and bone from fish and cut into short finger lengths. Sprinkle with salt lightly and rub with fresh ginger. Mix egg white into the fish. Let stand while making sauce.

Heat about a cup of oil in a wok. Toss pieces of fish in cornflour a few at a time, until lightly but completely coated. Fry a few pieces at a time over medium heat for a few minutes, until just done. Do not overcook the fish or it will become dry. Drain on absorbent paper, pour sauce over and serve immediately with rice.

Sauce: Seed and finely slice chillies, shred pickles into fine strips. Heat pickle juice, water, sugar and salt in a small saucepan and when boiling stir in cornflour mixed with cold water and stir until thickened and clear. Stir in pickles and chillies, set aside, keeping warm.

GWOO LO YUE LAU
CRISP-SKIN FISH WITH SWEET SOUR SAUCE

Serves: 3-4
1 x 750 g (1½ lb) whole snapper
1 teaspoon salt
½ teaspoon five spice powder
oil for frying
1 egg, beaten
¼ cup cornflour

Sweet Sour Sauce:
1 carrot
3 tablespoons frozen peas
1 small onion
1 tablespoon light soy sauce
1 tablespoon Chinese wine or dry sherry
3 tablespoons tomato sauce
2 tablespoons vinegar
2 tablespoons sugar
¾ cup water
1 tablespoon cornflour
3 tablespoons cold water
2 tablespoons peanut oil
1 clove garlic, crushed
¼ teaspoon finely grated fresh ginger
2 tablespoons preserved melon shreds, optional

Clean and scale fish, but leave head and tail on. Wash well and wipe dry with paper towels. Slash flesh of fish diagonally on both sides and then slash in opposite direction to form diamond shapes. Mix salt and five spice powder together and rub well into all surfaces of the fish, including slashes. Now prepare sauce.

Sweet Sour Sauce: Peel carrot, cut into thin slices, and bring to the boil in a little lightly salted water. Add the peas, boil for 2 minutes, drain and drop into cold water to set the colour. Peel the onion, cut into quarters lengthways, then cut each quarter across into two. Separate layers of onion.

Combine soy sauce, wine, tomato sauce, vinegar, sugar and water and stir until sugar dissolves. Mix cornflour smoothly with the cold water. Heat oil, add garlic, ginger and prepared vegetables and fry for 2 minutes. Add combined sauce mixture, bring to the boil, then stir in cornflour and cook, stirring until thickened. Remove from heat and stir in melon shreds. Keep warm while frying fish.

To fry fish: Heat oil in a wok or frying pan and while it heats, dip fish into beaten egg and then into cornflour, making sure all surfaces are coated. When oil is smoking hot, dust off excess cornflour and lower fish gently into the wok. With a ladle pour oil over the uppermost side of the fish. Fry for 4 minutes, then turn fish and continue to cook, spooning the oil over. Fish should be cooked through in 8-10 minutes. Drain on absorbent paper, put on dish and serve at once, accompanied by a bowl of the sweet sour sauce.

SZE CHUEN YAU JAR YUE
DEEP-FRIED FISH, SZECHWAN STYLE

Serves 4 as a main dish
4 whole firm white-fleshed fish about
 375 g (12 oz) each
2 tablespoons Chinese wine or dry sherry
2 tablespoons light soy sauce
2 teaspoons cornflour
1 tablespoon cold water
2 tablespoons dark soy sauce
2 tablespoons Chinese wine or sherry
1 teaspoon sugar
oil for frying
1 tablespoon finely grated fresh ginger
5 cloves garlic, finely chopped or grated
2 tablespoons hot bean sauce (see
 Glossary)
1 cup water
4 spring onions, finely chopped

Clean the fish thoroughly, leaving head and tail on. Trim spines with kitchen scissors. Wash well and dry on paper towels. With a sharp knife or chopper score the fish vertically, making parallel cuts about a finger's width apart and almost through to the bone to allow seasonings to penetrate. Combine wine and light soy and marinate the fish in the mixture, making sure it goes in all the cuts.

Mix cornflour with cold water, then stir in dark soy, wine and sugar. Set aside.

Heat half cup oil in a wok or large frying pan until very hot. Drain away any excess marinade, add the fish (two at a time should fit in a 35 cm or 14 inch wok) and deep fry about 3 or 4 minutes on each side or until the fish is dark brown. Turn fish once only when cooking. Drain on slotted spoon and put fish on a heated serving platter. Pour off oil in wok, but leave about 4 tablespoons and fry the ginger and garlic over medium heat, stirring constantly, until garlic starts to turn golden. Add the bean sauce and stir, then add water. Stir the sauce ingredients once more to distribute the cornflour evenly, add to wok and stir constantly until mixture comes to a boil, clears and thickens. Add spring onions and stir well. Pour sauce over fish and serve immediately with white rice.

FUN YUE
FRAGRANT FRIED FISH

A popular way of preparing fish, it is easy because it may be prepared well beforehand, unlike most fish dishes. It should be served at room temperature.

Serves: 6
1 kg (2 lb) firm white fish fillets
3 spring onions, finely chopped
1 tablespoon finely grated fresh ginger
1 teaspoon five spice powder
6 tablespoons light soy sauce
2 tablespoons Chinese wine or dry sherry
¼ teaspoon salt
2 teaspoons vinegar
½ cup fish stock (page 416)
2 teaspoons sugar
1 cup water
2 tablespoons sugar
oil for frying

Remove any small bones from the fillets. If they are large divide them in two, then cut crossways into finger width slices. Take one teaspoon each of the chopped spring onions and ginger and put into a deep plate for marinating the fish. Mix in the five spice powder, soy sauce, wine or sherry and salt. Add the fish to this marinade, mix well, cover and chill for 3 hours or longer. Just before starting to cook drain the fish well, squeezing out excess moisture. To the marinade add vinegar, stock and 2 teaspoons sugar.

Put the water and 2 tablespoons sugar into a saucepan and stir over low heat until sugar is dissolved. Leave simmering on low heat. Heat the oil in a wok and when very hot deep fry the fish pieces, a few at a time, for 1 minute or until they are golden. Remove from the oil on draining spoon and put into the simmering syrup. Add more pieces of fish to the oil and just before they are ready, remove fish from the syrup with another draining spoon, then add the next batch of fried fish. Fish should fry very quickly and simmer in the syrup for only a minute. When all the fish has been cooked, discard syrup left in the pan.

Pour off all but 2 tablespoons of oil from the wok, add reserved onion and ginger. Stir fry over medium heat for 1 minute. Add fish pieces and toss gently. Add the reserved marinade mixture, bring to the boil, then remove from heat. Arrange on serving plate, pour juices over and allow to cool to room temperature before serving.

GAI CHOY CHOW HAR KAU (stir-fried prawns with mustard cabbage) *recipe page 384*

SAI LAN FAR CHOW HAR KAU
CORAL AND JADE PRAWNS *(picture page 2)*

Serves: 4
12-16 large raw prawns
1 head firm, fresh broccoli
1 tablespoon peanut oil
½ teaspoon finely grated fresh ginger
¼ teaspoon salt
4 tablespoons water
1 tablespoon Chinese wine or dry sherry
1½ teaspoons cornflour
1 tablespoon cold water
1 tablespoon shredded red ginger
  (see Glossary)

Shell and de-vein prawns, leaving tails on. With point of a sharp knife make a small slit through underside of prawn. Wash broccoli, divide into florets, taking care to keep a length of tender green stalk on each piece. If florets are large, slice with a sharp knife, cutting through stem as well. Pass the end of the stem through the slit in the underside of the prawn so that the floret rests within the curve of the prawn.

Heat wok, add oil and when oil is hot add ginger and prawns threaded with broccoli. Stir fry for 2 minutes. Add salt, water and wine, reduce heat to simmer, cover and cook for 3 minutes. Push prawns to side of wok, add cornflour mixed with water, stir until thick. Serve at once, garnished with shredded red ginger and accompanied by white rice.

CHING CHOW HO YAU HAR YAN
STIR-FRIED PRAWNS WITH OYSTER SAUCE

Serves: 3-4
250 g (8 oz) raw prawns
2 tablespoons oil
1 clove garlic, crushed
½ teaspoon finely grated fresh ginger
1 tablespoon oyster sauce
2 tablespoons Chinese wine or dry sherry
½ cup fish stock (page 416) or water
2 teaspoons cornflour
1 tablespoon cold water

Shell and de-vein prawns. Heat oil. Fry garlic and ginger on low heat until soft and golden. Add prawns and stir fry on medium heat until colour changes. Add sauce, wine or sherry, stock or water and bring to the boil. Cover and simmer 2 minutes, then stir in the cornflour mixed with the cold water and cook, stirring, until liquid thickens and becomes clear. Serve at once with white rice.

If liked, vegetables can be added to this dish. Stir fry about 3 cups mixed vegetables or just one kind, cut into bite-size pieces, after frying the ginger and garlic. Remove them from pan before adding prawns and return vegetables to pan to reheat after the sauce has been made. Vegetables and prawns must not be overcooked.

GAI CHOY CHOW HAR KAU
STIR-FRIED PRAWNS WITH MUSTARD CABBAGE *(picture page 383)*

Serves: 3-4
250 g (8 oz) large raw prawns
1 Chinese mustard cabbage
2 tablespoons peanut oil
1 clove garlic, crushed
½ teaspoon finely grated fresh ginger
3 tablespoons water
1 tablespoon light soy sauce
1 tablespoon Chinese wine or dry sherry
¼ teaspoon five spice powder
½ teaspoon salt
1½ teaspoons cornflour
1 tablespoon cold water

Shell and de-vein prawns. Cut mustard cabbage into bite-size pieces, using the thick stems and only the tender part of the leaves.

Heat oil in a wok and add garlic, ginger, prawns and mustard cabbage and fry for 2 minutes over high heat, stirring constantly. Add water mixed with soy sauce, wine and seasonings and cover and simmer for 5 minutes. Add cornflour mixed smoothly with cold water and stir until sauce boils and thickens, about 1 minute. Serve at once with rice or noodles.

Note: If buying frozen prawns that are already shelled, 125 g (4 oz) will be sufficient.

SZE CHUEN CHOW HAR KAU
SZECHWAN-STYLE PRAWNS WITH DRIED CHILLIES

I have made this recipe using equal quantities of prawns and cooked shelled crab claws (in large pieces, not flaked), and it has been delicious. If you do it this way, add crab to marinade with the prawns and cook for the same length of time.

Serves: 6
500 g (1 lb) raw prawns
1 cup cold water
½ teaspoon salt
2 teaspoons cornflour
1 tablespoon water
½ egg white, beaten slightly
½ teaspoon salt

Seasonings and Sauce:
8-10 large dried chillies
1 teaspoon cornflour
2 teaspoons cold water
1 tablespoon light soy sauce
2 teaspoons Chinese wine or dry sherry
1½ teaspoons honey or sugar
1 teaspoon white vinegar
½ teaspoon salt
¼ teaspoon black pepper
3 tablespoons oil
2 spring onions, finely chopped
1 teaspoon grated or chopped fresh ginger
2 cloves garlic, crushed

Shell and de-vein prawns, put into a bowl and add cold water and salt. Stir and leave for 2 minutes, then rinse under cold tap for 1 minute. Drain well.

Make the marinade by mixing cornflour with cold water then adding egg white and salt. Add prawns, mix well, leave for 30 minutes.

Prepare seasonings and sauce. Break or cut tops off chillies, shake out and discard seeds. Mix cornflour and water in small bowl, then stir in light soy, wine, honey, vinegar, salt and pepper. Set aside.

Start cooking about 5 minutes before serving, for this is one dish that must be served immediately it is cooked. Heat a wok over medium heat, add the oil and heat again, swirling wok to coat inside with oil. Fry the chillies over medium heat until they are almost black. This takes only a few seconds, and they should be stirred and turned all the while. Remove chillies from wok and drain on absorbent paper.

Drain any excess marinade from prawns, add prawns to wok and stir fry over high heat. The prawns must not be overcooked. Ten to 20 seconds is enough for very small prawns, 35 to 40 seconds for large prawns. Add spring onion, ginger and garlic and stir fry briefly. Stir seasonings mixture again to blend the cornflour smoothly, add to the wok, stirring constantly until cornflour boils and thickens. Turn off heat. Return chillies to the wok, stir to mix and serve immediately with white rice.

Note: For a less hot result, discard oil in which the chillies are fried and heat fresh oil for frying the rest of the ingredients.

HO LAN DAU CHOW HAR KAU
FRIED PRAWN BALLS WITH SNOW PEAS

Serves: 4-6
1 quantity of prawn balls (page 420) with 1 clove garlic, crushed, added
sesame oil, optional
peanut oil for deep frying
250 g (8 oz) snow peas, strings removed
½ cup fish or chicken stock (page 416)
2 teaspoons cornflour
1 tablespoon cold water
1 tablespoon oyster sauce
½ teaspoon sugar

Make prawn ball mixture as described. Lightly grease hands with sesame oil and form mixture into small balls about 2.5 cm (1 inch) in diameter. You can use peanut oil if sesame oil is not available, but sesame oil gives a delightful flavour to the prawns.

Heat oil in a wok or small deep frying pan and, when hot, put in about 4 or 5 of the balls at a time. Fry, turning with a perforated spoon, for about 3 minutes, until golden. Lift out of oil and drain on absorbent paper. Keep warm.

When all the prawn balls are fried, pour off all but 1 tablespoon of the oil in the wok, and on a high heat, toss the snow peas in the oil until they turn bright green. This takes about 1½ minutes. Push peas to side of pan, pour in stock, add cornflour mixed with water and cook, stirring, until clear and thickened, about 1 minute. Stir in oyster sauce and sugar. Stir in snow peas. Arrange prawn balls on a dish, spoon snow peas and sauce over and serve immediately.

Note: This dish cannot be made with cooked prawns. If snow peas are not available, substitute sliced broccoli, sliced celery or sliced Chinese mustard cabbage.

SEE JUP GOOK HAI
FRIED CRAB IN BLACK BEAN SAUCE *(picture opposite)*

This is perhaps the most popular shellfish preparation in Chinese restaurants in Australia. To be enjoyed to the fullest the crab should be picked up in the fingers and eaten. That is the only way to make sure all of the delicious, sweet flesh is prised from the shell.

Serves: 4

1 fresh medium-size crab
1 tablespoon canned salted black beans
1 large clove garlic, crushed
1 tablespoon light soy sauce
1 teaspoon sugar
4 tablespoons peanut oil
extra clove garlic, cut in two
2 slices fresh ginger
2/3 cup hot water
2 teaspoons cornflour
1 tablespoon cold water
3 spring onions, chopped
1 egg, slightly beaten

Wash crab well, scrubbing away any mossy patches on the shell. Remove the hard top shell and fibrous tissue or 'dead men's fingers' and also discard stomach bag attached to shell below the eyes. With a heavy cleaver chop body of crab into 4 or 6 pieces, leaving legs attached. Separate large claws from body and crack shell of claws so sauce can penetrate.

Rinse black beans in a strainer under cold water for a few seconds, then drain. Mash beans well and mix well with crushed garlic, soy sauce and sugar.

Heat oil in a wok or large frying pan and fry halved clove of garlic and slices of ginger until they start to brown, then remove from pan. Over high heat fry the pieces of crab, stirring and turning them constantly for 4 or 5 minutes or until shells are bright red. Remove crab pieces from pan. Add black bean mixture to the oil and fry for 1 minute, then add hot water and crab pieces, stir well, cover pan and cook for 3 minutes. Stir in cornflour mixed with cold water, stir until sauce boils and thickens, then add spring onions and egg and stir until egg sets. Serve at once with steamed white rice to soak up the salty sauce.

SEE JIU CHOW LOONG HAR
QUICK-FRIED LOBSTER IN HOT BEAN SAUCE

Serves: 6

500 g (1 lb) raw lobster tails
1 small green or red capsicum
3 tablespoons oil
2 cloves garlic, crushed
½ teaspoon finely grated fresh ginger
1-2 tablespoons hot bean sauce (see Glossary)
salt to taste
½ cup chicken stock (page 416) or water
2 tablespoons Chinese wine or dry sherry
1 egg, beaten
2 teaspoons cornflour
1 tablespoon cold water
few drops sesame oil, optional

Chop lobster tails into sections and remove shells. Remove and discard seeds and centre membrane of capsicum and cut into squares. Heat oil until very hot and fry lobster pieces for 1 minute or until just cooked. Remove from oil. Add capsicum and fry for 1 minute on high heat, remove. Reduce heat, add garlic and ginger to oil and stir fry briefly, add bean sauce and stir for a few seconds. Add salt, stock and wine and bring to the boil, then dribble beaten egg into the sauce, stirring to form shreds.

Mix cornflour smoothly with cold water and stir quickly into the sauce until it boils and thickens. Add sesame oil, return lobster pieces and capsicum and heat through. Serve with white rice.

CHOW LOONG HAR KAU
STIR-FRIED LOBSTER WITH RED SAUCE

Serves: 2-3
250 g (8 oz) raw lobster tails
½ egg white
2 teaspoons Chinese wine or dry sherry
½ teaspoon salt
2 teaspoons cornflour
3 tablespoons oil

Sauce:
1 small clove garlic, crushed
½ teaspoon finely grated fresh ginger
¼ cup tomato sauce
1 teaspoon chilli sauce
¼ cup water
1 tablespoon Chinese vinegar or 2
  teaspoons cider vinegar
2 teaspoons sugar
2 teaspoons cornflour
1 tablespoon cold water
½ cup cooked peas, optional

Chop lobster tails into sections and remove shells. Cut lobster meat into bite-size chunks and marinate in a mixture of slightly beaten egg white, wine or sherry, salt and cornflour. Set aside for 20 minutes. Heat oil in a wok and when very hot put in pieces of lobster and fry, turning to cook all sides. These should be done in about 2-3 minutes, depending on size of lobster chunks. Remove lobster from oil and set aside.

Sauce: Pour off all but about a tablespoon of the oil in which the lobster was fried. On low heat stir fry garlic and ginger until just beginning to turn colour. Add tomato sauce, chilli sauce, water, vinegar and sugar and stir until sugar is dissolved. When sauce boils add the cornflour mixed smoothly with cold water and stir until thickened. Return lobster to wok, add green peas and heat through. Serve immediately with rice.

HO YAU CHANG DAU DEW PIN
SQUID WITH GREEN PEAS IN OYSTER SAUCE *(picture page 379)*

Squid is one of the most subtle of sea foods and is best served with a lightly flavoured vegetable. This dish combines it with tender young peas and a sauce that tastes of the sea.

Serves: 6
500 g (1 lb) tender small squid
1½ cups fresh or frozen peas
2 tablespoons peanut oil
½ teaspoon finely grated fresh ginger
½ cup fish or chicken stock (page 416)
1 teaspoon light soy sauce
1 tablespoon oyster sauce
2 teaspoons cornflour
1 tablespoon cold water

Wash squid well. On chopping board, put blunt edge of knife at point where head joins body and give a tug to separate tentacles and head from body. Cut just where tentacles start and reserve these. Discard head and inside of squid. Slit body of squid lengthwise and if large cut into pieces. Rinse well and on inner surface make shallow slits with sharp knife in a pattern of squares or diamonds. If using frozen peas, thaw.

Heat 1 tablespoon oil in a wok, add ginger and squid and stir fry for 2 or 3 minutes. Turn on to dish. Add remaining oil and toss peas in it for a few seconds, then add stock, soy, and oyster sauce. Stir and allow to come to the boil. Mix cornflour smoothly with cold water and stir into sauce. Return squid and heat through. Serve on a bed of braised lettuce (see page 412).

HO LAN DAU CHOW DAI TZE
SCALLOPS WITH SNOW PEAS

This delicate dish must not be overcooked, so have seasonings measured and cornflour mixed with water in readiness for adding to pan. Serve immediately.

Serves: 2-3
250 g (8 oz) scallops
2 leeks
125 g (4 oz) snow peas
2 tablespoons peanut oil
½ teaspoon finely grated fresh ginger
2 teaspoons cornflour
¼ cup water
1 teaspoon light soy sauce
½ teaspoon salt

Wash scallops and dry well. Wash leeks thoroughly to get rid of all sand and grit. Cut white part of leeks into thin diagonal slices. Remove strings from snow peas.

Heat oil in wok or frying pan and fry the leeks and ginger for 1 minute over medium heat. Add scallops and fry on high heat, stirring, for 1 minute. Add snow peas and toss with other ingredients for just 1 minute longer. Push to side of pan, add cornflour mixed with water and soy sauce and stir until thickened, about 1 minute. Stir in scallops and vegetables, sprinkle with salt and serve immediately.

Note: If leeks are not available, substitute the white part of 10 spring onions cut into 2.5 cm (1 inch) lengths.

CHAN PEI FUN GAI
SMOKED TANGERINE CHICKEN

Serves: 4-5
1 x 1.5 kg (3 lb) roasting chicken
1 tablespoon light soy sauce
1 teaspoon salt
1 teaspoon sugar
1 tablespoon Chinese wine or sherry
1 piece dried tangerine peel about the size
  of a rose leaf
1 whole star anise
3 tablespoons brown sugar
heavy duty foil
fresh coriander leaves to garnish

Wipe chicken inside and out with paper towels. Combine soy, salt, sugar and wine and rub inside and outside the chicken. Allow to marinate for 20 minutes, then put in a steamer and steam for 15 minutes.

In mortar and pestle crush the tangerine peel and star anise as finely as possible and mix with brown sugar. Take a stout saucepan with a well-fitting lid, large enough to hold the whole chicken. Line the base of the pan with heavy duty foil, bringing it a little way up the side of the pan. Sprinkle sugar and spice mixture evenly over foil, then put a trivet or wire rack in pan and put chicken on it. Cover pan tightly, put over medium heat and when smoke starts escaping under lid turn heat very low and smoke chicken for 15 minutes or until done.

This chicken dish can be served hot, at room temperature, or cold. Slice the flesh off the bones and arrange on a platter, or chop through bones into small serving pieces. Garnish with sprigs of coriander.

CHU HAU JEUNG MUN GAI
CHICKEN WITH BARBECUED OYSTERS

Serves: 4-5
500 g (1 lb) chicken breast meat
2 teaspoons cornflour
1 teaspoon five spice powder
1 teaspoon salt
oil for frying
1 clove garlic, crushed
½ cup chicken stock (page 416)
2 teaspoons extra cornflour
2 tablespoons cold water
1 can barbecued oysters

Cut chicken meat into small dice, removing any skin and bones. Toss in a mixture of cornflour, five spice and salt. Heat 2 tablespoons oil in a wok with the garlic for a few seconds. Add chicken and stir fry over high heat for 2-3 minutes or until chicken starts to colour. Push chicken to side of wok, add stock, then stir in extra cornflour mixed with cold water. Stir over medium heat until it boils and thickens, then add oysters and toss all together until heated through. Serve with rice.

LING MOONG GAI
LEMON CHICKEN

Serves: 4-6
1 x 1.5 kg (3 lb) roasting chicken
2 tablespoons dark soy sauce
2 teaspoons finely shredded fresh ginger
1 large lemon
1 cup water
1 tablespoon sugar
1 teaspoon sesame oil
1 teaspoon cornflour
1 tablespoon cold water
spring onions and lemon slices to garnish

Cut chicken into quarters, dry with paper towels and rub with 1 tablespoon of the soy sauce, particularly on the skin. Leave aside while preparing other ingredients.

To shred ginger for this recipe, cut 3 or 4 large thin slices from a knob of fresh ginger which has had the brown skin scraped away. With a sharp knife cut the slices into fine shreds. Peel lemon very thinly, taking only the yellow portion of the rind, none of the white pith. Chop the rind finely. Squeeze lemon and measure ⅓ cup of the juice.

Combine lemon juice, remaining tablespoon soy sauce, water, sugar, sesame oil and lemon rind. Stir to dissolve sugar.

Heat oil in wok, fry chicken pieces skin side down, then turn and brown other side. Add shredded ginger and continue to fry for 1 minute. Add lemon juice mixture, bring to the boil, then turn heat very low, cover and simmer for 15 minutes or until chicken is tender but not falling off the bone. This can be prepared ahead up to this stage, transferred to a dish and left until required. Do not leave it in the metal wok. At serving time return to pan and heat through, lift out chicken and cut into bite-size pieces. Mix cornflour smoothly with cold water, add to sauce in pan and stir until it boils and thickens. Spoon over the chicken, garnish with spring onions and lemon slices and serve with white rice.

HO YAU MUN GAI
COLD CHICKEN IN OYSTER SAUCE

Serves 4 as a main dish, 8-10 as part of an hors d'oeuvre tray
500 g (1 lb) chicken breast or half a roasting chicken
few celery leaves
1 small onion
2 tablespoons honey
1 tablespoon oyster sauce
1 tablespoon light soy sauce
½ teaspoon salt
⅛ teaspoon five spice powder
3 tablespoons finely chopped spring onion
3 teaspoons finely grated fresh ginger
2 tablespoons toasted sesame seeds

Put chicken breasts or half chicken into a saucepan with cold water to cover, celery leaves and onion for flavour, and bring slowly to the boil. Cover and simmer on very gentle heat for 10 minutes, turn off heat and allow to cool in liquid. Take chicken from liquid, remove all skin and bones and slice the meat thinly. Arrange on a plate.

In a bowl mix together the honey, oyster sauce, soy sauce, salt and spice powder, then spoon over the chicken. Cover and leave for 30 minutes. Before serving sprinkle all over with spring onion and ginger mixed together, then with the sesame seed.

Note: To toast sesame seed put into a dry frying pan and shake or stir constantly over medium low heat for 5 minutes or until seeds are golden brown. Remove from pan immediately or they will darken and become bitter.

SZE CHUEN JAR GAI (fried chicken, Szechwan style) *recipe page 393*

YUEN SAI LING JUP LAHNG GAI
COLD LEMON CHICKEN WITH FRESH CORIANDER

Serves 4 as a main dish, 8-10 as part of an hors d'oeuvre tray

500 g (1 lb) chicken breast or half a roasting chicken

few celery leaves

1 small onion

2 tablespoons Chinese lemon sauce

1 tablespoon barbecue sauce or dark soy sauce

3 tablespoons finely chopped fresh coriander leaves and stems

1 teaspoon finely grated fresh ginger

Cook chicken as in preceding recipe. Cool and slice as described. Combine lemon sauce and barbecue sauce or soy sauce. Marinate chicken in this mixture at least 30 minutes, and arrange on serving dish. Sprinkle with finely chopped coriander and ginger mixed together.

MUT JUP MUN GAI YIK
HONEY-SOY BRAISED CHICKEN WINGS

Serves: 5-6

1 kg (2 lb) chicken wings

2 tablespoons peanut oil

⅓ cup dark soy sauce

2 tablespoons honey

2 tablespoons Chinese wine or dry sherry

1 clove garlic, crushed

½ teaspoon finely grated fresh ginger

Cut each chicken wing into 3 pieces and reserve wing tips for stock. Heat oil in wok and fry the larger joints on high heat for 3-4 minutes, or until browned. Add soy, honey, wine, garlic and ginger, stir well. Reduce heat to low, cover and simmer about 30 minutes or until chicken wings are tender. Towards end of cooking stir frequently and make sure the sweet glaze does not burn. Serve warm or at room temperature, either with white rice or as an appetiser.

Note: This recipe can use a whole chicken, cut up, instead of only the wings.

TZE GHEUNG MUN GAI
BRAISED GINGER CHICKEN WITH LILY BUDS

Serves: 4-6

1 x 1 kg (2 lb) chicken

20-30 dried lily buds

1 piece tender fresh ginger

1 clove garlic

pinch salt

10 pieces Szechwan pepper or black peppercorns

2 tablespoons peanut oil

⅓ cup Chinese wine or dry sherry

1 tablespoon honey

¼ cup light soy sauce

1 segment star anise

Cut chicken into bite-size serving pieces. Soak lily buds in hot water for 20 minutes and drain, then pinch off tough stem end and cut buds into 2 or 3 pieces each. Scrape brown skin off ginger and cut into very thin slices, then into fine shreds until you have a tablespoonful. Crush the garlic with a sprinkling of salt. Heat the Szechwan pepper or peppercorns lightly in a dry pan, then crush with pestle or handle of Chinese chopper.

Heat wok, add oil and fry ginger and garlic over low heat just until pale golden. Add chicken pieces, raise heat to medium and fry until chicken changes colour. Add drained lily buds, pepper, wine or sherry, honey, light soy sauce and star anise. Cover and simmer over low heat for 25 minutes, adding a little hot water toward end of cooking if necessary.

HAI YOOK PAR GAI
FRIED CHICKEN WITH CRAB SAUCE

Serves: 4-6
1 small roasting chicken, about 1 kg (2 lb)
1 teaspoon salt
2 teaspoons five spice powder
3 tablespoons cornflour or chestnut flour
about 2 tablespoons cold water
peanut oil for deep frying

Crab Sauce:
125 g (4 oz) crab meat
2 tablespoons peanut oil
½ teaspoon finely grated fresh ginger
6 spring onions, finely sliced diagonally
¾ cup chicken stock (page 416)
pepper to taste
1 egg white, slightly beaten
2½ teaspoons arrowroot or cornflour
1 tablespoon cold water

Cut chicken into serving pieces. Sprinkle with salt and five spice powder combined, rub well into all parts of chicken and leave for 30 minutes (while chicken is marinating, make sauce).

Mix cornflour or chestnut flour with enough cold water to form a thick paste. Heat oil until very hot, dip chicken pieces in the flour paste, drain excess and drop a few pieces at a time into the oil. Fry quickly until chicken changes colour and is cooked. Drain on absorbent paper. When all the chicken has been fried arrange on serving plate, pour sauce over and serve immediately.

Crab Sauce: Flake crab, removing any bony tissue. Heat oil in a small saucepan and fry ginger and spring onions on a low heat for a minute, not allowing them to brown. Add stock, bring to the boil. Add crab meat and season with pepper, and when sauce returns to the boil, dribble in the egg white, stirring with a fork. It will set in shreds similar to chrysanthemum petals. Stir in arrowroot mixed with cold water. Cook, stirring, until clear and thick.

SZE CHUEN JAR GAI
FRIED CHICKEN, SZECHWAN STYLE *(picture page 391)*

Serves: 6
500 g (1 lb) chicken breasts
4 tablespoons cornflour
1 teaspoon salt
½ teaspoon five spice powder
½ cup chicken stock
2 teaspoons sugar
1 tablespoon light soy sauce
½ teaspoon sesame oil
1 teaspoon vinegar
2 teaspoons Chinese wine or dry sherry
extra ¼ teaspoon five spice powder
¼ teaspoon ground black pepper
2 teaspoons cornflour
1 tablespoon cold water
½ cup oil for frying
15 dried red chillies, seeded
2 cloves garlic, finely chopped
2 teaspoons finely chopped fresh ginger
4 spring onions, chopped in 5 cm (2 inch)
   lengths

Bone chicken breasts and cut meat into bite-size pieces. Mix together the cornflour, salt and five spice powder and toss chicken pieces in the mixture, then dust off excess cornflour. Mix stock, sugar, soy, sesame oil, vinegar, wine, five spice and pepper together. In another small bowl mix the cornflour and cold water.

Heat oil in a wok and when very hot add chicken pieces, a third at a time, and fry on high heat, tossing chicken to brown all over. As each batch is fried drain on absorbent paper and let oil return to high heat before adding next batch. When chicken has been fried pour off all but 2 tablespoons of the oil. Add chillies, garlic and ginger and fry until garlic and ginger are golden and chillies turn dark. Add spring onions and toss for a few seconds, then add stock mixture and bring to the boil. Stir the cornflour again to mix smoothly and add to the pan, stirring constantly until it boils and thickens. Add chicken and toss to heat through. Serve immediately with white rice.

TZE BAO GAI
CHICKEN FRIED IN PAPER *(picture opposite)*

Makes approximately 24
500 g (1 lb) chicken breasts
1 teaspoon light soy sauce
2 teaspoons oyster sauce
1 teaspoon sesame oil
1 tablespoon Chinese wine or dry sherry
1 teaspoon sugar
¼ teaspoon salt
1 tablespoon tender ginger shreds
4 spring onions, sliced thinly
24 snow peas, optional
1 packet rice paper
oil for deep frying

Remove skin and bones from chicken breasts and cut meat into thin slices. If slices are long, cut them to bite size. Put chicken into a bowl with sauces, sesame oil, wine, sugar and salt and mix well. Leave for 30 minutes to 1 hour before cooking.

Divide rice paper into squares approximately 13 cm (5 inches) and put filling off centre. Each piece of paper should contain a slice or two of chicken, one or two shreds of ginger, a slice or two of spring onion and, if liked, a snow pea. When snow peas are out of season simply omit them — do not use another vegetable in their place.

Fold up paper as shown, tucking in the flap of the 'envelope' securely. When they are all folded, heat sufficient oil in wok to deep fry the paper-wrapped chicken. When oil is hot put in about 8 envelopes at a time and fry on high heat for about a minute and a half. Lift out with slotted spoon, drain on absorbent paper and when all are fried, serve hot.

Note: When rice paper is used, chicken can be eaten envelope and all, but if rice paper is not obtainable use greaseproof paper. The paper is then opened at the table, using chopsticks, and the contents lifted out and eaten, perhaps with a sauce.

SHIU NG HEUNG GAI
OVEN-ROASTED SPICED CHICKEN

This method of preparation is particularly suitable for chicken drumsticks, thighs or wings. If it is not possible to buy selected joints, a whole chicken can be used. See variation at end of recipe.

Oven temperature: 170-190°C (350-375°F)
Cooking time: 45 minutes to 1 hour
Serves: 6-8
1.5 kg (3 lb) chicken pieces
⅓ cup light soy sauce
¼ cup peanut oil
1 tablespoon Chinese wine or dry sherry
1 clove garlic
½ teaspoon salt
½ teaspoon finely grated fresh ginger
2 teaspoons five spice powder

Wash chicken pieces, dry well on paper towels. In a large shallow dish mix soy sauce, oil and wine. Crush garlic to a pulp with salt and add to soy mixture with ginger and five spice. Mix well. Put chicken joints in marinade and turn to coat all sides. Cover and marinate for 1 hour or more.

Remove chicken from the marinade, put in a roasting pan in one layer and spoon about 2 tablespoons of the marinade over. Roast in a moderate oven for 45 minutes to 1 hour or until chicken is brown and crisp, basting every 20 minutes with the marinade. Serve hot or cold.

Wings need about 45 minutes roasting time, drumsticks from 45-55 minutes and thighs 1 hour. Thighs should be roasted skin side uppermost.

Variation: Make a marinade as above and rub it well all over a 1.75 kg (3½ lb) roasting chicken. Spoon some of the marinade into the cavity of the chicken as well. Marinate for 1 hour, then roast as above, turning the chicken first on one side and then on the other so it is browned all over. Baste frequently. Finish cooking chicken breast upwards. It should take about 1 hour 45 minutes. To serve, carve chicken as for red-cooked chicken (page 396).

TZE BAO GAI (chicken fried in paper) *recipe above*

SEE YO GAI
RED-COOKED CHICKEN

'Red cooking' is the term applied to cooking in dark soy sauce. The liquid that remains after cooking is called a 'master sauce', and can be frozen or refrigerated for future use. It should be used to cook meat or poultry at least once a week to keep it 'alive'. Cook chicken drumsticks this way for taking on picnics or serving at buffet parties. Fragrant with ginger and anise, red-cooked chicken will surely become one of your favourites.

Serves 8-10 as part of a large menu, 4-5 as a main meal with rice

1 x 1.75 kg (3½ lb) roasting chicken
1½ cups cold water
1½ cups dark soy sauce
¼ cup Chinese wine or dry sherry
5 cm (2 inch) piece fresh ginger, peeled
  and sliced
1 clove garlic
10 sections star anise
1½ tablespoons sugar
2 teaspoons sesame oil

Wash chicken well. Choose a saucepan into which the chicken will just fit so that the soy liquid covers as much of the bird as possible. Put chicken into saucepan, breast down, then add all the ingredients except sesame oil. Bring slowly to the boil, then reduce heat, cover and simmer very gently for 15 minutes. Using tongs, turn chicken over, replace lid and simmer 20 minutes, basting breast with liquid every 5 minutes.

Remove from heat and leave covered in the saucepan until cool. Lift chicken out of sauce, put on serving platter and brush with sesame oil. This gives the chicken a glistening appearance as well as extra flavour.

Traditionally the chicken is put on a chopping board and cut in two lengthways with a sharp cleaver. Each half is chopped into 3.5 cm (1½ inch) strips and reassembled in the original shape. If this proves too much of an undertaking, simply carve the chicken into joints. Serve at room temperature with some of the cooking liquid as a dipping sauce.

BAW LAW GAI
CHICKEN WITH PINEAPPLE

Serves: 4-6

Half a small ripe pineapple or 1 x 425 g
  (15 oz) can unsweetened pineapple
250 g (8 oz) chicken breast meat
1 tablespoon cornflour
½ teaspoon salt
½ teaspoon ground Szechwan pepper or
  black pepper
1 tablespoon light soy sauce
2 teaspoons sesame oil
1 small clove garlic, crushed
1 tablespoon peanut oil
6 spring onions, sliced
fresh coriander leaves to garnish

Sauce:
2 teaspoons cornflour
½ cup pineapple juice
1 tablespoon light soy sauce

Skin pineapple, cut away all eyes and cut lengthways into triangular wedges. Trim away core from each wedge, then cut across into slices. Bone and skin the chicken and slice the flesh thinly. Toss chicken meat in a mixture of cornflour, salt and ground pepper until well coated (pulverise Szechwan pepper in mortar and pestle, then pass through a fine sieve, discarding the husks left in the sieve.) Add soy sauce, sesame oil and garlic to chicken and mix well.

Heat peanut oil in a wok, add chicken and fry just until the colour changes. Add pineapple, reduce heat, cover and simmer 3 minutes. Add sauce mixture, stir until thickened, toss in spring onions and mix thoroughly, spoon on to serving dish. Garnish with sprigs of fresh coriander. Serve with rice or noodles.

Sauce: Add pineapple juice gradually to cornflour, mixing until smooth. Stir in soy sauce.

SAI LAN FAR GAI PIN TO YAN
CHICKEN WITH WALNUTS AND BROCCOLI *(picture page 366)*

Serves: 6
750 g (1½ lb) chicken breasts
3 teaspoons cornflour or chestnut flour
½ teaspoon five spice powder
½ teaspoon salt
oil for deep drying
1 cup peeled walnuts (see glossary)
4 tablespoons extra oil
100 g (4 oz) tender broccoli
1½ teaspoons finely grated fresh ginger
1 small clove garlic, crushed
2 tablespoons Chinese wine or dry sherry
1 tablespoon light soy sauce
1 teaspoon sugar
2 teaspoons cornflour
2 tablespoons cold water

Bone chicken breasts and cut flesh into small pieces, about 12 mm (half inch) square. Sift cornflour, five spice and salt over chicken and mix well. Set aside. Heat oil and deep fry walnuts over a moderate heat until golden. Lift out and drain on paper.

Heat 2 tablespoons of the extra oil in wok and quickly stir fry the broccoli over high heat for 3 minutes until barely tender. Lift on to plate. Add remaining oil to wok, fry ginger and garlic for a few seconds, then add chicken and fry, stirring constantly, over a high heat until chicken changes colour (this will take only a minute or two). Add remaining ingredients mixed together and stir over heat until liquid boils and thickens. Remove from heat, mix in walnuts and broccoli and serve immediately.

SEEN GOO GAI LAU TO YAN
CHICKEN AND WALNUTS WITH STRAW MUSHROOMS *(picture page 422)*

Serves: 4
2 whole chicken breasts
3 teaspoons cornflour
1 teaspoon salt
½ teaspoon five spice powder
6 spring onions
1 x 430 g (15 oz) can straw mushrooms
1 canned bamboo shoot
oil for deep frying
1 cup peeled walnuts or blanched almonds
½ cup stock
1 teaspoon light soy sauce
1 teaspoon extra cornflour
1 tablespoon cold water

Remove skin from chicken breasts and with a sharp knife cut flesh from bones. Skin and bones can be simmered in a little water and used for stock. Cut chicken meat into small dice. Combine cornflour, salt and five spice powder and sprinkle over chicken. Toss to coat. Cut spring onions into bite-size lengths. Drain straw mushrooms and cut each mushroom in half. Dice bamboo shoot.

Heat oil and deep fry walnuts or almonds until golden. Drain and set aside. Fry chicken pieces, a third at a time, in deep oil over high heat just until they change colour. This takes about 1 minute for each lot. As they are fried, lift them out with a slotted spoon and drain on absorbent paper.

Pour off all but 2 tablespoons oil. Add vegetables to pan and stir fry over high heat for 1 minute. Add stock. Mix soy and extra cornflour with cold water, add to pan, stir until it thickens. Add chicken pieces and heat through. Turn off heat, stir in nuts and serve immediately with rice or noodles.

SAI LAN FAR GAI PIN HAR KAU
CHICKEN AND PRAWNS WITH BROCCOLI

Serves: 4-6

1 whole chicken breast
375 g (12 oz) shelled raw prawns
½ teaspoon five spice powder
½ teaspoon salt
1 cup broccoli sprigs
2 tablespoons peanut oil
1 clove garlic, crushed
½ teaspoon finely grated fresh ginger
2 teaspoons light soy sauce
1 tablespoon Chinese wine or dry sherry
2 tablespoons chicken stock (page 416) or
   water
1 teaspoon arrowroot or cornflour
2 teaspoons cold water

Bone chicken breast and remove the skin. Slice flesh thinly and mix with five spice powder and salt. De-vein prawns and if very large cut in halves. Mix with chicken and set aside.

Bring a little lightly salted water to the boil and drop in the broccoli sprigs. If there are any thick stems peel away the skin, cut into slices and drop into the water 1 minute before adding the florets. When water returns to the boil cover pot and simmer for 3 minutes, then drain and run cold water over the broccoli. This keeps the colour bright and prevents overcooking.

Heat oil in a wok and add garlic and ginger. Stir fry for 30 seconds, then add chicken and prawns and toss over high heat until chicken turns white and prawns pink. Add soy, wine, stock or water and allow to simmer for 2 minutes. Mix arrowroot smoothly with cold water, add to liquid in pan and stir until it thickens. Add drained broccoli and toss gently to mix and heat through. Serve hot with rice.

SO JAR FOR TUI GAI GUEN
CHICKEN AND HAM ROLLS *(picture page 419)*

Serves: 4-8

2 whole large chicken breasts
1 slice ham 12 mm (½ inch) thick
1 teaspoon salt
¼ teaspoon pepper
¼ teaspoon five spice powder
1 small clove garlic, crushed
2 eggs, beaten
2 tablespoons plain flour
4 spring roll wrappers (see note, page 424)
oil for deep frying

Sauce:
½ cup liquid from Chinese mixed pickles
½ cup water
1 tablespoon tomato sauce or pinch red
   food colouring (see Glossary)
2 tablespoons sugar
1-2 tablespoons white vinegar
¼ teaspoon salt
¼ cup chopped Chinese mixed pickles
2 teaspoons arrowroot
1 tablespoon cold water

With sharp knife remove skin and bones from chicken breasts. Cut each breast in two down the middle. Remove fillets (the small cylindrical pieces of meat that lie next to the bone) and reserve for another recipe. Put large pieces of breast meat between two sheets of plastic or wax paper, and pound until thin using a meat mallet. Meat should be thin; but take care not to tear it. Cut ham into 12 mm (half inch) strips the length of the chicken breasts.

Combine salt, pepper and five spice. Mix garlic clove with quarter teaspoon of the salt and spice mixture and spread each piece of breast with the merest trace of it. Put stick of ham on the chicken and roll up, covering the ham completely and moulding the chicken flesh to seal.

Dip in beaten egg seasoned with half teaspoon salt and spice mixture, then in plain flour. Put diagonally on spring roll wrapper, roll over twice, then enclose corners by folding in, envelope fashion. Seal with a little beaten egg mixed to a thick paste with flour.

Heat oil in wok until it starts to form a haze, but it should not be too hot. Fry rolls over medium heat for 3½ minutes, turning them so they brown evenly. Drain on absorbent paper. Put on serving dish, on a bed of shredded lettuce if liked, and serve with following sauce.

Sauce: Combine first 6 ingredients in a small saucepan, bring to the boil, stirring to dissolve sugar. Add pickles and the arrowroot mixed smoothly with cold water. Cook, stirring, until sauce boils, clears and thickens. Serve in a bowl. If liked, the pickles can be omitted and the sauce based on pineapple or orange juice. In this case, increase vinegar and salt content to taste.

BUCK GING NGAP
PEKING DUCK

One duck yields three separate dishes, for after the crackling crisp skin is eaten with mandarin pancakes (this is the most important course and what is meant by 'Peking duck') the flesh is served separately and the bones used to make a rich soup. But of course the soup needs long simmering and cannot be served at the same meal. Having had a demonstration in Hong Kong of how to make and how to carve this famous dish by the chef and head waiter respectively of the Peking Garden Restaurant, I decided that, delicious though it is, it is too time-consuming to prepare too often. But for those who, like me, are willing to try anything at least once, here's the story. Try to get a duck complete with head — not easy to find in these days of politely packaged frozen poultry devoid of all extremities; if you have access to a Chinese delicatessen, however, they may be purchased there. The vodka is not traditional, but it works!

Serves: 6
1 x 2.5 kg (5 lb) roasting duck
2 teaspoons salt
⅓ cup vodka
3 tablespoons honey
3 cups water
6 slices fresh ginger
pinch red colouring powder, optional

For serving:
mandarin pancakes (page 431)
spring onion brushes
hoi sin sauce
1 cucumber, peeled and cut in slivers

Wash duck, drain well and dry thoroughly with paper towels, inside and out. Rub salt inside body cavity and put the duck on a large plate. Spoon vodka over and rub all over the duck. Leave for 4 hours, turning the bird from time to time so all the skin is in contact with the vodka. Dissolve honey in the water and add the tiniest pinch of red colouring powder. Rub this mixture into the skin of the duck, not missing any places. Truss the bird and tie a string around its neck, then hang the duck in front of an electric fan or, if the weather is cool enough, in a breezy place. Leave it to dry for at least 4 hours. (The Chinese chef inflated the skin of the bird, before hanging it, by blowing through a tiny hole in the skin of the duck's neck just above where he would tie the string. He did it as effortlessly as if blowing up a child's balloon, but I imagine it isn't as easy as it looked. No, I haven't attempted this!)

Preheat oven to moderately hot 190°C (375°F). Put duck on a rack in roasting pan with hot water in it. The duck must be well above the water. Cook for 30 minutes, then turn heat to slow, 150°C (300°F), and continue roasting for 1 hour. Turn heat to original temperature again and continue roasting until skin is crisp and brown all over and duck is tender.

Remove from oven and serve with accompaniments. The duck is carved at the table, only the skin being cut away in thin pieces. These are put on a flat plate and presented ungarnished to the guests. Each guest places a piece of skin on a pancake, dips a spring onion brush into hoi sin sauce and brushes it over the pancake and duck, then wraps the spring onion and a few cucumber slivers into the pancake and eats it.

The duck meat can also be carved and served on a separate plate for eating with the pancakes. Alternatively, the flesh of the duck is cut away from the bones in slivers, quickly stir fried with sliced spring onions, strips of red or green capsicum or fresh bean sprouts, and served as a separate course.

Note: To make brushes cut spring onions into 7.5 cm (3 inch) lengths and with a sharp knife make two parallel cuts about 2.5 cm (1 inch) deep in each end. Then make two more similar cuts, intersecting the first. Soak in iced water and chill until ends turn outwards.

LUT TZE MUN NGAP
BRAISED DUCK WITH CHESTNUTS *(picture page 410)*

Serves: 6
125 g (4 oz) dried chestnuts
1 x 2 kg (4 lb) duck
2 cloves garlic, crushed
1 teaspoon finely grated fresh ginger
1 tablespoon light soy sauce
1 tablespoon Chinese wine or dry sherry
½ cup peanut oil
3 tablespoons red bean curd (see Glossary)
2 teaspoons sugar
4 spring onions
tomato or chilli flower to garnish,
   optional

Pour boiling water over dried chestnuts in a bowl and allow to soak for 30 minutes. Pour off, replace with more boiling water, soak a further 30 minutes. Drain off water before using.

If duck has been frozen, allow to thaw completely, rinse and wipe inside and out with paper towels. Combine garlic, ginger, soy and wine and rub all over duck, inside and out.

Heat oil in a wok and brown duck all over, turning it frequently. Remove duck to a dish and pour off the oil, leaving only a little. Return duck to wok. Add bean curd mashed with the sugar. Pour in hot water to come halfway up the duck. Add chestnuts. Bring to the boil, then reduce heat, cover wok and simmer duck and chestnuts until duck is tender, about 1¼-1½ hours. Turn duck during cooking and add more boiling water if necessary. Lift duck on to a wooden board and cut into pieces with a sharp cleaver, Chinese style. Arrange duck on a serving platter, spoon chestnuts and gravy over and garnish with short lengths of spring onions. If liked, use a tomato or chilli flower for garnish as well.

Note: Chinese yam or even the humble potato can be used to replace the dried chestnuts. In either case, peel and cut into cubes, then add to the simmering gravy 30 minutes before duck is completely cooked.

SZE CHUEN SHIU NGAP
SZECHWANESE-STYLE ROAST DUCK

Oven temperature: 170-190°C (350-375°F)
Cooking time: 2 hours 20 minutes
Serves: 4-5
1 x 3 kg (6 lb) roasting duck
3 teaspoons salt
3 teaspoons black peppercorns or
   Szechwan pepper
1 whole fresh coriander plant
1½ teaspoons finely grated fresh ginger
4 spring onions, chopped
½ teaspoon five spice powder
1 tablespoon honey
1 tablespoon Chinese wine or dry sherry
2 teaspoons sesame oil
1 tablespoon light soy sauce
½ teaspoon red food colouring

Remove neck and giblets of duck from body cavity, wash duck inside and out and dry thoroughly with absorbent kitchen paper. Pick off any pin feathers or quills that remain. Rub all over with salt.

Roast the pepper in a dry pan for a few minutes, then crack coarsely with mortar and pestle or rolling pin. Wash and dry fresh coriander, chop leaves and stem. Reserve the well-washed root. Combine all seasonings and the red colouring and rub well inside and outside duck. Put any coarse leaves of spring onion and the coriander root inside the bird. Cover with plastic wrap or foil and refrigerate overnight, or at least 4 hours.

Preheat oven to moderate. Half-fill a roasting pan with hot water and put a rack in the pan; the water should not reach the rack. Put duck on rack, breast upwards, and roast in a moderate oven for 30 minutes. Cover with foil and continue cooking for another 30 minutes. Reduce heat to 150-160°C (300-325°F), turn duck breast downwards, put foil over duck and roast for a further 30 minutes. Turn duck breast upwards again and continue cooking for 30 minutes, then remove foil and allow duck to brown for 15-20 minutes. Carve duck and serve with mandarin pancakes, plum sauce and spring onions cut into 5 cm (2 inch) lengths and fringed to form brushes. The sauce is rubbed on the Mandarin pancakes with the 'brush', a piece of meat placed on it, the spring onion placed on the meat, and the whole thing rolled up in the pancake and eaten in the style of Peking duck.

PEI PAR NGAP
BARBECUE-STYLE ROAST DUCK *(picture page 415)*

Serves: 4
Oven temperature: 170-190ºC (350-375ºF)
Cooking time: 1¾ hours
1 x 1.75 kg (3½ lb) roasting duck
1 clove garlic, crushed
1 teaspoon finely grated fresh ginger
1 teaspoon hoi sin sauce
1 teaspoon sesame paste (see Glossary)
1 tablespoon honey
1 tablespoon light soy sauce
1 teaspoon salt
½ teaspoon pepper

Wash duck inside and out, remove neck and giblets and reserve for making stock. Combine all other ingredients in a small saucepan and heat gently until honey melts and all are smoothly incorporated. Simmer for 2 minutes, adding a spoonful of water if it seems too thick, and use as marinade.

Rub marinade all over duck, inside and out. Reserve remaining marinade to serve as a sauce. After 1 hour, put duck into oven bag or wrap in foil. If using oven bag follow manufacturer's instructions and do not fail to make 3 or 4 holes in top of bag near the tie.

Turn duck breast downwards in roasting pan and cook in a moderate oven for 45 minutes. Turn duck breast up and cook for a further 45 minutes to 1 hour. Remove from bag, carve duck and serve hot with reserved marinade, mandarin pancakes (page 431), spring onions and plum or hoi sin sauce.

HEUNG SO NGAP
STEAMED AND DEEP-FRIED DUCK

Serves 4 as main dish, 6-8 as part of a
Chinese meal
1 x 2 kg (4 lb) duck
1½ teaspoons salt
¼ teaspoon ground Szechwan pepper or
    ground black pepper
1 tablespoon light soy sauce
2 teaspoons Chinese wine or dry sherry
1 teaspoon five spice powder
⅛ teaspoon red colouring powder (see
    Glossary)
2-3 teaspoons cornflour
oil for deep frying
spring onions or fresh coriander leaves to
    garnish

Wash duck well, dry inside and out with paper towels. Combine salt, pepper, soy, wine, five spice and red colouring powder. Rub all over duck, inside and out. Let duck marinate for at least an hour, then put on steamer rack and steam for 1¼-1½ hours, until tender. Dredge duck with cornflour.

Heat oil in wok and when very hot gently lower duck into the oil. Keep ladling hot oil over the top of the duck if duck is not immersed. Turn duck when underside is done and fry other side in the same manner until skin is crisp. Drain, chop duck into bite-size pieces. Garnish with spring onions or fresh coriander leaves and serve hot with plain white rice.

JING NG FAR NAM
STEAMED FIVE-FLOWERED PORK

Fragrant with spice, this delicious pork dish is
so rich that it must be eaten with plenty of
white rice, and is certainly better served in
cold weather.

Serves: 6
1 kg (2 lb) lean belly pork
4 tablespoons dark soy sauce
2 tablespoons Chinese wine or dry sherry
½ teaspoon five spice powder, optional
1 clove garlic, crushed
½ cup uncooked rice

Ask butcher to remove skin from pork. Cut pork into large squares and marinate in a mixture of soy sauce, wine, five spice powder and garlic for at least an hour, preferably longer.

Roast uncooked rice in a heavy frying pan over medium low heat, stirring constantly, for 15 minutes or until the grains are golden in colour. Put into container of electric blender and blend on high speed until ground to powder. If blender is not available, pound a little at a time using a mortar and pestle.

Roll pieces of pork, one at a time, in the rice powder and put them into a heatproof dish. Steam over rapidly boiling water for 2 hours or until the pork is so tender it can easily be broken with chopsticks. Serve hot, accompanied by steamed white rice.

CHA SHIU
BARBECUED PORK

Serves: 4-6
Cooking time: approximately 45 minutes
Oven temperature: 200-230°C (400-450°F)
500 g (1 lb) pork belly or fillet
3 cloves garlic
1 teaspoon salt
½ teaspoon finely grated fresh ginger
1 tablespoon light soy sauce
1 tablespoon honey
1 tablespoon Chinese wine or dry sherry
½ teaspoon five spice powder

With a sharp knife remove rind from pork, or ask butcher to do this for you. Cut pork into strips the length of the piece and about 2.5 cm (1 inch) wide. Crush garlic with salt and combine with all other ingredients in a large bowl. Put in the pork, mix well together so that pork is covered on all sides with mixture. Allow to marinate for 15 minutes or longer.

Half fill a roasting pan with hot water and put a wire rack across the top of the pan. Put pork on rack and roast in hot oven 30 minutes. Turn pork strips over, brush with remaining marinade and cook further 15 minutes or until well glazed and lightly touched with dark brown on the spots where the honey marinade has caramelised. Cut in slices to serve. Serve immediately, with plum sauce or hoi sin sauce for dipping.

GWOO LO YOOK
CRISP FRIED PORK WITH SWEET SOUR SAUCE *(picture opposite)*

Pork can be fried once and set aside with ingredients for sauce prepared beforehand. At serving time make the sauce and fry pork briefly once more.

Serves: 4-6
500 g (1 lb) pork fillet or pork chops
1 tablespoon light soy sauce
1 tablespoon Chinese wine or dry sherry
½ teaspoon salt
¼ teaspoon pepper
¼ teaspoon five spice powder
1 cup plain flour
¾ cup warm water
1 tablespoon peanut oil
1 egg white
extra peanut oil for deep frying

Sweet Sour Sauce:
1 tablespoon light soy sauce
1 tablespoon Chinese wine or dry sherry,
   optional
3 tablespoons tomato sauce
2 tablespoons white vinegar
2 tablespoons white sugar
¾ cup water
1 tablespoon cornflour
1 tablespoon water
1 small onion
2 tablespoons peanut oil
1 clove garlic, crushed
¼ teaspoon finely grated fresh ginger
½ cup sliced water chestnuts
1 red capsicum, diced
3 tablespoons frozen or fresh green peas
2 tablespoons preserved melon shreds,
   optional

If using pork chops, remove rind. Cut pork into 12 mm (½ inch) slices, then into 2.5 cm (1 inch) squares. Mix with soy sauce, wine, salt, pepper and five spice powder. Refrigerate while preparing batter.

Mix flour and warm water to a smooth batter with a wooden spoon, stir in oil, allow to stand for 30 minutes. Beat egg white until stiff and fold in.

Heat oil. Dip pieces of pork in batter and deep fry a few at a time over medium heat until pork is cooked and batter golden. Drain on absorbent paper and set aside. Make sauce.

Shortly before serving, reheat oil and once more fry pork, a few pieces at a time, on high heat for just a few seconds. This second frying makes the batter very crisp. Drain on absorbent paper. When all the pork is fried arrange on a plate, pour hot sauce over and serve immediately.

Sweet Sour Sauce: Combine soy sauce, wine, tomato sauce, vinegar, sugar and water in a bowl and stir until sugar dissolves.

Mix cornflour smoothly with about 1 tablespoon cold water. Peel onion, cut into four lengthways, then cut each quarter across into two. Separate layers of onion. Heat oil, add garlic, ginger and all the vegetables and fry for 2 minutes. Add combined sauce mixture, bring to a boil, then stir in cornflour and cook, stirring constantly, until thickened. Remove from heat and stir in melon shreds.

GWOO LO YOOK (crisp fried pork with sweet sour sauce) *recipe above*

LUT GEE HOONG SHIU JU YOOK
BRAISED PORK WITH CHESTNUTS

Serves: 4-6
750 g (1½ lb) pork belly
2 cloves garlic, crushed
1 teaspoon salt
1 tablespoon light soy sauce
1 tablespoon Chinese wine or brandy
125 g (4 oz) dried chestnuts
2 tablespoons peanut oil
2½ cups hot water
2 teaspoons cornflour
2 tablespoons cold water
spring onions to garnish, optional

With a sharp knife remove skin from pork, or ask butcher to do this. Cut pork into thin slices, then into small dice. Mix with garlic crushed with salt, soy sauce and wine or brandy. Marinate for 1 hour. Pour boiling water over dried chestnuts in a bowl, allow to soak for 30 minutes. Pour off water and replace with more boiling water. Soak for a further 30 minutes. Drain off water before using.

Heat oil in a wok and fry marinated pork, stirring constantly, until brown. Add chestnuts and stir well, then add hot water, cover and simmer for 35-40 minutes. Mix cornflour with cold water. Push pork and chestnuts to side of pan and add cornflour mixture to liquid in pan. (There should be about 1 cup cooking liquid. If not, make up quantity with water.) Cook until thick, stirring constantly. Garnish, if liked, with pieces of spring onion. Serve with rice.

JU YOOK MA TAI CHOW HAHM SUEN CHOY
PORK AND WATER CHESTNUT DISCS WITH SWEET AND SOUR VEGETABLES

Serves: 8
500 g (1 lb) minced pork
1 cup chopped water chestnuts
1 clove garlic, crushed
1 teaspoon salt
1 tablespoon cornflour
3 tablespoons finely chopped spring
   onions
½ teaspoon five spice powder, optional
1 egg, beaten
oil for deep frying
fresh coriander leaves, or tomato
   flowers to garnish

Batter:
½ cup plain flour
¾ cup water
2 teaspoons oil

Sweet and Sour Vegetables:
1 cup canned pineapple pieces
¾ cup juice from canned pineapple
1 small can chow chow preserves
¼ cup white vinegar
3 tablespoons sugar
10 spring onions, including green leaves
1 carrot
2 tablespoons sliced water chestnuts
pinch red colouring powder (see Glossary)
¾ teaspoon salt
1 tablespoon arrowroot
1 tablespoon cold water

Combine pork with water chestnuts, garlic, salt, cornflour, spring onions, five spice and egg. Mix thoroughly, form into three rolls about 17 cm (7 inches) long, put on a lightly oiled heatproof plate and steam, covered, for 20-25 minutes. Cool completely and chill for a short while if possible. While pork rolls are cooking and cooling prepare batter and sweet and sour vegetables.

Cut rolls across into 2 cm (¾ inch) discs. Dip slices in batter and deep fry until golden. Drain on absorbent paper, then arrange on heated serving platter, pour sweet and sour vegetables over, garnish, serve.

Batter: Put flour into a bowl, pour in oil and water and beat until smooth. Allow batter to stand for 30 minutes.

Sweet and Sour Vegetables: Combine pineapple juice in saucepan with 2 tablespoons syrup from chow chow preserves, vinegar, and sugar.

Cut chow chow preserves into large pieces, spring onions into bite-size lengths, carrot into thin slices or matchstick strips. If sliced water chestnuts are not available, cut whole canned ones into 2 or 3 round slices.

Bring combined liquid in saucepan to a boil. Add the tiniest pinch of red colouring powder — the colouring should be a bright, clear flamingo pink, not deep red. Add salt, pineapple pieces and vegetables, return to boil. Mix arrowroot with cold water and stir into boiling mixture over low heat. Stir constantly until thick and clear. Pour over fried pork discs, garnish with sprigs of fresh coriander, chilli or tomato flowers, and serve hot.

CHOW YOOK PIN
TWICE-COOKED PORK

A rich dish suitable for winter eating, this comes from north China.

Serves: 3-4
250 g (8 oz) boiled pork loin
1 tablespoon Chinese wine or dry sherry
1 tablespoon light soy sauce
1 teaspoon sugar
1 large or 2 small green capsicums
pinch salt
3 spring onions
3 tablespoons oil for frying
1 teaspoon finely grated fresh ginger
3 cloves garlic, crushed or finely chopped
1 tablespoon hot bean sauce (see Glossary)
1 tablespoon hoi sin sauce

Cut the pork into very thin slices no thicker than a cracker biscuit. The fat is important in this dish, so do not remove it. It helps to chill the pork well before cutting it. Mix wine, soy and sugar together.

Cut capsicum into bite-size pieces, discarding seeds and centre membrane. Cut spring onions into 2.5 cm (1 inch) lengths.

Heat oil in a wok until very hot. Add capsicum and sprinkle with a little salt. Toss for a few seconds on very high heat until capsicums are coated with oil and turn a brilliant green. Remove from pan, spoon off 2 tablespoons oil and add pork to small amount of oil left in pan. Toss over medium heat for 1 minute, add garlic and ginger and continue to stir fry until the pork is nicely brown. Add spring onions, capsicums, wine, soy and sugar, and two sauces. Toss to mix well and heat through. Serve hot with white rice.

NGAU YOOK JU YOOK YIN
BEEF AND PORK BALLS WITH RICE COATING

Serves: 4-6
1 cup short grain rice
6 dried Chinese mushrooms
250 g (8 oz) minced lean topside
250 (8 oz) minced pork
3 spring onions, finely chopped
½ teaspoon finely grated fresh ginger
1 clove garlic, crushed
2 teaspoons salt
1 egg, beaten
¼ cup finely chopped water chestnuts

Soak rice in cold water to cover for at least 2 hours, then drain well, spread on kitchen paper towels and leave to dry while preparing meat balls.

Soak mushrooms in hot water for 30 minutes. Squeeze out excess water, discard stems and chop the caps finely. Put into a large bowl with all the remaining ingredients and mix very well with the hands. Shape into balls about 2.5 cm (1 inch) in diameter, rolling them between your palms.

Roll each ball separately in the rice with enough pressure to make the rice stick and coat the ball.

Line a steamer rack with greaseproof paper and put the balls on it, leaving space between so the rice can swell as it steams. Steam over boiling water for 30-35 minutes, from the time the water comes to a fast boil. If necessary add more boiling water during this time. If you do not have a steamer, any large pan with a well-fitting lid will do. Put an upturned heatproof bowl in the pan and pour water into pan to come halfway up the bowl. On this put a plate that is slightly smaller than the pan so that steam can rise and cook the meat and rice balls.

The rice will swell and the balls will be covered with pearly grains when done. There are two names for this recipe — one is pearl balls and the other porcupine balls, because the rice grains stick out like the quills of a porcupine.

NG HEUNG NGAU YOOK SZEE
SHREDDED FIVE SPICE BEEF

Serves: 4-6
500 g (1 lb) tender beef
1 clove garlic, crushed
1 teaspoon salt
½ teaspoon finely grated fresh ginger
1 tablespoon dark soy sauce
½ teaspoon five spice powder
2 teaspoons cornflour
2 tablespoons peanut oil
3 tablespoons water or stock

Partially freeze and slice the beef very thinly, then cut slices into shreds. Crush garlic with salt. Mix garlic, ginger and soy into the beef. Combine spice powder and cornflour and sprinkle over beef. Toss to distribute evenly.

Heat oil in a wok and when hot add the beef and fry over high heat, stirring and tossing constantly, until meat changes colour. Add water, stir well and allow liquid to boil up and thicken. Stir, then serve immediately with rice or noodles.

Note: This recipe, or beef in black bean sauce (below), can be adapted to combine with vegetables. Use the same weight of vegetables as of beef, perhaps a combination of Chinese white cabbage or mustard cabbage, beans, broccoli, onion, cauliflower or celery. If using beans, cauliflower or broccoli, blanch them in boiling water for 2 minutes and drain before adding to the dish, but other vegetables can be added raw and stir fried for 2 minutes. Cauliflower and broccoli should be sliced finely or divided into small sprigs. Beans, cabbage and celery should be sliced in thin diagonal slices. Onions should be cut in eighths and the layers separated.

SEE JUP NGAU YOOK
BEEF IN BLACK BEAN SAUCE

Perhaps the all-time favourite among Chinese beef dishes, and one of the easiest to cook.

Serves: 4-6
500 g (1 lb) lean rump or fillet steak
1½ tablespoons canned salted black beans
1 tablespoon dark soy sauce
¼ cup water or stock
1 teaspoon sugar
1 teaspoon cornflour
2 teaspoons cold water
2 tablespoons peanut oil
1 teaspoon sesame oil, optional
2 cloves garlic, crushed

Trim off any fat and freeze beef for an hour or just until firm enough to cut into paper-thin slices. Cut slices into narrow strips. Put black beans into a small strainer and rinse under cold tap for a few seconds. Drain, then mash with a fork, and combine with the soy sauce, water and sugar. Mix cornflour with cold water and set aside.

Heat wok, pour in oil or oils and swirl to coat the wok. Add beef and fry over high heat, tossing and stirring constantly until the beef loses its redness. Add garlic and toss for a few seconds longer, then add bean mixture. Bring to the boil. Lower heat, cover and simmer for no more than 5 minutes. Stir in cornflour until clear and thick and serve immediately with white rice.

Note: Cheap cuts of lean meat such as round steak or blade steak may be used for any stir fried dishes, but because of the extremely short cooking time, they should be tenderised by the Chinese method. Shred or slice meat as directed. For 500 g (1 lb) of meat, dissolve half teaspoon bicarbonate of soda in 3 tablespoons hot water. Add to meat and knead well or beat with chopsticks until meat absorbs all the liquid. Cover and refrigerate for 2 hours or longer, overnight if possible. Proceed with the recipe in the usual way. This method is used in many Chinese restaurants, making cheaper cuts of meat as tender as the choicest fillet.

LIN NGAU CHOW NGAU YOOK
BEEF WITH LOTUS ROOT

Serves: 3-4
250 g (8 oz) fillet or rump steak
1 tablespoon light soy sauce
½ teaspoon salt
1 clove garlic, crushed
½ teaspoon finely grated fresh ginger
¼ teaspoon five spice powder
2 tablespoons peanut oil
½ cup beef stock (page 417) or water
1 tablespoon cornflour
2 tablespoons cold water
12 slices canned lotus root

Cut meat into paper-thin slices. Sprinkle with soy sauce, salt, garlic, ginger and five spice powder, mix well by hand to season all the pieces of beef.

Heat oil in a wok or large frying pan. When hot, add the beef and toss over high heat until colour changes. Add stock, stir in cornflour mixed with cold water and boil, stirring, until gravy becomes thick and clear. Add sliced lotus root and heat through. Serve with boiled rice.

HO LAN DAU CHOW NGAU YOOK
BEEF WITH SNOW PEAS *(picture page 407)*

Serves: 4-6
500 g (1 lb) rump steak
2 tablespoons light soy sauce
½ teaspoon salt
6 dried Chinese mushrooms
250 g (8 oz) snow peas
3 tablespoons oil
4 spring onions, in 2.5 cm
  (1 inch) lengths
1 tablespoon Chinese wine or dry sherry
½ teaspoon sugar
½ cup beef stock (page 417)
3 teaspoons cornflour
1 tablespoon cold water

Trim off fat and discard. Cut lean meat into fine shreds. Sprinkle with soy and salt, mix and allow to marinate 30 minutes. Soak mushrooms in hot water 30 minutes, then trim off stems and slice caps into thin strips. String snow peas and blanch for 2 minutes in lightly salted boiling water.

Heat 2 tablespoons oil in wok and when very hot add beef and stir fry over high heat until colour changes. Remove to a dish and wipe out wok. Heat remaining 1 tablespoon oil, add mushrooms and the spring onions. Fry 1 minute. Add wine, sugar and stock. Bring to boil, add cornflour blended smoothly with cold water, stir until it clears and thickens. Return beef and snow peas to wok, stir and heat through and serve immediately with rice or noodles.

SEE YO NGAU YOOK
RED COOKED BEEF

Here is how to use an economy cut of beef to make a superbly spiced, really special dish. Cooked in a master sauce, it makes a silk purse out of the sow's ear known as gravy beef! Serve hot, or let it cool in the sauce, slice thinly and serve cold.

Serves 8-10 as part of a Chinese meal with other dishes
1.5 kg (3 lb) shin of beef in one piece
3 cups cold water
1½ cups dark soy sauce
¼ cup Chinese wine or dry sherry
6 large slices fresh ginger
2 whole cloves garlic, peeled
2 whole star anise
2 tablespoons sugar
1 tablespoon sesame oil

Put beef in a saucepan just large enough to hold it. Add all the remaining ingredients, bring to the boil, then turn heat low so that it simmers very gently. Cover and simmer for 3 hours or until beef is very tender. Test by piercing with a skewer, which should penetrate easily. Turn beef once or twice so that every part of it is immersed in the liquid at some time during cooking. Uncover pan and cook for a further 15 minutes, spooning sauce over the beef every 5 minutes. Slice and serve hot, or let the beef cool in the sauce, turning it over after an hour. Chill until serving time, then put on a board and with a sharp Chinese chopper cut into very thin slices. Arrange overlapping slices as part of a selection of cold hors d'oeuvre.

Note: Save the master sauce, as the cooking liquid is now called, and freeze it for future use. A spoonful added to a dish in place of stock will give a rich, delicious flavour. If whole star anise is difficult to obtain, use about 16 of the broken sections.

SEEN LO SHUN CHOW NGAU YOOK
STIR-FRIED BEEF WITH FRESH ASPARAGUS

Serves: 4-6
375 g (12 oz) lean steak
2 teaspoons light soy sauce
1 clove garlic, crushed
½ teaspoon salt
1 bunch fresh tender asparagus
2 medium onions
4 tablespoons peanut oil
2 teaspoons Chinese bean sauce
  (see Glossary)
¼ cup water or beef stock (page 417)
1 teaspoon cornflour
1 tablespoon cold water

Trim off all fat and discard. Cut steak across the grain into paper-thin slices, then cut into bite-size strips. Sprinkle with soy, mix in garlic crushed with salt. Leave aside while preparing asparagus and onions.

Wash asparagus well in several changes of cold water, making sure all the fine sand has been removed from the tips. Cut off tough ends of stalks and peel away the skin from the base to within an inch or so of the tender tops. With a sharp knife cut into thin slices on the sharp diagonal so the slices are quite long and oval shaped. Keep the tips whole and set aside.

Peel onions, cut in half lengthways, then cut each half into 4 or 6 wedges. Cut the wedges in two crossways. Separate layers of onion.

Heat 2 tablespoons oil in a wok. Fry meat over high heat until colour changes. Remove it to a bowl. Wipe out pan, heat remaining 2 tablespoons oil and on high heat stir fry the sliced asparagus stalks for 3 minutes. Add onion and fry for 1 minute longer. Add bean sauce and water or stock, and stir. Add the asparagus tips. Reduce heat, cover and cook for 5 minutes or until asparagus is tender but not mushy.

Push vegetables to side of pan. To the pan liquid add cornflour mixed smoothly with cold water. Stir and cook for 1 minute or until liquid boils and thickens. Return beef to pan, stir gently and cook only until heated through. Serve immediately with white rice.

DOONG GWOO CHOW NGAU YOOK
STIR-FRIED BEEF WITH ONIONS AND MUSHROOMS

Serves: 4
6 dried Chinese mushrooms
250 g (8 oz) lean beef steak, thinly sliced
¼ teaspoon five spice powder
½ teaspoon salt
1 clove garlic, crushed
½ teaspoon finely grated fresh ginger
3 tablespoons oil
2 onions, cut in eighths
2 tablespoons dark soy sauce
2 teaspoons sugar
¼ cup water or beef stock (page 417)
2 teaspoons cornflour
1 tablespoon cold water
spring onions to garnish

Soak mushrooms in hot water for 20-30 minutes. Cut off and discard stems, slice caps thinly. Slice beef paper-thin in bite-size lengths. Sprinkle with five spice powder and salt, add garlic and ginger and mix well.

Heat 1 tablespoon oil in wok, fry onions and mushrooms for 2-3 minutes. Add beef and fry on high heat, stirring and tossing, until beef changes colour. Add soy, sugar and stock, bring to the boil, then thicken with cornflour blended with cold water. Serve garnished with spring onions.

CHU HAU JEUNG MUN WAN YEE
CLOUD EARS IN HOI SIN SAUCE

Serves: 4
½ cup dried wood fungus (wan yee)
2 teaspoons hoi sin sauce
2 tablespoons light soy sauce
1 small clove garlic
2 teaspoons peanut oil
1 teaspoon sesame oil
¼ cup water
1 teaspoon cornflour
1 tablespoon cold water

Wash wood fungus and soak in hot water in a large bowl for 1 hour. Fungus will swell to many times its original size. Rinse and cut off any gritty parts, then cut large pieces into bite-size bits. Mix hoi sin sauce and soy sauce. Crush garlic. Heat both oils and fry garlic over low heat for half a minute. Add sauces and water, wood fungus and stir until heated through and boiling. Thicken liquid with cornflour mixed with cold water and serve immediately with rice or noodles.

HUNG SHIU DOONG GWOO
BRAISED MUSHROOMS

To be served as part of the cold hors d'oeuvre platter.

Serves: 6-8
125 g (4 oz) dried Chinese mushrooms
3-4 cups hot water
2 tablespoons dark soy sauce
2 tablespoons sugar
1 tablespoon sesame oil
3 tablespoons peanut oil

Wash mushrooms well in cold water. Put in a bowl, pour hot water over and soak for 20 minutes. With a sharp knife, cut stems off and discard. Squeeze as much water as possible from mushrooms, reserving the liquid. To the reserved liquid, add some of the water in which the mushrooms were soaked, enough to make 1½ cups. Add soy sauce, sugar, sesame oil and stir to dissolve sugar.

Heat peanut oil in a small wok and fry mushrooms over a high heat, stirring and turning, until the undersides are browned. Add liquid mixture, reduce heat, cover and simmer for approximately 30 minutes or until all the liquid is absorbed and the mushrooms take on a shiny appearance. Towards end of cooking time, it is advisable to stir occasionally. Serve hot or cold.

Note: Braised mushrooms can also be added to other dishes, either whole or sliced.

JING YEUNG BUCK GWOO
STEAMED MUSHROOMS WITH PORK FILLING

Makes about 24
250g (8 oz) fresh button mushrooms
250g (8 oz) lean minced pork
6 water chestnuts, finely chopped
1 tablespoon cornflour
1 tablespoon light soy sauce
¾ teaspoon salt
½ teaspoon finely grated fresh ginger
½ teaspoon sugar
sesame oil
fresh coriander leaves to garnish

Choose mushrooms of an even size, about 4 cm (1½ inches) in diameter. Wipe mushrooms with damp kitchen paper. Do not peel. Remove stems carefully with a little twist, leaving caps intact. Reserve stems for another use.

Put pork, water chestnuts, cornflour and all seasoning ingredients into a bowl and mix thoroughly. Put a teaspoonful of the mixture into each mushroom cap, mounding it very slightly and firming the filling into the cap. Put in a heatproof dish lightly coated with sesame oil, cover dish tightly with foil, and steam mushrooms for 25-30 minutes. Allow to cool slightly and serve, garnished with a few sprigs of fresh coriander leaves if liked.

If mushrooms are being served as appetisers, save liquid in plate for adding to soups or sauces. If they are part of a meal, thicken liquid slightly by bringing to the boil in a small saucepan (adding more stock or water if necessary) and thickening slightly with cornflour mixed smoothly with cold water. Pour over mushrooms on serving dish and serve with white rice.

PAR SAY SAW
MIXED BRAISED VEGETABLES

Use a mixture of white Chinese cabbage,
mustard cabbage, leeks, cauliflower, spring
onions, beans, in any combination or
proportions. Weigh after trimming and slicing.

Serves: 4-6
2 tablespoons peanut oil
1 teaspoon sesame oil
1 large clove garlic, crushed
1 teaspoon grated fresh ginger
750 g (1½ lb) sliced vegetables
½ cup hot water or light stock (page 416)
1 tablespoon oyster sauce
2 teaspoons light soy sauce
½ teaspoon salt
½ teaspoon monosodium glutamate, optional
2 teaspoons cornflour
1 tablespoon cold water

Heat oils in a wok with garlic and ginger, add vegetables and fry, stirring, for 2 minutes. Add hot water or stock and sauces, salt and monosodium glutamate mixed together. Cover and simmer for 4 minutes. Push vegetables to side of wok, add cornflour mixed with cold water, stir until thick. Toss vegetables in sauce and serve immediately with boiled rice.

HUNG SHIU SAY SAW
HEAVENLY BRAISED VEGETABLES *(picture page 6)*

Serves: 4
12 dried Chinese mushrooms
3 tablespoons dried wood fungus (wan yee)
1 x 238 g (8½ oz) can bamboo shoot
1 x 425 g (15 oz) can young corn cobs
2 tablespoons peanut oil
1 tablespoon sesame oil
2 tablespoons soy sauce
1 tablespoon sugar
2 cups mushroom liquid

Soak mushrooms in 3 cups hot water 30 minutes. Remove and discard stems, squeeze out excess moisture from caps. Reserve mushroom liquid. Soak fungus in water 10 minutes, rinse and drain, then cut each piece in two. Slice bamboo shoots thinly. Drain corn.

Heat oil in a wok and fry mushrooms until brown, about 5 minutes on high heat, stirring all the time. Add remaining ingredients, except wood fungus. Add mushroom liquid, cover and simmer over low heat for 25-30 minutes. Add wood fungus and heat through. Serve with rice.

CHOW SAHNG CHOY
BRAISED LETTUCE

Serves: 2-4
1 large, firm head of lettuce
1 tablespoon peanut oil
1 small clove garlic, crushed
¼ teaspoon finely grated fresh ginger
2 tablespoons light stock (page 416) or water
1 teaspoon sugar
pinch salt
2 teaspoons light soy sauce
1 teaspoon cornflour
1 tablespoon cold water

Wash lettuce, drain and dry well. Cut into halves lengthways, then cut each half twice lengthways and twice crossways. This will give chunky pieces of convenient size.

Heat oil in wok, swirl wok around so oil covers as much of inner surface as possible. Add, all at once, the garlic, ginger and lettuce. Stir fry, tossing leaves lightly, for 1 minute. Add stock or water, sugar, salt and soy. Push lettuce to side of wok and stir the cornflour blended with cold water into the liquid in the wok. When it boils and thickens toss the lettuce in and dish up immediately.

LO HAN CHAI
BRAISED VEGETABLE COMBINATION

Serves: 6

125 g (4 oz) dried bean curd or
   gluten steak or dried soy
   bean protein
12 dried Chinese mushrooms
30 dried lily buds
2 tablespoons dried wood fungus
1 canned bamboo shoot
1 canned lotus root
1 small can white nuts or sliced water
   chestnuts, optional
3 tablespoons peanut oil
2 tablespoons light soy sauce
2 tablespoons hoi sin sauce
1½ cups mushroom soaking liquid
3 sections star anise
2 teaspoons sesame oil
2 teaspoons sugar
2 teaspoons cornflour
2 tablespoons cold water

Break bean curd into bite-size pieces and soak in cold water 20 minutes. Drain, pour boiling water over and allow to stand for a further 20 minutes. Drain well. Wash mushrooms and soak in hot water 30 minutes. Drain, remove stems, squeeze out excess moisture from caps. If large, cut caps in halves. Soak lily buds in hot water 30 minutes, drain, pinch off tough stem ends if necessary and either tie a knot in each one or cut in halves.

Soak wood fungus in hot water 10 minutes, drain and cut in bite-size pieces. Cut bamboo shoot and lotus root into thin slices, then into bite-size pieces. Drain white nuts.

Heat a wok, pour in peanut oil and swirl to coat wok. When very hot add bean curd, mushrooms and lily buds and stir fry for 4 minutes over medium high heat. Add the soy and hoi sin sauces stirred into the mushroom liquid. Add star anise. Bring to the boil, turn heat low, cover and simmer 15 minutes. Add bamboo shoot, lotus root, white nuts, sesame oil and sugar, stir well, cover and simmer 10 minutes longer. If liquid evaporates too rapidly add more mushroom liquid or hot water.

Mix cornflour smoothly with cold water and stir into liquid. Cook until it becomes clear and thickens. Add wood fungus and push other vegetables to side of pan, allowing fungus to heat through. Serve hot with rice.

Note: Prepare gluten steaks or dried soy bean protein according to instructions on label. The bean curd or substitute may be replaced with 250 g (8 oz) beef or pork cut in small cubes.

JUN JU SHUN HO LAN DAU CHANG GWA
YOUNG CORN COBS AND SNOW PEAS WITH CUCUMBER

Serves: 4

1 x 440 g (15 oz) can young corn cobs
250 g (8 oz) snow peas
1 cucumber
1 tablespoon peanut oil
1 teaspoon sesame oil
¼ teaspoon crushed garlic
¼ teaspoon finely grated fresh ginger
salt to taste

Drain liquid from can of corn. Remove stems and strings from snow peas. Peel and cut cucumber into thin slices. Heat peanut oil in a wok, add sesame oil, garlic and ginger and stir once, then turn in corn and snow peas. Stir fry for 1 minute over high heat. Add cucumber slices and cook 2 minutes longer. Serve at once.

CHOW DAU KOK
QUICK-FRIED LONG BEANS

Serves: 4

500 g (1 lb) long beans
2 tablespoons peanut oil
1 small clove garlic, crushed
½ teaspoon finely grated fresh ginger
1 teaspoon sesame oil
½ teaspoon salt
½ teaspoon monosodium glutamate,
   optional

Wash and cut beans into 5 cm (2 inch) lengths. Heat oil in a wok or frying pan and add garlic, ginger and beans and fry, stirring constantly over high heat, for 2 minutes. Stir in sesame oil, salt and monosodium glutamate. Serve at once.

CHU HAU JEUNG MUN DAU FU
BEAN CURD IN BARBECUE SAUCE

Serves: 3
2 tablespoons oil
6 squares fresh bean curd
2 tablespoons barbecue sauce or marinade
   as for barbecued pork (page 403)
¾ cup light stock (page 416) or water
1 cup cooked peas or chopped spring
   onions

Heat oil and gently fry the bean curd for a few minutes, turning once. Mix marinade with stock or water and add to pan. Simmer for 3 minutes. Add peas or spring onions and heat through. Serve with boiled rice or noodles.

HAI YOOK PAR DAU FU
BEAN CURD WITH CRAB SAUCE

Serves: 4
125g (4 oz) fresh, frozen or canned crab
   meat
2 tablespoons peanut oil
6 spring onions, roughly chopped
½ teaspoon finely grated fresh ginger
¾ cup chicken or fish stock (page 416)
small pinch pepper
2½ teaspoons cornflour
1 tablespoon cold water
8 squares fresh bean curd
salt to taste

Drain and flake crab and pick over to remove any bony tissue. Heat oil in a small pan and gently fry spring onions and ginger for a minute or so, stirring, until ginger starts to turn golden and onions are softened. Add stock, cover and simmer for 3-4 minutes. Add crab meat and heat through. Season with pepper, then stir in cornflour mixed to a smooth cream with water. Stir over medium heat until sauce boils and thickens. Add bean curd, spoon sauce over and heat until just about to come to the boil. Do not overcook. Taste and add salt if necessary, serve immediately with rice.

SEE JUP YEUNG FU GWA
STUFFED BITTER MELON IN BLACK BEAN SAUCE

Serves: 2-3
2 bitter melons
1 large bream fillet
125g (4 oz) raw prawns
¾ teaspoon salt
½ teaspoon finely grated fresh ginger
1 tablespoon egg white
1 teaspoon cornflour
4 tablespoons peanut oil

Sauce:
2 tablespoons canned salted black beans
1 clove garlic, crushed
1 teaspoon sugar
½ cup light stock (page 416) or water
1½ teaspoons cornflour

Cut bitter melon into 4cm (1½ inch) sections, discarding stem end and pointed tip. With a small, sharp knife remove spongy centre and seeds and discard, leaving small tubular sections of melon.

Using a Chinese chopper remove skin from fish. Chop fish very finely, discarding any bones. Shell, de-vein and chop prawns finely. Mix fish and prawns with salt, ginger, egg white and cornflour. Fill sections of melon with this mixture, rounding the filling slightly on one end of each section. Heat oil in a wok or frying pan and fry the melon rounded side down, until fish is just starting to brown. Turn over and fry on other side. Use a frying spoon to lift pieces of melon on to a plate.

Sauce: Rinse salted beans in a strainer under cold water for a few seconds, then drain off liquid, put beans on a wooden board and mash well with a fork. Mix with crushed garlic. Fry this mixture in the oil remaining in wok, add sugar and stock or water and bring to the boil. Return pieces of melon to pan, rounded side upwards, cover and simmer over very low heat for 20 minutes. Lift stuffed melon on to a serving plate. To mixture in pan add cornflour mixed with a little cold water and stir over medium heat until it thickens. Pour over the melon and serve with rice.

PEI PAR NGAP (barbecue-style roast duck) *recipe page 401*

JAHP SIK CHOY
CHINESE SALAD

Salads are rare in Chinese cuisine, but they do exist. Here is a delicious combination that may be served as a vegetable accompaniment or as a main dish.

Serves: 4-6
1 large can winter bamboo shoots
500 g (1 lb) fresh bean sprouts
half a white Chinese cabbage
1 can lychees, optional
2 tablespoons lightly toasted sesame seeds

Dressing:
½ teaspoon finely grated fresh ginger
1 clove garlic, crushed
1½ teaspoons salt
1 tablespoon light soy sauce
2 tablespoons Chinese wine or dry sherry
4 tablespoons sweet Chinese vinegar or
    other mild vinegar
½ cup peanut oil
2 tablespoons sesame oil

Drain winter bamboo shoots and cut across into thin oval slices. Winter bamboo shoots are smaller, whiter and much more tender than ordinary bamboo shoots. If they are not available use the larger variety but after slicing into bite-size strips, bring to the boil in lightly salted water, simmer for 8 minutes, then drain and cool.

Wash the bean sprouts thoroughly, removing any skins and pinching off straggly brown 'tails'. Make sure the sprouts you buy are really crisp and fresh. Drain well. Wash and finely shred the Chinese cabbage. If using lychees for a touch of sweetness in the salad, drain well.

Put shredded cabbage in a bowl and arrange other vegetables on top in concentric circles. Pile lychees in the centre. Sprinkle with sesame seeds, cover with plastic wrap and chill until serving time, then pour dressing over, toss and serve right away.

Dressing: In a shaker bottle (or screw-top jar) put ginger, garlic crushed with salt, soy, wine and vinegar and shake well. Add both kinds of oil and shake again. Just before using shake the jar very well.

YUE SHEUNG TONG
BASIC FISH STOCK

fish heads and trimmings or prawn heads
    and shells
8 cups cold water
10 black peppercorns
3 slices fresh ginger
1 carrot
2 stalks celery
1 large onion
2 stalks fresh coriander leaves

Wash fish trimmings, or prawn heads and shells, thoroughly. Put into a large pan with cold water to cover, add remaining ingredients and bring to the boil. Cover and simmer 1 hour or longer. Strain stock and use in soups or as part of the liquid in seafood recipes.

GAI SHEUNG TONG
BASIC CHICKEN STOCK

chicken bones and trimmings (giblets,
    neck, feet, etc.)
8 cups cold water
10 black peppercorns
2 small stalks celery with leaves
1 onion
few stalks fresh coriander
2 slices fresh ginger
salt to taste

Put bones and trimmings in a saucepan, add water and other ingredients, bring to the boil. Cover and simmer 45 minutes to 1 hour. Strain. Skim if necessary. The stock is now ready for use in soups and sauces. If stock is fatty, chill until fat congeals and discard.

JU YOOK SHEUNG TONG
BASIC PORK STOCK

500 g (1 lb) pork bones
8-10 cups cold water
3 slices fresh ginger
¼ teaspoon whole black peppercorns
1 onion or 2 spring onions
1 stick celery with leaves
1 carrot
few stalks fresh coriander if available
light soy sauce and salt to taste

Put pork bones into a large saucepan with cold water to cover, bring to the boil, reduce heat and simmer. As fat and froth rise to the surface skim them off. Add spices, vegetables and herbs and simmer, covered, very gently for 2 hours or longer. Add soy sauce and salt to taste and allow stock to cool. Strain. Refrigerate stock and remove fat from top when it congeals before using stock for soup. If there is no time for this skim off all fat from surface, then wrap ice cube in muslin or teatowel and pass across the surface to remove the last drops of fat.

NGAU YOOK SHEUNG TONG
BASIC BEEF STOCK

1 kg (2 lb) soup bones
500 g (1 lb) gravy beef
8 cups cold water
1 onion
1 celery stalk with leaves
1 whole star anise
4 fresh coriander or parsley stalks
3 teaspoons salt

Put bones and beef into a large pan with water to cover. Add all other ingredients. Bring to the boil, then cover and simmer for 2 hours. Strain and allow to cool, then chill. Remove fat from surface. Use as a base for soup or as part of the liquid in sauces for beef, chicken or pork dishes.

YUE CHI TONG
SHARK FIN SOUP

Serves: 6
1 can shark fin
6 cups chicken stock (page 416), chilled
   and defatted
1 cup chopped cooked chicken
2 tablespoons light soy sauce
salt to taste, optional
2 tablespoons Chinese wine or dry sherry
1 tablespoon cornflour
2 tablespoons cold water
2 egg whites, slightly beaten
6 spring onions, finely chopped

Combine shark fin and chicken stock and bring to the boil. Add chopped chicken meat, soy, wine and if necessary add salt to taste. Mix cornflour smoothly with cold water and stir into simmering soup until it boils and thickens very slightly. Add egg white to the soup, stirring with chopsticks so that it sets in small shreds. Remove soup from heat, pour into tureen, sprinkle spring onions over and serve.

YUE TONG MIN
FISH SOUP WITH NOODLES

Serves: 5-6
1 tablespoon peanut oil
1 clove garlic, crushed
1 teaspoon finely chopped fresh ginger
6 cups fish stock (page 416)
500g (1 lb) fillets of white fish
2-3 bundles egg noodles, boiled
few drops sesame oil
2 tablespoons chopped fresh coriander
　　leaves

Heat oil in a saucepan and fry garlic and ginger over low heat for a few seconds. Add fish stock and bring slowly to the boil. Add fish cut into bite-size pieces, cook 5 minutes, then add noodles and return to the boil. Stir in sesame oil and garnish with coriander leaves. Serve at once.

HAI YOOK DAHN GUNG
CRAB AND EGG SOUP

I remember a Chinese restaurant in Colombo that specialised in this soup. Their chef made it with fresh crab and it was a soup to remember. But canned or frozen crab meat can be substituted if fresh crab is difficult to obtain.

Serves: 5-6
1 large fresh crab or 2 x 185g (6½ oz) cans
　　or 375g (12 oz) frozen crab meat
6 cups fish or chicken stock (page 416)
4 eggs, lightly beaten
2 tablespoons cornflour
4 tablespoons cold water
6 spring onions, finely sliced

If using fresh crab, cook in water with seasoning as for fish stock (page 416) for 10 minutes. Cool, then pick out flesh and reserve. Discard shell and fibrous tissue from stomach. Flake crab meat, discarding any bony tissue.

Bring stock to the boil. Slowly dribble in beaten eggs. Stir gently. After 2 minutes stir in cornflour smoothly mixed with cold water, return soup to the boil and stir constantly until it is clear and slightly thickened.

Add fresh, canned or frozen crab meat and heat through. Serve immediately, sprinkled with spring onions.

DAHN FAR TONG
EGG FLOWER SOUP

This simple, nourishing soup can be made in a few minutes, using chicken stock cubes. The beaten egg will set when poured into the boiling soup and look like chrysanthemum petals.

Serves: 4-5
4 cups chicken stock (page 416)
2 tablespoons Chinese wine or dry sherry
1 teaspoon sesame oil
salt to taste
3 eggs, beaten lightly
3 tablespoons chopped spring onions

Bring stock to the boil, add wine and sesame oil. Taste and add salt if necessary.

Season beaten eggs with half teaspoon salt, pour slowly into the boiling soup. Stir once or twice. Serve at once, sprinkled with chopped spring onions.

SO JAR FOR TUI GAI GUEN (chicken and ham rolls) *recipe page 398*

GAY LIM SOOK MI GAI TONG
CHICKEN VELVET AND SWEET CORN SOUP

Chicken velvet is the name given to a purée made from chicken meat (usually white meat from the breast). This is minced or very finely chopped so it is smooth in texture. The delicate golden soup combines the purée with creamed corn.

Serves: 4-5
1 large chicken breast
½ teaspoon salt
2 tablespoons cold water
2 egg whites, beaten until frothy
5 cups chicken stock (page 416)
1 x 250 g (8 oz) can creamed corn
1½ tablespoons cornflour
3 tablespoons cold water
1 teaspoon sesame oil
2 tablespoons Chinese wine or dry sherry
2 thin slices smoked ham or bacon, finely
    chopped

Bone the chicken breast. Remove skin, and chop the flesh very finely until it is almost a paste. Add salt and water, mixing well. Fold in egg whites. Strain chicken stock into a saucepan, bring to the boil, add corn.

Bring slowly to the boil again, then stir in cornflour mixed with a little cold water. Return to boil, stirring, and cook until thickened, about 1 minute. Stir in sesame oil, wine or sherry and the chicken velvet. Stir and simmer for 2 or 3 minutes. Serve at once, sprinkled with finely chopped ham.

JU YOOK HAR KAU DOONG SHUN TONG
PORK AND PRAWN BALL SOUP WITH BAMBOO SHOOT

Serves: 6
Pork Balls:
500 g (1 lb) minced pork
¼ teaspoon finely grated fresh ginger
1 clove garlic, crushed
1 teaspoon salt
2 tablespoons finely chopped spring onions

Prawn Balls:
500 g (1 lb) raw prawns
¼ teaspoon finely grated fresh root
    ginger
½ teaspoon salt
1 slice soft white bread, crumbed
1 egg yolk
1 teaspoon cornflour

Soup:
6 cups pork or chicken stock (pages 416-417)
3 tablespoons canned bamboo shoot, sliced
1 tablespoon Chinese wine or dry sherry
3 teaspoons cornflour
2 tablespoons cold water
½ teaspoon sesame oil
2 tablespoons finely chopped spring onions
    to garnish

Pork Balls: Combine all ingredients, form into balls the size of a large marble. Bring stock to the boil, drop in balls and bamboo shoot (see 'soup' below) and return to the boil. Simmer for 15 minutes. Meanwhile make prawn balls.

Prawn Balls: Shell and de-vein prawns and chop very finely. Combine with all other ingredients, form into balls the same size as the pork balls and drop into simmering stock after pork balls have cooked 15 minutes. Return to simmering point, cook for a further 7 minutes. Remove pork and prawn balls, set aside. (This recipe is not successful with cooked prawns.)

Soup: Stir Chinese wine or dry sherry into the stock, then cornflour mixed with cold water. Boil, stirring until soup is clear and slightly thickened, about 1 minute. Stir in sesame oil. Return pork and prawn balls to soup and serve, garnished with finely chopped spring onions.

SZE CHUEN TONG
SZECHWAN SOUP

Serves: 6-8

2 cups soaked cellophane noodles
15 dried Chinese mushrooms
1 tablespoon dried wood fungus
1 tablespoon oil
½ cup finely chopped cooked pork
1 tablespoon dark soy sauce
2 teaspoons sugar
¼ cup hot water
½ cup chopped cooked prawns
½ cup fresh bean curd, chopped
6 cups chicken or pork stock (pages 416-417)
1 tablespoon light soy sauce
1 tablespoon Chinese sweet vinegar or
   other mild vinegar
1 tablespoon Chinese wine or dry sherry
1 teaspoon chilli oil
2 eggs, beaten
1½ tablespoons cornflour
6 tablespoons cold water
salt and pepper to taste

Cut soaked noodles into short lengths. Soak mushrooms in hot water for 30 minutes. Cut off and discard stems, then slice mushroom caps finely. Soak wood fungus in water for 10 minutes to soften, trim off any gritty portions and cut remaining fungus into small pieces. Set aside.

Heat oil in a saucepan and fry mushrooms and pork, stirring constantly, until they start to turn slightly brown. Add dark soy sauce, sugar and ¼ cup water and simmer, covered, until mushrooms have absorbed almost all the liquid. Add prawns and bean curd and stir fry for 1 minute. Add stock and noodles, bring to the boil, then reduce heat and simmer for 3 minutes. Add light soy, vinegar, wine, chilli oil. Dribble beaten eggs into simmering soup, stirring constantly so that egg separates into fine shreds. Mix cornflour smoothly with cold water, then add to soup away from heat. Return to heat and stir constantly until soup is thickened. Season to taste with pepper and salt.

Put a spoonful of wood fungus in the bottom of each soup bowl and pour a ladle of the boiling soup over. Serve immediately.

SUAN-LA TANG
SZECHWANESE HOT AND SOUR SOUP

Serves: 6

6 cups pork or chicken stock (pages 416-417)
60 g (2 oz) cellophane noodles, soaked
1 cup finely chopped cooked pork or
   chicken, or mixture of both
4 dried Chinese mushrooms, soaked and
   chopped
1 small canned bamboo shoot, chopped
1 teaspoon finely grated fresh ginger
1 tablespoon cornflour
4 tablespoons cold water
1 egg, slightly beaten
1-2 tablespoons tomato sauce
1 tablespoon light soy sauce
½ teaspoon salt or to taste
1 tablespoon vinegar
ground black pepper to taste
pinch of chilli powder, optional
2 teaspoons sesame oil
2 spring onions, finely chopped

Strain stock, chill and remove fat from surface. Bring to the boil in a large pan and add noodles cut in short lengths, pork or chicken, mushrooms, bamboo shoot and ginger. Stir the cornflour and the cold water together to blend thoroughly and add to simmering soup, stirring constantly until it boils and clears. Dribble the beaten egg into soup, stirring rapidly with chopsticks or fork so that it sets in fine shreds.

Remove soup from heat, add remaining ingredients and mix well, taste and correct seasoning as required. The taste should be quite sour and hot, but not overpoweringly so.

JAHP WUI TONG MIN
COMBINATION LONG SOUP

Serves: 6

6 dried Chinese mushrooms, soaked and cut in strips
2 eggs, beaten
salt and pepper to taste
few drops sesame oil
250 g (8 oz) fine egg noodles
8 cups chicken stock (page 416)
250 g (8 oz) lean pork or chicken
2 tablespoons peanut oil
1 clove garlic, bruised
2 slices fresh ginger
3 cups white Chinese cabbage, cut in strips
1 canned bamboo shoot, diced
2 tablespoons light soy sauce
2 tablespoons Chinese wine or dry sherry
salt to taste
1 teaspoon sesame oil

Soak mushrooms in hot water 30 minutes, discard stems and slice caps finely.

Season eggs with a little salt and pepper. Heat an omelette pan, grease lightly with few drops of sesame oil, and pour in half the beaten egg to make a thin omelette. Repeat with remaining egg. Slice omelettes finely and set aside.

Cook noodles for 2 minutes in plenty of lightly salted boiling water. Drain in colander and run cold water over to separate. Drain again. Heat chicken stock.

Shred pork or chicken very finely. Heat peanut oil in a wok, fry garlic and ginger and discard when brown. Add pork or chicken to flavoured oil, fry quickly, stirring, until colour changes. Add cabbage and bamboo shoot, fry 2 minutes longer.

Add fried mixture and noodles to chicken stock, return to the boil. Add soy sauce, wine and salt to taste. Stir in sesame oil. Serve immediately, garnished with omelette strips.

CHANG DAU NGAU YOOK SEE TONG
SHREDDED BEEF AND GREEN PEA SOUP

Serves: 4-5

250 g (8 oz) lean beef
5 cups cold water
½ teaspoon salt
1 whole star anise
1 teaspoon finely chopped fresh ginger
1 tablespoon Chinese wine or dry sherry
250 g (8 oz) frozen peas
2 teaspoons cornflour
extra 2 tablespoons cold water
2 eggs, lightly beaten
4 spring onions to garnish

Cut beef into thin slices, then into shreds. Put beef, water, salt, star anise, ginger and wine into a saucepan and bring to the boil. Cover and simmer 15 minutes. Add frozen peas, cook 5 minutes. Discard star anise. Mix cornflour with extra cold water and stir into soup. When it boils, stop stirring and dribble in eggs. Cook 1 minute, add more salt if necessary. Serve, garnished with short lengths of spring onion.

WONG NGA BAHK TONG
PALE GREEN SOUP

Serves: 4-5

1 tablespoon peanut oil
½ teaspoon finely grated fresh ginger
1 clove garlic, crushed
5 cups hot chicken stock (page 416)
1 cup boiled rice
750 g (8 oz) white Chinese cabbage, finely shredded
4 spring onions, finely chopped
1 tablespoon Chinese wine or dry sherry
½ teaspoon sesame oil

Heat oil, and fry ginger and garlic over low heat for 1 minute. Add hot stock and boiled rice and simmer for 30 minutes or until rice is very soft. Add cabbage and spring onions, simmer uncovered for 5-7 minutes. They will turn bright green when they first come to the boil, then cook to a paler shade of green. At this point stir in wine and sesame oil, and serve.

SEEN GOO GAI LAU TO YAN (chicken and walnuts with straw mushrooms) *recipe page 397*

WOO DIP HAR
BUTTERFLY PRAWNS

Serves: 4-6

12 large raw prawns
1 tablespoon Chinese wine or dry sherry, optional
2 tablespoons light soy sauce
1 small clove garlic, crushed
¼ teaspoon salt
½ teaspoon finely grated fresh ginger
½ cup cornflour
1 large egg, beaten
breadcrumbs for coating
peanut oil for deep frying

Shell and de-vein prawns, leaving tails on. With a sharp knife slit prawns along curve of back but do not cut right through. Combine wine, soy sauce, garlic crushed with salt, ginger. Marinate prawns in this mixture for 15 minutes.

Dip prawns into cornflour, shake off excess flour, then dip into beaten egg and finally into breadcrumbs. Press gently to flatten prawns and firm on the crumb coating.

Heat oil and fry prawns, 2 or 3 at a time, until golden brown, about 2 minutes. Drain on absorbent paper and serve hot with chilli sauce if desired.

DAI TZE GUEN
MINIATURE SCALLOP ROLLS

Makes 20-24

185 g (6 oz) scallops
3 dried Chinese mushrooms
6 canned or fresh water chestnuts, roughly chopped
2 spring onions, finely chopped
¼ teaspoon finely grated fresh ginger
½ teaspoon salt
1 teaspoon light soy sauce
1 teaspoon sesame oil
5 or 6 spring roll wrappers
1 egg
1½ tablespoons plain flour
peanut oil for deep frying

Beard scallops, rinse and drain on absorbent paper, then cut into small pieces. Soak mushrooms in hot water 30 minutes, cut off and discard stems, chop caps finely. Mix scallops and mushrooms with the chestnuts, spring onions, ginger, salt, soy sauce and sesame oil.

Cut each spring roll wrapper into quarters. On each quarter put a teaspoonful of filling, near one end. Fold pastry over filling, then fold sides in to enclose filling, and roll over again as for first fold. Beat egg until frothy, add flour and beat to a smooth, thick paste. Smear end of spring roll pastry with this paste and press gently to seal.

When all are made, fry in deep oil over medium heat until golden brown all over, about 1½ minutes. Drain on absorbent paper and serve hot.

Note: Frozen spring roll pastry is sold in Chinese stores. Thaw before attempting to separate wrappers.

JAR YUE HAR GUEN
DEEP-FRIED FISH AND PRAWN ROLLS

Serves: 4

12 raw prawns
500 g (1 lb) fish fillets (see note)
1 egg, beaten with 1 tablespoon water
¼ teaspoon finely grated fresh ginger
½ teaspoon salt
plain flour
dry breadcrumbs
oil for frying

Shell and de-vein prawns. Using a sharp knife, skin the fish fillets. Depending on the size of the fillets, they may be cut into two, three or four strips. Wrap each strip around a prawn and fasten with a wooden toothpick. Mix egg with ginger and salt. Dip fish rolls into plain flour, then into beaten egg and finally into breadcrumbs.

Heat about half cup oil in wok. When it starts to form a haze add fish rolls, about 6 at a time. Fry until golden brown all over, approximately 3 minutes. Drain on absorbent paper. Fry remaining rolls. Serve hot with soy or chilli sauce for dipping.

Note: Choose flat fillets of firm white fish. They should be thin, for they have to be rolled around the prawns.

SO JAR HAR YUEN
LOTUS FLOWERS

Crisp outside, meltingly soft inside, these are served as an appetiser at a Chinese meal or as a between-meal snack.

Makes about 15
500 g (1 lb) raw prawns
10 fresh or canned water chestnuts
2 spring onions
½ teaspoon finely grated fresh ginger
½ teaspoon salt
1 teaspoon Chinese wine or dry sherry
1 egg white
1 teaspoon cornflour
oil for deep frying

Shell and de-vein prawns, and chop finely. If fresh water chestnuts are used, peel and wash. Finely chop the chestnuts. Chop spring onions very finely. Mix prawns, water chestnuts, spring onions, ginger, salt and wine in a bowl, mixing thoroughly. Beat egg white until stiff, fold into mixture together with cornflour. Make walnut-size balls.

Heat oil in a wok or frying pan and deep fry the balls for 2 or 3 minutes until golden. Drain on absorbent paper and serve immediately.

SO JAR GAI YUEN
GOLDEN BLOSSOMS

Makes 12-15
250 g (8 oz) chicken breast
250 g (8 oz) raw prawns
3 spring onions, chopped
¾ teaspoon salt
2 teaspoons cornflour
½ cup drained whole kernel corn
2 tablespoons finely chopped barbecued
   pork (page 403), optional
1 small clove garlic, crushed

Batter:
¾ cup plain flour
1 tablespoon cornflour
½ teaspoon salt
¾ cup water
2 teaspoons peanut oil
½ teaspoon finely grated ginger, optional
1 egg white, stiffly beaten
oil for deep frying

Bone and skin chicken breast, reserve bones for stock. Chop breast meat very finely. Shell and de-vein prawns, chop very finely. Combine all ingredients thoroughly. Form mixture into balls, dip into batter and deep fry in hot oil until puffed and golden. Fry only a few at a time. Drain on absorbent paper. If not serving immediately, heat oil again until very hot and fry the golden blossoms briefly to crisp and heat just before serving.

Batter: Sift flour, cornflour and salt into a bowl, add water and beat to a smooth batter with wooden spoon. Stir in oil and ginger, allow to stand for 30 minutes. Just before using, beat egg white until stiff and fold in.

LAHNG POON
COLD HORS D'OEUVRE

Serves: 6-8
1 x 455 g (1 lb) can abalone
braised mushrooms (page 411), ½ quantity
200 g (8 oz) barbecued pork
1 cooked chicken breast
2 pairs dried red Chinese sausages (lap
   cheong)
6 tea eggs (page 433), quartered
1 large cucumber, thinly sliced
1 large radish, thinly sliced

Marinade
4 tablespoons light soy sauce
1 tablespoon sugar
1 tablespoon Chinese wine or dry sherry
1 tablespoon sesame oil
½ teaspoon finely grated fresh ginger

Drain abalone and discard liquid from can. Cut abalone into very thin slices and put in marinade. Slice braised mushrooms thinly. Cut barbecued pork and chicken breast in thin slices. Steam sausages for 10 minutes or until plump, cool and cut in paper-thin diagonal slices. Drain abalone slices and reserve the marinade.

Arrange ingredients attractively on a large serving plate and serve marinade in a small bowl as a dip.

Marinade: Mix all ingredients together.

DOONG GWOO LAP CHEONG JING JU YOOK
MUSHROOM, PORK AND CHICKEN SAUSAGE

Cooking time: approximately 50 minutes
Oven temperature: 170°C (350°F)
Serves: 8-10

8 dried Chinese mushrooms
500 g (1 lb) chicken breast
125 g (4 oz) barbecued pork
1 canned bamboo shoot or small can
   water chestnuts
1 large clove garlic, crushed
1 teaspoon salt
½ teaspoon finely grated fresh ginger
2 tablespoons light soy sauce
1 tablespoon Chinese wine or dry sherry
¼ teaspoon pepper
1 teaspoon sugar
3 teaspoons cornflour
1 tablespoon sesame oil
1 tablespoon barbecue sauce
length of sausage skin, large size

Soak mushrooms in hot water for 30 minutes. Cut off stems with sharp knife and keep for adding to stock, or discard. Chop mushroom caps finely. Bone and skin the breast of chicken and cut flesh into small dice. Dice barbecued pork. Drain bamboo shoot or water chestnuts and chop finely. Crush garlic with the salt, mix ginger and garlic together, and add to all the chopped ingredients. Add soy sauce, wine, pepper, sugar, cornflour, sesame oil and barbecue sauce, and mix well to combine ingredients and seasonings thoroughly.

Using a funnel, push filling into the sausage skin. Tie a knot in the skin about a metre from where you start. When you have filled the skin, you will have a handsome sausage, which you coil around and put on a wire rack. Prick the sausage with a very fine sharp skewer to prevent bursting. Put the rack over a roasting tray with an inch of hot water in it. Roast in a moderate oven for 25 minutes, turn over and roast until brown on the other side too. Cut into short lengths to serve. If liked, you may twist the sausage skin at intervals, while filling, to form small sausages.

Note: Try to buy barbecued pork with a fair amount of fat on it. When buying the sausage skin from your butcher, emphasise that you need the large one. (My butcher once gave me the small size by mistake, and you should have seen the fun I had getting the filling in.) The skin should be thoroughly cleaned and ready for use, but if liked, soak it in salted water at home while preparing the filling, then fit one end of it on the cold water tap and run water through it.

HAR KAU or K'AU CHE (prawns in transparent pastry, *top right*) *recipe page 432;*
SIEW MAI (steamed prawn dumplings, *top left*) *recipe page 428;*
CHA SHIU BAO (barbecued pork buns, *bottom*) *recipe page 428;*
MA YUNG BAO (steamed sweet bean buns, *bottom, with smooth tops*) *recipe page 433*

DAI BAO
DOUGH FOR STEAMED BUNS

This dough is used with a variety of fillings, both savoury and sweet.

Makes: 8-10 buns
2½ cups plain flour
3½ teaspoons baking powder
3 tablespoons caster sugar
2 tablespoons softened lard
about ½ cup lukewarm water
½ teaspoon white vinegar

Sift flour and baking powder into a bowl, stir in sugar and rub in lard with fingertips until evenly distributed. Add water and vinegar mixed together and knead to a fairly soft dough. Shape into a smooth ball, cover and rest dough for 30 minutes.

To make buns, divide dough into 8 or 10 portions and mould each into a smooth ball. Roll out on a very lightly floured board to a circle about 10 cm (4 inches) across. Put a heaped teaspoonful of filling in centre of circle and gather edges together, folding and pleating to make a neat join. Twist dough to seal. Put each bun, join downwards, on a square of greaseproof paper lightly brushed with sesame oil. Put in steamer, cover and steam for 20 minutes. Serve warm. The cooked buns can be refrigerated overnight and reheated by steaming for 3 minutes before serving.

CHA SHIU BAO
BARBECUED PORK BUNS *(picture page 427)*

Makes: 6-8 buns
185 g (6 oz) barbecued pork
2 teaspoons peanut oil
1 small clove garlic, crushed
¼ teaspoon salt
⅓ cup hot water
2 teaspoons light soy sauce
½ teaspoon sesame oil
1 teaspoon oyster sauce
3 teaspoons cornflour
1 teaspoon hoi sin sauce
1 teaspoon sugar
small pinch red colouring powder
  (see Glossary)
1 quantity steamed bun dough (above)

Dice pork very small. Heat oil in a pan, add garlic crushed with salt and cook very slowly, not allowing garlic to brown. Add hot water, soy sauce, sesame oil and oyster sauce. Mix cornflour with a tablespoon of cold water and stir in, then cook stirring until thick and clear. Remove from heat, stir in hoi sin sauce, sugar and red colouring. Cool, then stir in pork. Mould and steam buns as described above.

SHIU MAI
STEAMED PRAWN DUMPLINGS *(picture page 427)*

Makes about 24
500 g (1 lb) small raw prawns
6 dried Chinese mushrooms
6 canned water chestnuts, chopped
3 tablespoons canned bamboo shoots,
  chopped
3 spring onions, chopped
250 g (8 oz) minced pork
1½ teaspoons salt
1 tablespoon light soy sauce
1 tablespoon Chinese wine or dry sherry,
  optional
1 teaspoon sesame oil
1 egg white
125 g (4 oz) wonton wrappers

Peel prawns, reserve about 24 for garnish and chop the remainder. Soak mushrooms in hot water 20 minutes, then slice off and discard stems. Chop mushroom caps. Combine all chopped ingredients with pork, salt, soy, wine, sesame oil and egg white. Mix well together and put 1 heaped teaspoon of mixture in the centre of each wonton wrapper. Gather the wrapper around filling and press it close to give the shape of a little money bag, open at the top. Press a prawn on top of each for decoration. Lightly oil a steamer and put siew mai in a single layer on perforated tray. Cover tightly and steam over boiling water for 20 minutes. Serve hot or cold with a dipping sauce if liked.

WONTON
TINY SAVOURY DUMPLINGS

*Wonton are little squares of noodle dough
enclosing a savoury meat mixture. They may be
deep fried and served as a crisp snack or they
may be boiled in soup. Wonton are the main
ingredient in 'short soup'. Wonton wrappers are
sold in Chinese grocery stores.*

Makes about 40
6 dried Chinese mushrooms
3 tablespoons finely chopped bamboo shoot
125 g (4 oz) raw prawns, finely chopped
4 spring onions, finely chopped
250 g (8 oz) minced pork
1½ teaspoons salt
1 tablespoon light soy sauce
1 teaspoon sesame oil
250 g (8 oz) wonton wrappers
peanut oil for deep frying

Soak mushrooms in hot water for 30 minutes, squeeze out excess moisture, trim off and discard stems and chop mushroom caps finely. Blanch bamboo shoot in boiling water for 1 minute, drain, then chop finely. Combine all chopped ingredients with minced pork and seasonings.

Put a small amount of filling (about half a teaspoonful) in the centre of each wonton wrapper, moisten edges of dough with water, fold over to a triangle with points slightly overlapping and press together. Then bring the two ends together, dab with a little of the filling mixture where they join and press to seal. When all are made, deep fry a few at a time on medium heat until golden (about 2 minutes). Serve as an appetiser or as part of a meal with sweet sour sauce.

CHAI DIM SUM
VEGETARIAN DIM SUM

Makes about 36
4 cups cooked and minced gluten (see
   opposite column)
6 dried Chinese mushrooms
3 tablespoons peanut oil
¼ cup finely chopped spring onions
1 clove garlic, crushed
1 teaspoon finely grated fresh ginger
2 cups finely sliced cabbage
½ cup finely chopped bamboo shoot and/
   or water chesnuts
2 tablespoons light soy sauce
2 teaspoons sesame oil
3 teaspoons salt
1 teaspoon monosodium glutamate,
   optional
2 tablespoons cornflour
2 eggs, beaten
250 g (8 oz) wonton wrappers

To make gluten: Measure 2 cups water into a large mixing bowl. Sprinkle in 2 cups gluten flour, mix well and knead until smooth, then leave for an hour or more. Bring water to a boil in saucepan, cut pieces of gluten dough off and drop into the water. Return to boil, then simmer for 30 minutes or until they rise to the surface. Drain and cool, then chop or mince finely.

Stuffing mixture: While making gluten, soak mushrooms in hot water for 30 minutes. Then remove and discard stems, chop caps very finely. Heat peanut oil in a wok or large frying pan and fry spring onions, garlic and ginger on low heat for a minute or two. Add cabbage and continue to fry, stirring, until cabbage is soft. Add bamboo shoot, water chestnuts, mushrooms, gluten and cook for a minute or two longer. Remove from heat, put into a large bowl and add seasonings, cornflour and enough beaten egg to bind the mixture together.

Take a wonton wrapper in the palm of your hand. Put a tablespoonful of mixture in the centre and gather up the pastry to enclose filling. With the back of a teaspoon, press points of the dough down to cover. Squeeze dumpling firmly to make dough adhere to filling. Put in an oiled steamer and steam for 10 minutes.

These may be served at once, or refrigerated for a day or two and deep fried, or reheated by further steaming before serving.

POK PANG
MANDARIN PANCAKES

These delicate crepes are traditionally served with Peking duck, but are also used to enclose a variety of fillings such as egg foo yong, shredded pork or chicken. The filling is seasoned with a dab of rich flavoured sauce, sprinkled with finely shredded spring onions, then rolled up and eaten as a snack.

Makes 20 pancakes to serve 4-5
2 cups plain flour
¾ cup boiling water
1 tablespoon sesame oil

Measure unsifted flour into bowl. Bring water to the boil and pour at once on to the flour, stirring with chopsticks or the handle of a wooden spoon for a few minutes. As soon as it is cool enough to handle, knead for 10 minutes until the mixture is a soft, smooth dough. Put dough on a board and cover with a bowl, then let it stand for at least 30 minutes.

Roll dough into a cylindrical shape and cut into 10 slices of equal size. Keep covered with plastic wrap to prevent drying out. Take one slice at a time and cut in two equal pieces. Roll each to a smooth ball, then roll out on a lightly floured board to a circle about 8 cm (3 inches) in diameter. Brush one circle lightly with sesame oil, taking it right to the edge of the circle. Put second circle on top of the first one and roll again, both circles together this time, until the pancakes are about 17 cm (6 or 7 inches) across. They must be very thin. Cover each pancake with plastic as it is made. When they are all rolled out, heat a heavy frying pan or griddle and put pancakes one at a time on the ungreased surface. Cook over low heat until pancake develops small bubbles. Turn frequently so that it cooks on both sides. A few golden spots will appear.

Remove from pan and gently pull the two circles apart. The sesame oil they were brushed with makes this quite easy. Pile the pancakes on a plate and cover tightly or they will dry out. Pancakes should be soft and pliable, not brittle. To serve, fold each pancake in quarters.

To reheat, arrange pancakes in a steamer lined with a clean tea towel, cover and put over simmering water for a minute or two.

JEUNG
SAUCES

SEE YAU GHUNG JEUNG

Ginger Soy Sauce:
For any kind of fried seafood or steamed dumplings.

Combine 1 teaspoon very finely grated fresh ginger with ½ cup light soy sauce.

SEE YAU LAHT JIU JEUNG

Chilli-Soy Sauce:
For fried prawns, dim sum, kau che, hot or cold hors d'oeuvre.

Combine 2 tablespoons Chinese chilli sauce and ½ cup soy sauce.

DAU SEE SHEUNG JING JEUNG

Black Bean Sherry Sauce:
Subtle enough for delicate seafood like crab and scallops.

Rinse and mash 1 tablespoon canned salted black beans, then combine with 3 tablespoons Chinese wine or dry sherry, 1 teaspoon sugar and a few drops of sesame oil.

SUEN TAU DAU SEE

Black Bean Garlic Sauce:
Good with pork or duck.

Rinse and mash 2 tablespoons canned salted black beans, crush 1 small clove garlic. Mix beans and garlic with 2 tablespoons each of light soy sauce and Chinese wine or dry sherry.

CHA YIP DAHN (tea eggs or marbled eggs) *recipe page 433*

SOO MUI JEUNG, SHIU HAU JEUNG

Plum and Barbecue Sauce:
Serve with roast duck, barbecued pork.

Combine 6 tablespoons each plum sauce and red barbecue sauce. Stir in half teaspoon ginger juice, 2 tablespoons light soy sauce and, if a hotter dip is preferred, 1 teaspoon chilli sauce or to taste.

TIM SUEN JEUNG

Sweet Sour Sauce:
Serve with hot hors d'oeuvres or fried wonton.

Make sauce as for crisp fried pork (page 403) but omit the vegetables. If liked, stir in a teaspoonful of chilli sauce at the end.

WAH YIM

Salt and Five Spice Mix:
Serve with crisp fried chicken, roasted duck or pork.

Mix 2 tablespoons salt with 1 teaspoon five spice powder.

GOO YUET FUN YIM

Roasted Pepper and Salt Mix:

Roast 2 tablespoons black peppercorns in a dry pan over medium heat, shaking pan or stirring, until pepper gives off a pleasant smell. This takes 4 or 5 minutes. Allow pepper to cool slightly, them pound with a mortar and pestle and mix with 3 tablespoons salt. If this is more than you need for one time, store mixture in an airtight bottle.

HAR KAU or KAU CHE
PRAWNS IN TRANSPARENT PASTRY *(picture page 427)*

These steamed savouries with a delicately seasoned prawn filling are a speciality on the menu of some Chinese restaurants. The filling is enclosed in thinly rolled, semi-transparent dough shaped like miniature Cornish pasties.

Makes about 20
Filling:
185 g (6 oz) raw prawns
2 tablespoons chopped ham or bacon fat
2 tablespoons finely chopped bamboo
   shoot
2 spring onions, finely chopped
½ teaspoon finely grated fresh ginger
3 teaspoons cornflour
1 teaspoon sesame oil
1 teaspoon salt
1 teaspoon sugar

Dough:
1 cup Chinese wheat flour
3 tablespoons cornflour
⅞ cup water
1 tablespoon lard
sesame oil for brushing

Filling: Shell and de-vein prawns and cut into small pieces. Combine with all other ingredients, mixing thoroughly. Set aside while making dough.

Dough: Mix Chinese wheat flour and cornflour together in a bowl. Put water and lard into a small saucepan, bring to the boil, cool while counting 20 seconds, then pour onto flour. Mix well with chopsticks or the handle of a wooden spoon and as soon as it is cool enough to handle knead to a smooth, pliable dough. Divide into two equal portions and mould each into a cylinder approximately 12.5 cm (5 inches) long and 2.5 cm (1 inch) in diameter. Keep dough wrapped in plastic film to prevent surface drying out.

On a smooth surface (a laminated pastry board is ideal) cut 12 mm (half inch) slices from one of the rolls of dough and flatten with the lightly greased blade of a wide Chinese chopper or a metal spatula. Roll out to a thin circle about 10 cm (4 inches) in diameter.

Put a teaspoonful of filling on the dough and bring edges together. Pinch to seal, at the same time fluting the joined edges as for decorating a pie crust. When the dough from one roll is used up, brush the kau che lightly with sesame oil, put on squares of oiled greaseproof paper and steam for 12 minutes. Repeat with remaining dough and filling. Serve hot with sauces for dipping if desired.

CHA YIP DAHN
TEA EGGS or MARBLED EGGS *(picture page 430)*

*Serves: 12-18 as part of a selection
of hors d'oeuvres.*

6 eggs
4 cups water
3 tablespoons tea leaves
1 tablespoon salt
1 tablespoon five spice powder

Put eggs in a saucepan, cover with cold water and bring slowly to the boil, stirring gently (this helps to centre the yolks). Simmer gently for 7 minutes. Cool eggs thoroughly under cold running water for 5 minutes. Lightly crack each egg shell by rolling on a hard surface. Shell should be cracked all over, but do not remove.

Bring 4 cups water to the boil, add tea leaves, salt and five spice powder. Add cracked eggs. Simmer, covered, for approximately 30 minutes or until shells turn brown. Let eggs stand in covered pan for 30 minutes longer (overnight if possible). Drain, cool and shell. The whites of eggs will have a marbled pattern on them. Cut into quarters and serve with a dipping sauce.

TIM SUEN JEUNG
SWEET SOUR PICKLE SAUCE

Makes about 2 cups sauce
½ cup Chinese pickles
½ cup pineapple pieces
⅓ cup juice from pickles
⅓ cup juice from pineapple
⅓ cup white vinegar
pinch red food colouring powder
   (see Glossary)
2 tablespoons sugar
½ teaspoon salt
1 small clove garlic, crushed
3 teaspoons cornflour
2 teaspoons cold water

Cut pickles into medium-sized pieces. Combine with pineapple pieces and set aside. Put juice from pickles and pineapple into a small enamel saucepan with vinegar, red colouring powder, sugar, salt and garlic. Bring to the boil, reduce heat and simmer for 2 minutes, then add the pickles and pineapple and bring once more to boiling point. Stir in the cornflour mixed with cold water and stir constantly until boiling, thickened and clear.

MA YUNG BAO
STEAMED SWEET BEAN BUNS *(picture page 427)*

These steamed buns with sweet bean paste filling are a between-meal snack rather than a dessert and are eaten by the Chinese much as Western people nibble cookies and candy.

Makes: 10
1 quantity bun dough (page 428)
1 x 255 g (9 oz) can sweet bean paste
   (dow saah)
1 tablespoon sesame oil for brushing

Divide dough into 10 equal portions and roll each into a circle about 8 cm (3 inches) in diameter. Put a teaspoonful of bean paste in the centre of each circle and mould and steam buns as described on page 428. Serve warm or at room temperature.

JAR WONTON
DEEP-FRIED SWEET WONTONS

Makes about 50
250 g (8 oz) dates without pits
¼ cup chopped walnut kernels, cashews
  or almonds
rind of 1 large lemon, finely grated
1 tablespoon orange juice or as required
250 g (8 oz) wonton wrappers
oil for deep frying
icing sugar for dusting

Chop dates finely, combine with chopped nuts, lemon rind and orange juice. Mix thoroughly, adding more orange juice if the mixture is too dry to hold together. This will depend on the quality of the dates — some may not need much juice at all, others may need quite a lot. Form the date mixture into small cylinders about as thick as your little finger and half as long. On each square of wonton pastry put a roll of date mixture, placing it diagonally. Pick up corner of pastry and place it over the filling, tucking point under. Roll up the wonton into a tube so that filling is completely enclosed, then twist the ends of the pastry tube, putting a finger in the end to keep the shape like a Christmas cracker. When they are all made heat oil in a wok and when very hot fry about 8 wontons at a time, turning them, until they are golden brown all over. This should take about 2 minutes. Lift them out with a slotted spoon and drain on absorbent paper. When cool, sprinkle with icing sugar, and arrange on serving plate.

Note: These wontons can also be prepared with a canned lotus nut filling.

HUNG YUN DAU FU
ALMOND BEAN CURD

Serves: 6-8
4 cups water
4 teaspoons powdered agar-agar or 1 cup
  soaked and drained agar-agar strands
1 can sweetened condensed milk
2 teaspoons almond essence

Put water into a saucepan, sprinkle agar-agar over and bring to the boil. Boil and stir until agar-agar is dissolved. Powdered agar takes only a couple of minutes to dissolve, strands take longer. Add condensed milk and almond essence and stir well. Pour into a large shallow glass dish or a large cake tin. Allow to cool and set, then chill. Cut into cubes or diamond shapes and serve by itself or with canned fruits or melon balls.

DOONG FONG SIK GOW LAHM
ORIENTAL FRUIT BASKET *(picture opposite)*

Take a medium-size watermelon and cut off the top third. With a melon-baller scoop out melon flesh, discarding seeds. Combine melon balls with any of the following: canned lychees, longans, loquats, mandarin segments. Mix with some of the syrup from the cans. Cover and chill at least 3 hours. If liked, a few canned or bottled chow chow preserves can be added. Before serving, arrange fruits in the watermelon shell and spoon some of the syrup over.

DOONG FONG SIK GOW LAHM (oriental fruit basket) *recipe above*

KOREA

I thought I knew about fine slicing and shredding, having cooked Chinese food for years, but until I was taught how to make some Korean specialities by Mrs Soojin Kim I had no idea just how finely food should be shredded for cooking in the Korean way. Fascinated, I watched her deft, graceful hands turn out strips of beef, vegetable and omelette that were incredibly fine. It was done at impressive speed, yet the strips were quite uniform in thickness and length. I was learning how to make *guchulpan,* or Nine Varieties (page 450), a traditional Korean dish.

Small pancakes are piled in the centre of a tray (preferably a compartmented tray). All around are a selection of ingredients for filling the pancakes, each one shredded finely, stir fried with very little oil, and seasoned with pepper and salt; where it will not spoil the colour, a little soy sauce is added during the cooking. The ingredients are picked up with chopsticks and put in the centre of a pancake, which is rolled around the filling, dipped in a special sauce and eaten.

Guchulpan is usually served as a prelude to a meal or as something to nibble with drinks. I have found it

can be a complete dinner — but one of those informal occasions where guests participate more than usual because they become involved in choosing their own fillings, and test their skill at completing the whole operation using chopsticks. Because *guchulpan* is served at room temperature, it is ideal for advance preparation.

Mrs Kim also showed me jars of bean paste that are a staple of Korean cooking. The nearest equivalent would be Chinese bean paste or Japanese *aka miso* (red bean paste), but the Korean version, *dhwen-jang,* has more flavour. According to Koreans it has more nutritional value too.

Another large stone jar held *gochujang,* a very salty chilli paste that was surprisingly mellow and did not catch the throat as most chilli preparations do. *Silgochu,* thread-fine strips of dried red chilli, are also widely used in Korean cooking.

It is traditional for soybean pastes and sauces to be made in the spring, and most people make them at home. Equally important is the autumnal pickle-making season when jars of *kimchi,* the famous Korean pickle based on *baechu* (variously known as

Korean cabbage, Chinese cabbage, celery cabbage) are put down in readiness for winter and the year ahead. Radishes and cabbage are the favourite vegetables for pickling and large quantities are made, for *kimchi* appears on the table at every meal, even breakfast.

In Korea, rice is served at every meal. At breakfast it is sometimes served as gruel, especially for elderly people and children. At other meals steamed rice, cooked by the absorption method, is accompanied by soup, meat, fish, vegetables and, of course, *kimchi.* Rice is of such importance that meals are described as consisting of rice and *panch'an,* a term that takes in whatever else is served with the rice.

Sometimes the rice is combined with other grains such as barley and beans. Among the beans used are dried lima beans, *azuki* beans (red beans) and soy beans, or soybean products such as bean curd, bean pastes and soy sauce.

Korea has an abundance of fish and other seafood, and often the fish is combined in surprising ways with meat or poultry (see Sin Sul Lo, page 446). Like the Japanese, Koreans use seaweed, especially the dried laver seaweed known as *nori* by the Japanese and *kim* by the Koreans. It is used as a relish. Mrs Kim says that in order to give it a delicious flavour it should be liberally brushed with sesame oil and sprinkled with salt on one side; the thin sheet is passed back and forth over a hotplate or gas fire until it becomes crisp, then cut into small squares and served with steamed rice. The rice is wrapped in the seaweed by each diner and rolled up with chopsticks.

Beef is the most popular meat in Korea. Pork and chicken are also used, but mutton never. Beef is not usually cooked in one big piece. It is very thinly sliced and cut into bite-size pieces; sometimes the slices are beaten out for extra thinness. The beef is then kneaded well with a marinade and left for 2-4 hours so that it is tenderised and flavoured.

While Koreans charcoal grill or broil such meals as *bulgogi* or *bulgalbi,* everyday cooking includes boiling, steaming, stir frying and deep or shallow frying; baking is not one of their cooking methods, for few Koreans have ovens.

The seven basic flavours of Korean food are garlic, ginger, black pepper, spring onions, soy sauce, sesame oil and toasted sesame seeds. The sesame seeds are crushed before being added to marinades or mixed with cooked dishes, thus releasing their full flavour — and it is amazing what a difference the toasting makes to the flavour of sesame. Thus, the Middle Eastern *tahini* (sesame seed sauce), made with untoasted sesame seeds, seems to have no relationship to the sauces of Korea, which are made

after the seed has been roasted, giving them a rich nutty flavour.

Here are the quantities of basic flavourings sufficient for marinating 500 g (1 lb) of beef.

½ teaspoon finely grated fresh ginger
1 teaspoon finely chopped or crushed garlic
1 teaspoon finely chopped spring onion
1 teaspoon sesame oil
1-2 teaspoons toasted, crushed sesame seed
4 teaspoons light soy sauce
2 teaspoons honey or sugar
¼ teaspoon ground black pepper

SERVING AND EATING A KOREAN MEAL

Silver chopsticks and spoons are used for Korean meals because silver discolours in the presence of poison, so they are considered the safe way to eat. A formal dinner setting will also have silver bowls for rice and soup. Expensive, but the silverware is usually part of a bride's dowry. Everyday settings are of brass or china. Nowadays stainless steel is more popular than brass because it does not need the polishing that brass does.

The food is served and eaten from bowls, not plates. Everything is put on the table at once — rice, soup, fish, chicken, beef, hot sauces, sweet and sour sauces, vegetables prepared in several ways and *kimchi* of various kinds. There are numerous varieties of *kimchi,* some prepared with the addition of dried shrimps or salt fish, and elaborate versions including rare fruits and vegetables. Some are very strong while others are quite mild.

The meal does not end with sweets. Sometimes fresh fruits are served, but this is not the everyday pattern of eating. Korean fruits include apples, Korean pears (different from the varieties we know) oranges, grapes, cherries, plums and persimmons.

UTENSILS

The traditional Korean kitchen featured wood fires, but modern times have brought gas and electric stoves. Most of the cooking is quite simple. A good heavy frying pan, a *wok* and some saucepans or flameproof casseroles will see you through any of the Korean dishes in this chapter. The only other unusual vessel you need is the traditional pot used in 'steamboat' or 'firekettle' meals if you want to serve Sin Sul Lo in true Korean fashion. This pot has a central chimney surrounded by a moat, which holds the food. It cooks and keeps hot at the table

because the chimney is filled with glowing coals. Get the coals ready an hour or more beforehand in an outdoor barbecue, an *hibachi* or a metal bucket so they will be well alight and glowing when needed.

The food can be arranged in the pot well ahead of serving time and the whole pot placed in the refrigerator. Just before starting the meal the moat is filled with boiling stock, the cover put on the pot to ensure particles of coal don't fall into the food, and the coals or briquettes (which should be alight and glowing) are transferred to the chimney with tongs. To protect the table, put the pot on a heavy metal tray and put the tray on a thick wooden board. After the broth has simmered for a while, and the contents of the pot are heated through, guests pick out food with chopsticks and eat it with rice and a dipping sauce. At the end of the meal the stock is served as soup.

These pots are usually sold at Chinese stores. While some models in polished and ornate brass are quite expensive, the modest anodised aluminium versions are cheap and work just as well. In Korea the pots are either individual-size silver ones, or larger stainless steel versions. Of course you can always substitute an electric frypan or deep fryer or *wok,* three quarters filled with stock; or use any fairly deep pan on an efficient table burner.

YOUR KOREAN SHELF

black pepper, ground
cayenne pepper or chilli powder
chilli sauce (substitute for *gochujang,*
    Korean chilli paste)
bamboo shoots, canned
dhwen jang (bean sauce) or *mein chiang* (Chinese
    bean paste) or *aka miso* (Japanese red bean paste)

dried mushrooms (Oriental variety, not
    Continental)
dried shrimps
peanut oil
rice wine or dry sherry
sesame oil
sesame seeds
soy sauce, light and dark
white vinegar

In addition to these items, which keep indefinitely, there are the all-important garlic, ginger and spring onions. Garlic of course can be bought anywhere, but fresh ginger root is not so common. If you buy fresh ginger in a large quantity when available it is a simple matter to preserve it for months by scraping away the brown skin, cutting into knobs or small sections and putting it in a clean, dry bottle. Pour over dry sherry until the ginger is completely immersed, cover tightly and store in the refrigerator. Mature ginger root will keep quite well for about a month in a paper bag in the crisper section of the refrigerator; or, as many people do in the East, bury it in a patch of damp soil about 10 cm (4 inches) below the surface.

Toasted, crushed sesame seed is such an essential item of Korean seasoning that it is useful to prepare a fair amount and store it in readiness for use.

Put 1 cup white sesame seed in a heavy frying pan and cook over medium heat, stirring constantly, until sesame is golden brown. As soon as it has acquired the right colour and smells cooked; turn it out of the hot pan onto a plate or it will darken too much and turn bitter. When slightly cool, crush the seeds with mortar and pestle (much used in Korea) or pulverise in an electric blender. Cool completely and store in a screw-top jar.

SONG-I BAHB
RICE WITH MUSHROOMS

Serves: 6
250 g (8 oz) fresh mushrooms
1 tablespoon vegetable oil
1 tablespoon sesame oil
2 medium onions, finely sliced
½ cup finely shredded lean steak
500 g (1 lb) short grain rice
3 cups hot water
1 teaspoon salt
2 tablespoons light soy sauce
¼ teaspoon ground black pepper
2 tablespoons toasted ground sesame seeds

Wipe over the mushrooms and slice. Heat the oils together in a large saucepan and fry onions, steak and mushrooms for 2 minutes, then add rice and stir-fry for a further minute. Add all remaining ingredients and bring to the boil. Turn heat very low, cover tightly and cook for 20 minutes. Do not lift lid or stir at all during this time. Serve hot with pickles or vegetable dishes.

GUCHULPAN (nine varieties) *recipe page 450*

BOKUM BAHB
CRAB AND PORK FRIED RICE

Serves: 4
2 tablespoons oil
1 clove garlic, finely grated
1 teaspoon finely grated fresh ginger
½ cup flaked cooked crab meat
½ cup chopped cooked pork
4 cups hot cooked rice
½ cup chopped spring onions
1 teaspoon salt or to taste

Heat oil in a wok and put in garlic, ginger, crab and pork at once. Stir fry until very hot, add rice and continue stir frying until rice is fried. Add spring onions and sprinkle salt over. Toss well to mix, taste and add more salt if necessary. Serve hot.

GUN SAENGSUN
GRILLED FISH

Serves: 6
6 small fish or 12 small fillets
3 tablespoons soy sauce
2 teaspoons sugar
3 tablespoons toasted, crushed sesame seeds
1 tablespoon sesame oil
1 medium clove garlic, crushed
1 teaspoon finely grated fresh ginger
½ teaspoon chilli sauce, optional

Buy fish cleaned and with heads removed, but leave them whole. Trim fins and tail. Combine remaining ingredients for sauce.
   Turn each fish over in the sauce, put on oiled griller tray and grill under medium heat until fish is cooked through to the centre bone. Better still, grill over glowing coals. Brush fish with sauce during cooking to keep flesh moist. Do not overcook.

TUIGIM SAENGSUN
FRIED FISH

Serves: 6
6 small fillets of fish
2 tablespoons light soy sauce
2 tablespoons toasted, crushed sesame seeds
pinch ground black pepper
2 tablespoons finely chopped spring onions
2 teaspoons sesame oil
2 tablespoons vegetable oil

Wash and dry fish. Combine soy, sesame seeds, pepper, spring onions and sesame oil. Dip fish in the mixture and fry in hot oil until it is cooked through and golden brown on both sides. Serve soon after cooking.

DAK JIM
CHICKEN STEW

Serves: 4-6
1 x 1.5 kg (3 lb) roasting chicken
¼ cup light soy sauce
2 tablespoons sesame oil
1 tablespoon finely chopped garlic
½ teaspoon chilli powder or cayenne
   pepper
3 spring onions, very finely chopped
¼ teaspoon salt

Cut chicken into small serving pieces. Put into a large heavy pan, add all remaining ingredients and mix well so that all the chicken comes in contact with the flavourings. Leave for 2 hours at room temperature then put on low heat and cook, covered, until chicken is tender. Serve with hot rice and kim chi (page 446).

DAK BUSUT JIM
BRAISED CHICKEN AND MUSHROOMS

Serves: 4-6

10 dried Chinese mushrooms
1 x 1 kg (2 lb) chicken
3 tablespoons light soy sauce
1 tablespoon sesame oil
2 cloves garlic, crushed
½ teaspoon cayenne pepper or chilli
  powder
½ teaspoon ground black pepper
2 tablespoons vegetable oil
1 large onion
2 canned winter bamboo shoots
4 spring onions
2 tablespoons toasted, crushed sesame
  seeds

Soak mushrooms in hot water for 30 minutes. Discard stems, cut caps into thin strips. Cut chicken into joints, then chop into small pieces, cutting through the bones with a heavy cleaver. Mix together the soy sauce, sesame oil, garlic, cayenne pepper and black pepper and rub well over chicken. Marinate chicken in this mixture for 30 minutes.

Heat vegetable oil in a wok and stir fry the well-drained chicken over medium heat until brown. Add mushrooms strips, half cup of liquid in which mushrooms soaked and the remaining marinade from chicken. Cover and simmer for 15-20 minutes or until chicken is tender. Meanwhile, cut onion into 8 wedges, divide each wedge in halves crossways and separate layers of onion. Cut bamboo shoots into quarters, then into slices. Cut spring onions into bite-size lengths, using green portion as well as white. Add to simmering chicken and cook for a further 2 minutes. Garnish with sesame seeds and serve with white rice.

YUKKAE JANG KUK
BEEF STEW

Serves: 6

1 kg (2 lb) skirt or flank steak
2 teaspoons salt
½ teaspoon ground black pepper
24 spring onions, sliced
1 teaspoon sugar
125 g (4 oz) rice vermicelli
2 tablespoons sesame oil
2 teaspoons chilli powder (or to taste)
2 eggs, lightly beaten

Put whole piece of steak into a saucepan with salt, pepper and just enough water to cover. Bring to the boil, cover and simmer until steak is very tender. Allow to cool, then shred with fingers into fibres. Return to the pot, add spring onions and sugar and simmer for 10 minutes. While simmering, soak rice vermicelli in hot water for 10 minutes, then drain. Add to simmering pot. Mix sesame oil and chilli powder together and add to stew. The rich red oil will float on top. Drizzle the beaten eggs into the bubbling stew, stirring so that it cooks in shreds. Serve with hot white rice.

BULGALBI
BARBECUED SHORT RIBS OF BEEF *(picture page 443)*

Serves: 8-10 as an appetiser, 4 as a main dish

2 kg (4 lb) beef short ribs
½ cup soy sauce
½ cup water
4 tablespoons finely chopped spring
  onions
2 teaspoons finely grated garlic
1 teaspoon finely grated fresh ginger
1 tablespoon sugar
½ teaspoon ground black pepper
2 tablespoons toasted, crushed sesame seeds

Ask butcher to saw through the bones to make cubes of about 5 cm (2 inch) size. Hold pieces on board, bone downwards, and with a sharp knife cut halfway through meat in small dice to let marinade penetrate. Combine the remaining ingredients in a large bowl, add the short ribs and mix well. Cover and chill overnight, or at least 4 hours.

Prepare domed grill or hibachi well ahead of cooking time so coals have an hour or more to achieve the steady glow necessary for successful cooking. Put meat on grill with bone side downwards and cook until brown. Turn and cook other side until well done. Turn pieces frequently, so that all sides are grilled brown and crisp. The short ribs are intended to be picked up with the fingers for eating.

Note: Bulgalbi can also be cooked under a preheated griller or oven-roasted. Short ribs should be in one layer in roasting pan. Roast in moderately hot oven for 1 hour, turning pieces over halfway through cooking.

BULGOGI
FIERY BEEF

Serves: 10-12 as an appetiser, 6-8 as a main dish
1 kg (2 lb) lean rump or fillet
marinade ingredients as for bulgalbi
(page 441) in half quantities

Cut steak into very thin slices. Beat them out very flat, cut into medium-size squares. Make up the marinade and leave meat to soak for 3 hours (longer in the refrigerator). When ready to serve, grill briefly over glowing coals and serve with white rice, accompanied by bulgogi sauce (below).

YANGNYUM KANJANG
BULGOGI SAUCE

3 tablespoons soy sauce
2 teaspoons sesame oil
1 teaspoon mein chiang (Chinese bean paste), optional
2 tablespoons water
2 tablespoons rice wine or dry sherry
1 teaspoon toasted, ground sesame seeds
2 teaspoons finely chopped spring onion
½-1 teaspoon chilli sauce, optional
1 small clove garlic, crushed
salt to taste
2 teaspoons sugar

Put soy sauce and sesame oil in a small bowl and stir in next 6 ingredients. Crush garlic with salt and sugar to a fine paste. Stir in, mix well and serve in small individual sauce dishes.

GOGI BOKUM
DEEP-FRIED BEEF SLICES

Serves: 3-4
500 g (1 lb) lean rump or fillet steak
1 spring onion, finely chopped
1 tablespoon finely chopped leek
1 clove garlic, finely chopped
½ teaspoon sugar
3 tablespoons light soy sauce
2 teaspoons sesame oil
few drops hot chilli sauce
½ cup peanut oil
1 quantity bulgogi sauce

Cut steak into very thin slices and beat them quite flat. Arrange in a single layer on a dish and sprinkle with spring onion, leek and garlic. Mix sugar, soy sauce, sesame oil and chilli sauce together. Spoon over the beef. Marinate for 2 or 3 hours, or longer in the refrigerator.

Heat peanut oil in a wok and when very hot fry the beef slices a few at a time for only a few seconds. Drain briefly then serve at once with rice and bulgogi sauce (above). Steak is dipped in the sauce and eaten, accompanied by white rice.

BULGALBI (barbecued short ribs of beef) *recipe page 441*

CHICHIN GOGI
BRAISED MEAT WITH ONIONS

Serves: 4-6

750 g (1½ lb) lean steak, round or topside
24 spring onions, white part of
3 tablespoons toasted sesame seeds
1 clove garlic
½ teaspoon finely chopped fresh ginger
¼ cup light soy sauce
½ teaspoon chilli powder or cayenne
    pepper
2 tablespoons vegetable oil
6 dried mushrooms, soaked and sliced

Slice meat and cut into bite-size squares, then beat until very thin. Slice spring onions thinly and set aside. Put sesame, garlic, ginger, soy and chilli powder into a bowl and combine with beef, kneading seasonings into beef. Heat oil in a wok and stir fry meat and mushrooms on high heat until cooked. Remove from wok and fry onions, adding a little more oil if necessary. Scatter onions over the meat and serve immediately. This should be eaten with bowls of hot rice.

GOGI BUSUT BOKUM
STIR-FRIED BEEF WITH FRESH MUSHROOMS

Serves: 2-4

250 g (8 oz) lean steak
1 small clove garlic, crushed
½ teaspoon finely grated fresh ginger
½ teaspoon salt
250 g (8 oz) fresh mushrooms, thickly
    sliced
2 tablespoons oil
¼ cup stock or hot water
1½ teaspoons cornflour
1 tablespoon cold water

Cut beef into paper-thin slices across the grain. Mix garlic, ginger, and salt with beef, distributing the seasoning evenly. Heat oil in a wok and stir fry beef over high heat until colour changes. Add mushrooms and continue stirring and frying for a further minute, then add stock, reduce heat, cover wok and simmer for 2 minutes.

Push beef and mushrooms to side of wok, stir in cornflour mixed smoothly with the cold water and keep on stirring until it boils and thickens. Serve immediately with white rice.

SANJUCK
SKEWERED BEEF AND MUSHROOMS

Serves: 4-5

250 g (8 oz) lean rump or round steak
2 tablespoons sesame oil
1 tablespoon soy sauce
2 teaspoons toasted, crushed sesame seed
1 clove garlic, crushed
½ teaspoon sugar
pinch ground pepper
½ teaspoon crushed fresh chilli
185 g (6 oz) fresh mushrooms
12 spring onions
plain flour for dipping
2 large eggs, beaten
oil for frying

Cut slice of steak into 6 mm (¼ inch) strips, then cut strips into 5 cm (2 inch) lengths. Combine oil, soy sauce, sesame seed, and garlic crushed with sugar, pepper and chilli. Pour mixture over the meat in a bowl, mix and leave to marinate while preparing other ingredients. Slice mushrooms thickly if large, or cut into halves if small. Wash and trim spring onions to where the green leaves start to separate, then cut the solid part into 5 cm (2 inch) lengths. On bamboo skewers thread alternately pieces of meat, onion and mushrooms. Cut skewers in half if they are too long to fit into your frying pan, but thread two lots of ingredients on before you cut them so you have the pointed end for easy threading.

Dip skewers in flour, then in beaten egg. Heat enough oil to cover base of frying pan. Oil should be hot, but not smoking. Put skewers in pan and cook until brown and crisp, 2 or 3 minutes on each side. Serve immediately with white rice.

GALBI JIM
SPARERIBS BRAISED WITH SESAME SAUCE

Serves: 4-5
1.5 kg (3 lb) pork spareribs
1 tablespoon oil
2 tablespoons soy sauce
2 teaspoons sesame oil
3 spring onions, finely chopped
2 cloves garlic, crushed
1 teaspoon finely grated fresh ginger
2 tablespoons sugar
2 tablespoons rice wine or dry sherry
1 tablespoon toasted, ground sesame seeds
1 cup hot water
1 teaspoon cornflour
1 tablespoon cold water
spring onions for garnish

Ask butcher to chop spareribs across into short lengths of about 5 cm (2 inches). Separate them with a sharp cleaver, heat oil in a wok and brown spareribs over high heat. Combine all other ingredients (except cornflour and cold water) and add to pan, bring to the boil, then cover and simmer 40-45 minutes. Add cornflour mixed smoothly with cold water and stir constantly over medium heat until gravy boils and thickens. Dish up and garnish with spring onions either thinly sliced or split and curled in iced water. Serve with white rice.

SONG-I BUSUT JIM
STEAMED MUSHROOMS WITH PRAWN AND CHICKEN

Serves: 4
250 g (8 oz) fresh mushrooms
125 g (4 oz) peeled raw prawns
1 medium chicken breast
6 canned water chestnuts, chopped
2 tablespoons chopped bamboo shoot
2 tablespoons finely chopped spring onion
1 tablespoon cornflour
1 tablespoon light soy sauce
1 teaspoon oyster sauce
½ teaspoon salt
½ teaspoon finely grated fresh ginger
few sprigs fresh coriander leaves, optional

Choose mushrooms at the button or cup stage about 3.75 cm (1½ inches) in diameter. Wipe with damp paper towels and remove stems with a little twist, leaving caps intact. (Save stems for another purpose.) De-vein prawns and chop finely. Skin and bone chicken breast and chop finely. Combine with all other ingredients in a bowl, mixing thoroughly. Fill into mushroom caps, mounding filling slightly and pressing into a neat shape. Put mushrooms on a lightly oiled heatproof plate and steam for 20 minutes. Garnish with fresh coriander sprigs and serve at room temperature.

OYI JIKAI
STIR-FRIED CUCUMBERS WITH BEEF

Serves: 4
250 g (8 oz) lean rump or fillet
2 teaspoons sesame oil
1 tablespoon light soy sauce
½ teaspoon salt
½ teaspoon sugar
¼ teaspoon cayenne pepper
2 large green cucumbers
1 tablespoon vegetable oil
2 tablespoons toasted, crushed sesame
  seeds

Freeze the beef for a short time to make it firm enough to cut into paper-thin slices. Slices should be about 5 cm (2 inches) long and 12 mm (½ inch) wide. Put beef in a bowl and add sesame oil, soy, salt, sugar and cayenne. Mix well with the hand so flavourings penetrate meat.

Peel cucumbers, leaving a thin strip of green skin at intervals for decorative effect. Cut in halves lengthways, scoop out seeds then cut crossways into medium-thin slices.

Heat the oil in a wok, swirl wok to coat with oil, add beef and stir fry on high heat for 1 minute. Add cucumbers and toss for a further minute, then let mixture simmer until cucumber is half cooked. It should be tender but still crisp. Garnish with sesame seeds and serve hot with white rice.

SIN SUL LO
BANQUET FIREPOT (*picture opposite*)

In Korea, this version of the famous Steamboat is served on special occasions. All the food is arranged in the pot before it is brought to the table to finish cooking. It is also sometimes served in individual pots with coals in the central chimney to keep the broth simmering throughout the meal.

Serves: 6
500 g (1 lb) fillet steak
2 medium onions, peeled and sliced
250 g (8 oz) white fish fillets
250 g (8 oz) calf's liver
3 eggs, separated
plain flour
vegetable oil for frying
4 spring onions
1 carrot
6-8 cups beef stock (page 452)
½ cup each walnuts and pine nuts
sesame seed sauce (page 451)

Partially freeze steak, then cut into paper-thin slices. Put beef and onions into sin sul lo pot (opposite) or individual pots. Slice fish into bite-size pieces. Slice liver very thinly into pieces of similar size. Season both fish and liver with pepper and salt. Beat the yolk of 1 egg and dip slices of liver in it, then in flour. Slightly beat the white of the egg and dip fish slices in it, then in flour. Heat just enough oil to cover the base of a frying pan and quickly saute the pieces of fish and liver until just cooked. Put these in the pot on top of the beef and onions.

Beat remaining 2 egg yolks and make a flat omelette with them, turn out on a plate to cool. Do the same with the remaining egg whites. On a wooden board cut the yellow and white omelettes into strips just long enough to fit across the moat of the firepot. Do the same with the spring onions. Slice the carrot thinly and cut into strips of the same size. Arrange these over the beef, fish and liver, then garnish with walnuts and pine nuts. The recipe may be prepared up to this point, covered and refrigerated.

At serving time carefully ladle boiling stock into the moat without disturbing the arrangement of the food. Replace cover on pot and with tongs put glowing coals into the chimney. Bring to the table and allow broth to simmer for a few minutes and heat the contents of the pot thoroughly.

Remove cover and let guests help themselves from the pot with chopsticks. They dip the food in individual bowls of sesame seed sauce before eating. Boiled rice is served with this meal and at the end the stock is served as soup.

KIM CHI
PICKLED CHINESE CABBAGE

Kim chi is one of Korea's national dishes, with as many versions as there are cooks. This is a combination of three recipes, and while it may have an unorthodox touch in the Japanese dashi stock, it is a very tasty version of kim chi — one that would appeal to most people.

1 large white Chinese cabbage
common salt (not iodised)
cayenne pepper
6 spring onions, finely chopped
6 cloves garlic, finely chopped
3 fresh red chillies, finely chopped
3 teaspoons finely chopped fresh ginger
2 cups dashi stock (page 476)
2 teaspoons light soy sauce
pinch monosodium glutamate

Cut base off cabbage, then slice lengthways into 6 segments. Dry in the sun for half a day, cut each segment in halves crossways, then put into an unglazed earthenware pot alternately with good handfuls of salt and a sprinkling of cayenne pepper, making several layers. Cover with a wooden lid just small enough to fit inside the pot so that it rests directly on the cabbage. Weight it down with a heavy stone and leave for a week, then rinse the cabbage thoroughly under cold running water. Squeeze out as much moisture as possible. Slice into 2.5 cm (1 inch) sections or chop more finely if preferred and put into the rinsed-out jar, this time layering with the onions, garlic, chillies and ginger. Fill pot with the dashi stock mixed with the soy and monosodium glutamate. Cover with wax paper, put lid back on top and refrigerate. After 4 or 5 days the kim chi is ready for eating. Serve with hot white rice and a dash of soy sauce.

Note: In cold weather kim chi does not require refrigeration, but when weather is warm, store in refrigerator for up to 3 weeks.

SIN SUL LO (banquet firepot) *recipe opposite*

SAEWOO BOKUM
GREEN BEANS WITH PRAWNS

Serves: 6
500 g (1 lb) small prawns or shrimps
500 g (1 lb) tender green beans
2 tablespoons vegetable oil
1 tablespoon sesame oil
1 medium onion, sliced thinly
3 tablespoons light soy sauce
1 teaspoon sugar
3 teaspoons toasted, crushed sesame seeds

Shell and de-vein prawns, chop them roughly and set aside. Top and tail the beans, remove strings and with a sharp knife cut into thin diagonal slices. Heat oils in a wok and stir fry the onion and prawns together for 2 minutes, add beans and stir fry for 3 minutes. Add seasonings and mix well, cover and simmer on low heat for 6-8 minutes or until beans are just tender. They must not be overcooked. Serve at once with rice.

SIKUMCHI KUK
BRAISED SPINACH WITH PORK

Serves: 6
2 bunches fresh spinach
250 g (8 oz) pork fillet
2 cloves garlic
2 tablespoons oil
2 tablespoons light soy sauce
¼ teaspoon ground black pepper
5 spring onions, finely chopped
1 egg, beaten
3 tablespoons toasted, crushed sesame seeds

Wash spinach well, remove the tough stems and break leaves into large pieces. Dice the pork very small. Chop garlic finely. In a wok heat the oil and fry the pork and garlic, stirring constantly, until pork changes colour. Add spinach and toss well, season with soy sauce and pepper. Cover and simmer on low heat until spinach is tender. Add spring onions and egg and stir well over medium heat for 2 minutes, then sprinkle with sesame seed and serve hot with rice.

CHAP CHYE
STIR-FRIED MIXTURE

Serves: 4-6
250 g (8 oz) fillet of beef
1 teaspoon sugar
1 tablespoon soy sauce
2 teaspoons finely chopped spring onion
1 teaspoon finely chopped garlic
1 teaspoon ground sesame seeds
¼ teaspoon ground black pepper
1 tablespoon sesame oil
125 g (4 oz) white Chinese cabbage cut in thin strips, optional
125 g (4 oz) carrots, cut in matchstick strips
125 g (4 oz) bamboo shoots, finely sliced
125 g (4 oz) onions, finely sliced
2 cucumbers, finely sliced
1 bunch spinach, cooked and shredded
omelette strips (page 451)
60 g (2 oz) cellophane noodles
soy sauce, sugar, salt, pepper to taste
¼ teaspoon monosodium glutamate, optional

Cut beef into paper-thin strips and put in a bowl with next seven ingredients. Set aside for 30 minutes while preparing vegetables.

Soak noodles in hot water for 20 minutes, then drain and cut in 7-10 cm (3-4 inch) lengths.

Stir fry all ingredients *separately* until just cooked. Mix together on a large plate, season to taste with soy, sugar, salt, pepper and add monosodium glutamate if liked. Serve very hot.

MU SAINGCHAI
WHITE RADISH SALAD

Serves: 4
2 giant white radishes
1 or 2 crisp cooking apples
juice of half lemon
3 spring onions

Dressing:
3 tablespoons light soy sauce
1 tablespoon salad oil
2 teaspoons sesame oil
3 tablespoons mild vinegar
3 teaspoons sugar
1 teaspoon salt
1 tablespoon toasted, crushed sesame seeds
1 fresh hot red chilli, seeded and finely
   chopped

Peel radishes and cut into matchstick strips. Peel apples and cut into similar strips, and soak in cold water with a good squeeze of lemon juice to prevent discolouration. Slice the spring onions very finely, including white and green portions. Combine all remaining ingredients and toss with the radish, well-drained apple and spring onion. Cover and chill before serving.

OYI NAMUL
CUCUMBER SALAD

Serves: 6
2 large green cucumbers
3 teaspoons coarse salt
1 cup water
2 tablespoons mild vinegar
1 teaspoon sugar
¼ teaspoon cayenne pepper
1 clove garlic, finely chopped
1 spring onion, finely chopped
3 teaspoons toasted, crushed sesame seeds

Peel cucumbers thinly and cut across into thin slices. Put in a bowl, sprinkle with salt and add water. Soak for 15 minutes, then drain off all liquid. Combine other ingredients, pour over cucumbers, mix well and serve chilled.

KONG NAMUL
BEAN SPROUT SALAD

Serves: 6
500 g (1 lb) fresh bean sprouts (mung or
   soy)
1 tablespoon sesame oil
1 tablespoon salad oil
1 tablespoon crushed, toasted sesame seeds
3 tablespoons light soy sauce
1 clove garlic, crushed
2 spring onions, very finely chopped
1 teaspoon honey or sugar
dash of chilli powder or cayenne pepper

Wash bean sprouts. Bring a pan of lightly salted water to the boil, drop in the bean sprouts and return to the boil. Boil for 1 minute if using mung beans, longer for soy beans. The sprouts should be just tender, never overcooked. Drain at once and cool under cold water. Drain well. Combine all other ingredients for the dressing and toss with bean sprouts. Chill before serving.

GUCHULPAN
NINE VARIETIES *(picture page 438)*

Shredded omelettes, stir-fried shredded beef, various stir-fried vegetables, surround a pile of small pancakes. Fillings are rolled in the pancake, dipped in sauce and eaten.

Serves: 6 as a main dish, 12 as an appetiser
Pancakes:
1½ cups plain flour
¼ teaspoon salt
2 eggs, beaten
1 cup milk
1 cup water
vegetable oil for frying
few pine nuts and parsley sprigs, optional

Fillings:
10 dried Chinese mushrooms
3 eggs, separated
250 g (8 oz) fillet of beef
vegetable or sesame oil for frying
soy sauce to taste
ground black pepper to taste
3 tender carrots
salt to taste
12 spring onions
1 giant white radish
250 g (8 oz) zucchini
sprinkle of sugar

Dipping Sauce:
¾ cup soy sauce
3 tablespoons mild vinegar
3 tablespoons crushed, toasted sesame
  seeds
2 tablespoons finely chopped spring
  onions

Pancakes: Sift flour and salt into a bowl. Mix beaten eggs with milk and water. Make a well in the centre of the flour and add liquid, stirring rapidly with a wooden spoon. Beat until smooth and let the batter stand while preparing fillings.

Heat a large frying pan and grease very lightly with oil. Pour in a ladle of the batter, sufficient to make a fairly thin pancake. Cook on medium-low heat so pancake does not brown. Turn and cook other side, then turn on to a large board. When all the pancakes have been made, cut into small circles with a 7.5 cm (3 inch) round pastry or cookie cutter and pile pancakes in centre of tray or dish. Decorate with a few pine nuts and a sprig of parsley if desired.

Fillings: Soak dried mushrooms in hot water for 30 minutes.

Beat egg yolks and egg whites separately and cook separately in a lightly greased frying pan to make large, flat omelettes. Do not allow to brown. Turn out on plate or board and allow to cool, then shred into very fine strips.

Shred the beef very finely. It is easier to do this if the beef is partially frozen first. Heat about a tablespoon of oil in a pan and stir fry the beef, adding soy sauce and ground black pepper to taste. Beef should be well done and any liquid should be evaporated.

Scrape the carrots, cut into very thin slices, then cut slices into thin shreds, finer than matchsticks. Stir fry in very little oil, adding salt and pepper to taste. Cut spring onions into similar size lengths and stir fry briefly. Peel and shred radish and stir fry until wilted. Season with salt. The aim is to keep the natural colour of the vegetables so cook for only a short time and do not allow anything to brown. Do not peel zucchini — the green skin adds to the appearance of the dish. Slice finely, then cut into fine strips and stir fry for a few minutes, season with salt.

Squeeze out water from the mushrooms, cut off and discard tough stalks, then shred the caps into thin slices. Heat very little oil and stir fry, then add soy sauce and pepper and a sprinkling of sugar and half cup of the water the mushrooms soaked in. Cover and cook 15-20 minutes or until mushrooms are tender and liquid absorbed.

Arrange all the filling ingredients in separate piles around the edge of a plate or in a compartmented tray, leaving the centre for the pancakes.

Dipping Sauce: Blend together ingredients and divide between individual sauce bowls.

GANGHWE
APPETISERS

2 eggs, separated
sesame oil
375 g (12 oz) fillet of beef
basic seasonings (page 437)
thin strips of dry red chilli (silgochu)
very fine young spring onions or large
    chives

Beat egg yolks and whites separately with a fork. Lightly grease a heavy frying pan with oil and pour in the beaten yolks. Swirl frying pan to make a paper-thin omelette; when set, turn and lightly cook other side. Turn on to a plate. Repeat with white of eggs. Cut yellow and white omelettes into fine strips. Slice beef into very fine shreds, marinate in basic seasonings for 20 minutes, then stir fry in heated wok without any oil or cook on an ungreased pre-heated griddle for just a few minutes.

Cut off white portion of spring onions and save for salads, etc. Pour boiling water over spring onion leaves to make them pliable. Drain off water after 1 minute, then make little bundles of egg strips, beef strips and strips of chilli. Bind them tightly with the onion leaves, leaving strips of egg and beef showing at either end. Dip in sesame seed sauce (below) and eat.

BINDAE DUK
BEAN PANCAKES

Makes about 20
1 cup mung dhal (dried mung bean halves
    without skin)
1 cup water
2 eggs, beaten
125 g (4 oz) pork mince
1 small onion, finely chopped
1 spring onion, finely chopped
2 cloves garlic, crushed
1 teaspoon salt
¼ teaspoon ground black pepper
1 teaspoon finely grated fresh ginger
½ cup fresh bean sprouts, chopped
½ cup kim chi or shredded white Chinese
    cabbage
2 tablespoons sesame oil

Wash mung dhal and soak in cold water overnight. Rinse and drain well, then put into container of electric blender with 1 cup water. Blend until smooth. Pour into a bowl, add all other ingredients and mix well. Heat a griddle or heavy frying pan and drop tablespoonfuls of the mixture on the hot surface. Cook until golden brown underneath, turn and cook other side. Serve hot or cold.

CHO KANJANG
SESAME SEED SAUCE

Serve this sauce with cooked or raw vegetables. It may be made and kept for a few days, or longer in the refrigerator.

½ cup sesame seeds
1 tablespoon sugar
3 tablespoons vinegar
4 tablespoons light soy sauce

Toast the sesame seeds in a dry frying pan over medium heat, stirring constantly, for 5 minutes or until they are a toast-brown colour. Crush with mortar and pestle or in electric blender. Mix in sugar, vinegar and soy sauce. Store in a bottle and serve with hot or cold vegetables or as a sauce for meat.

TANG
BEEF STOCK

2 kg (4 lb) beef rib bones
1 kg (2 lb) shin beef
4 large slices fresh ginger
1 teaspoon salt
cold water

Put well-washed bones into a large pan with beef, ginger, salt and sufficient cold water to cover. Bring to the boil. Remove any scum from surface, then lower heat, cover and let stock simmer for 2-3 hours on very low heat. Cool, strain stock and chill. Remove any trace of fat from surface. Use as basic stock in soups.

GORIGOMTANG
OXTAIL SOUP

Serves: 6-8
1.5 kg (3 lb) oxtail, jointed
8 cups water
2 slices fresh ginger
1 teaspoon salt

Sauce:
3 tablespoons light soy sauce
1 tablespoon sesame oil
1 tablespoon toasted, crushed sesame seeds
¼ teaspoon ground black pepper
3 tablespoons finely chopped spring
  onions
3 teaspoons finely chopped garlic
1 teaspoon finely chopped ginger

Put oxtail into a large pan with water, ginger and salt. Bring to the boil, then reduce heat and simmer until meat is tender. Take off any froth and scum that forms on the surface; this may take about 2 hours. If a pressure cooker is used, it should take about 45 minutes. Liquid should be reduced to about 6 cups. Combine remaining ingredients and serve with soup as a dipping sauce for the pieces of oxtail.

GOGI KUK
BEEF AND VEGETABLE SOUP

Like many Korean dishes, this soup has a hot tang from the bean sauce.

Serves: 4-6
6 cups beef stock (above) or water
250 g (8 oz) round or chuck steak
3 spring onions
2 cloves garlic
2 tablespoons oil
4 dried mushrooms, soaked and sliced
1 teaspoon hot bean sauce, or more as
  required
2 tablespoons light soy sauce
1½ teaspoons salt
1 tablespoon rice wine or dry sherry
½ teaspoon black pepper
1 teaspoon sesame oil

Stock should be strained and cleared of fat (see above). Cut steak into small dice. Cut spring onions into 5 cm (2 inch) lengths and cut each length in half lengthways. Chop garlic finely. Heat oil in a large pan, add beef and stir fry until browned. Add onions, garlic and mushrooms and fry for a minute longer, then add bean sauce, stock, soy sauce and all the other seasonings except sesame oil. Bring to the boil, stir well, turn heat low and simmer for 10 minutes. Taste and add extra seasoning as necessary. Add sesame oil, stir and serve.

MANDOO
DUMPLING SOUP

Serves: 6

9 cups basic beef stock (opposite)
2 tablespoons light soy sauce
salt to taste
omelette strips to garnish
toasted, crumbled nori (page 437) to
    garnish

Dumplings:
2 tablespoons oil
125 g (4 oz) pork mince
125 g (4 oz) lean beef mince
½ cup water
250 g (8 oz) fresh bean sprouts
half a small white Chinese cabbage
1 square fresh bean curd
3 spring onions, finely chopped
1 tablespoon toasted, crushed sesame seeds
1 clove garlic, finely chopped
½ teaspoon salt
¼ teaspoon ground black pepper
125 g (4 oz) wonton pastry

Prepare and clear beef stock. Add soy sauce and salt, have garnishes ready. Prepare dumplings, cover with plastic wrap and have ready (they may be made 2 or 3 hours before required). Bring stock to the boil, drop in the dumplings one at a time, taking care they do not stick together. Depending on size of the pot, it may be necessary to cook them in two or three batches. Simmer for 10 minutes or until dumplings come to the surface and are cooked. Serve immediately in small bowls.

Dumplings: Heat oil in saucepan and fry pork and beef until colour changes. Add half cup water and simmer gently until liquid evaporates. Set aside. Boil bean sprouts in lightly salted water for 3 minutes, drain and chop. Boil cabbage for 5 minutes, drain well and chop finely. Mash the bean curd. Mix all these ingredients with the spring onions, sesame seeds, garlic, salt and pepper. Taste for seasoning. Put a teaspoonful of the filling in the centre of each square of wonton pastry, dampen edges with water and press together to form a triangle. Cover so they do not dry out before cooking.

KONG NAMUL KUK
SOUP OF SOYBEAN SPROUTS

Serves: 6

500 g (1 lb) soy bean sprouts
375 g (12 oz) lean steak
1 tablespoon soy sauce
1 tablespoon sesame oil
¼ teaspoon ground black pepper
2 cloves garlic, crushed
8 cups water
finely chopped green leaves of 2 spring
    onions

Wash and drain bean sprouts, pinch off straggly tails. Roughly chop the sprouts if they are very long. Shred meat into fine strips and marinate in soy sauce, sesame oil, pepper and garlic. Heat a wok, put in beef and stir fry until it changes colour. Add water and bean sprouts, bring to the boil, cover and simmer for 30 minutes. Remove from heat, add spring onion leaves and cover for 5 minutes. Add more soy sauce or salt if necessary and serve hot.

JAPAN

Japanese food stands apart from all other Asian food because of its simplicity and purity. It is memorable not for its spicing or richness or complex blending of flavours, but because it emphasises basic ingredients and trains the palate to accept and appreciate food in its most natural state.

To those brought up in a tradition of cooking that prides itself on subtle sauces or spice blends that tantalise and defy analysis, this sparseness of seasoning comes as something of a shock. But once Japanese food has been approached without prejudice, and sampled with good appetite and open mind, it wins admirers from all culinary backgrounds.

My regret is that I didn't discover it until quite recently — now I'm really converted, and consider Japanese food to be some of the most delicious in the world. To think I imagined I wouldn't enjoy raw fish! It is one of the delicacies of a cuisine that makes delicacies of most foods.

What is the special quality of Japanese cooking? Is it the beautiful presentation? Is it the small quantities in which food is served so that one appreciates the appearance, aroma, taste and texture in a special way?

I think it is all these — and a certain attitude the Japanese have towards food. It is considered not only fuel for the body but also food for the soul. There is as much attention given to the right bowl or plate on which to present the food as to the preparation of the food itself. The surroundings in which a meal is eaten are also carefully chosen so that a peaceful atmosphere prevails. An alcove in the room will provide a setting for a simple flower arrangement, a scroll or some other beautiful object.

Great emphasis is placed on freshness, quality and foods in season. Japanese wives shop every day so they are certain of the freshness of ingredients. The first of any seasonal food is always greatly prized, and they are prepared to pay high prices for the privilege of tasting the first strawberries, *matsutake* mushrooms or other seasonal treats.

Comparing Japanese cooking with other Asian cooking, another difference is that most traditional Japanese cooking is done in or over water, while other cuisines use oil as a cooking medium. Water-based cooking gives a lightness and delicacy of flavour that is most appealing. Steaming means that the pure flavours of the food and most of the food value are retained. As a result, the Japanese are a slim, healthy race, and heart disease has never been a problem — although since hamburgers, ice-cream, cheese, butter and other Western foods have become popular, overweight Japanese are not as rare as they used to be.

Most people who have been exposed to the food of Japan do not just accept it, but become happily addicted to the Japanese style of eating. I have seen Westerners sitting at *tempura* counters or *sushi* bars, relishing *sushi, tempura, yakitori, sashimi* and other dishes.

Sashimi or *otsukuri* the famous (and often dreaded) dish consisting of various kinds of raw fish, is often avoided without being given a chance to vindicate itself. But for the diner who dares, what a wonderful surprise awaits. There are no strong, fishy tastes to offend because only the choicest portions of the freshest fish are used. It is truly a dish for the connoisseur with a discerning palate, the dipping sauce of soy and *wasabi* (green horseradish) adding flavour without disguising the fish itself.

Seaweed may not be everyone's cup of *dashi,* but when used as a flavouring for rice, stock and other dishes, it is so subtle as to be hardly discernible. On the other hand, toasted *nori,* a great favourite in Japan, is prized for its strong flavour. *Wakame,* a seaweed popular in soups and other simmered dishes, has an unmistakably marine smell and taste.

Tofu or soy bean curd, low in calories and high in protein, is a mainstay of the Japanese diet. It is served at breakfast, lunch and dinner. Its flavour is so delicate that it might be mistaken for a custard that is neither sweet nor savoury, but once someone takes a liking to this food, it becomes almost a fetish. A recent innovation is 'instant tofu' sold in powder form and which, when heated and combined with a coagulating agent, makes very good *tofu* in very little time. What's more, this instant *tofu* will keep under refrigeration for a week or longer, whereas fresh *tofu* bought readymade will keep for only a day or two. *Miso* (bean paste) and *shoyu* (soy sauce) are two more soy bean products that are fundamental to Japanese food. Japanese soy sauce is the most universally used seasoning and who, having savoured the wonderful difference it makes to all kinds of food, would be content to do without it?

Perhaps the best feature of Japanese food is that it is so light. Even deep-fried foods such as *tonkatsu* or *tempura* are renowed for their lightness. The batter that covers *tempura* has no relationship at all to the coating batter used in a fish-and-chip shop. *Tempura* batter is feather-light and so thin it is almost transparent, providing a crisp coating which helps the food cook both in the hot oil and in it sown steam within the fragile batter covering. Pure vegetable oil is used for frying, and is usually a mixture of different oils such as corn oil, olive oil and a proportion of sesame oil to give flavour. It is heated to just the right temperature to keep fried food digestible and non-greasy.

Although *tempura* is so widely known, and is one of the most popular Japanese dishes, it is a comparatively recent addition to Japan's cuisine, having been introduced by the Portuguese in the sixteenth century. On days when, as Catholics, they were forbidden to eat meat, they asked for shrimp fried in batter. What the Japanese did with the basic idea was to refine it, create a batter of exquisite lightness and make the cooking and serving of it a triumph of split-second timing. At Japan's many *tempura* restaurants, customers sit around the bar where a chef dips seafood and vegetables in ice-cold, freshly made batter, fries it for just the right length of time, drains it briefly and serves it within seconds so it is eaten at its best.

Tonkatsu (fried pork schnitzel), introduced by the Germans, is said to be the Far Eastern version of *wiener schnitzel;* and deep-fried chicken is only one example of the Chinese influence on Japanese cooking. But in each case Japanese chefs have given the dishes a delicacy that makes these foreign ideas fit comfortably into the rest of Japan's aesthetic cuisine.

And 'aesthetic' is the word that must be used in describing Japanese food, because next to freshness and flavour is an awareness of how the food must look, how it should be presented. This changes with the seasons of the year. The Japanese don't try to impress with out-of-season foods, but use the foods nature provides and emphasise with a seasonal motif the changing moods of nature. A slice of carrot may be shaped like a blossom in springtime, while in autumn it will be carved to resemble a maple leaf. Summer foods, cool and light, are set off by green leaves and delicate plates, while winter brings on steaming *nabemono* foods such as *shabu-shabu* and *sukiyaki,* to be cooked and eaten at the table. Even the dishes to serve and eat on are chosen for their seasonal suitability. This awareness of the changing of the seasons permeates Japanese culture and thinking, and the choice and presentation of food. The Japanese word for it is *kisetsukan*—'seasonal feeling'.

It is virtually impossible for someone who has not lived in Japan to absorb and express this kind of awareness. But it is possible, without too much trouble, to be able to cook Japanese food and enjoy it.

Great importance is attached to the cooking of rice, for if there is one thing the Japanese housewife must be able to do, it is to cook rice — and cook it perfectly. Nowadays, automatic rice cookers are widely used, but for centuries rice has been cooked without these modern marvels and has always been cooked well. The absorption method is used; though slightly different from the methods used in other Asian countries, the recipe (page 458) is simple and always gives good results. Apart from being the staple food of Japan, rice is the foundation of many favourite dishes such as *tendon, oyako donburi,* and *sushi* — Japan's popular version of an open sandwich (page 480).

Fortunately for me, I had excellent guidance when discovering Japanese cuisine. My first encounter was arranged by Mrs May Leong, who knows Japanese food well and who also knows the Japanese chefs at a first class restaurant. The menu was so well chosen that I enjoyed every taste of the many dishes.

Back in Australia, Tetsu Kurosawa helped me further. Tetsu is a self-taught Japanese chef who has quite a clientele in one of Sydney's better Japanese restaurants.

Best of all, I was introduced to Mrs Keiko Terada, a magnificent cook in the true Japanese tradition —

see an example of her work in the tray of *sushi* on page 482. She is friendly and extremely willing to teach me, and it doesn't seem to matter that her English is limited and my Japanese is non-existent (except for the names of ingredients and dishes), for we both enjoy our encounters tremendously. When one wishes to learn and one is ready to teach, even a language barrier cannot spoil the sense of accomplishment.

It is not my aim to convert everyone to seaweed, rice and raw fish, because there is much more to Japanese food than that. Rather, I have chosen for this chapter some of the most outstanding and delicious Japanese dishes that will appeal to Western tastes.

SERVING AND EATING A JAPANESE MEAL

Unlike Chinese meals where the effect is lavish, with large serving dishes holding quantities of food, Japanese meals are usually served on individual dishes in small servings. Sometimes a tray is set in front of each diner, with all the food served at one time, but each dish is on its own carefully chosen plate or bowl.

Soup is served in covered bowls. Japanese lacquer bowls with covers keep the soup hot but must be handled carefully, for the steam forms a seal; to release the seal, squeeze the bowl gently or the soup will spill while you try to prise off the cover. Chopsticks are used to pick up any ingredients added to the soup, then the bowl is lifted to the lips with both hands. No spoons are used for any Japanese food except *chawan mushi* (steamed savoury custard). Japanese chopsticks are more pointed than Chinese ones, and are generally made from lacquered wood. In most restaurants, however, wooden chopsticks *(waribashi)* are used; they come sealed in a paper envelope, and are thrown away after use.

Although rice is of prime importance, noodles of various kinds are sometimes served instead; chilled noodle dishes are especially popular in summer. Buckwheat noodles, with a packet of instant dipping sauce and a packet of *wasabi* powder, are sold as a packaged instant meal; it is only a few minutes' work to cook the noodles, mix the sauce concentrate with water and blend the *wasabi* with a little water to make a mustard-like paste. When Mrs Terada showed me how to prepare this (the instructions on the packet are only in Japanese, which is a disadvantage) she stirred a few finely chopped spring onions into the dipping sauce, added a few slices of *chikuwa* (fish cake) — there was a light luncheon as delicious as it is simple.

Sake or tea is served with meals. In summer a popular beverage is *mugicha,* iced 'tea' made not with tea but with roasted unhusked barley brewed like tea. It is refreshing and, though the first sip may taste strange, it is a drink most people grow to like. It is also very popular in Korea, and I have been served it both in Japanese and Korean homes.

When *sake* is served in winter, the bottle or flask is put in hot water until it warms up to about 43ºC (110ºF). Tiny cups called *sakazuki* are used for drinking the sake, but liqueur glasses may be used instead. In summer the *sake* may be served chilled.

UTENSILS

While there are special utensils traditionally used in Japanese cooking, it is reassuring to know that modern Japanese housewives prefer to use electric frypans and automatic rice cookers. Heavy saucepans with well-fitting lids and other good quality cookware normally found in any Western kitchen cope adequately with any of the Japanese dishes in this chapter. The one pan that would not be found in a Western kitchen is the rectangular omelette pan used for making rolled omelettes. It is naturally easier to achieve an even roll in one of these than in a round pan, and if you're keen on buying one, some Japanese stores sell them. A sharp chopper or really good kitchen knife, and other utensils you are most at home with, are the best ones to use. For cooking at the table there are now available many useful and decorative pans.

YOUR JAPANESE SHELF

See Glossary for descriptions of these ingredients.

aburage (keep frozen)
bean curd or *tofu* (instant variety)
beni shoga
dashi (instant variety)
katsuobushi
kombu
mirin or *sake*
miso
noodles of various types
wasabi (powdered green horseradish)
short or medium grain rice
shoyu (Japanese soy sauce)
sesame oil
sansho (Japanese pepper)

GOHAN
RICE

White rice cooked by the absorption method is the staple food of Japan, and short or medium grain varieties are preferred. Rice is made up into other dishes with vegetables, fish or meat but most often is served as the mainstay of the meal with which other dishes are eaten. The modern Japanese housewife often uses an automatic rice cooker which ensures perfectly cooked rice every time, but just as reliable is this traditional method.

Serves: 6
2½ cups short or medium grain rice
3 cups cold water

Wash rice several times in cold water. Let it drain in a colander or sieve for at least 30 minutes. Put rice in a heavy-based saucepan with a well-fitting lid, add cold water and bring rapidly to the boil. Cover pan, turn heat low and cook for 15 minutes without lifting lid. Turn heat high for 20 seconds and, still without lifting lid, remove pan from heat and allow to stand for 10 minutes before serving.

MUSUBI
RICE BALLS

In Japan, rice takes the place of sandwich bread, hamburger buns and hot dog rolls. Rice balls are usually taken on picnics and are sometimes filled with pieces of fish, raw or smoked. They may also be very simply flavoured with sesame seeds or seaweed.

hot cooked rice
goma sio (black sesame seeds and salt) or
    powdered nori (seaweed)
raw or smoked fish, optional

Cook rice and when cool enough to handle take about half cup rice and, with wet hands, roll into firm balls about 7.5 cm (3 inches) in diameter. If using fish cut it into very thin strips and push a strip into the centre of the rice ball, moulding the rice around it. Roll the rice balls lightly in goma sio or powdered nori.

OYAKO DOMBURI
PARENT AND CHILD DOMBURI

Domburi means an earthenware bowl, but the name also applies to the food served in it, generally rice with toppings of meat, eggs, poultry, vegetables, or a combination of ingredients. Oyako domburi is so called because it is made from chicken and eggs served over rice.

Serves: 6
2½ cups short grain rice
1 large chicken breast or thigh and
    drumstick
2 cups chicken stock
3 tablespoons mirin or dry sherry
5 tablespoons Japanese soy sauce
6 eggs
¼ teaspoon salt
6 spring onions, thinly sliced

Cook rice according to gohan recipe (above) and keep warm. Skin and bone the chicken, then cut flesh into small dice. Heat chicken stock with mirin and soy sauce. When boiling add chicken, return to the boil, cover and simmer for 8 minutes. Meanwhile, beat eggs slightly, adding salt. Add eggs and three quarters of the spring onions to the simmering stock. Without stirring let mixture return to the boil, then turn heat very low, cover and cook for 3 or 4 minutes until eggs are set but still soft.

Spoon rice into a heated earthenware bowl, then pour hot chicken and egg mixture over. Garnish top with remaining spring onions. Serve immediately.

OBORO (rice with chicken and mushrooms) *recipe page 460*

OBORO
RICE WITH CHICKEN AND MUSHROOMS *(picture page 459)*

Serves: 6
2½ cups short grain rice
8 dried mushrooms (shiitake)
4 tablespoons Japanese soy sauce
4 tablespoons mirin or dry sherry
2 tablespoons sugar
375 g (12 oz) boned chicken breast, thinly
    sliced
2 eggs, beaten
⅛ teaspoon salt
1 cup cooked green peas

Wash rice well and let it drain in a colander for 30 minutes. Pour boiling water over the mushrooms and allow to soak for 30 minutes, then cut off and discard stems and put caps in a small saucepan with half cup of the soaking water and half each of the soy, mirin and sugar. Bring to the boil, cover and cook until liquid is almost completely evaporated. Remove mushrooms from pan and allow to cool.

Into same saucepan put remaining soy, mirin, sugar and about a quarter cup mushroom liquid. Add sliced chicken and bring to the boil, turn heat low, cover and simmer gently for 3 minutes. Turn off heat and leave covered.

Put rice into a saucepan with 3 cups water, bring to the boil, turn heat very low, cover pan and cook for 20 minutes without lifting lid or stirring.

While rice is cooking beat eggs slightly with salt and cook in a lightly greased frying pan to make 2 or 3 large, flat omelettes, taking care not to brown them. Turn onto a flat plate and when cool cut into narrow strips.

When rice is cooked spoon it into a large domburi or earthenware bowl with lid, spread chicken over surface of rice and spoon the liquid in which the chicken was cooked over the rice. Slice mushrooms and spread them over chicken. Decorate top with omelette strips and green peas and serve hot.

KITSUNE DOMBURI
RICE WITH FRIED BEAN CURD

Kitsune is the Japanese word for fox and this dish is so named because according to Japanese folklore that animal has a great fondness for fried bean curd which, with rice, is the chief ingredient in this dish.

Serves: 6
1 quantity cooked rice (page 458)
4 sheets aburage (fried bean curd)
2½ cups dashi (page 476) or chicken stock
½ cup Japanese soy sauce
½ cup mirin or dry sherry
1 tablespoon sugar
6 spring onions, finely sliced diagonally

While rice is cooking pour half a kettle of boiling water over the aburage in a colander to make it less oily. Cut each sheet in halves lengthways, then cut across into strips the width of a pencil.

Put the dashi, soy, mirin and sugar into a pan with strips of bean curd and bring to the boil, reduce heat and simmer for 10 minutes. Add sliced spring onions, simmer covered for 1 minute.

Put the rice into one large bowl or six individual bowls and ladle the hot soup over. Serve hot.

YAKITORI DOMBURI
RICE WITH FRIED CHICKEN

Serves: 6

1 small roasting chicken
½ cup Japanese soy sauce
½ cup mirin or dry sherry
2 cloves garlic, crushed
1 teaspoon finely grated fresh ginger
3 cups water
2½ cups short grain rice
¼ cup vegetable oil
3 teaspoons sugar
3 spring onions, finely sliced

Cut chicken into joints and marinate in a mixture of soy, mirin, garlic and ginger for 30 minutes. Use chicken back and wing tips to make a stock. There should be 3 cups stock.

Wash the rice, drain well and cook as described on page 458. Drain pieces of chicken well, reserving marinade. Heat oil and fry chicken until golden brown, allow to cool slightly, then cut meat into bite-size pieces.

Arrange hot cooked rice in a large bowl or individual bowls and put chicken pieces on top of rice. Add reserved marinade to the stock, bring to the boil with sugar. As it comes to the boil stir in the spring onions. Pour over the rice and chicken and serve immediately.

TENDON
TEMPURA DOMBURI

This is the way Japanese housewives use up leftover tempura ingredients. Often, though, pieces of fried fish are substituted for tempura.

Serves: 4

hot cooked rice
12 pieces cooked tempura (page 464),
   including prawns or fish
oil for frying

Sauce:
¼ cup mirin or dry sherry
¼ cup Japanese soy sauce
¾ cup dashi (page 476)
pinch monosodium glutamate, optional

While rice is cooking, heat oil and re-fry tempura very briefly. Drain on absorbent paper. Make sauce and allow to cool to room temperature. To serve, put rice in individual bowls, top with 3 pieces tempura each and serve with sauce, which is spooned over to taste. Serve hot.

Sauce: Heat mirin or sherry in small saucepan and ignite it with a match. Shake pan gently, away from heat, until the flame dies out. Stir in the dashi, soy sauce and monosodium glutamate if used. Cool and pour over rice.

ZARU SOBA
CHILLED NOODLES

Serves: 4

200 g (7 oz) soba (buckwheat noodles)
1 sheet nori (dried laver seaweed)
1 tablespoon finely grated fresh ginger
3 spring onions, very finely sliced

Dipping Sauce:
2 cups dashi (page 476)
½ cup Japanese soy sauce
½ cup mirin or dry sherry
salt or sugar, optional

Bring a large saucepan of water to the boil and add noodles. When water returns to the boil add 1 cup cold water. Bring to the boil again and cook until the noodles are just tender. This does not take long, about 2 minutes, so keep testing and stop cooking as soon as they are tender enough to bite. Drain in a colander and hold under running cold water until they are quite cold. Drain well.

Toast sheet of nori over gas or electric burner or under griller until crisp. Put noodles on plates and crumble the nori over.

Mix ginger with spring onions and put a small portion on each plate. Pour dipping sauce into individual sauce dishes for each person. The ginger mixture is stirred into the sauce and the noodles are dipped in the sauce before eating.

Dipping Sauce: Put ingredients into a small pan and bring to the boil. Remove from heat and cool. Taste and add salt or sugar as desired.

KINOME YAKI
GRILLED MARINATED FISH

Serves: 4
2 large fish steaks (tuna, mackerel or
   other oily fish)
4 tablespoons Japanese soy sauce
2 tablespoons mirin or dry sherry
2 tablespoons sake
2 teaspoons finely grated fresh ginger
1 tablespoon sugar

Garnishes:
pickled ginger or
   2 spring onions, shredded or
   1 large cucumber
3 tablespoons white vinegar
3 tablespoons sugar
1 teaspoon Japanese soy sauce
1 teaspoon salt

Wash fish, dry well and cut each steak into 4 pieces. Combine soy, mirin and sake.

Squeeze juice from ginger into mixture and discard fibres. Add sugar and dissolve. Marinate fish in this for about 30 minutes.

Preheat griller and cook fish about 10 cm (4 inches) away from heat source for 5-7 minutes, brushing two or three times with the marinade. Turn fish and grill other side. The fish should have a rich glaze of marinade. Serve immediately, garnished with pickled ginger, spring onion shreds or cucumber sticks marinated in mixture of vinegar, sugar, soy sauce and salt.

YOSENABE
SIMMERED SEAFOOD AND VEGETABLES *(picture opposite)*

Other varieties of fish or vegetables as available may be substituted for those in the recipe.

Serves: 6
500 g (1 lb) snapper or bream fillets
1 lobster tail
1 cup cooked cellophane noodles
8 cups dashi (page 476) or chicken stock
2 tender carrots, sliced
small piece kombu, optional (see Glossary)
soy sauce to taste
few young spinach leaves
6 fresh mushrooms, sliced
6 spring onions, cut in bite-size lengths

Wash fish fillets and cut into 2.5 cm (1 inch) pieces. With a sharp cleaver cut lobster tail into slices, then cut each large slice into halves. Drain cellophane noodles and cut into short lengths, put into a saucepan with the dashi, bring to the boil. Reduce heat and simmer for 5 minutes before adding carrots, kombu and soy sauce. Simmer a further 2 minutes, then add fish and lobster, spinach, mushrooms and spring onions and continue to cook for 5 minutes or until everything is just done. Serve in soup bowls accompanied by small dishes of dipping sauce as served with zaru soba (page 461).

SAKANA NO GINGAMI YAKI
SEAFOOD AND VEGETABLES IN FOIL

Serves: 4
4 fillets of firm white fish
½ teaspoon salt
1 tablespoon sake
8 large raw prawns
4 large dried mushrooms
12 ginkgo nuts

Wash fish well, dry it, sprinkle lightly with salt and sake and let it marinate for 10 minutes. Remove prawn heads and cut along the back of the shell with a sharp knife so that the vein can be removed without shelling the prawn. Soak mushrooms in very hot water for 30 minutes, then cut off and discard stems and slice the caps finely.

Take pieces of foil about 25 cm (10 inches) square and lightly oil one side. Put a fish fillet, 2 prawns, a mushroom and 3 ginkgo nuts on each square of foil. Fold foil to form a parcel and bake in a moderate oven, 170°C (350°F), for 20 minutes or cook over coals on a barbecue or under a griller. Serve hot in the foil parcel.

YOSENABE (simmered seafood and vegetables) *recipe above*

TEMPURA
DEEP-FRIED SEAFOOD AND VEGETABLES *(picture page 475)*

Perhaps the most popular of all Japanese dishes among Western people, good tempura should be crisp, light, the batter a mere wisp that covers the food. It should never be the heavy coating found on fried fish as in 'fish and chips'. A Japanese chef told me that the secret is to have both food and batter very cold and that the batter must be freshly made and not allowed to stand for too long. Tempura is best served the moment it is ready, so cooking at the table in an electric wok or deep fryer is particularly suitable.

Serves: 4
12-16 medium-sized raw prawns
500 g (1 lb) fish fillet
1 canned lotus root
1 can baby corn cobs
3 canned winter bamboo shoots
canned ginkgo nuts
8 spring onions
250 g (8 oz) fresh mushrooms
4 tablespoons grated white radish
2 tablespoons finely grated fresh ginger
3 cups vegetable oil
½ cup sesame oil

Tempura Batter:
1 egg
1 cup ice-cold water
pinch bicarbonate of soda
¾ cup unsifted plain flour or tempura
   flour

Tempura Sauce:
3 tablespoons mirin or dry sherry
3 tablespoons Japanese soy sauce
1 cup dashi (page 476)
pinch salt
pinch monosodium glutamate

Shell prawns, leaving tails on. Remove the vein, wash and dry well on kitchen paper. Slice fish fillet into thin, bite-size slices. Drain all the canned vegetables thoroughly and dry them on kitchen paper. Cut lotus root crossways into thin slices, slice bamboo shoots and if large cut in halves. Winter bamboo shoots are smaller and much more tender than ordinary bamboo shoots, and if they are not available the larger shoots will have to be cut in suitably sized pieces.

Thread 2 or 3 ginkgo nuts on wooden cocktail picks. Wash and trim spring onions and cut into bite-size lengths. Wipe mushrooms clean with damp kitchen paper and cut in halves or quarters according to size.

Arrange all ingredients attractively on a tray, cover and refrigerate until serving time.

Set before each place a plate lined with a paper napkin, a small bowl for dipping sauce and another small bowl with a tablespoon of grated white radish and 2 teaspoons of grated fresh ginger.

Prepare sauce and have ready. No more than 10 minutes before serving, make batter and stand the bowl in a larger bowl containing ice. Heat both oils to 190°C (375°F). If sesame oil is not available it may be omitted, but it gives a delicious and distinctive flavour to the food.

When guests are seated, dip pieces of food one at a time into the batter and drop into the oil. Do not fry more than about 6 pieces at a time, as the temperature of the oil must be kept moderately high for best results. As each piece turns golden (this should take only a minute) lift it from the oil with a perforated spoon, drain for a few seconds on absorbent paper, then serve immediately to guests, who dip each piece in the sauce and eat it while crisp and hot. The radish and ginger are mixed into the sauce to suit individual taste.

Tempura Batter: Break egg into bowl of iced water and beat until frothy. Add bicarbonate of soda and flour and beat just until flour is mixed in. Do not overbeat. Batter should be thin. If it seems too thick, add a few drops of iced water.

Tempura Sauce: Heat mirin in a small saucepan, remove from heat and ignite with a match. Shake pan gently until flame dies, add all other ingredients, bring to a boil quickly. Cool to room temperature, taste and adjust seasoning if necessary.

Note: Ready-to-use tempura sauce may be purchased in bottles if preferred.

HARUSAME TEMPURA
DEEP-FRIED SEAFOOD

Harusame are fine, translucent noodles, the Japanese equivalent of cellophane noodles. In this version of tempura, the ingredients are dipped first in cornflour, then in egg whites and finally in harusame noodles snipped into small pieces. When deep-fried the noodles expand in spectacular fashion and form a crisp coating for the seafood. Good as an appetiser.

Serves: 4
500 g (1 lb) fillets of bream or other firm
   white fish
12 small to medium-size raw prawns
1 tablespoon Japanese soy sauce
1 tablespoon mirin or dry sherry
½ teaspoon salt
½ cup cornflour
1 or 2 egg whites, beaten until frothy
1½ cups finely snipped harusame noodles
vegetable oil for deep frying
tempura sauce (page 464) or salt for
   dipping

Remove all bones and skin from fish fillets and cut fillets lengthways into narrow strips, then into bite-size lengths.

Shell and de-vein prawns, leaving tails on. Marinate fish and prawns in soy, mirin and salt for 30 minutes.

Roll each piece of seafood first in cornflour, dusting off excess, then in egg white, then in harusame noodles. The noodles should be cut with kitchen scissors, a few strands at a time, to pieces not more than 12 mm (½ inch) long.

Heat oil to about 170°C (350°F) and fry a few pieces at a time. Harusame will puff and swell immediately on being immersed in the hot oil. If it does not, it means the oil is not hot enough and the harusame will be tough and leathery instead of crisp and crackling. Fry for half to 1 minute, and remove from oil with a slotted spoon before the colour changes. Drain on absorbent paper and serve with tempura sauce or sea salt for dipping.

SASHIMI
RAW FISH

This is considered a great delicacy in Japan — and many non-Japanese who have tasted this 'way-out' dish have been, in most cases, instantly converted. Far from being strong or fishy, the flavour is indescribably delicate. Wasabi or green horseradish is served with the fish and each person mixes some with soy sauce for dipping the fish in before eating.

For each serving:
125 g (4 oz) very fresh tuna, salmon,
   bream, bonito, kingfish, mackerel or
   jewfish
1 tablespoon grated giant white radish
1 tablespoon grated carrot
1 teaspoon prepared wasabi (see Glossary)
Japanese soy sauce
mirin or dry sherry

Fish for sashimi must be absolutely fresh, and preferably whole; shop-bought fillets are unsatisfactory, and frozen fish is disastrous. Fillet the fish, removing all bones. Carefully cut away the skin.

With a sharp knife, and handling the fish as little as possible, cut the fillet into thin slices and arrange on serving plate. Tuna and bonito are preferable cut in small cubes; cut small fish or squid in thin strips.

Serve with grated daikon (white radish) and grated carrot, decorate with a sprig of watercress and accompany each serving with a dab of wasabi and a sauce dish holding Japanese soy sauce or a mixture of soy and mirin or dry sherry.

SABA NO SUTATAKI
MACKEREL IN VINEGAR MARINADE *(picture opposite)*

Serves: 4
500 g (1 lb) mackerel fillets
salt
½ cup mild white vinegar
2 tablespoons cold water
2 tablespoons sugar
4 tablespoons grated white radish
4 tablespoons grated carrot
sprigs of watercress or parsley

Dipping Sauce:
1 teaspoon grated fresh ginger
3 tablespoons Japanese soy sauce
2 tablespoons mild white vinegar
1 tablespoon sugar

Rub mackerel fillets liberally with salt and refrigerate about 3 hours or overnight if more convenient. Remove any bones, rinse off excess salt, then slice fish thinly and marinate in a mixture of vinegar, water and sugar for about 30 minutes.

Arrange fish slices on individual plates, put a tablespoon each of grated radish and carrot on each plate and garnish with watercress or parsley. Serve accompanied by small bowls of dipping sauce and wasabi.

Dipping Sauce: Combine ginger, soy, vinegar and sugar, stirring until sugar dissolves.

TORI TERIYAKI
GRILLED MARINATED CHICKEN

Serves: 6
1 x 1.5 kg (3 lb) roasting chicken
½ cup Japanese soy sauce
½ cup mirin or dry sherry
2 tablespoons sugar
1 clove garlic
pinch salt
1½ teaspoons finely grated fresh ginger
few drops sesame or vegetable oil

Joint the chicken and then, with a heavy cleaver, cut each drumstick and thigh in halves. Cut breast in halves lengthways, then cut each half across into three pieces. Wings are cut in three at the joints and the tips discarded or put into the stock pot. The back may be cut across into four pieces, or used for stock if preferred.

Combine soy sauce, mirin and sugar in a large bowl. Crush garlic with a good pinch of salt and add to bowl together with ginger and sesame oil. Put chicken pieces one at a time into the marinade, turning them so they are coated all over. Let them stand in the marinade for at least 1 hour, turning them two or three times, or marinate overnight if more convenient.

Preheat oven to 200°C (400°F). Oil a large baking dish and put pieces of chicken in a single layer in the dish. Roast in hot oven for 15 minutes, then turn each piece over with tongs and roast for 10 minutes longer. Turn oven down to moderate, 170°C (350°F), pour away fat from the baking dish, and spoon some of the marinade over the chicken.

Return chicken to oven for a further 20-25 minutes, basting with marinade every 10 minutes, until chicken is tender, well glazed and browned. Serve hot with rice, or cold as an appetiser or picnic food.

Note: To cook chicken teriyaki in a frying pan, drain the pieces of chicken well, reserving marinade. Dry chicken on absorbent paper and pierce the skin a few times with a fork. Heat 2 tablespoons oil in a large, heavy frying pan and put in chicken pieces, skin side down. Brown on one side, then turn with tongs and brown other side. Pour away oil, add half the marinade to pan, turn heat low. Cover and cook for 15-20 minutes or until chicken is almost tender. Uncover and cook for a further 5 minutes or until chicken is well glazed and brown and marinade is quite thick.

TATSUTA AGE
MARINATED FRIED CHICKEN

Serves: 4
500 g (1 lb) boned chicken
3 tablespoons Japanese soy sauce
2 tablespoons sake
2 teaspoons sugar
4 tablespoons cornflour
oil for deep frying

Cut chicken into bite-size squares and marinate in a mixture of soy, sake and sugar for at least 1 hour. Drain chicken, roll pieces in cornflour and set aside for 10 minutes.

Heat oil in a deep pan to 170°C (350°F) and fry chicken in small batches for about 2-3 minutes or until golden brown and crisp. Drain on absorbent paper and serve hot.

GOMA YAKI
FRIED CHICKEN WITH SESAME

Serves: 4
1 tablespoon white sesame seeds
2 medium-size chicken breasts
4 tablespoons sake
1 teaspoon salt
1 teaspoon Japanese soy sauce
1 tablespoon sesame oil
4 crisp lettuce leaves

In a dry frying pan toast sesame seeds over medium heat, stirring constantly, until they are evenly golden. Turn on to a plate to cool.

Bone the chicken breasts and cut each breast into halves lengthways. Prick skin several times with a fork. Mix sake, salt and soy sauce together and dip chicken in the mixture on both sides, then set aside for 30 minutes.

Heat oil in a frying pan and fry chicken, browning the pieces on both sides. Reduce heat and cook 4 or 5 minutes until done. Cut each piece in slices and put back together in shape. Sprinkle with sesame seeds and serve each half breast on a lettuce leaf.

DASHIMAKI TAMAGO
ROLLED OMELETTE

Japanese omelette pans are rectangular. If you can get one it will make your rolled omelettes easier to handle and neater in appearance, but a round pan can be used quite successfully.

Serves: 4
5 eggs
2 teaspoons sugar
¼ teaspoon salt
½ cup dashi (page 476)
2 teaspoons Japanese soy sauce
vegetable oil for cooking
parsley sprigs for garnish

Beat eggs until well mixed. Dissolve sugar and salt in the dashi, stir in soy sauce, then mix with beaten eggs.

Heat omelette pan and grease with a few drops of oil. Pour in a third of the egg mixture and tilt pan so it covers entire surface. Cook on low heat (omelette must not brown) until it is set, then roll the omelette away from you.

When omelette is completely rolled up, lightly grease pan again, slide omelette towards you and grease that part of the pan where omelette was. Pour in half the remaining mixture and lift the egg roll so the uncooked egg can cover the base of pan. Cook as before and roll again, this time rolling the first omelette within the second one.

Repeat as before, using the remaining beaten egg. Turn the omelette on to a sudare (bamboo mat) or a clean cloth and roll the omelette firmly. Leave it for 10 minutes, then remove mat and cut the rolled egg into thick slices. Serve garnished with parsley.

TORIMAKI
CHICKEN OMELETTE

Serves: 2
3 eggs
2 tablespoons dashi (page 476) or water
½ teaspoon salt
1 teaspoon soy sauce
vegetable oil for frying

Filling:
½ cup finely chopped cooked chicken
2 teaspoons Japanese soy sauce
2 teaspoons mirin or dry sherry
1 teaspoon sugar
1 teaspoon finely grated fresh ginger

Beat eggs and add dashi, salt and soy. Heat omelette pan and grease lightly with a few drops of oil, pour in the egg and cook until set on the bottom, but liquid on top.

Put chicken filling in a neat line across the omelette and roll the egg mixture firmly around it, away from you. Turn on to a plate, cut in two and serve immediately.

This chicken omelette may also be rolled in a bamboo mat (sudare), left until cool and firm, then unrolled, sliced and served as an hors d'oeuvre.

Filling: Flavour chicken with soy, mirin, sugar and juice pressed from the grated ginger.

CHAWAN MUSHI
STEAMED EGG CUSTARD WITH SEAFOOD

This savoury egg custard is regarded as a soup in Japan and is ideal as a light lunch or supper dish. If you want to make a single portion, beat the egg in the cup in which it will be cooked (Japanese cooks use chopsticks for this), pour in stock to three-quarters fill the cup and add salt, soy and sake to taste. Add other ingredients as available — a good way to use up a few prawns or oysters.

Serves: 4
4 dried mushrooms
2 tablespoons Japanese soy sauce
1 tablespoon sugar
4 small prawns or 8 slices canned
  kamaboko (fish cake)
4 fresh oysters or 4 small slices fresh tuna

Custard:
4 eggs
2½ cups dashi (page 476)
1½ teaspoons salt
1 tablespoon Japanese soy sauce
2 tablespoons sake, mirin or dry sherry

Soak mushrooms in hot water 30 minutes, cut off and discard stems and simmer the caps in a small saucepan with 1 tablespoon of soy and the sugar for 8-10 minutes. Shell and de-vein prawns. If tuna is used, marinate for a few minutes in remaining tablespoon of soy sauce.

Into each chawan mushi cup (or custard cup or ramekin) put a mushroom; a prawn or 2 slices of kamaboko; an oyster or a slice of tuna. Fill cups with custard mixture and put in a saucepan with hot water to come halfway up the sides of the cups. If chawan mushi cups with lids are not available, cover the top of each cup with foil, pressing it close to the outside of the cup. Cover saucepan with a folded tea towel and then with the lid and bring water to the boil. Lower heat and simmer 15 minutes or until set. Serve hot. In summer these custard soups may be served cold. They are the only soups that are eaten with a spoon.

If more convenient the chawan mushi may be baked in a moderate oven, standing them in a baking pan with hot water to come halfway up the cups. An electric frypan is also a convenient method of steaming chawan mushi, with the cups standing in water as in previous methods.

Note: If preferred, substitute thinly sliced chicken breast for the seafood. You will need 1 small or half a large chicken breast, skin and bones removed, for this quantity.

Custard: Beat eggs, then mix in all other ingredients. When mixture has been poured into cups, carefully skim off the bubbles on the top of the mixture.

KUYA MUSHI
STEAMED EGG CUSTARD WITH TOFU

Serves: 4

250 g (8 oz) bean curd (tofu)
1 cup sprigs of watercress or young
    spinach leaves
8 small button mushrooms

Custard:
4 eggs
2½ cups dashi (page 476) or chicken stock
1½ teaspoons salt
1 tablespoon Japanese soy sauce
2 tablespoons sake, mirin or dry sherry

Drain tofu of liquid by putting on kitchen paper towels for 10 minutes, then turning over on fresh dry paper towels. Cut tofu into 8 equal squares and put two in each custard cup.

Wash watercress or spinach very well and remove any tough stems. Cut into 5 cm (2 inch) lengths and blanch for 1 minute in lightly salted boiling water, drain at once and run cold water over, then dry well on kitchen paper. Press into 4 neat portions. Wipe mushrooms clean with damp paper and cut into slices.

Put mushrooms into cups. Strain custard and pour over, skim off bubbles, cover cups with lids or foil and steam as described for chawan mushi. After 10 minutes add a portion of the blanched watercress or spinach to each cup, pushing it under the surface of the custard. Replace covers and continue steaming until custard is firm. Serve hot.

Custard: Beat eggs slightly just until whites and yolks are mixed, mix in stock, salt, soy sauce and sake.

SUKIYAKI
QUICK-COOKED BEEF AND VEGETABLES *(picture opposite)*

Serves: 6

1 kg (2 lb) tender steak in one piece
12 spring onions
1 small can winter bamboo shoots
500 g (1 lb) fresh mushrooms
2 medium onions
250 g (8 oz) fresh bean sprouts
1 small white Chinese cabbage
1 packet shirataki or 60 g (2 oz)
    cellophane noodles
6 pieces bean curd (tofu), optional
piece of beef suet
Japanese soy sauce
sugar
sake
beef stock
6 eggs, optional

For this dish choose well-marbled steak — Scotch fillet is ideal. Freeze the steak for an hour or until just firm enough to cut in very thin slices. Wash and trim spring onions and cut into bite-size lengths using part of the green portion as well as the white. Drain bamboo shoots and slice thinly. Wipe over mushrooms and cut in halves or quarters according to size.

Peel and cut onions in eighths. Wash bean sprouts and remove brown 'tails'. Wash Chinese cabbage and cut into bite-size pieces, discarding any tough leaves.

Cook noodles in boiling water for 10 minutes, drain and cut into short lengths.

Heat a heavy frying pan and rub over with beef suet until well greased. Add half of each vegetable to pan and fry on high heat for a minute or two until slightly soft. Push to side of pan and add slices of meat in one layer. When cooked on one side (this should not take long because meat is so thinly sliced) turn and cook other side. Sprinkle with soy sauce, sugar and sake to taste, add a little stock to moisten all the meat and vegetables. Mix in noodles and tofu (if used) and heat through. Serve immediately, each person helping himself from the pan.

Traditionally, each diner breaks an egg into his bowl and beats it lightly with chopsticks, then dips the hot food in it before eating, but some prefer to omit this step. Serve hot white rice with sukiyaki.

More ingredients are added to the pan and cooked only after the first batch has been eaten and guests are ready for second helpings. Add more stock, sauce, sake and sugar to pan and simmer ingredients as required.

Note: A Japanese housewife cooked sukiyaki for me and other guests in an electric frypan, right at the table, and said that its size and easy heat control made it ideal for table-top cooking.

Ingredients for SUKIYAKI (quick-cooked beef and vegetables) *recipe above*

GYUNIKU TERIYAKI
GRILLED MARINATED BEEF

Serves: 6

6 slices fillet steak
1 small clove garlic
½ teaspoon sugar
½ teaspoon finely grated fresh ginger
6 tablespoons Japanese soy sauce
6 tablespoons mirin or dry sherry
2 tablespoons oil
2 teaspoons sugar
4 tablespoons water or dashi (page 476)
1 teaspoon cornflour
cold water

Trim excess fat off beef. Crush garlic with sugar and mix with ginger, soy sauce and mirin. Dip each steak into the marinade on both sides and leave for about 30 minutes. Heat a heavy griddle plate or frying pan, spread oil over the cooking surface and when hot put steaks on the griddle for 1 minute before turning to brown other side. Turn heat down and continue cooking until done.

Put remaining marinade in a small pan with sugar and water or dashi, bring to the boil, then stir in cornflour mixed smoothly with very little cold water. Stir until it boils and becomes clear, then spoon glaze over the steaks. Serve steaks immediately. For easy eating with chopsticks the steaks should be cut into slices and assembled again in their original shape.

TEPPAN YAKI
MEAT AND SEAFOOD ON THE GRIDDLE

Serves: 4

500 g (1 lb) fillet or other tender steak
1 small clove garlic
1 teaspoon sugar
½ teaspoon finely grated fresh ginger
3 tablespoons Japanese soy sauce
8 large prawns
1 dozen fresh oysters
1 large green capsicum
1 small eggplant
vegetable oil for cooking

Dipping Sauce:
½ cup Japanese soy sauce
¼ cup mirin or dry sherry
3 teaspoons sugar
1 teaspoon finely grated fresh ginger

Slice beef very thinly. Crush garlic with sugar and mix with ginger and soy sauce. Marinate meat in the mixture for 30 minutes. Shell and de-vein prawns. Drain oysters. Cut capsicum into strips, discarding seeds and centre membrane. Cut eggplant into thin round slices.

Heat griddle or individual steak platters and grease lightly with oil. Cook eggplant and capsicum first as they require longer cooking. Add slices of beef, prawns and oysters as required, cooking only just until done. Do not overcook. Dip in sauce and eat with hot white rice.

Sauce: Combine soy, mirin, sugar and ginger, stirring to dissolve sugar. Divide among individual sauce bowls.

GYUNIKU NO KUSHIYAKI
BEEF AND ONIONS ON SKEWERS

Serves: 4-6

500 g (1 lb) fillet or rump steak
6 spring onions
4 tablespoons Japanese soy sauce
2 tablespoons mirin or dry sherry
1 teaspoon sugar
4 tablespoons plain flour
1 egg, well beaten
1½ cups dry breadcrumbs
oil for deep frying

Trim beef and cut into bite-size cubes. Cut spring onions into pieces just a little longer than the beef cubes. Thread beef and spring onions alternately on oiled bamboo skewers, 3 or 4 pieces on each skewer. Marinate in mixture of soy, mirin and sugar for at least 30 minutes, longer if possible. Turn skewers a few times while meat marinates.

Drain, dust lightly with flour, shaking off excess. Dip into beaten egg and then roll in breadcrumbs.

Heat oil to 170°C (350°F) and fry skewers of meat and spring onions, a few at a time, until golden brown all over. Drain on absorbent paper and serve at once, accompanied by bowls of hot white rice.

SHABU-SHABU
SIMMERED STEAK AND VEGETABLES

Shabu-shabu is the Japanese version of Mongolian 'fire pot' or Singapore 'steamboat'. Guests cook their own meal at the table, holding pieces of steak and vegetables with chopsticks and dipping them into boiling stock. The name comes from the gentle swishing sound made as the food is cooked.

Serves: 6-8
1 kg (2 lb) fillet steak
1 small white Chinese cabbage
12 spring onions
2 tender young carrots
500 g (1 lb) button mushrooms
8-10 cups chicken stock

Sesame Seed Sauce:
4 tablespoons sesame seeds
2 tablespoons mild white vinegar
¾ cup Japanese soy sauce
3 tablespoons finely chopped spring onion
2 teaspoons finely grated fresh ginger

Cut steak in very thin slices. (It is easy to do this if you partially freeze the meat, slice it while frozen, then thaw in the refrigerator.)

Cut cabbage into short lengths. Cut spring onions into bite-size lengths. Cut carrots in round slices, parboil and drain. Wipe mushrooms with damp kitchen paper, trim ends of stalks and cut in halves unless they are very small. Arrange food on serving platter, cover and refrigerate.

At serving time, pour stock into shabu-shabu cooker, put lid on and fill the chimney with glowing coals. Or use a table-top cooker or electric pan. Heat and place in the centre of the table, within easy reach of everyone. Keep stock simmering throughout the meal, adding more as necessary.

Set each place with a bowl, chopsticks and individual bowl for sauce. Also set a large bowl of hot white rice on the table so guests can help themselves.

Ingredients are picked up with chopsticks and held in the boiling stock until just done, then transferred to individual bowls, dipped in sauce and eaten with rice. Care should be taken not to overcook meat and vegetables. Steak should be pale pink when cooked and vegetables tender but still crisp.

When all the meat and vegetables are eaten the stock is served as a soup. The bowls should be lifted to the lips, Japanese fashion, rather than using a spoon.

Sesame Seed Sauce: Lightly brown sesame seeds in a dry pan over moderate heat, stirring constantly with a spoon or shaking pan. This should take about 5 minutes. Turn on to a plate to cool, then crush in a mortar and pestle. Combine with remaining ingredients. Alternatively, put ingredients in container of electric blender and blend on high speed for a few seconds.

TONKATSU
PORK CUTLET

'Ton' means pork, and 'katsu' is the Japanese pronunciation of cutlet. This is not a traditional dish, but one that has become tremendously popular in recent years. It is said that the Germans introduced this to Japan.

Serves: 4
4 slices pork fillet or bolar blade, cut as
    for schnitzel
4 tablespoons Japanese soy sauce
4 tablespoons mirin or dry sherry
1 clove garlic, crushed
pinch of sansho (Japanese pepper) or
    ground black pepper
1 egg, beaten
1 tablespoon finely chopped spring onion
1 cup soft white breadcrumbs
oil for shallow frying
shreds of pickled ginger (shoga)

Marinate pork in mixture of soy, mirin, garlic and pepper for 30 minutes. Mix egg and spring onion together. Dip pork in egg and then in breadcrumbs, pressing them on firmly. Chill for 1 hour or longer.

Heat oil in a large, heavy frying pan and fry crumbed slices over medium heat until golden brown on both sides. Drain on absorbent paper, cut each one in slices and assemble again in original shape.

Serve on white rice and garnish with pickled ginger. A tempura-style dipping sauce may be served separately.

SUNOMONO
VINEGARED CUCUMBER

Serves: 4
1 green cucumber
3 tablespoons mild white vinegar
1 tablespoon water
2 teaspoons sugar
½ teaspoon salt
½ teaspoon finely grated fresh ginger

Peel cucumber, cut in halves lengthways and remove seeds. Slice crossways into thin slices. Combine all other ingredients and marinate cucumber in the mixture for at least an hour. Serve small helpings as a side salad or relish.

AWABI GOMA ZU
ABALONE IN VINEGAR AND SESAME

Thinly sliced abalone and cucumber marinated in a sesame and vinegar dressing may be served as a side salad or an appetiser.

Serves: 6-8
1 can Japanese abalone
1 green cucumber
salt

Dressing:
2 tablespoons sesame seed
1 tablespoon sugar
6 tablespoons mild white vinegar
2 tablespoons water

Drain abalone and cut in paper-thin slices. Peel cucumber, cut in halves lengthways and remove seeds. Cut crossways in thin slices. Put cucumber into a bowl, sprinkle with about half teaspoon of salt and leave for 20 minutes, then drain off liquid that collects and rinse briefly in cold water. Drain well. Combine abalone and cucumber, pour dressing over and chill. Taste and add salt if necessary. Serve relish-size helpings in the small deep bowls used for vinegared dishes.

Dressing: Toast sesame seed in a dry pan over medium heat for a few minutes until golden, stirring constantly. Turn on to plate to cool, then crush slightly with mortar and pestle or in electric blender. Combine sugar, vinegar and water. Stir in sesame seeds.

HIJIKI NITUKE
SEAWEED AND VEGETABLE SAUTE

Before you turn away from the possibility that you may actually like eating seaweed, try this simple vegetarian dish and be prepared for some surprises. The flavour is subtle, the combination pleasing. The fried bean curd is optional.

Serves: 4
½ cup dried hijiki (dried seaweed)
2 sheets aburage (fried bean curd),
   optional
2 medium carrots
2 medium onions
1 tablespoon vegetable oil
2 teaspoons sesame oil
2 tablespoons Japanese soy sauce
4 tablespoons dashi (page 476) or water
1 tablespoon sugar

Wash seaweed and soak in cold water for 30 minutes. Drain. Pour boiling water over the fried bean curd in a colander to remove some of the oil, then cut into fine strips. Cut carrots into matchstick strips and onions into very thin slices.

Heat vegetable oil and sesame oil in a frying pan and saute seaweed, bean curd, carrots and onions for a few minutes. Add soy, dashi and sugar, cover and simmer 5 minutes or until seaweed and vegetables are tender but not mushy. Serve with white rice.

NAMASU
RADISH AND CABBAGE SALAD

Serves: 6
1 giant white radish (daikon)
¼ firm white cabbage
1 tender carrot
kimizu dressing (below)

Peel radish and cut into very fine strips. Shred cabbage finely, discarding leaf ribs and tough stalks. Scrape carrot and cut into very fine strips. Chill in iced water for 1 hour or until crisp. Drain well and serve with dressing.

KIMIZU
SALAD DRESSING

Makes about 1¼ cups
3 egg yolks
¼ teaspoon salt
1 tablespoon sugar
3 tablespoons white vinegar
¾ cup water
1 tablespoon cornflour
1 teaspoon prepared wasabi (see Glossary) or mustard

Put all ingredients into container of electric blender and blend until smooth, about half a minute.

Pour into a small saucepan and cook over very low heat, stirring constantly with a wooden spoon, until mixture thickens and coats back of spoon. Do not allow it to approach simmering point or it will curdle, and keep stirring until it is half cool. Chill and serve with sliced raw or crisp-cooked vegetables as a salad.

DASHI
BASIC STOCK

Dashi is basic to Japanese cooking and is quickly and easily made. It may be kept refrigerated for 2 days. Even simpler to make (and useful to have on hand) is instant dashi, sold in packets.

6 cups water
5 cm (2 inch) square kombu (dried kelp)
3 tablespoons katsuobushi (dried flaked bonito)

Bring water to the boil. Wash dried kelp under cold tap and add to the water as it comes to the boil. Stir and let boil for 3 minutes, then remove from water and add flaked bonito. Allow to come to the boil and remove from heat immediately. Leave for a few minutes until flakes settle, then strain and use as required.

CHICKEN STOCK

When a different flavour is preferred, or if ingredients for dashi cannot be obtained, use this Japanese-style chicken stock in place of the more traditional dashi.

half a chicken and bones from other half of chicken
3 or 4 large slices of fresh ginger
1½ teaspoons salt
8 cups water
2 spring onions

Put chicken and bones into a large saucepan with all the other ingredients and bring to the boil. Reduce heat, cover and simmer for about 1 hour, skimming surface as necessary.

Cool to lukewarm, strain through muslin and then chill so that any fat solidifies on the surface and can be removed. The stock should be very clear.

SAKANA USHIOJIRU
FISH BROTH

Serves: 4

500 g (1 lb) bones, head and trimmings of
    any delicate fish
6 cups water
2 slices fresh ginger
1 spring onion, cut into 4 pieces
1 tablespoon Japanese soy sauce
1 tablespoon sake
salt to taste
3 tablespoons finely sliced spring onions
4 slices raw fish, optional

Put fish into saucepan with water, ginger and cut spring onion. Bring to the boil, then reduce heat and simmer, skimming surface as necessary.

Cook for 10-15 minutes, then cool slightly and strain into a clean pan and stir in soy sauce, sake and salt.

To serve, heat soup to boiling and stir in sliced spring onions. Remove from heat immediately and serve. If liked, a thin slice of raw fish can be put in each bowl and the boiling broth ladled over.

MISO SHIRU
BEAN PASTE SOUP

Serves: 4

5 cups dashi (page 476)
2 tablespoons aka miso (red bean paste)
4 cubes of tofu (bean curd)
2 spring onions, sliced diagonally
2 sliced mushrooms

Bring dashi to the boil, then mix some of the hot liquid with the bean paste in a small bowl, stirring until smooth. Pour mixture back into saucepan, stir well, add bean curd and spring onions and return to the boil. Simmer for a few seconds only.

Ladle into bowls, garnish each with a slice or two of mushroom, and serve hot.

SUMASHI WAN
PRAWN AND BEAN CURD SOUP

Serves: 6

1 small carrot
6 cups dashi (page 476)
6 medium-sized prawns
6 cubes tofu (bean curd)
sprigs of watercress for garnish

Peel carrot and cut off both ends so you are left with a straight cross-section. With a sharp cleaver remove narrow V-shaped strips the length of the carrot at regular intervals, then slice across very thinly to make flower shapes. Drop into boiling water for 1 minute, then drain and refresh in iced water. Set aside for garnish.

Bring dashi to the boil, drop in shelled and de-veined prawns and simmer for 1 minute. Add bean curd and let stock once more return to the boil. Remove from heat and ladle carefully into soup bowls, putting a prawn and a cube of bean curd in each bowl. Fill bowls with stock, then garnish each with a sprig of watercress and one or two carrot slices. Serve immediately.

KAKEJIRU
SOUP FOR NOODLES

This is the basic stock in which noodles of all kinds may be served. If preferred, clear chicken stock may be substituted for the dashi.

6 cups dashi
½ cup mirin or dry sherry
½ cup Japanese soy sauce

Put the prepared dashi, mirin and soy sauce in a saucepan and bring to the boil. Reduce heat, cover and simmer for 10 minutes. Taste and add extra salt if necessary. Half a teaspoon of monosodium glutamate may be added if desired.

NABEYAKI UDON
HEARTY NOODLE SOUP

Serves: 6
6 shiitake (dried mushrooms)
500 g (1 lb) udon (thick wheat noodles)
1 can kamaboko (fish cakes)
1 large chicken breast
2 spring onions
6 cups kakejiru (page 477)
fried prawns to garnish

Soak the mushrooms in very hot water for 30 minutes. Remove stems and slice caps thinly. Bring a large saucepan of water to the boil and add the noodles. When the water returns to the boil add 1 cup cold water. Bring to the boil again and cook until noodles are just tender, being careful not to overcook. Drain in colander and let cold water run over the noodles to cool them. Drain well.

Slice the fish cakes. Bone chicken breast and cut into thin bite-size slices. Cut spring onions into thin diagonal slices. Bring the kakejiru to the boil, add mushrooms and chicken and simmer for 3 minutes. Add noodles and heat through, then garnish top with fish cake, fried prawns and spring onions, cover and allow a further minute or so for the prawns to heat through. Serve immediately.

KENCHIN-JIRU (1)
CHICKEN AND VEGETABLE SOUP

Serves: 6
4 dried mushrooms
7 cup dashi (page 476) or chicken stock
1 small carrot
1 stalk celery
half a giant white radish
½ cup chicken meat, diced small
salt to taste

Soak mushrooms in very hot water for 30 minutes, then discard stems and cut mushrooms into thin slices. Put into pan with stock, cover and cook for 10 minutes.

Cut carrot, celery and radish into fine matchstick strips and add to pan with chicken. Cook for 5 minutes, taste and correct seasoning. Serve hot.

KENCHIN-JIRU (2)
CHICKEN AND VEGETABLE SOUP

More suited to Western tastes than the previous recipe, this version of kenchin-jiru is based on chicken stock and uses fresh mushrooms instead of dried.

Serves: 6
125 g (4 oz) button mushrooms
1 small chicken breast
3 spring onions
few sprigs watercress
6 cups chicken stock

Wipe mushrooms clean with damp kitchen paper, slice or, if very small, leave whole. Remove skin and bone from chicken breast, cut into dice with a sharp knife. Wash and trim spring onions and cut into bite-size lengths, using part of the green portion as well as the white. Wash watercress and break small leafy sprigs for garnish. The thick stalks may be simmered in the stock and strained out.

Heat chicken stock, which has been previously strained and cleared of all fat. Add chicken and simmer for 3 minutes, then add mushrooms and spring onions and return to the boil.

Divide among soup cups and garnish each with a sprig of watercress.

A selection of Japanese soups *Recipes pages 476-480*

KAKITAMA-JIRU
EGG FLOWER SOUP

Serves: 4

5 cups dashi (page 476) or chicken stock
8 snow peas or ¼ cup sliced celery
2 tablespoons Japanese soy sauce
2 eggs
½ teaspoon salt

Bring stock to the boil and add snow peas, strings removed, or the sliced celery. Cook for 1 minute after liquid returns to the boil, then add soy sauce. Beat eggs slightly with salt and pour slowly into boiling stock, stirring gently. Ladle into soup bowls and serve immediately.

SUSHI

Sushi is the Japanese equivalent of the open sandwich. Rice flavoured with a vinegar and sugar dressing takes the place of bread, and is topped with various kinds of raw fish; rolled around fillings of fish, pickles, mushrooms or other vegetables; and in some cases enclosed in omelettes or bean curd.

A selection of sushi can make a complete lunch.

Among the most popular types of sushi are nigiri zushi (rice with raw fish), norimaki zushi (rice rolled in seaweed), fukusa zushi (rice wrapped in omelette), inari zushi (rice in fried bean curd) and chirashi zushi (rice with seafood and vegetables).

SUSHI
RICE WITH VINEGAR AND SUGAR

2½ cups short or medium grain white
  rice
2½ cups cold water
5 cm (2 inch) piece kombu (dried kelp),
  optional

Dressing:
4 tablespoons rice vinegar or mild white
  vinegar
3 tablespoons sugar
2½ teaspoons salt
2 tablespoons mirin or dry sherry

Wash rice several times in cold water and allow to drain for 30 minutes, then put into a saucepan with measured water. If dried kelp is used, wash it well in cold water and add it to the pan. Bring to the boil quickly, cover pan, turn heat very low and steam for 15 minutes without lifting lid. Remove from heat and let it stand, still covered, for a further 10 minutes. Discard kelp and turn rice into a large bowl. Have ready the dressing ingredients, mixed together until sugar dissolves completely. Pour over the rice. Mix gently but thoroughly and cool quickly to room temperature.

INARI-ZUSHI
SUSHI IN FRIED BEAN CURD

In Japanese groceries you can buy aburage, sheets of fried bean curd. These form 'bags', which are filled with sushi and are a favourite snack in Japan.

The sushi can have additions as in chirashi-zushi, or be flavoured simply with toasted sesame seeds or a sprinkling of gomasio, black sesame seeds and salt. They are particularly tasty when the rice is mixed with dried mushrooms cooked as for oboro (page 460).

Use half as many sheets of aburage as the number of inari-zushi you want, because each sheet makes two. Put aburage in a colander and pour 3 or 4 cups of boiling water over to remove excess oil. Press out most of the water by rolling in kitchen paper and sprinkle aburage with a few drops of soy and mirin or dry sherry to give it flavour. Alternatively, simmer the aburage in half cup dashi or chicken stock with 2 tablespoons soy, 1 tablespoon mirin or dry sherry and 1 tablespoon sugar until liquid is absorbed by the bean curd. Press out excess moisture by rolling in kitchen paper, cut the sheets in halves across the centre and pull the sides apart.

Fill each half three-quarters full with rice mixture, then fold the cut ends over to enclose the filling. Put folded end down on serving tray.

CHIRASHI-ZUSHI
RICE WITH SEAFOOD AND VEGETABLES *(picture page 454)*

There are no hard and fast rules for making this Japanese version of a rice salad — add whatever ingredients are readily available for a colourful and easy main dish.

Serves: 6
1 quantity sushi (page 480)
4 dried mushrooms
1 tablespoon Japanese soy sauce
1 teaspoon sugar
½ cup cooked crab or prawns
½ cup finely sliced raw fish, optional
2 eggs
pinch salt
vegetable oil
½ cup finely shredded bamboo shoot
½ cup cooked green peas
1 piece canned lotus root, sliced
1 tablespoon pickled kombu (kelp), thinly sliced
1 tablespoon takuan (pickled radish), thinly sliced
few shreds beni shoga (pickled ginger root) for garnish

Prepare sushi and cool. Soak mushrooms in boiling water for 30 minutes, remove and discard stems, slice caps thinly and simmer 10 minutes in half cup of the soaking water with soy sauce and sugar. Flake crab or slice prawns. Remove any bones from fish.

Beat eggs slightly, season with salt and cook in a lightly oiled pan to make a thin omelette, taking care not to let it brown. Cool, then cut in thin shreds.

Toss rice gently with all the ingredients, reserving a few of the most colourful for garnish. Serve cold.

NIGIRI ZUSHI
RICE WITH RAW FISH

Makes about 24
3 cups sushi (page 480)
2 tablespoons sushi dressing (page 480)
500 g (1 lb) very fresh fillets of tuna, snapper, bream or other suitable fish (see note below)
2 teaspoons wasabi powder (see Glossary)
2 teaspoons cold water
pickled ginger, in strips

Prepare rice according to recipe on page 458 and reserve 2 tablespoons of dressing from the quantity made for flavouring the rice.

Skin the fish and cut into very thin slices with a sharp knife, angling the knife so that the slices are larger than they would be if cut straight. Cover with plastic wrap and refrigerate until just before required.

Mix reserved sushi dressing with 2 tablespoons cold water and use it to moisten your hands before starting to shape the rice. Take a rounded tablespoon of sushi at a time and form each into a neat oval shape. They should be a little smaller than the slices of fish, so that the fish completely covers one side of the rice. Spread each slice of fish with a little wasabi dressing (made by mixing the powder with the cold water) and put it, dressing downwards, on the rice. Mould to a neat shape. Arrange on tray, garnish and serve with a few strips of pickled ginger.

Note: Similar open sandwiches can be made with cooked prawns, shelled, de-veined and opened out butterfly fashion by slitting through the inside curve.

If squid is used, remove and discard everything in the body cavity and wash well under running water, rubbing off the skin. Slit squid down one side and lay it flat, then cut into pieces just large enough to cover the mounds of rice. Blanch in boiling water for 1 minute. Drain, cool and place over the rice. Decorate with a strip of nori (dried laver seaweed).

NORIMAKI ZUSHI
SUSHI ROLLED IN SEAWEED

Vinegared rice with a filling of simmered mushrooms, pickled radish, cucumber, egg, raw fish, singly or in combination, is rolled neatly in a sheet of seaweed and cut into small cylinders.

Makes about 36
1 quantity sushi (page 480)
4 dried mushrooms
2 tablespoons Japanese soy sauce
1 tablespoon sugar
2 eggs
¼ teaspoon salt
few drops vegetable oil
1 green cucumber
1 small piece takuan (pickled radish)
125 g (4 oz) raw tuna, bonito or kingfish
1 teaspoon prepared wasabi (see Glossary)
6 sheets nori (dried laver seaweed)

Prepare sushi. While it cools, soak mushrooms in hot water for 20 minutes. Cut off and discard stems, shred the caps into very thin slices and simmer in half cup of the soaking liquid mixed with soy and sugar until liquid is almost all evaporated.

Beat eggs with salt and cook in lightly oiled pan like a flat omelette. Cool, then cut in thin strips. Peel cucumber thinly, leaving a trace of green. Cut lengthways in strips the size of a pencil. Drain the takuan and cut in similar sized strips.

Remove skin and bones from fish, cut in strips and smear with wasabi.

Toast sheets of nori by passing them back and forth over a gas flame or electric hotplate a few times.

Put a sheet of nori on a bamboo place-mat, or on a clean linen napkin. Divide the rice into six equal portions and spread one portion evenly over two-thirds of the sheet of nori, starting at the end nearest you. In a row down the middle of the rice put one of the ingredients or a combination of ingredients.

Roll up sushi in the mat, keeping firm pressure on the rice so that a neatly packed cylinder results. Let the rolls rest for 10 minutes before cutting into about six pieces. Arrange on a tray, decorate with tiny leaves or green paper cut in fancy shapes. Serve cold.

FUKUSA ZUSHI
SUSHI WRAPPED IN OMELETTE

Makes 8 or 9
half quantity chirashi-zushi (page 481)
4 eggs
2 tablespoons cold water
½ teaspoon salt
few drops vegetable oil
thin strips of nori (dried laver seaweed)

Press chirashi-zushi firmly into a square or rectangular casserole or cake pan to a depth of 2.5 cm (1 inch). Weight down and leave while cooking wrappers.

Beat eggs lightly, add water and salt and cook in small, lightly oiled pan to make 8 or 9 very thin omelettes. Cook on low heat and do not allow omelettes to brown.

Cut pressed sushi into 8 or 9 pieces about 5 cm (2 inches) square. Put a square of sushi in the centre of an omelette and roll up or fold, envelope fashion, to enclose the rice. Wrap a thin strip of nori around the parcel and put on serving plate with joins underneath. Repeat with remaining sushi and omelettes. Serve cold.

A selection of sushi can make a complete lunch.

EQUIVALENTS OR SUBSTITUTES

Most culinary terms in the English-speaking world can cross national borders without creating havoc in the kitchen. Nevertheless, local usage can produce some problems. Just as Americans ride in elevators and walk on sidewalks, and Australians take lifts and walk on footpaths or pavements, so there are differences in cookery usage — the Australian biscuit is a cookie to an American, but an American biscuit is an Australian scone!

The following list includes names of ingredients and cookery terms that are commonly used in Australia (and in this book), but which may be less than familiar to North American readers. Explanations of Asian ingredients are to be found in chapter introductions and in the glossary that begins on next page.

AUSTRALIAN	AMERICAN
absorbent paper	paper towels
almond essence	almond extract
baking powder	double-acting baking powder
baking tray	baking sheet
bicarbonate of soda	baking soda
belly pork	fresh pork side
biscuits	cookies
boiling chicken/fowl	stewing chicken
bonito	skipjack, bone jack, horse mackerel
bream	sole
cake tin	cake/baking pan
capsicums	sweet or bell peppers
caster sugar	fine granulated sugar, superfine sugar
celery stick	celery rib
chicory	Belgian witloof
choko	chayote, christophenes
chuck steak	round steak, stewing steak
chump (lamb)	leg steak
cornflour	cornstarch
crumpets	British crumpets
curly endive	chicory
cutlets	chops
desiccated coconut	shredded coconut
essence	extract
eggplant	eggplant, aubergine
fillet (of meat)	tenderloin
frying pan	skillet
glacé (fruits)	candied
gravy beef	stew beef
greaseproof paper	wax paper
green prawns	raw shrimps
grill/griller	broil/broiler
groper	salmon
ground rice	rice flour
hard-boiled egg	hard-cooked egg
icing sugar	confectioners' sugar

AUSTRALIAN	AMERICAN
jewfish	halibut
John Dory	Porgy, scup
king prawns	jumbo shrimps, scampi
kitchen paper	paper towels
mince/minced (meat)	ground
okra	gumbo, ladies' fingers
papaw, pawpaw	papaya
pastry	pie crust
peperoni	preserved sweet peppers
pinch (of salt)	dash
plain flour	all-purpose flour
pork fat	fat back
prawns	shrimps
rasher (of bacon)	slice
rockmelon	cantaloupe
rose essence	rose extract
rump steak	sirloin
Scotch fillet	sirloin
self-raising flour	self-rising flour
semolina	farina
(to) shell	(to) shuck, hull
shin (of meat)	shank
sieve	strain/strainer
(to) sift	(to) strain
silver beet	Swiss chard
skirt steak	flank steak
snapper, schnapper	sea bass
snow peas	sugar peas, mange-tout
spring onions	scallions, green onions
stock cubes	bouillon cubes
stone, seed, pip	pit
sultanas	seedless raisins
tailor	blue fish, snapping mackerel
tea towel	dish towel, glass cloth
tomato sauce	tomato catsup
vanilla pod	vanilla bean
(to) whisk	(to) whip, beat

GLOSSARY

ABURAGE

Japanese-style fried bean curd. Unlike the Chinese type (*dow foo pok*) which comes in cubes, *aburage* is prepared in thin sheets, square or rectangular, and is sold frozen. It can be kept frozen for months.

AGAR-AGAR
Chinese: *dai choy goh*
Japanese: *kanten*
Burmese: *kyauk kyaw*
Sinhalese: *chun chow*

A setting agent obtained from seaweed. Widely used in Asia, for it sets without refrigeration. Available in powder form from chemists or in packets from Chinese grocers or health food stores. It is also sold in strands. Gelatine can be substituted, but texture will be different and the amount used varies.

AJOWAN
Bot.: *Carum ajowan*
Fam.: *Umbelliferae*
Hindi: *ajwain*

Of the same family as parsley and cummin, the seeds look like parsley or celery seeds, but have the flavour of thyme. It is used in Indian cooking, particularly in lentil dishes that provide the protein in vegetarian diets, both as a flavouring and as a carminative. It is one of the seeds used to flavour the crisp-fried snacks made from lentil flour. *Ajwain* water is used as a medicine in stomach ailments.

AKA MISO

Red bean paste. See *miso.*

AMCHUR

Dried green mango, usually available in powder form. Used as an acid flavouring ingredient in Indian cooking.

ANISE PEPPER (CHINESE PEPPER SZECHWAN PEPPER)
Bot.: *Xanthoxylum pipesitum*
Fam.: *Rutaceae*
Chinese: *faah jiu, hua chiao*
Japanese: *sansho*

One of the ingredients of five spice powder, it is made from the dried berries of a small tree and is reddish-brown in colour. Roast for a few minutes over heat in a dry pan, pound, sift and mix with salt for a salt-and-pepper seasoning. It gives a tingling sensation when placed on the tongue.

ANNATTO SEEDS

Also called *achuete,* these are small red seeds used for colouring and flavouring Filipino food. Substitute paprika and turmeric in given amounts (see The Philippines introduction).

AROMATIC GINGER

see galangal, lesser

ASAFOETIDA
Bot: *Ferula asafoetida*
Fam.: *Umbelliferae*
Hindi: *hing*
Tamil: *perunkaya*
Burmese: *sheingho*

Used in minute quantities in Indian cooking, its main purpose is to prevent flatulence. It is obtained from the resinous gum of a plant growing in Afghanistan and Iran. The stalks are cut close to the root and the milky fluid that flows out is dried into the resin sold as *asafoetida.* Although it has quite an unpleasant smell by itself, a tiny piece the size of a pea attached to the inside of the lid of a cooking pot adds a certain flavour that is much prized, apart from its medicinal properties.

ATTA

Fine wholemeal flour used in making Indian flat breads. Substitute fine wholemeal sold in health food stores. *Atta* flour can be bought from stores specialising in Asian foods.

BAGOONG

see shrimp paste

BAMBOO SHOOT
Chinese: *suehn*
Japanese: *takenoko*
Malay: *rebong*
Indonesian: *rebung*

Sold in cans, either water-packed or braised. Unless otherwise stated, the recipes in this book use the water-packed variety. After opening can, store in a bowl of fresh water in the refrigerator, changing water daily, for up to 10 days. Winter bamboo shoots are much smaller and more tender, and are called for in certain recipes; however, if they are not available, use the larger variety.

BARBECUE SAUCE

A reddish sauce, very salty and at the same time heavily sweetened. Use as a dip or as an ingredient in barbecue marinades. Keeps indefinitely in a covered jar.

BASIL (SWEET BASIL)
Bot.: *Ocimum basilicum*
Fam.: *Labitae*
Hindi: *babuitulsi*
Thai: *horapa*
Lao: *phak itu lao*
Malay: *selaseh, kemangi*
Indonesian: *kemangi*

Used in Indonesian cooking, the leaves add distinctive flavour to those dishes requiring it.

BAY
Bot.: *Laurus nobilis*
Fam.: *Lauraceae*

Almost universally used in European cooking. There is a rather similar leaf, known as *tej pattar,* used in Indian cooking.

BEAN CURD
Chinese: *dow foo*
Japanese: *tofu*

Fresh bean curd, made from soy beans, is available refrigerated, ready to use, and will keep for 2 or 3 days in the refrigerator. Immerse in cold water, which should be changed daily. A high-protein food prized by the Japanese and Chinese, its flavour is delicate and its texture smooth and soft like baked custard. Japanese bean curd, *tofu,* is sweeter and more delicate than *dow foo; tofu* is also sold in instant powdered form, easy to prepare.

Yellow bean curd, also fresh, is firmer and has a different flavour. Store in refrigerator for 2 or 3 days. No substitute.

Dried bean curd is sold in flat sheets or rounded sticks, and needs no refrigeration. It has to be soaked before use. The sticks need longer soaking and cooking.

Red bean curd is much more pungent than fresh bean curd, and has a flavour like strong cheese. It is used in certain sauces. Sold in cans.

BEAN SPROUTS

Green *mung* beans are normally used for bean sprouts. They are sold fresh in most Chinese stores and in certain supermarkets and health food stores. The canned variety is not recommended. Substitute thinly sliced celery for a similar texture but different flavour. Fresh bean sprouts can be stored in a refrigerator for a week in a plastic bag; alternatively, cover with water and change water daily.

BENI SHOGA

Pickled ginger, coloured red, and sold in plastic packets or in bottles. Used as a garnish or for flavour.

BESAN (CHICK PEA FLOUR)

Available at most stores selling Asian foods. Pea flour from health food stores can be substituted, but if it is coarse pass it through a fine sieve before using. Alternatively, roast yellow split peas in a heavy pan, stirring constantly and taking care not to burn them. Cool, then blend at high speed in an electric blender or pound with a mortar and pestle. Sift, then store the fine flour in an airtight container. *Besan* has a distinctive taste, and ordinary wheat flour cannot be substituted.

BLACHAN

The commercial spelling of *blacan.* See dried shrimp paste.

BLACK BEANS, SALTED
Chinese: *dow see*

Made from soy beans, heavily salted and sold in cans and jars. Rinse before using to avoid over-salting recipes. Substitute extra soy sauce for flavour though not for appearance. Store in covered container in refrigerator after opening. It will keep for 6 months or longer. Add a little peanut oil if the top seems to dry out.

BOMBAY DUCK

Not a bird, despite its name, this is a variety of fish that is salted and dried. It is sold in packets and should be cut into pieces no more than 2.5 cm (1 inch) long. Deep fried or grilled, it is served as an accompaniment to a meal of rice and curry, and should be nibbled in little pieces.

A selection of Japanese ingredients

CANDLE NUT
Bot.: *Aleurites moluccana*
Fam.: *Euphorbiaceae*
Malay: *buah keras*
Indonesian: *kemiri*

A hard oily nut used to flavour and thicken Indonesian and Malaysian curries. The name arises because the nuts, when threaded on the midrib of a palm leaf, are used as a primitive candle. Use Brazil kernels as a substitute, though their flavour is sweeter than that of the candle nut.

CARDAMOM
Bot.: *Elettaria cardamomum*
Fam.: *Zingiberaceae*
Hindi: *illaichi*
Sinhalese: *enasal*
Burmese: *phalazee*
Thai: *kravan*
Malay: *buah pelaga*
Indonesian: *kapulaga*

Next to saffron, the world's most expensive spice. Cardamoms grow mainly in India and Ceylon, and are the seed pods of a member of the ginger family. The dried seed pods are either pale green or brown, according to variety. Sometimes they are bleached white. They are added, either whole or bruised, to pilaus and other rice dishes, spiced curries and other preparations or sweets. When ground cardamom is called for, the seed pods are opened and discarded and only the small black or brown seeds are ground. For full flavour, it is best to grind them just before using. There is one brand of 'ground decorticated cardamom' that seems to preserve extremely well the essential oils and fragrances of this exotic spice, but if you cannot buy a really good ground cardamom, crush the seeds in a mortar as required.

CASHEW NUT (CASHEWS)
Hindi: *kaju*
Malay: *gaju*
Sinhalese: *cadju*

A sweet, kidney-shaped nut. In countries where the cashew tree is not grown, it is not possible to get the milky sweet fresh cashews. However, it is possible to buy raw cashews (as distinct from the roasted and salted cashews sold as snacks); nut shops, health food stores and grocers specialising in Asian ingredients stock the raw cashews.

CELLOPHANE NOODLES or
BEAN THREAD VERMICELLI
Burmese: *Kyazan*
Thai: *woon sen*
Malay: *sohoon, tunghoon*
Chinese: *bi fun, ning fun, sai fun, fun see*
Japanese: *harusame*
Indonesian: *sotanghoon*
Tagalog: *sotanghon*

Fine, transparent noodles made from the starch of green *mung* beans. May be soaked in hot water before use, or may require boiling according to the texture required. It is also deep-fried straight from the packet, generally when used as a garnish or to provide a background for other foods.

CHILLI POWDER

Asian chilli powder is made from ground chillies. It is much hotter than the Mexican-style chilli powder, which is mostly ground cummin.

CHILLI SAUCE

There are two different types of chilli sauce. The Chinese style is made from chillies, salt and vinegar, and has a hot flavour. The Malaysian, Singaporean or Sri Lankan chilli sauce is a mixture of hot, sweet and salty flavours generously laced with ginger and garlic and cooked with vinegar. It is easy to buy both types.

CHILLIES, BIRD'S EYE or
BIRD PEPPERS

Very small, very hot chillies. Used mainly in pickles, though in some cases added to food when a very hot flavour is required (as in Thai food). Treat with extreme caution.

CHILLIES, CAPSICUM or PEPPERS
Bot.: *Capsicum frutescens* or *capsicum annum*
Fam.: *Solanaceae*
Sinhalese: *malu miris*

A much milder though still flavourful variety of chilli with a long pod large enough to stuff with spiced meat or fish mixtures.

CHILLIES, GREEN
Bot.: *Capsicum spp.*
Hindi: *sabz mirich*
Sinhalese: *amu miris*
Thai: *nil-thee-sein*
Malay: *chilli, cabai hijau*
Indonesian: *lombok hijau*

Used like fresh red chillies. Sometimes ground into sambals. The seeds, which are the hottest parts, are usually (though not always) removed. See page 12 for advice on handling.

CHILLIES, KASHMIRI
Hindi: *degi mirich*

A red pepper of Kashmiri origin. The chillies are dried, the seeds discarded and the pods ground and sieved. They are less pungent than red chillies.

CHILLIES, RED
Bot.: *Capsicum* spp.
Hindi: *lal mirich*
Sinhalese: *rathu miris*
Burmese: *nil-thee*
Thai: *prik chee pha*
Tamil: *kochikai*
Lao: *mak phet kunsi*
Malay: *cabai, chilli*
Indonesian: *lombok*

Used fresh for flavouring, either whole or finely chopped; or sliced for garnishes. See page 12 for handling.

CHINESE BEAN SAUCE

There are two types of bean sauce. One is a ground bean sauce (*mor sze jeung*), which is smooth and can be used as a substitute for Korean bean sauce, served as a relish with Korean meals. The other type (*min sze jeung*) is similar to Malaysian *taucheo* or *tauceo,* and is a thick paste of mashed and whole fermented soy beans. Substitute mashed salted black beans, sold in cans. Both these bean sauces are too thick to pour. Their flavours are almost identical, the main differences being texture. Whenever bean sauce is an ingredient in recipes from Malaysia, Singapore and China, use *min sze jeung* if possible.

CHINESE SAUSAGES

Lap cheong are dried sausages filled only with spiced lean and fat pork. Steam for 10-15 minutes until soft and plump and the fat is translucent. Cut in thin slices to serve, or include in other dishes.

CHINESE-STYLE FISH CAKES

Sold ready to use at Chinese provision stores. They can be kept for a few days under refrigeration, and need no further cooking apart from heating through.

CHOW CHOW PRESERVES

A mixture of fruits and vegetables in a heavy syrup flavoured with ginger, which is also one of the ingredients. Sold in cans or jars, it keeps indefinitely in the refrigerator after opening.

CHRYSANTHEMUM

see pyrethrum

CINNAMON
Bot.: *Cinnamomum zeylanicum*
Fam.: *Lauraceae*
Hindi: *darchini*
Sinhalese: *kurundu*
Thai: *op chery*
Burmese: *thit-ja-boh-gauk*
Malay: *kayu manis*
Indonesian: *kayu manis*

True cinnamon is native to Sri Lanka. Buy cinnamon sticks or quills rather than the ground spice, which loses its flavour when stored too long. It is used in both sweet and savoury dishes.
  Cassia, which is grown in India, Indonesia and Burma, is similar. It is much stronger in flavour, and is cheaper, but it lacks the delicacy of cinnamon. The leaves and buds of the cassia tree have a flavour similar to the bark and are also used for flavouring food.
  For sweet dishes especially it is best to use true cinnamon. Look for the thin pale bark, sun-dried to form quills that are packed one inside the other. Cassia bark is much thicker because the corky layer is left on.

CLOVES
Bot.: *Eugenia aromatica*
Fam.: *Myrtaceae*
Hindi: *laung*
Sinhalese: *karabu*
Burmese: *ley-nyin-bwint*
Malay: *bunga cingkeh*
Indonesian: *cengkeh*

Cloves are the dried flower buds of an evergreen tropical tree native to Southeast Asia. They were used in China more than 2,000 years ago, and were also used by the Romans. Oil of cloves contains phenol, a powerful antiseptic that discourages putrefaction, and the clove is hence one of the spices that helps preserve food.

COCONUT MILK

Not the water inside the nut, as is commonly believed, but the creamy liquid extracted from the grated flesh of fresh coconuts or from desiccated (shredded) coconut (page 11). When coconut milk is called for, do try to use it, for the flavour cannot be duplicated by using any other kind of milk.

CORIANDER
Bot.: *Coriandrum sativum*
Fam.: *Umbelliferae*
Hindi: *dhania* (seed), *dhania pattar*, *dhania sabz* (leaves)
Sinhalese: *kottamalli* (seed), *kottamalli kolle* (leaves)
Burmese: *nannamzee* (seed), *nannambin* (leaves)
Thai: *pak chee*
Lao: *phak hom pom*
Malay: *ketumbar* (seeds), *daun ketumbar* (leaves)
Chinese: *yuen sai*
Tagalog: *kinchay*

All parts of the coriander plant are used in Asian cooking. The dried seed is the main ingredient in curry powder, and although not hot it has a fragrance that makes it an essential part of a curry blend.

The fresh coriander herb is also called Chinese parsley or cilantro. Although it may take some getting used to because of its pungent smell (the name comes from the Greek *koris*, meaning 'bug'), Southeast Asian food is not the same without it. It is indispensable in Burma, Thailand, Vietnam, India and China where it is also called 'fragrant green'. If you have difficulty obtaining it, grow fresh coriander yourself in a small patch of garden or even a window box. Scatter the seeds, sprinkle lightly with soil and water every day. They take about 18 days to germinate. Pick them when about 15 cm (6 inches) high and do not allow plants to go to seed.

CUMMIN or CUMIN
Bot.: *Cuminum cyminum*
Fam.: *Umbelliferae*
Hindi: *sufaid zeera* (white cummin), *zeera*, *jeera*
Sinhalese: *sududuru*
Thai: *yira*
Malay: *jintan puteh*
Indonesian: *jinten*

Cummin is, with coriander, the most essential ingredient in prepared curry powders. It is available as seed, or ground. There is some confusion between cummin and caraway seeds because they are similar in appearance, but the flavours are completely different and one cannot replace the other in recipes.

CUMMIN, BLACK
Bot.: *Nigella sativa*
Fam.: *Ranunculaceae*
Hindi: *kala zeera, kalonji*

Although the Indian name *kala zeera* translates as 'black cummin' this is not true cummin and the flavour is different. Aromatic and peppery, *Nigella* is an essential ingredient in *panch phora*.

CUMMIN, SWEET

see fennel

CURRY LEAVES
Bot.: *Murraya koenigii*
Fam.: *Rutaceae*
Hindi: *kitha neem, katnim, karipattar*
Sinhalese: *karapincha*
Tamil: *karuvepila*
Burmese: *pyi-naw-thein*
Malay: *daun kari, karupillay*

Sold dried, they are as important to curries as bay leaves are to stews, but never try to substitute one for the other. The tree is native to Asia, the leaves are small and very shiny, and though they keep their flavour well when dried they are found in such abundance in Asia that they are generally used fresh. The leaves are fried in oil, until crisp, at the start of preparing a curry; they can also be pulverised in a blender; and the powdered leaves can be used in marinades and omelettes. Substitute *daun salam*.

CURRY POWDER

Rarely used in countries where curry is eaten daily (the word comes from the Tamil *Kari,* meaning 'sauce'). It is preferable to roast and grind the spices separately. **(pages 34 and 125)**.

DAIKON

see giant white radish

DASHI

A clear soup made from dried bonito flakes and seaweed. Instant *dashi*, sold in Japanese stores, is made from *katsuobushi* (powdered dried bonito) and *kombu* (seaweed). It is essential for Japanese cooking, for in addition to being served as a soup it is used as a cooking stock or as part of a dipping sauce.

490

DAUN PANDAN

see pandanus

DAUN SALAM

An aromatic leaf used in Indonesian cooking, it is larger than the curry leaf used in India and Sri Lanka, but has a similar flavour. Substitute curry leaves.

DILL
Bot.: *Anethum graveolens*
Fam.: *Umbelliferae*
Sinhalese: *enduru*
Lao: *phak si*

Much used in Russian and European cooking, this herb is also very popular in Sri Lanka where it gives a distinctive flavour to minced-meat mixtures, *frikkadels,* fish cutlets, and so on. Similar in appearance to fennel, it is much smaller and grows only to 45-90 cm (1½-3 feet) in height; the leaf is feathery and thread-like.

DOW FOO POK

Chinese-style fried bean curd, sold by weight in Chinese provision shops. It comes in large cubes and is sold fresh, not frozen, but can be kept under refrigeration for about a week.

DRIED FISH
Hindi: *nethali*
Sinhalese: *haal masso*
Thai: *plasroi*
Malay: *ikan bilis*
Indonesian: *ikan bilis*

These tiny sprats or anchovies should be rinsed and the intestines removed (if this has not already been done) before use. Avoid soaking them, or they will not retain their crispness when fried. Dry on paper towels before frying.

DRIED SHRIMP PASTE
Burmese: *ngapi*
Thai: *kapi*
Malay: *blacan*
Indonesian: *trasi*
Vietnamese: *mam tom*

A pungent paste made from prawns, and used in many Southeast Asian recipes. It is sold in cans or flat slabs or cakes and will keep indefinitely. If stored in a tightly closed jar it will, like a genie in a bottle, perform its magic when required without obtruding on the kitchen at other times! It does not need refrigeration. Commercially sold as 'blachan'.

DRIED TANGERINE PEEL

see tangerine peel, dried

FENNEL
Bot.: *Foeniculum vulgare*
Fam.: *Rutaceae*
Hindi: *sonf*
Sinhalese: *maduru*
Burmese: *samouk-saba*
Malay: *jintan manis*
Indonesian: *adas*

Sometimes known as 'sweet cummin' or 'large cummin', it is a member of the same botanical family and is used in Sri Lankan curries (but in much smaller quantities than true cummin). It is available in ground or seed form. Substitute an equal amount of aniseed.

FENUGREEK
Bot.: *Trigonella foenum-graecum*
Fam.: *Leguminosae* (papilionaceae)
Hindi: *methi*
Sinhalese: *uluhaal*
Malay: *alba*

These small, flat, squarish, brownish-beige seeds are essential in curries, but because they have a slightly bitter flavour they must be used in the stated quantities. They are especially good in fish curries, where the whole seeds are gently fried at the start of cooking; they are also ground and added to curry powders. The green leaves are used in Indian cooking and, when spiced, the bitter taste is quite piquant and acceptable. The plant is easy to grow, and when at the two-leaf stage it makes a tangy addition to salads.

FISH SAUCE
Vietnamese: *nuoc mam*
Burmese: *ngan-pya-ye*
Thai: *nam pla*
Tagalog: *patis*

A thin, salty, brown sauce used in Southeast Asian cooking to bring out the flavour in other foods. A small variety of fish is packed in wooden barrels with salt, and the liquid that runs off is the 'fish sauce'. Substitute light soy sauce, adding to each cup one teaspoon of dried shrimp paste, which has been wrapped in foil and grilled for 5 minutes on each side and then powdered. Stir well and bottle. Shake bottle before use. There are different grades of fish sauce, the Vietnamese version being darker and having a more pronounced fish flavour than the others.

FIVE SPICE POWDER
Cantonese: *heung new fun, hung liu, ngung heung fun*

Essential in Chinese cooking, this reddish-brown powder is a combination of ground star anise, fennel, cinnamon, cloves and Szechwan pepper.

FRIED BEAN CURD

see *aburage* and *dow foo pok*

GALANGAL, GREATER
Bot.: *Alpinia galanga*
Fam.: *Zingiberaceae*
Thai: *kha*
Lao: *Kha*
Malay: *lengkuas*
Indonesian: *laos*

The greater galangal is more extensively used in Southeast Asian cooking than the lesser, and is more delicate in flavour. It is a rhizome, like ginger, and beneath the thin brown skin the flesh is creamy white; the flesh of lesser galangal has an orange-red hue.

GALANGAL, LESSER
Bot.: *Kaempferia pandurata* or *Alpinia officinarum*
Fam.: *Zingiberaceae*
Sinhalese: *ingurupiyali*
Thai: *krachai*
Malay: *zeodary* or *kencur*
Indonesian: *kencur*
Chinese: *sa leung geung, sha geung fun*

Also known as 'aromatic ginger', this member of the ginger family cannot be used as a substitute for ginger or vice versa. It is used only in certain dishes, and gives a pronounced aromatic flavour. When available fresh, it is sliced or pounded to a pulp; but outside of Asia it is usually sold dried, and the hard round slices must be pounded with a mortar and pestle or pulverised in a blender before use. In some spice ranges it is sold in powdered form. The plant is native to southern China and has been used for centuries in medicinal herbal mixtures, but it is not used in Chinese cooking.

GARAM MASALA

A mixture of ground spices used in Indian cooking (see page 35).

GARLIC
Bot.: *Allium sativum*
Fam.: *Liliaceae*
Hindi: *lasan*
Sinhalese: *sudulunu*
Burmese: *chyet-thon-phew*
Malay: *bawang puteh*
Indonesian: *bawang putih*

Almost universal in application, and vital in Asian cooking (although Kashmiri Brahmins eschew it as inflaming baser passions), garlic is not only a flavouring but is also prized for its health-giving properties. There are many varieties — some with large cloves, some very small; some white in colour, some purplish; some easily peeled, and some with a skin that sticks so closely that it has to be prised off; and some is very strong in flavour, while other types can be quite mild.

GHEE (CLARIFIED BUTTER)

Sold in tins, *ghee* is pure butter-fat without any of the milk solids. It can be heated to much higher temperatures than butter without burning, and imparts a distinctive flavour when used as a cooking medium. See page 22 for details on making *ghee*.

GIANT WHITE RADISH
Chinese: *loh bahk*
Japanese: *daikon*

A very large white radish — 30-38 cm (12-15 inches) long — with a mild flavour. It is sold in Oriental greengrocers' shops, but substitute white turnip if not available.

GINGER
Bot.: *Zingiber officinale*
Hindi: *adrak*
Sinhalese: *inguru*
Burmese: *gin*
Thai: *khing*
Malay: *halia*
Indonesian: *jahe*
Chinese: *jeung*
Japanese: *shoga*

A rhizome with a pungent flavour, it is essential in most Asian dishes. Fresh ginger root should be used; powdered ginger cannot be substituted for fresh ginger, for the flavour is quite different. To prepare for use, scrape off the skin with a sharp knife, and either grate or chop finely (according to recipe requirements) before measuring. To preserve fresh ginger for long periods of time, scrape the skin from the rhizome, divide into sections and pack in a well-washed and dried bottle. Pour dry sherry over to completely cover the ginger, cover tightly and store in the refrigerator.

GINKGONUT
Bot.: *Ginkgo biloba*
Fam.: *Ginkgoaceae*
Chinese: *bahk gwoah*
Japanese: *ginnan*

The kernel of the fruit of the maidenhair tree, which grows in China and Japan. It has an individual flavour, and is eaten roasted as a nut or used to give its flavour to foods. Usually sold canned.

GOMAIRI-HATAGORASHI
Red pepper, leaves and sesame seeds combined in a relish to be served with rice as part of a Japanese meal, much as sambals and *chatni* are served with Indian meals.

GOMASIO
A seasoning of black sesame seeds, coarse salt and monosodium glutamate used in Japanese cooking.

GRASS JELLY
Chinese: *leung fun*
Sold in cans at Chinese grocery stores, this black jelly made with seaweed is used exclusively in sweet drinks throughout Burma, Malaysia, Singapore and China. It tastes and smells faintly of iodine, reassuring proof of how good it is to eat, as those who use it believe.

GROUND RICE
see rice, ground

HIJIKI
A type of seaweed used as a vegetable by the Japanese. In its dried state it looks like coarse black wire, and must be soaked before cooking.

HOI SIN SAUCE
A sweet, spicy, reddish-brown sauce of thick pouring consistency made from soy beans, garlic and spices. Used in barbecued pork dishes and as a dip. Keeps indefinitely in a covered jar.

HOT BLACK BEAN SAUCE
Also called 'chilli bean sauce', it is a mixture of fermented soy beans and ground hot chillies. Substitute bean sauce or mashed black beans mixed with Chinese chilli sauce.

JAGGERY
see palm sugar

KAMABOKO
Japanese fish sausage, sold in cans.

KATSUOBUSHI
Dried bonito, the favourite flavouring ingredient in Japanese cooking. It can be bought already flaked; this is by far the most convenient, for dried bonito is extremely hard and needs a special tool for flaking it. Keeps indefinitely.

KEMIRI NUTS
see candle nut

KEWRA
see *Pandanus odoratissimus*

KOMBU
Japanese kelp seaweed, available dried in broad, greyish-black ribbons. It is used to flavour *dashi* and rice for *sushi*. It will keep indefinitely, and is also pickled to be used as a relish.

KURI YOKAN
Bean jelly. The variety in the photograph of Japanese ingredients (page 487) includes chestnuts and is quite delicious. This type of sweetmeat is served with Japanese tea, not as a dessert.

LAOS
Bot.: *Alpinia galanga*
A very delicate spice, sold in powder form, *laos* comes from the dried root of the 'greater galangal'. It is so delicate in flavour that it can be omitted from recipes. See galangal.

LEMON GRASS
Bot.: *Cymbopogon citratus*
Fam.: *Gramineae*
Hindi: *sera*
Sinhalese: *sera*
Burmese: *zabalin*
Thai: *takrai*
Lao: *Bai mak nao*
Malay: *serai*
Indonesian: *sereh*
This aromatic Asian plant also grows in Australia, Africa, South America and Florida (USA). It is a tall grass with sharp-edged leaves that multiply into clumps. The whitish, slightly bulbous base is used to impart a lemony flavour to curries. Cut just one stem with a sharp knife, close to the root, and use about 10-12 cm (4-5 inches) of the stalk from the base, discarding the leaves. If using dried lemon grass, about 12 strips dried are equal to one fresh stem; or substitute 2 strips of very thinly peeled lemon rind.

LETTUCE
Thai: *pak kad*
Malay: *daun salat*
Indonesian: *daun salada*
Chinese: *saang choy*

Asian lettuce is rather like Cos lettuce (UK) or Romaine lettuce (USA); in Australia it is known by both names.

LILY BUDS
Cantonese: *khim chiam*

Also known as 'golden needles' or 'lotus buds', these long, narrow, dried golden buds have a very delicate flavour and are said to be nutritious. Soak for half an hour or longer in hot water, and cut in half crossways for easier eating.

LIME, SMALL GREEN
Bot.: *Citrus microcapa*
Hindi: *nimboo*
Sinhalese: *dehi*
Thai: *ma now*
Malay: *limau nipis, limau kesturi*
Tagalog: *calamansi*

The juice of this fruit is used in Asian countries for adding a sour flavour to curries and other dishes. Lemons may be used as a substitute.

LOTUS ROOT
Chinese: *lien ngow*
Japanese: *renkon*

Sometimes available fresh; peel, cut into slices and use as directed. Dried lotus root must be soaked at least 20 minutes in hot water with a little lemon juice added to preserve whiteness. Canned lotus root is readily available, and can be stored in the refrigerator for a few days after being opened.

MACE
Bot.: *Myristica fragrans*
Fam.: *Myristicaceae*
Hindi: *javatri*
Sinhalese: *wasa-vasi*

Mace is part of the nutmeg, a fruit that looks like an apricot and grows on tall tropical trees. When ripe, the fruit splits to reveal the aril, lacy and bright scarlet, surrounding the shell of the seed; the dried aril is mace and the kernel is nutmeg. Mace has a flavour similar to nutmeg but more delicate, and it is sometimes used in meat or fish curries, especially in Sri Lanka, although its main use in Asia is medicinal (a few blades of mace steeped in hot water, the water then being taken to combat nausea).

MALDIVE FISH
Sinhalese: *umbalakada*

Dried tuna from the Maldive Islands, used extensively in Sri Lankan cooking. It is sold in packets, broken into small chips, but needs to be pulverised further before use. Substitute dried prawn powder or Japanese *katsuobushi*.

MINT
Bot.: *Mentha viridis*
Fam.: *Labiatae*
Hindi: *podina*
Sinhalese: *meenchi*
Lao: *pak hom ho*
Malay: *daun pudina*

Although there are many varieties, the common, round-leafed mint is the one most often used in cooking. It adds flavour to many curries, and mint sambal is an essential accompaniment to a *biriani* meal or as a dipping sauce for *samoosa*. Mint is also used in Laotian fish dishes.

MIRIN

Japanese rice wine, sweeter than *sake* and used only for cooking. Dry sherry can be substituted.

MISO

A paste made from cooked, fermented soy beans. There are various types — white, red, brownish and beige. There are also varying degrees of saltiness. Japanese thick soups are mostly based on *miso* stirred into *dashi,* the usual proportion being one tablespoon to one cup of stock.

MONOSODIUM GLUTAMATE (MSG)
Chinese: *mei chen*

White crystals like coarse salt, MSG is an extract of grains and vegetables with no flavour of its own; it acts as a catalyst on the taste buds to enhance other flavours. If food is of good quality and cleverly seasoned it is not necessary to use this additive. Although some cooks use it as extensively as soy sauce in Chinese cooking, I prefer not to.

It is also well known under the brand names 'Vetsin' and 'Aji-no-moto'.

MUNG BEAN FLOUR

Extremely fine, smooth flour made from *mung* beans, it is available either white or coloured a delicate pink or green, and is used in the making of sweets. When mixed with water and brought to the boil it becomes clear and thick like arrowroot or cornflour (both of which are suitable substitutes).

MUSHROOMS, DRIED CHINESE and JAPANESE
Bot.: *Lentinus edodes*
Thai: *hed hom*
Malay: *cindauwan*
Chinese: *doong gwoo, leong goo*
Japanese: *shiitake, matsutake*

Also known as 'fragrant mushrooms', the flavour of these mushrooms is quite individual. They are expensive but give an incomparable flavour. Soak before using. Dried Continental mushrooms are quite different — there is no substitute.

MUSHROOMS, JELLY or WOOD FUNGUS

see wood fungus

MUSHROOMS, STRAW
Bot.: *Volvariella volvacea*
Chinese: *chao gwoo*
Japanese: *nameko*
Burmese: *hmo*

Also known as 'paddy straw mushrooms'. Especially popular in Japan, this tiny, cultivated mushroom consists of a sheath within which is the mushroom. Available canned, bottled or dried. Very delicate flavour. Substitute champignons.

MUSHROOM SOY

Soy sauce flavoured with mushrooms during the last stage of processing. Substitute ordinary light or dark soy sauce.

MUSTARD, BLACK
Bot.: *Brassica nigra*
Fam.: *Crucilerae*
Hindi: *rai, kimcea* (brown mustard)
Sinhalese: *abba*
Malay: *biji sawi*

This variety of mustard seed is smaller and more pungent than the yellow variety. Substitute brown mustard seed *(juncia)*. Alba or white mustard is not used in Asian cooking.

NOODLES, JAPANESE

The kinds of noodles most commonly used in Japanese cooking are:

Harusame: Fine noodles, made from bean starch, that are translucent when soaked and boiled. When deep fried from the dried state they become crisp, white and opaque, and puff up. They are the equivalent of China's *fen szu* or 'cellophane noodles'.

Soba: Very fine buckwheat noodles.

Somen: Very fine white wheatflour noodles. As a substitute use very fine vermicelli.

Udon: Thick wheat flour noodles. Substitute spaghetti.

(See also the section on noodles in the Chinese chapter pp 373, 374 and 376.)

NORI

Dried laver, a type of edible seaweed that is one of the most popular flavourings, garnishes and decorations in Japanese cooking. It is sold in paper-thin sheets, shiny purple-black in colour, and must be warmed and crisped before use.

NUTMEG
Bot.: *Myristica fragrans*
Fam.: *Myristicaceae*
Hindi: *jaiphal*
Sinhalese: *sadikka*
Malay: *buah pala*
Chinese: *tau kau*
Indonesian: *pala*

Not widely used as a curry spice, but used to flavour some sweets and cakes, and sometimes used in *garam masala*. For maximum flavour, always grate finely just before using. Use sparingly, for large quantities (more than one whole nut) can be poisonous.

ONION
Bot.: *Allium cepa*
Fam.: *Liliaceae*
Hindi: *peeaz*
Sinhalese: *lunu*
Malay: *bawang*
Thai: *hom hua lek*
Lao: *phak boua nyai*

Onions come in many varieties, but those most commonly used in Australia are the brown or white onions.

ONION, RED
Bot.: *Allium rubrum*

The most commonly used onions in Asia.

OYSTER SAUCE
Cantonese: *ho yau*

Adds delicate flavour to all kinds of dishes. Made from oysters cooked in soy sauce and brine, this thick brown sauce can be kept indefinitely without refrigeration.

PALM SUGAR
Hindi: *jaggery*
Sinhalese: *hakuru*
Burmese: *tanyet* (Palmyrah), *chandagar* (cane)
Malay: *gula Melaka (Malacca)*
Indonesian: *gula Jawa*

This strong-flavoured dark sugar is obtained from the sap of coconut palms and Palmyrah palms. The sap is boiled down until it crystallises, and the sugar is usually sold in round, flat cakes or two hemispheres put together to form a ball and wrapped in dried leaves. Substitute black sugar, an unrefined, sticky sugar sold in health food stores, or use refined dark brown sugar sold at supermarkets.

PANCH PHORA

Panch means 'five' in Hindi, and *panch phora* is a combination of five different aromatic seeds. These are used whole, and when added to the cooking oil impart a flavour typical of Indian food. Ingredients are described in the introduction to the Indian chapter, page 22.

PANDANUS or SCREWPINE
Bot.: *Pandanus latifolia*
Fam.: *Pandanaceae*
Sinhalese: *rampe*
Thai: *bai toey*
Malay: *daun pandan*
Indonesian: *daun pandan*

Used as a flavouring in rice, curries; and as a flavouring and colouring agent in Malay and Indonesian sweets. The long, flat, green leaves are either crushed or boiled to yield the flavour and colour. In Malaysia and Indonesia especially the flavour is as popular as vanilla is in the West.

PANDANUS ODORATISSIMUS
Hindi: *kewra*

Another variety of screwpine. The male inflorescence has a stronger perfume than roses or jasmin. It is used mostly in Indian sweets, and is obtainable as an essence or concentrate. It is so strong that only a drop is needed (or, more discreetly, a small skewer dipped in the essence is swished in the liquid to be flavoured). On special festive occasions, rose essence and kewra essence are used to flavour the rich rice dish, *biriani*.

PAPRIKA PEPPERS
Bot.: *Capsicum tetragonum*

These are canned or bottled as *pimiento*, or dried and powdered for paprika. Good paprika should have a mild, sweet flavour and brilliant red colour. Although it is essentially a European flavouring, particularly used in Hungary, it is useful in Asian cooking for imparting the necessary red colour to a curry when the chilli tolerance of the diners is not very high. In Asia, the colour would come from 20 to 30 chillies!

PEPPER, BLACK
Bot.: *Piper nigrum*
Fam.: *Piperaceae*
Hindi: *kali mirich*
Sinhalese: *gammiris*
Burmese: *nga-youk-kaun*
Lao: *phik noi*
Malay: *lada hitam*
Indonesian: *merica hitam*

Pepper, the berry of a tropical vine, is green when immature, and red or yellow when ripe. Black pepper is obtained by sun-drying the whole berry. It is only used in some curries, but is an important ingredient in *garam masala*.

PEPPER, WHITE

This comes from the same plant as black pepper, but the ripened berries are soaked in stagnant water for some days until the outer covering or pericarp rots, when the berries are washed to remove the pericarp and make them white. They are then dried. Rarely used in curries, its main use is in white sauces in which it looks better than black pepper.

PEPPERS, RED and GREEN
Bot.: *Capsicum grossum*
Sinhalese: *thakkali miris*

Also known as 'capsicums' and 'sweet' or 'bell' peppers, this large, rounded variety is very mild and sweet in flavour, and is used as a vegetable or salad ingredient.

PETIS

see shrimp sauce

PLUM SAUCE

A spicy, sweet, hot Chinese sauce made from plums, chillies, vinegar, spices and sugar. Use as a dip. It keeps indefinitely in a covered jar.

POPPY SEEDS
Bot.: *Papaver somniferum*
Fam.: *Papaveraceae*
Hindi: *khas-khas*

Used in Indian curries mainly for thickening gravies since flour, corn-flour or other starches are never used for thickening. The seeds are ground to a powder for this use.

PRAWN POWDER

Finely shredded dried prawns or shrimps, sold in packets at speciality food shops and at Chinese grocery stores.

PRESERVED MELON SHREDS

Also known as 'sweet pickled cucumber', these are thin shreds of melon preserved in a ginger-flavoured syrup. They keep indefinitely in a covered jar.

PYRETHRUM
Bot.: *Chrysanthemum cinerariaefolium*
Fam.: *Compositae*
Chinese: *kung choy, tung ho*
Japanese: *shungiku*

This terms covers all varieties of the common chrysanthemum, which is frequently used in China and Japan as a vegetable. The plants are not poisonous, and the leaves and flowers can be used safely when required.

RAMPE

see pandanus

RED COLOURING POWDER

A brilliant red powder sold in Chinese grocery stores and used very sparingly to give the distinctive colour seen in barbecued pork. Substitute a bright red liquid food colouring.

RED GINGER

Preserved ginger slices coloured a deep red. Add to Chinese food as a garnish and flavouring.

RED MISU

see miso

RICE, GROUND

This can be bought at many grocery stores, health food stores and super-markets, and is slightly more granular than rice flour. It gives a crisper texture when used in batters or other mixtures.

RICE, ROASTED AND GROUND

This cannot be bought, but is easy to prepare. Lighty brown the rice in a dry pan over low heat for about 15 minutes, stirring constantly so that it does not brown unevenly or burn. Grind to a powder in an electric blender.

RICE VERMICELLI
Chinese: *mei fun*
Malay: *beehoon, meehoon*
Thai: *sen mee*

Sometimes labelled 'rice sticks', these are very fine rice flour noodles sold in Chinese grocery stores. Soaking in hot water for 10 minutes prepares them sufficiently for most recipes, but in some cases they may need boiling for one or two minutes. When deep fried they swell up and turn white. For a crisp result, fry them straight from the packet without soaking.

RICE WASHINGS

The water in which rice has been washed; used as a cooking liquid in the Philippines.

ROASTED GROUND RICE

see rice, roasted and ground

ROSE WATER

A favourite flavouring in Indian and Persian sweets, rose water is the diluted essence extracted from rose petals by steam distillation. It is essential in *gulab jamun* (page 109) and *ras gula* (page 111), and is also used in *biriani*. If you use rose essence or concentrate, be careful not to over-flavour — count the drops. However, with rose water a tablespoon measure can be used. Buy rose water from chemists or from shops specialising in Asian ingredients.

ROTI FLOUR

Creamy in colour and slightly granular in texture, this is ideal flour for all unleavened breads; unlike *atta* flour, it is not made from the whole grain. Sold at some health food and Chinese grocery stores.

SAFFRON
Bot.: *Crocus sativus*
Fam.: *Iridaceae*
Hindi: *kesar*

The world's most expensive spice, saffron is obtained by drying the stamens of the saffron crocus. The thread-like strands are dark orange in colour and have a strong perfume; it is also available in powder form. Do not confuse it with turmeric, which is sometimes sold as 'Indian saffron'. Beware also of cheap saffron, which in all probability will be safflower or 'bastard saffron' — it looks similar, and imparts colour, but has none of the authentic fragrance. Saffron is used more extensively in northern India than anywhere else in Asia.

SAMBAL BAJAK

A combination of chillies and spices used as an accompaniment to rice and curry meals. Sold at stores specialising in Indonesian products, at Chinese grocery stores and at some delicatessens. Some Dutch-manufactured brands still use the old Dutch-Indonesian spelling, 'sambal badjak'.

SAMBAL ULEK

A combination of chillies and salt, used in cooking or as an accompaniment. The old Dutch-Indonesian spelling, still seen on some labels, is 'sambal oelek'.

SAKE

Pronounced 'sahk-ay', Japan's famous rice wine is usually served warm — about 44°C (110°F), easily achieved by immersing the wine's container in very hot water for a short time. It is also used as an ingredient in sauces and marinades, when brandy or dry sherry can be substituted.

SEMOLINA

A wheat product known as 'farina' in the USA and packaged as 'Breakfast Delight' in Australia, it comes in coarse, medium and fine grades. Recipes stipulate the correct grade to use, but a different grade can be substituted although there will be some change in texture.

Breakfast Delight is a coarse grade; the bulk semolina sold in health food stores is medium grade; and the packaged semolina sold in Italian grocery stores is either medium or very fine. A little experimental shopping is recommended, for the grade of semolina is seldom labelled.

SESAME SEED
Bot.: *Sesamum indicum*
Fam.: *Pedaliaceae*
Hindi: *till*
Sinhalese: *thala*
Malay: *bijan*
Chinese: *chih mah*
Japanese: *goma*
Indonesian: *wijen*

Used mostly in Korean, Chinese and Japanese food, and in sweets in Southeast Asian countries. Black sesame, another variety known as *hak chih mah* (China) or *kuro goma* (Japan), is mainly used in the Chinese dessert, toffee apples, and as a flavouring *(gomasio)* mixed with salt in Japanese food.

SESAME OIL

The sesame oil used in Chinese cooking is extracted from toasted sesame seeds, and gives a totally different flavour from the lighter-coloured sesame oil sold in health food stores. For the recipes in this book, buy sesame oil from Chinese stores. Use the oil in small quantities for flavouring, not as a cooking medium.

SESAME PASTE

Sesame seeds, when ground, yield a thick paste similar to peanut butter. Stores specialising in Middle Eastern foods sell a sesame paste known as *tahini*, but this is made from raw sesame seeds, is white and slightly bitter, and cannot be substituted for the Chinese version — which is made from toasted sesame seeds, and is brown and nutty. A suitable substitute is peanut butter with sesame oil added for flavour. Sesame paste is sold in cans or jars, and keeps indefinitely after opening.

SHALLOTS
Bot.: Allium ascalonicum

Shallots are small, purplish onions with red-brown skin. Like garlic, they grow in a cluster and resemble garlic cloves in shape. The name 'shallots' in Australia is generally (and incorrectly) given to spring onions.

SHIRATAKI

These translucent noodles, used in *sukiyaki*, are made from the starch of a tuberous root. They are usually sold in cans or plastic packets, ready to use in Japanese cooking.

SHRIMP PASTE or SHRIMP SAUCE
Tagalog: *bagoong*
Indonesian: *petis*

Although not widely distributed as *bagoong* or *petis*, this is sold at Chinese grocery stores as 'shrimp sauce' or 'shrimp paste'. Thick and greyish in colour, with a powerful odour, it is one of the essential ingredients in the food of Southeast Asia. Substitute dried shrimp paste (blachan) or anchovy sauce.

SHRIMP PASTE, DRIED

see dried shrimp paste

SILVER FUNGUS
Chinese: *sit gnee*

Also known as 'white wood fungus', this is so rare and expensive that it is used only in special festive dishes. Almost flavourless, it is prized for its crunchy texture and pretty appearance, and is also a 'prestige' food used to honour special guests. It is sold dried, by the gram; or in cans, cooked in a sweet syrup. However, the home-made version is infinitely preferable to the canned silver fungus, which loses its texture through processing. Silver fungus is said to be very beneficial to pregnant women.

SNOW PEAS
Chinese: *ho lan dau*
Japanese: *saya endo*
Indonesian: *kacang kapri*

These are also known as 'sugar peas' or 'Chinese peas', or by their French name, *mange-tout*. They are small, flat pods containing embryonic peas, are bright green in colour, and are cooked for only a minute or two before being eaten whole (including the pod). They can be stored for a few days in a plastic bag or a bowl of water in the refrigerator.

SOY SAUCE

Indispensable in Asian cooking, this versatile sauce enhances the flavour of every basic ingredient in a dish. Different grades are available.

Chinese cooking uses light soy and dark soy. The light soy is used with chicken or seafoods, or in soups where the delicate colour of the dish must be retained.

Always use *shoyu* or Japanese soy sauce in Japanese cooking.

In Indonesia, *kecap manis,* a thick, dark, sweetened soy, is often used. As a substitute, use dark Chinese soy with black or brown sugar added in the proportions given in recipes.

All types of soy sauce keep indefinitely without refrigeration.

SPRING ONIONS (SCALLIONS or GREEN ONIONS
Bot.: *Allium cepa* or *Allium fistulum*
Fam.: *Liliaceae*
Lao: *phak boua sot*
Malay: *daun bawang*

This member of the onion family is known as 'shallot' in Australia, but is correctly called a spring onion almost everywhere else (though the term 'scallion' is popular in the USA). Spring onions are the thinnings of either *Allium cepa* or *A. fistulum* plantings that do not form a bulb. They are white and slender, with green leaves, and are used widely in China and Japan.

SPRING ROLL PASTRY

Thin white sheets of pastry sold in plastic packets and kept frozen. Thaw and peel off one at a time (unused wrappers can be re-frozen). Large wrappers of the *wonton* type cannot be substituted.

STAR ANISE
Bot.: *Illicium verum*
Fam.: *Magnoliaceae*
Malay: *bunga lawang*
Chinese: *baht ghok*
Indonesian: *bunga lawang*

The dried, star-shaped fruit of an evergreen tree native to China, it consists of 8 segments or points. It is essential in Chinese cooking.

STRAW MUSHROOMS

see mushrooms, straw

SWEET BEAN PASTE
Chinese: *dow saah*

Made from soy beans and sugar, this paste is used in sweet steamed buns or Chinese moon cakes.

SZECHWAN VEGETABLE

Mustard cabbage *(gai choy)* preserved in brine, with chilli added. It can be used as a relish, or included in dishes requiring piquancy and tang. Sold in cans.

TAKUAN

Pickled *daikon,* the giant white radish so widely used in Japanese cooking.

TAMARIND
Bot.: *Tamarindus indica*
Fam.: *Leguminoseae*
Hindi: *imli*
Sinhalese: *siyambala*
Lao: *mal kham*
Malay: *asam*
Indonesian: *asam*
Thai: *som ma kham*

This acid-tasting fruit of a large tropical tree is shaped like a large broad bean and has a brittle brown shell, inside which are shiny dark seeds covered with brown flesh. Tamarind is dried, and sold in packets. For use as acid in a recipe, soak a piece the size of a walnut in half a cup of hot water for 5-10 minutes until soft, then squeeze it until it mixes with the water and strain out the seeds and fibres. Tamarind liquid is used in given quantities.

TANDOORI MIX

A blend of hot and fragrant spices including cardamom, chillies, turmeric, saffron, and *garam masala*. If commercial brands are not available, substitute the following mixture: 2 teaspoons turmeric, 1 teaspoon paprika, ½ teaspoon chilli powder (optional), 1 teaspoon *garam masala* (page 35), ½ teaspoon ground cardamom, ⅛ teaspoon powdered saffron. A half teaspoon of garlic powder can be added, but this is not necessary if fresh garlic is used in the recipe.

TANGERINE PEEL, DRIED
Chinese: *gom pei*

Sold in Chinese grocery stores, this gives an incomparable flavour to food. Substitute fresh tangerine or mandarin peel, or orange rind.

TRASI

see dried shrimp paste

TSUKUDANI

A sweet and salty Japanese relish made from flaked dried fish, tiny shrimps, soy sauce and sugar. Serve in small quantities to accompany rice meals.

TSUYU NO MOTO

Concentrated soup stock. Dilute one part stock with two parts water and use as a dipping sauce with noodles.

TULSI
Bot.: *Ocimum sanctum*
Hindi: *tulsi*
Sinhalese: *kus kus*

This is the tiny black seed of a plant of the Basil family. The seeds look like poppy seeds when dry, but when soaked in water they develop a slippery, translucent coat. They are floated on cool, sweet drinks, for they are said to cool the body (a highly regarded attribute in hot countries); and, although without flavour, they add an intriguing texture.

TURMERIC
Bot: *Curcuma Longa*
Fam: *Zingiberaceae*
Hindi: *Haldi*
Sinhalese: *Kaha*
Burmese: *Fa Nwin*
Indonesian: *kunyit*
Thai: *kamin*
Chinese: *wong geung fun*

A rhizome of the ginger family, turmeric with its orange-yellow colour is a mainstay of commercial curry powders. Though often called Indian saffron, it should never be confused with true saffron and the two may not be used interchangeably.

WAKAME

A type of seaweed with long, narrow, ribbon-like strands. Sold dried, it must be soaked before use in Japanese cooking. It is used in soups or vinegared relishes.

WALNUTS

Walnuts used in Chinese dishes should be the peeled walnuts sold in Chinese grocery stores, for the thin skin (which turns bitter with cooking) has been removed. If peeled walnuts are not available, use the canned, salted walnuts also sold at Chinese stores; they do not need further cooking.

WASABI or WASABE

Pungent green horseradish used by the Japanese. It is available in dried, powdered form in tins, and is reconstituted (like dry mustard) by the addition of a little cold water.

WATER CHESTNUTS
Chinese: *mah tai*
Japanese: *kuwai*

Sometimes available fresh, their brownish-black skin must be peeled away with a sharp knife, leaving the crisp, slightly sweet kernel. They are also available in cans, already peeled and in some instances sliced. After opening, store in water in refrigerator for 7-10 days, changing water daily.

WINTER BAMBOO SHOOTS   see bamboo shoots

WOOD FUNGUS
Bot.: *Auricalaria polytricha*
Chinese: *wun yee*
Japanese: *kikurage*
Malay: *kuping tikus*
Indonesian: *kuping jamu*
Thai: *hed hunu*

Also known as 'cloud ear fungus' or 'jelly mushrooms', wood fungus is sold by weight, and in its dry state looks like greyish-black pieces of paper. Soaked in hot water for 10 minutes, it swells to translucent brown shapes like curved clouds or a rather prettily shaped ear — hence the name 'cloud ear fungus'. With its flavourless resilience it is a perfect example of a texture ingredient, adding no taste of its own but taking on subtle flavours from the foods with which it is combined. Cook only for a minute or two.

WONTON WRAPPERS

Small squares of fresh noodle dough available at Chinese grocery stores. They can be refrigerated for up to a week if well wrapped in plastic, or can be wrapped in foil and frozen. Sold by weight, there are approximately 90 wrappers to the half kilogram (one pound).

YELLOW BEANS, SALTED

Very similar to canned salted black beans, but lighter in colour. Use in dishes in the same way as salted black beans. See Black beans, salted.

YELLOW BEAN PASTE

This paste is not really yellow, but brown. Use it in recipes where a lighter sauce than black bean sauce is needed. Sold in cans.

YOGHURT

Cultured yoghurt. For recipes in this book, use unflavoured yoghurt (preferably one with a pronounced acid flavour) such as Greek yoghurt or goat's milk yoghurt

INDEX